Globalization and Change
in Fifteen Cultures

Globalization and Change in Fifteen Cultures

Born in One World, Living in Another

George Spindler   and   Janice E. Stockard
Stanford University   *Mills College*

✳ Case Studies in Cultural Anthropology: George Spindler and Janice E. Stockard, Series Editors

THOMSON
WADSWORTH

Australia • Brazil • Canada • Mexico • Singapore
Spain • United Kingdom • United States

Globalization and Change in Fifteen Cultures:
Born in One World, Living in Another
George Spindler and Janice E. Stockard

Publisher: *Eve Howard*
Anthropology Editor: *Lin Marshall*
Assistant Editor: *Leata Holloway*
Technology Project Manager: *Dee Dee Zobian*
Marketing Manager: *Lori Grebe Cook*
Marketing Assistant: *Teresa Jessen*
Marketing Communications Manager: *Linda Yip*
Project Manager, Editorial Production: *Emily Smith*
Creative Director: *Rob Hugel*
Art Director: *Maria Epes*
Print Buyer: *Linda Hsu*
Permissions Editor: *Kiely Sisk*

Production Service: *Sara Dovre Wudali,*
  Buuji, Inc.
Photo Researcher: *Sue Howard*
Copy Editor: *Heather McElwain*
Illustrator: *Jill Wolf, Buuji, Inc.*
Compositor: *Interactive Composition*
  Corporation
Cover Designer: *Laurie Anderson*
Cover Image: *Nathan Stockard,*
  writer/illustrator
Text and Cover Printer: *Thomson/West*

Printed in Canada
2 3 4 5 6 7 09 08 07 06

Thomson Higher Education
10 Davis Drive
Belmont, CA 94002-3098
USA

For more information about our products,
contact us at:
Thomson Learning Academic Resource Center
1-800-423-0563

For permission to use material from this text or
product, submit a request online at
http://www.thomsonrights.com.
Any additional questions about permissions
can be submitted by e-mail to
thomsonrights@thomson.com.

Library of Congress Control Number: 2005935130

ISBN 0-534-63648-9

This photograph of Louise and me was taken in June 1974 at Davis Lake in Oregon. We were on our way to Canada for a summer of fieldwork with the Kenai (Blood Indians) in Alberta.

    Like me, Louise was an anthropologist. All her life she was ready for adventure. She was a courageous and loving person. We were together for more than fifty years and made dozens of field trips. We worked not only with the Blood, but also with other Native Americans, including the Cree in Canada and Menominee in Wisconsin. In other major projects, we conducted fieldwork in schools, among teachers and students, in small towns in Wisconsin and Germany.

    To have known Louise is to miss her. This anthology is dedicated to the memory of my wife, Louise Schaubel Spindler (1917–1997).

—George Spindler

Contents

Preface   xv

Introduction   xix

**PART I   CHALLENGES TO IDENTITY
            AND POWER   1**

**Chapter 1   Continuity and Change in Aztec Culture:
                From Imperial Lords to Royal Subjects   1**
                Frances F. Berdan

Setting the Stage: Some Themes   2
The Aztec Empire on the Eve of the Spanish Conquest   2
  Imperial Strategies   3
  Political and Territorial Organization: the Altepetl   4
  Social Stratification   5
  Commerce   6
  Religion   7
The Stage Is Set   8
New Lords of the Land   8
Aztecs to Nahuas: Continuity and Change in the New Order   9
  Demographic Disaster   9
  The Altepetl and Cultural Identity   10
  Social Stratification: Disintegration Over Time   11
  Occupations and Commerce   13
  Taking Advantage of New Things and Ideas   15
  Religious Syncretism   18
Conclusion   20
References   21
Notes   22

**Chapter 2   Change in the Lives of a Brazilian Indigenous People:
                To Pluck Eyelashes (or Not?) among the Canela   24**
                William and Jean Crocker

The Canela Today   28
Some Background to the Current Canela Situation   29
Tracing Culture Change Through Individuals   31
  Basket Lifter and her Son, Speechless   32
  Hard Bed   35

Anaconda 38
Ângelo Carampei 41
Edible Vine 44
Summary: Factors in Culture Change   48
References   50
Notes   51

**Chapter 3   Cultural Identity in China: The Rising Politics
of Ethnic Difference   53**
Dru C. Gladney
The Soviet Union as China's Prologue?   54
Nationality in China   57
Han Nationality as Invented National Unity   59
Identity Politics and National Minorities   60
Internal Divisions among the Han Majority   63
Internet Cafés, Discos, and Democratization?   65
Conclusion: National Disunity?   67
References   70
Notes   71

**Chapter 4   The Vice Lords Today: Sociocultural Change
in an African American Street Gang   73**
Lincoln Keiser
References   95
Notes   96

PART II   CHANGE IN GENDER HIERARCHIES   97

Chapter 5   Sambia Gender, Sexuality, and Social Change   97
Gilbert Herdt and Birgitta Stolpe
Precolonial Sambia Society   98
Traditional Gender Roles and Initiation   100
Social Hierarchies among the Sambia   102
Marriage and the Traffic in Women   103
Social Change and Resistance   105
Schools and Gender Change   107
Change over the Past Decade   109
Conclusion   115
References   116
Notes   116

**Chapter 6   Mothers to Daughters: Social Change and Matrilineal
Kinship in a Minangkabau Village   117**
Evelyn Blackwood
Minangkabau and Their Houses   120
Reconfiguring Daughters' Desires   123

    Education   124
    Marriage Rights   125
  Models of Domesticity   127
  Contradictory Housewives   130
  Social Change and Small Houses   132
    Households, Demographics, and Migration   132
    Residence and Matriliny   133
    Daughters Who Leave   134
    Daughters' Claims   135
  Matriliny in Single-Family Households   137
    Husband and Wife Contributions   138
    Reconstituting Single-Family Households   139
  Conclusion   140
  References   141
  Notes   142

**Chapter 7   The Ju/'Hoansi at the Crossroads: Continuity
and Change in the Time of AIDS   144**
    Richard B. Lee
  Four Decades of Change   146
  Nyae Nyae: A Struggle for Survival   150
  Ju/'Hoansi in the Twenty-First Century: Progress and Poverty   154
    Botswana   154
    Namibia   155
  Regional Developments: From the End of Apartheid
    to the Coming of AIDS   156
  AIDS and the Ju/'Hoansi   156
  The Ju/Hoansi's Lower Rates: Macro and Micro Factors   158
  Ju/'Hoan Women's Autonomy   159
  Forces Driving the Epidemic   161
  The Larger Social Framework of AIDS Risk   163
  The Tsumkwe Junior Secondary School   164
  The Old-Age Pension Affair   165
  Craft Buying as Income Generation   166
  The Kashipembe Crisis   166
  The Wider Nyae Nyae and Dobe Region   167
  Conclusion: Back from the Brink?   168
  References   169
  Note   171

**Chapter 8   From Field to Factory and Beyond: New Strategies
for New Realities in a Yucatecan Village   172**
    Cindy L. Hull
  Theoretical Perspective   173
  Yucatán and the World System: Historical Perspective   174
  Yucatán and the Modern World System   179
  Yaxbe   179
  1990s—The Fall of the Ejido: New Strategies for New Realities   181

Economic Diversification in the Village   182
  Agriculture   182
  Nonagricultural Occupations   183
  Women and Income Production Within the Home   184
  Women and Income Production Outside of the Home   186
  Women in Solidarity: The Horchateras   187
Commuting as Economic Strategy   190
  Factory Jobs   191
  Professional Occupations   191
  Other Occupations   192
  Men and Commuting   192
  Women and Commuting   193
Migration as Economic Strategy   193
Conclusion: The Impact of Globalization   195
References   196
Notes   197

**PART III   NEW PATTERNS OF MIGRATION
               AND MOBILITY   199**

**Chapter 9   The Yolmo People of Melemchi, Nepal:
                 Change and Continuity   199**

      Naomi H. Bishop

Melemchi: A Yolmo Temple-Village   200
  The Village   200
  Traditional Subsistence Strategies   201
  Social and Political Organization   204
  Religion and Worldview   204
Moving into the Twenty-First Century: 1971–2000   206
  Changes in the Subsistence System   206
  Changes in Circular Migration   207
  Incorporation into the Langtang National Park   209
  A Primary School in Melemchi   212
Melemchi in the Twenty-First Century: Challenges of the Future   214
  The Changing Demography of Melemchi   215
  Dependence on External Remittance   217
  Viability of the Village Subsistence System   217
  Maintaining Cultural Knowledge   219
Conclusion   220
References   223
Notes   223

**Chapter 10   The Mardu Aborigines: On the Road
                  to Somewhere   225**

      Robert Tonkinson

Introducing the Mardu Aborigines   225
Fieldwork among the Mardu   227
Conceptualizing Social Change and the Challenge to Analysis   229

The Mardu in a Wider Australian Context   232
Early Contacts with Europeans: Defining the "Whitefella"   235
The Mission and Its Aftermath: From Masters of the Desert to
    Children of the Devil   238
"Self-management": The Perils of Well-Meaning Government Policy   241
On Mobility, Dispersal, and Aggregation   243
The Mardu Today: On the Road to Somewhere   245
Conclusion   251
References   253
Notes   254

Chapter 11   From Local "Tribe" to Transnational Arab:
                 The "New" Rashaayda Bedouin of Sudan   256
                 William C. Young

Geographical and Historical Background   259
The History of "Tribal" Affiliations in Eastern Sudan   262
The Economic Internationalization of Eastern Sudan   262
International Politics and the Unstable National Border Between
    Sudan and Eritrea   265
  The War in Eritrea   266
  The War in Sudan   268
The Bani Rashiid in Saudi Arabia   272
The Bani Rashiid Campaign to Rework Genealogies and History   274
Conclusion   277
References   278
Notes   281

Chapter 12   Culture Change and Cultural Reproduction:
                 Lessons from Research on Transnational Migration   283
                 Leo R. Chavez

Why is Transnational Migration Important for Anthropologists?   285
A Love-Hate Relationship with Immigrants   287
Culture Change and Cultural Reproduction   292
Immigration and Culture Change   297
References   300
Notes   303

**PART IV EFFECTS OF ECONOMIC CHANGE
          AND MODERNIZATION   304**

**Chapter 13   Scottish Crofters: Narratives of Change
                 among Small Landholders in Scotland   304**
                 Susan Parman

Doing Fieldwork   308
Narratives about Crofting   309
Narratives about Speaking Gaelic   315

Narratives about the Free Church   319
Narratives of Home and Exile   323
Summary of Changes   326
References   331
Notes   332

Chapter 14   A Village in Greece: Vasilika Then and Now   334
         Ernestine Friedl
Migration and the Fates of Migrants   337
Gender Roles   345
Epilogue   346
References   349
Additional Works on Vasilika   350
Recommended Reading   350

**Chapter 15   Through Japanese Eyes: Culture Change
                in a Midwestern Town   351**
         Toshiyuki Sano and Mariko Fujita
Changing Eyes—From Analogue to Digital   352
Two Views of Downtown and the Public Square   353
A Tranquil Place and an Intense Site   358
Changes in Farming Practice   361
A Changing Ethnic and Economic Map   366
The Transformation of the Senior Center   367
Concluding Remarks   369
References   370
Notes   371

Index   373

INSTRUCTOR'S CHART TO CHAPTER COVERAGE

	Identity	Migration & Mobility	Globalization/ Economic Change/ Modernization	Gender & Sexuality	Marriage & Family/Kinship	Colonialism	Religion	Ethnicity	Power
Berdan Central America (Mexico)	●		●			●	●	●	●
Bishop South Asia (Nepal)	●	●	●				●		●
Blackwood Southeast Asia (Indonesia; Sumatra)	●			●	●		●		●
Chavez (Cross-Cultural)	●	●	●						●
Crocker & Crocker South America (Brazil)	●	●	●	●					●
Friedl Europe (Greece)	●	●	●		●				
Gladney East Asia (People's Republic of China)	●		●	●			●	●	●

	Identity	Migration & Mobility	Globalization/ Economic Change/ Modernization	Gender & Sexuality	Marriage & Family/Kinship	Colonialism	Religion	Ethnicity	Power
Herdt & Stolpe Pacific Oceania (Oceania)	●		●	●	●	●			●
Hull Central America (Mexico)	●	●	●	●	●				
Keiser North America (U.S.A.)	●			●			●	●	●
Lee Africa (Namibia, Botswana)	●	●		●	●	●			●
Parman Europe (Scotland)	●	●	●				●		
Sano & Fujita North America (U.S.A.)	●	●	●		●			●	
Tonkinson Australia	●	●	●	●		●			●
Young Africa (Sudan) Mid-East (Saudi Arabia)	●	●	●		●				●

Preface

The Case Studies in Cultural Anthropology series serves as the starting point for the chapters in this anthology. George and Louise Spindler launched the popular series with an initial six case studies, published in 1960. Since that time, more than two hundred have been published. Initially conceived as descriptive studies of culture and intended for classroom use, the case studies were designed to be accessible, short, and engaging, written by anthropologists who had "been there." Their goal was to introduce students to cultural differences, as well as to demonstrate the commonality of human lives everywhere. Each case study focused on a relatively bounded community—a cultural group, tribe, area—that could be distinguished by its own customs, beliefs, and values.

Today the case studies and the chapters in this anthology reflect a world changed by globalization, and an anthropology committed to documenting the effects of the vast cultural flows of people, information, goods, and technology, now in motion the world over. In the twenty-first century, the greater pace and reach of globalization has created an infinite number of meeting points for people and cultures, multiplying the sites and contexts for change.

The 15 anthropologists included in this anthology have each previously published a case study. In their chapters in this volume, they take students on a return visit to their field sites, the focus of their original case study work. For this visit, they return with new questions for a new era, but with perspectives seasoned by the first (and subsequent) experiences with the same people.

Each anthropologist reports on a field site that is to some extent still familiar (with its distinctive cultural characteristics recognizable) and yet is at the same time changed, transformed by global forces. Writing from wide-ranging field sites, their research documents four major dimensions in culture change: challenges to identity and power; changing gender hierarchies; new patterns of migration and mobility; the effects of economic change and modernization. The anthology is thus ideal for use in anthropology and other social sciences classes that focus on the "local" effects of globalization in communities and societies around the world. Its design recommends it for use as a core text, facilitating the integration of auxiliary ethnographies, original case studies, and other monographs.

An innovative feature of this anthology is the inclusion of a fieldwork biography at the beginning of each chapter. Employed as epigraphs, each biography introduces the student to the anthropologist whose field methods and experience provide the lens into cultural change for that chapter. These biographies serve to familiarize students with a broad spectrum of field experience, as well as with the signature methods of ethnographic research. In addition, the fieldwork epigraphs also personalize the research and perspectives presented in each chapter.

Finally, the availability of the original studies makes this anthology, with its new chapters, an unprecedented and rich learning experience. No other combination offers the opportunity to see simultaneously both what was and what now is. This anthology is an education in how the world is evolving. The chapters provide insight into how change—in some places partial, in other places transformative and seemingly total—is also about how people, through their culture, reconfigure its impact, in this way shaping local experience and the meaning of change itself.

Across 15 field sites, the repercussions of global transformation for local peoples are described by the anthropologists who study them: William Young documents how the Rashaayda Bedouin of Sudan, in forging new ties with their distant cousins in Saudi Arabia, have created a transnational Arab kinship. Among the Ju/'hoansi of Africa, Richard Lee finds that the renowned autonomy of women now serves to protect them from the worst ravages of HIV/AIDS, which has decimated other tribes in the region. In the Sambia tribe of New Guinea, Gilbert Herdt and Birgitta Stolpe discover a crisis in gender and a search for new models of masculinity. Cindy Hull reports from a Yucatecan village that global markets and factory work have transformed not only the everyday working lives of men and women, but their established domestic hierarchies, as well. From China, Dru Gladney analyzes how contemporary ethnic groups employ self-identification to navigate national and international politics and advance their own special interests. These and many more local accounts reflective of globalization await the reader of this anthology.

ACKNOWLEDGMENTS

The editors of an anthology owe an expression of gratitude to many people. First of all, we thank the people in all the places represented in this volume, for it is they who opened their hearts and minds so that we might learn about them—and the transformations affecting all of us.

Next we recognize our 15 contributing authors. All of them anthropologists, they are an experienced, dedicated group of professionals. Collectively, they have spent more than four hundred years studying, living among, and writing about the people they bring to you in the following chapters. As seasoned anthropologists, their perspectives on culture change and continuity are informed by multiple return visits to their field sites. With a practiced eye, they report on how diverse peoples respond, adapt, and resist changes instigated by the many facets of globalization. They have written thought-provoking chapters, and no one ever has had a better group to work with. We thank them profoundly.

We wish to express our heartfelt thanks to Lin Marshall at Wadsworth, who unrelentingly worked with us (and on us), as editors, to face our task with a strong heart and courageous spirit. As the editor of anthropology and with many other projects on her desk, Lin always had time for us, pushing us when we would have relaxed. Her editorial talents and expertise in anthropology proved to be an inspiration to us. To Lin we offer our special thanks.

Then we thank the people who put the raw writing into finished, polished text. The list is long, and includes colleagues, reviewers, copyeditors, and the talented team of production specialists: Emily Smith and Kiely Sisk of Thomson Wadsworth; Sara Dovre Wudali, Jill Wolf, and Virginia Aretz of Buuji, Inc.;

Sue Howard, Heather McElwain; and the folks at Interactive Composition Corporation.

Naturally, we wish to express our gratitude to our dear families and friends for their support along the way. Without them, we couldn't have done it. For their abiding interest in our project, across the several years of its development, we thank them.

And lastly, we thank each other for all the hard work and collegial comradeship, friendship, and faith. We can't imagine two editors better equipped to be the captains of this enterprise!

ABOUT THE EDITORS

The anthology coeditors, George Spindler and Janice Stockard, wish to take this opportunity to introduce themselves. George Spindler is an old-timer, with more than 50 years at Stanford University, dozens of field trips, and a long list of publications. He completed most of his anthropology in collaboration with his wife of 55 years, Louise Schaubel Spindler, who received her doctorate from Stanford University in 1956. George received his from the University of California at Los Angeles in 1952. Together they founded and edited the Case Studies in Cultural Anthropology series. Janice Stockard, coeditor of *Globalization and Change in Fifteen Cultures*, received her doctorate from Stanford in 1985. She has taught at Stanford University as well as at Connecticut College and Mills College. Janice is the author of two published books, *Daughters of the Canton Delta: Marriage Patterns and Economic Strategies in South China, 1860–1930* (Stanford 1989) and *Marriage in Culture: Practice and Meaning Across Diverse Societies* (Harcourt 2001). Her continuing research into gender, marriage, and technology has resulted in a new manuscript investigating silk production in early New England. Janice is co-editor of the Case Studies in Cultural Anthropology series.

In the chapters of *Globalization and Change in Fifteen Cultures: Born in One World, Living in Another*, we invite the reader to learn how diverse peoples and cultures experience and respond to the changes our world faces today.

George Spindler
Janice Stockard

Introduction

At the opening of the twenty-first century, vast cultural flows of people, information, goods, and technology are in motion around the globe. With this globalization has come an intensification and an acceleration in the frequency of "border crossings." In journeys both real and virtual, more people are now moving beyond their own nations and cultural territories, generating unprecedented levels of cross-cultural contact and encounter. Historically, these encounters (both benign and violent) constituted powerful moments of cultural challenge, generating the potential for change in institutions, practices, and meanings. In this contemporary era, the increased pace and reach of globalization has created an infinite number of meeting points for peoples and cultures, multiplying the sites and contexts for change.

In this volume, 15 anthropologists analyze the effects of globalization and change on cultures around the world.[1] Each of these anthropologists is also the author of an ethnography that has enjoyed outstanding success as part of the Case Studies in Cultural Anthropology series, edited by George and Louise Spindler.[2] In their chapters on cultural transformation and continuity, these anthropologists revisit their field sites, the people, and the communities that were the focus of their original case studies. For this visit, they return with new questions for a new era—but with perspectives seasoned by first (and subsequent) experiences with the same peoples and cultures in far-ranging societies: the Canela in Brazil, Yolmo in Nepal, Sambia in New Guinea, Mardu in Australia, Bedouin in Sudan, Ju/'Hoansi (!Kung San) in Namibia, Minangkabau in Sumatra, Scottish crofters, Greek villagers, Chinese minorities, the Aztecs and Yucatecans in Mexico, as well as among Mexican immigrants in the United States, African American gang members, and Wisconsin town residents.

Anthropologists offer a distinctive, critical perspective on "the local" in a global era, providing a window into how people in cultures around the world are affected by the processes of globalization, how they engage with these changes and (in some cases) turn them to their own advantage. This singular perspective is grounded in the nature of anthropology and its field arm, ethnography. Through field research sustained across many months (and even years), anthropologists achieve a cultural immersion experience, learning to live and work with the people they study. This commitment to the field, to the people, and their culture typically creates trust and intimacy, enabling the anthropologist to observe, participate, and interview with a perspective that approaches an insider's. From this angle of vision, anthropologists learn to ask the "right" questions, eliciting from the people they study their own account of society, culture, and life experience in the era of globalization and change.

THEMATIC OVERVIEW

In their chapters, the authors identify four general dimensions of culture change: **challenges to identity and power, changing gender hierarchies, new patterns of migration and mobility,** and the **effects of economic change and modernization.** Each of these dimensions of change is not simply an entry in the anthropologist's notebook; each also represents a fundamental rupture with the past for local people in diverse cultural settings around the world.

Every author documents **challenges to identity and power** arising from increased cross-cultural encounters generated by globalization and change. With differing emphases, they write about shifting identities and altered relations of power. The people they have lived with and studied are all experiencing new challenges to the established identities and hierarchies of the past.

Although the specific identities contested are distinctive to each society, the theme "challenges to identity" emerges as universal in the chapters in this volume. In some places anthropologists find people working to reaffirm traditional identity; in other places identities are invented, negotiated, resisted, and lost. Change in personal identity arises as the primary concern in some of the societies examined. In other places, people in villages and towns struggle to maintain or reestablish "local" identities. In some of these societies, the fundamental challenge to local identity is the threat to established kinship identities, based on the lineage or clan. Elsewhere, ethnic and indigenous people (members of minority groups and tribes) reaffirm traditional identities, or "discover" or reconstruct them in the wake of change. Finally, some of these chapters consider the politics, conflict, and violence arising from asserting ethnic identity over and against the identity of the greater nation-state. In addition, some describe the creation of new and powerful transnational identities in diaspora that cut across the borders of nation-states and challenge their power.[3]

The multiple dimensions of power—its changing form and face—emerges as another key "local" concern for people around the world in the era of globalization. As the accounts by anthropologists bear witness, in a world suddenly and dramatically altered by access to new information, goods, and technologies, people struggle both to retain the meaning of established cultural ways of living and thinking, and to re-imagine them in the face of new cultural possibilities. Access to the new transnational cultural archive brings change (and even rupture) to established hierarchies of power.

Changing in gender hierarchies is one of the major effects of globalization documented in these chapters. Some of the authors also describe shifts in other kinds of hierarchy, including changing relations of power between persons, generations, and kinship groups, ethnic and indigenous groups, regional and local groups, "nations" and minorities within nation-states, and transnationally constituted diasporic communities and groups.

Although their emphases differ, all of the authors contributing to this volume consider change initiated by increased cross-cultural contact and encounter, resulting from increased global movements of people, information, goods, and technology. In some chapters, the authors are concerned primarily with the effects of the movement of people themselves. In their chapters, they analyze the different outcomes of a broad spectrum in types of **migration and mobility.**[4] We learn about the consequences of transnational migration in the case of Nepal and Namibia—and in Sudan, where mass migrations are also considered. Internal and regional migration are the focus in the chapter on China, which also features the effects of international tourism and travel. Rural to urban and chain migration are analyzed in Greece. Circular and/or seasonal migration and their consequences are considered for the Bedouin of Sudan, Yolmo of Nepal, and Mardu of Australia, and the effects of new commuting practices among Yucatecan villagers are analyzed. Some chapters consider the effects and aftermath of another type of international movement among peoples and cultures, a more negative and violent order of cross-cultural "encounter," the colonial enterprise. The social and cultural legacy of colonialism is analyzed in the case of the Sambia of New Guinea, the Canela of Brazil, the Mardu of Australia, and in the Spanish conquest of the Aztecs.

Several authors consider the **effects of economic change and modernization.** In these chapters, although the migration or transnational movement of people themselves is one instigator of change, even more important is the transnational flow of information, goods, and technology. The specific agents of change—including the introduction of print and electronic media, the establishment of schools and missions, and the improvement of transportation—serve to introduce modernity by increasing exposure to Western (and other) cultural values and practices.[5]

Some authors analyze the profound cultural impact of still another aspect of modernization—the transition from traditional subsistence economies to a cash economy and by the incorporation of local labor and products into global markets. They document the cultural repercussions of several economic transitions: the effects of the shift away from hunting and horticultural practices among the Canela tribe of Brazil and the Sambia tribe of New Guinea; from hunting and gathering among the Mardu of Australia and the Ju/'Hoansi of Namibia; from alpine agro-pastoralism among the Yolmo in Nepal; from pastoralism among the Bedouin in Sudan; from subsistence agriculture and sheep raising to fish and wind farming in Scotland; and from mixed subsistence farming first to mono-cropping and then factory employment among villagers in Yucatan.

CHAPTERS IN BRIEF

In William and Jean Crocker's analysis of the cultural challenges facing the Canela tribe of Brazil (Chapter 2), we learn that in the wake of a host of dramatic and traumatic changes—including the alienation of much of their land, increasing absorption into external markets, the introduction of a cash economy, and the influence of government jobs—people today are increasingly concerned about personal and ethnic identity. In the Canela personal accounts, we hear several informants discuss the strategy behind their decisions to reconstruct (in whole or part) their Canela cultural identity, which they visually signal through the removal of some or all of their eyelashes and brows.

In their analysis of the cultural challenges confronting the Sambia tribe of the New Guinea highlands (Chapter 5), Gilbert Herdt and Birgitta Stolpe discover a contemporary crisis in gender identity. They argue that the combined effects of colonialism, missionary activity, the introduction of schools, and a growing dependence on out-migration for wage work have all contributed to a general undermining of Sambian male authority and ritual—and to a weakening of the traditional gender hierarchy that shaped the relations between men and women. In response to this crisis in gender, Herdt and Stolpe document Sambian efforts to construct a new masculinity.

Local and ethnic identity are the focus of Susan Parman's return to the crofters (small landholders) of Scotland, who have for generations enjoyed a reputation as a distinctive people (Chapter 13). This identity is based on their historical descent from Scots, as well as their heritage as traditional speakers of Gaelic and producers of tweed cloth, all attributes establishing them as a people apart from the English. In her analysis of the narratives of Scottish crofters, Parman maps the inroads made by modernity (including new technology and transportation), its assaults on the identity of the crofters as an independent and distinctive people, and charts the ways in which they seek to resist change and reassert their unique identity.

Another perspective on contemporary challenges to local identity is presented by Ernestine Friedl who returns to the Greek village where she first began fieldwork 50 years ago. Her analysis (Chapter 14) focuses on the effects of village out-migration and chain-migration, as youths leave Vasilika for Athens in search of wage work, a modern marriage, and consumer goods. Friedl analyzes the effects of these changes on gender relations, hierarchy, and power. The toll from frequent departures has left the village much diminished in population, but still resilient. Even as migration and a taste for modernity relentlessly claim the next generations, Friedl recounts efforts to reaffirm village identity by those remaining at home, as well as by migrants to Athens.

Local and ethnic identity are the lenses through which Toshiyuki Sano and Mariko Fujita examine culture change and continuity in a small Wisconsin town, the site of their original field research and case study (Chapter 15). As Japanese anthropologists, they bring a different perspective to the analysis of change in American culture. On their return visit they are confronted by changes in both the ethnic composition of the town, as well as in the occupation and livelihood of its residents and surrounding farm families. At once familiar and yet different, their Wisconsin town has experienced new waves of both immigration and out-migration and incorporation into global markets. These effects of larger transnational forces have thus achieved a cultural transformation that has challenged local identity, as well as disrupted traditional regional identity.

In the chapters by Keiser, Gladney, Bishop, and Young, we are introduced to cases in which ethnic groups and indigenous peoples in the United States (Chicago), China, Nepal, and Sudan struggle to reaffirm traditional identities. At the same time, in each case, people seek to reinvent themselves on a transnational level. Lincoln Keiser follows his original case study focused on an African American gang in Chicago (the Vice Lords) with an analysis of the several historical transformations in identity experienced by that group in recent decades

(Chapter 4). Originally, they based their identity on the extension of metaphoric kinship relationships that created a shared "brotherhood" of gang members. More recently, as part of their identification with the Nation of Islam, the gang has reinvented itself, in effect extending its kinship network to include their Muslim "brothers" in the wider transnational community.

In the People's Republic of China, Dru Gladney explicates the state system for classifying and establishing ethnic (minority) status (Chapter 3). Gladney analyzes both how the state constructs ethnic status and how ethnic groups employ self-identification to navigate national and international politics and advance their own group interests. Internal migration, international travel, and electronic media and communications are shown to be resources that ethnic groups exploit to enhance their own power and to resist state power and policy. Gladney shows how some ethnic and religious groups effectively create and strategically employ transnational diasporic identities to empower themselves in their struggles against the state.

In her analysis of cultural transformations in a village in Nepal, Naomi Bishop highlights the changes in traditional subsistence strategies that increased rates of permanent international migration (Chapter 9). She contrasts this new pattern of migration with traditional seasonal and circular patterns, and analyzes the differential effects of migration on Yolmo cultural life. Bishop considers how the incorporation of Yolmo youth into global labor markets and foreign factories has challenged cultural life at home in Nepal, while at the same time generating attempts to re-create village identity and ritual through membership in immigrant and transnational diasporic communities.

William Young analyzes the profound effects of recent national and international politics on the lives and culture of a Bedouin tribe in Sudan (Chapter 11). State policy, war, and the massive in-migration of refugees have disrupted Bedouin reliance on pastoralism. However, opportunities for wage work in Saudi Arabia have given rise to a new pattern of circular migration, from Sudan to Saudi Arabia and back. The economic profits of this new economic strategy have been employed as a resource by the Sudanese Bedouins to creatively chart a more powerful ethnic identity. In effect, they have recast traditional kinship identity to include Bedouins in Saudi Arabia, thereby creating a transnational Bedouin identity that serves to empower them in their resistance to the government in Sudan.

The migration of undocumented Mexican workers into Southern California, the focus of Leo Chavez's original case study, becomes a platform in his new chapter for a comprehensive analysis of culture change in the wake of increasing international migration (Chapter 12). Chavez takes cases of transnational migration in a variety of settings to examine the meaning of culture and change in an era of globalization. Specifically, he examines the cultural encounters resulting from transnational migration to explicate the general processes of cultural reproduction. Chavez turns to both history and theory in anthropology to map the meanings of culture and change across time, situating debates about immigration within the context of these meanings.

The resilience of ethnic identity and indigenous cultural practices in the face of new technologies and political realities is a theme Francis Berdan explores in her "return visit" to the historical Aztecs under Spanish colonial administration in the sixteenth century (Chapter 1). The cultural encounter of Aztecs and Spaniards was of course driven by Spanish conquest and colonial enterprise. In her original case study, Berdan analyzed the violent and traumatic consequences of the conquest for Aztec people and culture. In this chapter, Berdan focuses on the evidence of Aztec cultural resilience following the imposition of Spanish cultural institutions and practices. In the face of the overwhelming political and military power of their Spanish occupiers, Berdan finds that institutions key to the success of Spanish administration were in fact adaptations of Aztec ones, thus clearly demonstrating continuity with Aztec pre-conquest cultural structures. As Berdan's contribution reminds us, neither globalization nor cultural continuity and synthesis are new phenomena.

Change and continuity in gender hierarchies and power, central to the analyses by Gladney, Herdt, and Stolpe, also emerge as organizing themes in the chapters by Richard Lee, Cindy Hull, and Evelyn Blackwood. Richard Lee analyzes the devastating cost of increased levels of cultural encounter and accelerated change for the Ju/'hoansi (!Kung San) of Namibia and Botswana (Chapter 7). In his comparative analysis of the spread and toll of HIV/AIDS among several indigenous groups of southern Africa, Lee demonstrates how cultural continuity in the autonomy of Ju/'hoansi women has served to protect them from the terrible rates of HIV/AIDS infection that women of other ethnic groups have suffered. In those groups, women's traditional and contemporary status as dependents of men creates greater vulnerability to infection by male partners.

Cindy Hull finds less continuity in gender hierarchy in the Yucatan than did Lee in southern Africa, and more challenge to the traditional hierarchy (Chapter 8). Hull focuses in particular on the economic changes wrought by transnational markets and factories. She analyzes cultural transformations originating in the economic transition from village reliance on traditional swidden subsistence agriculture and the cultivation of diverse crops to dependence on monocultural farming (with its focus on one crop), factory work, and tourism. Hull considers the consequences of these economic changes, tracking their impact on newly emerging patterns of work for village men and women. Commuting beyond the village for men and wage work in village factories for women have brought change to women's economic and political participation and power, both in the family and larger public sphere.

In Chapter 6, Evelyn Blackwood considers shifts in another gender hierarchy. She focuses on the Minangkabau of Sumatra and the changing nature of the relationship between mothers and daughters in that matrilineal society. Blackwood analyzes how the incorporation of the Minangkabau into the Indonesian state has presented new models of domesticity that have served to empower daughters, giving them the ability to challenge their mothers' control over their choice of husbands and conjugal residential arrangements. The Minangkabau, who are Islamic, have successfully resisted pressures to abandon their matrilineal system in which females of the family inherit the land. However, the new national discourses on domesticity have created a historical moment when daughters find they can successfully resist the claims of their mothers, refusing to reside in their large communal houses, taking up residence instead with their husbands in smaller, nuclear houses nearby.

For the Mardu of Australia, ethnic identity and power within the nation-state emerge as key cultural concerns. In Chapter 10, Robert Tonkinson describes how the Mardu continue to live with the legacy of colonialism as they struggle to reestablish claims to traditional territories and to maintain the power and vitality of their customary law and cultural practices. Tonkinson depicts a people whose mobility, "dreaming" tradition, and sense of place run counter to the claims of the state, other nationalities, and resource developers as well.

CONCLUSION

As a collection, the chapters in this volume provide a critical, alternative perspective on the effects of globalization and change on peoples and cultures. The acceleration in pace and tempo of transnational flows in people, information, goods, and technology has generated infinite numbers of meeting points for people and cultures. Although we know that neither can remain unchanged by contact and encounter, the critical questions remain: In what specific ways will different peoples and cultures be affected? How will each respond to change?

Anthropologists are strategically positioned to answer these questions. The distinctive structure and process of ethnographic field research entails cultural immersion, face-to-face personal interactions and relationships, and long-term commitment to working within a particular local setting (group, community, lineage, or town). Ethnographic fieldwork permits the anthropologist to observe people and culture over time and to share the worldview of the people studied.[6] As near-cultural insiders, anthropologists are thus poised to observe both small, incremental cultural shifts, along with larger cultural ruptures and quakes. This distinctive angle of vision on the local enables anthropologists not only to recognize culture change—differentiating it from continuity or the simple mirage of change—but most important, to understand the full meaning of change and continuity for the people themselves.

Janice Stockard
George Spindler

NOTES

1. **About culture change:** Because cultures are neither static nor unchanging, anthropologists have been studying "culture change" for as long as they have been studying culture itself. Of course, culture change has been differently conceptualized in different historical eras. Comprehensive reviews by anthropologists on the subject at midpoint in the twentieth century include Louise S. and George Spindler's, "Culture Change" in the *Biennial Review of Anthropology* (1959), Felix Keesing's *Culture Change: An Analysis and Bibliography of Anthropological Sources to 1952* (1953), and June Macklin's "Culture Change" in the *Review of Sociology* (1957). At mid-century, key categories for research included urbanization, technological development, nativistic movements, values

and culture change, kinship and culture change, psychological processes and culture change, and acculturation.

Beginning in the late twentieth century and continuing to the present, most work on culture change has been incorporated within a new array of anthropological research topics, including globalization, transnationalism, postcolonialism, modernity and postmodernity, migration, diaspora, identity, and power. Most of these topics have emerged as critical dimensions of change analyzed within the chapters in this anthology, and indeed are employed as subheadings within its table of contents.

Although each chapter author directs readers to pertinent reading within these topic areas, a few general recommendations in each category can be made to the interested student:

On globalization and transnationalism:
An introduction to the fields of globalization and transnationalism studies within anthropology can be found in Michael Kearney's, "The Local and the Global: The Anthropology of Globalization and Transnationalism" in the *Annual Review of Anthropology* (1995), Marc Edelman and Angelique Haugerud's *The Anthropology of Development and Globalization* (1998), and Jonathan Xavier Inda and Renato Rosaldo's *The Anthropology of Globalization: A Reader* (2002). See also Eric Wolf's *Europe and the People Without History* (1982) and Arjun Appadurai's *Modernity at Large: Cultural Dimensions of Globalization* (1996). See also Linda Basch, Nina G. Schiller, and Cristina S. Blanc's *Nations Unbound: Transnational Projects, Postcolonial Predicaments, and Deterritorialized Nation-States* (1994) and Aihwa Ong's *Flexible Citizenship: The Cultural Logics of Transnationality* (1999).

2. As this anthology goes to press, one of our chapter authors, Evelyn Blackwood, is engaged in writing her case study. The other 14 anthropologists contributing to this volume are authors of published ethnographies in the Case Studies in Cultural Anthropology series, edited by George Spindler and Louise Spindler.

3. **On identity:** See the references to literature on identity within specific cultural contexts cited by the individual chapter authors. For general anthropological sources on contemporary issues in identity, see A. King's *Culture, Globalization and the World-System: Contemporary Conditions for the Representation of Identity* (1991); Edward Said's *Orientalism* (1978); Anthony Giddens' *Modernity and Self-Identity: Self and Society in the Late Modern Age* (1991); Dorothy Holland, William Lachicotte, Debra Skinner, Corole Cain's *Identity and Agency in Cultural Worlds* (1998).

4. **On migration:** General sources on the topic of migration in the era of globalization can be found in Note 1. Additional references include Louise Lamphere's *Structuring Diversity: Ethnographic Perspectives on the New Immigration* (1992) and Nancy Foner's *American Arrivals: Anthropology Engages the New Immigration* (2003).

5. **On modernization and modernity:** In addition to the anthropological sources on modernity referenced in Note 1, especially Eric Wolf's *Europe and the People without History* (1982) and Arjun Appadurai's *Modernity at Large:*

Cultural Dimensions of Globalization (1996), see also Anthony Giddens' *Consequences of Modernity* (1990); David Harvey's *The Condition of Post-modernity: An Inquiry into the Origins of Culture Change* (1989); and Greg Urban's *Metaculture: How Cultures Move Through the Modern World* (2001).

6. **On fieldwork practice:** Recommended sources on contemporary issues in fieldwork practice include Paul Rabinow's *Reflections on Fieldwork in Morocco* (1977); James Clifford and George Marcus (eds.) *Writing Culture: The Poetics and Politics of Ethnography* (1986); Mark Manganaro (ed.) *Modernist Anthropology: From Fieldwork to Text* (1998); Margery Wolf's *A Thrice-Told Tale: Feminism, Postmodernism, and Ethnographic Responsibility* (1992).

Fieldwork Biography
Frances F. Berdan

Dr. Frances F. Berdan is professor of anthropology and codirector of the Laboratory for Ancient Materials Analysis at California State University in San Bernardino. She received her PhD in anthropology at the University of Texas at Austin in 1975. Dr. Berdan has spent over 30 years researching the culture of the pre-Hispanic Aztecs of Mexico, along with their colonial experience and modern lives. She combines ethnohistory, ethnography, archaeology, and experimental archaeology in her research. She has authored or coauthored 11 books, an ethnographic simulation called EthnoQuest (on CD-ROM), and numerous articles.

1/Continuity and Change in Aztec Culture

From Imperial Lords to Royal Subjects

Continuity and change, trauma and transition, adaptation and assimilation: these common dualities highlight the complex and multifaceted nature of unexpected and shocking culture contact situations. One of the most staggering such occasions involved the encounter between the peoples of the eastern and western hemispheres, a true war of the worlds.

This chapter focuses on the consequences of one of the most significant, and also one of the best documented, of these cultural collisions: the conquest of the Aztecs and their extensive empire in 1521 by Spanish conquistadors under the banner of Charles V, king of Spain and Holy Roman Emperor. Although the event of conquest, and especially its aftermath, had significant repercussions on both sides of the Atlantic, this chapter emphasizes the native adaptations to the arrival and entrenchment of new lords of the land from Spain, particularly during the first century after contact.

SETTING THE STAGE: SOME THEMES

When the Spanish conquistador Hernán Cortés set foot on the coast of present-day Mexico in the spring of 1519, he encountered a well-established civilization, indeed an empire. This Aztec Empire,[1] although itself only 89 years old, drew on the accomplishments and institutional developments achieved by a succession of prior civilizations, dating from as early as 1600 B.C.E. This long history of cultural development, and of the rise and fall of cities, states, and city-states resulted in certain repetitive patterns and conditions of life in Mesoamerica[2] that became significant in the events following the Spanish conquest. Chief among these patterns and conditions were (1) large populations residing in cities and communities throughout the countryside that were especially dense in the lake-dominated Basin of Mexico; (2) the volatile nature of political and military relations among competing polities (city-states), commonly entailing warfare, conquest, and the establishment of rather uncertain alliances; (3) the presence of a considerable ethnic diversity throughout the land, based on language, territory, dynastic heritage, founding legends, patron deities, and an assortment of material attributes such as clothing, housing, weaponry, and ritual celebrations; (4) a hierarchical social stratification system firmly separating the "haves" from the "have-nots" through religious legitimacy, political power, economic control, and the display of overt symbols of social station; (5) widespread economic ties primarily based on commercial networks but also entailing politically based tribute and taxation systems; (6) a willingness, perhaps even eagerness to adopt new materials, ideas, and concepts from other groups; and (7) a polytheistic religion that tended to incorporate deities from conquered subjects, resulting in ever-expanding pantheons.

Two significant processes can be extracted from these attributes, particularly as they apply to the time of the Spanish conquest. First, the native peoples of Mesoamerica experienced an interplay between internal and external forces in their daily lives. Cultural and political traditions of community, and/or city-state loyalties, combined with ethnic ties tended to direct an individual's energies and allegiance inward. Simultaneously, that same individual's interests and motivations found outlets beyond the local polity, attracted by bustling marketplaces, the arrival of merchants and ambassadors from far-off lands, and engagement in wars in enemy territories. Second, an Aztec's life combined the old and the new, the familiar and the unfamiliar. After the arrival of the Spaniards, unusual objects and materials appeared in the marketplaces, uncustomary warrior regalia were brought home from faraway battlefields, and new deities and rituals were incorporated into the temples and ceremonial rounds. These dual themes (the exertion of internal and external forces, and the reliance on the familiar and an embracing of the unfamiliar) took center stage with the Spanish conquest and subsequent establishment of a new order on the land.

THE AZTEC EMPIRE ON THE EVE
OF THE SPANISH CONQUEST

Under Cortés, the Spaniards encountered a complex world that was at the same time firmly entrenched and under considerable stress. The Aztec Empire had aggressively expanded its political and economic dominion over much of central

Mexico during its brief history. This empire was built on a foundation of diverse city-states, depended on complex hierarchical social arrangements, was supported by extensive and lively commerce, and required active ritual participation in the maintenance of a precarious universe. These dimensions of life provide a backdrop against which the Aztecs and their neighbors reacted and adjusted to life under Spanish rule.

Central to these developments was a reliance on highly productive systems of agriculture, the result of centuries of botanical and technological innovations performed by the Aztecs' Mesoamerican predecessors. In central Mexico, the Aztecs mainly cultivated maize, beans, chilies, squashes, maguey, and a variety of vegetables and herbs, relying on both hillside dry farming and flatland irrigation agriculture.[3] The latter reached its productive peak with highly intensive *chinampas,* lands systematically built up in shallow lakebeds for cultivation and residence. These fertile agricultural plots were especially prominent in the densely populated Basin of Mexico, providing an important means of territorial expansion of the lakeside and island cities, and contributing to their impressive population sizes and densities. While famine and other disasters occasionally interrupted the general security that central Mexican agriculture afforded, the system was sufficiently reliable and productive to allow for considerable storable surpluses. These surpluses, in turn, contributed to the demographic, social, and economic complexities the Aztecs experienced, particularly dense urban settlements, a hierarchical social system, state-level political organization, and economic specialization.

Imperial Strategies

In developing and sustaining their empire, the Aztecs employed several successful strategies. They established political and military alliances with their neighbors as well as more distant polities to enhance their strategic position. These alliances were frequently cemented through carefully arranged elite marriages. They conducted persistent wars of conquest, establishing an additional layer of rule over city-states already governed by their own rulers. Typically, these conquered rulers were allowed to retain their traditional reigning positions as long as they adhered to the conditions negotiated with their new overlords. These conditions required that the city-state refrain from rebellion, assist Aztec troops that may trek through its lands in pursuit of more distant conquests, and pay tribute in kind on a specified schedule. That tribute was collected by locally unpopular imperial tribute collectors; their haughty demeanor, and perhaps the simple fact that they represented unwanted overlords, frequently raised the hackles of the subject peoples and their traditional rulers. Between alliance and conquest lay a gray area of clientship, whereby the Aztec rulers negotiated asymmetrical relations with city-states in strategically situated outlying areas: along hostile borderlands, astride active commercial routes, or in close proximity to critical natural resources (Berdan et al., 1996). These relationships provided "clients" to the empire who could maintain these volatile and exceptional areas at small expense to the Aztec lords. The domain of the Aztec Empire, therefore, consisted of both tributary and strategic (client) provinces (see Figure 1.1).

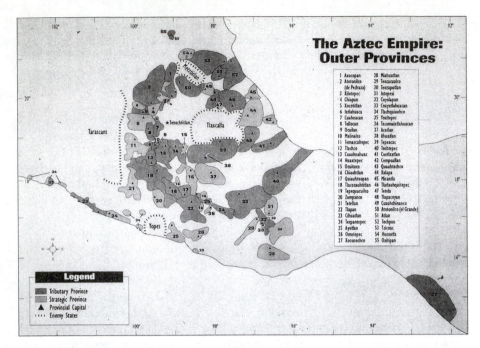

Figure 1.1 Map of the extent of the Aztec Empire on the eve of the Spanish conquest (Berdan et al. 1996, fig. A4–1, 324. Reproduced by permission of Dumbarton Oaks Research Library and Collection).

Despite these varied imperial strategies, unrest was rife in the empire, and unconquered groups such as the Tlaxcallans and Tarascans continued to foment rebellion and cause difficulties along contested borders. The Aztecs responded with the occasional replacement of a local ruler, the installation of imperial governors, and the establishment of military garrisons (ibid.).

Political and Territorial Organization: the Altepetl

The fundamental unit of political and territorial organization in central Mexico on the eve of the Spanish conquest was the *altepetl*. The term *altepetl* (literally, "water, hill") referred to the people occupying a particular territory, and also appears to have applied to the place itself (Lockhart 1992, 14). Best likened to a city-state, an altepetl was typically supported by a founding legend, patron deity, and legitimate ruling dynasty. Many altepetl also represented recognizable ethnic identities, were known for a specific occupational specialization or noteworthy market, or were famous as a pilgrimage destination. Typically, a city-state was structurally composed of a large community or city, divided into territorial subdivisions called *calpulli* or *tlaxilacalli*. Outlying communities were attached to the larger center, where the major administrative, economic, and religious activities of the city-state took place. These altepetl, with their subunits, served as the basic building blocks of Aztec political and territorial organization.

Social Stratification

Aztec society was decidedly hierarchical. The fundamental division between noble and commoner was based on divine prescription and hereditary rights. Rights of nobles included control over land and the commoners working those lands, access to exalted political positions, an elite education provided by the priesthood, and the several overt symbols of status such as residence in sumptuous palaces and prerogatives to wear exquisite clothing and elegant adornments of feathers, precious stones, and fine metals. The greatest among them were rulers of the land, high priests, military commanders, and high-ranking warriors. Nobles of lesser rank, also well educated, filled positions such as teachers, scribes, lower priestly ranks, and the myriad bureaucratic officials required of an expanding empire. Commoners, for their part, apparently could possess such expensive goods if they had sufficient economic means (Smith and Heath-Smith 1994), but apparently were at serious juridical risk if they wore such finery in public (Berdan 2005, 62). Commoners comprised the majority of the Aztec population: they tilled the soil, fished the lakes and rivers, and produced large quantities of utilitarian goods such as pottery, baskets, and stone implements. Residing at the bottom of the production pyramid, some of their surpluses were siphoned off as tributes to noble overlords or imperial rulers.

This brief characterization of Aztec social stratification suggests a rather static and easily delineated system. Quite to the contrary, this was a highly dynamic and complex set of social arrangements. Although social categories of noble and commoner appear to have been firmly and unequivocally established, there were means of mobility, both up and down the social ladder. All men were trained as warriors and any man might find himself on the battlefield. Valiant deeds, especially the capture of enemy warriors, gained that man specific social and economic rewards: rights to wear special cloaks and warrior costumes (see Figure 1.2). With the capture of four enemy warriors, a man was elevated to the ranks of the *tequiua*, a special grade of warriors who attended war councils and were eligible to serve in civil and military offices. Although commoners could achieve such a level, the highest positions were reserved for the nobility, who were also striving for acclaim with battlefield exploits. Another avenue for social mobility was commitment to the priesthood where special training provided the opportunity for advancement. As in the military realm, however, the highest positions again were the domain of the nobility. A third major opportunity for social advancement lay in the economic sphere. Successful commercial ventures enabled individuals to gain wealth beyond their social stations, creating ambiguous and uncertain situations in the social hierarchy. This was most obviously the case with the long-distance professional merchants (*pochteca*) and artisans of luxury goods (*toltecca*). Some of these ambitious individuals, working within the hierarchical framework of their occupational guilds, accumulated considerable wealth to the extent that they felt the need to conceal it from the established nobility (Sahagún 1950–82, 9:31). It is possible that the landed aristocracy viewed the emergence of a wealthy nonnoble class of people as threatening, although the Aztec rulers of Tenochtitlan (Mexica) esteemed these groups and granted them special rights, concessions, and responsibilities: the merchants served as

Figure 1.2 Aztec warriors were awarded specially designed cloaks and warrior costumes for their achievements (captures) on the battlefield (Berdan and Anawalt 1992, vol. 4, fol. 64r).

imperial spies and marketplace judges, and played dual roles as private entrepreneurs and state agents in their commercial treks. Luxury artisans provided the nobility with the very symbols of their exalted status, and had access to the royal treasure stores in producing their exquisite works. In its interest in assuring reliable supplies of status-linked preciosities, the imperial powers sometimes went to war over the assault or murder of their professional merchants in outlying regions; although after-the-fact actions, such responses by the state signaled political and military support of the merchants' endeavors.

Commerce

Life in 1519 central Mexico was highly commercialized. Virtually every need and desire could be purchased in the many marketplaces that characterized communities throughout the region. The Aztecs were not only accustomed to, but also apparently fond of, frequenting the markets. Attendance was essential not only to replace perishables and obtain other necessities and extras, but also to renew social relations and glean all the latest news and rumor of the land. From the vendor's point of view, markets provided a convenient and economically viable outlet for specialized production whether it be reed mats, fine feathers, wood products, herbs, or maize. The extent of commercialization in Aztec Mexico is affirmed by the presence of these bustling markets, the profitable ventures of professional long-distance and regional merchants, and the use of forms of money to facilitate transactions. Chief among these money forms was cacao, chocolate beans, providing a durable and low-value "denomination." Large white cotton cloaks served as higher value media of exchange, and as a standard of value and payment of debts. Overall, commerce in Mesoamerica on the eve of the Spanish conquest linked broad and diverse geographic and cultural regions into an extensive world system (Smith and Berdan 2003). Additionally, a wide range of cultural information accompanied the exchanges in material goods and was transmitted from group to group along these trade networks.

Religion

The Aztecs shared with other peoples of Mesoamerica an extensive and colorful pantheon of deities. Polytheistic religion was already well entrenched in central Mexico when the Mexica and other Nahuatl-speaking people arrived there in the thirteenth century. The Mexica had brought with them their patron deity Huitzilopochtli ("Hummingbird on the Left," or "Hummingbird of the South"), and readily adopted other deities from neighboring peoples. As they conquered city-state after city-state, they adopted those deities as well; by the time of the Spanish conquest their pantheon was well representative of the wide range of Mesoamerican gods and goddesses.

While the people of every city-state worshipped roughly the same range of deities, each such polity revered one particular god or goddess as its patron. Thus the Mexica of Tenochtitlan gave pride of place to Huitzilopochtli, the Tlaxcallans especially honored Camaxtli (a god of hunting), and Cholula had become famous as a pilgrimage site for the worship of Quetzalcoatl ("Feathered Serpent"). Similarly, each calpulli had its special temple and deity, as did specialized occupational groups and activities: the pochteca focused their ceremonies on the god Yacatecuhtli ("Nose-lord"), the metalworkers sacrificed to the god Xipe Totec ("Our Lord the Flayed One"), the midwives looked to the goddess Teteoinan ("Our Mother of Gods"), and the game of *patolli*[4] was overseen by the god Macuilxochitl ("Five Flower").

With as many as 200 named gods and goddesses (Smith 2003, 200), and with each deity requiring temples, ceremonies, and a cadre of priestly officials, it is easy to understand the extent to which religious activity permeated the daily life of the Aztecs and their neighbors. A temple was always in sight; the sounds, smells, and views of flamboyant ceremonies (often including human sacrifice) were continually in evidence; and participation in many rituals was required and universal. In addition, there was no separation of politics and religion here, no separation of church and state. Political and religious activities overlapped and melded into single purposeful events, encompassing both domestic and public spheres of social life.

These perpetual religious rituals were bolstered by a belief system grounded in fate and requiring an almost constant appeasement of the gods and goddesses through sacrifice. The Mexica in particular displayed an involvement in and active commitment to the maintenance of the universe and its repetitive cycles: they believed that propitiation and nourishment of the deities was required of them to ensure the continuation of a universe perpetually on the brink of destruction.

THE STAGE IS SET

Some of these Aztec institutions and practices did not seriously conflict with those the Spaniards employed as they established their imperial domain after 1521. There was much familiar to the conquered Aztecs in the new order: they and their subjects were no strangers to events of conquest and the entrenchment of new lords of the land. They were accustomed to either receiving or paying tribute, and their altepetl and calpulli, somewhat transformed, continued to serve as the political and territorial foundation of the Spanish administration. A strong social hierarchy was well entrenched in Aztec life, a concept clearly shared with Spanish social organization. Native commercial attitudes and inclinations fell quite readily into the Spanish commercial approaches. And religion was an all-pervasive feature of daily life, ordering the calendar and containing elaborate rituals that reinforced common beliefs and punctuated the daily round. In these broad generalities, then, the Aztecs found something of the familiar. Yet there was much that was both new and unexpected, and their lives were to become transformed by the relatively little things, such as the adoption of the chicken, to very large things indeed, such as the massive demographic trauma suffered from the ravages of unfamiliar contagious diseases.

NEW LORDS OF THE LAND

Cortés and the Spanish soldiers who accompanied him were not paid salaries for their efforts. Their rewards would come from a successful conquest and consequent booty, titles, and grants in the new land. Gold and souls were the banners, so it is not surprising that the first Spaniards to settle in New Spain were soldiers who received such rewards, and friars who came to spread Christianity to the native population. Both of these processes, the acquisition of gold and the enthrallment of souls, were already underway by Spaniards before the conquest was even complete: Cortés sought gold at every opportunity from all he met on his trek to Tenochtitlan, and his men bartered for it whenever they could get away with it (Díaz del Castillo 1963, 97). Similarly, the Spaniards before and during the conquest repeatedly attacked the native religion, at times instructing the natives in Christianity and at other times destroying idols and replacing them with images of the Virgin Mary and crosses (ibid., 62, 81, 83, 96, 237).

In the early years after the Spanish conquest, there were some patterns to the Spanish arrivals. First, they were almost exclusively male (although the notable exploits of María de Estrada as a conquistadora under Cortés should not be overlooked). It is estimated that in the period between 1520 and 1540, women constituted no more than one-seventh of the Spanish population in New Spain (Knight 2002, 110). Second, Spaniards were often attached to some formal bureaucratic or religious office. And third, they were normally granted rights to native labor, whether it involve entire communities given in *encomienda*[5] or labor drafts to build churches, public works, or estates.

Spanish men carrying other backgrounds, occupations, and goals also arrived in New Spain during the sixteenth century, some with wives and families. These included, for instance, farmers, herders, merchants, muleteers, entrepreneurs, and artisans. Yet even though some of these occupations required settlement in rural areas, the Spanish colonists uniformly preferred to live in cities. Although some of these attributes of the Spanish colonization (that is, urban preferences, government jobs, encomendero status) tended to detach them from the indigenous life around them, there were many points at which native and Spanish activities intersected. Whether directly or indirectly, the Aztecs as Spanish subjects now faced the need to deal with the requirements, expectations, and culture of the new lords of the land.

AZTECS TO NAHUAS: CONTINUITY AND CHANGE IN THE NEW ORDER

With conquest by the Spaniards, the Aztec Empire came to a sudden and dramatic end. The Aztec world of military dominance, with its concomitant avenues for social mobility, tribute support, and supply of sacrificial victims was suddenly over. A new order now prevailed, entailing familiar and unfamiliar aspects of life for both conquered and conqueror. Both natives and Spaniards coped with and adapted to these conditions with a mixture of creativity and stubbornness.

Emphasis in this chapter is on the adjustments the native peoples made to Spanish rule in New Spain.[6] At this point, it is reasonable to shift terminology, designating Aztecs as Nahuas (see Lockhart 1992, 1). They are the same people: but there is no longer an Aztec Empire, and while many aspects of life continued relatively unchanged, others became dramatically transformed. It would therefore be misleading to continue to refer to them as Aztecs after their conquest by Spain. Nahuas refers to Nahuatl-speaking peoples, who comprised the bulk of the indigenous population in the central valleys of Mexico during the first century of Spanish rule. True, there were also Otomí and other native groups, and their roles will also be considered here.

Demographic Disaster

Epidemic disease was sweeping the great city of Tenochtitlan even before it fell to the Spaniards and their allies. Cuitlahuac, imperial successor to Motecuhzoma Xocoyotzin, died of smallpox after only six months as *tlatoani*.[7] Famine accompanied the disease, as the Aztecs themselves reported: "There was death from hunger; there was no one to take care of another. . . ."(Sahagún 1950–82, 12:83). This same account states that the disease ravaged the city for 60 days, and then moved to other cities in the basin (ibid.).

During the first century of Spanish rule in New Spain, smallpox and other epidemic diseases—measles, influenza, and perhaps typhus—vented themselves in devastating waves on the native population (see Knight 2002, 21), which had no immunities to them. Successive epidemics from 1545 to 1547, 1576 to 1581, and 1629 to 1631 decimated the central Mexican native population, estimated at 13,839,000 at the time of contact (Denevan 1992, xxviii). Notwithstanding a number of somewhat conflicting calculations on population size and decline (see Borah and Cook 1963, Newson 1993, Sanders 1992, Whitmore 1992),[8] the disastrous loss of native people through disease and accompanying famine is undisputed. Indigenous survival was highest in the upland valleys and plateaus, and most precarious in the lowland tropical regions where some communities disappeared entirely. In the Basin of Mexico, current estimates of population loss range from one-half to five-sixths by less than 50 years after the conquest (Gibson 1964, 138). Some estimates for individual communities are illustrative: by 1563 Xochimilco in the southern Basin of Mexico had plummeted from 30,000 to between 6,000 and 7,000 inhabitants (ibid.); more than half the native population of Otumba in the northern Basin of Mexico died in the epidemic between 1576 and 1581 (Gerhard 1993, 208); and the community of Cuetlaxtlan in the Gulf Coast region of southern Veracruz plunged from an estimated 40,000 families at contact with approximately 800 to 900 tributaries[9] in 1560, to a mere 24 tributaries in 1569 (ibid., 342). For the Basin of Mexico itself, it is estimated that by the end of the 1576–1581 epidemic the Nahua population numbered a mere 200,000 people (Smith 2003, 281).

Such immense losses entailed not only physical and emotional strains, but social, economic, and political ones as well. The impact on daily life cannot be underestimated, especially in lowland regions where nearly entire communities disappeared, their few survivors seeking refuge in neighboring or more distant centers and possibly sacrificing their altepetl loyalties and ethnic identity in the process. In the more highly populated highland regions it was more feasible to retain basic social, economic, and political structures, although the impact was felt: for instance, lifetime political offices often ended prematurely and turned over frequently, and traditional nobles sometimes had difficulty maintaining sufficient laborers to work their lands[10] (Lockhart 1992, 32, 113).

The Altepetl and Cultural Identity

As the Aztec imperial structure disintegrated with the Spanish conquest, native political structure relied on its essential building block, the altepetl. This was not particularly novel, as the inhabitants of central Mexico had been basing their lives in these units for centuries (at least) prior to the Spanish arrival. Yet, with interminable conquests, these units were rarely autonomous, and were often required to answer to some more powerful authority. As administrative overlays, both Aztec and Spanish empires were structured to control and amass surpluses from their conquered polities; to manage this, each imposed somewhat different political arrangements on its subjugated populations.

Under Spanish rule, existing city-states provided the rough basis for parish delineations, encomienda grants, and the establishment of municipal governing councils (*cabildos*) in the Spanish manner. As a whole, these new institutions replaced the preconquest dynastic rulerships, and responsibilities of forming labor drafts, assessing and collecting taxes, overseeing public construction projects, maintaining order, and assuring spiritual well-being were transferred to the new lords and offices.

Encomiendas were grants awarded to privileged Spaniards and some high-ranking native nobles. Among the Nahua noble recipients was Tecuichpo, a favored daughter of Motecuhzoma (although other descendents of this ruler were not so fortunate). In 1526 she was granted Tacuba (formerly Tlacopan), along with some nearby villages and farms in encomienda: "By the late sixteenth century this was the largest surviving encomienda in the Valley of Mexico" (Thomas 1993, 594). Also by that time she had been married, successively, to three conquistadors.

The fortunate *encomendero,* Spanish or Nahua, received rights to the labor and tribute of native peoples occupying one or more city-states; therefore, the altepetl provided the basic territorial structure for this institution. Encomenderos, for their part, were required to offer protection and religious instruction (conversion to Christianity) to the people in their thrall. Tribute goods and labor owed to an encomendero may not have differed substantially from the demands of pre-conquest nobles on their commoner subjects: maize, chilies, salt, firewood, and household labor would have been familiar to the Nahuas; chickens sometimes replaced turkeys; occasionally payments in Spanish coin were also required. Beyond these demands, Nahua labor was also directed to agricultural labor and Spanish mining activities.

In pre-Hispanic times altepetl were in frequent competition with one another, forever engaging in ferocious wars or forming strategic alliances. Under Spanish dominion this style of competition ended, but nonetheless continued in a different form. Spanish courts were sometimes overwhelmed with native litigations over land rights and claims of hereditary territorial rights, often at the expense of their Nahua (or other ethnic) neighbors. In these external relations, as well as in internal affairs such as organizing labor drafts and maintaining order, the Spanish-style council or cabildo became a prominent altepetl institution. For the first century or so after conquest, the cabildo was the domain of traditional nobles, who struggled to maintain their traditional status and privileges. This was difficult, as they were pressured from above (by Spaniards) and threatened from below (by Nahua commoners).

In pre-Columbian as well as colonial times, ethnicity was used in contrasting one group to another, the "we" versus the "they." Before the arrival of the Spaniards, the altepetl typically provided the territorial contours for such designations. Even if members of neighboring communities also spoke Nahuatl and worshipped essentially the same pantheon of deities, subtle differences in dialect, dress, patron deity, founding myth, ritual, and other customs defined their loyalties. Although these altepetl distinctions continued in the early colonial period, new contrasts appeared. From the 1550s until the end of that century, Nahuas often referred to themselves as *nican titlaca* ("we people here"), and by around 1600, this term was basically supplanted by *macehualtin* (broadly defined as "human beings"). Though this term applied only to commoners in pre-Hispanic times, under colonial rule it came to refer to any native person (in contrast to a Spaniard, mestizo, or slave of African heritage), regardless of social station.[11]

Social Stratification: Disintegration Over Time

These erosions in the native social hierarchy resulted in a more homogeneous indigenous population by the end of the sixteenth century. Replacing the complex native hierarchy was an imported one, peopled by Spaniards. At the apex were the *Peninsulares,* Spaniards born in Spain and granted the highest political offices and favors. Peninsulares included "educated clergymen, genteel professionals, and high-ranking administrators of honorable descent and impressive political connections" (Berdan 2005, 188). Below them in social station were the *Criollos*, Spaniards born in New Spain and eligible for less exalted positions in the colonial administrative and religious world. Although denied the highest positions, many Criollos nonetheless became wealthy through agricultural, ranching, mining, and commercial ventures.

With the arrival of comparatively few Spanish women in the colony, many Spanish men acquired native wives and mistresses. Often these native women were of noble lineage and heiresses in their own right; their extensive dowries, often in land, made them particularly attractive as marriage partners (Carrasco 1997, 92). Whatever their social station, the offspring of these unions, *mestizos,* occupied a variable and often ambiguous social position in the colony during the first century after the conquest. Similarly, the relatively few African slaves in central Mexico frequently merged with the Spanish population; the most common unions were Spanish men with black women. As with mestizos, the social position of these children depended primarily on personal circumstances. Individuals of "mixed blood" in New Spain are described in some documents as troublemakers and indigent (Gibson 1964, 147), and even as "the lame, the destitute, the abandoned" (Lockhart 1976, 112), highlighting their ambiguous status.

While the Nahua social ladder was becoming compressed, its occupants were also being acculturated into the Spanish scheme of things. Early on some native elite were allowed to retain some of their titles and perquisites, but as time wore on they became "governors," obtained tribute through encomienda awards, and were granted Spanish-style privileges, such as carrying swords or riding horses with saddles and bridles (Gibson 1964, 155). Other cultural features associated with the native hierarchy were virtually dissolved: heredity gradually disappeared as a basis for rulership, elaborate native dress no longer symbolized rank or achievements, polygyny was no longer permitted as a perquisite of the aristocracy (or of anyone, for that matter), and success on the battlefield ceased to serve as a means of social mobility. Most of these changes affected the elite; the familiar and traditional life of the commoners exhibited greater persistence and tenacity.

None of these social levels existed in a vacuum. It was indeed the case that all, individually and generally as a group, had opinions of and interacted with the others. So, for instance, the Peninsulares considered the Criollos to be "innately lazy, effete, irresponsible, and lacking in both vigor and intelligence," and the Criollos attributed "arrogant, hypocritical, and rapacious" behavioral characteristics to the Peninsulares (Meyer and Sherman 1979, 207). On another dimension, although Spaniards generally occupied higher social status than Nahuas, this does not mean that their relationships were necessarily predictable. Take, for instance, the town council of Tlaxcalla: in the mid-sixteenth century this cabildo placed its valuable sheep herd in the hands of a Spaniard who agreed (by contract) to increase the herd's size. The council agreed, sternly, to renew his contract only if he was successful (Lockhart, Berdan, and Anderson 1986, 42, 56). Here the Spaniard was in the employ of Nahuas, and indeed under their close scrutiny. Social life is rarely (if ever) neat and tidy.

Occupations and Commerce

Preconquest Aztec occupations underwent certain transformations after 1521. Some specialized enterprises, particularly those luxury crafts geared toward native noble consumers, were short lived. Some of the esteemed featherworkers, whose artistry adorned palaces, temples, nobles, and valiant warriors, faced early unemployment. Those who made their living by tying feathers into flowing creations found few new consumers. Yet the feather mosaic artists were able to adapt to Spanish needs. Their meticulous techniques were applied to a new style of mosaics, becoming transformed in conformity with the changes wrought by the conquest: indigenous objects and iconography were replaced by Christian objects and iconography. So mosaic shields and warrior costumes disappeared, to be replaced by miters, triptychs and crosses. Likewise, depictions of indigenous deities and other symbols yielded to Christian imagery. Even with these new adaptations, some of the traditional-style feather handiwork survived, perhaps as heirlooms: in 1566, don Julián de la Rosa, a nobleman of Tlaxcalla, willed the following ornate objects to his descendents: a shield with 200 quetzal plumes, a monkey of feathers with a pheasant's head device, a coyote's head headdress with a crest device, and more quetzal feathers (Anderson, Berdan, and Lockhart 1976, 50–51).

The goldworkers similarly needed to find new outlets for their skills. Because gold served as a monetary standard in Spain, many gold adornments were melted down—the gold, not the artistry, carried value.[12] Yet newly constructed churches throughout the colony required highly ornate goldwork. Like the featherworkers, the goldworkers found new outlets for their well-honed skills.

Other crafts continued more successfully with less stress, and certain specializations continued to be associated with their traditional centers of production: silverwork in Azcapotzalco, pottery in Cuauhtitlan, masonry and woodworking in Coyoacan and Xochimilco, and fine stonework and lacquer work in Texcoco (Gibson 1964, 350–351). Crafts such as these found both indigenous and Spanish consumers, and as new styles and objects appeared, and metal tools became more common, Nahua artisans could nonetheless draw on materials and techniques developed long before the Spanish arrival and continue to produce these objects at least for another few generations.[13]

The Spanish market, generally speaking, did profoundly impact some areas of the indigenous economy. For instance, the tiny cochineal insect (which thrived on the pads of the prickly pear cactus) produced a deep red dye that became the rage in Europe. Its high demand made intensified output very attractive to the Nahua, who previously had produced the dye for indigenous consumption. In Tlaxcalla during the mid-sixteenth century, this developed into something of a social crisis: the native nobles of the town council decried the perceived deleterious effects of excessive (successful) cochineal production on the part of commoners of the town:

> And he who belonged to someone no longer respects whoever was his lord and master, because he is seen to have gold and cacao. That makes them proud and swells them up, whereby it is fully evident that they esteem themselves only through wealth (Lockhart, Berdan, and Anderson 1986, 81).

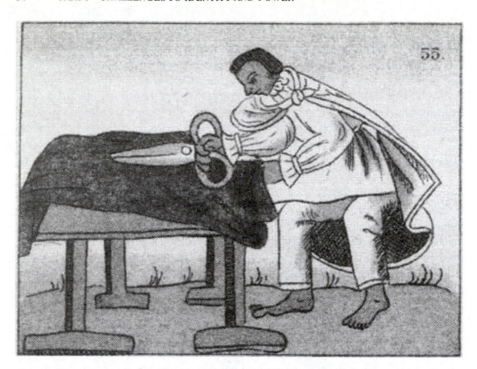

Figure 1.3 A native tailor in colonial times, using Spanish-introduced scissors. Observe the indigenous cape over the Spanish-style tunic and trousers (Sahagún 1950–82, Book 10, ill. 55. Reproduced by permission of University of Utah Press).

The nobles of this council continued this tirade about the "rise of the commoners," obviously threatened that these ambitious individuals were encroaching on their traditional perquisites, and feeling "themselves very grand because of it" (ibid., 82). In point of fact, these commoners were taking advantage of a new opportunity to gain wealth and the trappings of higher social position within their native community.

Specialized occupations that Spaniards brought to New Spain faced early competition from Nahua artisans, who learned the new trades quickly. According to Motolinía (1950, 241–242), the "skill and great cleverness of the Indians" allowed them to readily acquire skills as blacksmiths, tailors, saddlers, and in tooling leather, fashioning Spanish-style musical instruments, making silver cups, and manufacturing shoes of all kinds. The Nahua were apparently not hesitant about grasping these opportunities, and applying their traditional knowledge to new materials and objects (see Figure 1.3).

The highly commercialized economy of Aztec times provided a familiar context for adapting to the highly commercialized economy of the Spanish empire. The marketplace, or *tianquiztli*, remained a community's economic and social hotspot, continuing to perform its economic and social functions much as in pre-Hispanic times. Some adjustments did need to be made. If markets rotated among communities on a five-day basis, this system now faced a seven-day week. The most common solution was to retain the original five communities and allow two of them an extra market under the new calendrical system. It must have seemed odd to the Nahuas at first, yet was a boon to the favored towns. And marketplaces now contained a mix of native and Spanish wares, and in the colonial period served as the most widespread and effective means for moving goods from person to person. The consumer, in addition to seeing the customary reed mats, maize, and herbal remedies, also encountered Spanish goods such as candles, shirts, chicken eggs, and guitars (Lockhart 1992, 187–188). As in preconquest times, vendors and consumers came from near and far, and represented all rungs of the social ladder. Spanish coin also changed hands in these markets, often side-by-side with cacao beans, which long continued in use as a medium of exchange.

As the Aztec Empire collapsed and its political framework toppled, so too did the favored long-distance merchants, the pochteca. Although they no longer gained material wealth and political favor from an imperial head, they nonetheless had a history of successful entrepreneurship and a few such groups apparently retained some corporate status after the conquest and still engaged in extensive trade into the latter half of the sixteenth century:

> Indian merchants of the Valley of Mexico, Tlaxcala, and Cholula went on long expeditions, particularly to the south, to bring back tropical fruit, cacao, feathers, and other regional specialties, much in the manner of their predecessors (Lockhart 1992, 192).

A handful of others appeared clearly as traders, but their orbit of exchange and the relatively low value of their wares suggest that, even if they had been pochteca in the past, they were more like regional merchants now.

Taking Advantage of New Things and Ideas

The Spanish conquistadors had not yet moved inland when they had already taught the local native people how to make candles from beeswax found broadly in the countryside[14] (Thomas 1993, 213). This was possibly the first of a long list of novel material things and abstract ideas to greet the native peoples as the Spaniards entrenched themselves in New Spain. Long before Spanish rule, the Aztecs were accustomed to encountering new objects and ideas and incorporating them into their own material and symbolic repertoire. Now, as Nahuas, they brought forth that same tradition, ability, and adeptness in dealing with the Spanish novelties. Indeed, their adeptness was demonstrated in a native illustration of events of the Spanish conquest, in which an Aztec warrior was depicted wielding, quite expertly it would seem, a Spanish sword obtained from a Spanish casualty (see Figure 1.4; Sahagún 1950–82, 12: ill. 126).

Some of the most basic Spanish introductions fell into the realm of subsistence: new crops[15] such as wheat, grapes, sugarcane, and a variety of fruits; livestock such as cattle, horses, donkeys, mules, goats, sheep, domesticated pigs, and chickens; technologies such as iron machetes and the practical use of the wheel[16] in vehicles, the potter's wheel, and the spinning wheel. All of these were new, or at least new applications, to the Nahuas.

The arrival of these foodstuffs and technologies was met with variable enthusiasm by the native peoples. In general, the Spanish crops favored the Spanish

Figure 1.4 An Aztec warrior wields a Spanish sword during the conquest (Sahagún 1950–82, Book 12, ill. 126. Reproduced by permission of University of Utah Press).

palate, and the Nahuas continued to prefer their familiar diet of maize, beans, chilies, and squashes. Raising livestock, especially the larger animals, was most typically a Spanish endeavor throughout the sixteenth century; the Nahuas demonstrated little interest in raising cattle (and the entailment of a fairly large capital investment may have also been an inhibiting factor), and they were also faced with restrictions on their use of horses[17] and in the sizes of other animal herds.[18] Nonetheless, there were some significant adoptions. Chief among these was the chicken, whose resemblance to the native turkey most certainly facilitated its ready adoption by the Nahuas and their neighbors. Sheep were also somewhat popular, particularly for their wool. The sheep themselves were (and are today) called *ichcatl* ("cotton") in Nahuatl, and the wool was treated in a manner parallel to the well-known cotton fibers: wool was spun on a familiar spindle with whorl (although larger than that used for cotton), and the resulting thread was woven on a backstrap loom akin to the ones used for cotton weaving (see Figure 1.5). Although sheep and their wool became integrated into the

© Frances F. Berdan

Figure 1.5 Wool (a Spanish introduction) warped on a backstrap loom (a pre-Hispanic technology). Wool thread spun on a native spindle rests in a basket.

material lives of the Nahuas, the Spaniards for their part established commercial *obrajes* or textile workshops (with decidedly unpleasant working conditions), where wool was spun on spinning wheels and woven on large treadle looms. Here, then, were parallel production systems of the same item for different consumption goals of Nahuas and Spaniards.

There were some serious consequences of these livestock and crop introductions. One of the most significant was the appropriation of lands, previously the domain of traditional Nahua agriculture, to the cultivation of Spanish crops and livestock raising. At the same time, many Nahuas, owing labor to one or another Spanish encomendero, were expected to cultivate lands and work with animals in the Spanish manner—in this way they acquired a different set of skills. But the animals sometimes encroached on native fields, and the production of some crops for animal fodder meant less production for direct human (especially native) consumption.

Iron tools, indeed a wide variety of metal implements, came into ready and popular use among the Nahua. The multipurpose machete eased agricultural and other work considerably, and the Nahuas quite obviously saw its advantage over their traditional stone tools. The Spanish-style plough also arrived, but required draft animals and so early on was applied to Spanish agricultural production. Nonetheless, steel heads were manufactured for the traditional Nahua digging stick, or *uictli,* an essential farming tool still used today in some indigenous communities in Mexico. Similarly, Nahua artisans adopted implements such as metal knives and scissors as they undertook new occupations such as tailoring, at which they showed considerable facility.

Despite these adoptions, much of the material culture in Nahua homes retained much of its preconquest content: the Nahuas slept on reed mats, covered their houses with thatch, prepared maize with manos and metates, worked their fields with digging sticks and hoes, and walked to field and market. Nonetheless, any particular household could exhibit an interesting material eclecticism: one don Juan Tellez of Culhuacan (in the Basin of Mexico) included in his last will and testament some traditional baskets, old reed mats, gourd bowls, and colored cloth with rabbit fur, but also scissors, a lock, a green glass bottle, an axe, leather shoes, and white boots (Cline and León-Portilla 1984, 40–43). Clothing was another area where the old and the new formed special combinations. Spanish friars, "scandalized by the scanty attire of native men, insisted on the adoption of Spanish-style attire" (Berdan 1993, 187). Skimpy loincloths were replaced by trousers, and shirts and tunics came to replace the traditional cloak.[19] However, these elements were donned in every possible combination for several decades following the conquest. Women's clothing experienced less change, and many women continued to wear the preconquest-style tunic and skirt, although the Spanish-style blouse also became popular over time. In some areas, however, where it was common for women to wear rather revealing triangular shawls (*quechquemitl*), Spanish modesty insisted on the addition of a blouse underneath.[20]

In the material world, the Nahuas demonstrated an impressive persistence of indigenous inventions, materials, and styles, but also a canny ability to adopt new materials and objects and meld them with existing ones to fit their changing needs. They exhibited similar inventiveness and adaptability in the more abstract world of religious beliefs and rituals.

Religious Syncretism

Conflict over religious beliefs and rituals began early after the Spanish arrival. The Spaniards were unaccustomed to and at times horrified by indigenous ritual practices; indeed some of Cortés's conquistadors who observed human sacrifices said it was "the most terrible and frightful thing they have ever witnessed" (Cortés 1986, 35). Even before the conclusion of the conquest, the Spaniards had boldly thrown idols off temples, installed crosses and Christian images, forbade human sacrificial practices, and in general interfered with the ongoing religious celebrations of the Aztecs and their neighbors. It was not an auspicious beginning.

The two religions, Aztec and Christian, merged on several planes. Both believed in a sacred virgin birth, and both practiced some form of confession and baptism. Both had a professional cadre of priests, and both had centrally designated sacred places for worship. Yet there was also considerable divergence. Aztec religion was polytheistic, its pantheon inhabited by a wide range of colorful yet demanding deities. Christianity was monotheistic. Aztec religion was "accumulative," adding deities to its expanding pantheon as city-states were conquered or encountered on trading or diplomatic missions. Christianity was proselytizing, requiring conversion to a single god to the exclusion of others. Calendars of time generally and of religious events specifically were notably dissimilar, so the rhythms of sacred time followed different temporal rules. And there were more subtle conceptual differences as well: the nature of the afterlife, single or multiple world creations, free will versus fate, and the relationships between humans and the supernatural world. In this latter instance, the Aztec belief in their necessary involvement in maintaining world balance and cycles (especially through human sacrifice) contrasted sharply with the Christian notion of a deity independent of human support.

Christian Spain imposed an energetic spiritual conquest on its new colonies. This was the time of the Inquisition in Spain, so there was no lack of motivated religious practitioners to drive the goals of conversion. The people of New Spain, engaging in human sacrifice, practicing idolatry, and believing in a vast pantheon of "false gods" (to the Spanish mind) was fertile ground for the endeavors of friars and priests arriving in the sixteenth century.

Yet these conversion attempts were only partially successful, although the earliest friars exulted over their apparent successes. The native population readily accepted the Christian god, but on their terms: as expected, this god was assimilated into an expandable pantheon. The native gods were, for the most part, retained as well. Over time and under increased conversion pressure, the Christian god became more central; native deities, still not to be abandoned, became fused with the convenient repertoire of saints. This was particularly dramatic with the emergence of the Virgin of Guadalupe, a blending of the ancient mother goddess and the Virgin Mary. Assimilation of introduced rituals and beliefs into the native framework was the rule rather than the exception:

> Even where a relatively high degree of exposure to Christian teaching existed, it would have been fairly easy for the Nahuas to accept what appeared to be compatible with their own conceptions, and to ignore or reinterpret the rest. Despite the incorporation of many Christian elements, the belief system of the majority of Nahuas remained essentially untouched. (Burkhart 1989, 192)

The tenacity of the indigenous religion was found in numerous realms of ritual and belief. Many individuals continued to be named after the Aztec day of their birth, indicating a persistence of the native calendar and the fateful characteristics of its days. Patron saints supplanted patron deities, yet carried on the traditional patronage. Rituals themselves became syncretized: for example, in 1550 Tlaxcalla, the town council expressly prohibited its citizens from dancing about with feathers that were adorning a Christian litter and cross (Lockhart, Berdan, and Anderson 1986, 70–71). Obviously the citizens were doing just that.

Such blending of native and Christian elements in ceremonies and beliefs was the usual case in the dynamic realm of religion in sixteenth-century New Spain. Despite the rupture in their belief system and disjunction in their ritual rhythms, the Nahuas adhered as closely as possible to their ancient religious ways. A group of Nahua sages expressed this firm determination when confronting 12 Christian friars in 1524. Among their laments: ". . . allow us then to die, let us perish now, since our gods are already dead. . . ."; " . . . And now, are we to destroy the ancient order of life? . . ."; "We cannot be tranquil, yet certainly do not believe; we do not accept your teachings as truth, even though this may offend you. . . ." (León-Portilla 1963, 63–66).

CONCLUSION

Continuity and change, trauma and transition, adaptation and assimilation. Each of these terms accurately describes different consequences of the Spanish conquest on the native population of central Mexico during the sixteenth century. It is especially remarkable that among the conquered Nahuas there was considerable cultural persistence, even in the face of severe demographic collapse and new institutional impositions. Indeed, the first and most common response among the Nahuas was to maintain their cultural, social, economic, and religious frameworks, with the new Spanish introductions "being assigned to niches already existing in the indigenous cultural scheme" (Lockhart 1992, 202). This was the case in spheres of life ranging from the practical arena of household subsistence and marketplace transactions to the more symbolic and abstract realm of religion and worldview. In addition, Spanish political institutions were built on the fundamental structure of the altepetl, which continued to serve as a point of cultural and social reference for the Nahuas residing in them.

Yet these indigenous institutions, activities, and beliefs were nonetheless affected, in varying degrees, by the new lords of the land. In some cases novel traits initially slid rather smoothly into the existing patterns, such as the introduction of new commodities in the marketplaces, the application of metal tips to traditional digging sticks, or the addition of the chicken to the native diet. Initially too, the ready incorporation of the Christian god into the expansive Aztec pantheon fell into this pattern.

In other cases there were replacements, such as encomienda and cabildo control of native labor, in place of the ancient ruling dynasties. Yet the processes of labor drafts and tribute payments were not at all unfamiliar to the Nahuas. Over a longer span of time, other replacements became more obvious, such as the use of Spanish coin over cacao beans and cotton cloaks as money forms and the almost universal adoption of the machete as a multipurpose tool.

In still other instances, there emerged a blending of cultural forms, resulting in a remarkable tenacity of newly created cultural forms. This was nowhere more profound than in the religious sphere, where the vast Aztec pantheon of deities became fused with the numerous saints of the Catholic religion. But such blending also occurred at more mundane levels, such as the incorporation of wool onto hand spindles and backstrap looms, or the sacrifice of chickens in traditional rituals (see Sandstrom 1991).

There were also some redefinitions. Principal among these was the gradual erosion of the native social hierarchy. By the end of the sixteenth century, the Nahua nobility had effectively merged with other rungs of the indigenous ladder, essentially forming a more homogeneous social category beneath the hierarchical complexity of the Spanish colonial world. This becomes manifested in the emerging general use of the term *macehualli* to refer to all native peoples, not just commoners. And some redefinitions took perhaps unexpected turns. The definition of native clothing is one of these: today a Nahua man's traditional clothing is of Spanish colonial vintage, not pre-Hispanic.

In all of these patterns, the Nahuas demonstrated considerable ingenuity in retaining as much as possible of their ancestral way of life, and in effectively dealing with the incorporation and blending of those Spanish materials, customs, beliefs, and institutions either casually available or forcibly imposed. In some cases they had few or no choices, but in others they participated as active creators of new cultural forms, not simply passive recipients of an intrusive one.

REFERENCES

Anderson, Arthur J. O., Frances Berdan, and James Lockhart. 1976. *Beyond the Codices*. Berkeley: Univ. of California Press.

Berdan, Frances F. 2005. *The Aztecs of central Mexico: An imperial society,* 2nd ed. Belmont, CA: Wadsworth.

_____. 1993. Trauma and transition in sixteenth-century central Mexico. In *The meeting of two worlds,* ed. Warwick Bray, 163–195. Oxford: Oxford Univ. Press.

Berdan, Frances F., and Patricia Rieff Anawalt. 1992. *The Codex Mendoza.* 4 vols. Berkeley: Univ. of California Press.

Berdan, Frances F., Richard E. Blanton, Elizabeth Hill Boone, Mary G. Hodge, Michael E. Smith, and Emily Umberger. 1996. *Aztec imperial strategies*. Washington, D.C.: Dumbarton Oaks Library and Collections.

Borah, Woodrow, and Sherburne F. Cook. 1963. *The Aboriginal population of central Mexico on the eve of the Spanish Conquest*. Ibero-Americana 45. Berkeley: Univ. of California Press.

Burkhart, Louise M. 1989. *The slippery earth*. Tucson: Univ. of Arizona Press.

Carrasco, Pedro. 1997. Indian-Spanish marriages in the first century of the colony. In *Indian women of early Mexico,* eds. Susan Schroeder, Stephanie Wood, and Robert Haskett, 87–103. Norman: Univ. of Oklahoma Press.

Charlton, Thomas. 1972. Population trends in the Teotihuacan Valley, A.D. 1400–1969. *World Archaeology* 4:106–123.

Cline, S., and Miguel León-Portilla. 1984. *The testaments of Culhuacan.*

Los Angeles: UCLA Latin American Center Publications.

Cortés, Hernán. 1986. *Hernán Cortés: Letters from Mexico,* ed. and trans. Anthony Pagden. New Haven: Yale Univ. Press.

Denevan, W. M. 1992. *The native population of the Americas in 1492.* Madison: Univ. of Wisconsin Press.

Díaz del Castillo, Bernal. 1963. *The conquest of Mexico*. Baltimore: Penguin Books.

Durán, Diego. 1994. *The history of the Indies of New Spain,* ed. and trans. Doris Heyden. Norman: Univ. of Oklahoma Press.

Gerhard, Peter. 1993. *A guide to the historical geography of New Spain,* rev. ed. Norman: Univ. of Oklahoma Press.

Gibson, Charles. 1964. *The Aztecs under Spanish rule*. Stanford: Stanford Univ. Press.

Knight, Alan. 2002. *Mexico: The colonial era*. Cambridge: Cambridge Univ. Press.

Landa, Diego de. 1966. *Landa's relación de las cosas de Yucatan,* trans. Alfred M. Tozzer. Peabody Museum Papers. Vol. 18. Cambridge: Harvard University.

León-Portilla, Miguel. 1963. *Aztec thought and culture*. Norman: Univ. of Oklahoma Press.

Lockhart, James. 1976. Capital and province, Spaniard and Indian: the example of late sixteenth-century Toluca. In *Provinces of early Mexico,* eds. James Lockhart and Ida Altman, 99–123. Los Angeles: UCLA Latin American Center Publications.

_____. 1992. *The Nahuas after the Conquest*. Stanford: Stanford Univ. Press.

Lockhart, James, Frances Berdan, and
  Arthur J. O. Anderson. 1986. *The
  Tlaxcalan Actas: A compendium of
  the records of the Cabildo of
  Tlaxcala (1545–1627).* Salt Lake
  City: Univ. of Utah Press.
Meyer, Michael, and William L. Sherman.
  1979. *The course of Mexican history.*
  New York: Oxford Univ. Press.
Motolinía [Fray Toribio de Benavente].
  1950. *History of the Indians of New
  Spain.* Documents and Narratives
  Concerning the Discovery and
  Conquest of Latin America, ed. and
  trans. E.A. Foster. Berkeley: The
  Cortés Society.
Newson, Linda A. 1993. The
  demographic collapse of native
  peoples of the Americas, 1492–1650.
  In *The meeting of two worlds,* ed.
  Warwick Bray, 247–288. Oxford:
  Oxford Univ. Press.
Sahagún, Bernardino de. 1950–82.
  *Florentine Codex: General history of
  the things of New Spain.* 12 vols. Salt
  Lake City: Univ. of Utah Press.
Sanders, William. 1992. The population
  of the central Mexican symbiotic
  region, the basin of Mexico, and the
Teotihuacan Valley in the sixteenth
  century. In *The native population of
  the Americas in 1492,* ed. W. M.
  Denevan, 85–150. Madison: Univ. of
  Wisconsin Press.
Sandstrom, Alan. 1991. *Corn is our blood.*
  Norman: Univ. of Oklahoma Press.
Smith, Michael E. 2003. *The Aztecs,*
  2nd ed. Oxford: Blackwell.
Smith, Michael E., and Frances
  F. Berdan. 2003. *The postclassic
  Mesoamerican world.* Salt Lake City:
  Univ. of Utah Press.
Smith, Michael E., and Cynthia Heath-
  Smith. 1994. Rural economy in late
  postclassic Morelos: an
  archaeological study. In *Economies
  and polities in the Aztec realm,* eds.
  Mary G. Hodge and Michael E.
  Smith, 349–376. Albany, N.Y.:
  Institute for Mesoamerican Studies.
Thomas, Hugh. 1993. *Conquest:
  Montezuma, Cortés, and the fall of
  old Mexico.* New York: Simon and
  Schuster.
Whitmore, Thomas. 1992. *Disease and
  death in early colonial Mexico:
  Simulating Amerindian depopulation.*
  Boulder, CO: Westview Press.

NOTES

1. The Aztec Empire was headed by a tripartite alliance of three major Basin of Mexico peoples with their city-state capitals: the Mexica of Tenochtitlan, the Acolhua of Texcoco, and the Tepaneca of Tlacopan. It is also usual to find the term *Aztecs* used in specific reference to the Mexica, the most powerful member of the alliance. Because these people and many of their neighbors spoke the Nahuatl language, they are frequently referred to as Nahua in the postconquest setting.

2. Mesoamerica is a culture area extending from northcentral Mexico, south into Honduras and El Salvador, and stretching from the Gulf to the Pacific coasts. In the most general terms, it is characterized as an area of sedentary agriculture that exhibited the rise and fall of high civilizations.

3. Several important cultigens were produced in lowland or coastal regions, some of which the empire controlled. Especially important were cacao (for both the chocolate drink and as money), cotton, and a variety of fruits and sea products (see especially Durán 1994, 204–206). A good amount of time and energy was also devoted to the cultivation of flowers, in both highland and lowland regions, highlighting the important role of flowers in the endless cycle of religious rituals. Maguey, a dependable highland plant, provided a fermented drink (*pulque*) and fibers for clothing and netting. The people of Mesoamerica had few animal domesticates, among which the most prominent were the turkey and the dog, both used for food.

4. *Patolli* was a game played much like pachisi.

5. An *encomienda* was a grant of native labor and tribute, usually based on an existing altepetl structure. The *encomendero,* almost always a Spanish grantee, was obligated to protect and convert the natives in their encomienda (Lockhart 1992; Knight 2002, 14).

6. New Spain was the Spanish administrative designation for central Mexico.

7. Literally, *tlatoani* means "speaker." It was imperative that rulers be eloquent orators, hence their title. The plural is *tlatoque*.

8. The problem is complicated by the fact that these and other scholars use different sources, criteria, and methods for their calculations; they also deal with different areal dimensions (for example, Basin of Mexico, central Mexico—vague designations at best).

9. Tributaries were typically heads of households, so the comparison with families here is reasonable.

10. Lockhart relates a case in point: "In Tetzcoco in 1589, a noble widow complained that her late husband's scattered lands could no longer be cultivated because none of the dependents who worked them were left; all had died" (1992, 113).

11. Despite this more generalizing process, local-level overt expressions of ethnic identities are still obvious in Nahua and other indigenous communities today.

12. Even as the Spaniards were besieged in Tenochtitlan, before the Noche Triste, they were frenetically melting down golden treasure into ingots they could carry around their waists as they attempted their escape from the city.

13. Thomas Charlton (1972, 111) has uncovered archaeological instances of Aztec-style pottery in the city of Otumba in the northern Basin of Mexico into the 1600s, after which it eventually died out.

14. Beeswax was a significant trade item in Mesoamerica, especially among the Maya (Landa 1966, 94–95). It was used as an adhesive, in religious rituals, and in various medicinal concoctions.

15. Intrusive weeds such as thistles and bracken were also introduced from abroad (Thomas 1993, 593).

16. The concept of the wheel is ancient in Mesoamerica: wheeled toys or ritual objects in the shapes of various animals have been uncovered from Classic-period Veracruz sites. Yet the wheel was never set to more practical uses: the lack of beasts of burden most likely inhibited the development of wheeled vehicles, and spinning and pottery making already had tried and true technological devices.

17. Like so many rules (in cultures generally), these restrictions were not followed rigidly. So we find, in 1581 Culhuacan, separate cases of a Nahua man and a Nahua woman, each willing a horse to his/her descendents (Cline and León-Portilla 1984, 152–153, 188).

18. In the late sixteenth century, the legal limit for herds managed by native entrepreneurs was set at 250 goats and 300 sheep; nonetheless, some of these natively managed herds numbered in the thousands (Gibson 1964, 345).

19. In his earliest encounters with the indigenous peoples, Hernán Cortés presented many Spanish shirts to native men, who became familiar with these Spanish fashions early on (Díaz del Castillo 1963, 58, 94).

20. It is interesting to note that, today among Nahuas of the Sierra Norte de Puebla in eastern Mexico, the symbols of "Indianness" include clothing that is not pre-Columbian, but rather derived from colonial times. Thus, the native man's *traje* consists of white shirt and trousers, and the native women's costume requires an embroidered blouse, built on the sixteenth-century Spanish model. However, this latter is combined with a preconquest-style skirt and a mound of colored hair cords that have no parallel in colonial Spanish or modern Mexican fashion.

Fieldwork Biography
William and Jean Crocker

William Crocker is emeritus curator for South American ethnology in the Smithsonian Institution's Department of Anthropology (NMNH). He first went to the Canela of Central Brazil in 1957 in pursuit of his doctorate in cultural anthropology from the University of Wisconsin. The Canela adopted Bill into their tribe, where he now has great-great-nieces and -nephews in his adoptive family. The Canela have been the focus of Bill's research throughout his anthropological career, during which he has accumulated 74 months of fieldwork with them. Jean Crocker, a former secondary school English teacher, married Bill in 1987 and collaborates with him in his writing projects. In this photograph, Bill has been honored by Canela elders who have painted him with red resin and decorated him with white duck down.

2/Change in the Lives of a Brazilian Indigenous People
To Pluck Eyelashes (or Not?) among the Canela

The Canela Native Americans of Brazil inhabit "closed savannahs" (*cerrados*), a terrain including grasses with small bushes and trees usually spaced far enough apart to let a horse or even a jeep pass between them. These sandy savannahs cannot be cultivated by methods available to the Canela. In their area, thick tropical foliage lines six small streams that run parallel to each other from south to north. There are no rivers. Only in these stream-edge forests can the Canela prepare farms, through the same simple "slash-and-burn" procedures that have constituted a worldwide form of horticultural survival in tropical regions for both early and current human societies. Aboriginally, the Canela relied on stone tools for gardening sweet potatoes, corn, yams, peanuts, and bitter manioc but only to a small extent—maybe for 20 percent of their

Festial boys in plaza received meat on leaves, with part of the village circle of houses in background.

subsistence. More important to them was their hunting, fishing, and food collecting (gathering the seeds, fruits, and edible roots of the region when in season). Such an unreliable form of subsistence requires the control of an extensive area of land, maybe 5,000 square miles in the Canela case, essentially from the Corda to the Itapicuru rivers. Endemic warfare and individual revenge between tribes contributed to the precariousness of this existence. During surprise raids, one tribe killed as many men, women, and children of the other tribe as possible in the heat of battle. The Canela adaptation to these uncertain conditions involved sharing almost everything—possessions, food, sex, and identity—so that individuals lived more for the good and the survival of the tribe than for themselves.

Thus, when the Canela lost 95 percent of their lands to the Brazilian pioneers settling their area during the early part of the 1800s, they had to adapt their gardening to the more intensive form of slash-and-burn farming that Brazilians used with their metal axes, machetes, and hoes. The Canela converted from being basically food collectors—foraging an extensive countryside for their survival—to being largely food producers—growing various crops on large farms. Nevertheless, they retained the aboriginal practices of sharing everything even though they had left behind the precarious aspects of living—their intertribal warfare and their high dependency on food gathering. They continued their extraordinary practices of extramarital sex-sharing well into the 1980s, when the influx of material goods made them less willing to be generous in this way.

The Canela today manifest many indicators of culture change—change in the direction of the Brazilian culture. There has been change in the style of houses, for instance. Before pacification, the Canela lived in oval palm-thatch huts with pointed tops made of poles, like the tepees of the American Plains Indians. However, by the 1840s, they squared their thatched houses like the Brazilian settlers. By 1900, they used dried mud and sticks to form some of the walls of their huts, but these dwellings were still largely made of palm thatch, especially the roofs. By 2000, the Canela were baking clay bricks in the sun with which to build some of their walls, and now a few of them have concrete floors and red-tile roofs like urban Brazilians. Aboriginally, the Canela went naked, but by 1910 women started wearing wraparound cloth skirts and by 1963 men felt they had to wear shorts or pants. Personal adornment also has changed over the decades. Both sexes let their head hair grow long, but cut a horseshoe pattern running horizontally from the forehead to the occipital region, leaving the back part uncut. However, since the 1950s employees of the federal Indian service have usually cut their hair like Brazilians and most Europeans. This adaptation signified that they were aligning themselves with Brazilian culture, but only to a small extent.

In sharp contrast, abandoning the ancient practice of plucking the facial hair surrounding the eyes signifies that an individual is turning to Brazilian culture to a very significant extent. To this day, almost all Canela pluck their eyebrows and eyelashes, a custom that is distasteful to Brazilians. Nevertheless, a few Canela these days let their eye hair grow out, much to the consternation of most other Canela, who see this lapse as a kind of betrayal of the Canela cultural stance in their continuing struggle to preserve their identity—as a special people—against the overwhelming onslaught of Brazilian cultural life. To pluck, or not to pluck, eye hair raises the question of being Indian or not. It demonstrates publicly one's cultural stance by a deformation of one's face that may be felt to be "unnatural." Cutting head hair with scissors is an act that is easy to perform, involving no pain. However, plucking eyelashes has to be somewhat painful, or at least unpleasant, and even messy, so it is more of a sacrifice and therefore more of a statement.

This chapter, while examining other indicators of change, will furnish data and examples to facilitate the understanding of this highly emotional, and currently crucial indicator of change—the plucking, or not plucking, of eye hair. We present culture change largely through the lives of individuals. In contrast, the chapter's summary presents general factors in change from early to current times.

Bill is the field anthropologist and Jean was a teacher of English literature for over 20 years. Thus, Bill writes the chapter for his scientific colleagues, and then Jean reworks it thoroughly for lay and student readers. We will use the pronoun "I" to relate Bill's experiences in the field.

I first went to the Canela in 1957 to gather data for my doctoral dissertation at the University of Wisconsin at Madison. I chose the Canela Native Americans because I wanted to build on the excellent study already done on the tribe; I thought this would be the best way to study cultural change through a significant length of time. This previous study, called *The Eastern Timbira* (1946a), was

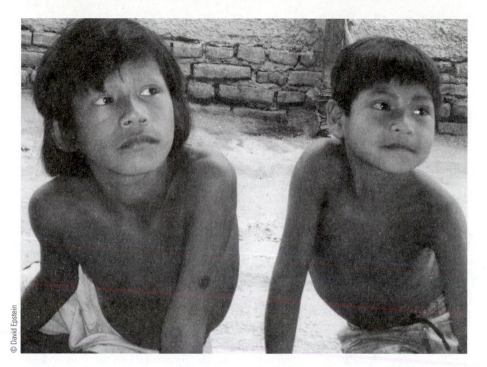

© David Epstein

Two Canela boys as students in the city, one with plucked eye hair and Canela haircut, the other with eye hair and city haircut.

written by Curt Nimuendajú, the foremost Brazilian anthropologist of the first half of the twentieth century. He had spent 14 months among the Canela between 1929 and 1936, so I was picking up his study of the Canela 21 years later. Employment by the Smithsonian as a research curator-scientist in 1962 made possible my repeated returns to the Canela over the years—21 visits in all, totaling 74 months in their villages. Besides a number of professional articles, the principal products of this long-term fieldwork have been a basic monograph in 1990, a video with Stephen Schecter in 1999, a website with Barbara Watanabe in 2003, and the second edition of a case study in the Spindler series with Jean Crocker in 2004.

I feel that the conditions of living among the Canela have been excellent, if not ideal, for an ethnologist. A Canela family adopted me in 1957, so every time I return I go back to the same family where I now have great-great-nieces for whom to bring toys. I go during their dry season, July through September, when the weather is mild and the mosquitoes are nonexistent. Besides my adoptive family, I have a team of 10 Canela who record diaries on audiotape and send them to me in the United States through my agent in Barra do Corda. This team of diarists keeps me up-to-date with news from the Canela for the long-term study and provides a set of well-oriented research assistants who can facilitate my research during each field visit. Three young men started writing these diaries for me in 1964. One wrote in Canela with a translation in Portuguese—a

Rosetta stone to help me learn their language. In 1970, two Canela started speaking on tape for me, and the practice continues to this day. In this chapter, I will use translated selections from recently received diaries to give the reader a sense of the involvement of Canela individuals in the cultural changes through which they are living today.

THE CANELA TODAY

The 1,400 Canela still speak a language classified as Gê, the second largest indigenous language family of Brazil, to which the languages of better-known tribes such as the Krahô, Apinayé, Xavante, and Kaingang also belong. Tupi, by far the largest indigenous language family of Brazil, includes the language of the Guajajara Indians (also known as the Tenetehara),[1] who are geographical neighbors of the Canela, living just north of them in the dry forests.

The Canela reservation is about 1,200 square miles. It lies close to 45 degrees west longitude and 6 degrees south latitude, near the center of the state of Maranhão, about 400 miles southeast of the mouth of the Amazon River. This location is east of the Amazon watershed by about 100 miles. The waters of the area flow north and enter into the Atlantic Ocean by São Luis, the state capital. The reservation is about 40 miles south of the city of Barra do Corda (population 55,000), but politically the Canela village of Escalvado lies in the neighboring *município* (township) of Fernando Falcão (population 5,000). The agency of the federal government called the FUNAI (National Foundation of the Indian), which we will refer to as the Indian service,[2] set up this reservation for the Canela between 1971 and 1982. During these years, the Indian service built a number of substantial buildings of cement and brick with red-tile roofs to help support the Canela—to give them needed encouragement. Currently, the Indian service employs seven Canela, employment that spreads significant income to their extended families. This infusion of wealth through the decades sets them apart and above many other families, and forms the basis for incipient classes. The medical agency of the federal government, the FUNASA (National Foundation of Health), which we will call the national health agency, has provided services since about 1998. Those services include visiting doctors and nurses, two resident nursing assistants, an ambulance on call in Barra do Corda by two-way radio, and the employment of three Canela. The national health agency put in a deep artesian well in 2001, so by 2003 most houses in the village had water faucets next to them.

The Canela village, Escalvado, is structured in the aboriginal way. The round central plaza, about 50 yards in diameter, serves as the meeting place for men, although both men and women sing, dance, and participate in ceremonies there. Straight pathways radiate some 100 yards out from the plaza to the family houses, which lie just beyond a circular boulevard about 20 yards wide. When seen from the air, a Canela village looks like a giant wagon wheel some 300 yards across: the plaza is the hub; the radial pathways, the spokes; the boulevard, the wheel's rim; and the houses, the studs on the wheel. The circle of houses constitutes the women's world, where they raise children and prepare food in extended family units. The village lies between two streams, which are used for bathing and washing clothes.

Between half a mile and 20 miles out from Escalvado in every direction, but mostly east and west, lie the family farms. Each woman over 16 or 18 years of age must have her own farm that her husband prepares and both genders cultivate. Near these family farms, clusters of houses form small villages in six to 10 regions of the reservation, depending on the year. However, 75 percent of the population spends much of its time in two large farm villages structured like Escalvado.

The Canela experienced four drastic messianic movements during the years 1963, 1980, 1984, and 1999, which they hoped would solve their economic problems through supernatural means and shamanistic transformations. During these movements, prophets predicted the ending of the world in different ways each time, with the Canela being saved only if they danced, sang, and carried out prescribed practices. Of course, these movements failed. In contrast, by 2003, the Canela had turned back to a more pragmatic reliance on extensive slash-and-burn agriculture, leaving behind their tendency to trust in supernatural solutions. Currently, the younger generations and even the elders of the tribal council have come to believe that their economic salvation and cultural solutions lie in formal Brazilian education. They hope that school graduates will return to the village and manage it well through their education, so that the outsiders will not be able to fool and cheat them any more. During August 2003, some 200 children and adolescents attended the first four grades in the village school, while about 30 children, adolescents, and adults attended four schools in Barra do Corda between the second and tenth grades. Approximately 80 Canela spouses, siblings, parents, and children lived in the Altamira suburb of Barra do Corda to accompany and support these students. Some parents attended the upper grades while their children studied in the lower grades. The most extreme cultural changes took place among the children, raised in the city away from their culture in the village. Some of them did not want to pluck out their eyelashes and eyebrows anymore—the most emotion-laden marker of Canela identity—because they had become ashamed of their culture and because they were afraid that their classmates would tease them.

SOME BACKGROUND TO THE CURRENT CANELA SITUATION

The Canela's ancestors, Timbira Indians, lived in groups of 1,000 to 1,500 people, or even 2,000, some experts hypothesize. Some 40 Timbira nations or tribes may have existed, spread out between the Tocantins and Parnaíba rivers and beyond to the east. Some Timbira nations raided each other seasonally; others formed loose alliances.[3] They subsisted largely on food collecting and only to a small extent on slash-and-burn gardens, which they established along the edges of streams and rivers, using stone axes. War and the uncertainties of hunting and gathering made existence precarious, so sharing almost everything, even their sexuality, was essential for survival. They traded between nations (tribes) minimally, mostly to obtain ceremonial items.

A Portuguese military expedition may have contacted the Canela's ancestors as early as 1694,[4] but contacts with outsiders began to have serious effects on their way of life beginning around 1780. Settlers from the east bringing cattle from Bahia state and farmers from the north around São Luis invaded the Canela area, driving them northwest into their hills for safety.[5] In 1814, decimated by the Cakamekra, a neighboring Timbira tribe, the Canela survivors surrendered to a military garrison at Pastos Bons.[6] During 1816, smallpox killed most of the Timbira people, and some time before 1838 the survivors of three Timbira tribes joined the Canela. The local ranchers and farmers allowed the Canela and their adherents to settle permanently in the northwestern corner of the Canela's former lands around 1838. Because the Canela had lost 95 percent of the land that they needed as hunters and gatherers, they had to shift from their old economic emphasis to more intensive slash-and-burn farming. They took over axes, machetes, and shotguns from the settlers and proceeded to adapt to their new style of life relatively successfully, though their values even to this day are not well suited to farming.

Between about 1838 and 1938, the Canela experienced 100 years of relative peace and development. However, as warfare and raiding disappeared, the need to train for it lost its rationale and internal changes gradually increased.[7] Elders began to lose their military control over the youths. In 1938, the federal Indian service (The Indian Protection Service) sent an agent and his family from Barra do Corda to live among the Canela to help protect them from the backland ranchers. These federal "intruders," though meaning well, further reduced the chiefs' and elders' authority and effectiveness as leaders. The economic system, which had depended on commands from these leaders, fell apart, and since 1947, the Canela have been economically dependent on the Indian service and other outsiders.

The Wycliffe Bible Translators maintained a missionary couple among the Canela between 1968 and 1990. They translated the New Testament and some Old Testament stories and left a much better understanding of the value of money and of buying and selling, including bargaining. However, the Canela never learned to put these new ideas into practice very well. The merchandise that the missionaries and the Indian service personnel brought in to trade for Canela artifacts seduced the Canela into believing that they had to have quantities of pots, pans, and household furniture. These items were too valuable to simply share or give outright to others, so the Canela began losing their generous ways of cooperation that had served them so well in earlier times, including the extensive sharing of each other in their extramarital sex system.[8] They were becoming "stingy" in their sharing of food and sex, just like the outsiders they had hated so much for this very characteristic. They changed from a society based on the commands of respected traditional leaders to a society based on money. By the 1980s, and certainly by the year 2000, no one would do anything significant for the chief or the elders unless these leaders paid them well for the service. However, the chief and the elders had no source of money to get tasks accomplished for the good of the whole, as the mayors of the broncos or "white"[9] communities had through taxation.

Taxation is the obvious answer for Canela leaders to regain their influence, and they have tried this way of raising money. The people do not trust the leaders, however, because such funds have "always" been diverted, they say, to purposes other than the intended ones. For instance, the leader's wife, nephew, or lover makes demands and the "generous" leader's resolve weakens so that he lends the money, which surely never returns to him. He finds it hard to be stingy. Some individuals will accuse him of spending the funds for his own purposes, whether or not he has allowed the funds in his charge to be diverted. Because the Canela do not like any leader to become too big, they must bring him down to average size, so such leaders invariably incur false accusations. The compulsions to share and to level political power reflect their earlier food-collecting values.

It is not that Canela families have too little money to make taxation possible. Most families have funds coming in from various government levels: national Indian service salaries, national health agency salaries, medical disability pensions, widow and widower benefits, maternity payments, child-in-school help, agricultural service retirement pensions, and social security. For reasons already described, these sources of income have not been amenable to taxation. Instead, they are used to support promising members of families, the young and those in their 30s—to get them through school, to help them to become future managers of the tribe. The Canela hope to solve the tribal problems in this way, instead of through messianic movements.[10]

I have always felt that the Canela are a dramatic and dynamic people, not small-minded and passive. They feel strongly about their future and are willing to take risks to shape it favorably. They are not fatalistic or blindly accepting. They believe deeply they deserve an economically rich future, which they have tried to bring about through messianic movements. In 1999, their mythical culture hero—originally named Awkhêê, but later conceptualized as Jesus—was to solve their economic problems forever in a manner that some might call magical, but I would term shamanic. This latest messianic movement devastated the Canela economically. Its leader, the younger Thunder, required them to abandon the planting of their crops and then dance and behave in traditional ways so that Jesus would come to their village to save them from a flood and bring them riches. Instead, Thunder brought them moderate hunger for almost two years due to the neglect of their fields. During 2000, the Canela turned passionately to their next movement to solve their problems: formal education in the world of the "whites." As the leader of the council of elders, Burnt Path, 63, spoke to me about his people in an October 2000 diary saying:[11]

> To know more about reading is the most important thing for them. They must have this road open so they cannot be left behind, isolated, like animals in the forest. . . . Parents and siblings must send their children to study and come to know things so that later they can learn professions and have the capacity to earn things.

This faith in education forms the framework for the most recent cultural changes in the individual stories to follow.

TRACING CULTURE CHANGE THROUGH INDIVIDUALS

The purpose here is to reveal problems of adjustment to cultural change through the stories of individual Canela—through my observations and through their own words. Selected Canela tribe members have been keeping diaries for me since 1964, first as written manuscripts and now as two-hour monthly talks on tape. Sometimes they become quite personal and almost confessional.

Three of these diarists as well as two other Canela clearly demonstrate the stresses of change. I will briefly introduce these five individuals.

Upon my return to the tribe in 2003, Khay-yalíya, or Basket Lifter, was becoming a small-time entrepreneur in a Canela world that had not previously practiced serious bargaining. In addition to adopting Brazilian commercial methods, she ensured that her son appeared acceptable to whites by refusing to pluck his eyelashes and eyebrows.

Pàl-tèy, or Hard Bed, the first Canela to marry a white city dweller, could not carry out his very important role as the first Canela Indian service post agent. Hard Bed could not live at the post with his family, because his wife refused to stay there.

Lo-'ti-'pôl, or Anaconda,[12] was elected by the Canela in 2002 as their first political representative to the municipality (township) of Fernando Falcão, the *município* in which the Canela reservation lies, but he could not communicate well enough with the mayor or with the other township representatives to be effective. He could not bring the "trophies" back to the Canela that they expected and wanted, such as better roads, electricity, and funds for projects.

Ângelo Carampei[13] wanted to train for modern skills, but was deeply distressed by the clash between Canela values of sharing and the modern cash economy.

Finally, a 18-year-old sensitive young woman, Kupaa-khà, or Edible Vine, is caught between village and city standards of living. Edible Vine could potentially betray the Canela and become culturally a white.

The common aspect in each case is whether the individuals pluck their eyebrows and eyelashes, the most emotionally loaded and telling marker of being Canela. Canela mothers pluck the eye hair of infants, children, and adolescents regularly. Canela mothers wait for their infants to sleep and then dip their wetted fingers in the ashes of the fireplace. They use the friction that the ashes provide to pluck deftly even the smallest eyelashes. If the babies wake, they are nursed. Then more plucking follows when they fall asleep again. It is a long procedure, but Canela mothers have time and patience. They do this grooming for their growing children and adolescents as well.

Canela individuals who stopped plucking their own eyebrows and eyelashes, or those of their children, showed many other signs of moving toward the white culture. Rejection of plucking seemed to correlate roughly with age and with physical distance from the tribe. Moving to the town for schooling, traveling in the white world, distancing oneself socially by employment in the Indian service or the federal health agency all resulted in various degrees of assimilation to the white culture and the desire to appear less Indian.

Basket Lifter and her Son, Speechless

The elders of the Canela had just honored me by having me decorated in white duck down and oily red paint. I was somewhat dazed from standing still for the hour-long ceremony and from smelling the resin that glued the feathers to my

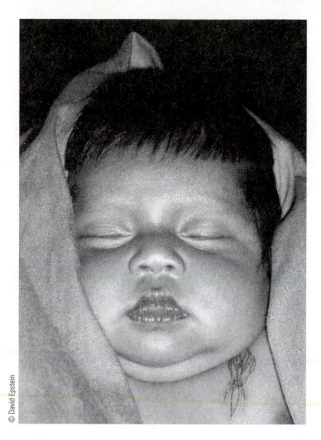

© David Epstein

Sleeping infant with already plucked eye hair.

skin. A Canela boy handed me a note that I read impatiently. It invited me to buy 100 *garafinhas,* which I assumed to be small bottles of cane alcohol. It appeared that Basket Lifter wanted me to buy alcohol for her people, alcohol that so often was their downfall. In my weakened condition the note left me so angry that I bellowed at the boy, very unprofessionally, that I would smash Basket Lifter's bottles of *kô tsè 'ti* (water bitter strongly) if she tried to sell them. I was bluffing, but hoped the bluff would deter her.

Soon the first chief of the Canela, Hõõkô or His Water,[14] strolled toward me across the plaza from the elders' spot. He threaded his way through about 200 Canela men, women, and adolescents. They had just finished dancing to honor my recent arrival. With Chief His Water approaching, I started thinking defensively. I had exceeded their customary norm of moderation with my outburst, so I wondered if he was about to scold me. However, His Water was my protégé; he had written diaries for me since 1979. I had known his father and mother since 1957, when I had first arrived as a young ethnologist to study the Canela. His Water ambled up to me calmly, and after pleasantries, asked if I knew what *garafinhas* were. I answered that, of course I did: they were little bottles (*garafas* = bottles) of *cachaça* (Brazil's rum). He laughed and said that they were little plastic bags containing flavored shaved ice. He added that Basket Lifter was selling them, but that it would help if I would buy the whole supply, so that she could give them out freely. Because the tribe had just honored me, I might return the honor, he suggested.

I pondered what was going on. Could a village with no electricity and no refrigerators have shaved ice? I had to investigate this new phenomenon. I walked the 100 yards from the plaza over to the house on the village circle of houses. I noted that a large group of adolescents and children had gathered there. As I expected, Basket Lifter was at the center of the commotion, standing by a white plastic cooler chest that held fist-sized plastic bags filled with yellow and red ice. Her son, Pël-nö, or Speechless, waved them in the air with both hands, while she took money from a buyer.

Seeing me coming, youths in shorts and young women with sarong-type skirts moved apart to let me in. One of them shouted, "*më imã 'nõ yakhô*" (buy us some). After some bargaining I paid Basket Lifter what she wanted for the *garafinhas,* but the face of her son, Speechless, kept drawing my attention. Speechless had *natural* eyebrows and eyelashes! This normal growth violated Canela custom. I was transfixed by this striking sign of culture change, change that was not usually that visible. Having lived with the Canela for 74 months over 46 years, I found the appearance of Basket Lifter's son, with eyebrows and eyelashes, distinctly strange.

Besides having brought crushed ice from the city to the village, Basket Lifter was selling it in the village for profit. She bargained with me—arguing vehemently—for the amount I should pay. The Canela have not customarily brought goods from the city to sell to other Canela in their village. The direction of their commerce ordinarily goes from the village to the city. They take traditional artifacts, such as mats and baskets, as well as farm products such as manioc flower and rice, to sell to certain dealers in Barra do Corda. For Basket Lifter to bring plastic bags of flavored ice into the village, she had to ride three hours on the Canela truck to traverse just 40 miles of unpaved road from Barra do Corda to the village.

Basket Lifter bargained to get as much as she could from me, much to my surprise. The usual Canela practice was to give something to please the other person and to expect something of greater value in return. Thus, in "giving" (that is, selling) things to me, they were likely to leave the price up to me, and they expected me to please them by giving in return more than was necessary. This practice of mutual giving, rather then buying and selling, came from their food-collecting economy. Basket Lifter's activities suggested that a new spirit of entrepreneurship was emerging among them.

Basket Lifter's son, the 13-year-old Speechless,[15] was chosen to be the leader of the Pepyê (warriors) festival in May 2003. The Warriors' initiation festival is staged every few years, and it takes about three months to pass through all the scenes and acts of the ceremony.[16] The festival traditionally trained 30 to 40 boys and adolescents to become warriors, but today the festival also disciplines these youths in obedience and respect for their traditions. The tribe elders appoint the leaders of this troop, whose members undertake a kind of schooling, preparing them for a lifetime of service together. The principal appointee of the elders is the file leader, the *mamkhyê'ti* (front pull greatly), who is believed to have shamanic abilities to help him foresee the best directions in which to lead his troops. He is supposed to set an example for them to follow. It was thus a great honor for Speechless to be chosen for this role.

In spite of this traditional honor, Basket Lifter refused to pluck her son's eyelashes and eyebrows for the festival. Reportedly, she was afraid that the adolescents in her son's school would tease him. Speechless is in the fourth grade in a city school, while his father Khen-tùk (mountain black), age 30, is in the tenth grade, expecting to become a nurse's assistant upon graduation.

Basket Lifter, with her husband and children, lives in the city in a house the Canela own for Canela students, their relatives remaining in the village. She buys food, cooks, and cleans for her family, and makes money crocheting and designing jewelry fashioned from beads. She also sews skirts and blouses for sale in the city stores, and makes skirts and bras for sale to the village women in addition to her trade in shaved ice. (Bras are an innovation; Canela women usually go topless when on their reservation.) Previously she was married to one of the three men whom a German nongovernmental organization (NGO) took to Germany for several weeks, so she has been exposed indirectly to international ideas. She is a great-granddaughter of the renowned Chief Hàk-too-kot (falcon-chick-green), who died in 1951, so the members of her family line have a sense of being special. All of these factors may have led to her strategy to let her son's eyebrows and eyelashes grow so that he could move ahead more easily in white society.

Hard Bed

Hard Bed is the only Canela male who has married a white woman, and he and his Canela family seem the most extreme in adopting the ways of the whites. Hard Bed is also the only Canela who is a high school graduate, though six others are in the *ensino médio,* or ninth through eleventh grades. (Brazilians have 11 high school grades in this area.) Hard Bed is the son of Mãã-tsè (ostrich smell), who was the chief of the tribe and an employee of the Indian service when Hard Bed graduated in 1997. Hard Bed's schooling and his father's influence qualified him for a number of positions in the Indian service; but the job of post agent on the Canela reservation, previously a white's job, happened to be open, so it was given to him. Hard Bed thus became responsible for administering the post, which involves registering births and deaths, keeping records of visitors and government expenditures, and maintaining the physical condition of the post and its several buildings. To help him with these duties, Hard Bed has five Canela Indian service employees. These men, varying in age from 20 to 70, seldom do any work for the post, because Hard Bed does not require them to do so. Receiving government pay and doing little if anything for it—a sinecure—is a common practice in this region of Brazil. In fact, Hard Bed himself is seldom at the post or in the village, because he spends most of his time in the city with his white wife Lady and their three children.

Lady grew up in a working-class family two blocks from the Canela's house in the Altamira suburb of Barra do Corda. She probably saw Hard Bed's government salary as a lifeline for survival, though Hard Bed was unquestionably strong and handsome. Lady almost never stays in the Canela village where her proper home should be, so Hard Bed is seldom there.

One of Hard Bed's principal roles as post agent, to improve the way of life and the physical welfare of his people, is simply not carried out. Hard Bed should be leading his people to put in larger farms to stave off the "partial hunger" (*meia fome*) they talk about so much. They put in farms one-quarter to one-third the size of backland farms of the region. Thus, when they have eaten their rice, manioc, beans, squash, pumpkins, sweet potatoes, yams, watermelons, and other produce by September, they beg or go partially hungry until the next harvest time from January into May. Fortunately, from late August through January, the South American ostrich (emu) lays its large eggs, the bees provide ample honey, and the fruit on numerous wild trees and domesticated ones ripen. Consequently, no one will die of starvation, though malnutrition is likely. Among large game, deer, wild boar, and ostriches still exist; however, because the young Canela are no longer sufficiently athletic to track them down, the game are harder to kill. Ironically, the deer population is increasing while their availability as a food source is decreasing. The young hunters, only males, are still able to kill small game. Fish are scarce, because only small streams flow through the Canela lands. The principal source of meat today is cattle bought from the backland ranchers. The Indian service used to help in this way, but underfunded as they have been since the early 1990s, they have left this role to outsiders, such as visiting scientists, politicians, clergy, and the personnel of NGOs. Salaried Canela also buy cattle and sell raw meat by the kilo (about 2.2 pounds) to their tribesmen.

Another one of Hard Bed's principal roles as post agent is to enhance relations between the Canela and the backlanders surrounding the Canela reservation. These largely poor and uneducated backlanders find it hard to justify the existence of the Canela. The backland families struggle hard to make a living from their farms or ranches. They sell produce in Barra do Corda or in other backland communities to buy cloth, medicines, and farming and hunting equipment. From the backlanders' point of view, the Canela work far less, produce insufficient foods to support their families, and contribute nothing to the area's economy. The backland farmers feel that the Canela mode of existence does not justify their occupation of so much land. This conviction is a rationale for the backlanders' desire to take over Canela lands, as they tried to do unsuccessfully in 1963.

It is important to understand how the Canela are seen by the backlanders, who are always a potential threat to Canela existence in these days of regional population growth. When I first arrived during the late 1950s and moved around among the backlanders to study them as background for researching the Canela, I became aware, much to my dismay, that these peasant families held the Canela in utter contempt. They referred to them as *bichos do mato* (animals of the forest) and they expected me to agree with them. They traveled on horseback between their farms and to the city along trails—there were no roads—bearing revolvers hanging on their right sides with machetes on their left or muzzle-loading shotguns slung across their backs. In contrast to the Indians, they referred to themselves as *cristãos* (Christians) or *civilizados* (civilized persons).

However, when I compared the Canela way of life to that of the backlanders, I felt that the Canela expressed a more humane way of living. The Canela taught their way of life to their young through the examples acted out in many festival-pageants like the Warriors' festival. They provided daily social dancing for the recreation of their adolescents. They also enriched all ages with spirited choral singing. The Canela resolved problems through twice-daily meetings of the elders and through frequent interfamilial trials. I was impressed by Canela self-reliance cultivated through dietary restrictions, and I was in awe of their prayerful singing to retrieve strength from the natural world.

The backlanders, on the other hand, lived isolated from each other on their family farms; they came together principally for annual religious festivals, and they played melancholy fife and violin music at their dances. Their dependency on folk Catholicism expressed in their much-used phrase, *se Deus quiser* (should God want it), suggested fatalism rather than the self-reliance of the older Canela.[17]

Hard Bed's failure to work with the backlanders became evident on my last day in Barra do Corda during September 2003. The Indian service official in charge of all the Gê-speaking tribes of the region, Sr. Raimundo Martins Franco, a white, had to drive for five hours to the western frontier of the Canela reservation to resolve a problem between a white rancher and a Canela family farmer. While the Canela family was in Barra do Corda receiving pension funds from the Banco do Brasil, the white rancher's cattle had broken through the fence around the Canela farmer's field. The cattle had eaten the green tops of the manioc and yam roots that remained in the ground from the previous year. Consequently, the Canela family would have little food to eat until the new harvests were available three to four months away. Formerly, they could have expected to receive food from their relatives, but currently kin keep their food stores to themselves—another significant change.

When I first arrived among the Canela during the late 1950s, the serious Canela complaint against the backlanders was that they did not share their stored food with hungry Canela. The Canela considered this lack of generosity to be stingy and evil. As a carryover from the Canela's largely food-collecting aboriginal existence, they still shared almost everything, enhancing their chances of survival. They expected the backlanders to do the same. They used to arrive at the door of a backland home, hungry, begging for food, and when the backland family refused, even though they had sacks of manioc flour in plain sight, Canela were incensed. People's possessions were to be distributed and shared with those in need. The Canela had no understanding of the backland family's own need to reserve their stores of food for themselves so that they would not go hungry before the products of the next harvest were available. The poor backland family could not afford to buy extra food supplies when their regular stores ran out.

Hard Bed failed to fulfill the hopes of the Canela as an educated leader who could help them with the backlanders and other problems. The older people forming the tribal council realize that they cannot handle tribal matters without young white-educated Canela as their leaders. Hard Bed should have fulfilled this expectation, but he was not doing it. The council of elders tried to remove him from his position several times, but his relatives have spoken so strongly against the move that the elders have had to abandon the effort.

Canela tribe members have told me that Hard Bed's family speaks only Portuguese in their home, so his three children are growing up to be whites. Hard

© David Epstein

Anaconda, representative to the municipal government, plucks eye hair.

Bed's Canela relatives talk to the children in Canela, hoping to teach them their father's language. As should be expected, none of Hard Bed's family members pluck or shave (a more recent method) their eyelashes or eyebrows.

Anaconda

Hard Bed is an example of a somewhat educated Canela who, although in a position to help his people immensely, is doing little for them. By contrast, the example of Anaconda shows a Canela who is trying to help his people. Anaconda has sent me poignant accounts of his attempts to learn some skills in the Brazilian world to bring back to his Canela village.

Anaconda claims that his grandfather was Curt Nimuendajú, the German-Brazilian ethnologist whose master study, *The Eastern Timbira,* was the impetus for my own study of the Canela.[18] Anaconda's mother, Pùt-khwèy (sun-woman), does not look at all white, however, so I have never accepted this Canela myth. I suspect, however, that this ethno-inheritance gives Anaconda a sense of superiority that may have contributed to his ascendancy among his people. Direct descent from famous and loved political leaders means much to certain Canela, and they boast about such an advantage in public.

Anaconda started his schooling in the Canela village when he was 16, after having worked on his parents' and then his father-in-law's family farms, as is usual for young men. His teacher for the first three grades was Risalva Cruz dos Santos, a cultural Brazilian who looked fully Indian, though not of the Canela heritage. She was brought up in a tribe living in a suburb of the city Rodelas, in the eastern state of Bahia. Her people had lost their indigenous language, because the Portuguese settlers first contacted them during the sixteenth century. The case of Hard Bed's children shows that the Canela language could suffer the same fate.

Risalva joined the federal Indian service as a teacher and was assigned to the Canela in 1977. I watched her enthusiastic style of teaching during my longest stay with the Canela during 1978 and 1979. Possibly because Risalva was of Indian descent, she had a special sympathy for her students. Anaconda continued into the fifth grade in 1990, living in Barra do Corda, which logistically and financially was very difficult in those days, so he had to terminate his education temporarily at this level.

I first became aware of Anaconda and his unusual talents when my diarist, Thunder, employed him as an account keeper during 1995. He may have been the first Canela to become adept with a calculator. Thunder was receiving funds to help establish a sustainable agriculture project over a five-year period, but could not keep track of the expenses on paper, while Anaconda could. Thunder let funds become diverted, because he could not resist being generous to certain individuals uninvolved in the farm, so the project collapsed with Anaconda sharply criticizing the reasons for its demise. The project failed also because Canela custom did not allow anyone to become much bigger than anyone else, so other Canela had to cut Thunder down to size with rumors and accusations regardless of what actually had occurred.

Soon after the breakup of the project, Anaconda asked me to fund a course in typing for him. Anaconda was so outstanding that I wanted him as one of my regular diarists. The first Canela to type effectively, he started transcribing and translating Canela myths for me and later began keeping a diary.

During 1997, Anaconda reentered and passed the fifth grade, and continued up the academic ladder. During 1999 he had to abandon his studies, however, as did all other Canela. This desertion of Barra do Corda occurred because Thunder, who was the tribal chief of those years, had assumed the role of a prophet and was predicting that the end of the world would occur on December 31, 1999. This was when their old culture hero, Awkhêê, would come to save all believers from a flood if they reverted to their ancestral practices. They were to dance each weekend, he dictated, to bring about this salvation. They had to sell most of their food sources (animals and crops) as well as their material possessions (guns, axes, and pots) to support the dancing. This effort to save themselves from the flood broke up any schooling plans and family farming activities. It disrupted village life for 2000 and most of 2001, increasing the condition of "half hunger" considerably. The Canela had experienced similar disorienting movements during 1963, 1980, and 1984. They were susceptible to choosing such otherworldly solutions to life's economic problems rather than this-worldly ones, such as trade, education, and agriculture. Thus, I was delighted to see Basket Lifter's efforts to introduce businesses to her village, and I was also encouraged that so many students were in the city. However, I was still waiting to find improved developments on the agricultural front, which would be so crucial for Canela self-sufficiency and respect in the backland world. Justification for their ownership of so much land would be their ultimate protection from attacks in a region where it is predicted that the populations of the neighboring groups will be growing considerably in the coming years.

During 2000, Anaconda reentered the eighth grade, but did not pass into the ninth until 2002, because of two events. First, on January 1, 2001, the Canela elected him to be their representative, the *vereador,* to the local government— equivalent to a U.S. county—in which the Canela reside, the *município* of Fernando Falcão governing an area of 3,000 square miles. This political position was another first for a Canela Indian. To continue as a student in Barra do Corda and also serve as the Canela representative to Fernando Falcão would have been geographically difficult. In the second event the Guajajara Indians had killed two whites near Barra do Corda, so all Canela Indians had to leave the city out of fear of reprisals. Nevertheless, by 2003 Anaconda was in the ninth grade, and soon hopes to pass the eleventh grade and then take a final year in a specialty—civil administration. After that he plans to get a job in the federal Indian service in Barra do Corda to help his people further.

Anaconda made it very clear to me that he was tired of politics and disillusioned by his service as a *vereador*. He said that his people blamed him for many things that he was not guilty of. In his October 2003 diary on tape he told me:

> Every year my people tell me, "You, Anaconda, will end your courses here and go on to get your bachelor's degree and never return to our village." . . . But, I know that I will always return to the village, to my people, Professor. However, here I am with a lot of doubt, so I do not know.
>
> The Canela community caught me as a child, like a child, not knowing anything. And then, they threw me in the [municipal] chamber, and there I became lost among the laws of the whites, being without [appropriate] thoughts. . . . That way was very difficult, but even in that way, I learned many things from them. . . . While taping for Professor, I become very doubtful about why the people are blaming me, and I speak to them, "Look, now, a dog could not break up a pack of many wild boar. It could not. Then, in the same way I could not break up a group of many whites, because, I alone could not break them up. But, I thought a lot and I spoke a lot to them so that it had the effect of opening up the situation for those [Canela] who will take my place, [a Canela] such as No Hands or His Water. Consequently, they would be able to speak up a lot more and thereby maybe obtain a project. They would be able to gain some things from the whites in the municipal chamber for their people. This would be very important, Professor, very important.
>
> This is why I am here, why I am studying here in Barra do Corda. I want to graduate later. Moreover, this is not just to clear myself, since another chance to clear myself could turn out well or badly for me, depending on the particular occurrences. I could talk a great deal. I could say certain things to the people so that the people could believe me. This is it, Professor.

Listening to this impassioned statement in my office at home near Washington, D.C., I could not help feeling very sorry for Anaconda. Like Thunder during his ascendancy as leader of the agricultural development project in the mid-1990s, Anaconda had become too big for the Canela to put up with. In keeping with their egalitarian orientation, they had to bring him down to size. Unconfirmed accusations of misuse of funds came in from other diarists and from Canela research assistants while I was in the field. Anaconda had not brought his people very much from the municipal chamber in Fernando Falcão to warrant his reelection. The mayor had made election promises to gain the Canela vote, but Anaconda had not been able to make the mayor carry out any of these promises, such as improving the road, building a better bridge, bringing in electricity, and installing a telephone system in the village.

In accord with his attempts to bridge the white and Canela worlds, Anaconda removed his brows and lashes for village festivals, but let them grow out when living in town. While in school one day Anaconda was called upon to defend the Canela eye-hair-plucking custom. In another part of his two-hour diary on tape for October 2003, he tells the following story:

> Often when I sit in my class in the middle school, male and female students ask me about my being Indian. . . . Teachers ask me as well. One said, "Anaconda, I have observed that those of you who are Canela are difficult to administer. . . . I have observed that you do not wear eyebrows and eyelashes. I find that this is your culture."
>
> Then I answered her, "Look, it is like this. It *is* our culture. Never will we forget our culture. It is because of this that we are Canela, and it is this that is difficult for you. We pluck our eyebrows and eyelashes. This is difficult for you."
>
> Then she spoke again and asked, "Does this not interfere with your sleep?"
>
> "No, it is custom. . . . They began to pluck when we were born." . . . When I answered her, she became like this, like this—very sad or very weak. No, not very sad, very amused, but I could not know her thoughts.

Ângelo Carampei

Ângelo was born in 1971 and first went to school under Risalva in the first grade in the village during 1980. Currently, after years of farming, he is finishing the eighth grade in the Catholic school Dom Marcelino de Milão, in Barra do Corda. In my research, Ângelo was outstanding in one respect; he consistently obtained part-time work in the city, which most Canela said was virtually impossible to find. Probably because of this diligence, Sr. Franco, the regional representative of the federal Indian service, arranged for a government agricultural training school (Escola Agrícola Federal) in São Luis to take Ângelo for three years of technical farm instruction, starting in February 2004. After this internship away from his family and tribe, he would return home as a *técnico agrícola* to help his people learn the modern techniques of mechanized agriculture. He is one of three Canela accepted for this training. Guajajara Indians have attended this school, but these three young men would be the first Canela. Hopefully, some five years from now, the Canela will be cultivating their first fixed and sustainable agriculture fields. Then they will no longer experience the specter of seasonal moderate hunger caused by the loss of their extensive territories, land needed to sustain their traditional hunting and foraging mode of subsistence, which they supplement with their horticulture.

© David Epstein

*Ângelo, the sensitive
student of bread baking,
plucks eye hair.*

Forays into the white world like Ângelo's projected internship in São Luis are actually part of an older Canela pattern. Even during the late 1950s, most of the men traveled in small groups to distant cities, such as Recife, Salvador, and Rio de Jañeiro. They traveled to bring back goods for their people, just as their food-collecting ancestors had gone on trek and returned with food. This ancestral pattern explains why Anaconda's people decried him, because he had not succeeded in obtaining projects for them from the mayor of Fernando Falcão.

In Ângelo's account of an earlier trip, he showed that such an attempt to learn the skills of the whites could be fraught with cultural misunderstandings. The Indian service administrator, Sr. Franco, sent Ângelo to Teresina in 2003 with another Canela man to receive training in baking bread. Sr. Franco was installing a bakery by the House of Canela Students in Barra do Corda to help them make money and to enhance their stature in the town. A Catholic order of Sisters partially supported the project, and one of the Sisters drove the two Canela to Teresina, where they stayed at the Sisters' convent there. Ângelo reported the following in his diary of September 2003:

> I am traveling to the city of Teresina to receive training in a bakery. When I arrived, . . .
> I was not yet used to the city of Teresina, which is hot; the temperature is too high. I
> am interning here and I am learning how to make bread. But, there is a Sister, Maria
> de Jesus, who is with us. She is responsible for us. She brought me and Thunder's
> nephew here. . . . But, there is one thing wrong, which is that the Sister, Maria de
> Jesus, is treating us very badly. . . . She is only giving us the value of five reais per day

on which to have lunch and dinner. [Three reais may equal one dollar.] And, these five reais are not enough for us to have a juice or anything. . . .

The owner of the bakery is called Leotardo Ferreira da Cruz. He gave us something to eat only once, lunch and dinner. But the next day, he did not want to give us anything any more, because he said that food is not given freely, not dinner and lunch. . . . But, it is Maria de Jesus, who brought us here, . . . who is to blame. . . .

The next day we went out in the car of Sister Tintina. Maria de Jesus was driving. We sat next to her. She did yet not know the local traffic practices. She drove up a one-way street the wrong way. She almost hit a bus in the street. I felt frightened. I had never seen cars crash. Thus, I almost died far away from my family here in the city of Teresina.

And when it was night, I felt very sad, lying down and thinking. It is just that I am spending time here learning about bread, and I almost died in an automobile accident away from my family. But, God is great. I escaped! God saved me. I did not die in a car crash.

The next day, Sister Maria de Jesus gave us 20 reais to pay for lunch and dinner, but I thought that she was not expecting to receive any change back. . . . And, we spent, Thunder's nephew and I, . . . 20 reais. At the end of the day, she asked for the change. She asked, "Where is my money? You have to give back some of the money that I gave you." I became frightened. I had thought that in giving us money, she was helping us. But, this Sister is very bad. I was just thinking [deeply] about it. (emphasis added)

But, as usual, I had brought with me a few artifacts, baskets. I sold them and raised some funds. If I had brought nothing along, how would I have paid her? But, as usual, I had brought a few baskets, so I sold them to the owner of the store that was next to the bakery, to Senhor Leotardo. . . . I returned her money, but I kept thinking about this.

And Franco, also, yes!—. The reason for my pondering began right away, before we even had started to travel. I asked Sr. Franco for some money. . . . to have a drink of something, coffee. And, he said, he became—wild in a way, very angry. He spoke to us, "Whether you want to go or not, the Indian service does not have any money for you." He spoke this bad way to me. I felt very ashamed. And, I went to chat with Climbing Ostrich (Mãã-jààpil) who works with Franco. And Climbing Ostrich went to speak with Franco. And, Franco spoke in the same way again: "If Ângelo does not want to go, he can stay. There is no money for this; the Indian service does not have any money." That was it! But, we traveled without money anyway.

This kind of pondering had begun soon in me, even before we had left Barra do Corda. And so, I kept mulling this over. And, I kept worrying about it until I finished the course. I certainly did learn to make bread. . . . And, later we traveled back . . . to Barra do Corda.

We can only sympathize with Ângelo, a sensitive young man, away from his family and people. The cultural differences could hardly be greater. Custom used to compel the Canela to be generous, and Ângelo is still that way. However, first Franco, then the Sister, and finally the baker—were mean and even angry about being expected to provide money, which might seem like an obligation under the circumstances. We have to understand that these Brazilians are very poor and are

Edible Vine, daughter of village and city culture, wears light eyebrows.

living in an economy that provides little. The Canela have even less, but they are generous in spirit as well as with the goods they happen to have. Ângelo finds this meanness of spirit incomprehensible. He is clearly depressed by his experience.

It was the feeling of being morally better human beings than the whites that preserved the Canela and their culture for so many years after the first devastating contacts during the first part of the nineteenth century. The old Canela of the 1950s, the ones whom I first knew, walked with great dignity and sense of self-importance. These individuals behaved like state dignitaries. They performed their roles with assurance and certainty. Sadly, they lost this dignified style of bearing when they lost their sense of superiority to the whites after the 1950s. Surely, this loss was one of the reasons they turned to messianic solutions.

Although he was raising children in the city and had been living there for five years, the conservative, timid, and older Ângelo still plucks his eyelashes and eyebrows regularly.

Edible Vine

Finally we examine an 18-year-old Canela woman struggling with two cultural homes—one urban and Portuguese-speaking, the other village and Canela-speaking. She has forebears of mixed heritage as well. Edible Vine, as she was named to protect her identity in our case study,[19] was born in 1986, a granddaughter of my long-term Canela research assistant, the younger Thunder.[20] Her mother was Three Streams, Thunder's second daughter. Thunder's first daughter,

Female One, married Twist It, a half-Canela. Edible Vine was raised partly in the village of Escalvado with her mother, Three Streams, and her grandfather, Thunder. However, because her real father, Dry Man, died while she was quite young, she also grew up in Barra do Corda with her mother's sister, Female One, and her foster father, Twist It.

Twist It claimed that whites kidnapped his Canela mother while she traveled from the tribal area with her husband and other Canela men. One of the whites kept her first as a servant and then as his common-law wife. She died when Twist It was young, so Twist It was raised by his father until he also died. This was when Twist It first visited the Canela during 1978. I saw him there as a late adolescent and well remember his first arrival in the village. He did not get along with the Canela. He could not run, sing, dance, or speak like them, nor could he endure the hardships of farming. The word *awkward* describes for me his postures and behavior in comparison with those of the Canela. Thus, the Canela named him Twist It (*to kayöt:* make twist).

When Twist It married Thunder's oldest daughter, the couple moved to the Altamira suburb of Barra do Corda, as a solution to his problems and as the first Canela couple to live there. Thunder liked this arrangement, I assume, because he had a place to stay in the city. He largely financed the couple at first from his Indian service salary, but later, Twist It earned money through a store he set up and by repairing items like bicycles. Currently, some 12 Canela houses are owned or rented near Twist It's house.

When I met Edible Vine for the first time during my 2003 visit to the Canela, my most marked memory was her striking intelligence. This observation should not have surprised me, because her father, Dry Man, and her mother's father, Thunder, were exceptionally bright. I brought in Thunder as one of my first three diarists in 1964, and during 1978 and 1979 Dry Man was my outstanding new diarist and translator. In addition to genetic contributions, Edible Vine's social conditioning may have contributed to her intelligence, because she grew up in a family of tribal leaders whose members exposed her to thought and discussion about the culture of the whites.

Edible Vine started her schooling in the Canela village at the unusual age of five (1991), but transferred to the city after two years to live with Female One and Twist It. She advanced to the fourth grade by 2000, but dropped out that year to get married at 14, which is almost old for Canela girls.[21] After two marriages, she is single again and is back to studying in the sixth grade (2003) in the state school. I believe that she is serious about what she said to me as a diarist in 2002: "I am married, but for me this does not make any difference. I want to bring about my dream of studying to be my life."[22] However, we must think of the profound problems that she faces as a woman in continuing her beloved studies. What would she do if she became pregnant? The Canela have neither contraceptives nor abortive practices. She would have the baby and would have to support it with or without a husband. Would this be financially possible? Maybe, but obtaining this assistance would be difficult as she got older.

Female One and Twist It were somewhat protected from having to share freely with the usually hungry and begging Canela, because any Canela living temporarily in Barra do Corda knew that the rules there were different. People could be stingy in the city, where it took money to obtain anything, unlike in the village where goods and food were still shared sometimes with those in need. Thus, Twist It and Female One were able to accumulate wealth over time. In 2001, they had a television set, couches, and chairs throughout the three-room house, an enclosed bedroom with a double bed instead of a hammock, a kitchen with dozens of implements, and a metal oven, which cooked with gas. Her mother Three Streams, as a widow, lived frequently with her older sister, Female One. This social proximity was enhanced by the Canela kinship system, according to which Edible Vine called her mother's sister (Female One), "mother," and her mother's sister's husband, "father." In my study of the sources of support for students in the city, it turned out that Edible Vine had received much money from her father, Twist It. Twist It spoke Canela with difficulty, because he had been learning it only since late adolescence. Thus Portuguese was largely the language of their household in the city, and this urban setting was Edible Vine's alternate home. Edible Vine speaks Portuguese fluently and correctly, unlike any other Canela her age or older, though Canela was the language of her extended family's set of houses when Edible Vine lived in the village to attend festivals.

In her diary spoken on tape for me during October 2003, Edible Vine was very clear about her loyalty to her Indian culture and to her Canela people. However, she may be caught between the two ways of life far more than she realizes:

> Look, Professor, I want to go in the direction of the culture of the Indian, because I have been an Indian since I was growing in the belly of my mother. I was born Indian, I was raised Indian, and I will die Indian. I will never cease to be Indian. I am proud of being Indian.
>
> There are many things that are important in my life. Some of these things are a kind of secret. I sing very well, but I am ashamed of singing [in the Indian way] (emphasis added). But, many people tell me not to be ashamed because the culture is ours. Moreover, it is for everybody who is a *mëhïï* [Indian]. No one has the right to depreciate our culture. . . .
>
> I want very much to speak about the culture of the *mëhïï*. The *mëhïï* are very significant indeed. They have a great deal of value. If it were not for the *kupë* [the whites], our value, our worth, would be greater. Moreover, our worth is greater than that of the whites, because our dances, our culture, our traditions are so very important. And, these things have much more worth than those of the *kupë*. . . . For this reason, I do not want to stop being Indian ever in my life.
>
> And plucking out eyelashes, I have no way of doing, because, Professor, when I pluck my eyelashes, I become feverish. And when I cut the hair of my head [the Canela way] (emphasis added), I come down with a fever, also. A person may think that I am lying, that I do not cut my hair and do not pull out my eyelashes without getting feverish. However, I am speaking the truth, Professor. For this reason, when I go to the village, I do not pluck my eyelashes and I do not cut my hair.
>
> But when I finish my studies, I will certainly return to the village. Then I will cut my hair, as I always used to cut it when I was ten years and 12 years old. I stopped cutting my hair when I was 15, because the last time I cut my hair like a Canela . . .

I had a fever. And since then—and my mother noted it—I have never cut my hair or plucked my eyelashes. However, I am not afraid to pluck them, because this is my culture, and I must not ever forget it, ever, because our ancestors left this for us, as if it were to be our identity. It is, as it were, our identity, itself. . . . The direction of my life is to go around in the Indian way—to paint myself, cut my hair and pluck my eyelashes.

But while I am here [in the city], I cannot do this, Professor, because . . . I get a fever. And so, my mother never lets me cut my hair, because she does not like to see me feeling badly. But there is one thing that I am never going to stop doing. When I arrive in the village, during vacations, I [body] paint myself and dance too. . . . I wrap cloth around myself. I do not like to remain dressed in shirts or blouses or shorts. I do not like these, so I take them all off, and I go around like an Indian indeed, because I am not a white. It is not for me to go around in the village all dressed up. But, while I am in Barra do Corda, I dress up in clothes and I only speak Portuguese. Moreover, in the house with my aunt, I speak my language, with my cousins, with my brothers. However, when I am in school, I only speak Portuguese.

There is a boy who studies with me. He is Indian also, Roger. We study in the same classroom, in the same grade. But, I find that he is ashamed of talking among those people in our language. I do not have trouble talking with him in Canela, but he told me, "Do not talk in our language." So I asked him, "Who do you think you are? Are you, in fact, a white or a *mëhïï*?" He did not answer at all. . . . Later, he said that he does not want to know anything, after he has graduated, about our culture. But, he is just talking big, because when he goes to our village, he has himself painted and he has his eyelashes plucked. He is just talking big. . . .

The culture of the whites, I have no way of following, Professor, because, later here in the city, there will be a lot of violence. And, we who study here, we have to go around carefully through the streets. Sometimes, when Canela get very drunk, they get boisterous, and they fight with the *kupë*. I have often seen this. And, they say that they want to go around as if they were *kupë*, but they cannot actually do this, Professor, because wherever they go, a *kupë* asks them if they are Indian. This is the question that the whites ask, because we do look like Indians, indeed. We cannot hide it, because we are not *kupë*. The ways of the *kupë* are very different. . . .

Look, Professor, I am not embarrassed to speak the truth to you, because you, sir, are my teacher, so I have to tell you everything. I am not ashamed to talk to you about anything in my life. . . . There are some Indians here that talk badly to me and say that I am losing my culture. I do not like this. They cannot reach into my heart to know what I really feel for my culture. . . .

If it were to happen some time in the future that I married a white, I would not leave—leave my culture because of him, no! If he were to accompany me, yes; but if he were not to accompany me, no! He would have to go away, because I *am* Indian. I have to fulfill myself through my culture. I will have to live close to my community for it to help me.

To listen to Edible Vine's diary on tape is to realize how deeply conflicted she is by the emotions aroused in her by her talking about her situation. She loves her city education, she thrives in white culture, but she feels profoundly loyal to her Indian roots. Student colleagues make her suffer for her relative success in appearing urban, which she vehemently believes she has to deny. Her case brings many questions to mind. Will she get pregnant? Will she finish her education? Whom will she marry, a Canela or a white man? She is so intelligent, so sensitive, and so enthusiastic about life now at 18 that we have to wonder how she will face the disillusionment and the lack of fulfillment that are likely to come her way, considering the limited opportunities for a Canela woman in Barra do Corda at this time. However, being a granddaughter of Thunder and a foster child of Twist It, her chances of receiving some financial support and due encouragement are better for her than for most young Indian women in similar positions in the region.

SUMMARY: FACTORS IN CULTURE CHANGE

We know little about pre-pacification Canela history and ethnography. What is aboriginal and what has evolved since the first contacts around 1700 is unclear. The major occurrences or situations that were major factors in bringing about cultural change from pacification (1814) to current times are clear, however.

By 1816, pioneers, tribal warfare, and smallpox had decimated the Canela, leaving only several dozen at the most out of around 1,500. Between about 1838 and 1938, the Canela kept adapting more and more to the loss of 95 percent of their lands, turning from food collectors into food producers and taking over the iron implements and some of the culture of the surrounding backlanders. They had to renounce warfare, and without a military goal, their quasi-military system of authority began weakening.

Between 1938 and 1980, intrusive Indian service personnel took over the Canela leadership structure, leaving it so weak by 1947 that the chief and secondary leaders retained little authority. This political weakness rendered inoperative the agricultural system, leaving the Canela dependent on outsiders for sufficient food to this day. The appearance of trucks, airplanes, and even the roles of some benevolent whites in Barra do Corda deprived the Canela of their firm belief that they were morally superior, leaving them little justification for not accepting the values of whites. About seven Canela Indian service salaries introduced wealth to certain extended families, contributing to the formation of a ceremonially based class and to differing standards of living. Indian service personnel and the Wycliffe Bible Translators traded for ethnographic artifacts in such large quantities that material possessions became increasingly valuable, instead of being of minimal value, as they were aboriginally; Canela had to be "stingy" with them. This emphasis on the ownership of possessions began to change trading from an attempt to please others to an act of bargaining. Similarly, valued possessions changed their practice of sharing in sexual relations to withholding and even the commercialization of sex.

Between 1980 and 2003, the increase in the number of government salaries, pensions, and other forms of support made the possession of money so pervasive that the chief and the council of elders could not accomplish anything for their people without paying for it. Without funds their power vanished almost

© David Epstein

Burnt Path writing names of deceased elders on their photos.

completely. With the failure of the messianic movement of 1999, the Canela turned to their next movement, as enthusiastically as ever, to solve the problem of their future economic support. They turned to education in Brazilian schools in significant numbers, both in their village and in the city, with the expectation that this solution would eventually provide able tribal leaders and managers. Money that could not be made to flow along the lines of political authority flowed instead through family lines to support promising young adults, adolescents, and children in schools.

During the last 10 years, situations that have stimulated Canela culture change the most include marriages to whites, travel away from the tribe, and both children and their parents studying in city schools.

Plucking eyebrows and eyelashes is a deeply emotional marker of Canela identity. It is practiced differently by those who strongly hold Canela tradition and those who hold it only weakly. Cultural conservatives (such as Ângelo) regularly pluck their eyebrows and eyelashes, while cultural moderates (such as Anaconda) do it only for attending the greater ceremonies in the Canela village. Those culturally committed to the white world (such as Hard Bed and Speechless), or those with mixed feelings (such as Edible Vine), do not pluck their eye hair at all.

REFERENCES

Crocker, William H. 2004. Canela. In *Encyclopedia of sex and gender: Men and women in the world's cultures,* eds. Carol R. Ember and Melvin Ember. Vol. 1, 345–355. Human Relations Area Files at Yale University. New York: Kluer Academic/Plenum Publishers.

———. 2003. War and peace among the Canela. *Antropológica* 99–100. Instituto Venezolano de Investigaciones Científicas. Caracas: Fundación La Salle de Investigaciones Científicas.

———. 2002. Canela "Other Fathers": Partible Paternity and its Changing Practices. In *Cultures of multiple fathers: The theory and practice of partible paternity in Lowland South America,* eds. S. Beckerman and P. Valentine, 86–104. Gainesville, FL: Univ. of Florida Press.

———. 1995. Canela relationships with ghosts: This-worldly or other worldly empowerment. In *Latin American Anthropology Review,* ed. J. Ehrenreich. *Journal of the Society for Latin American Anthropology* 5 (2) 71–78.

———. 1990. The Canela (Eastern Timbira) I: An ethnographic introduction. *Smithsonian Contributions to Anthropology,* no. 33. Washington, D.C.: The Smithsonian Press.

———. 1984. Canela marriage: Factors in change. In *Marriage practices in Lowland South America,* ed. K. Kensinger. Illinois Studies in Anthropology, vol. 14, 63–98.

———. 1982. Canela initiation festivals: "Helping hands" through life. In *Celebration: Studies in festivity and ritual,* ed. V. Turner, 147–158. Washington, D.C.: Smithsonian Institution Press.

———. n.d. The Canela extramarital sex system and its decline. Working paper.

Crocker, William H., and Barbara Watanabe. n.d. *The Canela of northeastern central Brazil.* [Online], www.mnh.si.edu/anthro/canela, "Literature". Republished: Crocker (1982; 1984; 1990; 1995) and Curt Nimuendajú (1946a).

Crocker, William H., and Jean G. Crocker. 2004. The Canela: Kinship, ritual, and sex in an Amazonian tribe. In *Case studies in cultural anthropology,* 2nd ed., ed. George Spindler. Belmont, CA: Wadsworth/Thomson Learning.

Hemming, John. 1987. *Amazon frontier: Defeat of the Brazilian Indians.* Cambridge, MA: Univ. of Harvard Press.

Melatti, Julio C. 1967. Índios e Criadores: A situação dos Krahó na área pastoril do Tocantins. *Monografias do Instituto de Ciências Sócias.* Vol. 3. Rio: Companhia Brasileiro de Artes Gráficas.

———. 1984. Myths numbered 98–112. In *Folk literature of the Gê Indians,* eds. J. Wilbert and K. Simoneau. Vol. 2. UCLA Latin American Center Publications. Los Angeles, CA: Univ. of California Press.

Nimuendajú, Curt [Curt Unkel]. 1946a. The Eastern Timbira. In *University of California publications in American archaeology and ethnology* 41. Trans. and ed. Robert Lowie. Berkeley, CA: Univ. of California Press.

———. 1946b. War and peace among the Canela. *Antropologica* 99–100 (13–29).

Schecter, Stephen, and William H. Crocker. 1999. *Mending ways: The Canela Indians of Brazil.* 49 min. Schecter Films and National Human Studies Film Archives, Smithsonian Institution. Princeton, NJ: Films for the Humanities and Sciences. (www.films.com, search "Canela.")

Wagley, Charles, and Eduardo Galvão. 1949. The Tenetehara Indians of Brazil: A culture in transition. *Columbia University contributions to anthropology,* no. 35. New York:

Columbia Univ. Press. Reprinted: New York: AMS Press, 1969.

Wilbert, Johannes, and Karin Simoneau, eds. 1984. Folk literature of the Gê Indians, Vol. 2. *UCLA Latin American Studies* 58. Los Angeles: UCLA Latin American Center Publications.

NOTES

1. For a classic monograph on these neighbors of the Canela, the Tupi-speaking Guajajara (that is, Tenetehara), see Wagley and Galvão (1969 [1949]).

2. I use the generic term *Indian service* to refer to the federal Indian Protection Service (SPI) of Brazil through 1968 and the National Foundation of the Indian (FUNAI) during and since 1968.

3. For warfare among the Eastern Timbira tribes during pre-pacification times, see Crocker (2003). For war stories, see Melatti (1984) in Wilbert and Simoneau (1984).

4. An early Portuguese military contact with the Canela's ancestors may have occurred during 1696. For such materials see, Nimuendajú (1946b, 3). This classic monograph is the masterpiece of the most prominent Brazilian anthropologist of the first half of the twentieth century, Curt Nimuendajú. This book is mostly about the Canela during the 1930s.

5. Melatti (1967) gives us a detailed account of Portuguese-Brazilian pioneers settling the region occupied by the Canela ancestors.

6. Hemming (1987, 185–186) provides an account of the Canela's ancestors, including their surrender to a military garrison in 1814.

7. See Crocker and Crocker (2004, 24) for the effects of the loss of military discipline.

8. For a more detailed account of the Canela extramarital sex system, see Crocker and Crocker (2004, 99–105) and Crocker (n.d.).

9. The Canela use the expression *whites* (*brancos*) to refer to non-Indian Brazilians, as is the current practice of Brazilian anthropologists in such interethnic contact situations. The Canela refer to themselves as Indians (*índios*), though they know they are Brazilians as well. I use the term *backlanders* for Brazilians living in the interior around the Canela reservation, an expression other authors use.

10. Priscilla R. Linn and William H. Crocker are writing a comprehensive monograph on the four major Canela messianic movements (1963, 1980, 1984, and 1999) and the six or seven minor ones. See Linn and Crocker (MS).

11. The passage is from Crocker and Crocker (2004, 27).

12. For more on Anaconda, see Crocker and Crocker (2004, 41).

13. Ângelo is the hero of the Canela video (Schecter and Crocker, 1999). See Crocker and Crocker (2004, 133) for another excerpt from his diary.

14. More about Chief His Water can be found in Crocker and Crocker (2004, 129).

15. Names of Canela individuals used here are real Canela names, but they are usually switched to disguise identity and preserve privacy.

16. For descriptions of and for understanding the Canela festivals, see Crocker (1982) and Crocker (1990, 269–289). Crocker (1982) and Crocker (1990) can be found in Crocker and Watanabe (2003).

17. For a study of Canela shamanism, see Crocker (1995) and Crocker (1990, 313–317; Crocker and Watanabe, n.d., Research and Collections, IV.D.1).

18. For how I came to study the Canela, see Crocker and Crocker (2004, xii–xv).

19. More on Edible Vine can be found in Crocker and Crocker (2004, 38).

20. For more on my long-term relationship with Thunder, see Crocker and Crocker (2004, 2, 32) and Crocker (1990) in Crocker and Watanabe (n.d., Research and Collections, I.G.4).

21. See Crocker (1984) for a full discussion of Canela marriage, and Crocker (2002, 96–97) and Crocker (2004, 353–354) for supplementary materials.

22. This passage is from Crocker and Crocker (2004, 38).

Fieldwork Biography
Dru C. Gladney

Dru C. Gladney has spent the last 25 years moving between Beijing and Istanbul conducting fieldwork among the mostly Muslim peoples who were dispersed over the last two millennia along the Silk Road. Focusing on Muslims who speak mostly Chinese, Turkic, and Mongolian languages, Dr. Gladney has examined the nexus of religion, identity, and nationalism. Currently professor of Asian studies and anthropology at the University of Hawai'i at Manoa, he has authored over 100 academic articles, as well as the following books: *Muslim Chinese: Ethnic Nationalism in the People's Republic* (Harvard University Press); *Ethnic Identity in China: The Making of a Muslim Minority Nationality* (Wadsworth); *Making Majorities: Constituting the Nation in Japan, China, Korea, Malaysia, Fiji, Turkey, and the U.S.* (Editor; Stanford University Press); and *Dislocating China: Muslims, Minorities, and Other Subaltern Subjects* (University of Chicago Press). Online articles and projects can be found at www.hawaii.edu/dru.

© Dru C. Gladney

3/Cultural Identity in China
The Rising Politics of Ethnic Difference

Foreigners and the Chinese themselves typically picture China's population as a vast monolithic Han majority with a sprinkling of exotic minorities living along the country's borders. This understates China's tremendous cultural, geographic, and linguistic diversity—in particular the important cultural differences within the Han population. This also ignores the fact that China is officially a multinational country with 56 recognized "nationalities." China argues that its minorities are involved in local and national governance, proving that China has a socialist system that represents the many peoples of the People's Republic of China (PRC) in a democratic system. More importantly, recent events suggest that China may well be increasingly insecure regarding not only these nationalities, but also its own national integration. The World Trade Center and Pentagon attacks of September 11, 2001, actually brought China and the United States closer together in an antiterrorism campaign that has made the case of Uygur separatism in China much more prominent in the Western press.

At the same time, China is now seeing a resurgence of local nationality and culture, most notably among southerners such as the Cantonese and Hakka, who are now classified as Han. These differences may increase under threats from ethnic separatism, economic pressures such as inflation, the growing gap between rich and poor areas, and the migration of millions of people from poorer provinces to those with job opportunities. Chinese society is also under pressure from the officially recognized minorities such as Uygurs and Tibetans. For centuries, China has held together a vast multicultural and multiethnic nation despite alternating periods of political centralization and fragmentation. But cultural and linguistic cleavages could worsen in a China weakened by internal strife, inflation, uneven growth, or a struggle over future political succession. The National Day celebrations in October 1999, celebrating 50 years of the Communist Party in China, underscored the importance of China's many ethnic peoples in its national resurgence. Recent crackdowns on antiseparatism and antiterrorism underscores China's increasing concern regarding national security and the integrity of its border areas.

Thus, just as the legitimacy of the Communist Chinese government has always rested on the construction of Han majority and of selected minority nationalities out of Sun Yat-sen's shifting "tray of sand," the prospects for and implications of democratization in China are closely tied to the ongoing constitution of collective identities. In China's increasingly assertive cultural diversity— intensely sharpened by economic liberalization—lies a new and perhaps precarious pluralism. As I argue below, it is too early to claim that this tolerance of diversity within authoritarian political unity carries the seeds of democracy. Nevertheless, it does reflect a heightened search for party–state legitimacy in the face of the increasing social, economic, and cultural strains brought on by globalization.

THE SOVIET UNION AS CHINA'S PROLOGUE?

At the beginning of the last decade, not a single observer of international politics predicted that the former Soviet Union would now be fragmented into a mélange of strident new nations and restive ethnic minorities. When Russian troops marched on Chechnya in hopes of keeping what remains of its former empire together, few analysts drew parallels to China's attempts to rein in its restive Muslim Uygur minority. Considering worldwide Muslim support for the liberation struggles of Muslims in Bosnia and Kosovo, and with growing support among world—notably Asian—Muslims for the Palestinian "anticolonial" struggle against Israel, it is not surprising to find growing Muslim concern regarding the plight of China's Muslims.[1]

China is thought to be different. It is rarely supposed to be shaken by ethnic or national disintegration.[2] Cultural commonality and a monolithic civilization are supposed to hold China together. Although ethnic nationalism has generally been absent from Western reporting and perspectives on China, the peoples of the People's Republic have often demonstrated otherwise. Continuing separatist

© Dru C. Gladney

*At 104 years old, Hui Hajji
is fluent in Arabic, Persian,
Turkish, and Chinese.
Hezhou City, Gansu, 1985.*

activities and ethnic unrest have punctuated China's border areas since a major
Muslim uprising in February 1996, which led to bombings in Beijing, and frequent eruptions on its periphery.[3] Quick and violent responses to thwart localized
protests, with 27 "splittists" reportedly killed in an uprising in December 1999
outside of Khotan in southern Xinjiang Uygur Autonomous Region, indicates
rising Chinese concern over the influence of separatist sentiment spilling over
from the newly independent Central Asia nations into China's Muslim areas. The
more than 20 million Turkic Uygurs, Kyrgyz, Kazakhs, and other Muslims who
live in these areas are a visible and vocal reminder that China is linked to
Eurasia. For Uygur nationalists today, the direct lineal descent from the Uygur
kingdom in seventh-century Mongolia is accepted as fact, despite overwhelming
historical and archeological evidence to the contrary, and they seek to revive that
ancient kingdom as a modern Uyguristan.[4] Random arrests and detentions continue among the Uygur, who are increasingly being regarded as China's
Chechens. A report in the *Wall Street Journal* of the arrest of Rebiya Kadir, a
well-known Uygur businesswoman, on August 11, 1999, during a visit by the

United States Congressional Research Service delegation to the region, indicates that China's suspicion of the Uygur people continues. Rebiya was sentenced to eight years' imprisonment. After pressure by several governments, her sentence was reduced by one year in 2003.[5]

China is also concerned about the "Kosovo effect," fearing that its Muslim and other ethnic minorities might be emboldened to seek outside international (read Western) support for continued human rights abuses. Just prior to its 50-year National Day celebrations in October 1999, the State Council hosted its first three-day conference on "the nationalities problem" in Beijing and issued a new policy paper, "National Minorities Policy and its Practice in China."[6] Though this White Paper did little more than outline all the "good" programs China has carried out in minority areas, it did indicate increasing concern and a willingness to recognize unresolved problems, with several strategic think tanks in Beijing and Shanghai initiating focus groups and research programs addressing ethnic identity and separatism issues.[7]

But ethnic problems in Hu Jintao's China go far deeper than the "official" minorities. Sichuanese, Cantonese, Shanghainese, and Hunanese cafés are actively promoting increased cultural nationalism and resistance to Beijing central control. As the European Union experiences difficulties in building a common European alliance across these linguistic, cultural, and political boundaries, we should not imagine China to be less concerned about its persistent multiculturalism.

If the Holy Roman Empire were around today, it would look much like China. Two millennia ago, when the Roman Empire was at its peak, so was the Han dynasty—both empires barely lasted another 200 years. At the beginning of the last millennium, China was on the verge of being conquered by the Mongols, and divided by a weakened Song dynasty in the south and the Liao dynasty in the north, whose combined territory was equal only to the five northern provinces in today's PRC. Indeed, it was the Mongols who extended China's territory to include much of what is considered part of China today: Tibet, Xinjiang, Manchuria, Sichuan, and Yunnan. Over the last two millennia China has been divided longer than it's been unified; can it maintain national unity until the next century? History suggests otherwise. Indeed, with the reacquisition of Macao in late 1999, China is the only country in the world that is *expanding its territory* instead of reducing it. Will China be able to continue to resist the inexorable forces of globalization and nationalism?

Just as linguistic diversity within China leads Chinese linguists such as John DeFrancis to speak of the many Chinese languages, attention to cultural diversity should force us to give further weight to the plurality of the Chinese peoples in national politics. A former American president once claimed to know the mind of the Chinese. This is as farfetched as someone claiming to know the European mind. Have any U.S. policymakers spent time talking to disgruntled entrepreneurs in Canton and Shanghai, impoverished peasants in Anhui and Gansu, or angry Central Asians in Xinjiang, Mongolia, and Tibet? Although ethnic diversity does not necessitate ethnic separatism or violence, growing ethnic awareness and expression in China should inform policy that accounts for the interests of China's many peoples, not just those in power. China policy should represent more than the interests of those in Beijing.

© Dru C. Gladney

Camel herder in Wu Zhong market, Ningxia, October 12, 1983. Camel meat is eaten and their coats are used for insulation.

NATIONALITY IN CHINA

Officially, China is made up of 56 nationalities: one majority nationality, the Han, and 55 minority groups. Initial results from the 2000 census suggest a total official minority population of nearly 104 million, or approximately 9 percent of the total population. The peoples identified as Han comprise 91 percent of the population from Beijing in the north to Canton in the south and include the Hakka, Fujianese, Cantonese, and other groups (MacKerras 1994, 25). A common history, culture, and written language is thought to unite these Han; differences in language, dress, diet, and customs are regarded as minor and superficial. The rest of the population is divided into 55 official minority nationalities that are mostly concentrated along the borders, such as the Mongolians and Uygurs in the north and the Zhuang, Yi, and Bai in southern China, near southeast Asia. Other groups, such as the Hui and Manchus, are scattered throughout the nation, and minorities dwell in every province, region, and county. An active state-sponsored program assists these official minority cultures and promotes their economic development (with mixed results). The outcome, according to China's preeminent sociologist, Fei Xiaotong, is a "unified multinational" state (Fei 1981, 20). But even this recognition of diversity understates the divisions within the Chinese population, especially the wide variety of culturally and ethnically diverse groups within the majority Han population (Honig 1992). These groups have recently begun to rediscover and reassert their different cultures, languages, and history (see Gladney 1998). Yet, as the Chinese worry and debate over their own identity, policymakers in other nations still take the monolithic Han identity for granted.

The notion of a Han person (*Han ren*) dates back centuries and refers to descendants of the Han dynasty that flourished at about the same time as the Roman Empire, but the concept of Han nationality (*Han minzu*) is an entirely modern phenomenon that arose with the shift from the Chinese empire to the modern nation-state (Duara 1995, 47). In the early part of this century, Chinese reformers had been concerned that the Chinese people lacked a sense of nationhood, unlike Westerners and even China's other peoples such as Tibetans and Manchus. In the view of these reformers, Chinese unity stopped at the clan or community level rather than extending to the nation as a whole. Sun Yat-Sen, leader of the republican movement that toppled the last imperial dynasty of China (the Qing) in 1911, popularized the idea that there were "Five Peoples of China"—the majority Han being one and the others being the Manchus, Mongolian, Tibetan, and Hui (a term that included all Muslims in China, now divided into Uygurs, Kazakhs, Hui, etc.). Sun was a Cantonese, educated in Hawaii, who feared arousing traditional northern suspicions of southern radical movements. He wanted both to unite the Han and to mobilize them and all other non-Manchu groups in China (including Mongols, Tibetans, and Muslims) into a modern multiethnic nationalist movement against the Manchu Qing state and foreign imperialists. The Han were seen as a unified group distinct from the "internal" foreigners— within their borders the Manchus, Tibetans, Mongols, and Hui—as well as the "external" foreigners—on their frontiers, namely the Western and Japanese imperialists. Dikotter (1992) has argued a racial basis for this notion of a unified Han *minzu,* but I suspect the rationale was more strategic and nationalistic—the need to build national security around the concept of one national people, with a small percentage of minorities supporting that idea. The Communists expanded the number of peoples from five to 56 but kept the idea of a unified Han group. The Communists were, in fact, disposed to accommodate these internal minority groups for several reasons. The Communists' 1934–35 Long March, a 6,000-mile trek across China from southwest to northwest to escape the threat of annihilation by Chiang Kai-shek's Kuomintang (KMT) forces, took the Communists through some of the most heavily populated minority areas. Harried on one side by the KMT and on the other by fierce barbarian tribesmen, the Communists faced a choice between extermination and promising special treatment to minorities—especially the Miao, Yi (Lolo), Tibetans, Mongols, and Hui—should the party ever win national power. The Communists even offered the possibility of true independence for minorities. Chairman Mao frequently referred to Article 14 of the 1931 Chinese Communist Party (CCP) constitution, which "recognizes the right of self-determination" of the national minorities in China, their right to complete separation from China, and to the formation of an independent state for each minority. This commitment was not kept after the founding of the People's Republic (Gladney 1996, 60–75). Instead, the party stressed maintaining the unity of the new nation at all costs. The recognition of minorities, however, also helped the Communists' long-term goal of forging a united Chinese nation by solidifying the recognition of the Han as a unified majority. Emphasizing the difference between Han and minorities helped to de-emphasize the differences within the Han community. The Communists incorporated the idea of Han unity into a Marxist ideology of progress with the Han in the forefront of development and civilization, the vanguard of the people's revolution (Gladney 1994a, 97). The more "backward" or "primitive" the minorities were, the more "advanced" and "civilized" the so-called Han seemed and the greater the need for a unified national identity. Cultural diversity within the Han has not been admitted because of a deep (and well-founded) fear of the country breaking up into feuding warlord-run kingdoms as happened in the 1910s and 1920s. China has historically been divided along north/south lines, into Five Kingdoms, Warring States, or local satrapies, as often as it has been united. Indeed, China as it currently exists, including large pieces of territory occupied by Mongols, Turkic peoples, Tibetans, for example, is three times larger than China was under the last Chinese dynasty, the Ming, which fell in 1644. Ironically, geographic China, as defined by the People's Republic, was actually established by foreign conquest dynasties, first by the Mongols and finally by the Manchus. A strong, centralizing Chinese government (whether of foreign or internal origin) has often tried to impose ritualistic, linguistic, and political uniformity throughout its borders. The modern state has tried to unite its various peoples with transportation and communications networks and an extensive civil service. In recent years these efforts have continued through the controlled infusion of capitalistic investment and market manipulation. Yet even in the modern era, these integrative mechanisms have not produced cultural uniformity.

HAN NATIONALITY AS INVENTED NATIONAL UNITY

Although presented as a unified culture—an idea many Western researchers also accept—Han peoples differ in many ways, most obviously in their languages. The supposedly homogenous Han speak eight mutually unintelligible languages (Mandarin, Wu, Yue, Xiang, Hakka, Gan, Southern Min, and Northern Min). Even these subgroups show marked linguistic and cultural diversity; in the Yue language family, for example, Cantonese speakers are barely intelligible to Taishan speakers, and the Southern Min dialects of Quanzhou, Changzhou, and Xiamen are equally difficult to communicate across (Norman 1988, 27). Chinese linguist Y. R. Chao has shown that the mutual unintelligibility of, say, Cantonese and Mandarin is as great as that of Dutch and English or French and Italian (1976, 83). Mandarin was imposed as the national language early in the twentieth century and has become the lingua franca, but, like Swahili in Africa, it must often be learned in school and is rarely used in everyday life in many areas. Cultural perceptions among the Han often involve broad stereotypical contrasts between north and south (Blake 1981). Northerners tend to be thought of as larger, broader-faced, and lighter-skinned, while southerners are depicted as smaller and darker. Cultural practices involving birth, marriage, and burial differ widely; Fujianese, for example, are known for vibrant folk religious practices and ritualized reburial of interned corpses, whereas Cantonese have a strong lineage tradition, both of which are almost nonexistent in the north. One finds radically different eating habits from north to south: northerners consume noodles from wheat and other grains, are open to consuming lamb and beef, and prefer spicy foods, whereas the southern diet is based upon rice, eschews such meats in favor of seafood, and along the coast is milder. It is interesting in this regard, that Fei Xiaotong (1989, 12) once argued that what made the Han people different from minorities was their agricultural traditions (specifically, minorities were traditionally not engaged in farming, though this failed to take account of groups like the Koreans and Uygur who have farmed for 1,400 years). Yet Fei never considered the vast cultural differences separating rice-eaters in the South from wheat-eaters in the North. This process of national unification based on an invented majority at the expense of a few isolated minorities is one widely documented in Asia and not unique to China (see Gladney 1998a).

IDENTITY POLITICS AND NATIONAL MINORITIES

China's policy toward minorities involves official recognition, limited autonomy, and unofficial efforts at control. The official minorities hold an importance for China's long-term development that is disproportionate to their population. Although totaling only 8.04 percent of the population, the minorities are concentrated in resource-rich areas spanning nearly 60 percent of the country's landmass and exceed 90 percent of the population in counties and villages along many border areas of Xinjiang, Tibet, Inner Mongolia, and Yunnan. While the 1990 census recorded 91 million minorities, the 2000 census is estimated to report an increase of the minority population to 104 million (Zhang Tianlu 1999).

Shortly after taking power, Communist leaders sent teams of researchers, social scientists, and party cadres to the border regions to "identify" groups as official nationalities. Only 41 of the more than 400 groups that applied were recognized, and that number had reached only 56 by 1982. For generally political reasons, most of the nearly 350 other groups were identified as Han or lumped together with other minorities with whom they shared some features. Some are still applying for recognition. The 1990 census listed almost 750,000 people as still "unidentified" and awaiting recognition—meaning they were regarded as ethnically different, but did not fit into any of the recognized categories. In recognition of the minorities' official status as well as their strategic importance, various levels of nominally autonomous administration were created: five regions, 31 prefectures, 96 counties (or, in Inner Mongolia and Manchuria, banners), and countless villages. Such autonomous areas do not have true local political control, although they may have increased local control over the administration of resources, taxes, birth planning, education, legal jurisdiction, and religious expression. These areas have minority government leaders, but the real source of power is still the Han-dominated Communist Party. As a result, they may actually come under closer scrutiny than other provinces with large minority populations such as Gansu, Qinghai, and Sichuan. While autonomy seems not to be all the word might imply, it is still apparently a desirable attainment for minorities in China. Between the 1982 and 1990 censuses, 18 new autonomous counties were established, three of them in Liaoning province for the Manchus, who previously had no autonomous administrative districts. Although the government is clearly trying to limit the recognition of new nationalities, there seems to be an avalanche of new autonomous administrative districts. Besides the 18 new counties and many villages whose total numbers have never been published, at least eight more new autonomous counties are to be set up. Five will go to the Tujia, a group widely dispersed throughout the southwest that doubled in population from 2.8 to 5.8 million from 1982 to 1990.

The increase in the number of groups seeking minority status reflects what may be described as an explosion of ethnicity in contemporary China. Indeed, it has now become popular, especially in Beijing, for people to "come out" as Manchus or other ethnic groups, admitting they were not Han all along. While the Han population grew a total of 10 percent between 1982 and 1990, the minority population grew 35 percent overall—from 67 million to 91 million. The Manchus, a group long thought to have been assimilated into the Han majority, added three autonomous districts and increased their population by 128 percent from 4.3 to 9.8 million, while the population of the Gelao people in Guizhou shot up an incredible 714 percent in just eight years. Clearly these rates reflect more than a high birthrate; they also indicate "category-shifting," as people redefine their nationality from Han to minority or from one minority to another. In interethnic marriages, parents can decide the nationality of their children, and the children themselves can choose their nationality at age 18. One scholar predicts that if the minority populations' growth rate continues, they will total 864 million in 2080 (ibid.). Reports regarding the 2000 census suggest that the minority population has increased to 104 million, amounting to 9.1 percent of the total population. China has recently begun to enforce the limits on births among minorities, especially in urban areas, but it is doubtful that authorities will be able to limit the avalanche of applications for redefinition and the hundreds of groups applying for recognition as minorities. In an important volume, Ralph Litzinger (2000, 238) has suggested that the "politics of national belonging" have led the Yao to willingly participate in the process of Chinese nationalization. Similarly, Louisa Schein's (2000, 30–31) book on the Hmong minority, argues that "internal Orientalism" has led to a resurgence of interest in the exoticized minority "Other."

Why was it popular to be officially ethnic in 1990s China? This is an interesting question given the negative reporting in the Western press about minority discrimination in China. If it is so bad to be a minority in China, why are their numbers increasing? One explanation may be that, in 1982, doubts still lingered about the government's true intent in registering the nationalities during the census. The Cultural Revolution, a ten-year period during which any kind of difference—ethnic, religious, cultural, or political—was ruthlessly suppressed, had ended only a few years before. By the mid-1980s, it had become clear that those groups identified as official minorities were beginning to receive real benefits from the implementation of several affirmative action programs. The most significant privileges included permission to have more children (except in urban areas, minorities are generally not bound by the one-child policy), pay fewer taxes, obtain better (albeit Chinese) education for their children, have greater

© Dru C. Gladney

These Bai Muslim women belong to the Hui nationality, in Eryuan county near Dali,
Yunnan, February 20, 1985.

access to public office, speak and learn their native languages, worship and practice their religion (often including practices such as shamanism that are still
banned among the Han), and express their cultural differences through the arts
and popular culture. Indeed, one might even say it has become popular to be ethnic in today's China. Mongolian hot pot, Muslim noodle, and Korean barbecue
restaurants proliferate in every city, and minority clothing, artistic motifs, and
cultural styles adorn Chinese bodies and private homes. In Beijing, one of the
most popular new restaurants is the Thai Family Village (*Dai Jia Cun*). It offers
a cultural experience of the Thai minority (known in China as the Dai), complete
with beautiful waitresses in revealing Dai-style sarongs and short tops, sensually
singing and dancing, while exotic foods such as snake's blood are enjoyed by the
young Han nouveau riche. As predicted, it is not unusual to learn of Han Chinese
prostitutes representing themselves as Thai and other minorities to appear more
exotic to their customers (Gladney 1994a). Surprisingly, the second-most popular novel in China in 1994 was *The History of the Soul (Xin ling shi),* which concerned personal and religious conflicts in a remote Muslim region in northwest
China and was written by Zhang Chengzhi, a Hui Muslim from Ningxia. This
rise of "ethnic chic" is in dramatic contrast to the anti-ethnic homogenizing policies of the late 1950s anti-Rightist period, the Cultural Revolution, and even the
late-1980s "spiritual pollution" campaigns.

Foreign policy considerations have also encouraged changes in China's
treatment of minority groups. China has one of the world's largest Muslim
populations—nearly 20 million, more than the United Arab Emirates, Iraq,
Libya, or Malaysia—and has increasing contacts with trade partners in the
Middle East and new Muslim nations created on its borders. China provides the

Middle East and Central Asia with cheap labor, consumer goods, weaponry—and increasing numbers of Muslim pilgrims to Mecca (Gladney 1994b). These relations will be jeopardized if Muslim, especially Uygur, discontent continues over such issues as limitations on mosque building, restrictions on childbearing, uncontrolled mineral and energy development, and continued nuclear testing in the Xinjiang region. Foreign policy considerations also argue for better treatment of Korean minorities, because South Korean investment, tourism, and natural resources have given China's Koreans in Liaoning and Manchuria a booming economy and the best educational level of all nationalities (including the Han). Another factor has been international tourism to minority areas, including the "Silk Road" tourism to Xinjiang and marketing packaged tours to the "colorful" minority regions of Yunnan and Guizhou for Japanese, Taiwanese, and southeast Asian Chinese tour groups. The most striking change in China's policy toward a single minority as a result of international relations has been the initiation, just after the improvement in Sino-Israeli relations in 1992, of discussions about granting official nationality status to the Chinese Jews (*Youtai ren*), once thought to have disappeared entirely. As Sino-Israeli relations improve, and China seeks increased tourism dollars from Tel Aviv and New York, one might imagine that the Chinese Jews will once again reappear as an official nationality in China.

The creation of several new nations on China's Central Asian frontier with ethnic populations on both sides of the border has also made ethnic separatism a major concern. The newly independent status of the Central Asian states has allowed separatist groups in Xinjiang to locate some sources of support, leading to over 30 reported bombing incidents in the Xinjiang Autonomous Region in 1999, claimed by groups militating for an "Independent Turkestan." At the same time, freer travel across the Central Asian borders has made China's Muslims well aware of the ethnic and political conflicts in Azerbaijan and Tajikistan, and also that many of them are better off economically than their fellow Muslims across the border. Several meetings of the "Shanghai Five" (PRC, Kazakhstan, Kyrgyzstan, Tajikistan, and Russia) since April 1997 have concluded treaties strengthening border security and the refusal to harbor separatist groups. In April 1999, Kazakhstan returned three Uygurs accused of separatism to China. Beijing's challenge is to convince China's Muslims that they will benefit more from cooperation with their national government than from resistance. In the south, a dramatic increase in cross-border relations between Chinese minority groups and Myanmar (Burma), Cambodia, and Thailand has led to a rising problem of drug smuggling. Beijing also wants to help settle disputes in Cambodia, Vietnam, and Myanmar because of the danger of ethnic wars spilling over the border into China. In Tibet, frequent reports of ongoing resistance and many arrests continue to filter into the media despite the best efforts of Beijing spin control.

INTERNAL DIVISIONS AMONG THE HAN MAJORITY

Not only have the "official" minorities in China begun to assert their identities more strongly, pressing the government for more recognition, autonomy, and special privileges, but different groups within the so-called Han majority have begun to rediscover, reinvent, and reassert their ethnic differences.

With the dramatic economic explosion in South China, southerners and others have begun to assert cultural and political differences. Cantonese rock music, videos, movies, and television programs, all heavily influenced by Hong Kong, are now popular throughout China. Whereas comedians used to make fun of southern ways and accents, southerners now scorn northerners for their lack of sophistication and business acumen. Mandarin-speaking Beijing residents will tell you that bargaining for vegetables or cellular telephones in Guangzhou or Shanghai markets is becoming more difficult for them due to growing pride in the local languages: nonnative speakers always pay a higher price. Rising self-awareness among the Cantonese is paralleled by the reassertion of identity among the Hakka, the southern Fujianese Min, the Shantou, and a host of other generally ignored peoples now empowered by economic success and embittered by age-old restraints from the north.

Interestingly, most of these southern groups traditionally regarded themselves not as Han but as Tang people, descendants of the great Tang dynasty (A.D. 618–907) and its southern bases (Moser 1985). Most Chinatowns in North America, Europe, and Southeast Asia are inhabited by descendants of Chinese immigrants from the mainly Tang areas of southern China and built around Tang Person Streets (*tang ren jie*). The next decade may bring the resurgence of Tang nationalism in southern China in opposition to northern Han nationalism, especially as economic wealth in the south eclipses that of the north. Also a newfound interest in the ancient southern Chu kingdom is key to modern southern success. Some southern scholars have departed from the traditional Chinese view of history and begun to argue that, by the sixth century B.C., the bronze culture of the Chu spread north and influenced the development of Chinese civilization, rather than this culture originating in the north and spreading southward. Many southerners now see Chu as essential to Chinese culture, to be distinguished from the less important northern dynasties—with implications for the nation's economic and geopolitical future. Museums to the glory of Chu have been established throughout southern China. There is also a growing belief that northerners and southerners had separate racial origins based on their different histories and contrasting physiogenetic types. This belief is underpinned by highly speculative 19th-century notions of race and Social Darwinism (see Mair 1999). An outpouring of interest in Hakka origins, language, and culture on Taiwan may also be spreading to the mainland. The Hakka, or "guest people," are thought to have moved southward in successive migrations from northern China as early as the Eastern Jin (A.D. 317–420) or the late Song dynasty (A.D. 960–1279) according to many Hakka (who claim to be Song people as well as Tang people). The Hakka have the same language and many of the same cultural practices as the She minority, but never sought minority status themselves—perhaps because of a desire to overcome their long-term stigmatization by Cantonese and other southerners as "uncivilized barbarians" (Blake 1981). This low status may stem from the unique Hakka language (which is unintelligible to other southerners), the isolated and walled Hakka living compounds, or the refusal of Hakka women during the imperial period to bind their feet. Nevertheless, the popular press in China is beginning to more frequently note the widely perceived Hakka origins of important political figures (including Deng Xiaoping, Mao Zedong, Sun Yat-sen, former party general secretary Hu Yaobang, and former president Ye Jianying). People often praise Zhou Enlai by stressing his Jiangnan linkages, Lee Kuan-yew as a prominent Hakka statesman. Even Chiang Kai-shek is lauded as a southerner who knew how to get money out of the United States.

INTERNET CAFÉS, DISCOS, AND DEMOCRATIZATION?

China's very economic vitality has the potential to fuel ethnic and linguistic division, rather than further integrate the country as most would suppose. As southern and coastal areas get richer, much of central, northern, and northwestern China is unlikely to keep up, increasing competition and contributing to age-old resentments across ethnic, linguistic, and cultural lines (see Wang, et al. 2000). Southern ethnic economic ties link wealthy Cantonese, Shanghainese, and Fujianese (also the majority people in Taiwan) more closely to their relatives abroad than to their political overlords in Beijing. Already provincial governments in Canton and elsewhere not only resist paying taxes to Beijing, but also restrict the transshipment of goods coming from across provincial—often the same as cultural—lines. Travelers in China have seen an extraordinary expansion of toll roads, indicating greater interest in local control. Dislocations from rapid economic growth may also fuel ethnic divisions. Huge migrations of "floating populations," estimated to total over 150 million nationally, now move across China seeking employment in wealthier areas, often engendering stigmatized identities and stereotypical fears of the "outsiders" (*wai di ren*) within China. Crime, housing shortages, and lowered wages are now attributed most to these people from Anhui, Hunan, or Gansu who are taking jobs from locals; these complaints are similar to those in West Germany about the influx of Easterners after reunification. Reports that 70 percent of those convicted of crimes in Beijing were outsiders have fueled criticisms of China's increasingly open migration policy (Fei Guo 1999). Eric Harwit has noted that the "digital divide" in China is closing, and the rapid expansion of Internet usage (up to 27 percent of all households are online in Beijing), has fostered wider communication and dissemination of news and information.[8]

As a result of all these changes, China is becoming increasingly decentered. This is a fearsome prospect for those holding the reins in Beijing and, perhaps, was a factor in the decision to crack down on the June 1989 demonstrations in Tiananmen Square. At that time central authorities had begun to lose control of a country they feared could quickly unravel. That such fears have not eased is shown by the increased calls for national unity during the National Day celebrations and new efforts to reduce corruption. Worker and peasant unrest reported throughout China cut across and may at times exacerbate cultural and ethnolinguistic differences between the haves and the have-nots, who in today's China are often and increasingly interacting along lines marked by multiethnic diversity.

Studies of democracy and democratization in China suggest that, at least at the village level, legitimate local elections are leading to a rising civil society and increasing pluralization (Brook and Frolic 1997). Nevertheless, few see this process advancing to the level of actually posing a serious threat to the rule of the

© Dru C. Gladney

Uygur textile market, Kashgar Bazaar, 1986.

Communist Party (Hu 2000). Most scholars locate China's increasing civil society, not in the political domain, but in those spaces created by the market economy that the state has difficulty controlling, such as the dance halls and discos (Schell 1988), the karaoke bars, massage parlors, and private businesses (Liu Xin 2001), and the free marketplace (Anagnost 1997).

Interestingly, scholars of Taiwan's democratization were equally skeptical of the democratic process ever dislodging the Nationalist Kuomintang Party, the wealthiest and most entrenched Chinese political party in history (Rigger 1999, 23). The recent reelection of Chen Shui-bian, suggests that local politics were the key to his winning the narrow vote, despite continuing controversy over the assassination attempt.[9] Comparisons between China and Taiwan suggest that democratization will never happen as a result of encouragement from the top, as it would only dislodge those in power, but only as an uncontrollable coalition of marginal groups (Dickson 1998, 82). Bruce Dickson (1998, 26ff) coherently argues that the Leninist system, though theoretically open to participatory governance, is inherently resistant to pluralist democratic processes due to the role of the Communist Party leadership as permanent leader of the proletariat. Nevertheless, it was the Leninist system that created a system of recognizing and legitimating separate nationalities, what many scholars suggest was the Soviet Union's ultimate undoing (see d'Encausse 1993, 31–47).

In the Taiwan case, Shelley Rigger (1999, 80–93) has argued forcefully for the role of marginal coalition politics in the rise of the Democratic Peoples Party (DPP), which Chen Shui-bian masterfully united to unseat the ruling Nationalist Party. The successful mobilization of women, temple organizations, Taiwanese nationalists, environmentalists, aboriginals, and disenfranchised workers helped to unseat a well-organized political machine. Rigger pays scant attention to the role of the minority aboriginal peoples in this process of "Taiwanization." Though small in number (about 2 percent of the total population), the Taiwan aboriginals (*yuanzhu min*) were a significant emblem of Taiwanese separate identity from mainland China, and enlisting their support was a pivotal symbolic move on the part of the DPP. Might not China's indigenous minority groups (numbering about 9 percent) also play a role in China's future democratization? Certainly, many of them are pushing at the seams of Chinese rule, and some, like the Uygurs and Tibetans, are receiving increasing international support. Only time will tell if they play an increasing role in Chinese affairs.

CONCLUSION: NATIONAL DISUNITY?

Although ethnic separatism on its own will never be a serious threat to a strong China, a China weakened by internal strife, inflation, uneven economic growth, or the struggle for succession after Deng's death could become further divided along cultural and linguistic lines. China's separatists such as they are could never mount such a coordinated attack as was seen on September 11, 2001, in the United States, and China's more closed society lacks the openness that have allowed terrorists to move so freely in the West. China's threats will most likely come from civil unrest, and perhaps internal ethnic unrest from within the so-called Han majority. We should recall that it was a southerner, born and educated abroad, who led the revolution that ended China's last dynasty; and, when that empire fell, competing warlords—often supported by foreign powers—fought for local turf occupied by culturally distinct peoples. Moreover, the Taiping Rebellion that nearly brought down the Qing dynasty also had its origins in the southern border region of Guangxi among so-called marginal Yao and Hakka peoples. These events are being remembered as the generally well hidden and overlooked "Others" within Chinese society begin to reassert their own identities, in addition to the official nationalities. At the same time, China's leaders are moving away from the homogenizing policies that alienated minority and non-northern groups. Recent moves to allow and even encourage the expression of cultural diversity, while preserving political unity, indicate a growing awareness of the need to accommodate cultural diversity. Further evidence of this trend was the 1997 incorporation of Hong Kong, a city that operates on cultural and social assumptions very different from those of Beijing, and that was granted an unprecedented degree of autonomy within China.

The construction of Chinese national identity has always been tentative. In June 1989, while China's future hung in the balance, there was significant concern over which armies would support Deng's crackdown: those based in Sichuan, Hunan, Canton, or Beijing, all with their own local concerns. The military has since been reshuffled and somewhat downsized, attempting to uproot any local attachments and professionalize the command structure (Lilley and Shambaugh 1999, 28). However, this only underlines the growing importance of regional and local ties. China, as of now, is a unified country militarily and, perhaps, politically. As a result of Hu Jintao's and Jiang Zemin's continuance of the Deng Xiaoping reforms, it is increasingly less unified economically. Yet how can

Young Hui women await the Ramadan procession to the local mosque, Hexhou city, Gansu, 1985.

China continue to withstand the forces of globalization and nationalism without a government legitimated through popular elections, transparency in the political process, adherence to the rule of law, and good governance?

In November 2000, an ambassador from one of China's friendliest Muslim nations remarked privately to me that by the end of the next decade China would be divided into nine republics. Historians debate whether a foreign threat has been the only thing that has held China together. Now that the encirclement doctrine, upon which Nixon and Kissinger built the Sino-American alliance, is no longer valid, and containment has been replaced by improving US-China relationship based on an "engagement" policy, China faces its only enemies from within. Certainly, the events of September 11, 2001, and China's participation in the war on terrorism have helped to further reign in China's separatist groups and further secure its borders (see Gladney, 2004, 238–57).

The Chinese press reported more than 5,000 organized social protests in 1998 alone, with many more in 1999, culminating in the widespread Falun Gong uprising and crackdown. Labor groups and peasant associations organized many of these protests, but increasingly ethnic and religious groups, such as the Falun Gong, have begun to speak out (see Chen 2003, 206–213). Provincial governments in Canton and elsewhere have continued to resist paying taxes to Beijing, as well as restrict the transshipment of outside goods across provincial and often cultural lines, to the extent that China is becoming dangerously decentered—a fearsome prospect for those holding the threads in Beijing, and perhaps the main reason for the rush to finalize international border agreements with Russia, Kazakhstan, Kyrgyzstan, Tajikistan, and Vietnam.

© Dru C. Gladney

*Father and son in mourning
dress for their deceased
elder, Xiji township,
Ningxia, 1984.*

Senator Daniel Patrick Moynihan once predicted that there would be 50 new countries in 50 years. The trend began with the Soviet Union in 1991 and has continued throughout much of Africa and Asia, particularly Indonesia. Why should China be immune from such global diversification? Although ethnic separatism alone will never be threatening enough to pull a strong China apart, a China weakened by internal strife, inflation, uneven economic growth, or the struggle for (un)democratic succession, could certainly fragment along cultural and linguistic lines. Ethnic strife did not dismantle the former Soviet Union, but it did come apart along boundaries defined in large part by ethnic and national difference. The generally well-hidden and over-looked "Others" within Chinese society, the Cantonese, Shanghainese, Sichuanese, and Fujianese, are beginning to reassert their own identities in addition to the official nationalities on China's borders. Increasing Taiwanese nationalism has caused great consternation in Beijing, an internal ethnic nationalism that few Chinese nationalists understand.

The rising politics of difference are of concern not only in Lhasa and Urumqi, but in Canton and Shanghai as well. The "Kosovo effect" may very well turn into the "Chechnya effect" where ethnic groups, especially Muslims in general (not just the Uygur), become stereotyped as internal threats and as separatists, and cleansing is launched as an internal affair. China also may link Uygur separatist actions to the issue of Tibet and Taiwan, leading to broader international ramifications of any crackdown. The problem for China, however, is that many of its internal threats may not come from official nationalities who are more easily singled out by race or language. China's Chechnya, like Indonesia's Aceh, may very well come from within its own people who seek economic and political advantage. The admission of China into the World Trade Organization (WTO) will mean an even further enrichment of the largely coastal and urban developed areas over the more rural central provinces and peripheral minority areas, exacerbating underlying tensions and cultural fault lines. The next decade promises to be as momentous for China as the last decade was for the United States, Europe, and Russia.

REFERENCES

Anagnost, Ann S. 1997. *National pasttimes: Narrative, representation, and power in modern China.* Durham, NC: Duke Univ. Press.

Blake, Fred C. 1981. *Ethnic groups and social change in a Chinese market town.* Honolulu: Univ. of Hawaii Press.

Brook, Timothy, and B. Michael Frolic, eds. 1997. *Civil society in China.* Armonk: M.E. Sharpe.

Chao, Yuen Ren. 1976. *Aspects of Chinese sociolinguistics.* Stanford: Stanford Univ. Press.

Chen, Nancy N. 2003. Healing sects and anti-cult campaigns. In *Religion in China today,* ed. Daniel L. Overmeyer, 199–214. Cambridge: Cambridge Univ. Press.

Dickson, Bruce. 1998. *Democratization in China and Taiwan: The adaptability of Leninist parties.* New York and London: Clarendon Press.

Dikotter, Frank. 1992. *The discourse of race in modern China.* Stanford: Stanford Univ. Press.

Duara, Prasenjit. 1995. *Rescuing history from the nation.* Chicago: Univ. of Chicago Press.

Encausse, Hélène Carrère d'. 1993. *The end of the Soviet Empire: The triumph of the nations,* trans. Franklin Philip. New York: Basic Books.

Fei, Xiaotong. 1989. *Zhonghua minzu de duoyuan jiti juge* (Plurality and unity in the configuration of the Chinese nationality), *Beijing Daxue Xuebao* 4, 1–19.

_____, ed. 1981. Ethnic identification in China. In *Toward a people's anthropology,* ed. Fei Xiaotong. New World Press: Beijing, China.

Gladney, Dru C. 2004. *Dislocating China: Muslims, minorities, and other subaltern subjects.* Chicago: Univ. of Chicago Press.

_____. 1998a. *Ethnic identity in China: The making of a Muslim minority nationality.* New York & London: Wadsworth Publishers.

_____, ed. 1998b. *Making majorities: Constituting the nation in Japan, Korea, China, Malaysia, Fiji, Turkey, and the United States.* Stanford: Stanford Univ. Press.

_____. 1998c. Internal colonialism and the Uyghur nationality: Chinese nationalism and its subaltern subjects. *CEMOTI: Cahiers d'études sur la Méditerranée Orientale et le Monde Turco-Iranien,* no. 25, 47–64.

_____. 1991/1996. *Muslim Chinese: Ethnic nationalism in the people's republic.* Reprint. Cambridge: Harvard Univ. Press.

_____. 1994a. Representing nationality in China: Refiguring majority/minority identities. *The Journal of Asian Studies* 53 (1): 92–123.

_____. 1994b. Sino-Middle Eastern perspectives and relations since the Gulf War: Views from below. *The*

International Journal of Middle Eastern Studies, 29 (4): 677–691.

Guo, Fei. 1999. *Beijing's Policies towards ethnic minority /rural migrant villages.* Paper presented at the Conference on Contemporary Migration and Ethnicity in China, 7–8 October 1999, Institute of Nationality Studies, Chinese Academy of Social Sciences, Beijing.

Harwit, Eric, and Duncan Clark. 2001. Shaping the Internet in China: Evolution of political control over network infrastructure and content, *Asian Survey* 41 (3): 377–408.

Honig, Emily. 1992. *Creating Chinese ethnicity.* New Haven: Yale Univ. Press.

Hu, Shao-hua. 2000. *Explaining Chinese democratization.* New York: Praeger Publishers.

Lilley, James R., and David L. Shambaugh, eds. 1999. *China's military faces the future.* Armonk: M.E. Sharpe.

Litzinger, Ralph A. 2000. *Other Chinas: The Yao and the politics of national belonging.* Durham: Duke Univ. Press.

Liu, Xin. 2001. *The otherness of self: A genealogy of the self in contemporary China.* Ann Arbor: Univ. of Michigan Press.

Mackerras, Colin. 1994. *China's minorities: Integration and modernization in the twentieth century.* Hong Kong, Oxford, New York: Oxford Univ. Press.

Mair, Victor, ed. 1999. *The Bronze Age and early Iron Age people of Eastern Central Asia.* Washington, D.C.: Institute for the Study of Man, Inc.

Moser, Leo J. 1985. *The Chinese mosaic: The peoples and provinces of China.* Boulder: Westview Press.

Norman, Jerry. 1988. *Chinese.* Cambridge: Cambridge Univ. Press.

Rigger, Shelley. 1999. *Politics in Taiwan: Voting for democracy.* London and New York: Routledge Press.

Schein, Louisa. 2000. *Minority rules: The Miao and the feminine in China's cultural politics.* Durham: Duke Univ. Press.

Schell, Orville. 1988. *Discos and democracy: China in the throes of reform.* New York: Anchor Books.

Shambaugh, David, ed. 2000. *Is China unstable: Assessing the factors.* Armonk: M.E. Sharpe.

Wang, Shaoguang, Hu Angang, Kang Xiaoguang. 2000. *The political economy of uneven development: The case of China.* Armonk: M.E. Sharpe.

Zhang, Tianlu. 1999. *Xiandai Zhongguo Shaoshu minzu renkou zhuangkuang* (Analysis of the Contemporary China minority nationality population situation). Paper presented at the Conference on Contemporary Migration and Ethnicity in China, 7–8 October 1999, Institute of Nationality Studies, Chinese Academy of Social Sciences, Beijing.

NOTES

1. The following are statements by Zainuddin, spokesman for the Indonesian Islamic Defenders Front: "Israelis are not welcome in Indonesia because their illegal colonization has killed thousands of Muslim people. . . . We are ready to go to war, a holy war, to defend Islam. . . . The Israelis are colonialists, and we are against what they have done to the Palestinians, therefore they should have been barred from coming to Indonesia" (Calvin Sims, "Islamic Radicals in Indonesia Vow Vengeance on Israelis," *New York Times* 15 October 2000: 11). For Xinjiang as an "internal colony of China," see Gladney (1998b, 47).

2. David Shambaugh's (2000) collection of essays entitled, *Is China Unstable,* dismisses the ethnic issue as minor and completely unlike the troubles the former Soviet Union encountered. For a recent work on the ways in which marginalized peoples help us to understand China in different ways, see Gladney (2004).

3. See Amnesty International's critical report, "Peoples Republic of China: Gross Violations of Human Rights in the Xinjiang Uygur Autonomous Region" (April 21, 1999), London.

4. The best "Uygur nationalist" retelling of this unbroken descent from Karakhorum is in the document "Brief History of the Uyghers," originating from the Eastern Turkestani Union in Europe, and available electronically at www. geocites.com/CapitolHill/1730/buh.html. For a review and critique, including historical evidence for the multiethnic background of the contemporary Uygur, see Dru C. Gladney's "Ethnogenesis and Ethnic Identity in China: Considering the Uyghurs and Kazakhs" in Victor Mair (1998, 812–34). For a discussion of the recent archeological evidence derived from DNA dating of the dessicated corpses of Xinjiang, see Victor Mair's "Introduction" in Victor Mair (1998, 1–40).

5. See *Wall Street Journal,* Ian Johnson, "China Arrests Noted Businesswoman in Crackdown in Muslim Region," August 18, 1999.

6. See China State Council, "National Minorities Policy and its Practice in China," Beijing, October 1999.

7. The China Institute for Contemporary International Relations (CICIR), under the State Council, has initiated a "Nationality Studies Project" to examine security implications of China's minority problems (Chu Shulong interview, November 14, 1999).

8. For a critical discussion of China's "digital divide" and the often surprising accessibility of many Internet sites, see Eric Harwit, "The Digital Divide of China's Internet Use." Paper presented at the Association for Asian Studies Annual Meeting, New York, March 28, 2003. See also his coauthored article, Eric Harwit and Duncan Clark (2001, 378–381).

9. For an excellent discussion, see the February 23, 2004, Brookings Institute Report, "Taiwan Elections 2004" http://www.brookings.edu/dybdocroot/comm/events/20040223.pdf.

Fieldwork Biography
Lincoln Keiser

Over the years many people have asked me how I was able to conduct a field research project with an African American street gang. It was really quite by accident. I was in the right place at the right time and thus met people I happened to connect with on a very personal level. Most of the data anthropologists collect comes from the personal relationships they form with the people they are studying. Without personal relationships the anthropologists can gain little understanding of an alien way of life.

I was fortunate to find in my research with the Vice Lords, and with the Kohistanis of Afghanistan and Pakistan, people who were very skillful at opening my eyes. The understanding I was able to achieve owes a lot to their skill. Through my work I attempt to provide readers with an understanding of what most interests me, and thus in the final analysis reflects how I came to be the person I am—both as an anthropologist and as a human being.

Lincoln Keiser is professor of anthropology at Wesleyan University.

4/The Vice Lords Today
Sociocultural Change in an African American Street Gang

It is generally stated that the Vice Lord Nation—referred to by Vice Lords as a "club" not a "gang"—originated in 1958 in what is usually called "Charlie Town," the Illinois State Training School for Boys at St. Charles, Illinois. In St. Charles the inmates lived in what are called "cottages." The Vice Lords began in Harding Cottage, which housed the toughest boys in the institution. The club was started in the Lawndale area of Chicago in the fall of 1958, following the release of several members (Keiser 1969).

Thirty plus years have passed since *The Vice Lords* first appeared. Although the Vice Lord Nation changed during that time, it is stronger now then ever. Anthropology changed too. Even though in some ways I changed with it, I remain most interested in what first drew me to anthropology—a fascination with figuring out how sociocultural systems work.

In *The Vice Lords* (1969) I tried to understand how their sociocultural system worked by focusing on structure and pattern—how the Vice Lords were organized, how this organization was regularized, systematic, how it fit with a system of meaning to form a coherent whole. At the time I was dissatisfied with how the social science literature generally dealt with groups like the Vice Lords—portraying them as loosely organized groups of delinquent boys. Although the literature was rich in theories of delinquency it seemed thin in ethnography. It didn't tell me what I wanted to know—it didn't tell me much about the nature of Vice Lord society and culture.

The delinquency approach still lives (for example, see Mark Fleisher, 1995); I find it just as dissatisfying now as I did then. But looking at the Vice Lords in terms of structure and pattern no longer satisfies me either. The Vice Lords have shed their skin. They are no longer a "club" organized to fight for territory and reputation. Now they form a mob or gang, an economic–political organization competing (often times violently) with similar groups for control both of the street-level drug trade and the underground prison economy.

To understand these new Vice Lords we need to underline what should be obvious to all—that African Americans (and the Vice Lords specifically) in the United States are trapped in a political and economic system that oppresses them. But simply diagnosing oppression and identifying the sites where it occurs (an endeavor that sometimes passes for analysis in contemporary sociocultural anthropology) doesn't help us understand very much in itself. Oppression is part of sociopolitical environments and we need to understand how Vice Lords adapt to the oppression that contorts their lives. This involves us in questions of power and resistance (although a resistance that is not necessarily by definition heroic).

Power and resistance, however, are never naked. Thus we must also analyze Vice Lord culture—the space defined by a sometimes-messy body of public beliefs, concepts, symbols, and meanings.

Moreover, we need to look at the Vice Lord Nation not as a structured sociocultural entity but as a process—that is to say, as a system of social relationships and meaning playing out through time. And we have to place this process in the wider political–economic contexts that affect it.

***

This chapter began for me in a rather strange place—on the basketball court at Wesleyan University where I work. Since 1975 I've played pickup basketball Monday, Wednesday, and Friday beginning at noon. Noon-ball, as it is called, has an interesting mix of players. Besides students, some of the regulars work at the university; some work in town at various professional and nonprofessional jobs, and some are street people who work sporadically, if at all. Besides a good workout, the best thing about noon-ball is the opportunity it affords me to connect across race and class lines. But this is not about noon-ball, although that would be a fascinating subject for the anthropological eye.

A few years ago Joe, an African American guy from town, brought a copy of a supermarket tabloid called *The Examiner* to the basketball court. Now Joe knew of my previous work on the Vice Lords (Keiser 1969, 1974). In this particular issue he had found an article called "Death of the Evil . . . Vice Lords",[1] with the subheading "America's most feared and wanted drug gang goes out with just a whimper." He thought I might be interested. I was. The article relates to how poverty in the inner city is rooted in oppressive political and economic inequalities, how popular culture creates meanings and understandings that obscure these roots, and how these meanings and understandings are produced and maintained (Gregory 1994, 42).

But the piece does more than this. It also resonates, if ever so faintly, with something that should be just as important to anthropologists working in the inner city, specifically, understanding how social actors create order and meaning in their lives in various urban contexts (Peletz 1995, 350). Thus this chapter suggests ways to go beyond merely diagnosing oppression and identifying the sites where it occurs. For oppression works in shaping both patterns of social relationships and the meanings and understandings that give them the degree of order and disorder they possess. And it works in complex ways, with often unexpected and unintended consequences. When we look at oppression in this light, as part of broad, political–economic contexts, we can begin to understand how groups like the Vice Lords, (started by a small group of friends in an Illinois juvenile detention facility some 40 odd years ago) got to be cats with so many lives.

But I should make clear at the outset that what I have to say is not based on any recent field observations. Although I speak with an authoritative voice, this piece is really a set of hypotheses, plausible guesses based on tantalizing bits of information from odd sources—newspaper articles, Internet web pages, and informant accounts. My conclusions need to be tested, clarified, and undoubtedly modified by focused field research.

So, *The Examiner* proclaimed the death of the Vice Lords, "Americas most feared and dreaded drug gang." But in the past 40 years, powers within mainstream society, such as the Chicago police and Chicago's daily newspapers, have declared many times the Vice Lords and other similar groups in Chicago to be dead. Yet, like a phoenix, the Vice Lord Nation has always risen from its ashes.

To understand why this is so let's begin by looking at the spin the media gives the Vice Lords, (as well as groups like the Black P-Stone Nation and the Gangster Disciples). *The Examiner* piece is particularly valuable in this respect because its hyperbolic, alien-gives-birth-to-two-headed-monster-on-crowded-disco-dance-floor approach to its subjects clarifies by its very exaggeration things often hidden by the more staid approach of traditional daily newspapers. The piece starts like this:

> In a stunning predawn raid, Chicago cops busted 21 top members of America's most powerful street gang—and broke their brutal hold on the city's crime-ravaged West Side. Their prize catch was kingpin Willie Lloyd, the arrogant, flamboyant boss of a multimillion-dollar crack cocaine dynasty that ruled the streets with an iron fist. When prosecutors finally convicted Lloyd on a weapons charge, it was a crushing blow to the 1,000-member Unknown Vice Lords, a savage criminal operation that forced kids and families into nightmare lives of coke, crime and degradation. "These people held a Chicago neighborhood hostage," says prosecutor Michael Smith. "They lived by none of society's rules. They lied, they cheated, they murdered and finally they turned on each other" (*Examiner,* August 9, 1994).

The piece goes on to tell how kingpin Lloyd "brazenly" spoke to his underlings over speakerphone while in jail, and even ran a snack shop and game room from his cell. (We'll come back to the snack shop later on.) Finally, the article tells with special relish how Lloyd was found having sex with his girlfriend in the jurors' bathroom during a court appearance.

The subnarrative in the *Examiner* article is clear. The ills of the inner city, (people living lives of coke, crime, and degradation) are caused by powerful criminal street gangs headed by evil tyrannical bosses that oppress entire urban communities. But the evildoers can no longer threaten the lives of everyday citizens if the guys in the white hats can smash these criminal organizations and put them away. This will go a long way toward curing the sickness of the inner city.

This same narrative underlies stories told in more mainstream newspapers, although the message there is more subtle. A few years ago the *Chicago Tribune* ran a series of articles about Larry Hoover and the Gangster Disciples, the group he heads.[2] The federal government had just indicted Hoover and other leaders of the Gangster Disciples on a variety of drug-related charges. Interestingly enough, the indictments came while Hoover was imprisoned in an Illinois correctional center.

These articles contain interesting ethnography, but what's most interesting here is the way the *Tribune* portrayed Hoover. Hoover is more difficult to demonize than Willie Lloyd, for he captured the imagination of many people in Chicago through his attempts to use the Disciples as a force for political change, both in the Illinois prisons and in the inner city. Hoover played a key role in forging peace agreements with the Vice Lords, and, as the *Tribune* reported, began a political action committee that registered many ghetto residents to vote. Moreover, his organization sponsored public rap concerts and his associates started a "legitimate" business, developing a line of clothing with designs created by Hoover himself. In prison he used his political power to maintain peace and to reduce rape.

Yet, the article minimizes this side of Hoover by portraying his enterprises as smoke screens designed to hide his real purpose: protecting and developing the Disciples' corner of the illegal drug trade. To quote the *Tribune,* articles noted the following:

> The indictment of Hoover and 38 others, including a Chicago police officer, on federal drug conspiracy charges was portrayed as a crippling blow to the Midwest's largest and most violent street gang. . . . "I guess I would say, I told you so," said Jack Hynes, an assistant Cook County state's attorney who has vigorously opposed Hoover's efforts for parole from a murder conviction for which he has spent the last 21 years in prison. "This indictment has kind of torn down the facade and exposed the gang for what they are" (*Chicago Tribune,* September 1–3, 1995).

So the guys in the white hats have once again helped make the inner-city streets safe by taking a guy who was behind bars, and well . . . putting him behind some more bars. It takes me back to the Hindu-Kush and one old Kohistani guy who threatened my research assistant with retribution if he ever told about the history of the village we were living in. "I'll find you in the afterlife and kill you!" he said. The logic in protecting the public by jailing a person already in jail didn't seem to bother the federal prosecutors and state's attorneys any more than killing a person who was already dead bothered the old Kohistani.

But state's attorneys and federal prosecutors are not stupid. Their actions (and the reporting of them in the media) are not just about keeping the streets safe from urban predators. No. It's also about maintaining a political hierarchy in which the power of ghetto residents is minimized. Thus it was no accident that when the Gangster Disciples began organizing themselves as a force in Chicago politics and developing a legitimate economic power base, the government made sure Larry Hoover would never see the light of day again. This, in other words, is oppression in action, for intertwined with the rhetoric of keeping the streets safe from drug dealers lies the reality of keeping the ghetto poor and nonthreatening to existing economic and political power arrangements.

What interests me in this case, however, is not simply that we oppress poverty stricken African Americans. We've been doing that forever (well, almost forever). It's old news. Nor is it even how oppression relates to hegemony and counterhegemony, to use jargon popular in contemporary anthropology. Rather what I find most interesting is how oppression shapes cultural forms in the inner city.

Okay, so politicians encourage the police to get the drug gangs off the streets by arresting and jailing their members, and instruct the courts to keep them in jail by passing laws requiring harsh, mandatory sentences. And the media supports all of this by giving our understanding of street gangs a particular spin. Not surprisingly, the police take their job very seriously, and, in the name of freeing the inner city from fear, arrest young ghetto males in huge numbers. The National Institute on Drug Abuse released figures a few years ago showing that on any given day one in three ghetto males between the ages of 20 and 29 is under the supervision of the criminal justice system, a figure vastly higher than accounted for either by their percentage of the population, or their rate of drug use.[3]

Undoubtedly this has many important consequences for ghetto men. For starters, young men in the ghetto obviously see what's happening around them and know that in all probability the continuity in their lives will involve regular movement between prison and the streets. In a piece called "Mobility, Continuity, and Urban Social Organization" David Jacobson (1971, 636) argued that for ghetto men, ". . . the prospects were those of moving between street life and prison, a pattern of circulation which can be seen to underlie the persistence of their relationships, since they expect to see each other again and again both in and out of jail."

By a rather circuitous route, this takes us back to Willie Lloyd and the snack shop he allegedly ran while in prison. Although some have criticized it, one of the best prison ethnographies I have seen is R. T. Davidson's (1974) *Chicano Prisoners: The Key to San Quentin*. What he says about underground prison shops (including snack shops) and how they operate in the underground prison economy is particularly illuminating. According to Davidson underground prison shops provided sources of goods that made life more tolerable for the prisoners of San Quentin; consequently, the control of their business was a major concern of the underground, prisoner power structure (1974, 101–147).

Obviously, San Quentin in the early 1970s does not equal the Illinois correctional facilities of today. Yet, material contained in the *Tribune* stories hints at a prison sociocultural system similar in many ways. Thus, according to the

Tribune article, "When inmates at Pontiac Correctional Center want a hot pizza, they can place an order and enjoy one fresh from the oven in the comfort of their cells, courtesy of a delivery man who also happens to be a fellow prisoner" (*Chicago Tribune,* September 1–3, 1995).

As we shall see, these "pizza huts" (and the snack shop run by Willie Lloyd as well) do business very much like the underground shops Davidson described. This is also the case with the production and circulation of illegal drugs and weapons in the Illinois prisons.

Like San Quentin, much of the political and economic power in prison society in Illinois lies in the hands of gangs (but unlike San Quentin, these are African American organizations rather than Chicano ones). As the *Tribune* reports, "So powerful are some inmate leaders in state prisons that they can provide contraband items to other prisoners. . . . The state prisons (are) run by the gangs that populate them" (*Chicago Tribune,* September 1, 1995, 7). As Magnus Seng, a professor of criminal justice at Loyola University in Chicago noted, prison officials ". . . couldn't run the prisons otherwise. . . . The inmates are running the place to some extent. There's a sub-rosa economy, a small town run by inmates." And, as Bobby Gore, a Vice Lord leader from the 1960s and once an activist with the Safer Foundation, noted, "That's the way it ought to be" (ibid.).

We can see how valuable gang membership is to ghetto men given political and economic conditions in the inner city. On the streets, gangs provide a way to make a living for men with few job skills, fewer job opportunities, and a fast-eroding welfare safety net. In prisons, gangs can make the difference between easy time and hard time, protecting their members from violence and predation, and organize the activities of the underground economy.

This double function is particularly important given the alternating pattern between the streets and jail that dominates the career paths of so many ghetto men. For gangs help make the transition both from the streets to jail, and from jail to the streets relatively smooth for their members. Consequently, gang membership is a valuable resource, one made even more valuable by the punitive and repressive policies currently in favor in our society. The more jails we build, the more ghetto men we fill them with; the more we tear down the welfare system and the more jobs we cut, the stronger and more vital groups like the Vice Lords, the Gangster Disciples, and the Black P-Stone Nation become. The very policies designed to destroy street gangs in fact strengthen them.

Federal prosecutors argue that arresting Larry Hoover and putting him behind federal bars will affect the Disciples' ability to function effectively because federal prisons are more restrictive on prisoners' movements, making it more difficult for Hoover to run his drug empire. In this light it's interesting to note a recent Associated Press release describing the growing influence of gangs in federal prisons.[4] If history is any indication, putting such a skilled political leader as Larry Hoover in the federal prison system is like putting a fox in the chicken coop. It could very well come back to haunt us.

So groups like the Vice Lords rise ever stronger from the ashes of their destruction. But to better understand why this happens we need to understand how the Vice Lords changed from a club modeled on working-class social clubs and focused on gang-fighting and building "rep" (reputation), to a mob modeled on organized crime organizations and focused on regulating the street-level drug trade and the underground prison economy. Then we need to understand Vice Lord cultural dynamics—especially the powerful symbolic and ritual system that underlies and supports the Vice Lord political economy.

First, though, I should describe my general approach to understanding the Vice Lords, for it differs both descriptively and theoretically from much of the social science work on gang phenomena. Most importantly my approach is primarily ethnographic—but ethnographic in its social anthropological sense. Ethnography has become fashionable in urban studies outside of anthropology and has long been a staple of the "Chicago school" of urban sociology. It's not uncommon to find social workers, criminologists, and sociologists all doing ethnography. Often—although not always—such ethnography involves simply describing a way of life from first-hand observations. For example, in *Crackhouse,* Terry Williams defines ethnography as an attempt ". . . to provide a detailed portrait of people in their own setting through close and prolonged observation" (1992, 5).

In social anthropology, however, an ethnography is a study of a particular society, culture, or community (rather than Society, Culture, Community writ large). And what is distinctive about such studies is that they are analytical rather than descriptive. Thus in his classic ethnography *The Nuer,* E.E. Evans-Pritchard writes, ". . . if it be said that we have only described the facts in relation to a theory of them and as exemplifications of it and have subordinated description to analysis, we reply that this is our intention" (1940, 261).

In social anthropology, therefore, ethnography orders and explains the facts in terms of theories of them. An ethnography is a theory of a society, community, culture, or group of people. It explains whatever it is that the observer observed by analyzing those observations in terms of theoretical frameworks.

Gang research has long been dominated by theories of delinquency. From Thrasher's classic study *The Gang* (1927) to Hagedorn's *People and Folks* (1998), theories of delinquency and criminality have shaped gang research. In the pages that follow, however, I do not address in any way why, or even if, the Vice Lords are or were juvenile delinquents or adult criminals. In contrast I ask a different kind of question: in spite of the overwhelming political power arrayed against it, how did the Vice Lords rise again? Why did the claims that victory was just around the corner in the war against gangs (like the Pentagon's claims about victory over the Viet Cong) turn out to be so hollow?

To answer this question I must identify and describe social arrangements that order Vice Lord social interactions. But these patterns are not entities locked in a timeless reality. They participate with one another in systems playing out over time within social contexts composed of political, economic, and cultural forces interrelated in complex ways. These forces, however, do not cause the course social interactions take; in contrast they shape them. At the same time the forces themselves are not stagnant, but change through time—and in changing, continually shape and reshape Vice Lord social arrangements. Thus our analysis must focus on the forces shaping Vice Lord social arrangements.

I've mentioned culture as one force shaping Vice Lord social interactions. In the social science literature on gangs, a recurring controversy concerns what role, if any, culture plays in gang phenomena. In 1969 Walter Miller proposed that lower-class culture was the primary force generating gang delinquency. Although Miller's explanation never won the day, the cultural explanation for gang delinquency continues to draw supporters. According to John Hagedorn, the basic argument is that gang violence (a form of gang delinquency) ". . . is an age old lower class cultural product—i.e., violence is caused by men acting out [the] internalized norms of their violent subculture" (1998, 179).

Unfortunately, this kind of cultural explanation for gang violence has serious problems. "Norms" can mean two distinct things. First, they can mean patterns abstracted from observations of behavior. In this sense norms are the patterns of behavior that reoccur and thus form what we think of as "normal" behavior.

Norms abstracted from patterns of behavior, however, can't explain anything, certainly not themselves, a point Elizabeth Bott made clear long ago in her study of family and social networks (1957, 218). In contrast, they are what need to be explained.

But some who use the normative explanation use it in a different way. Rather than forming brute behavioral patterns, norms are thought to be the beliefs and values people hold both about how they normally act and how they should act in certain situations. Thus internalizing normative beliefs and values results in people acting in terms of them. And when they do, norms emerge in the behavior patterns we observe.

Most importantly, these normative beliefs and values form the traits that define a culture. As cultural traits they are passed on through learning (the process of enculturation) and when internalized produce observable patterns of behavior. Although such culture traits may be related to wider social, economic, and political conditions, they cannot be reduced to them. Thus learning the traits of culture and then internalizing them best explains why people act in ways their compatriots consider "normal."

Yet, in his classic urban ethnography, *Tally's Corner* (1967), Elliot Liebow argued that the behavior patterns observed among ghetto African American men are generated by American middle-class norms twisted by wider political and economic conditions. Thus Leibow found no distinctive African American ghetto culture. What appeared to be distinctive was the result of oppressive economic and political conditions acting on what was basically middle-class culture (1967, 222). Cloward and Ohlin made a similar point with respect to gang delinquency, arguing that cultural explanations ignore the extent to which lower-class and delinquent cultures are predictable responses to conditions in our society rather than persisting cultural patterns (1960, 75).

Finally, in *People and Folks,* a study of gangs in Milwaukee (including the Vice Lords), John Hagedorn maintains that patterns of gang delinquency are best understood as the embracing of mainstream cultural values in contexts shaped by difficulties in achieving success. Thus, for example, Hagedorn understands gang drug dealing as an innovative response to blocked opportunities resulting from economic restructuring in the Midwest. The cultural value of making money by any means necessary is the same in the ghetto as it is on Wall Street. It's only the different economic conditions that produce differences in behavior (1998, 192).

Yet, such cultural explanations have their own problems. Take the following example: In November 2000 a "chalking" appeared on a sidewalk near the Malcolm X house at Wesleyan University where I teach. Chalkings are anonymous political messages written in chalk on campus sidewalks. Such messages are usually "smash mouth," with very confrontational, in-your-face tones.

This particular chalking consisted in part of the following phrases: "White chicks lose the head wraps"; "Stop masturbating our culture"; "Hoop earrings and nameplate necklaces did not originate from white chicks on 'Sex and the City.' Stop appropriating!"

If you argue that there is no African American culture (ghetto or otherwise), that what appears African American is just a twisted version of white middle-class culture, then obviously, you can't masturbate it. Thus someone should tell the chalking's author that white chicks wearing head wraps aren't masturbating black culture for there is no black culture to masturbate.

I suspect that the author would argue with such a statement. She (assuming it was in fact a woman who wrote it) knows she has a culture. And she knows her culture—her African American culture—is distinct in some ways from white middle-class culture. And I'd be willing to bet she'd have some choice words for any social scientist who tried to say otherwise.

So if she is right, what is the nature of the culture she has, and how can we understand why she was so upset about "white chicks" appropriating it? After all, wearing or not wearing hoop earrings sounds like a tempest in a teapot if there ever was one.

Yet clearly in this case it was not, for it elicited deeply felt passions that shaped behavior (in this case, the behavior of writing the message on the sidewalk in chalk). And what the kind of argument advanced by Hagegorn, Liebow, and others cannot do is explain incidents of shaped behavior like this.

The problem in all of this lies in how social scientists studying gang phenomena think about culture. I was a graduate student when *Tally's Corner* was first published (Liebow 1967), and I asked one of my professors what he thought of the book.

He responded by saying, "It's a good book, but Liebow doesn't understand culture."

According to him, Liebow thought about culture as patterns of behavior and the distinct values and norms that seemingly lay behind them—in other words, as a set of customs, a way of life. Moreover, he thought Liebow correctly saw that the patterns could not explain themselves, nor could they be explained by what on the surface appeared to be distinct values and norms.

But what Liebow did not understand was that you can understand more if you think of culture, not as brute patterns of behavior, but as meaningful action, as systems of significance. Thus in the controversy over the power of culture to explain gang phenomena, the problem lies in the fact that neither side understands what Clifford Geertz called the semiotic concept of culture—a notion that has come to dominate much of mainstream anthropological thought in the last three decades.

For Geertz, people live their lives trapped in webs of shared meaning that they themselves have woven. Geertz takes culture to be these webs (1973, 5). Yet cultural analysis cannot focus simply on shared meaning. As Jean and John Comaroff (1992) argue individuals are situated in contexts defined not only by shared meanings, but by power as well, an argument William Roseberry also makes in *Anthropologies and Histories* (1989).

Moreover, culture is sometimes as much about contention and disagreement as it is about shared understandings. Nevertheless, whether shared or contested, the meanings that comprise culture form semantic spaces ". . . in which human beings construct and represent themselves and others" (Comaroffs 1992, 27). And in this process of constructing and representing, cultural meanings shape both what people do and how they interpret what is done to them.

Thus culture is also shaped by people's experiences. Culture, in other words, is both constituted and constituting (Roseberry 1989, 28). And finally, all this takes place within situations themselves shaped by inequalities in power, differential access to resources, and brute features of the sociophysical environment.

This takes us back to the chalking mentioned earlier. Wearing hoop earrings means one thing to "white chicks"; it's primarily about aesthetics—about "looking good." But wearing hoop earrings to African American Wesleyan students means something different: it's a statement about political identity and as such has meaning in contexts shaped by struggles over inequalities in power. This particular chalking spoke out against white women appropriating a symbol of African American identity—an identity critical in the struggle for power and the fight against oppression.

We can think of culture as learned patterns of behavior. If we do, then both African American and white female students share the same culture trait: they wear hoop earrings. But then we cannot understand why this action aroused such strong emotions and triggered at least one person to take definitive action.

In contrast, if we think of culture as semantic space that both shapes action and is shaped by it, we can understand why wearing hoop earrings became a political issue. For although the behavior of wearing hoop earrings was the same no matter who wore them, the cultural significance of that behavior was very different for African American and white students.

Thinking of culture as semantic space is just as useful in understanding the Vice Lords. But how meanings both shape and are shaped by action is a process that plays out over time. Thus we must take a historical perspective and place our analysis of the Vice Lords in a historical context.

***

The Vice Lord Nation began its change from a club primarily concerned with its gang-fighting reputation to a mob primarily focused on controlling the underground drug economy during the late 1960s and early 1970s. It began with a basic change in political organization. Because of brute factors of the sociopolitical environment, the Vice Lords have been faced with problems of social control throughout their history. Mainstream American political institutions don't function very well in the ghetto. The police are often corrupt. And even when they are not, too often the police see ghetto inhabitants as "the enemy" and respond to their needs slowly and sporadically, if at all. Moreover, the Vice Lords have always seen themselves in opposition to mainstream

American political institutions and, consequently, challenge the legitimacy of their authority. Thus Vice Lords often speak of the police the same way they speak of the Gangster Disciples—as another enemy gang, just one with more firepower.

Consequently the Vice Lords have always felt threatened by external dangers, whether those dangers are the police or some other gang. And as we well know, when publicly recognized external dangers exist, groups strive for internal harmony and accord. Thus the Vice Lords have always been concerned with developing ways to minimize internal disaffection and disorder and to maximize harmony and accord. This was clearly the case in the late 1960s when Tex, one of the Vice Lord chiefs at the time, explained to me how the Vice Lords changed their political organization in an attempt to deal both with internal and external dangers. As he explained:

"See, that's where we came up with the idea of the board. First we said like this: 'Take the President and Vice President of the Midgets, you take the President and Vice President of the Juniors, and you take the President and the Vice President of the Seniors and then you got six mens there.

Alright you got six mens, the War Councilor take it up to seven, and then there would always be that outside guy—which would be Pep (the founder of the Vice Lords). Like I say, he never did have no office, but they always would put him in there, and that's where we made the seven for the board.

So we eliminated the idea of president. We kicking that clean out—period! What I mean is the president is not authorized to give no strict decision. It have to be the board together.

And the reason why we doing that is so no one get blamed for taking any decisions. That's the way we handled the problem with the law. See, we noticed how large the number was that was going in and out of jail, and we noticed that a lot of those guys that had these tall reputations were not actually what was best for the group. Like, for instance, you look at it from the side point: here a guy that participated in almost everything that happened, but he hasn't been busted.

Then you got guys that is hard-headed. After the fight is over they'll just stand there and say, 'Fellows, we going to stay here!'

And they argue and argue 'till maybe the Man pick them up and take them away.

So we said, 'Well, these guys are all right to be something like war councilor or something like this. But they's no good for leading the group because this putting too much pressure on the group. And actually this is wrong for the club.'

So make a lot of these guys war councilors or something like this, or maybe Sergeant of Arms. But we take them out of the position of leadership and put somebody in there that was more lenient when it come to fighting and better at considering ways out of it.

At the same time, 'cause you got a couple of guys—maybe five or six—in jail for maybe five years. So in five years' time if everybody go ahead like this there won't be no club. See, if you take all your heads and put them out there in the conflict, then when they gone you haven't got nothing but a body left. So then we had to feel as though if we did get cracked and go to jail somebody had to be left to hold this thing together. So that's when we came with the idea of the board.

The way the board would work is that the board members was strictly one thing, advisors, and that's all—guys that been out there up against it and know it and know what it's about, and know what it takes to hold it down, and know what it takes to really solve the problems out there. So they put them guys on the board and they would try to keep the fellows aware of what was going on.

Now we all Conservative Vice Lords, but you going to have branches. You going to have guys that speak of this here: Well, the guys across 15th down that way say, 'We 15th Street Lords.' The guys across 16th, so they would say, 'We in the City (Vice Lord City).'

So along with the board we pull one of the guys that was mostly accepted in this particular branch out of the branch to be with the board. So, therefore, you got guys that feel as though so and so from our neighborhood is with the board. And that make them feel as though they is really accepted 'cause one of they guys is with the board. And really he is a pretty nice guy, and they have discussed it and chosen him. So there's guys from The City, Monroe, 5th Avenue, Kedzie, Albany, California. The Warlords are up on Pulaski, and they also got some on 71st. That's really where the idea of the Warlords came from—out south (the South Side of Chicago). They wanted to call themselves the Warlords in order to determine what side (of Chicago) they from. And then there was the Violent Lords and some of the Maniac Lords out there in the projects around Wentworth. And you got Lake Street Lords up that way too.

What we doing, we forming what you call a group of lieutenants, and this will be from each branch. And they be responsible for their neighborhood. This is for all the Vice Lords. And if the lieutenant see something going on that he feel he can't handle you bring it to the board. And the board call a meeting and get the decision from the whole group.

And the only way they can get hung up is if the board see that the decision from the group is wrong. So now the board versus the group. Okay, now Al (Alfonso Alford), he president of the board; he hold a meeting of the board to make a better decision. The board bring it back to the group and that's the way it's settled.

By Al being president of the board, this actually make him leader of the group. And actually his job is to keep the board in line. If he controls the board, then he control the group. The board controls the lieutenants and the lieutenants control their branch."

So then, by organizing leadership in terms of a board of directors and a group of lieutenants, the Vice Lords attempted to deal with the problem of maintaining unity and cohesion under constantly changing conditions. Vice Lords moved from neighborhood to neighborhood and in and out of jail. New groups of Vice Lords formed, old ones died out, and groups split to form new groups. Organizing leadership in terms of the board gave the appearance of structure, stability, and cohesion to a highly dynamic and changing reality.

The Vice Lords also created a court to deal with problems that arose because of the rapid growth of the group. Tex explained the court to me as follows:

"We had a guy; he was out of the Imperials (the Imperial Chaplains—a rival of the Vice Lords). He had been with the fellows almost from the beginning. This guy, he would fight anybody but the Imperials. And by him leading a part of the group, this wasn't good because we be expecting them to do one thing and they did nothing.

They be left holding a bag. So that's when we formed something like a court to make decisions. In other words, the court is actually called together by the group to make a decision upon whether or not this man should keep office, or whether he should be kicked out.

And a lot of times we had guys that will use extreme brutality up on the Ladies (the Vice Ladies—female Vice Lords) or any other one of the fellows. And at any time if he hold any type of office and he something like this then you lose a lot of respect from different parts of the group. And, therefore, this is what the court is for— to make these decisions, to take him out of his position—because he can actually start confusion within the group that might even lead to some sort of conflict. And this is not good because this is one way to divide a group."

For a time the organization the Vice Lords created to counteract threats to their unity worked. Nevertheless, fault lines existed. A conflict between Wren and Trip, two Vice Lord Chiefs, actually split the group for a short time. Tex related the events as follows:

"At one time Ernest Wren and Trip was left on the streets together. The other chiefs was locked up. There's one thing about Trip. Trip, he don't necessarily care about fighting. All he wants is to be looked up to. You notice a lot of times when you hear him make a statement.

He say, 'I run the Vice Lords!'

But Wren is the type of guy like this: he never wanted to be a leader himself. He always wanted to be war councilor. . . . He liked violence. So what he would do, he didn't mind him saying he was Trip or he was the president.

But he didn't like the idea of him saying, 'Well, I run it!' 'cause he didn't want anyone to think that they could run him.

So this would always cause some sort of conflict between him and Trip. One time they busted the group in half and the group was actually feuding with each other. The only thing that stopped that was William Frazer came out of the joint in time to halt it. And then they got back together.

I doubt if actually you could ever put the fellows apart 'cause I feel as though the fellows are actually lost without fellows. See, they find so much refuge in each other. Like a lot of time a guy come out of the joint and didn't even know where he was going to get his rent from or something like that.

And one of the fellows might tell him something like, 'I made a little such and such and we'll raise a little money for you.'

So we get together and we all chip in a dollar or so, and we pay his rent. Or I might come out of jail and I don't know where I'm going to live at.

One of the fellows say, 'Well, I got two or three rooms. I just got paid up for a month, but for a month at least you know where you're going to live at.'

So it'll work on like that."

Ultimately, however, Tex was wrong. For the Vice Lords could not withstand the centrifugal forces that developed as a result of wider political–economic changes that enmeshed the group and the Conservative Vice Lord Nation shattered. Tex himself was a victim of these forces, shot down in the hallway outside his apartment. No one knew for sure who committed the murder, but many Vice Lords believed the shooting resulted from a power struggle within the Nation. According to some, Tex wanted the group to remain a social club whereas others wanted the Vice Lords to take control of the underground economy in Chicago's Lawndale area. When Tex opposed their plans he was killed.

Whether or not this is true, Tex's faction lost power after his death. And in the following years groups spun off from the Conservative Vice Lords to form their own independent groups. Albany and Monroe became the nucleus of the Unknown Vice Lords. The Travelers developed as an independent group, as did the Mafia Insane Vice Lords, the Maniac Vice Lords, and the Four Corner Hustlers, to name just a few. And these groups in turn spun off other groups. Thus the Cicero Insane Vice Lords split from the Mafia Insane Vice Lords to form a fully independent group.

Still the independent Vice Lord groups recognized a metaphoric kinship relationship among themselves and an opposition to groups centered around the Black Gangster Disciples. Now the Vice Lord Nation was called the Almighty Vice Lords, and the Conservatives were reduced to branch status along with the Unknowns, Travelers, Mafia Insanes, and so on. But, as we shall see, in the Illinois prison system Lords of all branches act together as a united group, the Almighty Vice Lord Nation.

To understand why the Conservative Vice Lords shattered along their fault lines we have to understand changes in both the nature of the resources the group controlled and how individuals gained access to these resources. In the mid-1960s the Vice Lord Nation owned primarily three kinds of resources—reputation, territory, and leadership. Leadership status was a scarce resource—only a few individuals had it. It was not, however, a source of money. Leaders were not paid salaries, nor were they able to use their position to make money. And the other resources—reputation and territory—were not scarce in the same way as leadership. Although reputation was scarce, any Vice Lord could get it through his own actions. Moreover, Vice Lords did not get reputations at the expenses of other Vice Lords. Thus reputation, although a scarce resource, was not zero-sum.

The group had a reputation as well, and all Vice Lords shared in it. The Nation did gain its reputation at the expense of other clubs. But no one in the Vice Lords had greater access to the group's reputation than anyone else.

Like group reputation, territory was also a shared resource. All Vice Lords moved freely within the Nation's territory without fear of physical violence from more than one person. A Vice Lord might threaten violence against another Vice Lord with whom he had a beef, but members did not fear group attacks.

Even the kind of resources that the club did not control were as important in maintaining its unity. The Vice Lords as a group owned few, if any, financial resources. Getting money was an individual's own responsibility; it was not an activity the club organized and controlled. Ruthless individual capitalism dominated the moneymaking sphere; Vice Lords tried to best one another (and anyone else) in the pursuit of wealth. They expected that when it came to money, everyone "whupped the game." But because the club did not own significant financial resources, conflicts over money did not lead to competition for power within the group. Individuals who gained the position of Vice Lord Chief did not gain financial advantages. To get money, members had to have either a job or a game (which included all kinds of hustles, from armed robbery to mail-order scams).

Getting money took on a new dimension, however, when major foundations, as well as the U.S. government, started programs granting grassroots community organizations funds for neighborhood development as part of the War on Poverty (a federal initiative President Lyndon Johnson started early in his administration). In 1969 *The Chicago Tribune* reported that the Vice Lords had received grants totaling $221,000. The Vice Lords (now the Conservative Vice Lords, Inc.) used this significant sum to initiate several projects, including opening a restaurant, an office, and an art center; launching a neighborhood beautification project, and beginning an employment referral service.

This was also a time when the Vice Lords became more involved in local politics. City aldermen had long sponsored picnics and concerts in exchange for Vice Lord support. But now political organizations paid Vice Lords for their help. For example, those organizing the civil rights fight against housing discrimination in Cicero hired Vice Lords as community organizers and paid the Vice Lord leadership for members' participation in demonstrations. And even though civil rights organizations moved on to other projects, the Vice Lords continued to fight bias in the construction industry and battle slum landlords. David Dawley's book, *A Nation of Lords* (1973/1992), documents in detail this time in Vice Lord history.

Before the War on Poverty the board provided leadership in managing conflicts with other gangs; with this new money, however, the board held the strings to a purse filled with hundreds of thousands of dollars. And although the board promised the club's financial resources would be distributed among all Vice Lord branches, this happened sporadically, if at all. The board members received salaries and some rank-and-file members got jobs. But most of the wealth stayed in Vice Lord City.

Money from grants was a significantly different kind of resource than reputation and territory. It was limited in supply; when some people within the club got it, other people did not. It made membership on the board a valuable financial resource because all board members received salaries.

This exacerbated the divisions between the City Lords and other Vice Lord branches because, not surprisingly, everyone wanted a share of the wealth. Vice Lords in the Henry Horner housing project decided to go their own way and procured a grant of $20,000 from a local hospital, as well as ownership of a former Catholic school that the hospital owned (Kotlowitz 1991, 37). The ties holding the Nation together were beginning to unravel.

In the early 1970s, as the war in Viet Nam intensified, the War on Poverty lost its momentum. At the same time the U.S. government began a series of investigations into alleged misuse of federal funds. No one in the Vice Lords was ever convicted. But politicians were running scared. The Vice Lords and groups like it were flexing too much political muscle and grants for grassroots community development ceased.

At the same time the Chicago police also began arresting gang leaders and rank-and-file members of all stripes in large numbers. Bobby Gore, one of the most powerful Vice Lord chiefs at the time, was convicted of murder and sentenced to a long term in the Illinois penitentiary. Both Rico and Sonny, core members of the 15th Street Lords, were sent to the penitentiary on robbery charges, and Jeff Fort, the leader of the Blackstone Rangers, was convicted of conspiring to misapply federal funds and sent to a federal penitentiary.

Jeff Fort was, according to a number of Vice Lords I knew, originally a Conservative Vice Lord, but when he and his family moved from Chicago's West Side to the South Side he started the Blackstone Rangers, at one time the most powerful street gang in Chicago. Others maintain, however, that Fort started the Rangers at roughly the same time as Pep started the Vice Lords (Knox 2000, 54).

In any case, the Rangers' main rival on the South Side was the Devils Disciples, which later gave birth to a number of other groups including the Black Gangster Disciples, now one of the most powerful street gangs in Chicago. The Rangers maintained a loose alliance with the Vice Lords, as did the Disciples with the various factions of the Egyptian Cobras.

In the federal penitentiary Fort began to learn the skills needed for organizing the underground economy. When he returned to the streets he moved the Rangers (later called El Rukens) into the underground drug trade. In 1983 he was convicted of drug trafficking and this time sent to the state penitentiary.

This was a critical time in Vice Lord history. Many of the old Vice Lord chiefs as well as rank-and-file members were either dead or in jail. As a consequence, much of the gang action switched from the streets to the penitentiary.

At the time Goliath, my main informant from earlier years, told me, "Ain't many Lords and Cobras on the street no more, but they still kicking strong in the Joint."

"Kicking strong" in the penitentiary meant fighting for control of the underground prison economy. Earlier, according to Bobby Gore, old white cons primarily controlled that economy. But as African American street gang members came to dominate the Illinois prison population, they had the numbers and organization to take control of this economy.

To do so, first they forged ties with potential allies. Because the Vice Lords had a long history of close relations with the Blackstone Rangers, the Rangers were obvious allies. I suspect that the general principle underlying allegiances among Pukhtun tribesmen in Afghanistan was at work here as well—"The enemy of my enemy is my friend," and its corollary, "The friend of my enemy is my enemy." In any case the Cobras soon allied with the Disciples in opposition to the Vice Lord/Ranger alliance. Other groups joined until the Illinois prison political system opposed two grand alliances, initially called "the People" and "the Folk." The Folk took the six-pointed Star of David as its symbol, the core symbol of the Black Gangster Disciples, and the People took the Islamic five-pointed star as its symbol, the core symbol of the Vice Lords.

Now, however, all the gangs "riding up under the five-pointed star" in the Illinois prison system form the Almighty Vice Lord Nation. Few refer to the confederation as the People any longer. Today the Almighty Vice Lords include the Unknown Vice Lords, Conservative Vice Lords, Traveler Vice Lords, Insane Vice Lords, Mafia Insane Vice Lords, Renegade Vice Lords, Imperial Vice Lords, Bloods, Four Corner Hustlers, and Black P-Stone Nation. It also includes the

Latin Kings and Simon City—noteworthy because the Latin Kings is a Latino gang whereas Simon City is white gang.

History, however, is not just "one damn thing happening after another." Events take place within changing political–economic contexts that shape them in critical ways. The decades following the enactment of civil rights legislation saw significant changes in Chicago's African American ghettos as middle- and working-class African Americans fled to middle-class and upscale, integrated neighborhoods. They left a vast and concentrated "underclass" behind.

At the same time the manufacturing base of many American cities began to erode in the face of economic globalization. Perhaps the most dramatic example is the demise of the steel industry that in the Chicago area affected other jobs as well, in a kind of trickle-down, domino effect. As a result many decent-paying, working-class jobs disappeared. And with the election of Ronald Reagan to the presidency of the United States, the welfare safety net so important to the survival of many destitute African Americans began to unravel. Finally, law enforcement in the ghetto remained as it always was—weak, to say the least.

All these together created conditions favorable to the growth and development of the illegal, underground drug industry. As gang leaders like Jeff Fort returned to Chicago ghetto neighborhoods they came equipped with know-how learned while running the underground prison economy. And they came to a socioeconomic milieu that favored putting this knowledge into play.

But successfully competing for control of the underground economy both in prison and on the streets required new social and cultural arrangements. The Vice Lords had to create a level of discipline and unity previously unknown, for without it they could not compete successfully in the underground economy.

To create discipline Vice Lord leaders had to create authority, and to imbue power with legitimacy. Power—the ability to force compliance—is critical to the success of political leaders. But without some degree of legitimacy, no system of political leadership can overcome rank-and-file resistance. Leaders can exercise force to ensure compliance, but ultimately if compliance is not given to some degree, political systems disintegrate.

Thus a few of the most politically astute Vice Lord leaders set out to secretly create a new political system, one in which leadership rested on authority and power depended on legitimacy. This system was to be applied both inside prison and on the streets. It both dressed traditional gang leadership in new clothing and created a new kind of political culture.

The new Vice Lord political organization rested on a distinction between Vice Lords with status and those without—between the "elites" and "foot soldiers" or "representatives," as they were later called. Initially, a complicated leadership hierarchy was put in place with 38 distinct ranks ranging from foot soldier to universal elite. Within this hierarchy, ranks were grouped into categories of one to five "stars." Within each category the Vice Lords also ordered sets of ranks hierarchically. Thus, for example, ranks consisted of one-star chiefs, one-star lieutenants, one-star appointed chiefs, one-star elites, one-star appointed elites, one-star supreme elites, and one-star generals. Following these were the two-star chiefs, two-star lieutenants, two-star appointed chiefs, and so on.

However, this leadership system proved too complicated and cumbersome to work effectively and a more streamlined system evolved. Now all members without rank are representatives. Those with rank are divided into two kinds, elites of a particular branch and universal elites, whose status transcends branch membership. There are four kinds of branch elites: three-star branch elites, five-star branch elites, princes, and kings. Elites whose status transcends particular branches are three-star universal elites, five-star universal elites, and supreme elites. Supreme elites who are also kings and princes of branches have authority over all Vice Lords regardless of branch membership and stand at the very top of the Vice Lord political hierarchy. Finally their ministers are modeled after the ministers of the Nation of Islam, and are charged with leading prayers and generally upholding and developing the religious dimension of Vice Lordism.

They also regularized and employed rules regarding how individuals can achieve status. To become a representative, a person must be "blessed" into the Vice Lords, either by a three-star or five-star branch elite. Such elites may send those wishing to be blessed into the branch on missions, such as killing someone in a drive-by shooting, for example. But according to Vice Lord law the mission must regard Nation and not personal business. After they accomplish the task the Branch Elite blesses them into the group.

Or alternatively individuals may be blessed into the group without fulfilling such missions. That is a decision branch elites make. Except for the blessing in ceremony itself, there is no formal, regularized initiation through which all new members must pass.

Although both three-star and five-star branch elites bless members into the group, only five-star elites can award stars (elite status) to representatives. If the five-star elite is a branch elite then the status he can award is branch elite status. If he is a universal elite, however, then he can award universal status. Like membership in the Vice Lords itself, elites often award status for accomplishing missions on behalf of the branch or nation.

Those creating the new Vice Lord political system faced a problem all political leaders face: how to imbue the political system with legitimacy. To accomplish this they borrowed from the symbols and ideology of the Moorish Science Temple and its offshoot, the Nation of Islam, and created Vice Lordism. As one rank-and-file Vice Lord told my research assistant who had grown up in the area, "We follow the Muslim belief. Yeah, we believe in Allah."

Vice Lordism is a version of Islam that most orthodox Muslims would not recognize. It is contained in a secret set of sayings called "The Lit" (Literature), which also includes Vice Lord Law—the rules for behavior, leadership hierarchy, leadership privileges, and the system of supporting sanctions. The parts of the Lit I reproduce in this chapter come from two sources. None of these parts, however, contain the exact words that are secret. Informants gave me some parts of the Lit, but altered words so as not to break their oaths of secrecy. The Vice Lord prayer came from *An Introduction to Gangs* (Knox, 2000). In this book Knox includes an appendix entitled "Constitution of the Vice Lords." Knox acquired this "constitution" from the Chicago Police who in turn got it from a gang informer (pers. comm.).

I have shown this prayer to several of my Vice Lord friends who say that in many ways it resembles real Vice Lord prayers. The wording is incorrect in key respects, however, and they did not recognize parts of it.

Although the exact wordings of the fragments of the Lit contained below are inaccurate, they nevertheless give the reader a feel for what the real Lit is like. See *An Introductions to Gangs* (Knox 2000) for a more complete version.

All Vice Lords know the general parts of the Lit. But only those with status know other parts. Finally, only the most senior leaders whose identities are often secret know still other sections. Vice Lords must commit to memory and be able to recite on command the four basic elements of the Lit that contain the principles of Vice Lord Law. The law is supposed to govern all aspects of Vice Lord social relationships—both relationships among Vice Lords and between Vice Lords and outsiders.

In theory no Vice Lord, regardless of rank, is above the Vice Lord Law and anyone who violates its tenants can be brought up on charges. This is to limit the power of those with status and protect representatives from abuse, especially when in jail. A young representative explained the following to my research assistant:

> "Because some of the brothers be bogus down there (in the penitentiary). Be on some garbo (garbage). Like I never been to the joint but all the older brothers be coming back and telling me that you can slip off on the motherfucker. They just be on some bullshit with you. He just don't like you. He send you off, man (send you on some personal errand) and you got to honor him 'cause he an elite. So you got to know your Lit. Motherfucker can't fuck with you if you know your law. You can get the motherfucker elite fucked up. If he don't bring you up right (bring you up on charges according to Law) you can reverse that shit. But you got to know that law. Law govern everything. Ain't no motherfucker bigger than the law. I don't care if you got the whole nation, he ain't bigger than the law. You got to go through the law to get what you want in this nation."

Behavior that breaks law is a "violation," and if a Vice Lord is found guilty of committing a violation he is violated or punished. Punishments range in severity from "beat downs" to executions. The eight basic principles of Vice Lord Law are practicing unity, respect, not lying or stealing from another Vice Lord, never taking another's word over a Vice Lord's word, always listening to elites and supreme elites, never putting anyone above leaders, never denying help to another Vice Lord, and always living by leaders' fruitful teachings.

The four basic articles of faith that contain these principles are "The Oath," "The Statement of Love," "The LaFaTiHa," and "The Holy Divine." The versions of the following reproduced fragments resemble the authentic versions but are inaccurate in their wording.

The Oath

As a member of the Almighty Vice Lord Nation, I swear, to never dishonor Vice Lord unity, my most sacred weapon. Nor under the threat of death will I forsake those standing beside me. I as a representative of the Vice Lord Nation, the Holy Order of Vice Lordism, will listen well to the truthful teaching of all Vice Lord Chiefs, and

Elites. While incarcerated I will use my time constructively so that I will become more useful to our Nation as a whole. So may the almighty Allah bear witness. I come as I am, I am as I come. Vice Lord, Almighty Vice Lord.

The Statement of Love

To you my Brother, To you my Sister, My love for you began at birth, has manifested through out our Heritage. Because of my skin, the color of yours, My Blood, My Flesh and My bones I am you, And you are me. Our minds are the same, Our effort is for our cause. Our souls are bound together for eternity. To our holy cause I give my unity, And all my vitality. To you my Brother, And my Sister, I give my love.

The LaFaTiHa

All praise to Allah, Lord of Lords, Master of the World. The Beneficient, the Merciful Master of the Day of Judgment. Thee do we serve and thee do we beseech for help. Keep us on the right path of those upon whom thou best bestowed favors. Not the path of those upon whom thy wrath is brought down, or on those who go astray.

The Holy Divine

On the Holy Divine Day we give praise to Allah, Creator of the Universe. We give thanks to our Chiefs and to our Elites for bringing Vice Lords to the light. All praise to our Blessed Leaders who strove against our enemies and gave their lives for our Nation. Our left hand is for Satan, the Beast, the Great Flying Snake. Our right hand is for Allah, Give thy blessing to the Five Points of the Golden Star—Love, Truth, Peace, Freedom, and Justice.

Finally, the Lit includes a number of prayers that all Vice Lords must know, including the following:

> In the name of Allah, We the righteous of the Almighty Vice Lord Nation give praise and honor to our Supreme Chief, righteous son of the Almighty and a divine Prophet of Vice Lord.
>
> Behold, Hear our prayers O'Lord of Lords, And give us your people the courage to represent our nation, So that the world will know that we are Vice Lord, And as such will never stray from our divine principals and concepts, The laws by which we the most righteous of our people live by.
>
> By your divine grace and generosity, You have instilled with us thy divine seed of love, Knowledge, Wisdom and Understanding. And as a representative of this Almighty Vice Lord Nation, It is our responsibility to apply these precious gifts to the interest of our beloved nation, And all poor and oppressed people of color world wide.
>
> Let our conduct O'Lord of Lords be judged by you according to our deeds, By Birth, In the Spirit, and through the heart core, Behold, Behold, We come as we are, Vice Lord (Knox 2000, 629).

What is striking about these fragments of the Lit, as well as the entire Vice Lord "Constitution" that appears in *An Introduction to Gangs,* is the language in which it is expressed. The Lit combines the kind of ritual language of fraternal orders, the language of sacred books, and the codified legalese of the U. S. Constitution. These linguistic forms in themselves constituted powerful symbols, saturated with emotional quality.

Just as important, the linguistic forms clothe assertions regarding the legitimacy of the Vice Lord political hierarchy and the importance of Vice Lord unity. And they do this by asserting that political leaders have the best interests of all Vice Lords at heart. When a Vice Lord says he listens to Willie Lloyd (the king of the Unknown Vice Lords) or honors Willie Lloyd, he is saying that he accepts Willie Lloyd as his leader and will follow whatever legitimate commands he might give. At the same time the words of the oath underline listening to the "fruitful teachings" of elites. This presents a reality in which representatives obey elites' commands because they are for the good of all. "Fruitful teachings" is a powerful cultural concept that forms the foundation of elites' political legitimacy.

Making the Lit secret is also important. As Fredrik Barth noted in his study of the Bakatman of New Guinea, the potency of ritual knowledge increases in inverse proportion to the number of people sharing it. "Thus deceit and exclusion seem to create the preconditions for deeper truth, i.e. knowledge with greater power" (Barth 1975, 217–18). Thus at each stage in an individual ascent in the Vice Lord hierarchy he is given four new, secret pieces of the Vice Lord Lit. Only the most supreme leader, whose identity is secret, knows the entire Lit. The secrecy of the Lit itself helps convince Vice Lords of a particular construction of reality—one in which a system of political hierarchy has legitimacy and Vice Lord unity becomes tangible and real.

But the power of symbols increases yet again when they are used in rituals, when they become the musical notes in a ritual score. Because symbols have the power to stir emotions, rituals use symbols to convince participants that the world is constructed in particular ways. Thus, according to Barbara Meyerhoff in her study of retired Jews in Venice, California:

> "(R)ituals are capable of making improbable, impossible claims. Because they are dramatic in form, rituals persuade us by our own senses. . . . We perform in rituals and doing becomes believing" (1980, 86).

The symbols were the language of the Lit itself. The problem was how to ritualize these symbols in ways that performed and thus made real the legitimacy of the political hierarchy and the unity of the group. Vice Lord leaders devised four ritual performances to accomplish this. The first was the blessing ritual. Individuals that elites are about to bless into the Vice Lords were given in writing the four basic elements of Vice Lordism—the Oath, the Statement of Love, the LaFaHiTa, and the Holy Divine. When they had memorized the elements they came to the elite and orally recited the exact words of each piece. In jail the initiate had four days to accomplish the task. If he could not recite the text after four days he was violated.

Many young ghetto men read poorly at best. Thus memorizing the elements of the Vice Lord Lit is a difficult struggle that consumes hours of painful concentration. It requires repeating the words over and over again, and in constantly repeating the words, doing becomes believing.

Although Vice Lords only say the words of the oath when they are blessed into the group, the LaHaFiTa, the Holy Divine, and the Statement of Love form elements in repetitive, group rituals, such as the rituals of goals, the ritual blessings that begin prison meals, and the rituals of violation.

Vice Lord meetings are called "goals." In prison, regular goals take place every Friday for all those living on a particular prison deck. The cultural model is the Muslim Friday mosque service. All active Vice Lords living on the deck are required to attend. Refusing to do so is a violation of Vice Lord Law. Goals begin with all those in attendance standing in a circle with their palms pointing upward. The circle symbolizes that all are equally Vice Lords regardless of rank and, as a consequence, united by bonds of love and commonality. A minister then recites the LaHaFiTa and the goal begins. If no minister is available a Vice Lord known for his speaking ability recites the LaHaFiTa.

Whoever has the responsibility of running the deck moderates the goals. Usually, those with status appoint representatives for the job. Sometimes, however, an elite takes on the responsibility if no able representative is available.

Regular Friday goals give the Vice Lords an opportunity to discuss issues that have arisen on the deck since the last goal. For example, sometimes the Vice Lord who has the deck establishes special quiet hours for those needing time to study legal issues related to their incarceration. Such quiet hours are announced at goals.

Goals also give elites the opportunity to monitor the well-being of all Vice Lords on the deck and especially to make sure they have basic amenities—cigarettes, soap, shaving cream, safety razors—available from the commissary. According to their law, each deck must maintain what is called a "box" and all Vice Lords must contribute commissary goods to it when they can. Unfortunate Vice Lords who do not have basic amenities and cannot purchase them from the commissary can get them from the box.

When all discussion is finished, those attending stand in a circle with their palms raised once again. The goal ends with a recitation of the Holy Divine.

In prison Vice Lords usually eat with other Vice Lords. Neutrons—those with no gang affiliation—however, often eat at tables dominated by gangs. At Vice Lord tables each meal begins with a prayer. No one, especially neutrons, can begin eating until the prayer has been said.

Finally, when a Vice Lord is formally judged guilty of being "out of law," or in violation of a Vice Lord law, he is "beaten down" in a ritually, circumscribed way. Of all the Vice Lord rituals, the ritual of violation is perhaps the most politically potent: First, violations are public, performed in front of group members at special kinds of goals. Second, violations last for prescribed periods of time, usually measured by the time it takes matchbooks to burn. Thus, for example, during a two-matchbook violation the guilty Vice Lord is beaten down for the length of time two matchbooks burn. Third, only Vice Lords specially appointed by elites can perform the actual violation. Moreover, there are rules regarding who these people can be. Only Vice Lords of the same rank as the miscreant can administer the violation.

Finally, violation cannot commence until someone recites the Statement of Love to the miscreant. This is critically important for the legitimacy of the political system. The Vice Lord political system cannot survive without some degree of order and order cannot be maintained without legitimately recognized sanctions. But individuals must be convinced that these sanctions are fair and administered according to standards that apply equally to everyone.

And just as important, when Vice Lords are violated for being out of law it must be done in a way that maintains their allegiance to the group. Reciting the Statement of Love at the beginning of the ritual emphasizes that the punisher and punished alike share a common identity and love for one another that transcends the punishment itself.

In this respect ritualized violations are made to resemble parental punishments. As parents love their children, so does the Vice Lord Nation love its members, according to the Statement of Love. As parents must punish their children for misbehavior, so must the Nation punish those who misbehave by breaking Vice Lord Law. And just as punishing children is a form of parental love, so is punishing Vice Lord miscreants an act of love the Nation shows all its members.

This helps explain why the Vice Lord political system works much more effectively in prison than on the streets. Because Vice Lord neighborhoods are densely populated, and their populations spatially mobile, most Vice Lords live significant portions of their lives away from other Vice Lords. Anonymity is a fact of life in the city and this makes it difficult to track individuals. If a Vice Lord knows he will be violated he can easily move to a new neighborhood, hide out, and refuse to attend goals. Alternatively, he can move from his old neighborhood and start a new Vice Lord branch with a group of followers. This makes violations, both as sanctions and as rituals, less effective.

In prison, however, most Vice Lords live in constant contact with other Vice Lords. Vice Lord inmates have little anonymity and few havens to which they can escape. Not only is it difficult to escape punishment, it is just as difficult to escape both administering and witnessing punishments. As a consequence, all Vice Lords must attend ritual violations, making the enactment of the political order that occurs during the rituals all the more convincing.

Vice Lord leaders face the problem of devising a workable political system and imbuing their creation with legitimacy. Symbols, and the rituals that employ them, help shape the belief in the system's legitimacy. But for the system to work leaders have to surrender themselves to their own creation. Thus the symbols and rituals they devised shape not only the behavior of the rank and file, but of the leaders themselves.

REFERENCES

Barth, Fredrik. 1975. *Ritual knowledge among the Baktaman of New Guinea.* New Haven: Yale Univ. Press.

Bott, Elizabeth. 1957. *Family and social networks.* London: Tavistock.

Cloward, Richard A., and Lloyd E. Ohlin. 1960. *Delinquency and opportunity: A theory of delinquent gangs.* New York: The Free Press.

Comaroff, John, and Jean Comaroff. 1992. *Ethnography and the historical imagination.* Boulder: Westview Press.

Davidson, R. Theodore. 1974. *Chicano prisoners: The key to San Quentin.* New York: Holt, Rinehart, and Winston.

Dawley, David. 1973/1992. *A nation of Lords: The autobiography of the Vice Lords.* 2nd ed. Prospect Heights: Waveland.

Evans-Pritchard, E. E. 1940. *The Nuer.* London: Oxford.

Fleischer, Mark. 1995. *Beggars and thieves: Lives of urban street criminals*. Madison: Univ. of Wisconsin.

Geertz, Clifford. 1973. *The interpretation of cultures*. New York: Basic Books.

Gregory, Steven. 1994. Time to Make the Doughnuts: On the Politics of Subjugation in the "Inner City." *Polar* 17 (1).

Hagedorn, John M. 1998. *People and folks: Gangs, crime and the underclass in a rustbelt city*. 2nd ed. Chicago: Lake View Press.

Jacobson, David. 1971. Mobility, continuity, and urban social organization. *Man* n.s., 6 (4).

Keiser, R. Lincoln. 1969. *The Vice Lords: Warriors of the streets*. New York: Holt Rinehart, and Winston.

———. 1974. Some Thoughts on Generative Models in Urban Anthropology. *Ethnos* 38: i–iv.

Knox, George W. 2000. *An introduction to gangs*. Peotone: New Chicago School Press Inc.

Kotlowitz, Alex. 1991. *There are no children here*. New York: Anchor.

Liebow, Elliot. 1967. *Tally's corner*. Boston: Little, Brown and Company.

Miller, Walter. 1969. Lower class culture as a generating milieu of gang delinquency. In *Delinquency, crime and progress*, ed. Donald R. Cressey and David A. Ward. New York: Harper and Row.

Meyerhoff, Barbara. 1978. *Number our days*. New York: Touchstone.

Peletz, Michael G. 1995. Kinship studies in late 20th century anthropology. In Vol. 24 of *Annual review of anthropology*, ed. William H. Durham. Palo Alto: Annual Reviews Inc.

Roseberry, William. 1989. *Anthropologies and histories*. New Brunswick: Rutgers Univ. Press.

Thrasher, Frederick M. 1927. *The gang: A study of 1313 gangs in Chicago*. Chicago: Univ. of Chicago.

Williams, Terry. 1992. *Crackhouse*. Harmondsworth: Penguin.

NOTES

1. "Death of the Evil . . . Vice Lords," *Examiner,* August 9, 1994.

2. The *Chicago Tribune* ran a series of articles about Larry Hoover and the Gangster Disciples, including the following: *"*U.S. Goes behind Bars to Indict 39 Gang Leaders," September 1, 1995; "Peace Can Have Its Price: Gang Leaders Often Keep Prisons in Tow," September 1, 1995; and "Gang Indictments May Be Double-edged Sword," September 3, 1995.

3. *"*More Blacks in their 20s Have Trouble with the Law," *New York Times,* October 5, 1995, A18.

4. "Gangs Tied to Prison Uprisings," Associated Press (in the *Middletown Press*), November 3, 1995.

Fieldwork Biography
Gilbert Herdt

Between 1974 and 1993 Gil Herdt worked among the Sambia in the remote Eastern Highlands of Papua New Guinea for a total of 13 field trips and four years in all, initially as a Fulbright scholar, then as assistant professor at Stanford University, and finally as professor at the University of Chicago. Herdt focused on sexuality, gender, and identity change in his fieldwork, collecting individual life stories in the mode of what Herdt and Stoller (1990) called "clinical ethnography," the application of clinical concepts and techniques to fieldwork. He observed more than 16 male initiation ceremonies, and conducted in-depth studies of the dreams, feelings, and beliefs of individual informants. A witness to tremendous cultural change, Herdt went on to study patterns of institutional and gender role change. This led to his role as consultant on the British Broadcasting Corporation (BBC) film, *Guardians of the Flutes,* which is also the title of his first book (1981).

© Gilbert Herdt

Fieldwork Biography
Birgitta Stolpe, PhD

Birgitta's Stolpe's research with the Sambia of Papua New Guinea involves the physical, psychological, social, and cultural transformation of girls into women. She worked with Sambia women in 1999 and 2000 for her dissertation research at the University of Chicago. Pioneering a new field that she calls "cultural endocrinology," Stolpe examined the manner in which cultural norms and institutions guide intimate social interactions, and how these in turn influence hormonal functioning. Among the Sambia using menarche as a marker, she compared the development of girls who more strongly adhered to traditional life with those who were less traditional. She speculated that profound cultural change is radically reorganizing social interactions, which helps to explain at least in part the remarkable significant epidemiological changes in the rates of Sambia physical development.

© Gilbert Herdt

5/Sambia Gender, Sexuality, and Social Change

Several decades have passed since Herdt began fieldwork with the Sambia of Papua New Guinea in the autumn of 1974. A young Fulbright scholar, Herdt was an American working from Australia on research to charter men's secret society and ritual practices (Herdt 1981). At the time of Herdt's initial fieldwork, warfare had been halted only six years earlier (in 1968), at about the time that missionaries entered the Sambia region and French anthropologist Maurice Godelier started his path-breaking studies of the Baruya people, a neighboring tribe. As Herdt recounted in his case study, *The Sambia: Culture and Gender in New Guinea* (1987), five years prior to that, Australian colonial officers and police had effectively ended Sambia tribal autonomy in 1964 when they rounded up a large number of Sambia men and youths, chained them together as a gang, and marched them two days over the mountains to the Patrol Post. There they were incarcerated, and eventually released. Over the next 30 years of dramatic cultural change, Herdt continued to conduct fieldwork.[1] Birgitta Stolpe began her fieldwork in 1999 as a graduate student at the University of Chicago. Stolpe focuses on female sexuality and adolescent maturation. In their chapter, Herdt and Stolpe document the rise of new narratives and practices of Sambia masculinity and seek to explain some of these changes by contrasting the traditional forms and means of becoming a man with newly emergent ones. This chapter thus records the resilience and continuation of Sambia society, while at the same time describing the remarkable changes that have occurred in gender and sexuality over the last three decades.

PRECOLONIAL SAMBIA SOCIETY

The Sambia are a mountain-dwelling people who inhabit extremely rugged high forest ranges of the Eastern Highlands of Papua New Guinea. Although their territory is vast, their numbers (around 2,300) are small, with population density ranging between five and ten people per square mile. Warfare dominated their precolonial existence. Traditionally hunters and shifting agriculturists, the Sambia were sedentary at the time of colonization by Australia in the 1960s.

The world of men in precolonial society can be summed up in three domains: warfare and hunting, arranged marriage, and the rituals of initiation that socialized men into the absolute secrecy of the men's house (Herdt 1981). The world of women was restricted to the lower status domains of food production and child care.

The Sambia men's secret society was best characterized as a military-type dominance hierarchy that centered around the men's house, its nerve center. Male initiation was the basis for socialization into the men's house, male solidarity, and collective masculinity. The men employed the practice of inseminating boys through oral intercourse, a practice once referred to as "ritualized homosexuality" but now better known as boy-inseminating rites (Herdt 1984; 1993; 1999). As we have known since the critical work of Kenneth E. Read (1954) who pioneered study of the men's house in the highlands of Papua New Guinea, this was the dominant institution of these societies. Indeed the strategic place of tabooed masculinity dominated the landscape of each Sambia hamlet. Virtually everywhere across the New Guinea Highlands, men and boys lived as a body apart from women and children (Langness 1974), creating the conditions for making reality and secret reality (Barth 1975), both of which were vital to these "great men societies" (Godelier 1986). Moreover, men's living-and-sleeping arrangements in the men's house was the basis for a special kind of utopian worldview; within the men's house, men sought to perfect the imperfect, messy arrangements of the secular world (Herdt 2003).

Sambia first-stage male initiation, 1975.

Hamlet social organization was centered around gender and gender segregation in men's and women's areas (Herdt 1987). The hamlet was symbolically divided between male and female spaces, including separate paths for walking. At the top of each hamlet, one or more male clubhouses offered a defensive surveillance of surrounding mountains and hamlets. The clubhouses also served as living quarters for male initiates until marriage. Elders and adult men also spent much of their time there, laying strategies for ritual, defense, and warfare. Women were forbidden to enter the clubhouses or, in general, the forests above them. Men and male initiates similarly avoided the women's menstrual huts and the areas surrounding them. Men and women and all initiates were restricted by the spatial segregation of the sexes, which was reproduced within the small enclosure of the family hut, where a man lived with his wife or co-wives, his unmarried daughters, and his uninitiated sons. The interior of the hut was divided into separate male and female sleeping areas. Women were forbidden to enter their husbands' area, or to step over the central hearth where meals were prepared. By observing these restrictions, women reduced the possibility of transferring to men what the Sambia view as female polluting fluids. These restrictions least affected children, and young children of both sexes slept in their mother's area.

Gender dominated all socialization. Though very young children mixed in early childhood, later play was based on gender distinctions reinforced through the role models of parents. Implicit and explicit communication of cultural rules and norms also redundantly emphasized the divergence of the sexes and their differential cultural goals. Following weaning, children were encouraged to play in same-sex groups. Sexual segregation remained informal, however, until late childhood (ages 7–10), when boys were initiated into an age-graded ritual society focused on secret male knowledge. In all, this male society performed six initiations collectively for hamlet clusters, taking the boys into adulthood and fatherhood, with final initiation in their early to mid-twenties (Herdt 1982a; 1982b).

A hamlet depended upon its youth as a power base and labor corvée. The bond created between mothers and their children was intense, and it is difficult to imagine more extreme attachments (Herdt 1981). This developmental condition was undoubtedly very singular in its effects on the inhibition of male agency and sexual subjectivity in boys. Boys were prevented from becoming separate agents empowered by the men's society, just at the moment—around age 10—that they were coming into an awareness of their prepubertal sexuality.

Such changes in the boy could only be achieved through gender segregation and secrecy, on the condition that the boys would be treated first as sexual objects, before they got the chance to be sexual subjects. These are separable elements of subjective development that are conflated as "sexual orientation" in the Western world, where they are also treated as part of the same "biological package." In particular, the ability to locate desire in the person—to be acted upon first as an object and then as a subject—regardless of the same-gender context of the Sambia, suggests that these desires and their expression are being acquired in the microcontexts of the men's house and erotically expressed in action more often than previously believed. It is a bit too simple to say that these attractions are learned, nor must we think that they can be "unlearned" in any simple manner without doing violence either to the integrity or mental health of the person. Ultimately, such subjectivities, when they are lived realities, must be anchored in the social traditions of the community.

TRADITIONAL GENDER ROLES AND INITIATION

Countervailing theories of male and female development underlie the differences in the structure and timing of initiations for both boys and girls. Feminine behavior and female reproductive capabilities were thought to be natural outcomes of women's anatomy and early socialization. Female initiations merely affirmed girls' natural and inevitable attainment of biological and social maturity. Male development, however, was regarded as problematic in two respects. First, unlike girls, boys were thought to be biologically incomplete. Their slower physical maturation was attributed to their inability to produce semen, the biological essence of maleness. Collective male initiations, and the insemination of boys that were central to them, were performed in part to correct this perceived biological deficiency and to aid their progress toward reproductive competence. Second, boys were believed to be at greater risk than girls, because their early and prolonged contact with women exposed them to dangers of what the Sambia perceived as pollution and contamination that ultimately could kill them. Through forcible separation of boys from their mothers, dramatic nosebleeding, and other purificatory rites, men sought to eradicate the harmful effects of women's early physical and psychological presence, and instill the discipline and knowledge needed to transform weak and undisciplined boys into aggressive hunters and warriors. Here, as Margaret Mead (1935) once noted, this was a difficult outcome to achieve, and it created large contradictions in masculinity (Herdt and Stoller l990; Stoller and Herdt l982).

Every three or four years neighboring hamlets created a truce to initiate a cohort of age-graded boys, ranging in age from 7 to 10. The boys were separated dramatically from their mothers and placed in the men's house. For months afterward they experienced a series of ritual ordeals and events that gradually removed all traces of women and the profane world from their bodies—and, the Sambia men hoped, from their psyches, too. This first ritual was secret, hidden from the women. Five additional years of initiations followed, leading up to their young adulthood. The first initiation, however, had two key rituals of rebirth: first, boys underwent nosebleeding rituals that were thought to remove the pollution of their mother's menstrual blood; and second, older bachelors inseminated the young initiates through oral intercourse, a ritual they themselves had undergone at an earlier ritual stage. The physical ordeal was accompanied by many powerful ritual moods and emotions, and the separation from mother and the secular world was absolute and complete for years to come. According to Sambia belief, this ritual culminated in the third-stage initiation, when the boy's body became biologically mature, at which time he showed all the secondary sex traits, including a mature glans penis.

Female initiations were performed at menarche (between ages 17 and 19). This initiation also often made allies of neighboring warring villages. During these ceremonies women became allies and men became the enemies. This may have been an easier end for the women to achieve than for the men because women often performed these rituals with matrilineal relatives (kin on the mother's side of the family) who had been separated from them through marriage.

These rituals were intended to transform girls into women. Although the Sambia believed that female physical development was natural and occurred spontaneously, intellectual and psychological development required ritual instruction. Girl and woman were distinct categories, and it was the "knowledge" of womanhood that was instilled during these initiations.

The rituals traditionally took place over several nights and included the older women as well as the recently initiated young women who had not yet given birth to their first or sometimes even second or third child. Men were prohibited from viewing or even listening to the ceremony because secrecy was as important to the initiation of girls as it was to the initiation of boys. Cloaked in the darkness of night their mothers and several of the older women prepared the female initiates for their ceremonies, painting the girls with bright yellow mud and dressing them in traditional garb of grass skirts and bark capes. The women prepared a fire in the middle of the ceremonial arena where they bathed the initiates in smoke, "cooked" them over the fire, and then ritually beat them with pieces of wood. After this preparation, the teachings began.

In an apparent paradox, the Sambia regarded female development as "natural" but still requiring ritual learning. The ritual teaching instilled knowledge that was critical to how women experienced their bodies, and this "body knowledge" was created without censure or intellectual reflection. To this end, the skin was perforated to allow the knowledge to enter the body directly. The natural world was the source of "natural" knowledge, hence indigenous plants were applied to the body after it was "prepared." Of the 10 or 12 plants used, each contained specific knowledge that the girls needed to acquire, but ultimately the goal of these rituals was to teach the girls to be industrious gardeners and obedient wives. The physical force with which natural objects were applied to their bodies was not only the means by which these objects transmitted their knowledge, but also served to prepare the young women for the pain of childbirth and the painful beatings from their future husbands (Stolpe 2003).

SOCIAL HIERARCHIES AMONG THE SAMBIA

Male hegemony and warriorhood were the forms of political and social economy, although descent through the father's line and residence in the locale of one's father or father's people (patrilocal residential arrangements) privileged the male descent line. Thus it is not surprising that the Sambia and similar sexual cultures were constitutive of objectified boys and women and in turn regarded men as the primary icons of beauty and sex appeal. Moreover, the phallic preoccupation of these mythological traditions, in which the culture hero might sport a gigantic penis that was the cause of fertility, great power, and endless trouble, was iconic of their masculine imagery and folk psychology. The Sambia have said, for example, that a woman could not help but admire a man who achieved the ideal of prowess in war, hunting, and sexual conquest, especially if he was a good supporter of family and dutiful in his sexual obligations to his wife. She did not have to like him, for to admire and to like are different things, and Sambia marriage was a political, not a romantic, union. Sons were expected, however, both to like and admire their fathers, and to eventually enter into the secret world their fathers shared with other men and youth. Also they expected to become comrades in a warriorhood dedicated to the removal of all signs of womanliness (for example, by nosebleeding rites and other dietetics of masculine performativity). The Sambia, and many similar cultures, asserted the need to implant external signifiers of manliness, such as boy insemination. Ultimately puberty and *jerungdu,* or strength in the sense of virility, provided for successful masculine careers.

Age was a fundamental marker of social rank and status in these societies—extending beyond to the South Seas and Australian Aboriginal groups. Melanesia shared the importance of age as a means of social organization with such culturally diverse world areas as West Africa and insular Southeast Asia. Kinship and marriage systems were marked by age-graded principles of social hierarchy in which age accorded respect and was treated as a sign of accumulated ritual knowledge, social experience, and power. Age also defined a critical aspect of the relationship between the genders in virtually all sexual and reproductive matters, including arranged marriages, but also in religious practice, body rituals, and substance beliefs. As K. E. Read recognized long ago, "egalitarian" ideas and practices—such as being a leader in a war or hunt, or having a striking personality in politics were also valued by the Sambia and attained the status of social principles for men. For women, skillful gardening techniques and high fertility were sources of status. Nevertheless, age was the more consistent and powerful social classifier in these societies.

MARRIAGE AND THE TRAFFIC IN WOMEN

The ritual complex of boy insemination was part of a larger social and cultural system that included assigned marriages and the creation of enormous barriers to sexual intercourse between the genders prior to the arrangement and consummation of political marriages. Marriage and the trafficking in or exchange of women were practices based upon notions of male descent, strongly marked at all levels of social grouping. Hamlets were composed of one or two great patri-clans founded on relationships traced on the father's side of the family. Separate, constituent clans could also claim membership in these great patri-clans. Secrecy and ritual knowledge characterized the internal organization of clan ritual. Another organization, the confederacy, linked nearby hamlets together as participatory units involved in the men's secret society. These localized confederacies sometimes cut across kinship groups, uniting otherwise enemy clans and hamlets— as in the Sambia Valley—and creating wider and somewhat more tenuous political alliances. Before pacification, the stylized bow fights between hamlets sometimes got out of hand, escalating into full-scale war after casualties had been inflicted on either side—a pattern that has been well described previously. These neighboring hamlets were united as a confederacy, however, by their shared fear of attack by true enemies from other tribes.

Sambia exchanged women in marriage through three traditional customs: sister exchange (direct exchange), infant betrothal (delayed exchange), and bride service. For the purposes of this text, however, we may exclude bride service, because it accounted for less than 2 percent of all Sambia marriages. In simple terms, delayed exchange of women between clans created temporary imbalances with expectations and demands for future exchanges, offset with gifts and promises. The Sambia configured marriage as a means by which one clan– hamlet took a woman as womb, or "garden," from another hamlet; the female offspring of the new union was returned to the donor hamlet as brides in the following generation, thus achieving over time a balance in the exchange of women between different hamlets. The residents of Sambia Valley hamlets intermarried in this way, creating shifting, unstable alliances that provoked mistrust at all levels of social arrangements, interjecting suspicion and often paranoia into the marital relationship, living arrangement, child care, and other related daily interests.

Symbolically these arranged marriages resulted in transfers of blood and semen in which blood and semen flowed in opposite directions across generations. Blood was the arranged marriage of a woman from her brother's group to her husband's, and semen was the fluid inserted into her brother to make him grow big and strong, and hence, able to consummate his own marriage when an adult. Thus, blood went one way and semen the other in marriage and boy-insemination practices.

However, to counterbalance this situation, the man who had taken a wife was expected in return to give his semen to a boy. So, when a man was the recipient

Sambia women and marriage ceremony, 1975.

of a womb-vagina, he donated semen both to the woman (his wife) and to her younger brother (an initiate in the men's house). His wife was expected to produce a baby; her brother was expected to produce the masculinity of physical growth and manliness embodied in the glans penis. In the third-stage initiation that celebrates social puberty, the growth and enlargement of the glans penis was likened to a ritual rebirth, symbolizing culmination of manhood. Sons of arranged marriages were divided in their loyalties and social interests. The offspring of Sambia couples were caught between two social worlds and political networks: sons were to be initiated as future warrior-comrades, and daughters were to be used as commodities in future marriage exchanges for their brothers or other clansmen. These arranged marriages created complex and sometimes contradictory religious and political alliances between hamlets. The symbolism of the secret male initiation ceremonies was intentionally aimed to merge the desires and developmental subjectivity of the growing boy with the larger project of training warriors through boy insemination. Secrecy was vital to create jural authority in the hamlet and hierarchy inside the men's society.

In the precolonial world of the Sambia (especially prior to 1964), the roles of men and women were highly polarized and politically opposed in the condition proverbially described as "sexual antagonism" (Langness 1974). The women who came as brides were from hamlets that were invariably hostile and sometimes enemies in war, and therefore wives were forever regarded as alien and mistrusted. The residential segregation of unmarried, vulnerable male initiates living in the men's clubhouse (while the women and children were restricted to the women's houses) symbolized this deep structure of perceived social and material difference in village life.

Sexual relations between men and women were loaded with avoidance, ritual, and conflicted feelings. As married couples bore children and aged, however, their interaction in the later years of life improved to the point of even being cordial. In the early years, however, many marital histories reveal jealousies, fears of sorcery and spell-casting, arguments, physical abuse, and sometimes (though rarely) suicide. But it is not as if women simply did whatever their husbands said. A woman had quiet means at her disposal to subvert and resist her husband's demands, such as "forgetting to prepare his food, refusing to make love, shouting and commenting on her husband . . . using sorcery or semen sorcery, and pollution poison in the food" Godelier (1986, 150). But she could also openly criticize him and even castigate him loudly in public, though she risked a beating for doing so. The women could not go beyond a certain point because it infringed upon the men's secret boundary. Men believed sexual intercourse of any kind should be spaced out in time to avoid depletion of masculinity and premature aging or death; yet they typically reacted in frustration, and sometimes anger, when they did not have sex with their wives. Many young men became jealous and vindictive of wrong moves made by their consorts. Couples normatively had sex every few days or as infrequently as once every two or three weeks, depending on age, length of marriage, and other factors. However, the postpartum taboo forbade sexual intercourse for some two years following birth. No overt contact between the sexes was permitted in public—a taboo that has changed radically with increasing westernization.

SOCIAL CHANGE AND RESISTANCE

Social change has strongly impacted Sambia gender and sexuality. Australian government officers initiated change through a critical historical episode in the early 1960s when they tricked Sambia war leaders and young adult warriors into capture. The humiliation of the Sambia men was complete when the Australian officers destroyed their weapons, especially their war shields and bows and arrows. For Sambia men, these events disrupted their feelings of mastery and control over their own destinies to such an extent that they forever after lived in the dread of repeated humiliation. Their manhood was tested and they were in this sense emasculated. This subjective experience of social capture led to a new era of modernization and political change by perforating the perceived invincibility of Sambia masculinity. The local community appointees—the tultuls and komiti men—were at first accepted as proxies for the colonial government. Later, however, the sense of collusion with the government began to creep in and has undermined some of their authority. Though not perfect models of the new masculinity for boys to emulate, they do provide alternates to traditional images of men in the village.

The formal end of colonialism brought immediate changes. National independence in 1975 quickly began to shift the government presence and influence around the district capital. A system of independent village councils, constituted of locally elected representatives, serves as the primary link between local communities and the national and district governments. This system (begun in 1973) is only partially successful, and has been increasingly taxed by the absence of regular government visits (such as census patrols) that are no longer conducted.

Missionary activity increased—Lutherans established the first presence in the area, though not directly among the Sambia. They constructed a mission in the Baruya area in the early 1960s (Godelier 1982). Located at Wonenara (then the district capital), the mission served as a satellite for Lutheran activities in other parts of the district.

Many local people had been educated at Lutheran missions schools, which sought to convert and "civilize" the indigenous populations. Using a pattern well known from elsewhere in New Guinea, the school's platform aggressively attacked customs such as male initiation, polygyny, and shamanism to successively undermine confidence in traditional systems of belief (see Herdt 2003).

The Seventh-Day Adventists were also active very early in this area. Ironically, although their regional headquarters were located outside the district, and their early influence was not as extensive as that of the Lutherans, they are now dominant in many areas of the region, and their religion is hegemonic among the Sambia. Today, most Sambia consider themselves to be Seventh-Day Adventists and practice their liturgical ceremonies.

The Seventh-Day Adventists established an extensive network of evangelists who, together with their families, lived and worked in villages throughout the district. They preached against boys' initiation and the "heathen" ways of ritual and introduced biblical dietary restrictions (based on the book of Leviticus)[2] that dramatically altered the indigenous diet.

Unlike the Seventh-Day Adventists, the Lutherans were quick to display their own material wealth and to demonstrate the benefits of a familiarity with Western marketing practices. The Lutheran mission established its own trade store at Wonenara station in 1968; the store was relocated to Marawaka station when the district capital was moved there. Backed by a commercial company, and owned by the expatriate-run Lutheran congregation, the store imported trade goods directly from Australia and Japan for sale to locals. The store quickly created a demand for items such as machetes, canned meats and fish, and other commercially produced articles. There is little doubt that the sense of material display undermined the traditional masculinity that figured so prominently with the Sambia and their neighbors. Masculinity could no longer be achieved through the production of local goods.

The new masculinity that could only be produced through the accumulation of Western goods has lead to out-migration and coastal work, creating upheavals in traditional social hierarchies. Sambia men began leaving the hamlet areas in the late 1960s and the level of out-migration of male laborers continued apace into the mid 1980s. Under the colonial administrator's Highland Labor Scheme, men were recruited for two-year contracts to work on coastal cocoa, copra, and rubber plantations. The scheme was discontinued in 1974, but many men continue to seek work on coastal plantations. The early cohorts who left the Sambia Valley were the first to see the wider country and to report back the stories of life outside. Some of these men (perhaps a high number of them) never returned to their hamlets. They chose to work and live in the coastal towns. Others returned in the 1970s and early 80s and brought back cash and goods. Still others live on

Traditional round houses favored by "old" people intermingled with "modern" cornered houses favored by "young" people.

the coast today and send back monies and goods to wives and relatives in the villages. Some of these men have secured marriages and are rearing their children in these distant towns. Their masculinity is now an issue of transition, a liminal betwixt and between tradition and citizenship in the town.

SCHOOLS AND GENDER CHANGE

In Highlands' societies, schooling may be valued for boys because of its perceived relation to the modernization of masculinity: schools promise access to valued opportunities within the larger state society, such as urban jobs in business or government. Traditionally, in many societies, men acquired status through successfully negotiating the various stages of male initiation; this was less emphasized for females. Initiations prepared boys to become warriors, and male war leaders served as models of esteemed masculine behavior. With the cessation of warfare, following Australian pacification of the Highlands, male initiations have declined in importance. Though initiation rites are still performed in some parts of the Highlands, they no longer hold the same promise of status and recognition. Consequently, schools have displaced initiation as a primary means for gaining access to valued positions with the expanding society.

The introduction of schools among the Sambia has followed a similar regional geographical pattern. The first mission school was established at the government station in 1964. Built with the encouragement of the Australian colonial administration, and financed by German and Australian Lutheran churches, the school was attended by children (predominantly boys) from the surrounding Wonenara Valley and other nearby areas. A larger mission school was established in Marawaka when the government outpost was relocated there in 1968. Sons and a few daughters of government employees attended the school. A few local boys also attended. Both schools emphasized religious instruction, and Bible study was a major component of the curriculum. Children were also taught to speak and write in local pidgin, and to perform simple math problems. Both government employees and local villagers initially received the schools well, as they expected concrete results in terms of jobs or further schooling; however, residents became increasingly disillusioned as they began to feel that the schools prepared the students only for menial jobs as laborers or clerks. At best, the schools were regarded as training ground for native evangelists (Godelier 1982).

With religious emphasis, the mission schools at Wonenara and Marawaka significantly impacted local communities by offering an alternative to traditional socialization. Nonetheless, by challenging traditional beliefs about how children should be educated, the schools helped to create an awareness of diversity in socialization practices. Among the Sambia, the mission school provided the primary alternative to traditional socialization until 1985, when the first government school was created in the Sambia Valley.

The schools directly challenged local ritual customs and beliefs, and broke down gender segregation in a number of ways. First, children who attended the schools came from all tribes in the Wonenara and Marawaka areas, thus disrupting traditional enmity between tribes. Second, the schools admitted girls as well as boys, allowing them access to the same knowledge, and forcing them to mix in the same classroom (albeit on different sides). Thus norms governing sexual segregation and men's privileged access to valued knowledge were violated and ultimately could not be repaired. Third, missionaries were openly critical and aggressively attacked ritual beliefs and customs. Children attending the schools were forbidden to participate in initiation rites or to observe traditional sex-avoidance rules. Those who were shy around the opposite sex could be shamed, for example, into being more aggressive or "Western-like" in cross-sex interactions. Though these practices antagonized many local residents, the school received initial support and approval from mission converts. It seems clear that all of these patterns reinforced internal resistance to ritual initiation norms and opened the way for a much broader form of social challenge that displaced ritual as the structure of authority.

The boys' resistance to initiation was growing (Herdt 1987; Herdt and Stoller 1990). Sambia boys, such as Moondi, traditionally resisted initiation rituals out of fear. They sometimes ran away into the forest, requiring search parties to track them and to bring them forcibly back. The boys were reluctant to go into the areas of warfare and forced nosebleeding. The presence of schools and missions exacerbated this resistance. As Moondi has described this so vividly, he feared that initiation would "change" or "freeze" his thinking, disabling him from going to school, get an education, or succeed in the coastal towns (Herdt 1987, 121). In short, he feared the rituals would ruin his chance to become a new man, with a new kind of modernized masculinity. Many boys who followed him have experienced a similar existential dilemma. We might call this the questioning of manhood, a social panic that was a crisis of masculinity among the Sambia in the transition to modernity.

Both the Lutherans and the Seventh-Day Adventists established "bush schools" in isolated parts of the district. These schools were usually small and poorly attended. New government primary schools were opened in the district: the first in 1977 and another in 1985 with more than 300 students from the surrounding villages. Remarkably, they began as male institutions, but within a five-year period, one-third of the students were girls. Both mission and government schools have contributed to changes in traditional socialization practices. Because of these constraints, many parents reject schooling for their children. Much of the evidence, however, suggests that parents value schooling as alternative socialization, particularly for the boys. With the cessation of warfare, and the increase of adolescent and adult male out-migration for work on coastal plantations, male initiation rites have been successfully undermined. Ceremonies that once took months to perform have been reduced to a few short weeks or abandoned. As initiation rites have been increasingly undermined, parents have come to view schooling as a desirable alternative to traditional masculinity.

Although, as elsewhere, schooling is still unequally distributed among boys and girls, more Sambia girls are attending school, both reducing the relationship between the new masculinity and schooling and increasing the social status of the educated woman through acquisition of the "new knowledge." Because the girls' labor in their mothers' gardens is extremely important to the survival of the family (and the status of the mother as a good provider of food), it is difficult to understand why any family would endure the expense of sending a daughter to school. Despite the girls' own assertions that they go to school if they want to, it appears that two major factors drive school attendance: proximity to a school, and proximity to an airstrip that presumably gives the girls (and their parents) greater contact with the outside world, thereby creating the need and the desire to communicate with others in the manner taught in school. These findings suggest that reduced investment (for example, a one-hour daily hike to and from school versus a four-hour hike) is a key factor in determining whether or not to attend school. But girls living furthest from the school, along the airstrip, also have a high rate of school attendance, suggesting social and cultural—as well as pragmatic—forces at work. Not only does the decision to attend school vary by location of the village, once a girl decides to attend school, the number of years she attends significantly correlates with her residence as well. Observed departure from traditional behaviors also follows this same pattern: the location of the village of residence strongly correlates with the level of education and influence of the outside world (Stolpe 2003).

CHANGE OVER THE PAST DECADE

As social change sped up, the men's secret society began to lose control of the women, children and the intergenerational transmission of knowledge in Sambia society. The processes of change quickly and strongly impacted the performance of ritual initiation. Within a decade—roughly between 1970 and 1980—the great system of collective initiations known as the *mokeiyu* was curtailed. The boys were no longer routinely initiated into the men's house. Indeed, by 1979 the boys refused to live in the men's house, in spite of the fierce punishments from their elders. Even many women did not approve of the boys' resistance to male initiation customs, as this had previously assured the reproduction of gender relations, hunting, and marriage arrangements. The end of age-structured homoerotic relations was also at hand, because the out-migration of young bachelors and married men created an imbalance in the men's house. There no longer was a cohort of older males to socially monitor the young boys and serve as their inseminators. The end of warfare also diminished the threat of violence and coercion that was effective in insuring the compliance of boys in the past.

During the period of rapid change in the late 1970s and early to mid-1980s, the elders finally decided they could not trust the boys to keep the secrets of the men's society and suspended the ritual of boy insemination. However, other aspects of the ritual teachings continued. For example, the nosebleeding rituals still constituted important ritual purification. The boys were still taught the importance of bleeding at the time of initiation to strengthen themselves and remove their mothers' pollution from their bodies. Also, they were being prepared for when as adults they would bleed themselves as protection during their wives' menstrual periods. However, so much conflict emerged during this period that some men decided not to initiate their sons into the men's secret society. Instead, they sent their sons to the local school, to aim toward future jobs, as well as to avoid the risk of having their ritual secrets revealed and thus destroyed.

These were not only structural changes—they were registered in the lives of individual Sambia as well. Some young boys who were undergoing initiation at this time were adamantly opposed to the old ritual beliefs, whereas others were merely disinterested. The initiates who also attended school openly discussed the decline or collapse of traditional customs. They seemed to point to a real change in the achievement of masculinity outside of the traditional village system of warfare and ritual as necessary and increasingly positive. The more they experienced social change and the longer they attended school, the more aggressive they became in referring to custom as "the old ways" or the "pagan" ways. They also used the disparaging pidgin term *kanaka,* meaning a country bumpkin, yokel, or hick in the English sense, one who is not worldly-wise. Today, they articulate a distinction between the "bad" parts of the traditional initiation ceremonies, those they have eliminated, and the "good" parts, those they have kept.

This discursive exploration of cultural meaning and cultural change is explored in two films from the Sambia area: *Guardians of the Flutes* (1993) and the earlier *Towards Baruya Manhood* (1972). Gender narratives and masculinity are prominent themes in both films. Looking back at *Guardians* now, it is clear that the Sambia view the domination of women as more problematic than they did a generation ago. Likewise, Baruya women do not simply accept male domination in any simple sense. *Towards Baruya Manhood* suggests a more complex picture of the realities of domination. "We must not suppose that women consent at all times and in every way to male domination," Godelier (1986, 149) writes. In addition to the refusal of food and sex, the Sambia women also used gossip, scandal (resulting from suspected adultery, for instance), and manipulation of the children to get what they want from their husbands. Sambia women in the BBC film, *Guardians of the Flutes,* strongly hint that women never fully accepted some male beliefs, including the idea that insemination was necessary to produce breast milk. Neither had they demonstrated complete compliance in the oral flexion of their husbands. Men's fears of female semen sorcery and menstrual blood sorcery are always reminders of the powers of women's bodies among the Sambia and indeed are never far from their husbands' minds when they attempt to dominate their wives (Herdt and Stoller 1990).

Beginning in the mid-1970s a new set of social stories (Plummer 1995) on masculinity began to circulate, reaching their peak in the mid-1990s. The new modernizing tradition of masculinity presented two different scenes in which these stories were being played out—in the village and out in the coastal towns. Men who went to the towns saw this as an alternative to ritual initiation, as a means of testing themselves and their manhood to the ordeals and dangers they once faced in the traditions of the men's house. Of course, they did this without the social support of their age-mates or without the collective strategy of secrecy vis-à-vis their enemies and women. The attraction of fast food, alcohol, sex with prostitutes, Western goods, and other elements of "modernity" posed great temptations to these budding young men. When they returned to the village they love, they boasted of their conquests and their survival of the ordeals—proof of their new masculinity.

The men who went away to the towns left a kind of vacuum in the villages necessitating a renegotiation of social structures. Some men have said: "If these men go away, and their wives go to other men, that's their problem! Why can't we men who stay in the village marry all of them? It is more for us! Perhaps as many as three or four wives?" However, other men warned: "Oh, the women are many here, and the men are few; you don't want them to overwhelm you, gobble you up, do you? That's what can result in the loss of all of your semen and strength" (Herdt 1987; Herdt and Stoller 1990). Thus the absence of the men and the availability of their women has introduced a new problem into the social definition of masculinity: Should a man attempt to steal other men's wives to fulfill the ideals of traditional masculinity as in the past? The whole attitude had changed toward this old-fashioned ethic. The new proportion of women to men was one of the components of the new social uncertainty.

Women didn't seem to mind their husbands going away and leaving them, possibly because some of the women had their own means, such as gardens and cash crops, whereas other more modern women didn't want to marry and had designs on attending school. Others were no doubt simply relieved to have one less mouth to feed, and perhaps have a reprieve from frequent beatings from their husbands. Still others joined the Seventh-Day Adventist church and decided to leave or rid themselves of their more traditional or pagan husbands. The women's taste for power grew so much that some men even gasped, "What if the women achieve political office?" This would be the final blow to masculinity.

During this time much was said about the men who remained in the villages, especially the men who were *woganya*—weak, cowardly, or even "feminine" in their comportment. As one man remarked, "Women don't follow orders very well anymore. And some men don't know how to order them. Those men are woganya. At that time they are afraid of their food being poisoned by their wives. Some of the women only know the old ways, but others are changing." This same man continued, saying the following:

> The younger women, and some of the older ones too, they only want men with money. They "rubbish" [or denigrate] the "poor men." Before in the old days, it was that they only wanted men who could hunt possum and bring home a lot of meat for the women and children. Women would spit on a man who couldn't hunt or bag game. They say that the women want men who have money and will buy them tinned fish and rice from the trade stores. A man without money can't give rice and fish. . . . money is possum to them. . . . women swallow their spit when thinking about money. For example, Oruko is such a young man. He has fucked the wife of Erumbei and another man. That's because he can offer them rice and fish, and has money. They think he is smart-looking. Some of the women even push their men into going to work on the coast to get money. (pers. comm.)

This man, however, whose wife sometimes pushed him like this, rejected the idea, and told her that she was "behaving in the manner of a sexually loose woman, like a whore, who wants her husband to be gone so that she can play around." (See also Herdt and Stoller 1990 on these points.)

Clearly, out-migration of men was one of the components of the cultural destabilization that resulted in rapid cultural change. Although the effect of these changes has been less dramatic on the everyday lives of women and girls, the stories of exotic places, novel conquests, as well as the material artifacts brought back have left their marks. There is an insurgent discourse among many (especially young) Sambia women regarding traditional beliefs and their societal roles. Today the women's lives are still busy with the hard work of gardening and child care. It is difficult for most Sambia women to shy away from the responsibility of gardening because they and their families will go hungry if they do not harvest enough food throughout the year. However, childbearing and child rearing have become domains in which women can assert some new power. Many young women today do not wish to have more than two children, despite the tremendous social, political, and economic benefit of large broods. With a Western understanding of human reproduction supplied by pamphlets that the missionaries distributed, the young women have eschewed traditional reproductive teachings and are now better able to control their pregnancies. Although monthly birth control shots are now available at the health clinic (up to a six-hour walk for many of the women at the upper end of the Sambia Valley), abstinence is by far the preferred method. Abstinence is also a means for exerting some control over the marital relationship, as well as expressing dislike for spouses whom they were not able to choose. The traditional marriage system of contracted marriages is now contrasted with a new concept, the idea of "love" marriages. No one currently living in the Sambia Valley has such a marriage, thus love marriages remain a highly romanticized ideal. In a larger sense, the mere desire for the agency implied by a love marriage signals a significant departure from the traditional sociocentric cultural devoir and falls under the linguistic umbrella of *laik,* the pidgin word meaning "like" or "want to." To what extent it is appropriate for individuals, especially women, to act upon their "laik" is at the heart of much current debate among the Sambia. In general, the younger people embrace the perceived greater freedoms of the "outside" world by renouncing traditional teachings—*laik* has become metonymic for this freedom. Repudiating cultural mandates requiring many children is a powerful (albeit risky) way for young women to exert their own power, to make their own decisions in such a way as to affect their destinies. It seems likely that in the Sambia Valley, as elsewhere, the young women who attend school will have fewer children in their lifetimes than the women who do not. The reasons for this phenomenon are poorly understood (Bledsoe and Cohen 1993), although within the context of the current discussion, it seems that one source of power—many children—may be supplanted by another—education—while simultaneously displaying newly appropriated power.

But practical reasons drive the desire for fewer children as well. Despite the many perceived benefits of Christian conversion, the biblical dietary restrictions the Seventh-Day Adventists imposed placed an even greater burden of food production on the women. Until the conversions, the Sambia diet consisted of food gathered from the surrounding forest, food the women produced in their gardens, and food the men hunted, as well as pigs slaughtered for ritual and celebratory occasions. The missionaries advocated total restrictions against eating animals with certain traits including those with cloven hooves, animals that perch, and benthic fish (that is, eels and other bottom-feeders found in the local rivers). Almost all of the animals that the Sambia men hunted (as well as the domesticated pigs) fell into one of these categories. Not only did the nutrition of the Sambia suffer through the elimination of virtually all sources of animal protein in an already protein-deficient diet, but the proportion of food provided by gardening and gathering increased significantly. Women were now almost the sole providers of food for their families, further emasculating the Sambia men for whom hunting had been an important social and political activity. This increased responsibility also conferred a slight increase in social power on the women. However, with this increased responsibility, each additional child became more and more of a burden, with two seeming to be plenty. "Children are work, work, work," the young women frequently lament.

In the past decade or so, the introduction of coffee as a cash crop has further reorganized the lives of both Sambia men and women. Coffee production presented the Sambia with a dilemma: garden work was women's work; pecuniary and extracultural interests were men's work. Coffee was both. How then should the labor of coffee be divided between the sexes? A similar dilemma occurred in Africa more than a century earlier with the introduction of agricultural tools. Gardening had been the domain of women; tools had been the domain of men. The resolution resulted in the shift of agricultural labor from women to men (Comaroff and Comaroff 1997). For the time being, the Sambia have blurred gender distinctions and men and women generally work together in their gardens. This may be the first time in Sambia history that gender cooperation has been attempted.

The income from these gardens has both directly and indirectly affected the lives of the women. With monies, they can purchase food, decreasing the stress of daily harvesting in the gardens and the very real fear of disease that can destroy entire gardens and result in starvation. These purchased goods, primarily

© Gilbert Herdt

Men and children drying coffee beans.

rice, tinned fish, and Maggi Noodles, also increases the dietetic variation of the family diet. Thus, families with more money to purchase more food have healthier diets. The healthier diet increases the woman's fecundity as well as fertility and, no doubt, reduces the likelihood of infant and child morbidity and mortality. The greater survivability of each child born makes the woman's agency in reducing her number of pregnancies more acceptable.

For most Sambia, these purchased foods constitute less than 10 percent of their diet, but nonetheless the slight decrease in dependency on gardening for survival has significantly impacted the lives of women and girls. With decreased pressure on gardening and with the profits from the coffee gardens, more girls are able to attend school, often filling girls with expectations of lives different than their mothers'. Many of these girls express desires to change the trajectory of their lives—to "do anything but work in the gardens," as one educated young woman laments. These dreams are seldom realized, as the women are still required to fulfill their social obligations of marriage and reproduction at puberty. The newly realized pecuniary benefit of daughters in terms of brideswealth paid in the local currency (kina) has reconfirmed the importance of women as commodities. Once paid in pigs, other foodstuffs, and weapons, monetary brideswealth (in the amount of 400K for a woman from within the valley, more for an exogenous woman) now constitutes a primary source of family income, and daughters are often talked about in terms of their cash worth. One man in the valley whose wife gave birth to their fifth daughter, was constantly teased that he was now the wealthiest man in the valley—his assets amounted to 2000K. Fear of the loss of the anticipated brideswealth payments is one reason why girls are not often educated beyond

Sambia elders instruct youth

grade school. The only woman in the Sambia Valley who had attended high school was "sold" by her parents before she completed her studies because they feared loosing their brideswealth payment if she did not return to the valley. Thus, the introduction of cash into the valley has eradicated certain traditional ways of being a Sambia woman and simultaneously strengthened others.

CONCLUSION

As anthropologists have long attested, social change in culture and gender is an uneven, sometimes brittle process, but with possibilities for improvement in the social rights and legal entitlements of some. Throughout Melanesia the process of change that followed colonialism and more recently globalization has brought about a growing recognition of the rights of women in traditional cultures. The end of the men's secret societies (Herdt 2003) is part of this long and relentless process, whereby the conditional masculinity of entrance into male initiation was purchased in part at the subordination and social suppression of women and children. More recently the import of fundamentalist Christianity into Melanesian cultures has come at the price of new restrictions and limitations on the full personhood and citizenship of women, at least in some cases. However the expansion of cash crops and the opportunities of increased transportation have opened new vistas for younger Sambia, especially women, who aspire to be educated and affirmed in twenty-first-century desires to be more equal to their brothers, fathers, sons, and husbands. The next chapter of change for the Sambia will come when old and new traditions allow for the companionate gender relations increasingly appearing on Papua New Guinea television programs and commercials that are broadcast for its growing middle class.

REFERENCES

Barth, Frederick. l975. *Ritual and knowledge among the Baktaman of New Guinea*. New Haven: Yale Univ. Press.

Bledsoe, C., and Cohen, B., eds. 1993. *Social dynamics of adolescent fertility in sub-Saharan Africa*. Washington DC. National Academy Press.

Comaroff, J. L., Comaroff, J. 1997. *Of revelation and revolution*. Chicago: Univ. of Chicago Press.

Godelier, Maurice. 1922. Towards Baruya Manhood. Ian Dunlop, filmmaker.

———. 1982. Social hierarchies among the Baruya of New Guinea. In *Inequality in New Guinea*, ed. Andrew Strathern, 3–34. New York: Cambridge.

———. 1986. *The making of great men: Male domination and power among the New Guinea Baruya*. Trans. Rupert Swyer, New York: Cambridge Univ. Press.

Herdt, Gilbert. 1981. *Guardians of the flutes: Idioms of masculinity*. Chicago: Univ. of Chicago Press.

———, ed. 1982a. Fetish and fantasy in Sambia initiation. In *Rituals of manhood: Male initiation in Papua New Guinea*, 44–98. Berkeley: Univ. of California Press.

———. 1982b. Sambia nosebleeding rites and male proximity to women. *Ethos* 10:189–231.

———, ed. 1984. Ritualized homosexual behavior in the male cults of Melanesia, 1862–1983: An introduction. In *Ritualized homosexuality in Melanesia*, 1–82. Berkeley: Univ. of California Press.

———. 1987. *Sambia: Ritual and gender in New Guinea*. NY: Holt, Rinehardt, and Winston.

———. 1993a. Introduction. In *Ritualized homosexuality in Melanesia*, ed. G. Herdt, vii–xliii, Berkeley: Univ. of California Press.

———. 1993b. *Guardians of the Flutes*. British Broadcasting Co. Film.

———. 1999. *Sambia sexual culture*. Chicago: Univ. of Chicago Press.

———. 2003. *Ritual secrecy: Perspectives on New Guinea*. Ann Arbor: Univ. of Michigan Press.

Herdt, Gilbert, and Robert J. Stoller. 1990. *Intimate communications: Erotics and the study of the culture*. New York: Columbia Univ. Press.

Langness, Lewis L. 1974. Ritual power and male domination in the New Guinea Highlands. *Ethos* 2:189–212.

Mead, Margaret. 1935/l968. *Sex and temperament in three primitive societies*. Repr. New York: Dell Publishing Co., Inc.

Plummer, Ken. l995. *Telling sexual stories*. New York: Routledge.

Read, Kenneth E. 1954. Cultures of the Central Highlands. *Southwestern Journal of Anthropology* 10:1–43.

Stoller, Robert J., and Gilbert Herdt. 1982. The development of masculinity: A cross-cultural contribution. *Journal of the American Psychoanalytic Association* 30:29–59.

Stolpe, Birgitta. 2003. *Cultural endocrinology: Menarche, modernity, and the transformative power of social reconfigurations*. Diss. Univ. of Chicago.

NOTES

1. Herdt conducted fieldwork in Sambia 1974–76, 1979, 1981, 1983, 1985, 1987, 1989, 1990, and 1993.

2. The Leviticus book of the Old Testament establishes dietary restrictions against eating pigs, eels, birds that perch, animals with paws, and animals that crawl, all previously important social and nutritional components of Sambia life.

Fieldwork Biography
Evelyn Blackwood

I conducted research in a rural Minangkabau village whose inhabitants engaged primarily in wet-rice farming. Using participant observation, household surveys, and individual interviews, I examined the transformation of gender, kinship, and labor relations as a result of agricultural development and nationalist policies. I lived with a family in West Sumatra for 16 months between 1989 and 1990. During a typical day I typed up my field notes on a manual typewriter first thing in the morning and then spent my time watching women work in the rice fields, locating people to interview, and attending ceremonial events. Although most ceremonial activities were sex-segregated, my status as a foreign researcher allowed me to move between the spheres of men's and women's activities. In some cases I quite literally sat between women's and men's ceremonial spaces.

© Evelyn Blackwood

6/Mothers to Daughters

Social Change and Matrilineal Kinship in a Minangkabau Village

The Minangkabau living in West Sumatra are the largest matrilineal group in the world, numbering approximately 3.8 million in 1990. They have intrigued generations of scholars because they are matrilineal and, since the 1700s, Islamic. To Western eyes, matrilineal systems appear incongruous because they seem to do kinship "in reverse." In matrilineal systems the father is not the patriarch of the family, nor does descent and inheritance pass from father to sons. Instead inheritance, such as houses, land, livestock, and other forms of wealth, passes from mothers to daughters. Children trace their lineage through the mother's side of the family, not the father's, and take the clan name of the mother's family. And rather than sons bringing their wives home to live with them and their parents, daughters bring their husbands home to their mothers' houses in matrilineal systems. In effect, matrilineal systems keep the daughters at home and send the sons out at marriage, whereas patrilineal systems send the daughters out and keep the sons at home. As with any kinship system, matriliny has no fixed and universal form, but these principles tend to be typical of matrilineal societies (see Schneider and Gough 1961).

Societies with matrilineal kinship systems are less common than those with patrilineal systems but can be found around the globe in Africa, Asia and the Pacific Islands, South America, and North America. Based on a world ethnographic sample of 565 societies, Murdock (1957) found that descent was traced patrilineally in 44 percent of the societies and matrilineally in 15 percent. These numbers are not necessarily reliable because of disagreement among scholars about what features must be present for a society to be considered matrilineal or patrilineal. Just a few of the matrilineal societies worldwide include the Mosuo of Yunnan province in China; the Nayar of Kerala, India; the Asante of Ghana, West Africa; and the Navajo, Hopi, Cherokee, and Pueblo Indians of North America. In all these societies descent is traced through the mother; other practices, however, may differ. Among the Mosuo, sisters and brothers live together in the family house, neither moving out nor contracting marriages. Asante husbands live duolocally at their mothers' and their wives' houses; husbands and wives keep their money separate and work closely with their own matrilineal kinfolk. Among some other African matrilineal societies, wives live with their husbands and work their husbands' land.

Although earlier scholars predicted the demise of matriliny due to the supposed tensions between brothers and husbands within the same households, matriliny continues to flourish, even under conditions of social change. Like other kinship systems, matriliny is flexible and resilient, adapting to changing conditions through shifts in practice. Not all these shifts are detrimental to women and their landholding rights. Some of the challenges that matrilineal societies face, however, include colonial and religious influences supporting men's dominance, urbanization and capitalism under conditions that favor men's rights to property, new technologies, and income-earning activities, and state preferences for a citizenry comprised of small families headed by men rather than large corporate kin groups. These factors work together to weaken the bonds of matrilineal kin groups, in some cases giving rise to patrilineal kinship practices that conflict with matrilineal kinship. Yet in other cases, such as the Minangkabau, matrilineal kinship is reconstituted in new ways to deal with life in a globalized world.

Because the father is not the patriarch in matrilineal families, matriliny presents a paradox to scholars. In the 1800s scholars argued that matrilineal societies were ruled by matriarchs. Anthropologists have found very little evidence of such societies; most of that evidence comes from ancient myths. By the 1900s most scholars took for granted that men were the authority in kin-based societies. These scholars asked how men wield authority when descent and inheritance pass from mothers to daughters. The answer, they decided, was that the mother's brother replaces the father as the head of the kin group. Given the wide variation in matrilineal systems, it is impossible to say with certainty that mother's brothers always have more authority than their sisters or mothers. In many cases both women and men are influential in the affairs of the kin group.

The extent of men's authority in matrilineal societies continues to be a contentious issue as anthropologists try to unravel the knotty problems of gender and power. The development of men's authority within matrilineal systems can be connected to the influence of colonialism and world religions, such as Islam and Christianity, that privileged the mother's brother and even the husband as leaders of their families. In West Sumatra, Dutch colonizers installed the highest-ranking man as village head in each village and used other men as assistants to the chief. Women were excluded from Dutch colonial administration (see Benda-Beckmann 1990/91; Kahn 1993). Conservative Islamic clerics also periodically attempted to rid West Sumatra of matrilineal inheritance practices that were said to be inconsistent with Islamic traditions (see Oki 1977), although these attempts have generally been failures.[1] Their efforts are credited, however, with a shift in the husband's role within his wife's house. Traditionally a husband only visited his wife's house at night and returned to his mother's house in the morning. During the 1900s husbands began to take up ongoing residence at their wives' houses and were expected to contribute financially to their children's needs. This shift led to an increase in men's involvement in their children's lives over time, but also points to the flexibility of matriliny.

The Minangkabau case provides compelling evidence to disprove any simple association between men and authority in matrilineal societies, either as husbands or brothers. A husband resides with his wife in her mother's household and works on his wife's land. Husbands are treated as permanent guests in their wives' houses. Because they are not members of their wives' kin groups, they do not take part in any of the decisions of that kin group. Among the men of the family, one son in a generation is given the title of the kin group. The son holds the title until his death, at which time it is passed on to the best candidate among his sister(s)' sons, who is chosen through kin group deliberation. These titled men (*penghulu*) are considered representatives of their lineages, but not chiefs, because they do not have the type of power associated with chiefs. Further, because sons leave before or at marriage to live with their wives, titled men are not present on a daily basis in the family household; they are called home to help with major family decisions, such as those concerning marriages, title inheritance, and ceremonial festivities. Family decisions are made through a consensus-building process; not even the most senior titled man has the right to make a decision unless he has the agreement of his sister. Without her agreement, nothing can be carried out.[2]

Women's authority in this matrilineal society is based in their control of ancestral property (*harta pusaka*), which can include rice lands, house land, and the big house or lineage house (*rumah gadang*). The practice of matrilineal inheritance of property means that only women and their daughters are heirs to and in control of matrilineal land. A son may be given rights to use his mother's land, if she has ample land and is willing to help him out, but he cannot pass on that land to his wife's children. This matrilineal practice gives the senior woman the control of the use, income, and disposition of the land (see also Pak 1986). In addition, the practice of matrilocal residence after marriage (residence at the wife's mother's house) means that women maintain possession of houses and keep their married daughters with them. Because these practices privilege women as possessors of land and houses, senior women have authority to make decisions about land, houses, titles, and the conduct of subordinate kin, in consultation with senior men.

Matrilineal societies continue to intrigue scholars today. They provide important evidence that human social relations take many different forms. Because most of the literature on matrilineal societies focuses on men, this chapter turns attention to women in matrilineal societies, looking specifically at the changes that have occurred in relations between mothers and daughters in the past 50 years. My discussion of matriliny in West Sumatra is based on research in the village of Taram located in the province of Lima Puluh Kota (literally, Fifty Cities). One of the original three provinces that form the core of the Minangkabau world, Taram had a population of approximately 6,800 in 1989. Taram is a stronghold of *adat,* the system of customs, beliefs, and laws pertaining to everyday and ritual life; it is also a major producer of rice for sale on the market.

MINANGKABAU AND THEIR HOUSES

In West Sumatra, Indonesia, families of several generations used to live together in a big house. Many women born since the formation of the Indonesian state in 1945, however, have set up their own nuclear households separate from their mothers. This chapter examines the younger generation of women to understand first, why daughters choose to live in their own households rather than in the prestigious big houses, and second, whether this change in household form has led to changes in the way their matrilineal system operates.

Houses are a familiar location for studies of women because of the strong association in academic literature between women and the "domestic" domain of households. Families, child rearing, and women often appear to be synonymous. The Minangkabau, however, disrupt the conventional assumptions about gender and kinship in rural households. Minangkabau households contain more than a group of people engaged in domestic tasks; they are the very center of kinship and community relations.[3]

The Minangkabau big house is an impressive wood-planked building, rising above ground level on large wood posts with elaborately carved wood siding and a soaring peaked roof made of corrugated metal (see Figure 6.1). In the past it usually contained an extended family of three to four generations, including a senior woman, her daughters, and their husbands and children. Sleeping compartments lining the back and one end of the big house are designated for mother and daughters, and the front half of the house is an open space or hall for public gatherings and ceremonies (see Figure 6.2 for a floor plan of the big house). The central post of the house, which is located between the main hall and the entryway is identified with the senior woman; she is called the "central pillar of the big house" (Reenen 1996). When several daughters live in the big house, the most recently married daughter and her husband take the prestigious end room of the house, and her sisters and mother move down the row of bedrooms in the back of the house. As in the past, sons leave the house at marriage (and usually well before), although they keep their ceremonial gear at their mother's house. Should a son or brother be divorced or become widowed and have to return home, he may use the room next to the kitchen end of the house, but kinsmen in such a situation usually prefer to sleep at a nearby prayer house (*surau*).

Figure 6.1 Minangkabau big house.

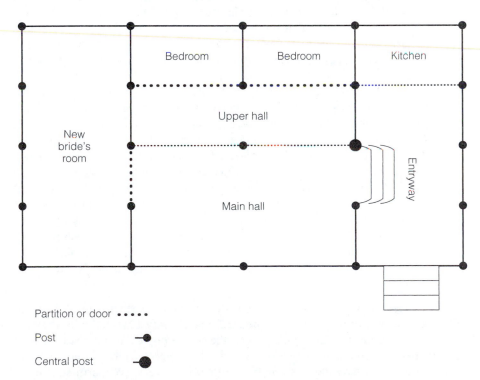

Figure 6.2 Floor plan of a big house.

Big houses are based on the bond between mothers and daughters; they persist from generation to generation as daughters are born, marry, bear children, and eventually achieve the position of senior women themselves. In the past mothers and their daughters shared all the land and its produce, and also shared the labor and expenses of the household with help from sons and brothers. For these kinswomen, it is one house and one cook pot:

> One of the wealthiest families in the village lives in a lively, bustling big house. It includes four generations: the elderly grandmother, the senior woman Hartati, who is widowed, her younger sister Siti and her husband, and two of Hartati's daughters, the married daughter Yetri, with her husband and two children, and an unmarried daughter. Another married daughter lives with her husband and children in Jakarta. Hartati and Siti have three brothers, one of whom is the titleholder. Yetri, the only married daughter at home, occupies the prestigious end room (*anjuang*).
>
> Outgoing and sure of herself, Hartati manages the household and rice lands. Her sister Siti never had any children, so Hartati, who is in her early 60s, was the logical choice to take over as senior woman. Although possessing a sizeable number of rice fields, no one in Hartati's family actually works in their fields. Hartati oversees sharecroppers who do the work of planting and harvesting the rice fields in return for half of the harvest. Yetri, the married daughter, has two small children who she stays home to care for. A stylish woman with shoulder-length black hair, Yetri is content with her place in the house and her expectations of becoming the next senior woman.
>
> Yetri described their house as a "collective household" (*rumah bersama*). The family pools their resources to maintain and improve their common assets—the house and land—and to hold life-cycle ceremonies. The ancestral property belongs to all of them and links the generations of mothers and daughters. Yetri told me, "The produce from our fields is brought home for food for all of us, mother, daughters, and children."
>
> When Yetri's children were born, the family hosted a large ceremony for each of them. Invitations were sent out to neighbors and kin throughout the village. Days before the ceremony, kinswomen came to the house to prepare the food, spending hours working, talking, and laughing together in the kitchen. On the day of the ceremony Yetri and her younger sister dressed in their most stylish dresses and sat with the baby in Yetri's bedroom to receive guests and gifts. Hartati oversaw the comings and goings of guests the whole day in the main hall of the big house, ensuring that they sat in the right places, according to their rank, and were served food and tea. In the early afternoon her kinsmen entered the hall with the local imam [Islamic cleric], who conducted the blessing. While Yetri's mother-in-law held the baby, who was wrapped tightly in a light blanket, the imam said a prayer and fed him bits of banana, welcoming him into the social world of the Minangkabau. (personal interview)

Big houses reflect the elite rank and status of the family that owns it. Only an elite family is allowed to build a big house.[4] It is not only a symbol of elite status but, more importantly, it is identified with the core group of matrilineally related kinswomen who live there (see also Ng 1993; Reenen 1996). Big houses vary in size, but an expansive and bustling big house with several compartments along the back that daughters occupy is a sure sign of the reproductive success, wealth, and good fortune of the family. The big house represents the "ideal" Minangkabau household; its structure signifies the preference for keeping daughters at home.

RECONFIGURING DAUGHTERS' DESIRES

Where big houses and extended families were the model for an older generation of women, many daughters born since the formation of the Indonesian state in 1945 have set up their own households separately from their mothers. In contrast to big houses, these contemporary-style houses are one-story buildings made with plaster and brick walls, cement floors, and slanted but not peaked corrugated metal roofs (see Figure 6.3). When the trend toward separate houses began, mothers at first built small units connected to the big house so that their daughters were still part of the big house. Over time, however, separate houses started to appear, although these single-family houses are quite often literally on the front steps of the mother's big house. As daughters started to move out, some of the big houses became empty, quiet buildings, occupied only by the senior woman with perhaps a granddaughter to keep her company.

Household composition in 1989 underscores the change in house style. The composition of the 115 households in Tanjung Batang that year varied widely from single-generation to extended-family units. Tanjung Batang is one of six hamlets in Taram. Based on my household survey, I found that two-generation families comprise 64 percent of households in Tanjung Batang. Three- and four-generation families, the extended households or matrihouses, comprise 26 percent of all households. I use the term *matrihouse* to refer to households with two or more generations of adult married women, that is, households with senior mothers and one or more adult daughters. Single-family, or nuclear, households—those composed of a wife, husband, and children—comprise 55 percent of two-generation households, or 36 percent of all households. The remaining households are comprised of a single generation, usually elderly. Although actual nuclear households are not in the majority, more families are living in single-family households than in extended-family households, and many more are doing so than in an earlier generation of families in the village.

If big houses reflect the matrilineal "ideal" of a household constituted around a core unit of mother and married daughter(s), why are daughters choosing to live in their own smaller, less prestigious houses? What factors could be working to reconfigure a daughter's desire for a house of her own, apart from her mother's? In the following I explore a number of factors that have shaped the views of women who have grown up in the postindependence era in Indonesia. Of particular relevance are state-sponsored education, state policies for women, the media, and Islamic fundamentalism. These processes converge to create a contemporary concept of Indonesian womanhood closely tied to domesticity. To document how these social processes have changed daughters' desires, I first examine the differences between women in the village who were born in the 1920s and 1930s and women born in the 1950s and 1960s. I focus on these two groups of women because those born in the 1920s and 1930s were the last group educated, if at all, under the old Dutch colonial system, whereas

Figure 6.3   Single-family house in front of mother's big house.

women born in the 1950s and 1960s were the first group educated under the new Indonesian state.

Education

For women born in West Sumatra in the 1920s and 1930s the only education generally available was a three-year elementary program. Education beyond that level required moving to and boarding at schools in the district capital. Over 85 percent of women born in those years had only an elementary school education or less, reflecting in part the reluctance of senior women to allow their daughters to leave the village. Many rural Minangkabau girls were not allowed to pursue higher education. An elite woman, who in the 1950s was the first of her generation to go to university, said the following:

> "Girls were not allowed to go to school if it meant going far away, or leaving the village. Before, Taram did not have a middle school, and students had to go to [the city of] Payakumbuh if they wanted to continue school. Parents were afraid to let their daughters leave home for two reasons. First, they were afraid their daughters would marry husbands from outside the village, and second, that they might not marry at all.
>
> I was stubborn and insisted that I be allowed to go [to the university]. My mother was very fond of me, she couldn't say no, and so she let me go. But my mother's decision made a lot of people in the village angry. At that time they still felt it was not right for a daughter to be so far from the village because of the concern that we would not return home." (personal interview)

Since Indonesian independence, the state has sought to improve education by building elementary and middle schools in local villages. As education became more accessible and public transportation more available, attitudes toward daughters leaving home for further schooling began to shift. Daughters no longer had to live away from home to attend high school, but could take public transportation each day to school. In some cases girls attended secondary schools located in towns far away from the village, especially if relatives with whom they could stay lived in that town. Over 40 percent of daughters born in the 1950s and 1960s graduated from high school versus only 2 percent in the earlier generation.

The shift in education rates reflects a shift in attitudes about the value of education for daughters. Many families now make sacrifices to put their children through high school. People articulate the belief that education is a key to obtaining a salaried job with a guaranteed income and pension. Villagers recognize the potential economic benefits of higher education and urban careers for women, especially when successful, educated daughters use their income to help out the family. For example, one elite daughter who worked in Jakarta for six years was able to save enough money so that she could build her mother a new house in the village. Although recognizing the importance of education for their children, rural Minangkabau are less willing to risk sending their daughters away to school than their sons. Yet the change in education rates between the two generations of women shows that, despite these concerns, daughters have been successful in contesting such restrictions. They have gained much greater access to higher education than was possible for an earlier generation.

While education for girls has become a desirable goal, education has served state interests by promoting national models of gender and modernity. The "modern" school system provides little validation for matrilineal practices, local customs, or the values of rural life. Schoolgirls are indoctrinated into the importance of becoming wives who serve their husband's needs. Schoolchildren wear uniforms that model the national dress code and reinforce gender difference: girls in skirts and blouses, boys in pants and shirts. On Fridays high school students wear more formal attire. Young women don woven sarongs and dress blouses, and young men wear jackets and (sometimes) ties, modeling the image of parents they are soon expected to be.

In addition to promoting a conservative gender ideology through the schools, the state promotes education as a way out of the village and a means to better, higher-status, salaried jobs. At an elementary school graduation ceremony I attended, the superintendent of schools encouraged the students to be successful. His idea of success was oriented toward the goals of change and development (*kemajuan*) that the state espouses. The village, he said, was changing but just beginning to be modern. He encouraged students to adopt "modern" values and strive for careers and jobs, which in the context of rural life means looking beyond the village for the source of success.

Marriage Rights

The right to choose when and whom they will marry has been another important issue for many women. Women of an earlier generation married according to their mother's will, even though they did not know or might not like their marriage partners. When I asked one woman what would have happened if she had refused the candidate her family chose for her, she replied, "I would have had to leave the house, even leave the village. I probably wouldn't have been given any rice fields." Between the generations of women born in the 1920s and 1930s and those born in the 1950s and 1960s, the age at marriage has increased from 17 to 19-and-a-half years old. Part of the reason for the change is the increased number of years women are attending school (the average age at graduation from secondary school is 19). As long as young women are in school, most families do not pressure them to marry. Some women wait until after they have secured a permanent job before they marry, particularly those seeking civil service jobs, which may add another two to three years before they start considering marriage.

Sentiment in the village has shifted somewhat with these changes. Whereas the older generation is concerned that their daughters marry good men of elite families, romantic novels and movies that encourage partner choice have influenced the attitudes of younger women about marriage partners. Reni, the only daughter of an elite family, is a good example of the complexities of young women's expectations and beliefs about marriage:

> After Reni graduated from high school, she had wanted to attend college like several of her friends, but her mother was unable to pay for both her son and daughter to attend college at the same time. Reni applied for a civil service job instead and sometimes took trips to visit her friends at the university. During this time, her attitude toward marriage was that she should choose her own husband. "Later on, parents die, and then we are left with their choices. If we follow them, who is happy? If you follow their choice and later divorce, and are unhappy, that's no good. We have to make ourselves happy first, we can't please our parents." She was not without long-term priorities, however. Reni felt that it was important to marry an educated man with initiative and desire to work, even if he was not elite. Echoing a sense of modern individualism, Reni felt that her own happiness was more important than following the wishes of the older generation to marry a husband with a title and blue blood.
>
> Around the time she married, however, Reni's ideas began to fall more in line with her mother's concerns. She told me how she finally decided on her husband. Her mother wanted her to marry a man who belonged to her father's lineage [*bako*], but Reni was never interested in him. For a time she was interested in a young man from Java, but her mother was adamantly opposed to him, so Reni eventually decided against pursuing that relationship. As she approached the age of 25, an age which is considered old for an unmarried woman, a woman friend suggested that her brother might be a good match. Within a couple months, Reni decided to marry him, although he was from another village. Her choice was not the best one according to her family, but one that was acceptable because they were able to verify that he was of elite rank.

The "romance" model of marriage has strong appeal for young women, but many daughters remain committed to the importance of "good" marriages for the future of their kin group. Consequently, many marry within the village or make accommodations to their kin's wishes. With the greater likelihood of daughters leaving the village for education and meeting men from outside the village, elite elders have had to loosen restrictions about marriage partners. In Reni's case marrying an elite man from outside the village accommodated some of the concerns of her mother. Such a partner would not diminish the standing of their family. The senior generation in their turn have ceded ground and allowed daughters more room to marry the ones they choose.

MODELS OF DOMESTICITY

Many young women grow up believing they are better off today under the patriarchal order of the Indonesian state because they can seek their own jobs and choose their own husbands. Indoctrinated in the values of the state and encouraged to seek opportunities for work away from the village, these young women find the older generation old-fashioned in many ways. With the increased availability of education, civil service, and other wage labor jobs, young women have demanded the right to pursue higher education and careers in urban areas.

Access to these options has exposed the younger generation of women to different models of family and household than those prevalent in rural Minangkabau villages. The Indonesian state, echoing Western development planners, has long trumpeted the importance of the nuclear family, women's role as housewife and mother, and men's role as head of the family. State programs promote the importance of motherhood and the idea that women are primarily responsible for their children and their family's health, care, and education.[5] All state family policies are oriented around a nuclear family defined as a husband, wife, and children, a definition of family that disregards the many forms of family found within the borders of Indonesia.

According to the state directive, a woman has five major duties (*panca dharma wanita*): (1) to be loyal backstop and supporter of her husband; (2) to be caretaker of the household; (3) to produce future generations; (4) to raise her children properly; and (5) to be a good citizen (Sullivan 1983, 148). Statements by high state officials (among others, the Minister for Education and Culture and the Minister for Social Welfare) reiterate the importance of women's roles as housewives. In a speech to wives of government officials, Mrs. Tien Suharto, wife of then President Suharto, declared:

> A harmonious and orderly household is a great contribution to the smooth running of development efforts. . . . It is the duty of the wife to see to it that her household is in order so that when her husband comes home from a busy day he will find peace and harmony at home. The children, too, will be happier and healthier" (quoted in Manderson 1980, 83).

This statement underscores the idea that within the domestic sphere of the "home," women have primary responsibility for children and household concerns.

Programs instituted for women by the state after 1966 implemented this new view of womanhood, focusing solely on women's roles in the family. The state created an organization of wives of civil servants, Dharma Wanita, in 1974. All wives are expected to participate according to the rank of her husband, even if she is a civil servant herself. In line with the previously stated directives, this group attended exclusively to domestic issues. Family Welfare Organization, another women's organization established in 1973, has had the most far-reaching

Figure 6.4 Cosmetics demonstration for village women.

effect. It is the main channel the government uses to reach women at the grass-roots level. Its leaders come from the wives of government officials. Holding offices according to the ranks of their husbands, these women are not elected or remunerated for their duties. Although they are under heavy pressure to take on these duties as good wives, their participation is considered voluntary. These two organizations strictly follow the dictates of the government regarding their structure and programs. Their members are kept busy with cooking and etiquette demonstrations, courses for sewing and flower arrangement, and family planning, health, and nutrition. Dharma Wanita regularly hosts events promoting different kinds of products, such as cosmetics, baby food, and clothes, among other things (see Figure 6.4). Even though some of the information provided is useful, these organizations propagate a middle-class view of womanhood and create a desire for items that reflect a middle-class status. They work together with state pronouncements about women's essential roles as wife and mother to reinforce the idea of women's domesticity within the nuclear household (see Tiwon 1996).

In addition to state policies and propaganda, women are inundated through national media with representations of urban, middle-class women. Advertisements in women's magazines and on television bombard women with the most fashionable clothes, skin care, and health care products necessary to make them successful women. Avon, Revlon, and Pond's are some of the non-Indonesian companies promoting this vision of femininity. The national dress code reflects this ideal of femininity—dresses, skirts, jewelry, and makeup are the only acceptable attire for women at work. Television shows also pick up the domestic theme.

On a popular television series that a government-owned television station produces, one of the themes illustrates that a good woman is a domestic person (Aripurnami 1996; Sen 1993).

Minangkabau newspapers published in West Sumatra for local readers are another source promoting femininity and domesticity for women. *Singgalang,* a daily paper published in Padang, the provincial capital, contains a women's section devoted to health, beauty tips, and heterosexuality. A columnist advises women not to worry if they are not beautiful; they can develop other characteristics that will still be attractive to men. Another columnist claims that men and women need each other; each sex is incomplete without the other: "Although it's not impossible for a woman to find meaning without a man," advised Fadlillah, "it gives women's lives new meaning when a man is there" (1996, 3, my translation). Another article admonishes women to be modest (*malu*), which is seen as the proper trait for a Minangkabau woman, and warns against too modern an attitude, "modern" here referring to the "loosened" values and morals of those in the cities.

Islamic fundamentalism in Indonesia is another principle agent promulgating domesticity. Islamic leaders, in Indonesia as elsewhere, have interpreted women's primary role to be wife and mother. They assert that motherhood is the natural role for women and the one they were born to. In an article on the status of women in Islam, an Indonesian Muslim scholar and intellectual of the modernist school of Islam developed this line of thought further:

> "Man is suited to face the hard struggles of life on account of his stronger physique. Woman is suited to bring up the children because of the preponderance of the quality of love in her. [W]hile the duty of breadwinning must be generally left to the man[,] the duty of the management of the home and bringing up of the children belongs to the women" (Raliby 1985, 36).

This view of womanhood closely corresponds to the one fostered by the Indonesian state. In fact, Islamic scholars and prominent Muslim women have interpreted the Qur'an to accommodate state views on women.

Statements by Indonesian Muslim women who are highly placed in government and those who are leaders of women's organizations support state policy on women. In an article on "Women and Career in Islam," the author, an Indonesian businesswoman, finds no contradiction between state directives for women and the Islamic emphasis on wifely duties. She states, "[T]he main duties of women are . . . family affairs, including the children's education matters. [O]ther duties, such as social and professional roles, are additional depending upon the condition of respective families" (Pramono 1990, 73). This statement suggests that woman's primary duty is to her family and only secondarily to her community. It echoes the terms of the state directive on women to educate children and provide support for their husbands. Support for women's careers "outside the household" is contingent on women's ability to maintain their families and homes in proper order.

State views of womanhood promote images of family and happiness that threaten the viability of extended-family households. By extolling a middle-class lifestyle, the state not only encourages smaller families but also emphasizes individualism and consumerism. In addition, market advertising of consumer goods, such as cosmetics, televisions, stereos, and automobiles, associate the consumption of goods with higher status. Encouraging the satisfaction of personal pleasures and the attainment of individual goals through consumption of goods, the market promotes a model of self-earned income for the earner's use alone, not for the extended family. Given these influences, daughters may have less incentive to live with and work for their mothers, and more incentive to focus their interests and income on their own families.

CONTRADICTORY HOUSEWIVES

The images of womanhood that are familiar to rural Minangkabau women in the 1990s underscore the values of domesticity and the nuclear family. Rural Minangkabau women have learned that in the "modern" world, staying home and taking care of the children represents the good life and accords with the state's view of women's lives. By contrast, working in the rice fields is represented as a dead-end, low-status job. The great majority of women in Taram, however, are farmers who spend many days a month working in the rice fields. Women do much of the rice production themselves, planting, weeding, and harvesting, while their husbands or brothers clear the harvested fields and prepare them for the next planting cycle. During the planting season, women go out early in the morning in small groups, carrying their tools and food with them, and work until mid-afternoon planting row after row of seedlings in flooded rice paddies. Traditionally, women in Taram did all the harvest work, cutting, winnowing, and threshing the rice plants by hand. They then carried the sacks of hulled rice home and placed them in the rice granary. With agricultural development, rice is no longer grown for subsistence but for sale on the market. Changes in technology have brought more men, along with the women, into the rice fields to cut and thresh the rice and carry it to the rice mill.

Despite the importance of their work and the pride many women feel in working their own rice fields, several women told me it was better to be a housewife and to not have to "work." Among them was Lina, who has been farming both for her elderly mother and as a paid laborer in other peoples' fields for several years. Lina said,

> "If you do other work, it's difficult. Your rice fields get less attention, your children get looked after less. If you sell things [at the market], then you're not often at home. You don't get home until night and that's tiring. If your husband is responsible [and makes money], then you can be the housewife."

Other women, who were busy farmers or active in community affairs, declared that it was more important to stay home and take care of the children than anything else they did.

Ironically, none of these women who claimed to be housewives (*ibu rumah tangga*) fit the stay-at-home housewife model. Each of them had work that took them outside the house and each had income from that work. Some of them were well-to-do farmers who did not have to do field labor. These women for the most part were owners/overseers, like Hartati; they hired others to work their fields for wages or hired sharecroppers to handle all the work (see Figure 6.5). One woman

Figure 6.5 Woman farmer (on left) overseeing her rice harvest.

owned a prosperous rice mill and another was a rice merchant buying and selling rice with her husband. The rice merchant told me that her husband does all the work of their business, but when I pressed her about it, she revealed that she is the one who buys the rice at harvest from her clients and has it brought to the mill; her husband handles the processing and sale of the milled rice.

Not all women in the village considered themselves housewives. Most women who worked their own rice fields generally considered themselves farmers, although in some cases they would say they were "just farmers" (*petani aja*), suggesting that their work was less prestigious than other types of work. Women who could actually be labeled housewives were mostly young married women who did not have their own sources of income and stayed at home taking care of their small children. Even these women did not fit the (Western) model of housewife because most of them were supported by their extended families and their husbands, not by their husbands alone.

The claim to and desire for housewife status reflected several processes at work: the devaluation of farming that occurs through education and the media, the official representation of women as housewives, and the notion of "work" as paid labor. In terms of the larger society, farming is seen as a low-status occupation; the preferred middle-class status is associated with a working husband and stay-at-home wife. Many women admire the image of the middle-class housewife found in cosmopolitan magazines and advertisements; her life seems preferable to work in the mud of the rice fields. By asserting that they do not work, women invoked the modern definition of work as something for which one gets paid, such as a job or career. By accentuating their domesticity as housewives, women aligned themselves with the state model for women.

Yet claiming the status of housewife was not simply a desire for middle-class status or a response to a state model. Many of these women maintained their own sense of what a "housewife" means. Like Lina, several women included work in their rice fields as part of being a housewife, thus creating a new definition of housewife that differed from the state model. As Lina explained about being a housewife, "Of course you go to your rice fields. But you don't have to leave the house for so long. To the rice fields in the morning and return home in the afternoon." Rural Minangkabau women incorporated their control of and labor on their rice fields into this new sense of themselves as "housewives." Although these women claimed to be housewives, they were not the housewives of state ideology.

SOCIAL CHANGE AND SMALL HOUSES

Several Minangkabau scholars have argued that the processes of capitalism and a global economy have led to a decline in the extended family form of Minangkabau households and the increase in nuclear households (Kato 1982; Naim 1985). The increase in smaller households in Tanjung Batang does seem to support that suggestion, reflecting a transition over time from big houses with extended families to smaller single-family units. Although older studies do not specify actual numbers of extended family households in rural Minangkabau villages, they do state that the typical residence included an extended family living in a big house (see, for example, Maretin 1961; Schrieke 1955). In 1962, the big house was the dominant style of house in Taram (Bachtiar 1967). Based on information from women of the senior generation in Tanjung Batang, most women born before 1940 lived with their extended families (84 percent), the great majority of which (80 percent) were housed in big houses.

Clearly more families are living in single-family households in Taram than in extended households and many more are doing so than in an earlier generation of families in the village. The increase in two-generation households may be suggestive of a pattern found in other rural areas where smaller households become more prevalent as peasant families are integrated into wage and commodity markets (see, for example, Kandiyoti 1990; Wilk 1989). Since the development of rice as a major cash crop in the early 1970s in West Sumatra, farm households have had greater access to cash, thereby increasing daughters' ability to build their own houses. But numbers do not tell the whole story. Other factors may account for the increase in single-family households.

Households, Demographics, and Migration

As was true for households of the older generation, the early death of the senior woman or the arrival of new families to the village explained a number of one- and two-generation households in 1990. In all likelihood, some of these households will become extended households in the next generation. Other single-family households resulted from failure to bear daughters. In households of this type sons moved out at marriage to live with their wives, leaving the senior generation alone in the house. In a few of these cases a son returned home to live with his

elderly mother after divorce or sent his young daughter to live with her grand-
mother and assist in domestic work.

Migrating in search of jobs or business (*merantau*) is another significant
factor in the number of one- and two-generation households. Migration is a common occurrence and long-standing tradition in West Sumatra (Naim 1985).
Many individuals migrate on a temporary basis, and others return to the village
permanently only after they have retired from work. Nearly one in four daughters (usually elder daughters) temporarily migrates from the village. In some
cases no daughters are left at home, accounting for 16 percent of one- and two-
generation households.

Although most of the scholarly attention to migration has focused on men,
judging from family genealogies in Taram and the numbers of women who migrated from the village in the 1920s and 1930s (7 percent), it was not uncommon
for daughters as well as sons to migrate to a different locale.[6] Daughters might
decide to leave due to lack of land to farm or overcrowded housing. This pattern
is still common today as migrants search for better opportunities elsewhere. The
change from the earlier generation is in the larger percentage of women who
migrate, reflecting the greater availability of jobs for women outside the village
than in the past. Villagers say that women leave to follow husbands who have
good jobs elsewhere or prospects of greater income than their wives, but many of
the current women migrants are educated, unmarried women who have obtained
permanent jobs elsewhere. As with sons, merantau siphons off additional daughters who are not needed at home or would cause too great a burden on ancestral
land if they stayed to make claims to it (see Naim 1985). Daughters who migrate
out have much weaker claims to lineage property. If they or their husbands are
successful in making a living, they are expected to refuse any claims on produce
from ancestral property, leaving it to the sisters who live in the village and manage the house and lands.

Residence and Matriliny

Some argue that the increase in nuclear families for rural Minangkabau reflects a
weakening of matrilineal kinship (see Maretin 1961). Residence patterns after
marriage, however, offer strong evidence of a continued commitment to matrilineality. Most daughters do not move out immediately after marriage but wait
until their younger sisters have married, spending the intervening years in their
mothers' houses. The average length of stay at home is almost 10 years for those
daughters in Tanjung Batang whose mothers are still alive and living in the village.
Those who move out usually live close by on matrilineal land or with close
kinswomen. Based on the residences of 81 adult married women born in Tanjung
Batang after 1945, nearly 73 percent live matrilocally.[7] Although they live in
their own houses, their proximity to mothers or kinswomen reflects their accommodation to matrilineal practice in the face of changing household form.

Of the remaining group of women, 18 percent live patrilocally with the father's
or husband's family and 9 percent live neolocally in the village on land that the
daughter and her husband purchase together. The presence of patrilocality in this
context might suggest a weakening of matriliny, but as in the case of migration,

it appears to be a long-standing practice related to the availability of economic resources. The cases of daughters living patrilocally (with husbands on husbands' mother's land, or near their fathers) are due in some cases to the poverty of the daughter's natal family or, in other cases, to the lack of a daughter in the husband's mother's household. If a husband has access to land or kin connections with wealthy elites, then a daughter might decide to live with her husband's relatives. In fact, most of the daughters who live with their husbands in Tanjung Batang come from commoner or low-income households. Tisra, who lives with her husband in a tiny house, comes from a village about an hour away. Her own family included her parents, six sisters, and two brothers. The fact that she had six sisters meant very little, if any, land was available to go around, making a move to her husband's village more desirable because he had access to land through his matrilineal kinswomen. Women who live patrilocally do so for the sake of better economic opportunities. Their actions do not portend the demise of matriliny because in other ways they maintain matrilineal kinship ties.

Clearly not all daughters remain at home in extended families but matrilocal residence continues to be the primary residence pattern for those who live in the village. Daughters draw on rights to land to build houses near mothers' houses, maintaining a strong connection with matrilineal kin. State views of nuclear families and middle-class lifestyles may be fueling daughters' desires to have their own separate households, but most do not move out precipitously or very far away.

Daughters Who Leave

As has been suggested, a number of reasons, both economic and demographic, explain why daughters end up in single-family houses not of their own choosing. But what about daughters who purposely choose to move out of their mothers' houses? Why would they leave the prestige of the big house for a smaller house with fewer hands to help in everyday house and farm tasks? How much have state and media representations of womanhood influenced their decisions?

To gain a better understanding of the pressures and conflicts at work in the lives of the younger generation of rural Minangkabau women, I examined 36 households of daughters and mothers living separately in the village, 20 daughter households and 16 mother households.[8] All daughter households in this group are nuclear (with a resident husband), except for two households where the husband is absent or was divorced, and one household without children. Mothers' households include all types of households from single woman only to nuclear to extended households with other daughters resident.

Despite the nearness of daughters' houses in many cases, mother and daughter households maintain separate resources and income (see Figure 6.6). Almost none of the mothers contribute income to their daughters on a regular basis, although they may share land and exchange labor. One daughter with her own household sharecrops her mother's land and splits the produce with her mother—shared land provides income for both of them. In most other cases the daughter manages her own household and relies on her own land and income along with her husband's resources and income to support the household. In the following discussion I asked

Figure 6.6 Mother (on left) and daughter in front of daughter's house.

first what claims daughters make about their reasons for moving to their own houses, and second, how much influence a husband has in his wife's small house.

Daughters' Claims

Daughters point to a number of reasons for wanting to live in their own houses, most of which center around tensions in the mother–daughter relationship and tensions over access to economic resources. Lack of generosity by a mother toward her daughters is one reason daughters give for moving out of mothers' houses. This claim draws on notions of mutual assistance (*tolong-menolong*) between family members for its validation. A mother who is perceived as ungenerous or unwilling to help out each of her daughters equally may create a rift in the relationship that causes a daughter to leave as soon as she is able to support herself.

> Nurani, who lives in her own house near her mother Yenita's big house, expressed resentment over the way her mother had treated her. Yenita's income from ample rice lands enabled each of her daughters to receive a high school education, but Yenita was very strict about who they married. Nurani was forced to marry a man she was not interested in and later divorced; she lived in her mother's house along with her siblings and their families for many years. She complains that her mother is stingy and never helps her as much as she does her younger sisters. According to Nurani, Yenita spoils the youngest daughter, who has a civil service job with her own salary. This daughter lives and eats with her mother and doesn't even have to cook. Even though she has her own salary and can buy whatever she wants to buy, she gets money for shopping from her mother. After the last harvest, Yenita bought a necklace

that the youngest daughter is now wearing. Nurani complained that she couldn't get any land from Yenita for her children. She wouldn't have had any, she said, if her father hadn't felt sorry for her and lent her some of his rice land [he was the last of his lineage]. For all these reasons, Nurani said, she worked hard and saved enough money from that rice land to build her own house down the path from her mother.

Nurani's story highlights the problems of a generation of daughters for whom money and income have become much more important and is much more closely scrutinized for the ways it circulates.

Other elite women emphasize their desires to get out from under their mothers' supervision after marriage. In their stories, they present their mothers' control over their lives as unwelcome interference in what they feel is their own affairs.

Lina lived in the big house with her mother Fitriani for several years after she got married until she and her husband saved enough money to build a house for themselves and their two children. Their house is just steps away from Fitriani's big house. In talking about her relationship with her mother, Lina stresses her need for independence from her mother and desire to be on her own. She told me,

"It's nice [being in my own house]. Because I don't depend on my mother or ask for help, she can't mix in my affairs. She can't tell me how to or how not to spend money. She can't ask, 'Why are you sleeping? What, no work to do, then come help me!' We would argue frequently if we were too close. So I earn my own money, I don't ask my mother. I'm on my own. If I wasn't, maybe my own house wouldn't have been built yet." (personal interview)

Lina's statement suggests that if she was still under her mother's supervision, she would not always get what she wanted. The money she earns allows her to buy things for herself. By living in her own house Lina can manage her own money and does not have to negotiate with her mother over how to spend it.

Reni, Nurani's daughter, had similar views about the desirability of living in her own house, although she has not yet been able to remain in her own house.

Reni spent her childhood living with her mother and brother, her two aunts, and their families in Yenita's big house. It was not until Reni was a teenager that her mother had her own house. Before Reni married, she told me that she would prefer going with her husband once she was married because she wanted to be on her own. She also remarked that according to Islam, a good wife must submit to the wishes of her husband, a religious sentiment that handily justifies her desire to move out of her mother's house. Not surprisingly, once Reni married, she moved with her husband to a town nearer her civil service job and his business.

They lived in an apartment building where, according to Reni, everyone worked and no one had any time to visit. She told me she liked living there without interference from other people. With the birth of her second child, however, she and her family moved back home with her mother again, a situation that has both good and bad aspects to it, she said:

"When I lived in town, I was busy all the time and tired. I got up early and cooked, swept, washed clothes, bathed, all before going to work, worked all day and then came home to cook some more, take care of my daughter, do more washing. Then I would just collapse early because I was so tired." (personal interview)

But when they lived in town, she was able to raise her daughter the way she wanted. At her mother's house, she said, although she gets help with taking care of her children, she can't control what goes on in the house. According to Reni, her daughter is getting spoiled but Reni does not argue with her mother over how to deal with her. To Reni, living in her own apartment was advantageous because she could run things as she wanted. Under her mother's roof, she defers to her mother.

Younger women such as Reni and Lina express a desire for independence and separation from the extended family, a desire that reflects in part state views about the nuclear family and woman's primary duty to her husband and family. Further, the view that village life is backward provides support for women in their resistance to the ideas of the older generation. In conversations with Reni, for instance, it was clear that she thought the older generation old-fashioned; she disagreed with their ideas about the relations between the sexes and also disapproved of the way her family treated her daughter. These points of difference encourage young married women to see their own small families as something that they, as wives and mothers, should be in control of, rather than their mothers, the senior women. Their attitude toward their kin group reflects the idea that the "modern" housewife should manage *her* household and *her* family on her own.

The tensions between mother and daughter over the mother's control of the household echo in claims about unfair use of household resources and unwanted supervision over daughter's family. Nurani, who was born in the mid-1940s, represents the first generation educated after Indonesian independence. Her desire to be on her own tends to reflect more of the local ideas about mutual assistance and generosity coupled with increasing concerns over cash income and its circulation. For Reni and Lina, two younger women born in the 1960s, their desire to have their own households reflects more strongly state ideology about marriage and family.

Based on a comparison of land controlled by daughters in their own households versus land controlled by their mothers, another reason for daughters to establish their own farm households was access to enough land of their own. Conversely, the ability of some households to hold onto daughters is closely related to the amount of land the mother controls. This pattern has interesting parallels in rural societies with patriarchal or patrilocal extended households. As a number of studies have shown, access to wage labor or cash income produces conflicts that loosen customary obligations within extended-family households and lead offspring to form their own nuclear households. As money becomes more important in peasant households, it undercuts existing concepts of equivalence or exchange (Kandiyoti 1990; Wilk 1989). In the Minangkabau case, if mothers have less land than daughters already have access to, daughters have less incentive to stay at home under their mothers' control and more incentive to live separately where they can make their own decisions.

MATRILINY IN SINGLE-FAMILY HOUSEHOLDS

The second question I explored about single-family households is the relationship between the husband and wife. As noted earlier, state policy recognizes nuclear households as the primary household type. Due to the influence of state policies, modern education, and Islamic views of family, rural Minangkabau men's responsibilities have shifted from their sister's children more toward their own children. Does state support for men as fathers and heads of households translate into husband's control over nuclear households? Have matrilineal practices been weakened in nuclear households?

Under the laws of the Indonesian state husbands are empowered as heads of households. The Indonesian Marriage Law of 1974 states that, "the husband is the head of the family and the wife is the mother of the household" (Salyo 1985, 20). Marriage law and state policy about households reach into rural villages not only through state education but also through a variety of other processes. State registration laws are one example of the way in which the state view of family is directly imposed on rural households. According to state law, all households must be registered with the village administrative office. Household registration forms allow families to register household head (*kepala keluarga*), wife (*isteri*), and children (*anak-anak*), a system that imposes a nuclear family form and predetermines the positions of the married couple. According to the form, household heads are men. Only women who are divorced or widowed can be listed as head of household.

When I asked people to identify the household head in their family, using the Indonesian term *kepala keluarga* (the Minangkabau do not have a similar term in their language), almost everyone responded with the name of a husband or male in-law, suggesting widespread recognition of the idea that men are heads of families. By identifying the nuclear unit with the household, the state in effect validates and prioritizes that unit at the same time that it diminishes the importance of the larger kin unit, the matrilineal unit, which is the basis of rural life.

The tendency of people to name a man as household head, however, has more to do with compliance to state directives than with a wholesale reconceptualization of family form. *Kepala keluarga* is an Indonesian term, not a cultural category for the Minangkabau. When I asked one woman why the husband is said to be the head of the household, she replied, "He is responsible for support, for providing sustenance for the family. He guides the children and takes care of his wife." This response was from a very wealthy woman whose husband has never been able to do more than help manage the family projects because he does not have his own source of income. In a way, she was correct: husbands do provide support, but so do wives. Another woman was more candid. After stating that the husband is the head, she said, "When we go to the village office (*kantor desa*) [to register a household], they ask who is the head of the household. The answer is, the husband, not the woman." Another young woman told me with a laugh, "My husband is only home now and again. But in the book [referring to the village registry], the husband is the head of household. It's forced on us (*terpaksa*)." Given a category that does not fit with Minangkabau practice, people are willing to pay lip service to state policies, but in so doing they are not necessarily representing their actual household relations or acquiescing to state dictates.

Husband and Wife Contributions

Another way to understand relations in single-family households is to look at the resources available to husbands and wives. A comparison of the amounts of land available to matrihouses versus the amount of land daughters control in their own houses highlights some interesting differences. Here I examined 20 daughter households separate from their mothers' houses in the village. As noted earlier, daughters who live in their own households have access to more land than do their mothers. They gain access to land primarily through their mothers, but also through their husbands, fathers, and kinsmen, as well as through their own efforts or in partnership with their husbands.

Women, who had redeemed land with assistance from their husbands, claimed that land as their own. In Lina's case, her mother Fitriani had pawned most of her family's ancestral land, leaving Lina with no land of her own except that which she shared with her mother. Both she and her husband are farmers and have worked together as sharecroppers and agricultural laborers for several years. They saved enough money in that time to redeem land that belonged to her matrilineage. Though her husband's labor and income was needed to allow them to save money, the land they redeemed with that money belongs to Lina. Overall, in single-family households the wife controls on average five times more land than that provided by her husband. Consequently, although husbands provide more land to women who live in their own households than to those in matrihouses, women still control more land than their husbands, ensuring that women maintain their dominance in single-family households even with husbands present.

Reconstituting Single-Family Households

So far these statements apply to the households of daughters whose mothers live in the village. What happens in the other single-family households (one or two generation) in the village in which a husband was present? Husbands in all nuclear households contribute 23 percent of land, compared to 8 percent in matrihouses and 15 percent in households of daughters living separately. Wives and husbands held an additional 13 percent of the land in common in these households, meaning that they had purchased it together out of pooled or joint income. Men thus provide greater access to land in nuclear households than in the other types. Yet across all nuclear households, women own or have access to 64 percent of household land, indicating that as in daughter households, women have greater control of resources than their husbands.

In single-family households husbands are more central and make a greater contribution than in matrihouses, which are under the rule of the senior woman. The husbands' greater prominence in single-family households, however, does not give him control over these households. In these households, both wife and husband contribute to household resources. They jointly control some of the land to which they have access, but both partners also have separate income or land resources, which they control themselves. Husband and wife consider nonancestral land that they buy or pawn through their combined efforts to be joint land during their lifetime. But even this land is reconstituted as matrilineal land at death and passed on to daughters. In like manner, whether their house is built by the husband or from joint earnings, the house is said to be for the wife or the daughter, and will be passed on to the daughter. In addition, a wife has a right to her husband's income but the husband does not have the same right in his wife's income. He has to turn to his family if he needs financial assistance. In the typical rural single-family household, both spouses have their own resources and income. Though poorer families have fewer resources, the resources they do have are passed on to daughters.

Although state efforts to prop up men as breadwinners and heads of households are well known to the Minangkabau, these single-family households remain firmly invested in matrilineal practices. Husbands do not assert claims to their wives' land nor to land that is redeemed through joint effort. Nor do they articulate rights to new houses that they help build with their earned income. Women assert rights to jointly built, single-family houses, maintain control of their own resources, and claim land for their matriline that was gained with husband's help. Some of these single-family households may even become matrihouses in their turn if a married daughter stays at home to raise her family. In the process of creating their own small households, women reinstitute matrilineality by incorporating new types of houses and new resources within matrilineal practice.

CONCLUSION

A number of historical processes have created different desires across generations of Minangkabau women without, however, leading to the demise of matrilineal kinship within both small and big houses. The old ideal of living in the big house is being replaced by desires for single-family households. Single-family houses reflect daughters' ideas about the importance of managing their own small families, having control of their own rice fields, and gaining independence from the senior woman. Although the younger generation of women has been influenced by the model of domesticity and nuclear families presented by state-sponsored education, state policies for women, the media, and Islamic fundamentalism, Minangkabau women are not replicating the dominant view of womanhood. Women have not become the stay-at-home housewives and mothers of national fantasy, even when some of them claim to be. Although over time the husband's contributions and responsibilities toward his wife's family have increased, rural Minangkabau husbands do not control their wives in single-family households. Rather than falling subject to husbands' wishes, women are reworking matrilineal kinship to create rights to their new smaller houses and maintain their rights over land and resources.

State and popular representations of motherhood and family do not dictate the shape of women's lives, but they do provide a means for daughters to challenge their mother's control of family interests. A daughter's desire to move out of her mother's household speaks to the extent of a mother's power over her household and offspring as well as the influence of state and market representations about work, consumption, and nuclear families. Through her position as senior woman of her kin group, the mother has the right to control family interests. She is the authority that a daughter must follow until the time that she takes over for her mother. The younger generation of women asserts the importance of their "own" (state-constituted) nuclear families as a way to move out of the big house and away from mother's direct control. A woman's desire for her own household reflects her desire for independence without subverting matrilineal bonds because mothers are not far away.

Because daughters continue matrilineal practices (of land and house owner-ship, inheritance, and matrilocal residence), the "nuclearization" of rural Minangkabau households does not portend the imminent collapse of matriliny or its replacement by state-defined categories of kinship and family. Rather the changes in household form suggest that mothers and daughters are reworking matrilineal kinship under current historical conditions to sustain their own material and social advantages. Daughters rework the state view of women's domesticity to create rights to their own small houses, ultimately reconstituting matriliny in new forms.

REFERENCES

Aripurnami, Sita. 1996. A feminist comment on the Sinetron presentation of Indonesia women. In *Fantasizing the feminine in Indonesia,* ed. L. Sears, 249–258. Durham: Duke Univ. Press.

Bachtiar, Harsja W. 1967. *Negeri* Taram: A Minangkabau village community. In *Villages in Indonesia,* ed. Koetjaraningrat, 348–485. Ithaca: Cornell Univ. Press.

Benda-Beckmann, Keebet von. 1990/91. Development, law and gender-skewing: An examination of the impact of development on the socio-legal position of Indonesian women, with special reference to Minangkabau. *Journal of Legal and Unofficial Law* 30/31:87–120.

Blackwood, Evelyn. 2000. *Webs of power: Women, kin and community in a Sumatran village.* Lanham, MD: Rowman & Littlefield.

Brenner, Suzanne A. 1998. *The domestication of desire: Women, wealth and modernity in Java.* Princeton: Princeton Univ. Press.

Fadlillah. 1996. Wanita, Malin Kundang, dan Feminisme. *Singgalang,* June 30, 3.

Kahn, Joel S. 1993. *Constituting the Minangkabau: Peasants, culture and modernity in colonial Indonesia.* Providence: Berg Publishers.

Kandiyoti, Deniz. 1990. Women and household production: The impact of rural transformation in Turkey. In *The rural Middle East: Peasant lives and modes of production,* ed. K. and P. Glavanis, 183–194. London: Zed.

Kato, Tsuyoshi. 1982. *Matriliny and migration: Evolving Minangkabau traditions in Indonesia.* Ithaca: Cornell Univ. Press.

Manderson, Lenore. 1980. Rights and responsibilities, power and privilege: Women's role in contemporary Indonesia. In *Kartini centenary: Indonesian women then and now,* 69–92. Monash Univ.

Maretin, J. 1961. Disappearance of matriclan survivals in Minangkabau family and marriage relations. *Bijdragen tot de Taal-, Land- en Volkenkunde* 117: 168–196.

Murdock, George P. 1957. World ethnographic sample. *American Anthropologist* 59: 664–687.

Naim, Mochtar. 1985. Implications of merantau for social organization in Minangkabau. In *Change and continuity in Minangkabau: Local, regional, and historical perspectives on West Sumatra,* ed. Lynn Thomas and Franz von Benda-Beckman, 111–117. Athens: Ohio University.

Ng, Cecilia S.H. 1993. Raising the house post and feeding the husband-givers: The spatial categories of social reproduction among the Minangkabau. In *Inside Austronesian houses: Perspectives on domestic designs for living,* ed. James J. Fox, 117–139. Canberra: Australian National Univ.

Oki, Akira. 1977. *Social change in the West Sumatran village: 1908–1945.* PhD diss., Cornell Univ.

Pak, Ok-Kyung. 1986. *Lowering the high, raising the low: The gender alliance and property relations in a Minangkabau reasant community of West Sumatra, Indonesia.* PhD diss., Laval Univ.

Pramono, Dewi Motik. 1990. Woman and career in Islam. *Mizan* 3 (1):72–75.

Raliby, Osman. 1985. The position of women in Islam. *Mizan* 2 (2):29–37.

Reenen, Joke van. 1996. *Central pillars of the house: Sisters, wives, and mothers in a rural community in Minangkabau, West Sumatra.* Leiden: Research School CNWS.

Reid, Anthony. 1983. Introduction: Slavery and bondage in Southeast Asian history. In *Slavery, bondage and dependence in Southeast Asia,* ed. Anthony Reid with Jennifer Brewster, 1–43. New York: St. Martin's Press.

Salyo, Suwarni. 1985. Islamic influences on the lives of women in Indonesia. *Mizan* 2 (2):1521.

Schneider, David M., and Kathleen Gough, eds. 1961. *Matrilineal kinship.* Berkeley: Univ. of California Press.

Schrieke, B. 1955. *Indonesian sociological studies: Selected writings of B. Schrieke, Part One.* The Hague: W. van Hoeve, Ltd.

Sen, Krishna. 1993. Repression and resistance: Interpretations of the feminine in New Order cinema. In *Culture and society in New Order Indonesia,* ed. Virginia Matheson Hooker, 116–133. Kuala Lumpur: Oxford Univ. Press.

Sullivan, Norma. 1983. Indonesian women in development: State theory and urban kampung practice. In *Women's work and women's roles: Economics and everyday life in Indonesia, Malaysia and Singapore,* ed. Lenore Manderson, 147–171. Canberra: Australian National Univ.

Suryakusuma, Julia. 1996. The state and sexuality in New Order Indonesia. In *Fantasizing the feminine in Indonesia,* ed. Laurie Sears, 92–119. Durham: Duke Univ. Press.

Tiwon, Sylvia. 1996. Models and maniacs: Articulating the female in Indonesia. In *Fantasizing the feminine in Indonesia,* ed. L. Sears, 47–70. Durham: Duke Univ. Press.

Wieringa, Saskia. 2002. *Sexual politics in Indonesia.* New York: Palgrave Macmillan/Institute of Social Studies.

Wilk, Richard R., ed. 1989. *The household economy: Reconsidering the domestic mode of production.* Boulder: Westview Press.

NOTES

1. The Minangkabau in West Sumatra today are considered devoutly Islamic. Identified with the Sunni branch of Islam, they generally see no conflict between *adat* and Islam.

2. See Blackwood (2000) regarding consensus decision making in Minangkabau families.

3. This study is based on my field experience in a rural Minangkabau village in West Sumatra, Indonesia, from 1989 to 1990 and in 1996. The complete ethnography based on this research is published in Blackwood (2000).

4. The lineage system in West Sumatra is a ranked system comprised of elite, commoner, and servant ranks. Elites are descendants of the original settlers of the village (*orang asli*). Because original settler clans have the highest status, I use the term *elite* to refer to them. The commoner rank designates newcomers to the village who are incorporated into the kinship system but lack the full rights of elite lineages. The servant rank is composed of families who are descendants of either debt bondsmen, who were unable to repay debts, or prisoners of war (Reenen 1996; Reid 1983).

5. See, for example, Brenner (1998), Manderson (1980), Suryakusuma (1996), and Wieringa (2002).

6. The figure is probably higher than 7 percent because people did not always tell me about kin who no longer lived in the village. In many cases I learned about older migrants only through casual conversation.

7. I exclude from this figure the women who have migrated to other areas of Indonesia. Having left the village altogether, their situation is somewhat different than that for women who remain in the village after marriage.

8. To make a comparison between the two types of households, I excluded households of women whose mothers are no longer living or whose mothers live outside of the hamlet of Tanjung Batang.

Fieldwork Biography
Richard B. Lee

Richard Borshay Lee first went to the Kalahari Desert in 1963, when Botswana was still under British colonial rule. His initial field research with the Ju/'hoansi (then known as the !Kung Bushmen, or San) focused on subsistence ecology and provided material for his 1965 doctoral dissertation at the University of California in Berkeley. *Man the Hunter* (1968) with Irven DeVore followed, bringing together hunting-and-gathering specialists from around the world. In the 1970s and 1980s, Lee made six more trips to the Ju/'hoansi focusing on social, economic, and political change, which resulted in several books including *Kalahari Hunter-gatherers* (1976), *The !Kung San* (1979), and *The Dobe !Kung* (1983, 1st ed.). Since 1996, Lee has been working mainly in Namibia on the social and cultural aspects of HIV/AIDS. This work has taken him to several field sites. One such site—which he visited in 2003 and 2005—is Tsumkwe, a subdistrict capital, where AIDS is becoming a major health problem.

7/The Ju/'Hoansi at the Crossroads
Continuity and Change in the Time of AIDS

Over the last 30 years the Ju/'hoansi—also known as the !Kung San or Bushmen—have become one of the classic cases in the anthropological literature, documenting the lifeways of a contemporary hunting-and-gathering society (Lee 1979; Lee 2003; Marshall 1976; Lee and DeVore 1976). They have also

Portions of this chapter have been adapted from a chapter that Richard Lee published with Megan Biesele in *Chronicling Cultures* (2002) Other portions of this chapter originated in a report that Richard B. Lee and Ida Susser presented at the annual meetings of the American Anthropological Association in a session titled, "Updating The San: Image and Reality of an African People in The 21st Century" (Lee and Susser 2003). Financial support for this research was received from the Fogarty Foundation for International Public Health, Columbia University, and the University of Toronto. The author wishes to thank Namibian collaborators Dr. Scholastika Iipinge, Pombili Ipinge, and Karen Nasheya, and North American collaborators Ida Susser and Megan Biesele, as well as Karen Brodkin, Polly Wiessner, and Robert Hitchcock. Special thanks goes to Donna Bawden, University of Toronto, whose research on the youth culture in Tsumkwe in August and September 2003 added valuable detail and insights.

© Richard Lee

Women at summer water hole. Nomadic patterns in the 1960s dispersed Ju/'hoansi to distant temporary water points, where gathered foods and game were abundant.

been the subject of extended inquiry into their historical status and the impact of contact and conflict with regional cultures and the colonial order (Solway and Lee 1989; Lee and Guenther 1991; Wilmsen 1988; Wilmsen and Denbow 1989). An informal group of scholars and activists, now centered around the Kalahari Peoples Fund of Austin, Texas, brought together anthropological work on diverse topics. The studies focused on change covering many spheres: the economic and political (Lee 2003), settlement patterns (Yellen 1990), demography (Howell 2000), kinship and marriage (Lee and Rosenberg 1994), health (Hansen et al. 1994), and religion and healing (Katz, Biesele, and St. Dennis 1997; with summaries in Hitchcock, Biesele, and Lee 1997, and Lee and Biesele 2002).

In the last 50 years the Ju/'hoansi have faced war, land dispossession, and internal violence fueled by alcohol, and they have survived. Less well documented is the fact that the Ju/'hoansi, straddling the border between Botswana and Namibia, are located in the heart of the world region hardest hit by AIDS. The most recent United Nations (UN) AIDS estimates put Namibia's HIV+ rates at 22.5 percent and Botswana's at 38 percent, the latter having the highest national rate in the world. How would the Ju/'hoansi, for all their renowned cultural resilience, fare in the geographical epicenter of the worst epidemic in world history?

This chapter will present an overview of the complex social and economic changes the Ju/'hoansi of Namibia and Botswana have undergone. This overview will examine how, in the midst of all these changes, the Ju are responding to what may prove to be their greatest challenge.

FOUR DECADES OF CHANGE

When I first encountered the Dobe Ju/'hoansi in 1963, perhaps three-quarters of them lived in camps based primarily on hunting and gathering, and the rest were attached to the cattle posts of their Herero and Tswana neighbors, Bantu-speaking Africans who had begun to settle in the Dobe area in the 1920s. It was the hunting-and-gathering or "foraging" camps that were the subject of sustained anthropological investigation in the 1960s (Lee and DeVore 1976). The foraging Ju/'hoansi relied on extensive mobility to sustain their way of life, moving camps frequently in the rainy season but always returning in the dry season to one of the nine permanent, naturally occurring water holes in the area. The Ju/'hoansi enjoyed an egalitarian lifestyle with relative equality between the sexes, aided in part by the strong contribution that women made to the group's subsistence. They possessed no domesticated animals except their hunting dogs. (In the 1960s a few of the settled Ju/'hoansi, not in the hunting-and-gathering camps, kept small herds of cattle and goats.) The large majority of their diet was dependent on wild plant foods (nuts, berries, roots) and game animals (small and large antelopes, hares, and game birds). The rest came from gifts of milk and meat from their cattle-keeping neighbors, the Herero and Tswana. Alcoholic beverages were unknown.

After Botswana's independence was declared in September 1966, the pace of change accelerated and has continued to accelerate to the present.

The Dobe area of 1964 had no trading stores, no schools, no clinics, no government feeding programs, no commercially drilled water sources (called boreholes), and no resident civil servants (apart from the tribally appointed headman, his clerk, and constable). By 2004 all these institutions were in place and the Dobe people had completed four decades of rapid social change; they had been transformed in two generations from a society of foragers—some of whom herded and worked for others—to a society of smallholders who eked out a living by herding, farming, and craft production, along with some hunting and gathering. The Dobe Ju/'hoansi today sit around their fires and smoke their pipes as before, but they also listen to their transistor radios, cook their store-bought "mealie meal" (ground cornmeal), brew home brew. . . and worry about the future.

Ju villages today look like other Botswana villages. The beehive-shaped grass huts are gone, replaced by semipermanent mud-walled houses behind makeshift stockades to keep out cattle. Villages ceased to be circular and tight-knit. Twenty-five people who lived in a space 20 meters by 20 meters now spread themselves out in a line village several hundred meters long. Instead of looking across the central open space at each other, the houses face the kraal where they keep their cattle and goats, inscribing in their living arrangements a symbolic shift from reliance on each other to reliance on property in the form of herds (Yellen 1990).

Hunting and gathering, which provided Dobe Ju with over 85 percent of their calories in 1964, now supplies perhaps 30 percent of their food. The rest is made up of milk and meat from domestic stock, store-bought mealie meal, and vast quantities of heavily sugared tea whitened with Nestlé powdered milk. Occasional produce from gardens and foraged foods makes up the rest of the

Men preparing meat at Dobe village, 1964. In the 1960s hunting and gathering provided over 85 percent of the Ju/'hoan diet, a third of which was from hunting.

Signs of change: After 1970 Dobe Ju/'hoansi began to build semipermanent mud-walled houses within fenced compounds. With the introduction of cattle, wage work, and craft production, subsistence dependency on hunting and gathering declined.

vegetable diet. For most of the 1980s and 1990s, government and foreign-aid drought relief programs provided a steady but monotonous diet. At some water holes so much was available that surplus was often fed to dogs.

When the government cut off general food distributions, the Dobe people at first were shocked and angry: but they quickly responded in creative ways. The mid 1980s saw a revival of hunting; men who hadn't hunted for years took it up again, and younger men who had never become skilled with bow and arrow, hunted from horseback with spears. In a single week in July 1987, five eland were killed, more than had been taken in the entire previous year. The possession of horses was the key to hunting success. One old couple sold six of their cows to buy one horse and then sent young men on horseback out to hunt for them. Hunting has continued to the present but with ever-diminishing frequency as the Government Wildlife Department continue to tighten game laws. Instead the government has offered waged employment to villagers on road crews and other make-work projects.

From as early as 1900 some Ju had been involved in boarding cattle for wealthy Tswana, in a loan cattle arrangement called *mafisa,* widespread in Botswana (Lee 1965; Hitchcock 1977). By 1973 about 20 percent of Ju families had some involvement as mafisa herders and the number grew through the 1970s; but in the 1980s people had become bitter about mafisa. They complained that cattle promised in payment for services rendered—usually one female calf per year—were not being paid, and without these beasts it was difficult to start one's own herd. Coupled with the withdrawal of government rations the lack of mafisa had soured some Dobe Ju/'hoansi about their prospects in Botswana.

The people saw what was happening in Namibia where the Nyae Nyae Development Foundation was helping Ju/'hoansi to drill boreholes and obtain cattle. Boreholes provided a reliable year-round source of clean water for people, animals, and for irrigating crops, all of which allowed people to reduce mobility and adopt a more settled lifestyle. Dobe area Ju wanted to obtain their own boreholes, and an overseas development aid agency (Norwegian NORAD) was favorably disposed to financing the project. But the Botswana government stonewalled an international proposal for five to eight boreholes, indicating that the government's once-liberal policies toward the San (known as Remote Area Dwellers or Basarwa) were taking on an increasingly regressive character. In 1987 some Dobe people started a movement to leave Botswana and cross the fence to their relatives in Namibia, and by 1994 some had actually made the move.

Some compensating developments have brightened this generally gloomy picture. From 1986 on, a small parastatal business enterprise, the Kung San Works, purchased increasing volumes of Dobe area crafts, primarily from Ju/'hoansi but also from Herero. This pumped considerable cash into the Ju economy, from a level of 400 to 500 Pula per month (US$200–250) before the marketing scheme, to P5000 to 7000 (US$2500–3000) per month at the peak of the scheme.

Unfortunately not many opportunities were available for productive investment of the proceeds in infrastructure such as plows, bicycles, cattle, or horses. Although some large stock were purchased, a distressing amount of cash was

© Richard Lee

Men playing cards and listening to the radio. After the first store opened in 1973, home-brew drinking became popular, accompanied by a rise in alcohol-related violence.

absorbed in buying beer, brandy, homebrew materials, bags of candies, and the ubiquitous sugar, tea, and Nespray powdered milk.

Schooling and the problems of youth were other areas of concern. When the first school opened at !Kangwa in 1973, some Ju parents responded quickly, registering their children, and scraping together the money for fees and the obligatory school uniforms. Most Ju parents however ignored the school or withdrew their children. They objected to the fact that the children were forbidden to speak their own language on school grounds or were subjected to the (mild) corporal punishment that is standard practice in the Botswana school system. Despite the efforts of parents, teachers, and the school board to encourage attendance, 40 to 60 percent absenteeism at the !Kangwa school continued into the 1990s.

In spite of these obstacles at least four of the Dobe area students did go on to secondary school in the 1980s. But even for these students—the first to get even this far in the educational system—the road has not been easy. For the large majority of Ju/'hoansi with no or little schooling, the job prospects were poor, and a life of odd jobs combined with heavy drinking was not uncommon. It was a bitter irony of underdevelopment that in the mid-1980s some Botswana youths were attracted to pre-independence Namibia under South African occupation where enlistment in the South African Army was the only job available.

Far more successful was the second and smaller of the two schools, at /Xai/xai, where a progressive headmaster wisely incorporated many elements of Ju/'hoansi culture into the curriculum, and was rewarded with strong parental and community support for the school and a low absentee rate. In 1986, the /Gwihaba Dancers, a troupe of /Xai/xai schoolchildren, won regional and national cultural competitions and performed at Botswana's 20th Anniversary of independence celebrations (Lee 2003, 201–205).

In the long run Dobe area Ju/'hoansi face serious difficulties. Since 1975 when wealthy Tswana wanted to expand cattle production they have formed borehole syndicates to stake out ranches in remote areas. With 99-year leases that can be bought and sold, ownership is tantamount to private tenure. By the late 1980s the borehole drilling approached the Dobe area. If the Dobe Ju did not form borehole syndicates with overseas help, their traditional foraging areas might be permanently cut off from them by commercial ranching. However it would be another decade before the borehole scheme finally came to fruition.

NYAE NYAE: A STRUGGLE FOR SURVIVAL

Although the Dobe people had to meet the challenges of declining foraging, sedentarization, and the cold bath of immersion in the market economy, the Ju/'hoansi of the adjacent Nyae Nyae had to deal with much more: massive resettlement, the imposition of apartheid, the loss of most of their land base, militarization, and finally the triumph and trauma of independence and post-independence Namibia.

The former German colony of South West Africa had been given to South Africa after the first world war as a League of Nations mandate. South Africa treated the mandate as a virtual colony and imposed policies of segregation and unequal treatment for the African majority (combined with some beneficial programs in public health and job-training, but not voting or civil rights). These largely repressive and unjust policies later became known as the apartheid system imposed throughout South Africa. These policies continued in their South West African colony from the 1920s right up to the late 1980s.

For the first half of that period, the Ju/'hoansi of Nyae Nyae, because of their remote location, continued their "traditional" lifestyle relatively unaffected by apartheid. Important studies of their hunting-and-gathering way of life were carried out from 1951 to 1958 (summarized in Marshall 1976). But in 1959, shortly after the Marshall expeditions had been completed, a South African civil servant arrived in Nyae Nyae to "civilize" the "wild" Bushman. Lured by promises of wage work, agricultural training, and medical care, the great majority of the foragers were assembled in the town of Tsumkwe in 1960. The settlement had been mandated only after the South African administration of the territory had ceded 70 percent of the traditional foraging areas of the Nyae Nyae Ju/'hoansi to other ethnic groups, 30,000 square kilometers of southern Nyae

© Richard Lee

Tsumkwe supermarket in 2000. With stores, a lodge, an airfield, and a secondary school in the district capital, the Namibian Ju/'hoansi in the 1990s were experiencing small-scale urbanization.

Nyae to Hereroland and 13,000 square kilometers of the north to Kavango and to the Kaudum Game Reserve.

For two decades 900 to 1,000 Ju/'hoansi were herded together under the watchful eye of South African authorities and missionaries, while weekly shipments of government rations supported the settlement, supplemented by some wage work, and occasional trips out for bush foods. The enforced idleness and unaccustomed crowding took a heavy toll: alcoholic drinks had never been a part of Ju/'hoan culture. In the space of a few years drinking became the focus of social life at Tsumkwe. Serious social problems—family violence and home-brew parties—became a regular feature of Tsumkwe life. Ironically after decades of forced settlement, rising alcohol consumption, and government paternalism, the South African filmmaker, Jamie Uys, came to Tsumkwe to film *The Gods Must Be Crazy,* which portrays the Ju/'hoansi as pristine hunter-gatherers so "untouched" that the mere appearance of a Coke bottle upsets the equilibrium of the society (Davis 1996).

John Marshall's excellent film *N!ai: the Story of a !Kung Woman* (1980) was a useful antidote to the *The Gods Must Be Crazy.* It documents the militarization, anomie, and Saturday-night brawling that characterized Ju/'hoansi life at Tsumkwe at this time; it even contains a sequence of the filming of *The Gods Must Be Crazy.*

In 1978 the South African Army began to recruit Nyae Nyae men into the South African Defense Forces (SADF) to fight the resistance fighters of the South West Africa People's Organization (SWAPO). Ultimately the 201 Battalion had about 700 Ju/'hoan soldiers, making the Ju/'hoansi one of the most heavily militarized peoples in Africa. The SADF recruitment campaign brought contradictory responses: the men were happy to have "work" (if you could call it that) and good pay; but the people were sharply divided on the morality of the war and which side to support. (Many Kung quietly supported SWAPO, and some soldiers even tried to warn SWAPO units of impending attacks.)

Engagements with "the enemy" were infrequent. Far more destructive was the sudden wealth in the hands of so many young men away from their families. Alcohol consumption increased further and drunken fights became more deadly. In a two-year period between 1978 and 1980, Marshall recorded six homicides, compared to an estimated four cases for the entire previous decade.

Even while the war was going on with all its dislocations, a new threat to their land base emerged: the Department of Nature Conservation within the South West African administration pushed strongly to have the Nyae Nyae area declared a game reserve from which all development, including livestock, was to be excluded. The administration wanted a few Ju/'hoansi to dress up in traditional clothes, dance, and sell curios to well-heeled tourists.

The Ju/'hoansi were appalled by this scheme and opposed it vehemently. The people were well aware that their traditional way of life had been seriously compromised. They knew their future lay not in being props in what John Marshall aptly labeled a "Plastic Stone Age," but in building up their herds and fields to establish themselves as smallholders with a mixed economy of foraging, farming, and wage labor. Happily, after years of protests, the scheme was abandoned.

The Ju/'hoansi won this victory in part because by 1988 the tide in Namibia was turning against South Africa; the SADF had suffered a military defeat in Angola at the battle of Cuito-Carnevale, and the momentum was gathering for a U. N.-sponsored plan for Namibian independence. In September 1989 elections, SWAPO won a clear majority and the independent nation of Namibia came into being in March 1990.

Despite the rejoicing at the end of 75 years of South African rule, independence for the Ju/'hoansi was not an unmixed blessing. To all intents the new nation was broke: the country was without developed energy sources; its minerals had been systematically extracted; and its former patron, South Africa, disappeared over the horizon. The hasty retreat was thrown into relief by the hundreds of demobilized Ju/'hoan soldiers, their livelihood vanished, lounging around their home communities suddenly with a great deal of time on their hands. At the same time neighboring ethnic groups began to cast their gaze in the direction of the pristine grasslands of Bushmanland as a place to graze their vast herds of cattle.

With all these forces arrayed against them, the Nyae Nyae Ju/'hoansi have had a major ally in the form of the Windhoek-based Nyae Nyae Development Foundation of Namibia (NNDFN). Founded by John Marshall and Claire Ritchie in 1981, the Foundation has lobbied hard in Namibia and internationally to preserve Ju/'hoansi land rights and community organization.

The Foundation arose in response to moves by some Ju/'hoansi to cut loose from the squalor of welfare capitalism that had been created for them at Tsumkwe. In the early 1980s, tiring of the incessant squabbling, hunger, and uncertainty, small groups of Ju/'hoansi began to move away to reestablish themselves on their traditional lands—called *n!ores*. Eight such groups had formed by 1986; thirty of these "outstations" had established themselves by 1991; and the number had stabilized at 37 by 1997. Drawing upon private donations and later international agencies, the NNDFN was able to provide funds to the newly formed Ju/wa Farmers' Cooperative (now known as the Nyae Nyae Conservancy) to drill boreholes and purchase small herds of cattle for these reassembled landholding n!ore groups.

Even with the Foundation's aid, the road to a semblance of self-reliance for the Nyae Nyae Ju/'hoansi has not been easy. First the Farmers' Cooperative had to fight interference from the South African bureaucracy that still controlled Namibia prior to 1990. Their small boreholes and cattle posts existed in the middle of what the administration still regarded as a vast game reserve. Between 1983 and 1986 lions decimated the herds of cattle; and elephants, seeking water, broke down several borehole pumps. At some villages the elephants were so destructive that the communities had to erect an electrified fence to keep them away from the wind pump and dam. The atmosphere of struggle and uncertainty is conveyed forcefully in Megan Biesele and Paul Weinberg's book *Shaken Roots* (1990) and in the epic five-part film series by John Marshall entitled *A Kalahari Family* (2003), covering a half-century of change among the Nyae Nyae Ju/'hoansi.

In the last few years and despite the uncertainties, the Ju people have made several steps forward. The Nyae Nyae Conservancy has developed into an effective representative of Ju/'hoan interests, standardizing the language with the help of a linguist, the late Patrick Dickens, and drawing up a constitution and bylaws in the Ju/'hoan language. These positive developments were facilitated during Megan Biesele's tenure as the Foundation's research director. It was during this period that the Ju/'hoansi made their voices heard and became actors in their own right on the national stage and at international forums.

The future of the Nyae Nyae people and their land rights took a significant step forward with the convening of the national Land Conference in Windhoek in June and July 1991. The Farmers' Coop and the NNFDN came to the conference armed with legal opinions, maps, and surveys of the 200 traditional n!ores (territories) into which the Nyae Nyae was divided, a complete set of bylaws and constitution for the NNFC in Ju/'hoansi and English, position papers, and other documents. The delegation was accompanied by lawyers, interpreters, a press kit, and two television documentaries about the Nyae Nyae people and the challenges they were facing. One of the most effective components of the NNFC presentation was a detailed discussion of the traditional n!ore tenure system and how it was being adapted creatively to the tasks of economic development. It urged that any land law that came into force should acknowledge these forms of tenure and their legitimacy. In the end the conference adopted most of the recommendations that the NNFC put forward, a major victory for the Ju/'hoansi. Sam Nujoma, the president of Namibia who instructed local authorities to respect Ju/'hoansi land rights, strengthened this with a subsequent visit to Bushmanland. This backing enabled the NNFC to peacefully remove neighboring pastoralists who, with their large herds of cattle, had illegally occupied southern Bushmanland in the euphoria and confusion following independence. The encroachment on Ju/'hoan grazing land by Herero pastoralists remains an ever-present threat.

The Nyae Nyae San are struggling against long odds to establish themselves as herder-foragers and as citizens in a modernizing state. But the legacy of decades of colonialism and forced acculturation is a bitter one: chronic drinking bouts and anomie are manifest. The 37 outstation communities vary widely in their economic well-being and sense of identity, from bustling villages of 100, to rural slums on the edge of hunger. It is too early to tell whether the Ju/'hoansi of Nyae Nyae will win the battle for self-reliance. However, if empowerment is the key to survival, then the Land Conference and its aftermath *do* offer a modest basis for optimism.

JU/'HOANSI IN THE TWENTY-FIRST CENTURY: PROGRESS AND POVERTY

Botswana

On recent visits to a Dobe village in the period between 2001 and 2004, observers noted some major changes. First, the long and twisting 90-mile road connecting the village to the rest of Botswana has been vastly improved, with travel time cut from six to seven hours to two-and-a-half hours. At a Dobe water hole, the 175 residents were living in eight small villages centered around a new borehole, engine, and water tank. The pride of the village though, was a soccer field, where teams of local and outside youths played a daily pickup game. Nearby, a preschool had been set up to give students two years of preparation before attending the main primary school as boarders 20 kilometers away, in !Kangwa. A dozen outsiders resided in Dobe: border guards who patrolled the frontier two kilometers to the west, as well as veterinary officials, teachers, and construction workers.

On the downside, home-brew sellers, formerly confined to !Kangwa, had arrived at Dobe, bringing daily drinking parties and social dysfunction. Dobe's most traumatic experience, however, had been in 1996 when a district-wide outbreak of bovine pleuropneumonia had necessitated destruction of the entire cattle population of the Northwest District. Some 140,000 head were slaughtered and bulldozers buried their carcasses, including several thousand in the Dobe area. Ju/'hoansi who had been slowly building up their herds since the 1970s, lost everything. Although herd owners were compensated, the process of rebuilding herds was slow.

Ecologists however were heartened at the welcome relief of pressure by the sudden withdrawal of bovine biomass on the fragile ecosystem. The new situation refocused attention on a prime preexisting "asset" of the Dobe area: the still abundant game populations. The creation of wildlife conservancies under the Community-Based Natural Resource Management Program (CBNRM) is an effort to combine environmental conservation with economic development. Small-scale wildlife conservancies have sprung up throughout Africa, with 28 projects in Botswana alone. At /Xai/xai, near Dobe, the Thlabololo Development Trust (TDT) has created a wildlife management area controlled by the Ju/'hoansi, with

Dutch overseas assistance. The Trust caters to tourists who want to experience Ju/'hoan life and see game, although limited subsistence hunting and gathering by Ju themselves is allowed.

The Ju of Dobe are in the process of setting up a similar trust under the guidance of the TOCADI Trust, a Botswana-based nongovernmental organization (NGO) with funding from Germany, Scandinavia, and the European Union. In preparation for the conservancy, a land-use and mapping project was instituted at Dobe making the most thorough study of local ecology since the intensive research of the 1960s. The Land Use Study has demonstrated the feasibility of the Kalahari People's Fund initiative of the 1980s to drill a series of boreholes on Dobe's outer margins. In April 2001 two drilling attempts—funded in part by a grant from the Kalahari Peoples Fund, based in Austin, Texas—produced water. The plan was to resettle Ju families and secure their land against the threat of land encroachment by Tswana cattle syndicates. As of this writing some of the legal obstacles are still being ironed out. The careful groundwork of Robert Hitchcock has been a key to implementation.[1]

Namibia

The Ju/'hoansi of Nyae Nyae have traveled a similarly rocky road of triumphs and failures. After the independence of Namibia and the successful National Land Conference, much discussion of development options for the people of Nyae Nyae ensued. After feasibility studies sponsored by the Nyae Nyae Development Foundation, the Nyae Nyae Wildlife Conservancy was set up in 1998. A bold initiative, the "Living in a Finite Environment" (LIFE) Project—funded by USAID—sought to combine conservation, game management, tourism, and rural economic development.

In 1996 the Tsumkwe Lodge opened offering accommodations and tours to selected Ju/'hoan villages. The Nyae Nyae Farmers Cooperative launched its own ecocultural tourism program around the same time.

The early 1990s were a stormy period for the NNFC and its funding source, the Nyae Nyae Development Foundation. Infighting among Foundation personnel over conflicting philosophies of change and management styles mirrored in some ways dissension within the cooperative itself. In a dramatic move in 1996 the Ju/'hoansi asked foundation personnel to withdraw to Windhoek and leave the running of the Coop to the Ju themselves. After a general shake-up of both organizations non-Ju staff were cut back and Ju took over most management positions. The results have been mixed and adjustments to the balance are ongoing. Despite the efforts of the LIFE project and the NNDFN, the 37 Nyae Nyae villages continue to vary widely in viability. In a 1998 study, Polly Wiessner evaluated the subsistence levels of a sample of villages and found over one-third experienced a serious shortfall in food supply (Wiessner 1998). At the Conservancy's Baraka headquarters, vehicles have been rolled and rendered undriveable.

The Village Schools Project (VSP) has been one of the bright spots in Nyae Nyae. The VSP offers three years of preschool training in their own language and in English for six- to eight-year-olds to prepare them for the government primary school at Tsumkwe. Initiated by Megan Biesele and colleagues in consultation with the Nyae Nyae communities in 1990, the project has assisted hundreds of Ju children in making the transition from village life to the culture shock of life in an African residential school.

REGIONAL DEVELOPMENTS: FROM THE END OF APARTHEID TO THE COMING OF AIDS

In the 1990s, southern Africa saw tumultuous changes to its political and social landscape: the independence of Namibia in 1989, followed closely by the release of Nelson Mandela from prison in 1990 and his coming to power in South Africa's first democratic elections in 1994. The Ju/'hoansi speak of the recent era as the time of "//xabe" or opening up, as new political and cultural spaces opened up for San peoples. The founding of the Working group for Indigenous Minorities of Southern Africa (WIMSA), an umbrella group based in Windhoek, has created a forum at which leaders from Dobe, Tsumkwe, Baraka, and many other San communities can come together to get a sense of common problems and lobby for change. WIMSA delegations have traveled to Geneva, London, Stockholm, and New York, and have received very sympathetic hearings from governments and NGOs. Wildlife conservancies and schools programs are just two of the kinds of grassroots programs receiving international support.

With the final overthrow of the apartheid regime the peoples of southern Africa were looking forward to a new era of progress and development. But a new threat was already looming on the horizon. Through the 1980s the disease labeled "Acquired Immune Deficiency Syndrome" (AIDS) ravaged populations in the developed world, affecting largely homosexual men. The disease spread rapidly to the rest of the world during the 1990s. Africa proved to be exceptionally vulnerable to the spread of HIV/AIDS, where it became a condition spread particularly by heterosexual contact, as well as from mother-to-child transmission (MTCT). Now sub-Saharan Africa has the world's highest rates of HIV incidence, with women comprising 55 to 60 percent of the victims.

AIDS AND THE JU/'HOANSI

Since 1996 I have been working in capacity-building projects to stem the tide of AIDS in Namibia and Botswana, in collaboration with Professor Ida Susser of the City University of New York. Although our main efforts have been to work in the society as a whole—conducting training workshops that involved over 200 students and health professionals over an eight-year period at the University of Namibia—we have combined this with regular tracking of the situation regarding HIV/AIDS among the Ju'hoansi. We visited the Tsumkwe/ Nyae Nyae area Ju/'hoansi in Namibia in 1996, 1997, 2000, and 2003 and the Dobe area Ju/'hoansi of Botswana in 1999 and 2001, first under a multiyear Fogarty Foundation grant to Columbia University and then supported by our respective universities.

As late as 1987, when I did fieldwork in the Dobe area of Botswana, no cases of AIDS had been reported. In that year a South African medical team, under the direction of Dr. Trefor Jenkins of the South African Institute for Medical Research, conducted a rapid nutritional and health assessment of about 140 Ju/'hoansi, a 20-year follow-up to an initial baseline survey in 1967 and 1968 (Truswell and Hansen 1976). During the research, Jeanette Peterson, a Danish doctor from the Maun Hospital toured the district to alert communities about a new sexually transmitted and invariably fatal disease. The Jenkins team joined her to present the AIDS story to a mixed audience of Herero and Ju/hoansi. The team decided to add HIV testing to the blood workups previously scheduled. Of the collected samples from close to 150 individuals in blind testing, not one sample returned positive. However Jenkins, working across the border in Namibia the following year, brought back two seropositive samples from Tsumkwe (Hansen et al. 1994).

Within a few years the national rates in both Botswana and newly independent Namibia had started their steep climb, approaching their record high levels by the mid-1990s. However, the situation in the Dobe and Nyae Nyae areas was still largely unknown. Interest in this question brought anthropologist Ida Susser and me together in 1996 to undertake research and training in Namibia and Botswana.

Six field trips have given us the opportunity to gauge a sense of the way the HIV/AIDS has entered the lives of the Ju/'hoansi. By 2001, we estimated from very fragmentary data, that about 50 cases had emerged in a total population of 2,500 Ju/'hoansi on both sides of the border. This number converts to a 3.3 percent seropositive rate in persons between 15 and 49 years. Compared to Botswana's 38 percent and Namibia's 22.5 percent, remarkably, this rate is about 60 to 90 percent lower than national averages. Recent statements by senior Namibian government officials—including statements by President Sam Nujoma himself—generally confirm this lower rate among the San peoples. In addressing the people of Tsumkwe on July 13, 2003, he said:

> "I am happy to report that Tsumkwe District does not have much AIDS. The people here are careful. They understand the risks and we want to keep it that way. The people from outside, from Windhoek, from Walvis Bay, from Caprivi are diseased. It is they who bring it here. Watch out for them when they come here. You can tell who they are they dress well."

Despite the problematic implications of this statement that people can blame outsiders for AIDS and tell if a person will transmit AIDS simply by their clothes, this statement recognizes that—for the moment—the Tsumkwe District has less HIV/AIDS than elsewhere in Namibia.

However, our most recent field trip to the San settlements of Tsumkwe and Baraka, Nambia, in July 2003, indicated that the nature of the epidemic was undergoing a transition and that there is a possibility that these rates could climb rapidly, approaching the levels observed in other parts of the region.

Given the long history of study of the Ju/'hoansi and our knowledge of them, how are we to explain these much lower AIDS rates among the Ju/'hoansi? And, what social and economic factors could account for what

© Richard Lee

Women in Tsumkwe, Jamibia at the "lokasie" (location) 1996.

appears to be the rapid growth in rates in the period between 2002 and 2004? And finally, what possibilities exist for turning the situation around so that a worst-case scenario doesn't materialize? In the remainder of the chapter I will address these questions.

THE JU/HOANSI'S LOWER RATES: MACRO AND MICRO FACTORS

In neither the Dobe nor the Nyae Nyae areas have the area's clinics made any attempts to survey the incidence of HIV by means of anonymous testing or sentinel surveys. People with AIDS may die without a definitive diagnosis. In the absence of serious survey data or even correct diagnoses, how do we know anything about the incidence of AIDS?

As noted above, Dobe, 20 kilometers west of the subdistrict capital of Qangwa, and only two kilometers from the Namibia border, had a resident population of about a dozen men from outside including border guards and livestock inspectors, and a similar number of unmarried young local women. If AIDS was present it might not be recognized as such, but the presence of a debilitating or incapacitating illness in persons in the age range between 15 and 49 would suggest the likelihood of the presence of the disease.

We undertook a house-to-house survey of all seven villages at the Dobe water hole in July 2001, moving from village to village and asking patiently and discreetly whether anyone in that village was incapacitated or had experienced bouts of debilitating illness. The survey revealed not a single case of any illness resembling AIDS in people of any age, in the village of Dobe with a population of 175 people.

In interviews, we asked repeatedly if anyone knew of other Ju/'hoansi living with AIDS or who had died of AIDS and the same three names kept coming up, all women across the border in Tsumkwe. Yet epidemiologists would agree that a survey in the year 2001, in a village of similar size elsewhere in Botswana, would have revealed dozens of examples.

In explaining the much lower rates among the Ju/'hoansi we have to invoke both macro and micro factors. Of the former, geographic isolation must play a role. Far from the urban centers and truck routes, the Ju/'hoan areas experienced low levels of interactions with outsiders. However since the 1990s a succession of civil servants, soldiers, workers in tourism, and traders, almost all male, has found its way into the interior. Additional factors for the low rates must be sought.

JU/'HOAN WOMEN'S AUTONOMY

Long before the AIDS crisis, ethnographic fieldwork in the 1960s and 1970s documented women's high status and freedom of action among the Ju/'hoansi. Young women could and did veto marriage plans. Women's voices were heard in the tribal councils. They provided 70 percent of the food and this economic autonomy was an important source of their strength. Ethnographic accounts of women's experiences of sex, work, and family provide us with a rich history on which to base our current understandings of Ju/'hoan response to the threat of HIV (Draper 1975; Marshall 1976; Shostak 1981; Rosenberg 1997).

Almost every observer of the African AIDS tragedy pinpoints the lethal combination of gendered inequality and poverty as the driving force in the epidemic. In our research among the dominant non-San ethnic groups elsewhere in Namibia, such as the Owambo, we noted that men more than women maintained multiple partners and women repeatedly voiced frustration at their powerlessness to insist on condom use with boyfriends and spouses. As noted, today women comprise 55 to 60 percent of people with AIDS in southern Africa as a whole (Lee 2004; Stein and Susser 2000; Preston-Whyte et al. 2000).

Based on Ju/'hoan women's history of autonomy one would predict that Ju/'hoan women differ in their sense of empowerment from women of other ethnic groups. In fact, in our interviews, women and young girls among the Ju/'hoansi revealed a greater degree of confidence in sexual negotiation with men, a sense of their own empowerment, than did the Owambo women (see also Stein and Susser 2000).

For example, we asked a young Ju/'hoan woman at Baraka in 1996 whether she would ask her husband to use a condom. She stated emphatically that, "Yes, I would ask him, and if he did not agree, I would refuse sex." Although Owambo women eagerly responded to demonstrations of the female condom and asked us where they could obtain them, Ju/'hoan women saw no particular advantage to the female condom, saying if they wanted a man to use a condom they would simply ask him to use a male one, distributed free at the local clinic.

© Richard Lee

Ida Susser interviewing Ju women in 2001. Unlike the national rates in Namibia and Botswana, the Nyae-Nyae Dobe areas have very low rates of HIV. But with added pressure, can they avert the looming catastrophe?

In a group discussion with young married women in Dobe in 2001, Ida Susser asked the women if they would be able to make use of a box of male condoms. "Give us some and we will teach our husbands how to use them," they said. Although this does not indicate whether actual behavior change would follow, the remarks of Ju/'hoansi women expressed a sense of entitlement and straightforwardness with respect to sexual decisions, which was not evidenced among the Owambo women. Nor was there the atmosphere of status-striving and peer pressure among girls that we observed with Windhoek high school and university students, traits that led to risky sexual liaisons with older men (Lee 2001; 2004).

When we interviewed young men in Dobe in 1999 and 2001 and in Tsumkwe in 2003, their responses corroborated the women's views. They talked as if women had the power to turn down sexual advances and they said that if a young woman were to accept such advances, they would see that as representing the opportunity to marry her, again in sharp contrast to the attitudes of young Owambo men. The terms in which young Ju men speak, coupled with the language used by young Ju/'hoan women—for example, seeing the opportunity to "teach" their boyfriends about condoms—suggests a kind of autonomy and a sense of self-confidence that could augur well for the future as Ju women encounter men from other ethnic groups.

Taken together these lines of evidence support the idea that women's autonomy is a powerful weapon against the spread of AIDS and may account in large part for the lower rates observed. Nevertheless we need to ask to what extent the rapid changes in recent years have affected San women's ability to retain control of their sexuality and their life choices.

FORCES DRIVING THE EPIDEMIC

In July 2003 we arranged to spend a period of fieldwork in the Namibian areas of the Ju/'hoan world. The town of Tsumkwe, population about 1,000, was once a remote San village, but is now the administrative center for the San region, and is connected to metropolitan Namibia by an all-weather road. The town includes a clinic, police station, stores, and rows of cement houses reminiscent of South African Bantustans. The town also has a coed boarding school, the Tsumkwe Junior Secondary School (TJSS), with a small primary school attached, housing 450 students ages between 7 and 19, half of them female. The Safari Lodge, opened in 1996, provides a base from which tourists can visit the San villages and witness healing rituals staged for their consumption. Recently the town was connected to the national telecommunications system with satellite phones powered by solar panels.

The town's population is divided roughly in two halves, with residents of Ju/'hoan ethnicity equaling the number of outsiders from several different Namibian ethnic groups, including Owambo, Kavango, Herero, and Damara. The Tsumkwe East Subdistrict includes some 1,200 other Ju/'hoansi dispersed at 35 settlements, located at distances from Tsumkwe ranging from10 to 50 kilometers. The Nyae Nyae Conservancy, the successor organization to the Nyae Nyae Farmers Coop, provides a loose cohesion to the far-flung settlements.

Founded during the apartheid era as a government station in 1960, the village of Tsumkwe has been the locus of massive state intervention in the lives of the Ju, accompanied by welfare dependency, rising interpersonal violence, and alcohol abuse. It also has—however faint—an aura of cosmopolitan sophistication, offering a taste of urban pleasures in a vast area of widely dispersed settlements. John Marshall's five-part film series *A Kalahari Family* (2003) chronicles the turbulent history of the Nyae Nyae area of which Tsumkwe is the principal settlement.

Apart from the shops, the health clinic, the Dutch Reformed Mission church and other grassroots informal churches, the most popular attractions by far are the *shebeens,* informal enterprises for the sale of alcohol. The 16 shebeens (one for every 60 residents of Tsumkwe) range in permanence from a few stools or benches in front of a woman's traditionally built mud-walled rondavel, to more substantial structures with pool tables and sound systems blaring the latest pop music. Shebeens offer home-brewed "tombo" beer for $N1.00 per pitcher (US$0.14), and commercially bottled beer for $N10.00 (US$1.40).

The shebeens are the main forums of social life for the people of Tsumkwe, sites for people of different social classes and ethnicities, insiders and outsiders, to mingle.

Were they also the sites where Ju/'hoan girls and young women went to drink and initiate liaisons with men from outside, with sex as the major transactional medium?

On our first trip to the area seven years earlier, we approached officials of the then Nyae Nyae Farmers Cooperative to conduct research on AIDS. The representatives (all men) were well aware of the nature of the disease, its lethality, and mode of transmission. But instead of implicating men as the main vectors of the disease, they believed that AIDS was introduced among them by Ju/'hoan women!

Given that it was the local women who had sexual relations with male outsiders from areas with high HIV rates, their perceptions were accurate if incomplete. At Tsumkwe it was common knowledge that nonlocal men—road crews, traders, civil servants—drank at shebeens, and then had liaisons with San women. Drinking was widely seen as the major problem.

Clearly Tsumkwe had a certain history as the main center for the spread of HIV; as discussed previously, South African Army units were based there in the 1980s. After the war's end and with the independence of Namibia, border guards and other administrative personnel replaced soldiers. Both in wartime and postwar, the men were posted far from home and sought the local nightlife. The good-quality gravel road and an airstrip further increased accessibility. On the Botswana side of the border, the administrative center, Qangwa, plays a similar role, though on a much smaller scale.

In contrast to Tsumkwe and Qangwa, other, more remote San villages had fewer outside visitors and home-brew shops. The Ju/'hoansi with whom we spoke in outer villages contrasted the drinking and sexual exchange at Tsumkwe with the situation in their home communities. One informant, a teenage girl at Dobe, said:

> "There is no AIDS here, but I know they have it at Tsumkwe. The girls over there told me not to sleep with the boys because they have that disease there. I am afraid of AIDS at Tsumkwe."

Nevertheless when we interviewed in Dobe in 2001 about the situation at Tsumkwe people could name only three people, all women who they believed had died of AIDS. We were told that one young woman died, unmarried, at age 20. The ages of the other two were estimated at 35 and 40. The two older women had young children, but there was no knowledge of children's deaths.

In our 2003 survey of Tsumkwe, we asked local Ju/'hoan informants to tell us about people they thought had died of AIDS, promising that we would observe strict anonymity. The informants gave us name after name, both men and women. They named fourteen in all, with mention of a few others. These were people in their twenties, thirties, and forties, struck down in the prime of life, usually coinfected with tuberculosis. When we asked the medical officer of health for the district that includes Tsumkwe East what kinds of numbers she had, Dr. Malita Boschoff (known throughout the district as Dr. Malita), came up with a figure of 17 and counting for the number of Ju people who had died of AIDS. The closeness of our tally with hers appeared to strengthen the quality of our data collection and the robustness of our own figures.

What does the number 17 represent as a proportion of the total Ju population and how did this compare to corresponding numbers of AIDS deaths in other parts of the region? Assuming that persons aged between 15 and 49 comprise about 50 percent of the total Ju population of Nyae Nyae (1,800), then the deaths due to AIDS represent 1.9 percent of the population at risk. This compares to a figure of 6.7 percent of AIDS deaths as a percentage of total population at risk for Namibia as a whole, based on the most recent United Nations AIDS epidemiological estimates.

A second part of our July 2003 research consisted of interviewing small groups of women in Tsumkwe about their knowledge of AIDS and, where possible, about sexual practices. Sa//gai, (name changed), an articulate single 21-year-old woman had an accurate knowledge of the disease, its mode of transmission, and means of prevention. When asked about how she was coping with problems of dating, she replied:

> "You must bring your own condom and not just trust the condom of your boyfriend . . . *If your boyfriend refuses the condom, then we know he has that disease and he wants to give it to you* (emphasis added)."

When we asked whether the girl must still have sex with the boy if he refuses to use a condom (a frequent theme in our Owambo interviews) Sa//gai replied, "No she can refuse and she will refuse."

The Ju/'hoansi use the term *Goba* to refer to non-San Africans generally. Our informants had strong views about dating Gobas, who were seen as very problematic. "Goba boys will give Ju girls drink after drink to make them drunk," said Sa//gai. "They don't give them gifts like food or soap or clothes."

We asked a group of Ju women if they knew of young women who had AIDS:

> "Yes, a young girl named //Ushe (name changed), only about 12 years old, had a Goba boyfriend; when he died she was tested for HIV and it came back positive but her parents tested negative. Then she died. Another member of the same family, an aunt, also had a Goba boyfriend. She too tested positive and both she and her boyfriend died."

Even with the 17 cases noted, the dimensions of the epidemic seemed to be well contained in 2003. However, recent changes in the Namibian economy threatened to make this situation worse, possibly much worse.

THE LARGER SOCIAL FRAMEWORK OF AIDS RISK

Although our 2003 fieldwork focused mainly on the drinking-sexuality nexus, our research quickly opened up additional lines of inquiry. In 2000, 10 years after independence, Namibia began to feel the stresses that neighboring Zimbabwe is currently undergoing. Ex-liberation fighters—promised land and jobs when SWAPO came to power—loudly expressed their disappointment with the government through marches and demonstrations in the capital. In response, the government of President Sam Nujoma made several moves to address the legitimate grievances of the veterans, moves that directly affected people in remote areas like Nyae Nyae. Thousands of government jobs were opened up to absorb some of the unemployed, including many in the Ministry of Environment and Tourism (MET) (formerly the Department of Nature Conservation) for game scouts and road and fencing crews. Tsumkwe, in the center of a vast game management area, received many dozens of job-seeking migrants, most from the overpopulated and HIV-endemic areas of the north and center of the country. As a result, old Tsumkwe residents estimate that the number of outsiders in Tsumkwe doubled between 2001 and 2003.

A significant proportion of these migrant workers were themselves HIV positive, and some were already sick with AIDS. One reliable source reported that in 2002 alone no fewer than 10 of the recent MET arrivals in Tsumkwe died of AIDS.

THE TSUMKWE JUNIOR SECONDARY SCHOOL

A second component in the mix that brought the AIDS epidemic to the Ju/'hoansi is the Tsumkwe Junior Secondary School (TJSS). In 2003 the school enrolled 452 students, most in Standards 8 through 10, with a smaller number in the primary grades 1 through 7, and 40 teachers and auxiliary staff. Students are housed in spartan dormitories and fed what appeared at least to us, to be a substandard diet served on the bare concrete slabs of the dining hall. Nevertheless when we interviewed students they appeared to be in good spirits.

Within the student body, local Ju/'hoansi youth match in numbers the students from outside the district; the teaching staff are almost all from outside. Interestingly, the presence of students from outside the district is explained in part by their parents' expressed desires to have their children spend their most vulnerable adolescent years in a remote area, far from the temptations of sex and alcohol in the larger towns of central and northern Namibia. But some of the incoming schoolgirls (and boys) brought with them a set of attitudes toward sexuality that included seeking liaisons with older men as acceptable practice. One also wonders if becoming caught up in the "sugar daddy" phenomenon is related to the fact that the school attendees are so materially deprived, with poor-quality food and living conditions, and harsh discipline inconsistently applied.

Despite the school's close supervision and policy against sexual harassment, our Ju informants (both students and adults), perceived the Tsumkwe Junior Secondary School as a hotbed of sexual impropriety, with male teachers having sex with their female students. A prominent theme of conversations with Ju informants was the after-school sightings of underage students at shebeens, one of which, the notorious "Baby Smile," was located only 50 meters from the school's main entrance. The enforcement of liquor laws—regarding hours of operation and legal drinking age—seemed lax to nonexistent. Thus added to the forces driving the AIDS epidemic was this volatile mixture of sexually active and materially deprived youth coming into contact with migrant workers with cash to spare and far from home. This combination is on a scale not seen in Tsumkwe since the days of the liberation struggle and militarization when the South African Army recruited San for "homeland security" at army bases (Lee and Hurlich 1982). However, during the last decades of the South African occupation in the 1970s and 1980s, liaisons with outside men was not complicated by the threat of AIDS which had yet to appear in this part of Africa.

Another curious anomaly in school policy has been observed at the times of school vacations. According to informants, no provisions are made for transport back home for those students whose home communities are distant from Tsumkwe. Nor are they allowed to remain in dormitories until transport is arranged. As a result some students have been forced to stand in front of the school, hitchhike on a road that might see only one vehicle per hour, and camp by the roadside overnight until obtaining a lift. The vulnerability of female students to sexual exploitation was so obvious that on one occasion the district medical officer, Dr. Malita, had to press her ambulance into service to rescue a group of stranded schoolchildren and deliver them to the bus station at Grootfontein, a distance of 300 kilometers to the west.

If girls "fall pregnant," it is school policy to suspend or expel them. The fact that several leave the school each year under this ruling suggests the magnitude of the problem of unprotected sex. Though certainly not all the pregnancies are the responsibility of teachers, epidemiologically one has to assume that the incidence of unwanted pregnancies is a proxy measure of unprotected sex and an indicator of the possibilities for HIV transmission.

THE OLD-AGE PENSION AFFAIR

The provision of old-age pensions might appear at first to be unrelated to the epidemiology of HIV/AIDS. Yet closer examination of the social situation at Tsumkwe reveals an unusual link. One of the more enlightened programs of Namibian social welfare, expanded under the postliberation SWAPO regime, is the provision of old-age pensions. In rural populations like the Nyae Nyae Ju/'hoansi, where fewer than 10 percent of adults have waged employment and petty commodity production such as handicrafts is still very limited, the pension for seniors may be the only source of income for entire families. Initially the Ju/'hoansi had to pick up their pension checks in Tsumkwe where they were delivered, a difficult trek for outlying villagers. In returning to their homes, pensioners and their relatives had to run the gauntlet of home-brew establishments, and much if not all of the pension monies could be dissipated if transport home was delayed.

In the mid-1990s the contract for delivering pensions was awarded to a retired civil servant who saw the difficulties families faced. He instituted a program for delivering the pension payouts directly to villagers, and allowed them to purchase essential foods and household goods at fair prices from his truck. By making the long trek to Tsumkwe unnecessary, he alleviated a major social problem—alcohol abuse—that was already severe in Tsumkwe and was in danger of spreading to outer villages as well.

However, in 2002 the contract expired and was awarded to a different company when it was put up for tender. The company stopped the payout trips to rural villages and announced that henceforth pension monies were to be picked up in town. Despite protests, once again pensioners and their families had to make the long trek to town. One observer described a typical outcome: while waiting for a lift home the pensioner, always accompanied by one or more younger family members, would stop at a shebeen, first for one drink then another and another. After a day or two of waiting for transport, much of the pension money would be gone. In addition local health workers have expressed concern that in the process, accompanying family members could be bringing HIV and other sexually transmitted infections (STIs) back with them to the villages.

CRAFT BUYING AS INCOME GENERATION

Another way rural areas generate income is through selling handicrafts. The Reverend H. Van Zyl and his wife Ellie of the Dutch Reformed Church (DRC) have been fixtures in the Tsumkwe community since the apartheid era. Their obvious commitment to the cause of the Ju/'hoansi has earned them respect by a range of stakeholders, both Ju and non-Ju. The Van Zyl's have combined prose-lytizing with income-generating projects. For several years they have conducted monthly craft buying trips to many of the 35 outlying villages of Nyae Nyae. They purchase bows and arrows, ostrich eggshell jewelry, richly beaded leather bags, and other items, and craft producers may take the cash or use it to purchase food, tools, household items, and clothing sold from the back of the truck. Tobacco products (but not alcohol) were available for purchase on the buying trips. The result is another way in which cash and resources are being pumped into the rural economy while permitting villagers to avoid the costly trek to Tsumkwe. Another consequence has been storerooms filled to overflowing with high-quality but unsold handicrafts at the reverend's home, forcing a temporary suspension of the monthly buying trips. Fortunately a Canadian craft marketing organization "Nharo!" run by Paul Wellhauser of Waterloo, Ontario, along with local partners, undertook negotiations with the DRC mission. In early 2004, the Canadian company purchased some of this accumulated inventory and is currently marketing it in North America (for details see their Web site www. nharo.com).

THE KASHIPEMBE CRISIS

Many of the tensions within the Tsumkwe community, between long-term residents and recent arrivals, came to a head with a series of events in March 2003 that became known as the *Kashipembe* crisis. *Kashipembe* is a distilled spirit, a form of moonshine that shebeen proprietors produce to increase profit margins. It is colorless, pleasant tasting, and is estimated to be 25 percent alcohol, making it at least 10 times more potent than *tombo* (home-brewed beer). The popularity of kashipembe, according our informants, has made the community's already serious alcohol-related social problems even worse.

The Tsumkwe town council, known officially as the Traditional Authority, is chaired by Samkau Toma, cofounder and former head of the Nyae Nyae Farmers Cooperative (later the Nyae Nyae Conservancy) and a leading figure in John Marshall's films (2003). The Authority was asked to address the kashipembe problem and they in turn enlisted the aid of the Reverend Van Zyl. When it turned out that a special permit was required to manufacture kashipembe and none of the shebeens were in possession of one, the Reverend, backed by the town council, went to the police demanding that the laws be enforced. But when the police went around the community confiscating equipment and dumping gallons of kashipembe on the ground, the shebeen owners and some of their influential backers, including members of SWAPO, the ruling party, expressed outrage.

A somewhat sinister figure, a middle-aged African man and minor SWAPO party official who went by the nickname Luborsky (after a heroic white SWAPO activist who was murdered by the apartheid regime during the liberation struggle) came from Grootfontein and orchestrated protest meetings targeting Reverend Van Zyl. He called him a racist and demanded that he be driven out of town. "Luborsky" presented a petition that he claimed San residents had signed, but it was quickly shown to be a crude forgery. A meeting of residents attended by over 70 people strongly backed the reverend and the stance of the Traditional Authority.

With strong community support, the reverend weathered the attacks and the situation was defused. However, soon after, the manufacture and sale of kashipembe quietly resumed and was actively on offer at shebeens during our July 2003 fieldwork.

For the local residents, the resumption of kashipembe production was seen as a pivotal battle lost in the fight against drunkenness in Tsumkwe and by extension in the struggle to prevent AIDS from spreading. They regard kashipembe as a "date rape" drug, the drink of choice for older men from outside, seducing the Ju women and girls. Francina Simon, an articulate Ju woman and vice-chair of the Traditional Authority said, "There is no way you can stop the shebeens; you must rely on condoms." Another woman added in exasperation, "If you could close the shebeens you would stop AIDS in Tsumkwe."

Dr. Malita, the medical officer of health, attested that rape is a serious problem, which is rarely prosecuted. Under Namibian law, sex with a girl under 16, even with consent, is statutory rape. The doctor related several cases of rape in which the victim became infected with HIV, but the families were bribed to keep quiet and not appear in court. Malita noted, "A Tsumkwe Ju/'hoan girl will never force an outside man to use a condom."

THE WIDER NYAE NYAE AND DOBE REGION

The situation elsewhere in the Ju/'hoan areas is more promising. Although the Ju are certainly poor by world standards, they maintain a strong sense of the value of their culture and lifeways. A Dobe area school dance troupe from /Xai/xai won a national dance competition in Botswana. Outside of Tsumkwe on both sides of the border, Ju/'hoan communities do not seem to be suffering the poverty of an underclass in which family and household relations are undermined and women and children are cast adrift to fend for themselves. Both men and women had access to small sums of money from government work programs and from craft production, such as beading and carving. In this situation, if people were poor, in terms of their clothes and their shelter, there were minimal differences between men and women and between higher and lower incomes. The strong tradition of the autonomy of women offered the opportunity for forthright sexual negotiations and mobilization to prevent the spread of HIV/AIDS. If asked what the major threat to their communities is, residents of the remote communities would probably cite elephants destroying their water pumps before mentioning AIDS or other sexually transmitted infections.

The border between the Namibia and Botswana had been officially closed from 1965 up to the end of the apartheid era in 1989. It remained closed for the first decade and a half of Namibian independence (1989–2003). The border was recently opened to vehicular traffic. Dr. Polly Wiessner of the University of Utah, who visited both sides of the Ju/'hoan world in 2003, commented on the relative prosperity and the absence of heavy drinking on the Botswana side when compared to the situation at Tsumkwe.

Dr. Elizabeth Yellen, a medical doctor, visited the Dobe area of Botswana, accompanying her parents, long-time Dobe observers, Drs. John Yellen and Alison Brooks (Yellen 1990, Brooks and Yellen 1992). Elizabeth Yellen interviewed the staff at the Qangwa clinic about HIV. She asked if the clinic tested for HIV. They replied that testing does occur but only on request. When Yellen asked for a rough estimate of how many HIV tests have come back seropositive, the head nurse responded that to her knowledge none of the Ju/'hoan patients had ever tested positive (A. Brooks, personal communication, November 2003).

However favorable conditions may be for the Ju/'hoansi in the Dobe area of Botswana and in Namibian areas beyond Tsumkwe, the fact remains that when the majority of Ju/'hoansi leave their villages, for work on road crews, on cattle ranches, and in regional centers, epidemiological factors alter sharply. They clearly become the "underclass" and their levels of risk for HIV/AIDS climb, as poor women find money through casual sex work or simply seek sexual relations with men who will provide gifts of food for themselves and their children. Professor Renee Sylvain of the University of Guelph has addressed this topic in her recent writings about the Omaheke farm San of the Gobabis District of Namibia 200 kilometers south of Tsumkwe (Sylvain 2001, 2002, 2003).

CONCLUSION: BACK FROM THE BRINK?

Returning to the focus on Tsumkwe and its current problems, here is a footnote to the shebeen issue. During recent fieldwork an affable and articulate young Goba man introduced himself to us as the AIDS educator for the town of Tsumkwe. He related all the efforts he was making to get the message out, through the "My Future, My Choice" national AIDS education program for youth, including free distribution of condoms at shebeens. Some of our enthusiasm for his good works was tempered however, when the district medical officer informed us later, that the same man is not only part-owner of one of the shebeens frequented by underage drinkers, but is notorious in the district for getting girls pregnant, seven at last count! Not a promising start to the campaign to defeat AIDS.

On the other hand, several signs do indicate some promise. The Tsumkwe Clinic, backed by the medical officer Dr. Malita, recently distributed 300 female condoms to women, Ju and non-Ju, who willingly accepted them. Male condoms are available free from clinics, shops, and at shebeens and are being used by the Ju/'hoan young men. Some Ju/'hoan mothers encourage their daughters to carry condoms at all times and they do. A well-established NGO, Health Unlimited, has been working at Tsumkwe for almost a decade and has engaged in health education and outreach throughout the Nyae Nyae. Finally the head of the nursing staff reported that in the recent voluntary testing and counseling program (VCT) at the Tsumkwe Clinic, seven people tested HIV-positive, but of these, six were outsiders and only one a Ju/'hoan.

In August–September 2003, a University of Toronto student, Donna Bawden, spent four weeks in Tsumkwe specifically to explore in more detail the involvement of Ju/'hoan men and especially women in the culture of drinking. She confirmed reports of young Ju women frequenting the bars and engaging in sex with men from the outside and added considerable detail to the picture.

What neither Donna Bawden nor Ida Susser and myself were able to ascertain is how widespread these practices are. Does the subculture of disco, kashipembe, and casual sex involve 5 percent, 10 percent or 50 percent of the young Ju/'hoan women of Tsumkwe? How strong are the countervailing forces within the community—such as the Traditional Authority and the church—in their efforts to educate the vulnerable, provide social support, and stop the practice? And are there stakeholders from the wider world, national and international, who are prepared to step in and offer assistance in stopping the spread of AIDS? What is the government stance on enforcing liquor laws? Given the international resources currently flowing into the continent of Africa to fight AIDS, how can income-generation projects targeting women reduce the necessity for women to engage in transactional sex with older "sugar daddies"?

The Kalahari Peoples Fund of Austin, Texas, under the direction of Dr. Megan Biesele, has initiated an education campaign in the Ju/'hoan language to alert Ju/'hoansi about HIV/AIDS (www.kalaharipeoples.org). Several NGOs have expressed interest in supporting this work. And the successful revival of craft marketing by the Canadian "fair-trade" organization Nharo! is another hopeful direction.

The answers to the questions raised will determine whether the AIDS epidemic among the Ju/'hoansi rises to national and regional high levels over the next five years, or whether the famed cultural resilience of the people will come to the fore and pull the Ju/'hoansi back from the brink.

REFERENCES

Biesele, Megan, and Paul Weinberg. 1990. *Shaken roots: The Bushmen of Namibia.* Johannesburg: EDA Publications.

Brooks, Alison, and John Yellen. 1992. Decoding the Ju/wasi past. *Symbols* (September 1992): 24–31.

Davis, Peter. 1996. *In darkest Hollywood: Exploring the jungles of cinema's South Africa.* Athens OH: Ohio Univ. Press.

Draper, Patricia. 1975 !Kung women: Contrasts in sexual egalitarianism in the foraging and sedentary contexts. In *Toward and Anthropology of Women,* ed. Rayna Reiter, 77–109. New York: Monthly Review Press.

Hansen, J. D., D. Dunn, R. B. Lee, P. Becker, and T. Jenkins. 1994. Hunter-gatherer to pastoral way of life: Effects of the transition on health, growth and nutritional status. *South African Journal of Science* 89:559–64.

Hitchcock, Robert. 1977. *Kalahari Cattle-posts.* Gaborone: Government of Botswana.

Hitchcock, Robert, Megan Biesele and Richard Lee. 1997 Three decades of ethnographic research among the

Ju/'hoansi of northwestern Botswana. *Botswana Notes and Records* 25:96–115.

Howell, Nancy. 2000. *Demography of the Dobe !Kung*. 2nd ed. Hawthorne NY: Aldine-DeGruyter.

Katz, Richard, Megan Biesele, and Verna St. Dennis. 1997 *Healing makes our hearts happy: Spirituality and cultural transformation among the Kalahari Ju/' hoansi*. Rochester VT: Inner Traditions.

Lee, Richard B. *Subsistence ecology of the !Kung Bushmen*. PhD diss. in anthropology, Univ. of California, Berkeley.

Lee, Richard B. 1979. *The !Kung San: Men, Women and Work in a Foraging Society*. Cambridge and New York: Cambridge Univ. Press.

Lee, Richard B. 2001. A fatal attraction: AIDS and youth in southern Africa. *Canadian Journal of Infectious Diseases* 12 (Supplement B): 91.

Lee, Richard B. 2003. *The Dobe Ju/' hoansi*. 3rd ed. Sausalito CA:Wadsworth/Thomson Learning.

Lee, Richard B. 2004. A tale of three communities: Anthropological insights into the African AIDS crisis. In *The university professor lecture series,* ed. Michael Goldberg, 69–85. Toronto: Faculty of Arts and Sciences, Univ. of Toronto.

Lee, R., and M. Biesele. 2002. Local cultures and global systems: The Ju/'hoansi-!Kung and their ethnographers fifty years on. In *Chronicling cultures*, ed. R. V. Kemper and A. P. Royce, 160–190. Walnut Creek CA: Altamira Press.

Lee, Richard B., and Irven DeVore, eds. 1976. *Kalahari hunter-gatherers: Studies of the !Kung San and their neighbors*. Cambridge MA: Harvard Univ. Press.

Lee, Richard B., and Mathias Guenther. 1991. Oxen or onions: The search for trade (and truth) in the Kalahari. *Current Anthropology* 32 (5): 592–601.

Lee, Richard, and Susan Hurlich. 1982. From foragers to fighters: South Africa's militarization of the Namibian San. In *Politics and history in band society,* eds. E. Leacock and R. Lee, 327–46. Cambridge and New York: Cambridge Univ. Press.

Lee, Richard B., and Harriet Rosenberg. 1994. Fragments of the future: Aspects of social reproduction among the Ju/'hoansi. In *Papers of the seventh conference on hunting and gathering societies, Moscow,* ed. L. Ellanna, 413–24. Fairbanks AK: Univ. of Alaska Press.

Lee, R., and I. Susser. 2003. *Confounding conventional wisdom: The Ju/' hoansi and the challenge of HIV/AIDS.* Paper presented at the annual meeting of the American Anthropological Association, November 19, 2003, Chicago, IL.

Marshall, John. 1980. *N!ai, the story of a !Kung woman*. Cambridge MA: Documentary Educational Resources (film).

Marshall, John. 2003 *A Kalahari family, parts I–V.* Cambridge MA: Documentary Educational Resources (film series).

Marshall, Lorna. 1976. *The !Kung of Nyae Nyae*. Cambridge MA: Harvard Univ. Press.

Preston-Whyte, Eleanor, Christine Varga, Herman Oosthuizen, Rachel Roberts, and Frederick Blose. 2000. Survival sex and HIV/AIDS in an African city. In *Framing the sexual subject,* eds. Richard Parker, Regina Maria Barbosa, and Peter Aggleton, 165–90. Berkeley: Univ. of California Press.

Rosenberg, Harriet. 1997 Complaint discourse, aging and caregiving. In *The cultural context of aging,* ed. Jay Sokolovsky, 19–41. New York: Bergin and Garvey.

Shostak, Marjorie. 1981. *Nisa: The life and words of a !Kung woman.* Cambridge MA: Harvard Univ. Press.

Solway, Jacqueline, and Richard Lee. 1989. Foragers, genuine or spurious: Situating the Kalahari San in history. *Current Anthropology* 31:109–46.

Stein, Zena, and Ida Susser. 2000. Culture, sexuality and women's agency in the prevention of HIV/AIDS in southern Africa. *American Journal of Public Health* 90 (7): 1042–48.

Sylvain, Renee. 2001. Bushmen, Boers and Baasskap: Patriarchy and paternalism on Afrikaner farms in the Omaheke region, Namibia. *Journal of Southern African Studies* 27 (4): 717–737.

Sylvain, Renee. 2002. 'Land, water and truth': San identity and global indigenism. *American Anthropologist* 104 (4): 1074–1085.

Sylvain, Renee. 2003. Class, culture and recognition: San farm workers and indigenous identities. *Anthropologica* 45 (1): 105–113.

Truswell, Stuart, and John Hansen. 1976. Medical research among the !Kung.

In *Kalahari hunter-gatherers: Studies of the !Kung San and their neighbors,* eds. Richard B. Lee and Irven DeVore, 166–94. Cambridge MA: Harvard Univ. Press.

Wiessner, Polly. 1998. Population subsistence and social relations in the Nyae Nyae area: Three decades of change. Unpublished MS: Department of Anthropology, Univ. of Utah, Salt Lake City.

Wilmsen, Edwin. 1988. *A land filled with flies.* Chicago: Univ. of Chicago Press.

Wilmsen, E., and R. Denbow. 1989. Paradigmatic history of San-speaking peoples and current attempts at revision. *Current Anthropology* 31:489–524.

Yellen, John. 1990. The transformation of the Kalahari !Kung. *Scientific American* 262 (4): 96–105.

NOTE

1. For details see the Kalahari Peoples Fund Web site www.kalaharipeoples.org and the recent special issue of *Cultural Survival Quarterly* devoted to the Kalahari San Spring 2002 issue.

Fieldwork Biography
Cindy L. Hull

I obtained my bachelor's degree in sociology from Grand Valley State University in Michigan in 1972, and my master's degree (1975) and doctorate (1980) in anthropology from Wayne State University in Detroit, Michigan. My husband and I lived in the village of Yaxbe (a pseudonym) between 1976 and 1977 while I conducted ethnographic research on economic change and migration related to the collapse of the henequen industry. I have returned to the village frequently (six times) since that time to update my data and to visit the families who have become a part of our lives. My research focus over the years has shifted from migration to women's participation in the economic and social sphere. Yaxbe is located in the Yucatán Peninsula of Mexico about 20 miles from the capital city of Yucatán state, Mérida.

When we return to the village, we often stay with the family shown in Figure 8.0. In this photo, they are looking over my shoulder as I work on my notes. The children in the photo are very close to us. The daughter, Carmen has visited us in Michigan, as did her father many years ago.

8/From Field to Factory and Beyond

New Strategies for New Realities in a Yucatecan Village[1]

In 1998, I walked down the newly paved road in Yaxbe, Yucatán, notebook in hand, to update my data on economic change. At house after house, I stopped outside the stone walls surrounding cement or stucco homes, waiting to be recognized and invited inside. No one home. . . . I remembered that in 1976 these same roads, dusty and unpaved, were a bustle of activity. Small children ran in and out of the enclosed *soláres* and led me excitedly to their mothers who worked at the back of the house, making tortillas, washing clothes or cooking dinner. I remembered the conversations, the confusion of voices as mothers simultaneously talked to me and instructed their daughters or scolded their sons, and the intrusions as neighbor women and female relatives happened by to visit while I was there. Then I remembered a cryptic statement that an elderly woman made to me in 1989: "We are a village of children and old people." Where is everyone?

In 2001, the daughter of our close friends from Yaxbe, Carmen, visited us in Chippewa Lake, Michigan. On a weekend excursion to Mackinac Island, we shopped in a small tourist mall. Here, she discovered a rack of Jerzees-brand sweatshirts with designs depicting local attractions—Mackinac Island and "Say 'ya' to da' UP, eh?" (a slogan for the Upper Peninsula of Michigan). She looked at the prices of the sweatshirts and did some calculations. She realized that her mother, who worked in a Jerzees factory near her village, would have to work nearly two full 12-hour days to afford to purchase the sweatshirt that she might have made.

These two vignettes illustrate the impact of globalization on one small village in the Yucatán Peninsula. I am sure that similar scenarios are playing out in small villages throughout the world as they become integrated into the global market-place. I have been conducting research in one such village, Yaxbe,[2] Yucatán, since the mid-1970s, documenting economic and social change. During this period, the economic structure of Yucatán state has shifted from monoculture sisal production to a wage economy, entrenched in the manufacturing and tourism industries. The consequences of economic transformations such as these affect all aspects of village life, encompassing domestic labor, social and economic networks, and a growing awareness of, and integration with, the larger world outside of the village. During more than 20 years of research in one community, I have been able to capture a historic episode in Yucatán: the bust cycle of one transnational mono-culture and the transition to another global episode, transnational manufacturing and tourism. I have been able to observe how families are currently bridging these two episodes, how the transition affects local economic strategies and social organization. In this chapter, I will explore the impact of the previously mentioned structural transformations on the lives of families in Yaxbe, located 20 miles from the capital city of Yucatán and 500 miles from the shores of the United States.

THEORETICAL PERSPECTIVE

Historically, because of our focus on community and culture, anthropologists have been primarily interested in events at the local level. Our research typically emphasizes the behavior of individuals within groups and how communities adapt to their physical and cultural environment.

As indigenous cultures become absorbed into the dominant society or eradicated altogether, and as the global economy begins to capture more of the world markets, anthropologists can no longer envision indigenous people as members of closed communities. Rather, it is imperative to examine local communities within a larger context, expanding outward from village to region to nation and to the international sphere. Ironically, the first step in this journey involves an understanding of the past political and economic relationships between colonial power and peripheral or emerging nations. This paradigm, known as the world systems theory (see Wallerstein 1974), focuses on how colonialism—or international, national, and state policies—transform local forms of production and social organization.

World systems theory envisions the world as comprised of three major spheres of global influence: (1) the core, composed of the major economic powers of the world that extract natural resources and exploit the labor from the periphery; (2) the periphery that supplies the core with these human and natural resources; and (3) the semiperiphery, functioning as a conduit for resources, ports, marketplaces, and other regions intermediary between the core and the periphery (Hopkins, Wallerstein, and Associates 1982, 93).

My research lies at the intersection between these two spheres, the local and the global. I am interested in human agency, that is, how families make decisions and adapt to changes in their lives, while attempting to maintain kin and community networks. I am interested in the processes of resilience as well as resistance, change, and adaptation as families and communities become embroiled in the global economy that is beyond their control.

YUCATÁN AND THE WORLD SYSTEM: HISTORICAL PERSPECTIVE

Globalization in the Yucatán Peninsula is not a recent phenomenon. In fact, the state of Yucatán has had direct contact with the Western world since the conquest of Mexico in the 1500s. More recently, however, Yucatán has experienced two epochs of globalization. The first occurred in the mid-nineteenth century and the second commenced 100 years later in the 1950s. Both of these epochs reinforced Yucatán's position firmly within the powerful sphere of its northern neighbor, the United States. While the first enslaved men and their families in the hacienda system, the second released them into a maelstrom of chaos and laissez-faire economics.

Yucatán state is wedged between two larger states, Campeche and Quintana Roo, that together comprise the Yucatán Peninsula. With the exception of the Puuc Hills in southwest Yucatán and northeast Campeche, the peninsula is flat and dominated by scrub forest that is replaced by rainforest south and east across the peninsula. This northern region boasts some of the major classic and post-classic Mayan civic centers: Uxmal, Chichén Itzá, Cobá, Tulúm, and Mayapán.

The environment of Yucatán state has shaped its history and influenced its place in the Mexican economic system. First, the region suffers from a lack of rainfall. Yucatán has a rainy season that is limited to four months, June through September, during which time 80 to 90 percent of the annual rainfall occurs (Roys 1943/1972, 10). Unfortunately, this concentration of precipitation does not guarantee ample moisture for all swidden farmers[3], because the amount of rainfall varies markedly from region to region, increasing to the south and east.

Unpredictable rainfall is exacerbated by a lack of surface rivers and streams. Instead of feeding natural bodies of water, the sparse rain that does fall is absorbed like a sponge into limestone karst that covers the peninsula. Consequently, the only source of potable water for the ancient Maya were *cenotes* (*dzonot* in Maya) that formed when the karst collapsed along fault lines, permitting water to rise from the water table below. Most Mayan ceremonial centers were built near these cenotes. Today, although some villages still rely on water from cenotes, most villages have either community wells or individual wells within each household, or *solár*.

A lack of soil cover, less than two inches in most areas, is another aspect of this uninviting topography. The challenge for the Mayan cultivator, then, is enormous. It is virtually impossible to grow many crops, including those such as wheat that require rich soils, and those whose fruit grows under ground. What is truly remarkable is the diversity of crops that are grown in this terrain: major food crops such as corn, beans, and squash (the trilogy), as well as a vast array of vegetable and fruit crops including tomatoes, chili peppers, cabbage, green peppers, oranges, grapefruit, bananas, and papaya.

Until the thirteenth century, the Yucatán Peninsula was part of the Mayan world, ruled by powerful decentralized city-states that extended from the modern states of Campeche to El Salvador. By the time of the conquest in 1519, these city-states were in disarray, warring against each other for hegemony. Yet, despite internal conflict, the Maya were able to resist the Spanish invaders for almost 30 years, finally succumbing to the Montejo family in 1542.[4] The conquest brought the Maya under the control of the Spanish Crown that exploited both the landscape and the people who lived in villages scattered throughout the peninsula. Friars and other religious leaders of the Catholic church established themselves in the villages, building churches from the rubble of Mayan temples and replacing Mayan gods with patron saints.

The inhospitable Yucatecan geography had little to offer the Spanish conquerors who sought gold, silver, and other valuable natural resources. Eventually, however, the peninsula found its place within the global world system as a link in the Spanish empire. Spain established cattle *encomiendas* that supplied Spain with beef and served as a trade commodity for Cuban sugar until Mexico gained its independence from Spain in 1821. Then, to replace its source of sugar, the Mexican government transformed the southern areas of Yucatán, heretofore isolated and sparsely populated, into sugar plantations. Ironically and tragically, it was to this region that thousands of indigenous families had fled from the brutal *hacienda* system in the north. Here, in the rainforest, they had settled into an existence as subsistence farmers. But they were being pursued and forced once again into servitude, tied to the sugar plantation by debt peonage. The Caste War, waged by the Maya Indians against the Mexican government (1847–1848), marked the end of the plantation system in the sugar zone and left a temporary void in the export economy of Yucatán and Mexico (see Reed 1964).

The Maya filled this void by farming henequen (sisal), and the hacienda system that accompanied it became the core of economic and political power in Yucatán. The Maya cultivated henequen (*agave fourcroydes*) in preconquest times, using the fibers for clothing, rope, and hammocks (Chardon 1961, 14–15) and its thorns for needles (Brockway 1979, 170–171). Because it is an agave, it is well adapted to the conditions of the northwest Yucatán, thriving in conditions of dry heat and poor soils. The transformation of henequen from a small-scale family crop to international monoculture occurred as a result of several related events.

© Cindy Hull

Henequen (agave four-croydes), *the "Green Gold" of Yucatán.*

The first event was the Yucatecan invention, in the mid-1800s, of a mechanized decorticator that strips the fibers from the thorny leaves (Brannon and Baklanoff 1987, 26). A second event was the invention in the United States of the McCormick Reaper that utilized the binder twine produced from the Yucatecan fibers. What resulted was a henequen boom that lasted until the mid-twentieth century (ibid., 26).

As with the cattle encomiendas and sugar plantations, the wealth produced by henequen production did not go to the producers. Henequen production, like cattle and sugar that preceded it, was part of an international system of exchange that used indigenous labor to fill government and private coffers. Also, like cattle and sugar, indigenous henequen laborers were assigned to haciendas that were owned by the local elite. Although there are subtle differences between plantations, encomiendas, and haciendas, they shared a philosophy that placed the indigenous population in a subordinate social and economic position, their daily lives, labor, and wages all controlled by the owners of the estate whose hegemony was reinforced and legitimized by the state. These indigenous laborers and the communities in which they lived were part of a periphery far distant from the economic centers of Mérida, Mexico City, and even the United States.

Henequen production, because of its life cycle and processing, was conducive to hacienda structure. The life cycle of henequen is unlike most other subsistence crops in that the plants require seven years of care before they produce their first viable leaves. This requires a long-term commitment, and ideally, the ability to produce multiple fields at various stages of maturity. Once the plant matures, it produces leaves for 10 to 12 years. However, unlike subsistence crops that do not require constant care, the Yucatecan "green gold" is a harsh taskmaster, requiring patience and skill for its exploitation. Plants must be continuously weeded, and their leaves, up to six feet long and lined with thorns, must be cut at the proper time to assure their quality. Overcutting results in the early death of the plant, and neglect results in inferior fibers. Once cut, the decorticating machines—which the hacienda owners owned—strip the fibers from the leaves. By owning the land, the crop, and the machinery, the hacienda owners controlled all stages of henequen production, thus reinforcing their economic and political hegemony in the rural areas. Likewise, the indigenous populations (as well as various imported groups) once again provided their labor to the large landowners. This system was maintained through various mechanisms. Benign institutions as the patron-client relationship[5] tied the worker economically and socially to the *hacendado* and his administrators. Blatant institutions such as debt peonage[6] tied the worker to the hacienda more directly and ultimately justified the murder of those who tried to escape it.

As the primary destination for Yucatecan twine and rope, the United States was able to control the prices of fibers imported from Mexico. Naturally, these prices remained low for the United States and International Harvester Corporation, the manufacturer of the McCormick Reaper. The Yucatecan elite, who owned the haciendas as well as the export houses, became wealthy and ultimately developed close cultural ties to the United States, often sending their children to school there (Brannon and Baklanoff 1987, 38–41).

As a result of the Mexican Revolution (1910–1914), extensive land reform policies seized land from the owners and returned it to villages and towns in the form of *ejidos*. Families held ejido land parcels in usufruct (use right); they passed the parcels on through inheritance, but could not sell them. Unused land reverted to the community. The goals of the Mexican Revolution were slow in coming to Yucatán. The strength of the wealthy oligarchy exceeded that of the reformers, and in Yucatán the hacienda still reigned in 1927 with 600 haciendas still owning or controlling more than 410,000 acres of henequen land (Simpson 1937, 5–6). Real land reform did not come to Yucatán until the presidency of Lázaro Cárdenas (1934–40). Bringing the spirit of the revolution to the henequen zone, Cárdenas began expropriating hacienda lands and privately owned decorticating plants from the owners and placing them in ejidos. By 1937, Cárdenas expropriated 80 percent of the land in the henequen zone, including the decorticating plants (Raymond 1968, 464).

Between 1937 and 1955, the henequen ejido system was modified to resolve certain problems inherent in henequen production: the long maturation cycle of henequen leaves, the rural mechanization process, and the difficulties of transportation from the periphery to the urban market. By the 1960s, there were two parallel systems of producing henequen: first, a modern system in which private individuals owned haciendas and hired villagers and resident laborers to plant the crop and work in the privately owned decorticating plant; and second, the henequen ejido in which men worked on village-owned land and were managed and reimbursed by the state. As will be seen, the Mexican government developed a system of state-owned decorticating factories that paralleled those owned privately.

Regardless of the system, henequen production was tightly controlled by the state, which determined the amount of henequen planted, harvested, as well as wages paid to the workers. Although peasant unions have been able to shape policies and direct wages somewhat, the dependence of laborers on monoculture production places them in a vulnerable bargaining position.

The henequen ejido and haciendas dominated Yucatecan landscape until the 1960s. According to Yoder[7] (1993, 328), Yucatán was producing 100 percent of the world's production of henequen in 1900; by 1950, the state was producing nearly the same amount of henequen but this only represented 14 percent of the world's total. This decline is due to a number of factors including increased worldwide competition in sisal production, the rise of the petrochemical industry, and the production of less expensive synthetic substitutes for binder twine and sisal rope. The precipitous drop in demand for Yucatecan henequen drastically transformed the economic landscape of the state that had been dependent upon monoculture production for approximately 100 years.

These factors have been exacerbated by events at the national level that have changed the face of rural Mexico forever. Economic decline, precipitated by the oil and debt crisis in the 1980s, resulted in closer economic ties to the United States, which loaned money and credit to Mexico. The year 1992 was a watershed year for Mexico as the major defining section of the postrevolutionary Mexican Constitution was amended to help pave the way for the impending North American Free Trade Agreement (NAFTA)[8]. President Salinas de Gortari, in justifying the "reforms" to Article 27, claimed that for Mexico to modernize, the peasantry must be transformed and absorbed into a more progressive agricultural system. To President de Gortari, part of this modernization included the privatization and commercialization of peasant-held land (Collier 1994, 85). As they were finally implemented, the reforms allow *ejidatarios,* through local agreement, to sell, buy, or rent land and legally hire laborers; further, ejidatarios can hold contracts or establish joint ventures with domestic and foreign private investors (Stephen 1994, 2). PROCEDE, the official program through which these reforms will be implemented, has been slow in arriving in Yucatán. In fact, during my 1998 visit, Yaxbe had its first introductory meeting of the Procuria Agraria, the government department responsible for educating peasants on the system of privatization.

The current history of Yucatán, that which is being written now in hundreds of villages like Yaxbe, is one of adaptation, survival, and a revival of old traditions. The henequen ejido is dead; it no longer exists. Its death knell sounded in June 1992. But even before that time, as already seen, the henequen era was waning. The question then is what can replace henequen as the livelihood of Yucatecan peasants? What is the next boom? As of now, it appears that the future of Yucatán and all the states of the Yucatán Peninsula will depend on two sources of foreign capital: the *maquila* (foreign-owned factories) industry and tourism. Both tourism and transnational investment have drawn Yucatecan villages into the national and international spheres.

YUCATÁN AND THE MODERN WORLD SYSTEM

Both the colonial relationship between Mexico and Spain and the later relationship between Mexico and the United States illustrate the power of global capitalism. In the case of modern world systems, transnational investment and cultural diffusion, spurred by NAFTA, have resulted in a proliferation of Western influences, from factories to fast food. The jobs that now accrue to the periphery are welcomed, both by governments and families seeking employment. However, they do not provide adequate wages or benefits that compensate for the loss of their land or natural resources. Factory or service jobs are insecure, and require a new and foreign set of cultural values, based on the clock rather than the agricultural cycle. They also enlist a different type of worker, preferring to hire young women instead of men, the latter who now find themselves marginalized economically and socially in their villages.

Likewise, tourism links formerly peripheral areas to a larger world system in unique ways. Instead of extracting labor and resources to support the core areas, tourism brings money and foreigners to the periphery. Development is local and has long-reaching consequences both to the communities that are transformed by it and to the region as a whole that becomes drawn into its web, through markets or labor. But like extractive industries, the profits from tourist development are concentrated in the hands of the major investors and the governments that sponsor them. Local residents may benefit from their labor or from local enterprise, but overall conditions of laborers seldom improve markedly, and evidence shows that tourism even has a detrimental impact on local economies and health (Daltabuit and Leatherman 2001).

In Mexico, tourism has emerged as a solution to severe economic crisis in the nation generally, and in the Yucatán, specifically. The development of Cancún and Cozumel as major tourist destinations, and the more recent development of the "Mayan Riviera," a strip of high-rise hotels and tourist restaurants on the Caribbean coast of the Yucatán Peninsula, has offered hope to regional and national planners. The costs and benefits of these tourist attractions to local communities, and to those who are migrating there to seek employment, are still being calculated. The impact of tourism on Yaxbe is indirect, as it draws individuals and families to the tourist markets of Cancún, Cozumel, and also to the state capitol, Mérida.

YAXBE

Yaxbe is located 20 miles from Mérida. It is the county seat and the only village in the *municipio* (county) of the same name. The other populations located within the municipio are haciendas, some abandoned and others still occupied by small clusters of people who gain their employment from agriculture or henequen production on privately owned parcels. The history and economic situation in

Yaxbe provides an illustration of the interaction between economic change and human agency. Until the 1960s, Yaxbeños patterned their lives around henequen production. Now that the monoculture production has collapsed, they are restructuring economic and social relations to adapt to these changes. Rather than viewing villagers as victims, I prefer to examine the means by which they endeavor to reshape their lives, the resourcefulness and flexibility with which they have seized the opportunities available to them, and how they have developed new strategies with which to address the new realities of their lives.

In 1977, Yaxbe had a population of 1750[9] comprised of 334 families. Over the course of my fieldwork year (1976–1977), I obtained detailed information on 286 families whose members (1,473 individuals) represented approximately 84 percent of the total population. At that time, 65 percent of the adult men designated agriculture as their primary occupation, and most of these men were employed in henequen production. *Henequeneros* worked primarily in the ejido, organized into work groups and supervised by a *socio delegado,* a locally elected official who set the work schedules and production quotas, and paid the workers. In addition to henequen, many farmers practice traditional agriculture, producing corn, beans, squash, and numerous other vegetable and fruit crops in small plots called *milpa*. Many families utilized a combination of ejido, milpa, and private parcels on which they cultivated their own food crops or henequen. Only a few local men, primarily merchants, held private parcels large enough to produce surpluses for the market.

Most other occupations in the village between 1976 and 1977 were associated with henequen production. In fact, 80 percent of the adult men in the village gained their primary income directly from the henequen industry, in the ejido itself or in henequen-related jobs, especially the trucking *sindicato* or the decorticating factories. The trucking sindicato included men who either owned trucks or worked for others, transporting henequen leaves and fibers to Mérida. The most highly valued job, however, was at the Cordemex factory, located at the outskirts of the village. Cordemex was a national corporation that owned all of the decorticating plants in the state of Yucatán (except those at the haciendas). These factories were located throughout the henequen zone. The local Cordemex factory served the *parcelarios*[10] of Yaxbe and surrounding villages. In 1977, Cordemex employed two shifts, each with 40 workers, most of whom resided in Yaxbe. The wages and benefits far exceeded that of any other local occupation; workers earned between US$60 and US$75 dollars a week and received seniority and benefits such as vacations. Cordemex workers formed the core of a new middle class, and in the 1970s comprised a new political faction powerful enough to elect several village presidents, a position previously dominated by wealthy merchants.

During the henequen era, women had very little involvement with henequen or milpa production. Although women may have assisted their husbands in the milpa from time to time, henequen production is very arduous and requires many hours of labor far from home. The women's realm was the home and the village. Within these confines, however, women had considerable influence and made significant economic contributions to the family.

Although few women earned wages in 1977, most of the families I interviewed reported that at least one resident female provided income to the family.

These sources of income included hammock weaving, sewing, selling fresh produce or prepared foods, as well as pensions received as a result of their husbands' work in the ejido. Women also raised domesticated animals such as turkeys, chickens, and pigs for their by-products and for meat. The number of women making these informal and undocumented contributions was certainly higher than reported because many women or their husbands did not consider such contributions "economic."

Economic contributions of younger household members were also crucial to the economic success of the family unit. Several adult male dependents worked at the Cordemex factory, drove trucks for the sindicato, or worked in local stores. Even boys and young men who attended school regularly were expected to contribute in some way, through agriculture or through wage-earning jobs. Young women were also economically productive, not only earning money in home-centered activities such as sewing and hammock weaving, but also outside the home, as sales clerks or babysitters.

It is important to recognize that the key for economic survival was, in the past, and still is, diversification. Most, if not all, henequeneros supplement their incomes in a variety of ways: working on milpa and private henequen parcels, selling produce, or working construction or in family stores. Every child over age 10 contributes in some way to the family labor pool. Few families can survive on what the husband earns in the henequen ejido, and no households in the village depend on a single income.

1990s—THE FALL OF THE EJIDO: NEW STRATEGIES FOR NEW REALITIES

I have returned to Yaxbe six times since that first research year. Each time, I have noted a shift away from henequen production to other forms of subsistence. In 1977, 80 percent of the men were involved in henequen-related occupations; only 20 percent were employed in other occupations. By 1990, these percentages were reversed. The henequen market had collapsed as the demand for Yucatecan sisal disappeared. In 1992, while I was in the village, the local Cordemex factory closed. Although it opened again by 1995, it reopened as a privately owned factory with a different name. The owners operated only one shift, paid the workers minimum wage with no benefits, and offered only yearly or six-month contracts.

As I made frequent visits to the village, I expected to see evidence of economic decline. Instead, I found, at least superficially, improvements in the infrastructure and appearance of the village. Since 1989, the local government has built a new municipal market, a Conasupo (government-subsidized grocery store), a library, and a medical clinic staffed by two part-time doctors and a nurse. In addition to buildings, other improvements in infrastructure are evident: an expanded system of paved roads leading from the village center to its perimeter, and an expansion of electrical services and potable water. However, in stark contrast, the village still has only a single telephone line that connects to a pay phone in the president's office. Until 2001, a long-distance call home necessitated a 20-minute drive to the neighboring town where I waited in a small room of a private home for my call to go through. If I was lucky, the proprietor of the long-distance office was home, there was no special local festivity, and the connection was good. However, if I was not lucky—or if my family was not home to answer the phone—then I had wasted my time as well as the gas and time of the villager who transported me there. Today, several villagers have cellular phones in their homes, and I have been able to call home with much more ease. In Mérida, I can send e-mail home from one of several Internet cafés.

Houses have become larger over the years, with separate rooms, modern appliances, and furniture. The demand for video machines and cameras has increased, as has the number of families who own cars or trucks. A few families have home computers, but without telephone lines, the Internet is still outside of their experience.

Underneath the superficial appearance of affluence lay an ominous sense of foreboding and fear. Women living in stucco houses complained about "the crisis," young people and married men left the village at dawn to work in urban factories, and married women added babysitting to their daily chores. The juxtaposition of this apparent affluence and the unkempt henequen fields and abandoned Cordemex factory presented a paradox and forced a question: Why was there such a contradiction between the economic deterioration and the apparent growth and prosperity of the village? Where was the money coming from that built these houses and purchased these material goods? How can a village, wrought by economic depression, support a growing population?

The answer to these questions is complex and related to various economic strategies that have emerged for men and women in the past 20 years: (1) diversified sources of income and the increased participation of women in the wage economy; (2) commuting; and (3) out-migration.

ECONOMIC DIVERSIFICATION IN THE VILLAGE

Agriculture

When critical changes occur in an economic system, they do not affect all individuals in the same way. This is true in the Yucatán. Middle-aged married men have limited options given the decline in the agricultural sector. Displaced ejidatarios are especially disadvantaged, as they do not have the training or education necessary to take up a skilled or semiskilled occupation. These men who are not able to continue in henequen production have begun to invest in other forms of agricultural labor, such as vegetable production or raising domesticated animals. Older men, in their fifties and sixties, are particularly vulnerable. Unable to find new work, they often work as laborers for younger village men who have private parcels, in family gardens, or possibly for their children who now own stores. Although this type of diversification illustrates their industriousness and flexibility, the reality is that these local sources of income pay very poorly and often offer only part-time employment.

Justo Chan and his sons are the epitome of the new farmer. Justo and Jesus both worked in the ejido in 1976. Justo also owned a *parcela* on which he cultivated additional henequen. In 1992, Justo solicited the *socio delegado* for former ejido land. He was granted about three acres of land that he holds in usufruct. Although other men abandoned their henequen fields or allowed them to be overrun with weeds, the Chans planted henequen and maintained three immaculate fields at different stages of maturity. In 1995, they planted a field of young plants (called *hijos*) in a field they had recently burned. A group of men worked in each row, lining up the plants, digging the holes, placing the plants, and securing each with rocks.

By 1998, Justo and Jose were joined by Daniel, Jose's brother, who had recently returned from working in Cancún. Together, they had greatly expanded their farm. They now raised various fruit and vegetable crops: watermelon, sweet potato, tomatoes, and squash. In addition, they owned 100 head of cattle and 30 pigs. The latter were Daniel's contribution to the family enterprise, and he had just completed a small barn with 10 stalls to house his animals. In addition to the cattle corral and pig barn, they built a caretaker's house, sparsely furnished with farming equipment and a hammock. An impressive flock of turkeys and chickens pecked and foraged freely among the abundant fruit trees and fragrant herb bushes. Finally, the area surrounding the house and food crops was planted with a variety of grasses for their cattle. The henequen fields were thriving. They now had several fields of mature henequen plants, ready for cutting. The hijos I watched them plant three years ago were thriving. He had since planted more hijos. Interspersed with these younger plants was his milpa, the corn stalks now brown and bent down in Mexican fashion to protect the corn from birds and the heat of the sun. As lush as this farm appeared, it is the exception to the rule in agricultural diversity, as few families have the resources to invest in this type of enterprise.

Although some families have attempted to maintain family fields such as the Chan's, few are able to do so. Other men have maintained ties to agriculture by forming cooperatives. Cooperatives were not very successful in the early years of my research, as they were incompatible with the demanding routine of henequen production. However, beginning in the 1990s, village men began to form cooperatives, sponsored by national peasant organizations. The supporting organizations assist the men in dynamiting wells and in purchasing seeds. The men share the labor of planting, weeding, harvesting, and guarding the fields. Unfortunately, these cooperatives continue to be only marginally successful, and do not promote real development. They must constantly address problems such as theft of their produce, malfunctions of their wells, water shortages, and conflicts among the men that center on the fair distribution of labor. Because the cooperatives are generally supplemental to other forms of employment, men are often unable or unwilling to put the necessary time and labor into them. Those men for whom the cooperatives are a primary source of income often complain about the lack of commitment from the others.

The most interesting development in the village since the early 1990s is the initiation of women's agricultural and factory cooperatives that have allowed women to supplement family incomes. These cooperatives will be discussed later.

Nonagricultural Occupations

As a large village, Yaxbe has always had a diverse economic structure. In 1976, 16 percent of adult men worked in nonagricultural occupations, such as construction, tailoring, and as merchants. In 1998, 70 percent of the men in my sample worked in nonagricultural positions. Innovative villagers with access to capital have developed new strategies that allow them to pursue entrepreneurial alternatives to agricultural labor. The source of capital for these local businesses has been, ironically, the severance pay allotted to workers laid off from the ejido and from Cordemex. Although both ejidatarios and factory workers received severance pay, Cordemex workers received substantially more, thus catapulting the factory worker far beyond the average villager and entrenching his position in the new middle class.

Several farsighted men used part of their severance pay to purchase private parcels or *soláres* in the village. The most obvious change in the village in my 1989 visit, however, was the proliferation of small housefront stores, financed primarily by severance payments. These enterprises, often secondary sources of income, are managed on a daily basis by the members of the immediate and extended family. Other men invested in vans that formed the core of the taxi service. Another purchased a flatbed truck and started his own transport business. Those who did not start businesses added to the material prosperity of the village through the construction of new homes or the purchase of the consumer goods already described. All of these short- or long-term investments attest to the continued commitment of families to the village.

Shifts in economic participation of women are also remarkable. In 1976, only 12 percent of the women earned an income from their labor. In contrast, by 1998, 21 percent of the women I interviewed earned an income or participated in a family business. Women's participation is much more difficult to gauge because a substantial percentage of their income is earned in the home, sewing or weaving hammocks. Nevertheless, the numbers reflect a marked increase in the contributions that women make to the family income.

Women and Income Production Within the Home

Women have always earned income through a variety of means within the household, including hammock weaving and the raising and sale of produce and domesticated animals. These strategies still exist for many women, and even those who have jobs outside of the home continue to earn money in these ways, as do other female household members: daughters, mothers, and sisters. I lived in their homes, and this afforded me the opportunity to observe various supplemental economic activities. At one home where I lived in 1998, a steady stream of neighborhood children purchased soft drinks, ice pops, and ice from the family refrigerator. At another house, I peeled, sliced, and packaged papaya and watermelon; and weighed tomatoes, limes, and chili peppers to sell to women and children who came to the door while my hostess did laundry or ran errands. This informal economy is not lucrative in and of itself, but compounded, provides additional income to the family.

The household responsibilities of many women had been expanded in many homes where men invested their severance pay into housefront stores. Although men do the purchasing and dedicate some hours to the store, it is often their second source of income, supplementing a factory job or agricultural labor.

Estéban and his wife Berta bought their store with his severance money from Cordemex. They now live on Cozumel with their children.

Instead, the women and children contribute the bulk of the labor to the store, sharing housework and taking turns helping customers. The success of this endeavor depends largely on the life cycle of the family: the age of the children, the time available to the mother, and the cooperation of the husband and his family members.

In my initial research, hammock weaving was a major source of income for women. Hammock weaving was conducive to the daily routine of women whose "free" time was fragmented into short segments in between household and child-care duties. The exploitative nature of this enterprise cannot be ignored. Alice Littlefield (1978, 1979, 1990) has written extensively on the nature of such cottage industries and how they exploit not only women's labor but that of children as well. The women in Yaxbe and hundreds of other villagers were (and some still are) subcontractors in the hammock enterprise, and thus are an integral part of this "putting-out" system. They obtained the skeins of fiber from women who represent the major distributors in Tixkokob, a town in a nearby municipio. In 1977, weavers were paid piecemeal for each hammock completed, earning between US$2 to $3 per hammock depending on size. Meanwhile, young men from Tixkokob carried their brightly colored bundles daily to the capitol or distant port towns and sold them for an amazing range of prices (US$20 to $50), depending on hammock size and on the gullibility and language skills of the buyer. The same hammocks cost even more in the English-speaking tourist stores.

Between 1995 and 1998 I noticed that few homes had hammock looms. I was surprised to see unused looms hanging from the beams of houses or leaning against dilapidated outbuildings. In response to my inquiries, I learned that women now saw the hammock putting-out system as an inefficient means of income production. Increasingly sophisticated about the value of their labor, women realized that the hammock contractors and distributors had been taking advantage of them. "We know how much they sell for in Mérida," was a common response.

The hammock industry is reliant upon a compliant and indigent workforce. Currently, in Yaxbe, only the poorest families continue to pursue this option. One exception is a hammock cooperative that several elderly village women formed. These women bypass the contractors; they purchase their own skeins, and weave and sell their own products. Their hammocks are huge, and made of the best materials. Best of all, the women are being rewarded for the value of their labor.

Women and Income Production Outside of the Home

Although the transformation of women's production from household to village and beyond has its roots in the overall shifting economic conditions, outside forces have also affected the direction of women's participation. Women in Yaxbe and elsewhere have become involved in various government-sponsored cooperative programs that have altered women's roles within the village and in the household.

The Mexican government has long provided a myriad of social and economic programs designed to ameliorate the poverty in the rural areas. Although none of these programs provides real economic development, many have positively impacted rural life. Some of these such as the DIF and PACR[11] have provided milk and nutritional programs; other agencies have brought the health clinic, the library, and potable water. Since the late 1980s and the early 1990s, the federal government has intensified its investment in rural areas for purposes of supplementing the incomes lost during the instigation of the land reform (Collier 1994, 141). I am intrigued by two of these programs in particular. The first is *Solidaridad* (Solidarity), an antipoverty program administered as part of an umbrella program called PRONASOL. Solidarity consists of four packages of programs that target a menu of social and economic ills, education, health, agricultural training and development, and rural infrastructure. Programs also target specific groups, one of which is Women in Solidarity (Collier 1994, 139–141; Laurell and Wences 1994).

The second program is the Women's Agro-Industrial Unit (UAIM) that allows women to form cooperatives within the structure of the ejido to farm collectively or carry out small development projects. Obtaining UAIM status allows women to receive land equivalent to that held by one ejidatario (Stephen 1994, 16; see also Robles, Aranda, and Botey 1993). This program is often the only way women can gain access to land under the new privatization procedures, which do not guarantee a woman's joint rights to her husband's land during his life or upon his death (Stephen 1994, 28–29). Yaxbe has one women's cooperative, sponsored by UAIM.

Because these programs were developed by the PRI[12] after the 1992 reforms, critics argue very effectively that they further reflected the attempts by the government at that time to deflect the opposition parties and increase the dependence of the poor on government programs. Critics also argue that the underlying agenda of these programs was to compensate the rural poor for eliminating economic subsidies and for increasing poverty that resulted from the massive privatization efforts associated with NAFTA. Yet, regardless of the national agenda, women in Yaxbe have taken advantage of these initiatives and have organized four cooperatives. I will discuss one of these cooperatives, the most successful and the one that best illustrates the resilience and power of local women to seek and achieve their goals despite resistance from the local political leaders.

Women in Solidarity: The Horchateras

In the early 1990s, a government promoter came to Yaxbe to recruit women to start an *horchata* factory in the village. Horchata is a beverage made from rice and caramel that rural families substitute for cow's milk. Several women attended the meeting and ultimately 14 women initiated a cooperative through the *Mujeres en Solidaridad* (Women in Solidarity) Program. The government provided them with a *molino* (mill to grind the rice) and an initial supply of ingredients. At first, the women produced the milk in the home of one of the women, Doña Paula, the current president of the cooperative. Later, they were allowed to put their molino in the *casa del pueblo,* in the same room where my husband and I lived between 1976 and 1977.

By 1995, the factory was in full operation. Fourteen women worked three days a week, grinding the rice in the molino, mixing in the other ingredients, stirring (with their hands), and finally straining the liquid into cleaned liquor bottles that they had solicited from friends and relatives. Although not physically demanding, the work was challenging. They worked long hours in a hot room, fighting flies that were drawn to the sweet liquid. During one visit, I purchased two fans that allowed them to circulate the air without opening the windows to the flies, but it was a minor improvement as the room was small, cramped, and unbearably hot.

At 6:00 p.m., their work was still not completed. After the bottles were filled, the women departed in different directions to sell their milk. Some traveled by bicycle to nearby haciendas and villages, bottles rattling in metal bike racks. Others traveled by bus and taxi to villages more distant. After one woman was injured in a bicycle accident and was stranded on a lonely road for several hours, the women started traveling in pairs, a less efficient but much safer option for them. Then, after working a long and exhausting day, the women returned home to do their household chores.

In 1998, all but one from the original group still worked in the factory. One elderly woman had to quit for health reasons, but another woman, age 72, was still active. The group had divided into two shifts by 1998, solving the dual problem of having too many women in the small factory room at once and not having enough work to keep all 14 women busy. The groups worked 10-hour shifts on alternate days, producing horchata six days a week, instead of three, and their business expanded all the way to Mérida. They produced 500 bottles a week, and

© Cindy Hull

*Sara, president of the UAIM
cooperative, first woman to
run for village president
and first woman to hold
public office in Yaxbe.*

finally, they began to purchase new, sterile bottles as well as their own label. They also obtained a small truck (*camioneta*) from the government that they used to transport their horchata to other villages. That none of the women knows how to drive is an insignificant problem, as husbands take turns transporting the women on their rounds.

When I arrived in 1998, the women were preparing to move to a new building about one block away. Their account of how this move came about provides an excellent example of the perseverance of these women. Once their business began to thrive, the women became concerned about the size of their factory, and the fact that it had no ventilation. They approached the village president for assistance in soliciting the state governor for a larger facility or money to expand the size of the current building. The president was not responsive to the women's proposals, canceling meetings and ignoring their requests. In a mood of frustration and determination, the women took a very brave step on their own behalf . . . they went directly to the governor. All 14 women took the bus to Mérida and coaxed each other into the intimidating entrance of the governor's palace, a daunting colonial structure guarded by

The author's house in 1976 and the women's horchata factory in 1998.

soldiers with semiautomatic rifles. They all entered the governor's office without an appointment and requested a meeting. Despite the secretary's insistence that the governor was busy, they decided to wait. And wait they did, middle-aged women with *huipiles* (white cotton shifts with embroidered neckline and hem) and their hair tied in tight buns at the back of their heads, younger women in worn polyester skirts and plastic shoes, sitting in the governor's waiting room.

Finally, they did see the governor, and they explained their predicament and what they wanted to do. The governor gave the women money for their lunch and transportation and promised that he would send someone out to look at their building and assess their need. The women, skeptical and not very hopeful, returned to the village. They were very surprised when a man did come about one week later and agreed that their factory was inadequate. Inquiries within the village resulted in the purchase of a *solár* and building across the street from their current location. The governor bought the building and *solár* for Mex$20,000 and paid for half of the cost of a new roof and other construction necessary to meet the requirements of the new factory. The women were to pay the remaining cost for the roof and build a bathroom in the back. When I returned to the village in 2001, the factory was in operation. The women had a well-lit and amply ventilated factory, and their business was thriving. Today the women laugh when they tell the story. They are very proud of their accomplishments and are very critical of the president who spurned their requests. They speak affectionately of Don Vicente, the governor, who calls the women "his *horchateras de Yaxbe*."

Members of one horchata *group with their new delivery truck.*

COMMUTING AS ECONOMIC STRATEGY

In the predawn hours, an ancient ritual is replicated. Workers stumble down poorly lit, rock-strewn roads toward the center of town where transportation to their jobs awaits them. In 1976, these workers were men climbing onto the bed of pickup trucks or onto horse-drawn wagons that took them to the henequen fields at the outskirts of the village. Today, these workers have a very different appearance and destination. Instead of wagons and trucks, buses line up along the plaza to await the new workers. Many of the workers converging on the plaza from all directions are women. Some climb on the bus that will take them to the foreign-owned brassiere factory in Mérida; others board the bus that takes them to the American-owned Jerzees factory in Tixkokob. The men board a bus that will take them to a concrete factory on the highway to Mérida. The ritual repeats itself in the early evening, when the buses return and release their exhausted passengers to return to their homes. In addition to the company-owned buses, public buses and taxis also provide transportation for the new workers, as men and women leave the village daily to work in restaurants, stores, hospitals, schools, and urban offices.

From 1976 to 1977, only 14 of 197 households (7 percent) had at least one family member commuting from the village. By 1998, Yaxbe had become a bedroom community, with more than half of the households sending at least one member out of the village to work. These daily commuters represent a vital transformation in village economics and family dynamics. In this section, we will examine the impact of commuting on village life.

Factory Jobs

Wage labor is not a new development in Yucatán, as we have seen. Because henequeneros have earned wages for their labor since the 1930s, the shift from reciprocal exchange to market economies is not a recent one. What is new is the shift in the relationship between the worker and employer. Whereas, historically, the henequen workers were employees of the paternalistic state, modern laborers work for private corporations. As such, they are invisible laborers often far removed geographically and/or experientially from their employers.

Whereas the ejido and Cordemex employed only men, factory work today is defined largely as female work. This is also true in Yaxbe. Of 59 villagers who worked in factories outside Yaxbe in 1998, 22 (37 percent) were women and 16 of these were single. Men are primarily employed in two factories, one that produces rugs and another that produces cement blocks. The factory that employs the most women is a brassiere/lingerie factory near Mérida. Here, women and other employees work from 7 a.m. to 5 p.m., five days a week with a half-hour lunch and two breaks. They earn a base wage and additional pay for anything produced beyond their daily quota. They also earn a bonus every year and have a one- or two-week paid yearly vacation. As with many piecemeal systems, however, the quotas are constantly being raised and the women earn a minimal amount of money for their time in the factory. One young woman told me in 1995 that she earned between 116 and 120 pesos per week. In 1995, this equated to roughly US$20–$25 per week. In comparison, a henequen farmer, working every day, earned about 150 pesos (US$30) per week. Although painfully inadequate, the income a young woman earns can greatly augment a family income or pay for her own education.

By 2001, even more factories have proliferated in the countryside, providing low-paying jobs for villagers and high profits for their parent companies. Another example illustrates this point: In 2001, my friend Sonia was employed at Jerzees, a factory that produces casual clothing, shirts, and sweatshirts. She worked a shift cycle called a four-by-four in which women work four straight 12-hour days and then have four days off. These 12-hour days don't include travel time between Yaxbe and Tixkokob where the factory is located, about 30 minutes each way. For a four-day shift, Silvia earned 500 pesos (about US$45), or less than US$1 an hour (including lunch).

Professional Occupations

Between 1976 and 1977, few children attended school beyond primary, or sixth grade. Secondary school (equivalent to junior high) or *prepa* (high school) attendance was limited to those children whose families could afford the loss of their labor, as well as their transportation and/or living costs. After the secondary school was built in the village, attendance increased. Improved access to transportation has likewise increased the number of children who now attend high school or technical school. Consequently, numerous villagers today have earned degrees in higher education and vocational licenses.

The most common professions for men are in business, accounting, and administration; for women, they are in teaching and nursing. Professional careers run the gamut: a woman from Yaxbe is now a doctor, a man became a veterinarian, and another woman plays violin in the Yucatán State Symphony Orchestra. Because few opportunities are available for professionals in the village, most educated villagers must either migrate or commute to their jobs. In the past few years, more of the local teachers are Yaxbeños, including the director of the secondary school and several of the elementary school-teachers, public and Seventh Day Adventist (SDA). In one exceptional family, five of the seven children (four daughters and one son) are all teachers: two of the daughters live and teach in the village, two live and teach elsewhere, and the son lives in the village and commutes to a nearby town.

Other Occupations

The proximity of Yaxbe to the capital city of Mérida offers additional opportunities for wage employment. Nonfactory employment in Mérida centers on the tourism industry, as Mérida is a major destination for tourists visiting the many archaeological sites that surround it. Many young people seek employment in the restaurants, hotels, and tourist shops. If they can learn a little English, they can earn good money in this industry. More will be discussed concerning tourism in the next section. Besides tourism, factories, and the professions, Mérida offers opportunities in many semiskilled and service industry jobs, including construction, trucking, and for women, jobs as domestics and nannies.

Although commuting has become a dominant employment pattern for both married and unmarried men and women, the meaning of work is not identical to all categories of workers. For women, the work itself is a novelty, a vast and dangerous leap into new economic and social territory where the ramifications to self and family are just beginning to be felt. For men, commuting is an extension of their previous wage labor that nevertheless necessitates a shift in their economic and social ties to the larger society. In this section, I will discuss briefly the different meanings attached to work and commuting for men and women in Yaxbe.

Men and Commuting

Growing from 2 percent of working men in 1976 to 44 percent in 1998, it is apparent that commuting is expanding as a strategy for both married and single men. For married men, commuting represents a less risky alternative to migration that will separate them from kin and their established social networks. In the village, one lives within walking distances to family, friends, church, school, and stores. Men and women all assert that they prefer to live in the village where life is "quiet and agreeable." For most men, commuting is less disruptive to their families and it preserves the desired quality of life. It follows then that commuting is a strategy chosen most often by married men. In fact, in 1977 only 10 men commuted (five married, five single); today, approximately 65 percent of those who commute are married, divorced, or widowed—in other words, men who have obligations and connections to the village.

The sources of employment for unmarried and married men depend upon their level of education and skills. Both unskilled married and unmarried men are likely to find work in one of the factories where skills are learned on the job. Men who have learned a skill, such as carpentry or mechanics, are able to obtain higher paid employment in the urban areas. Young men often strive to find employment in the tourist area of Mérida, in the hotels, restaurants, and stores. These jobs pay well, but the employees must have a working knowledge of English and perhaps a little French or German. For young men (and women), the ability to speak English is a growing avenue out of the unskilled job market and into a more lucrative and enviable occupation.

Women and Commuting

One day as I waited in the plaza for the taxi, I realized that all of those waiting with me were women. An informal poll showed that most of these women were on their way to work or school. Several were on shopping expeditions. I have found that commuting is an important new strategy for women. In 1976 only 12 percent of working women commuted to their jobs, compared to 52 percent in 1998.

As we have already seen, women have limited means available for earning money within the village, and the income earned in these endeavors is insufficient to meet the growing economic needs of the family. For unmarried women, the opportunities for employment in the village are few, because businesses such as stores and *tortillerías* employ family members before tapping the local labor pool. Although the potential exists for a future market in child care and housekeeping, these responsibilities are still primarily fulfilled within the family.

Contrary to what we might expect, half of the commuting women in both 1976 and 1998 were married, divorced, or widowed, and half were single. However, married and unmarried women differed in the types of jobs they obtained. Because of their flexibility and lack of family commitments, most unmarried women found jobs in the factories. Surprisingly, the married women who commuted from the village tended to be educated, professional women, such as the teachers and nurses already described. As we have seen, village women do not suffer the angst that many U.S. women feel leaving their children with strangers or day-care centers. Most working women in Yaxbe know that their mothers or mothers-in-law are loving (and inexpensive) caregivers. Additionally, most villagers, even the more cosmopolitan-oriented women, agree that it is better to raise one's children in the village where they are loved and where they learn the proper values.

MIGRATION AS ECONOMIC STRATEGY

The single most important reason for out-migration is tourism. In the 1970s, when Cancún and the tourist islands of Cozumel and Isla Mujeres were being developed, many opportunities were available for men in carpentry, masonry, and other skilled and semiskilled trades. Many men, young and middle-aged, learned valuable skills during these years that they were able to apply when they returned to the village. Now, the resorts continue to draw young people and families who seek employment in the restaurants, hotels, and tourist shops there.

© Cindy Hull

Justo, a veterinarian, commutes to work daily so his wife and daughter can stay close to her family Yaxbe.

Cancún and Cozumel are only a one-day journey from Yaxbe, so workers frequently return home on the weekends and for special occasions. They are able to maintain ties with the village, and also procure jobs for their relatives, resulting in a continuous flow of people back and forth.

To leave one's village of birth is a major decision, one that is not taken lightly. The decision to migrate and the strategies employed depend on such variables as gender, age, and marital status. Most migrants, especially young people, leave the village with the intent to return. They live with relatives while they attend high school, vocational school, or university. Others leave to pursue jobs. Parents prefer that their children stay within the Yucatán Peninsula so that they can return home on weekends, maintain their ties to family and friends, and share their wages with their parents. Despite their best efforts, however, some young people stray further away in search of better jobs, or to follow someone that they met. The longer that a migrant stays away, the more likely that temporary migration stretches into years and the young person becomes lost to the family and community.

Chain migration is a very common pattern in many parts of the world, and this is also true in Mexico. It is most common for the oldest child to leave, establish herself with other family members, and send for younger siblings. One by one, they follow the leader, live together, share expenses, and often work at the same location. This pattern becomes complete when the parents leave the village to join their children.

Once this occurs, it is likely that migrants will remain permanently in the receiving area, returning only for occasional visits. This was especially true in the past when the village offered little in terms of employment that could lure villagers back home. Consequently, the most highly educated and skilled individuals became lost to the village. This pattern is reversing itself as the village expands and as communication and transportation between Yaxbe and the outside world improve. Slowly and cautiously, young professionals and skilled workers are returning to the village.

One such man earned an accounting degree. He and his family lived and worked in Mérida until he was appointed by a newly elected village president to be the village civil registrar. Another young man moved to Valladolid after finishing veterinary school. However, his wife, also from Yaxbe, was homesick and unhappy. Attempting to please her, he eventually obtained a position as an animal inspector, traveling throughout the region, inspecting domesticated cattle and goats, and giving inoculations. He was thus able to move his family back to Yaxbe and use the village as his home base.

Migrant remittances have always been considered an important contribution to rural households. Although most families noted that their migrant relatives send money, they always added that it was not a lot of money. Numerous resident families complained that their children sent little if any money home because of the expense of living in Cancún and Cozumel. The longer that the family members are gone, and once they become established with families of their own, the less they send home and the more tenuous the bonds become. This is even truer in cases where the emigrant marries a person from the receiving area or from another region of Mexico. Connections become strained, networks are neglected, and families lose touch.

CONCLUSION: THE IMPACT OF GLOBALIZATION

It is evident that the long history of globalization has had a tremendous impact on the daily lives of Yaxbeños for many generations. It is critical to explore this impact from a variety of levels, as I have been so fortunate to do for more than 20 years. The macro approach, examined from the framework of the world systems theory, allows us to understand the global issues of globalization, transnational industrialization, and tourism, and their impact on national international economic and governmental policies; the micro or regional approach gives us a valuable glimpse into the impact of these policies on individuals and families. Some of these effects are subtle, the shift from ejido to private farming and ranching. Others, though gradual, are more obvious, such as increases in entrepreneurship, commuting, and migration, and the dramatic visibility of women in the economic sphere.

To summarize, I would like to outline several principles of culture change that I have observed over the years and that illustrate the interaction between the global and the local:

1. *Current economic and social conditions and patterns of culture change are enmeshed in history and must be understood within a larger context of shifting*

political policies and decisions related to the allocation of land and the exploitation of natural resources. The world system perspective allows anthropologists, political scientists, economists, and others to envision the impact of global economics on peripheral areas and rural people. In this chapter, I have attempted to demonstrate how the local and the current must be understood within the context of the global and historic.

2. *Within this larger context, individuals and groups are agents of change, shaping their own futures and adapting to events beyond their control.* Anthropologists attempt to locate and assess the local within the global to understand how people perceive of themselves and their place in the larger social and economic system, and to examine how they act within the constraints of that larger system. In Yaxbe, villagers patterned their lives around henequen production; now that the system has begun to unravel, they are restructuring their economic and social relations to adapt to these changes. In my work, I have seen how villagers—instead of being "victims" to outside forces—actively engage with these changes, adapting and reshaping their lives.

3. *Human responses to events and conditions are not identical or predictable in all places.* Human agency is based on many factors both within the family and within the social structure of the community. Poor families do not have the same options as wealthier families; women's options differ from those of men; those of the uneducated differ from those of educated individuals. All social action is also performed within the context of ethnicity, social class, wealth, religion, age, and gender. In addition, all individuals and families perceive their own potential and options in diverse ways. In this chapter, we have explored how individuals and families are agents of both change and resistance while simultaneously acting within the context of events that are beyond them, geographically and politically.

REFERENCES

Brannon, Jeffery, and Eric Baklanoff. 1987. *Agrarian reform and public enterprise in Mexico: The political economy of Yucatán's henequen industry.* Tuscaloosa: Univ. of Alabama Press.

Brockway, Lucille. 1979. *Science and colonial expansion: The role of the British Royal Botanical Gardens.* New York: New York Academic Press.

Chardon, Roland. 1961. *Geographical aspects of plantation agriculture in Yucatán.* National Research Council Publication 876. Washington, DC: National Academy of Sciences.

Collier, George. 1994. *Básta! Land and the Zapatista rebellion in Chiapas.* With E. Lowrey Quarantiello.
Oakland, CA: Institute for Food and Development Policy, Food First Books.

Daltabuit, Magalí, and Thomas L. Leatherman. 2001. Biocultural impact of tourism on Mayan communities. In *Building a new biocultural synthesis,* ed. Alan H. Goodman and Thomas L. Leatherman, 317–337. Ann Arbor: Univ. of Michigan Press.

Hopkins, Terence K., Immanuel Wallerstein, and Associates (Robert L. Bach, Christopher Chase-Dunn and Ramkrishna Mukherjee). 1982. *World-systems analysis: Theory and methodology.* Beverley Hills: Sage Publications.

Hull, Cindy L. 2004. *Katun: A twenty-year journey with the Maya.* Belmont, CA: Thomson/Wadsworth.

Joseph, Gilbert M. 1982. *Revolution from without: Yucatán, Mexico, and the United States, 1880–1924.* Cambridge: Cambridge Univ. Press.

Laurell, Asa Cristina, and Maria Isabel Wences. 1994. Do poverty programs alleviate poverty? The case of the Mexican National Solidarity Program. *International Journal of Health Services* 24 (3): 381–4.

Littlefield, Alice. 1978. Exploitation and the expansion of capitalism: The case of the hammock industry in Yucatán. *American Ethnologist* 5 (August): 495–508.

———. 1979. The expansion of capitalist relations of production in Mexican crafts. *Journal of Peasant Studies*, 6:471–488.

———. 1990. The putting out system: Transitional form or recurrent feature of capitalist production? *The Social Science Journal* 27 (4): 359–372.

Raymond, N. 1968. Land reform and the structure of production of Yucatán. *Ethnology* 7:461–470.

Reed, N. 1964. *The caste war of Yucatán.* Stanford: Stanford Univ. Press.

Restall, Matthew. 1998. *Maya conquistador.* Boston: Beacon Press.

Robles, Rosario, Josephina Aranda, and Carlota Botey. 1993. La mujer campesina en la epoca de la modernidad. *ElCotidiano* 53 (March-April): 25–32.

Roys, Ralph. 1943/1972. *The Indian background of colonial Yucatán.* Norman: Univ. of Oklahoma Press.

Simpson, E. 1937. *The ejido: Mexico's way out.* Chapel Hill: Univ. of North Carolina Press.

Stephen, Lynn. 1994. *Viva Zapata: Generation, gender and historical consciousness in the reception of ejido reform in Oaxaca.* Transformation of Rural Mexico, #6. Ejido Reform Project. Center for US–Mexican Studies. San Diego: Univ. of California.

Thompson, J. Eric. 1970. *Maya history and religion.* Norman: Univ. of Oklahoma Press.

———. 1966/1975. *The rise and fall of Mayan civilization.* Norman: Univ. of Oklahoma Press.

Wallerstein, Immanuel. 1974. *The modern world system: Capitalist agriculture and the origins of the European world economy in the sixteenth century.* New York: Academic Press.

Yoder, Michael. 1993. The Latin American plantation economy and the world economy: The case of the Yucatecan henequen industry. *Fernand Braudel Center for the Study of Economies, Historical Systems, and Civilizations* 16 (3): 319–337.

NOTES

1. Material in this chapter was drawn from a 2004 monograph, "Katun: A Twenty-Year Journey with the Maya."

2. A pseudonym

3. Swidden farming is also known as slash and burn agriculture in which gardens are cleared and burned in the dry season and seeds planted just before the rainy season.

4. A vast literature exists on the ancient Maya and their conquest. See J. E. Thompson (1970, 1966/1975), R. Roys (1957, 1943/1972), and M. Restall (1998).

5. Patron-client relationships are unequal relationships in which the foreman or owner of the hacienda (patron) provides loans or gifts to the workers (clients) in return for their loyalty.

6. Debt peonage is an institution in which workers are tied to the hacienda by the debts to the owner or incurred in the hacienda store. Workers cannot leave the hacienda until these debts are paid,

and these debts pass from parent to children.

7. Statistics based on data published by Gilbert Joseph (1982).

8. The North American Free Trade Agreement (NAFTA) links the United States, Mexico, and Canada in interlocking trade arrangements. It went into effect January 1, 1994.

9. This is my estimated calculation.

10. *Parcelarios* are men who own private parcels that are dedicated to henequen production.

11. Desarrollo Integral de la Familia (DIF) is a family services agency. Programa del Alimentación Complimentaria Rural (PACR) is a rural food and nutritional program.

12. The Institutional Revolutionary Party (PRI) ruled Mexico from 1946 to 2000 when Vincente Fox, the candidate from the National Action Party (PAN) won the national election.

Fieldwork Biography
Naomi H. Bishop

Naomi Bishop is a physical anthropologist with an aversion to hot climates—hence, her choice of the Himalaya as a field site for studying the effects of environment on the social behavior of primates. The village of Melemchi provided not only a population of langur monkeys, but also a welcoming community of people who shared both their resources and their life stories. Naomi and her filmmaker husband, John Bishop, have returned again and again over the years since their first visit in 1971 (Bishop and Bishop 1978; 1998). The switch from primatologist to cultural ecologist was prompted both by living with two children in the field and by the attraction of learning about and documenting the centuries-old practical knowledge of how to make a life in this challenging environment.

© John Bishop

9/The Yolmo People of Melemchi, Nepal
Change and Continuity

My association with the village of Melemchi began in the fall of 1971 when I arrived with my photographer husband to study langur monkeys and how they change their social behavior and organization in response to the rigors of living in a high, mountainous environment. At that time, Ibe Pasang Buri was the oldest living person in the village. She was 86 years old, the mother of ten children, five of whom were alive at that time. Although she died one year after we met her, today she has more than 124 direct descendants. Her house in the village remains empty, and is looked after by her daughter who lives next door. The house belongs to Ibe's youngest son who is now 82 years old and lives in the Kathmandu Valley with his oldest daughter. His youngest daughter currently lives in New York City where she recently gave birth to her second child, the first U.S. citizen descended from the Melemchi village. His youngest son is a Khempo, a Tibetan monk and teacher who is of sufficient renown and entrepreneurial skill to have a small international following, a Web site, and a storefront temple in lower Manhattan. And in sad contrast, another of Ibe's descendants died last year, a drug addict in Kathmandu.

The opportunity to track the Melemchi story over an extended period of time offers a unique perspective on culture change, continuity, and challenges. The lives of more than one hundred families have been followed from the time of lived memory dating back to the 1920s and 1930s and forward into the new century. Like the descendants of Ibe Pasang Bulti, the story of Melemchi today reaches far beyond the boundaries of place and culture that first captured our attention in 1971.

MELEMCHI: A YOLMO TEMPLE-VILLAGE

The people of the temple-village[1] Melemchi in east-central Nepal are descendants of Tibetan Buddhists. These descendants came over a high Himalayan pass from the area around Kyirung, Tibet, into the Yolmo Valley[2] of Nepal sometime in the middle of the nineteenth century. These settlers founded temples, or *gomba,* along the high ridges, and built up villages around them. The lamas who built these temples were members of Tibetan Buddhist sects that did not form monasteries; they were allowed to marry and live as householders. The settlers from Tibet intermarried with Tamang people who lived in the river valley and lower slopes, spoke a different but related language, and shared many similar cultural values. Today Yolmo culture shares attributes with both Tibetan and Tamang culture.

Yolmo-*wa* (people) speak a dialect of Tibetan known only in this valley, but which is similar to the Tibetan dialect spoken by Sherpas elsewhere in Nepal. The Yolmo language is part of the Tibeto-Burmese language family, and is completely unrelated to Nepali, the national language of Nepal, which is an Indo-European language like Hindi.

The Village

Melemchi is situated at 8,500 feet on a north-south spur of the Thare massif. In 1971, 30 houses were interspersed with fields planted in wheat, barley, or potatoes, whereas today more than 100 houses can be found. Melemchi is the most northern village in the Yolmo Valley, and it is a two-day walk from the nearest road. The Nepalese capitol, Kathmandu, is about 50 miles to the southwest. Surrounding Melemchi, forested slopes lead north to higher mountains and the Langtang Valley. Just north of the Langtang Valley lies Tibet.

Houses in the village are built from stone and mud with roofs of wood shingles, although in the past 10 years, nearly everyone has replaced their wooden roofs with sheets of tin. The family lives on the second floor in a large L-shaped room. Against one wall, all the cooking takes place on a one-yard square in the floor, lined with mud. Firewood is arranged like spokes over a central depression, and cooking pots sit on an iron stand over the fire. Careful arrangement of the roof shingles encourages smoke to drift up to the ceiling and out the roof. Around 1990, families began to replace the open cooking fires with airtight stoves, venting the smoke out a metal pipe through their roofs. The stoves are efficient for cooking but don't provide as much heat as the open fire. Families in the village may own several water buffalo or cows to provide household milk and butter, as

Melemchi village at 8,500 feet altitude. Every small clearing surrounding the village is a pasture for Melemchi herders. (1986)

well as manure for the fields. The animals are kept under the second story and are fed grass and leaves gathered every day from the hillsides and forest.

A pipe carries water from high on the mountain into a tank in the village; there it is piped to spigots located near clusters of houses. Residents still have to bring the water into their houses with jugs but it is a great improvement over hauling it from the spring below the village, as they did until 1971. Before they received electricity in 1993, people depended on kerosene lights (a wick in a tin can of kerosene) for light in the evenings. Now, there is electricity every evening for a limited period. Every household has an outdoor latrine; twice a year, household members clean out the latrines and they till the composted waste into the fields to fertilize the crops.

Many Melemchi residents also own land in Tarke Dau, a satellite community located 1,000 feet down the hill. Corn grows better at that altitude, and until the early 1980s, Melemchi residents moved down to Tarke Dau in winter where there was less snow, and then moved up to occupy their houses in the village after the corn was harvested in May or June. During the winter of 1972, just six families stayed in the village with us; the rest lived lower down in Tarke Dau or out with their herds.

Traditional Subsistence Strategies

The traditional subsistence strategy in Melemchi has always been agro-pastoralism (nomadic herding combined with growing crops in the village). The primary source of food and income was a family dairy herd of *zomo* (<u>Dzo</u>'-mō), a hybrid animal whose mother is a cow and father is a yak. In addition, most families

Zomo (female), *left; yak* (male), *right. (1986)*

owned fields in the village where they grew wheat, barley, and/or potatoes to supplement their income and diet. *Zomo* dairy herding was and still is common at middle altitudes (between 7,000 and 12,000 feet) throughout the Himalaya, where animals produce enough milk to sustain an economy based on dairying. Other agro-pastoralist strategies were also practiced in Nepal. Below 7,000 feet, the Melemchi agro-pastoralists focused more on agriculture—they kept herds of cows or water buffalo mainly to fertilize the fields. Households set up temporary shelters for themselves on the fields, so that the manure from their grazing animals provided the extra nutrients needed for intensive agriculture in poor mountain soils (Metz 1994; Panter-Brick 1986).

Above 12,000 feet, the Melemchi again emphasized livestock raising, the yak being the best-adapted animal for such altitudes. Yak herds provide milk, dung for fuel, and hair for blankets, but they are most valuable as pack animals for long-distance trade. In the region around Mount Everest, Sherpa herders move their herds of yak or hybrids up and down several times during the year (Brower 1991). At these altitudes, agricultural productivity is limited due to climate and soils. Although Melemchi plant potato and barley crops in small, scattered fields, some as high as 16,000 feet, their emphasis is on maintaining livestock for carrying loads.

Whereas herds of sheep and goat need only a shepherd to look after the flock, zomo herding is a household production system, requiring two adults to manage it. In Melemchi, a boy receives part of his father's zomo herd, as well as access to the family pastures, at marriage. He and his wife move with their herd, as high as 14,000 feet in the summer and as low as 7,000 feet in the winter. The herders bring the herd to the village usually just once in the fall to fertilize the wheat/barley fields before planting. They milk the zomo twice daily and make butter from the milk, which they sell to others and use for food. Cheese (fresh and dried) is made from the leftover buttermilk. Butter is sold to others and used for food and ritual. Because families move with their herds, houses in the village are used only to store things, and most herding families don't build houses until later in their marriages. As they grow older, the wives stay in the village houses more, while the husbands continue to herd with the help of their youngest sons, or they help their married sons with their herds.

Zomo herding created wealth in Melemchi; stories are told about the "millionaire" zomo herders in the 1940s and 1950s who had huge herds and invested their butter profits in land and fields downriver. In the 1970s, zomo herding was still the primary source of income for many families, and nearly all residents in the village at that time had lived for part of their lives with a zomo herd. Agriculture only supplements herding at this altitude. Herding families arrange their routes to be nearer to their fields when work needs to be done. It takes complex coordination to manage both agriculture and pastoralism, especially when they must move the herds at frequent intervals. Large families ensure plenty of children to help manage the crops and the animals, and selecting your mate from a fairly limited pool of families also results in many relatives who can be called upon to assist.

In the mid-1940s, a few Melemchi men joined others from Yolmo and traveled to India to find work on road-building projects in the Indian Himalaya. This started a pattern of circular migration for wage labor in India that continues to this day, and which has replaced zomo herding as the primary basis for subsistence in this community. Men, women, families, and even children move between the village and several communities in North India, bringing or sending back money to family members in Melemchi. Melemchi migration tends to be a temporary or *circular* migration—people leave for wage labor in India and return to their residences in Melemchi. They are not looking to change their permanent residence. It is also *external* migration, or migration beyond national boundaries. It provides an infusion of capital that can sustain households in the hills without requiring the upheaval of permanent relocation. It is not a simple seasonal deployment of men who move back and forth between their village and a work site. Rather, it encompasses complex arrangements of family members through time and space between two countries, in response to a variety of needs and opportunities that shift all the time. It is "a lifecourse strategy which both recognizes the long-term nature of some mobility strategies, and which provides a framework for understanding unfolding sequences of migration" (Bailey and Hane 1995, 173). It involves individual and household information networks; people go where others already are or have been, and they use social networks to obtain work.

As will be seen later in this chapter, the income streams from outside Nepal have been crucial in fostering the shift from a subsistence economy to a cash economy in Melemchi, as well as in bringing new cultural values and experiences into the village and the Yolmo Valley.

Social and Political Organization

Melemchi is a temple-village: the temple, or *gomba,* sits in the middle of the village—literally and figuratively, the center of Melemchi life. Those who own land in the village are the members of the gomba. The political, social, and religious life of every Yolmo temple-village is intertwined as men hold simultaneously the positions of lama (priest), taxpayer, and landowner. Every householder in a Yolmo temple-village is expected to participate in the rituals of the gomba—in this way, every man can be considered a priest. Those who can read Tibetan read the books, while others prepare the ritual statues made of barley flour dough with colored butter decorations for the altar in the gomba, or assist in performing the rites. Men are expected not only to participate in the activities surrounding the rituals, but every household must also provide grain, butter, and money to support the ritual cycle, proportionate to their landholdings. In addition, every member of the gomba is eligible to serve a term as one of the group of village headmen. This group of five men is responsible for ensuring that the rituals in the gomba are performed properly; for collecting land, wood, and fodder tax; for regulating forest use; and for settling local disputes. In 1993, 84 men were listed as gomba members; by 2000, that number had risen to almost 100.

Yolmo is a patrilineal, patrilocal society organized around clans. Descent is traced through the father's line—the children belong to the father's lineage. (American society is bilateral—children belong to both the mother's and father's descent lines.) At marriage, the couple lives with or near the groom's family. A man chooses a wife from a clan different from his own (clan exogamy[3]). Although a woman retains her own clan membership throughout her life, her children will belong to the clan of her husband. Five clans are represented in Melemchi; altogether, the Yolmo region has fourteen clans. Clans in Yolmo function primarily to regulate marriage. Cross-cousin marriage is preferred, wherein a person marries either mother's brother's or father's sister's child or descendant. This marriage practice creates close-knit alliances among a small set of clans. Marriage partners are almost always chosen from within Yolmo. Capture marriage, in which friends of the groom surprised the bride and forced her to marry him, was traditional in Melemchi until the mid-1980s. In a capture marriage, the boy and his family may have arranged the marriage in advance with the girl's parents, but without telling the girl. Marriages arranged by the couple themselves have largely replaced capture marriages. However, a couple still may ritually enact the marriage-by-capture, with the girl being dragged to the home of the groom's father for the marriage, while she pretends to fight back and protest.

Religion and Worldview

Mountain dwellers face uncertainty, danger, and separation in their daily lives. The environment is unpredictable; families are separated and dispersed across pastures, villages, and outside Nepal in India; and both animals and people are at risk of disease and disaster with no outside assistance available. Religion provides one of the frameworks within which people organize, understand, and try to control their world.

© John Bishop

Karpu Bombo, 1986. He dances and drums while in trance, wearing a harness of bells, calling the local deities to speak through him.

Yolmo people are Tibetan Buddhists. They seek the services of monastically trained lamas for divination of the future, and officiating at funerary rites and gomba rituals. The village bears many signs of devotion to Tibetan Buddhist practice: the gomba with its statuary, prayer wheels and Buddhist murals; the prayer flags in front of every house; the absence of animal butchery by villagers (although everyone eats meat that is killed by non-Buddhists); and the rites and rituals of the Buddhist religious calendar. Although every man in the village is expected to participate in rituals, only trained religious practitioners can preside over them. Increasingly, young Melemchi men are being encouraged to obtain some religious training, if not a lifetime vocation. Travel periods of study in monasteries in Kathmandu and more recently, South India, are becoming more common.

Yolmo people also consult shamans, called *bombo,* who deal with the immediate effects of the spirit world. Usually several men in the village have learned how to contact local gods, demons, or witches—and can help alleviate human suffering by going into trance, communicating with these spirits, and transmitting advice. The shaman is at odds with Buddhist doctrine. The shaman uses blood sacrifice to appease the spirits, usually a chicken but sometimes a goat, whereas lamas do not shed blood. The shaman handles immediate problems of the human body and spirit, whereas lamas focus on keeping society balanced as a whole and into the afterlife (reincarnation). Because the shaman "loses control" through trancing, some stigma is attached to the position, whereas a lama is universally esteemed.

MOVING INTO THE TWENTY-FIRST CENTURY: 1971–2000

The Melemchi we knew in 1971 changed greatly over the years, just as Melemchi in 1971 differed from its pre-World War II state. The most pervasive transformation between 1971 and the turn of the century is a shift from a subsistence economy to a cash economy. Nearly every documentable change in the village and lives of Melemchi residents can be linked in some way to this transition. It is even reflected in the ways Melemchi residents talk about themselves. In 1971, people described their situation in terms of "luck"—people who were poor had bad luck. Success—for instance, having bigger fields or bigger herds or better pastures—was seen to be the result of good luck. Today, people talk about their successes or lack thereof in terms of money: "People don't live in *gode* now because no one made *money* in a *gode*"[4]; "You can't make *money* in Melemchi, so you have to go to India/Taiwan/America"; "If one zomo dies in a year, you lose all your *profit*."

Although the shift from dependence on agro-pastoralism to circular migration and a cash economy was underway in 1971, it accelerated in the 1980s and 1990s. Herd numbers dropped, new herd types were adopted, and circular migrants found new kinds of jobs in new locations. All of this contributed to increased affluence and new types of relationships to the village for residents, young and old. In addition the village itself was thrust into a new relationship with the national government. New opportunities for Melemchi residents to interact more directly with the national government came with the incorporation of Melemchi into the Langtang National Park in 1986, the opening of a government primary school in the village in 1984, and political changes in the mid-1980s that allowed villagers to obtain title to their land and receive citizenship papers. By 1993, Melemchi people were the beneficiaries of a government-sponsored electrification project that made it possible for them to watch television in their homes (albeit only one channel). By 2000, the village had a satellite telephone. When a call came in, a child was dispatched to run across the village and find the recipient who then had to run to the house with the phone—a process that often took up to 20 minutes!

Changes in the Subsistence System

DECLINE IN AGRO-PASTORALISM   In 1971, nearly everyone in Melemchi had been or was being raised in a zomo-herding family. However, even at that time, many adults no longer lived with herds. A number of families had given up herding and were pursuing periodic wage labor in India, Assam, or Sikkim. Although they retained their houses and fields in Melemchi, and even built and bought new ones, it was clear in 1971 that most of their children would never herd zomo. Those families who still owned zomo herds and lived out in the pastures often had several children living in India, sending back money when possible and returning only to visit.

The abandonment of zomo herding for wage labor took place over many years. Increasing numbers of young men chose to sell off their inherited live-stock and set out for India. Some returned periodically, bought herds with their savings, and herded for a while, but the majority left the herding lifestyle for good. In 1971, 24 gode were associated with Melemchi; the numbers dwindled over the years to 20 in 1986, 18 in 1989, 11 in 1993, 8 in 2000, and 6 in 2003.

SHIFT FROM ZOMO HERDING TO ZOMO PRODUCTION   In 1971, 23 of the village's 24 herds were zomo herds (the other was a sheep herd). Zomo were purchased from breeders north or far to the east of the village where yak were plentiful. By 1987, the village had eight herds of a new type: cow-yak herds. The cows are bred to the yak to produce the hybrid offspring, zomo. Cow-yak herds produce zomo for sale, not butter. Raising zomo calves leaves no milk for dairying, so these herders don't make butter. The Melemchi men who started this in the mid-1980s were all over 55 years old, and were seeking respite from the rigors of managing a dairying operation. They explained that managing a zomo herd is much more difficult: the daily work of milking and butter making is hard and the high pastures are isolated and uncomfortable. With cows, herders can stay lower in altitude and closer to the village; they don't need women to milk the animals so wives could stay in the village more of the year. In earlier times, these men passed some of their livestock on to their sons when they married, and either stayed to help them or kept their own small herd. Now their sons didn't want the animals, but the men weren't ready to retire. Living in a cash economy, they sought a way to make cash money without the hard life of a dairy herder. Nearly all tried wage labor in India for a while. However, as elder men who had spent much of their lives herding zomo, many didn't speak Nepali or Hindi and found it difficult to find unskilled jobs. They also preferred to be in and around Melemchi. The solution of a cow-yak herd presented a new challenge, a source of cash income, and the opportunity to maintain their family pastures in the event that one of their sons returned to herding. Ultimately, most men who tried man-aging this new type of herd abandoned it. It turned out to be difficult to manage yak and cow in the same herd, given their physiological adaptations to different altitude zones, plus the herders suffered larger losses of livestock and produced fewer zomo calves than anticipated.

Some retirees in the village tried producing zomo on a smaller scale. They took their household milk cow up to a high pasture to breed with one of the herder's yaks, in the hopes of producing a zomo that they could sell. The sale of even one zomo provided a nice supplement for an elderly couple living in the village on their savings and largesse from children outside Nepal. As another village-based strategy, seniors combined this occasional breeding with managing tourist trekker lodges in the village, a good source of income.

Changes in Circular Migration

NEW OPPORTUNITIES IN TRADITIONAL LOCALES   The Melemchi men who worked in India, Burma, Assam, and Sikkim in the 1960s and 1970s performed unskilled labor: they carried mud, broke up rocks into gravel, and carried supply loads for road-building projects throughout the Himalayas. They were acclimated to the altitude and able to work well under difficult conditions. The pay was meager, the working conditions brutal, and often they returned home with little to show for their time and labor. Women either carried loads or more commonly, provided food and liquor for the workforce.

In the 1980s, Melemchi people gained the contacts and skills to obtain work in India as contractors. This paid better with fewer risks. Road contractors "bought" a piece of the road to be built from the government; they were responsible for completing that job. Instead of backbreaking work, they supervised and subcontracted the projects. Other skilled work was found in the building trades, such as carpentry or stone masonry. Several carpenters in the village learned their skills in India; new houses built in Melemchi since reflected the shaped stone techniques learned in India. Although the basic motivation for working in India has always been economic, it is possible to see that the pull away from Melemchi has become both economic *and* social as new generations participate. Today's young men and women see life outside the village as both lucrative and exciting, a chance to participate in the world, whether it be Kathmandu, India, or beyond.

JOINING THE GLOBAL DIASPORA   Cultural and environmental factors were important in initially shaping the patterns of migration of Melemchi people. Yolmo residents followed friends and relatives to several parts of the Indian Himalaya, where work was available building outposts for the Indian army and later, other construction work. These sites were located in high-altitude regions of India where other Tibetan Buddhist populations lived. The most common areas to find Melemchi migrants, both in the past and today, are the western Himalayan regions of Ladakh, Tsopema (Riwalsar), Lahaul, Spiti, and Kulu in Himachal Pradesh, or in the eastern Himalayan town of Bamdila in Arunachal Pradesh, near the borders of Bhutan and Tibet. Culturally comfortable in these locales, Melemchi residents are also physiologically adjusted to the high thin air, and are used to long days of physical labor through lifetimes spent in subsistence activities.

Changes in Taiwan's immigration law in 1990 opened the door to a few Melemchi young people to work in Taiwan garment factories as guest workers. This work paid much better than the types of work available in India. Visas were difficult to obtain and the work and living conditions were severe. It was impossible to take children along, and the time limitation on the length of stay was firm. However, those few who had this opportunity returned to Nepal with significant savings. A few others found similar work in South Korea. From these tentative beginnings, young adults from Melemchi found additional international opportunities, so that by the mid-1990s, people from Melemchi lived and worked in places as far-flung as the United States, Abu Dhabi, Germany, and Belgium.

As global citizens, Melemchi residents are now able to send money back home from these countries, while putting in long hours and living the frugal lifestyle of guest workers. The benefits can be great, but so are the costs. Children are often left behind with grandparents, sometimes for years. As people travel longer distances, the circulation pattern changes. They can't go and come, like they do from India. Once they obtain a visa, the expense of travel and the problems of visa requirements mean that they must stay until they are ready to return permanently. These young adults miss the childhoods of their children, their parents' old age, and family rites of passage, including weddings and funerals. One couple in the United States showed us photos of their house in Boudhanath, in which they have never lived. It was built with money they sent back. Their two children live there but they haven't seen their parents in six years; the youngest one hardly remembers her mother.

Incorporation into the Langtang National Park

Although the shift to a cash economy put Melemchi villagers increasingly in contact with the world outside Nepal, their relationship with forces inside the country simultaneously changed. Through accidents of history and geography, Melemchi residents knew almost nothing about the national government of Nepal when we first lived there in 1971. As a *guthi*[5] of the Chini Lama of Boudhanath, they paid their allegiance and taxes to him, not to the King. But in the 1980s, Melemchi residents finally succeeded in founding a school in their village, while at the same time, the government succeeded in making Melemchi into a national park. These two experiences with the national government changed life in the village in significant ways.

The Langtang National Park was officially gazetted in 1976—it covers 66,023 square miles, and includes the western slopes of the Trisuli River Valley, the high dry inner valley of Langtang along the southern border of Tibet, and the humid mountain region south of Langtang along the upper slopes of Yolmo. The southern border in Yolmo was the last to be negotiated—those villages not included in the park would not have access to resources within it; therefore, heavy incentives urged villagers to participate, despite the costs of being under the rules and regulations of the park. Melemchi was incorporated into the park by the end of 1986.

The park had two administrative centers and an outpost; the outpost and one center were in Yolmo, although not near Melemchi. The park administration included park wardens who negotiated rules and Nepalese army units that enforced them. Inhabited national parks pose special problems for both governments and residents. In the famous example of Yellowstone Park in the United States, the government summarily removed the people living there, in one of the most shameful episodes involving native people in U. S. history. But, in Nepal, initial attempts to do that had been disastrous, so the government negotiated an uneasy truce with local residents in later parks such as Langtang.

Melemchi people reacted to the park with caution in the winter of 1989. They were concerned about having an administrative agency of the government in their midst as well as its enforcing arm, the Nepalese army. Although Melemchi people had no major complaints about the way they had been treated by the park administration, it was undeniable that living in a national park changed their way of life. The national park regulated the cutting of trees for fuel wood, timber, or fodder, and imposed fees as well as insisted on regulating access. The park administration implemented an annual fee of 25 rupees per year to cut and gather dead wood for fuel. Park regulations on cutting fodder allowed people to cut leaves and branch tips from trees and shrubs anywhere in the park, but not the tops of the tree, whole branches, or the entire tree. In an attempt to establish good community relations, the national park suggested early on that all fees be returned to the village for the gomba fund; in fact, the villagers themselves often collected the fees because the warden was not nearby.

The park administration also reserved the right to regulate grazing within its boundaries. The only actual restriction in effect prior to the winter of 1989 was in an area of bamboo forest important to the maintenance of the red panda (*Ailurus fulgens*). This area was so far from Melemchi that no Melemchi herders were affected; furthermore, it turned out to be more difficult to enforce than anticipated, so ultimately, the regulation was lifted. Additionally, park restrictions forbade situating godes near tourist trekking lodges in areas of the park, which affected Melemchi herders who owned lodges as well and wanted to manage both simultaneously.

The park assumed the right to operate services for tourists, including lodges, restaurants, teashops, and stores. Prior to the national park, Melemchi residents took paying guests into their homes or small attached guesthouses, providing lodging and food. This was mainly an option for those who spoke Nepali or even a little English, and whose houses were located near the trekking paths. The national park required villagers to purchase permits to operate businesses for the public within the park. Both an application fee and an annual fee were required, which limited lodge operation to those who had wealth. Lodge owners were given time limits for making improvements, such as installing metal roofs. The national park set the rates for food and lodging, with variable rates depending on the distance the supplies must be carried. It also instructed lodge owners in standards for cleanliness, hygiene, and manners for dealing with tourists, and punished those who did not maintain standards.

Finally, the park imposed a number of rules concerning activities and behavior within the park. Rules prohibited hunting, fishing, or firing a gun without park permission. As Tibetan Buddhists, most Melemchi men aren't hunters although many have old rifles for protection. With the park prohibitions, the wild boar population grew in the park and became a widespread nuisance and growing menace, especially to families isolated in gode. Finally, the warden permitted the killing of boar "by any traditional means other than guns." Specifically bow and arrow were permitted, which provoked mirth among Yolmo people who have never been archers.

Joking about the rules was one manifestation of fear about the park. People claimed that park rules about noise pollution—which outlawed radios, tape recorders, or musical instruments at any place within the park other than at hotels, lodges, restaurants, religious places, or residences—included a prohibition against whistling or shouting. They warned that the army would arrest anyone who shouted in the national park. Park rules regarding killing animals in the park were jokingly reinterpreted to mean that a fine would be charged for each leech or head louse killed in the national park!

The main response in 1989 to the presence of the national park was a general fear among residents about loss of autonomy and control. Heretofore, "the king," a distant and unknown power, embodied their conception of the national government. Now park wardens and army officers entered their houses at will, quoting rulebooks that the illiterate residents could not read. Rumors were rampant about terrible things that had happened in other villages within the park, most involving the army that enforced the regulations in the park. These rumors had two main themes: people were either wrongfully accused and punished, or were harassed or plundered by soldiers, especially in gode.

People were also concerned about loss of property or decline in its value. Gode owners felt that restrictions on fodder cutting and woodcutting, as well as the *possibility* of restrictions on herd size and pasturing locations, would make it difficult to maintain a gode. Melemchi men who "own" their pastures wondered where they would take their animals if denied access to their family pastures. With a complex subsistence strategy, involving frequent buying and selling of livestock, living in the park introduced the possibility that they would experience arbitrary interference in their management of options, such as limiting herd size or composition, or setting price controls on butter. In the winter of 1989, two-thirds of the Melemchi herders said they wanted to sell their herds because of the national park. They were certain that it would become more and more difficult to keep a herd and they wanted to sell before there were no longer any buyers. Especially in low-altitude winter pastures where overgrazing made it necessary to supplement grazing with fodder, these herders felt vulnerable to park regulations about what and where they could cut. Herder after herder, young and old, said they wanted to get out.

Today, Melemchi remains in the Langtang National Park and in the years since 1989, many of the concerns of the villagers have been addressed or never surfaced. In point of fact, the park has been difficult to administer, leaving villages essentially in control of enforcing the rules for themselves, something they had always done. Fines and taxes are all held in the village and used for the common good. By 2000, the few remaining herd owners said that the national park has actually been very good for herding families. With a small annual grazing fee, they can graze in any pastures they wish, rather than only in those owned by their families. Although there are fewer zomo gode today than there have been in the past twenty-five years, it is not at all clear that any of the decline is due to the park. Certainly the park has not interfered with herd management and prices as the Melemchi herders had anticipated. The reduction in numbers of herds has released the pressure on park resources for the remaining herds, so the future looks good. Melemchi men occasionally work for the park, clearing and constructing paths, and controlling fires. The national park has had an influence on life in the village, especially in the early years of its development. It put a face on "the king," bringing villagers into contact with the national government. The park administrators were instrumental in explaining to residents how to have their land surveyed and registered in their own name, as well as helping the village residents to extricate themselves from their feudal ties to the Chini Lama in Boudhanath. Contact with the park improved the quality of the tourist services the villagers provided, resulting in increased opportunities for revenue-generating activities. And, through validating traditional village regulations and enforcing sustainable practices, it could be said that the park administration bolstered local attempts to conserve forest resources and environments. It must be acknowledged that the diminished role of the army, once the park was established, also contributed to a reduction in anxiety about the effects of the park on the lives of local residents.

A Primary School in Melemchi

Beginning in 1975, free primary education was established in Nepal, with the government providing teachers, facilities and educational supplies. Although it was compulsory, there was no way of ensuring that all children in Nepal actually had access. In fact, in 1984, figures indicate that only 52 percent of school-aged children in Nepal were enrolled (Shrestha 1993). Due to an oversupply of teachers in nearby Tarke Ghyang in 1984, a 17-year-old Nepalese schoolteacher was assigned to teach in the Melemchi village and the first primary school was opened there.

Primary education in Nepal includes the first five years of school, followed by another five years of secondary school, prior to university. When the primary school opened in Melemchi, few children had any experience with formal education; even those young children who had spent time in India were rarely educated there, or else attended sporadically as the family moved. Most of the time, children in India stayed home to help their parents, conserving money to bring back to the village. The schoolmaster rented a vacant house and opened the school in the adjacent room. Starting with about 20 students, he struggled that first year under difficult conditions. A year later, he moved the school down to the social room next to the gomba, which had enough space for different classes to sit separately, an outdoor play area, and good natural light. In 1989, the village built a new school building using donations from tourist trekkers for labor and the roof. The building was a simple structure, furnished only with benches. The teacher moved from group to group, teaching five grades in all subjects. He rarely finished by 3:00 p.m. when school ended; often he worked with student groups until 5:00 p.m. and then tutored in the evening.

In the Melemchi School, children are taught to read and write in the Nepali language. The national primary school curriculum begins with Nepali language and mathematics, adding science, English, history, Sanskrit, and health and morals in grades 4 and 5. The teacher in Melemchi never attended college, himself; and although he was an education student in his village school south of Kathmandu, he had no actual instruction in pedagogy. His fellow teachers in Tarke Ghyang helped him with curriculum and materials. In his early years, he taught in Nepali, but by 1989, he was fluent in the Yolmo language and used it in the classroom as needed.

In general, people agree that it is beneficial for both boys and girls to attend when they live in the village. Children living in gode are usually too far from the village to commute. In some cases, families have arranged for their children with a particular aptitude or interest in school to live with relatives or friends in the village. In some cases, several young siblings live together in their family house in the village, fending for themselves while their parents tend the herds. In 2000, several sets of grandparents kept their grandchildren in the village while the

© John Bishop

Melemchi couple with children (theirs as well as children of his brother with whom they share pastures) standing in front of their portable shelter made of bamboo mats over a wood and stone frame in 2000. They have herded zomo since marriage.

parents worked in India. All said it was a wonderful arrangement—the children taught their grandparents what they learned in school and helped with chores that had become difficult for them. This served to guarantee that their parents returned more frequently. Some parents initially were not supportive of the school; they needed their children to work or their children didn't want to attend school. But over the years, villagers have become increasingly proud of the school and the progress shown by the village children in their studies. Many feel that the Melemchi School is better than the schools available to their children in India. It is a source of pride and comfort to many parents that their children can be well educated and live in the healthy surroundings of the village, with good food and water available.

The government pays the teacher's salary, but the parents pay for copybooks and supplies. After grade five, students must leave the village and pay room and board. Very few have done so. A few go on to enroll in school in Kathmandu, a few enroll in India where the family works, but most stop school altogether once they get old enough to be employable.

The school has been an agent of change in Melemchi. Several residents mentioned to us that the school curriculum socializes their children in the broadest sense, introducing them to new ideas about health, hygiene, and the world outside Melemchi. This reinforces the experience so many have when they live for periods in India. The teacher explicitly teaches children basic health—to wash their hands, comb their hair, and brush their teeth every day, to bathe once a week, to keep their books and bag clean, and to cover their mouths when they cough. In physical education, along with Nepali dances and songs, sports are taught, providing access to the only sports equipment (volleyballs) in the village. Village social gatherings have changed since the schooling began. The school picnic is a new institution. Spontaneously organized by the schoolteacher and some of the older students, picnics are open to all villagers who gather at the school where a huge meal is cooked. Everyone who comes donates a little money to pay for the food (another example of the impact of cash in the village). Sanitation and hygiene has improved. Where formerly dishes were washed with cold water and sand or ashes, now soap and water are used. The school picnics offer additional opportunities for the community to gather outside the ritual cycle. And with initial encouragement from the teacher, activities for teenagers and young adults in the village have expanded to include parties with dancing to Hindi pop music.

In 1989, the schoolmaster participated in a pilot program sponsored by the Department of Education, to provide adult literacy classes to illiterate villagers in Melemchi. After a month's training, he offered a six-month course. Each week, he taught literacy for six evenings. On the seventh evening he taught life skills such as building and maintaining latrines, oral rehydration therapy, and personal hygiene. Both men and women took his classes, at least 40 residents in all. Eventually, there were not enough eligible people in the village, so the classes stopped.

The school has been rebuilt and expanded twice since it started, and the staff has grown to three teachers. It is still remarkably primitive, both in curricular materials available and in the physical space. The literacy skills obtained are rudimentary and are overshadowed by the impact of what the school represents symbolically to the village and its citizens. Exposure to the national primary school curriculum has explicitly introduced ideas, behaviors, and skills that transform the way Melemchi residents interact with each other and with the world external to the village. Even limited literacy skills allow some residents to read and write documents. As speakers and writers of the national language, they can participate as citizens in the national agenda. At the same time, education, even in the limited form in which it exists in Melemchi, may also contribute to the exodus of children from the gode and Yolmo itself, as it provides the skills and opportunities that make this possible.

MELEMCHI IN THE TWENTY-FIRST CENTURY: CHALLENGES OF THE FUTURE

Melemchi faces the twenty-first century with the village intact, although the resident middle-aged population is smaller than in the past, and the elderly and the very young predominate. Residents are using the fields, maintaining houses, and building new ones (eight since 2000); the infrastructure of water pipes and electrical power is working, and money is coming into the village in a steady stream. A visitor to Melemchi today would find the annual ritual cycle being performed, daily agricultural and domestic tasks underway, and a lively social scene. At the same time, a satellite community has sprung up in the Kathmandu Valley around the Boudhanath stupa, a pilgrimage site for Tibetan Buddhists worldwide and the entry/exit point for the Yolmo Valley. Although a few Melemchi people have always lived there (it is the second guthi of the Chini Lama and also the center for all Tibetan Buddhists in the Kathmandu Valley), a small number of young adults from Melemchi chose to settle and raise their families there beginning in the mid-1990s. They remain closely connected to their family members and friends in the village, hosting them when they come to get medical care, shop, or just visit. With telephones, televisions, and Internet access, they serve as a tracking system for news and information between the village and its far-flung residents. Most of these urban pioneers also have houses in the village but they don't live in them. They visit to escape from the noise, pollution, and summer heat of the Kathmandu Valley, but they do not stay. Some send their children up to the village to live for a while, attend school, or help relatives. These young adults do not see a future in village life, and are in growing numbers choosing to establish households in Boudhanath or to join temporarily the Melemchi expatriate community, which includes those who circulate annually for wage labor in India and those long-term international migrants who stay away for years.

What is the future for the village of Melemchi itself? Can a viable community be forged and sustained? On the one hand, people today extol the virtues of the village—especially the older folks. They say Melemchi is a healthier, more beautiful, more spiritual place in which to live than it used to be. On the other hand, all but the youngest sons are choosing to spend significant amounts of time away from the village. Certainly this question is being asked elsewhere in Yolmo as well. There, the answer to the latter question seems to be no. Once-thriving villages such as Tarke Ghyang and Sermathang are becoming ghost towns. Through quirks of geography, these villages have had no access to forest resources for a long time, and therefore have longer histories of migration involving a greater percentage of their population than Melemchi. So, what are the prospects for Melemchi in the twenty-first century?

The Changing Demography of Melemchi

One element that enables us to understand and predict the future of the Melemchi village is that its population dynamics, or demographics, change over time. How many people have rights to the resources of the village, and is the population growing or shrinking? Data collected over the years between 1971 and 1993 suggest that population growth in Melemchi has been declining since the 1970s when we first lived there. In 1971, 349 individuals belonged to Melemchi village. The Melemchi population pyramid[6] for 1971 is widest at the bottom and narrows as it moves to the top, indicating a rapidly growing population, with many more individuals in the younger age cohorts than in the older ones. In fact, in 1971, 47.3 percent of the Melemchi population was under the age of 20 years. This is close to the 50-percent figure that is characteristic of rapidly expanding populations of the developing world.

By 1993, the total population of Melemchi was 483. However, the age-sex structure of the village population was no longer a pyramid shape. The sides did not slope progressively inward as they did in 1971, and the largest cohort was not at the bottom (the youngest). In 1993, the largest cohorts were those aged 15 to 24 years of age, suggesting that the last big period of high fertility in this population occurred between 1968 and 1973. The percentage of the population under the age of 20 years has dropped to 35 percent, supporting the conclusion that although the Melemchi population in 1993 was still growing, the speed of growth diminished substantially in the 22 years between 1971 and 1993.

In an agro-pastoral system, large family size is desirable. Children of all ages provide useful labor that, in turn, produces the food necessary to feed them. More children can take care of more plants and animals that can then feed more children, etc. In Melemchi, where livestock of various kinds were managed simultaneously with year-round agriculture in the village, flexibility in household size, composition, and location was essential. Family members were deployed in a constantly changing array of jobs and locations, including wage labor in India. The slowing of population growth in Melemchi relates to the increase in dependence on migration for subsistence. Families who want to work in India or beyond view large families as a burden rather than a benefit—their children can't earn a wage, they feel pressure to educate them, and they need more money to support them in India, unlike in the village. The international birth control campaigns of the 1970s coincided with increased migration and a desire for smaller families in Melemchi, providing the means for achieving that goal.

In the past 10 years, a small but steady exodus of young Melemchi men have traveled to monasteries where they study to become monks. In some cases, parents have sent them as small boys, although most are men in their twenties who have chosen a life course that reflects their assessment of the options open to them: marriage, a life spent outside Nepal doing hard labor, managing a herd near the village, or the constant pressure to find some other way to make a living. As with external migration, boys go to monasteries where their friends have gone—one Melemchi boy went to Penar Rinpoche's monastery in South India, and most of the others followed after him, although a few study at monasteries in the Kathmandu Valley. This interest in the monastic life is probably related in some way to the resurgence of religious practice in the Yolmo region in general. As individual wealth has grown through successful participation in the labor market, people have more disposable income to spend on public displays of piety, such as sponsoring a religious rite or participating in a meditation retreat. Families can also now afford to support a member in the pursuit of monastic life. Service as a monk or nun is viewed as a credit both to an individual and the family. The demographic implications of this are linked to the monastic practice of celibacy. If an interest in monastic life increases, it may eventually help to slow population growth in Melemchi by further reducing the number of marriageable men who need land and resources to begin a family.

Today in Melemchi we can see the last of the traditional large families; the parents are now in their sixties or seventies, a few with as many as 10 living adult children. With such large families, it is still possible for one child to reside in the village and help the parents, while others live in Boudha or India. This sustains the viability of the village while simultaneously providing a family-based economic safety net for all. But, what of the next generations? These adults have only two or three children. Will it be possible for them to pursue a mixed economic strategy that will support residence in the village? Can the village remain large enough to sustain a community?

Dependence on External Remittance

Mountain populations the world around depend on support from outside the local environment, in addition to local subsistence activities, to sustain themselves. Tin mining in Bolivia, army service in Switzerland, pensions from Ghurka army service for villages in western Nepal—all provide external income to supplement the efforts of mountain villagers to live in difficult environments. For Melemchi, it is clear that to a greater or lesser extent, the villagers depend on income from wage labor to maintain life in the village itself. It is true that presently resources and support are available for anyone wishing to continue the traditional subsistence activities in Melemchi, but the younger generations have little to no interest to stay and do it. Circular migration, especially beyond India, is perceived today to be far more lucrative and certainly preferable to staying in the village. But exactly how viable this will be in the future is unclear.

Today Melemchi citizens are dispersed over longer distances and for longer periods of time than ever before. Unlike in the past when Melemchi residents crossed and recrossed the permeable boundaries between India and Nepal whenever they wanted to do so, today's migrants to areas outside South Asia are subject to international immigration policies that are beyond their control. Many young people who want to emigrate for work are unable to obtain the financial backing or the visa to do so. The first wave of international travel by Yolmo residents to Taiwan and Korea took advantage of the world sympathy directed toward Tibetans and their situation of exile. But today only a few individuals are able to obtain visas to places far away from Nepal. Immigration policies and their enforcement can change rapidly, leaving carefully made plans impossible to carry out. The difficulties of getting abroad and staying abroad mean that people stay for long periods of time. They work extraordinarily long hours with no time off, live in crowded conditions, and are vulnerable to all types of exploitation. Their entire existence is devoted to working and sending money home. In Taiwan they are restricted to the confines of the factory and the factory housing; in the United States they can move around freely, but they have no time or money for recreation or travel. Guest workers operate under the radar screen most of the time, but as we have seen in the United States following September 11th, international events can change that suddenly.

Migration across local borders is far easier, especially for circular migrants who want to cross often. The permeability of the India–Nepal border has supported two generations of Melemchi residents in life course strategies that, although less lucrative than today's international options, are more flexible and easier for individuals to control. Income from India has been flowing into Melemchi for over 50 years and is likely to continue. Other external sources are far less predictable.

Viability of the Village Subsistence System

Mountain populations around the world succeed by pursuing a flexible, mixed strategy, in which householders have multiple options simultaneously from which they continually adjust their choices depending on circumstances. For instance in Melemchi, herders and householders take advantage of opportunities to buy and sell livestock, to move their households between the village and pastures or between the village and India, and to invest in a number of different economic activities all at the same time. They derive their livelihood from several different production zones: they grow corn during spring at around 7,000 feet, grow wheat and potatoes the rest of the year at 8,500 feet, rent out a rice field down valley at 5,000 feet and split the proceeds with the tenant farmer, and herd zomo at pastures as high as 13,500 feet during summer months. They protect themselves against environmental changes that they cannot control, such as disease, bad weather, or landslides, by always having several options to fall back on.

Today most village residents subsist primarily on money from family members outside the village, supplemented by what they grow and income from managing lodges for trekkers or selling calves from their household cow or water buffalo. Although this mirrors the multiple strategies of the past, it obscures the fact that dependence on remittances from abroad overshadows all other sources of support.

A number of the residents are concerned about the lack of economic options within the village today and the future this portends. Various schemes have been proposed to make the village economically viable: setting up a hostel to house and care for elders in the Yolmo Valley who want to live in a beautiful place and meditate, building a regional secondary school for the valley or taking in boarders, and organizing trekking services in a more coherent fashion. People have also made individual attempts to develop new economic options within the village. Apple orchards have revitalized other regions of Nepal at these altitudes, but they have not done well in Melemchi. The high concentrations of wildlife make it difficult to protect orchards from depredation, and those apples and peaches that the deer and monkeys do not eat are small and tasteless. One enterprising individual has experimented with several new crops, including tea, without success. After all, traditional subsistence systems are the result of centuries of trial and error learning, as well as biological adaptation to a local environment. A few people have tried to improve the output of household cows by buying expensive European hybrid cows from nearby areas. Unfortunately, these cows are much larger than the local hill cattle, and require huge amounts of fodder, which taxes the elderly residents who thought this would make an easy source of income. The hybrid cows get sick at these altitudes, and ultimately everyone who has tried this lost money. The presence of the National Park eliminates the possibility of harvesting natural resources for profit. For example, it is impossible to make paper, or gather forest products such as mushrooms, bamboo shoots, or wood for sale. It isn't just a matter of finding the right ideas. Unreliable electricity, poor access to roads, and more lucrative options in India are probably bigger factors in thwarting new subsistence options in Melemchi.

Of course, it is always possible that the global marketplace will come to Melemchi. In 1995, construction began on a major water project that will tap the water from the Melemchi River just south of the village and take it via a 27-kilometer tunnel through the mountains into the Kathmandu Valley. Plans include a road from Kathmandu that will nearly reach Melemchi. The people of Melemchi have no control over the development of the Greater Kathmandu

Water Supply Project and have no experience upon which to base any concern. It is likely that the existence of a year-round road that brings trucks up into this isolated area will change the lives of Melemchi people in ways difficult to predict today. Although roads provide access to markets for forest products, they also provide access to forest products for outsiders who want to exploit them. Resource extraction by governments or international companies often operates on a scale that can destroy the local environment for those living there. Mountain people worldwide are vulnerable to outside exploitation of the few resources they depend on: hydropower, timber, minerals, water, and space. For example, historian Richard Tucker (1987) describes the wholesale deforestation of vast forest tracts in India during the nineteenth century to build the Indian railway system, the summer hill stations for the British Raj, and roads. Hydroelectric projects that dam up major rivers displace whole communities, change water availability and supply, and alter ecosystems dependent on that water.

Finally, the viability of the village has always been sustained by the fact that at any particular time, only some of those who have rights to village resources are actually living in the village and exercising those rights. As long as the availability of work and good wages in India and elsewhere continues, the local population will place low demand for park resources. But this can change in the future, and if all those with a claim on village resources were to return, it would be difficult for the local ecosystem and the national park regulations to accommodate those needs.

Maintaining Cultural Knowledge

Melemchi adults over 50 years of age today are culture bearers of a way of life that has sustained humans in this mountain region for hundreds of years. They know things that are necessary to sustain life in that place. They know how to tell when a zomo is ready to breed, how to distill whiskey, how to make their own rope, paper, and baskets, how to build a house out of stones, how to thresh wheat, how to find wild food at any season, how to be a midwife to a cow or a human, and how to carry a load of over 100 pounds on their back up a mountainside without hurting themselves. They can conduct Tibetan Buddhist rituals, remember the words and tunes for hundreds of songs known only to the local community, and recount the birth years and names of most of the children born in the village during the past 50 years.

Their children and their grandchildren share some of this knowledge, especially if they have spent time in the village. In addition, these younger generations speak the Nepali language, and some Hindi or English. Although young adults in Melemchi today sport stylish haircuts, tee shirts with rock band logos, and baseball caps, and can dance the latest Hindi movie dance numbers, those who have grown up or spent significant amounts of time in the village hold much of the traditional knowledge and can function as competent adult members of the community.

The greatest concern to Melemchi residents of all ages is how to maintain this cultural knowledge for the growing numbers of Melemchi residents who live outside the country. Those who have relocated permanently outside Nepal are a lost cause,[7] but many do return to Nepal and to Melemchi periodically, and most young people today say they intend to return permanently, at least to Bhoudanath, when they finish their work abroad. Of course, there is no way for anyone to know if this will happen, but the intention is clear. Our Melemchi friend, whose baby was born a U.S. citizen in New York, describes her imagined future this way: "I will stay six months every year in Melemchi and six months in Kathmandu. When we get older, sometime we will visit our daughter, Tenzin, in New York."

The knowledge at stake for these people is not only the traditional subsistence knowledge, but also the cultural traditions and language. The widespread availability of tape recorders, video cameras, and still cameras helps maintain cultural contact, providing both residents and migrants with the opportunity to stay in touch. Tibetan New Year celebrants in Melemchi make videotapes to exchange with Melemchi guest workers in New York City who celebrate in a social hall, so everyone can see each other and affirm that the traditions are being observed. Inexpensive long-distance phone calls through the Internet, as well as e-mail, are other ways that villagers stay connected with Melemchi people overseas and those living in Kathmandu. Maintaining connections is the first step in ensuring return of these people, and the opportunity for exchanging and maintaining cultural traditions. This is pursued at a more explicit level as well. In the past five years, two organizations have been founded that are dedicated to the preservation of Yolmo culture. With headquarters in the Yolmo enclave of Boudhanath in the Kathmandu Valley, young Yolmo men who want to preserve Yolmo traditions and language head these organizations. They are social centers where events are held for the urban Yolmo community, as well as service organizations that help members of the community in need. Even the expatriate community in New York collects money to support these efforts.

Yolmo villages have visibly changed as the result of participation in a global market economy. The widespread availability of cash has spawned new technology and practices in Melemchi. Traditionally, bartered wealth was invested in agricultural fields or herds. Now, cash buys tin roofs, airtight stoves, VCRs, televisions, and for some families, satellite dishes. Children wear school uniforms; little girls play in fancy frilly dresses. Although these changes may signal the demise of Melemchi culture to some, certainly Melemchi residents don't view them in that light. Tin roofs don't need to be replaced as often as wood shingle roofs, and someone can be hired to carry the tin up to the village from Kathmandu rather than cutting and hauling all that wood every four years. Airtight stoves produce much less smoke, freeing women from the respiratory illnesses of the past. Participating in the world marketplace, through consumption of images (video and television), information (news), and goods (dresses), makes residents feel less isolated and backward, fostering pride in their village and a reason to remain.

CONCLUSION

In my case study, *Himalayan Herders* (Bishop 1998), I emphasize the importance of historical factors, geographic/ecological factors, and cultural factors in understanding the village of Melemchi and its position within Yolmo. These factors influenced the ways in which the Melemchi culture developed and changed over time. They will also influence its future, but the future for Melemchi will also be negotiated within yet new parameters—across extended boundaries that are even hard to define today.

How would I have ever thought in 1971 that I would ride a New York subway train one day with three friends from Melemchi? On our way to see the Empire State building, I realized that the other people in the subway car had no idea that these three young men were talking in a language that exists only in one small river valley in the Nepal Himalaya. In the international amalgam of New York City, these young men fit in with everyone else in the car. And in all likelihood, languages from several other river valleys were being spoken in that car at that very moment too. At one point, one of my friends turned to me and said, "You know, you are probably the only American on this train."

We were in New York to attend the Sonam Losar (Tibetan New Year) celebration with approximately 150 people from the Yolmo Valley who had somehow ended up in the United States. In the village, Sonam Losar is celebrated by spending a day in each household in the village, or with each family of close relatives, for up to eight or nine days of visiting and celebration, including reciprocating the hospitality in your own house. At each house or gode, guests are fed a special ritual meal as well as a second meal late in the afternoon. The point is to visit with your relatives, to feed each other special foods, and to relax during a time of year when little work needs to be done.

In the United States, Sonam Losar is centered around one big party. Everyone saves up vacation time, and a few brave souls quit their jobs if the boss doesn't agree to let them attend. A committee spends all year working on the arrangements; they hire a hall, arrange an Indian caterer for the meal, and plan every detail of the event. People start arriving in early afternoon and the party lasts until well after midnight. The ritual aspects of the food are maintained, with slight variations, whether in Melemchi, Boudhanath, or New York. First, drinks are served, in a particular order: salted butter tea, then sweet tea or coffee, then alcohol. In the village the alcoholic beverage would be fermented grain beer or homemade distilled liquor; in Boudhanath and New York, guests are offered a choice of Budweiser, whiskey, or cream sherry. With drinks come plates of pounded rice. After a few hours, the formal part of the evening begins. Everyone receives the ritual plate of Losar food, with three fried rice flour breads, two fried whole wheat breads twisted into a double figure eight, meat curry, and potato/radish curry. Butter, or tub margarine in New York, decorates the breads and the plate. Once everyone is served, a Yolmo lama offers a blessing, which is followed by a speech of welcome from the head of the organizing committee. Then the *sholgar* is performed, in which selected men lift the blessed bottles of beer high in the air and chant. While everyone eats their plates of food, community members entertain with a music and dance show. Groups of older men and women begin the show with traditional Yolmo line dancing and singing. Then the program moves on to young men and women who dance and lip-synch to Nepali or Hindi pop songs. One year, two young men performed a lengthy skit involving a call home to the village. As one man pretended to talk to various family members (all played by his partner), the audience roared with laughter at the

© John Bishop

Proud father and son with the first satellite dish installed in Melemchi by them next to their house in 2000.

linguistic misunderstandings, the village "types" who got on the phone, and the awkwardness of family relationships conducted over long-distance phone calls. The show ends with more contemporary Hindi dance routines and a raffle. At that point, someone starts the Yolmo line dancing and singing that characterize every festival or wedding in the villages of Yolmo. This goes on for several hours. Yolmo expats have developed subtle variations on the traditional songs, often ad-libbed to much hilarity, and with mostly young participants, the tempo is faster than at home. Around 11:00 p.m. the music switches to a DJ and disco music for dancing, and the party goes on into the early morning hours.

Although the ceremonial bread is daubed with soft margarine, the salted butter tea is made in a blender, and we are entertained by a talent show featuring teenagers and young adults miming Hindi film songs and dances or break dancing, the essential elements of Losar are preserved. The Losar celebration in New York includes specific food, gathering and homecoming, visiting, and presentation of a ritual plate of food to friends and family. The added elements of a rented hall, a talent show set to commercial Indian and Nepali music, and traditional Yolmo singing and dancing do not occur in Melemchi, but represent an accommodation to the size, ages, and available resources of the diasporic community. Sonam Losar provides a once-a-year opportunity to see friends, reenact shared cultural patterns, and celebrate identity. And Yolmo people aren't alone in this. The talent show at the New York Sonam Losar mirrors those performed at Hindu Dassai celebrations organized by Nepalis all over the United States. Combining traditional and popular forms of entertainment and aesthetic expression, these shows are hugely popular with Nepalis away from home.

Our friends in New York are breaking new ground and it is difficult to imagine just what the future holds for the Melemchi village and those who have claim to it. Attempts to make sense of the present and visualize the future can only partially rely on our understanding of the past. Melemchi people never predict the future, whether it involves which day they will leave on a journey or whether their children will live in a gode when they grow up—I can see now that perhaps they are on to something.

REFERENCES

Bishop, John, and Naomi Bishop. 1978. *An ever-changing place*. New York, NY: Simon and Schuster.

Bishop, John, and Naomi Bishop. 1998. *Himalayan herders*. Film. 75 min. Distributed by Media Generation (http://www.media-generation.com).

Bishop, Naomi. 1998. *Himalayan herders*. Fort Worth, TX: Harcourt Brace College Publishers.

Bailey, Adrian J., and Hane, Joshua G. 1995. Population in motion: Salvadorean refugees and circular migration. *Bulletin of Latin American Research* 14 (2): 171–200.

Brower, Barbara. 1991. *Sherpa of Khumbu: People, livestock, and landscape*. New Delhi: Oxford Univ. Press.

Metz, John. 1994. A framework for classifying subsistence production types of Nepal. *Human Ecology:* 17 (2) :147–176.

Panter-Brick, Catherine. 1986. The "Goths" of Salme, Nepal: A strategy for animal husbandry and working behavior. *Production Pastorale et Société*, no. 19:30–41.

Shrestha, Nanda R. 1993. Nepal: The society and its environment. In *Nepal and Bhutan: Country studies,* ed. Andrea Savada, 53–100. Washington DC: Library of Congress.

Tucker, Richard. 1987. Dimensions of deforestation in the Himalaya: The historical setting. *Mountain Research and Development* 7 (3): 328–331.

NOTES

1. For information about the village of Melemchi (trekking information, sacred sites, photographs, etc.) see the Melemchi Web site: http://www.melemchi.org.

2. This region of Nepal is also called Yermu by local people, or Helambu by the Nepal government.

3. Exogamy refers to the practice of marrying outside the group—in this case, *clan exogamy* means that a man must marry a woman from a clan different from his own. Marrying someone from within one's clan is considered incestuous.

4. The word *gode* literally refers to the living shelter made of bent poles covered with bamboo mats that is carried from pasture to pasture when the herd moves. It also is synonymous with being a herder and owning a herd. To say, "I live in a *gode,*" or "I have a *gode,*" means that I own a herd and live out year-round with my herd—I follow the herding lifestyle.

5. A *guthi* is a form of land grant given as patronage by the king in support of a religious institution. In 1859 the Chini Lama of Boudhanath was given the Melemchi gomba as a guthi. He had the right to share in the produce of the land attached to it, to enact and receive taxes from the residents, to receive unpaid labor from the residents, and to dispense justice within the village. Nepal

abandoned most guthi grants by 1971, but the Melemchi guthi was an exception.

6. A population pyramid is a diagram of the population at a certain point in time, organized by age and sex. The population is divided into five five-year age cohorts, starting at the bottom: the number of males and females in the population who are between 0 and 4 years old, then the number of those between 5 and 9 years old, then the number of those who are between 10 and 14 years old, etc. Males are on the left side of the center vertical line and females are on the right side. A population that is growing should be widest at the bottom (lots of births) and should gradually taper off into a peak at the top—a pyramid shape. Growing populations have many babies born, and thus the largest cells at the bottom of the pyramid.

7. In 1971, some individuals who had gone to work in India had either disappeared, or had made the decision to stay permanently outside Nepal. Although a few of these people have returned to visit an aged parent once or twice since 1971, they are to all intents and purposes Indian residents and no longer part of the village population.

Some Yolmo people have lived their whole lives outside Nepal. For them cultural identity takes on a more complex guise. We received a poignant e-mail from a young man in college in India. He had seen our Web site on Melemchi and wrote to us. He explained that he was the grandson of an old village friend of ours, the son of a man already working and living in India when we arrived in Melemchi in 1971. This young man referred to himself as "from Melemchi" but acknowledged he had never been there, did not speak the language, and was attending a computer course in a small college in northern India. He had no idea about life in the village and thanked us for helping him learn about "his" culture.

Fieldwork Biography
Robert Tonkinson

© Bob Tonkinson

Most of Bob Tonkinson's fieldwork among desert Aborigines in Western Australia's arid central-north has been done at Jigalong, initially when it was still a Christian mission in the 1960s, and later when it became an incorporated self-managing Aboriginal community. He also accompanied several expeditions into the desert interior in the early to mid-1960s, when contacts were made with the few remaining groups of nomads still living traditionally. In 1965, he served as anthropological advisor during the making of Film Australia's *Peoples of the Australian Western Desert,* a series of documentary movies about desert culture. Since 1963, he has returned countless times, spending a total of more than four years in the Western Desert and documenting several decades of social change. His wife, fellow anthropologist Myrna Ewart Tonkinson, has also worked with the Mardu people, beginning in 1974. They are currently in the midst of a major study of social trauma and coping strategies. Both researchers are affiliated with the University of Western Australia and continue to write on issues affecting the Mardu people; they remain in close contact with Mardu friends, whose basic optimism and keen sense of humor continue to bolster them in their continuing struggle for social justice.

10/The Mardu Aborigines
On the Road to Somewhere

INTRODUCING THE MARDU ABORIGINES

The Mardu today number about one thousand and live in several Aboriginal communities and small towns in the northwest of Western Australia. "Mardu," meaning "person" or "persons," is a collective name now used by several groups whose ancestral homelands surround Lake Disappointment (Kumpupintil), a large salt lake straddling the Tropic of Capricorn on the west side of the Western Desert (see Figure 10.1). This vast region covers about half a million square miles, or one-sixth of the Australian continent, which is almost the same size as continental United States (excluding Alaska). Topographically, it is a mosaic of surprisingly diverse ecozones: parallel sand ridges, gravelly plains, prairie-like expanses of spinifex (grass), dry riverbeds lined with large eucalyptus trees, stony breakaway country, gorges with pools and subtropical plant regimes, clay-pans, and salt lakes. Yet surface water is rare and ephemeral, and this region has been aptly described as "probably the most undependable and impoverished habitat anywhere in the world where people have succeeded in living entirely off

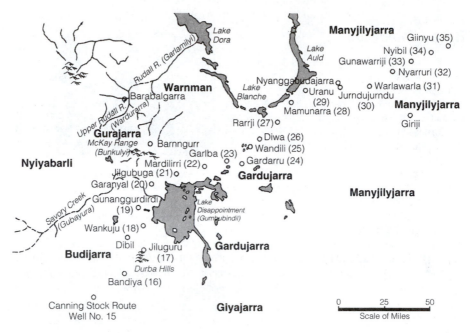

Figure 10.1 Mardu territory.

the land" (Gould 1969; 1971, 145). Certainly, Europeans tend to see it this way, especially during its furnace-like summers. Archaeological evidence suggests that the ancestors of the desert Aborigines first occupied the region more than 20,000 years ago (O'Connor et al. 1998).

After British colonization, the Mardu and their neighbors were protected from invasion and settlement by the desert's daunting aridity, which, when combined with highly erratic patterns of precipitation, rules out pastoralism and agriculture. Not surprisingly, this was the last Australian frontier, which ended in the desert in the 1960s when the last previously uncontacted groups walked or were taken into fringe settlements, almost two centuries after British settlement began, near where Sydney now stands. By this time, of course, those Aborigines whose homelands were in "settled" Australia had been thoroughly dispossessed, dislocated, and to a large extent submerged by the British invaders.

As members of Aboriginal Australia's largest single cultural bloc, known as the Western Desert, the Mardu shared basically the same language, social organization, religion, and value system (Berndt 1959). They were part of a vast regional system whose members numbered only several thousand and lived in small dispersed groups, obliged by ecological circumstances to be scattered thinly across great expanses and to pursue a nomadic hunter-gatherer mode of adaptation. Nonetheless, they were interlinked and integrated into a single society by multiple chains of overlapping cultural connections, forged via kinship, marriage, shared religious responsibilities and values, and a fundamentally homogeneous worldview. Ecological circumstances made it inevitable that spatial boundaries would be highly permeable to maximize access to the territories of neighboring groups in times of prolonged drought, and that cultural values favoring cooperation and mutuality would predominate over tendencies toward local ethnocentrism or competitive behaviors (see Tonkinson 1988b). Amid almost constant movement, Western Desert "society" writ large achieved its maximum visibility only periodically, and even then only for brief durations, during "big meetings" (*japal*). These prearranged assemblies brought large numbers of people from contiguous areas together for an intensely social and exciting occasion, lasting a week or two. At such times, much vital social and religious business was transacted. They publicly settled outstanding disputes, arranged betrothals, carried out a range of initiatory activities for young men, performed numerous other rituals, exchanged religious and secular property and knowledge, elevated men and women within the ritual status hierarchy, planned for further gatherings, and so on. Aboriginal societies were not at all centralized, so the big meeting was a crucially important manifestation of regionalism. It reminded people that, despite living in small local groups with very strong attachments to their heartlands, they were in fact part of a larger moral universe "out there." Later, the settlement situation would become something akin to a permanent "big meeting" site, but one in which their more settled existence permitted them not merely to greatly increase the body of pooled religious knowledge but also to deepen and strengthen it. This was true in the earlier years, at least, before the distractions of an evermore intrusive "whitefella business" began to affect what many Aborigines in rural and remote areas have come to refer to as "Law business."[1]

FIELDWORK AMONG THE MARDU

I began anthropological research among the Mardu in 1963. Over the past 40 years I have made many return visits, prompting much reflection about their society and culture, and the unrelenting pressure placed upon them as a consequence of their embeddedness within a remote and largely unknowable nation state. My first monograph about them, *The Jigalong Mob* (1974), was one of a number of anthropological case studies about the powerful impacts of Westernizing pressures on small-scale societies, with a particular focus on the coping strategies that indigenous peoples inevitably develop when confronted by unprecedented change. That study concerned a particular period (1946–1969) in the postcontact history of the Mardu, when they were engaged in a lengthy and sometimes bitter struggle against fundamentalist missionaries who had come to convert them to Christianity. In 1974, I spent almost a year back in the settlement of Jigalong (this time accompanied by my wife, who is also a social anthropologist). During that time, I largely responded to whatever the Mardu asked of me as I witnessed the initial impacts of a major change in federal government policy towards Aborigines. Subsequently, I wrote a number of papers about the accelerating rate of social and cultural change that was testing the adaptive capacities of the Mardu.

In a 1978 case study entitled *The Mardudjara Aborigines* (revised and published as *The Mardu Aborigines* in 1991), I depicted the society prior to the encroachment of Europeans. In the 1970s, much of Mardu worldview was still structured in terms of continuities with their traditional past, because most of the adult generation had been raised in the desert away from any direct contact with whites. In reconstructing the traditional society, I thus had much ethnographic data to work with. In addition, I questioned older people who still remembered aspects of Mardu society and life in the desert that had been a part of their lived reality. Not wishing to leave readers of the second monograph with an impression that the Mardu had remained frozen in a time warp, I rounded off the case study with an overview of the era since European intrusion and settlement triggered a cascade of irreversible changes in Mardu lives.

For more than a decade since 1990, my association with the Mardu was dominated by my role as the consultant anthropologist for a native title claim they had lodged over their traditional homeland areas. Until the 1970s, they had been living in ignorance of the fact that they did not still own their ancestral lands. Then exploratory and proving activities associated with mineral resources development (carried out without consultation with the relevant Aboriginal groups) led to damage to some of their religiously significant sites. Ever since this revelation, the Mardu became more and more concerned about protecting their country against such desecration. In recent decades, relationships between Aborigines and the mining industry have improved markedly nationwide, and the Mardu are now more amenable to resource development, though they remain firmly opposed to the development of a uranium mine on their lands.

Following the historic Mabo decision of Australia's High Court in 1992, which affirmed that British conquest had not fully extinguished indigenous Australians' native title, and the subsequent Native Title Act of 1993, the Mardu redoubled their efforts to gain ownership of their ancestral lands by lodging a native title application.[2] The Mardu claim was very strong because of their continuing and close association with these lands (some of the Mardu settlements lie within the claim boundaries), as evidenced by the huge body of "law and customs" that constitute the basis for native title. My task was to assemble and review all available anthropological data on the claim area, undertake several field trips to elicit additional supportive material, and then compile a "connection report" attesting to the veracity of past and continuing Mardu associations with the claimed territory. The regional Land Council duly submitted this report to the state government in September 2002, and native title was granted to most of the land sought. Missing was the Rudall River National Park, which, also unbeknown to the Mardu at the time, had been gazetted over a large area of their homelands in 1977. Following recent negotiations between the Mardu and the relevant authorities, however, it now seems likely that the Mardu will obtain substantial control over this land as well.

Since 2002, my wife and I have been engaged in a joint research project that is investigating how the Mardu have coped with more than three decades of severe social trauma, in large part a consequence of immense changes in the way Mardu live in the postcolonial era. One of the most obvious changes is the increasing accessibility of alcohol to the Mardu, and a rapid escalation of alcohol-related deaths. In addition, deaths from Western lifestyle diseases such as diabetes, renal and liver failure, and hypertension have risen, as have the levels of violence and motor vehicle accidents attributable to drunken driving. In the current project we aim to identify the ramifications for surviving Mardu of the loss and disruption that death, disease, and changed conditions are imposing. We are also attempting to assess in general the impact that television, videos, improved transportation, education, and greater knowledge of the outside world have on their worldview, values, ambitions, possible future movements, and their attitudes to religion. Evidence we have collected so far points to the continuing power of kinship, location, and community norms in shaping their sense of self and cultural conservatism, even though young Mardu appear to be experiencing a great deal more exposure to Western values and influences from the outside than preceding generations.

CONCEPTUALIZING SOCIAL CHANGE AND THE CHALLENGE TO ANALYSIS

Before embarking on this account of the Mardu, I would like to say something in general anthropological terms about how social and cultural change may be approached to illuminate its dynamics over time and space. Today, we live in an age of mass communications, with distances shrinking and the distinction between "local versus global" becoming ever more blurred in the face of pervasive Westernizing pressures. These are some of the many factors that have moved anthropologists to urgent debate over the future of our central concept of "culture" (see Cerroni-Long 1999) and the relevance of the "small-scale society" as a research locale. It seems, though, that as long as our fieldwork continues to yield evidence of resistance to outside influences and the persistence of difference, the concept of culture will retain its centrality for us as social scientists. Although we now live in an era of "moving populations, multilocal social worlds, displaced allegiances, and circulating meanings" (Appadurai 1997, 115), human social life is still played out through "the practices of intimacy—the work of sexuality and reproduction, the webs of nurture and of friendship, the heat of anger and violence, the nuance of gesture and tone" (ibid., 116).

Contemporary anthropological views of culture are frequently event-centered, stressing its fluid characteristics of contestation and negotiability. Such views have a tendency to focus more on the internal heterogeneity of culture rather than unity and harmony—or, in the words of A. F. C. Wallace (1961), more on "the organization of diversity" than on "the replication of uniformity" as keys to our understanding of social coherence. Of particular note in anthropological attempts to understand the vital connection between individual decision making and systemic social change has been the work of the American anthropologist, Clifford Geertz (1973). His symbolic interactionist approach shifted focus from structures and systems by depicting culture as constituted in and from the experiences of daily life. This provided its human creators and carriers with both "models of" and "models for" social reality. Another prominent scholar, Sherry Ortner (1984), noted in an influential essay on theory in anthropology, that such approaches accept that the system in which the action takes place has important constraining effects on human action and the shaping of events, but social scientists seek to discover where the "system" comes from, how it is produced and reproduced, and how changes occur.

In attempting to explain the often-devastating impacts of the spread of European "civilization" on the rest of the world, many observers have lamented the "collapse" of small-scale societies, depicting them as essentially brittle things. For example, "technologies introduced from a more instrumentally powerful culture into traditional society 'burn like a cigarette on a silken fabric' into the wholeness of the cultural patterns that existed before" (Hill 1988, 75). However, anthropologists have long been wary of "collapse" theories. For instance, Hogbin, in his discussion of social change processes, employs a metaphor similar to that of Hill yet offers a very different perspective: "Although the social fabric of the traditional culture is being unraveled, the threads are not lying in a completely disordered tangle. Some of them have been gathered up in an attempt to weave a new cloth based on a different set of patterns" (1958, 51). Almost 70 years ago, American anthropologist Ralph Linton (1936), discussed cultural borrowing, by far the most common source of innovation. He pointed out that the transfer that occurs is almost exclusively of form, but that alien elements inevitably undergo transformations in meaning, functions, and contexts of use when borrowed by members of a different society. Back in 1958, Ian Hogbin reminded us that societies confronted by sudden alien incursion simply do not disintegrate—unless of course, they are physically exterminated. Rather, from the moment of initial contact with foreigners the society's members have no option (other than taking flight) but to struggle ceaselessly to reintegrate their lives around newly negotiated, and often conflicting, understandings of what is happening to them. In other words, as things begin to fall apart under conditions of extreme inequality in power relations, the people affected must generate from their own intellectual resources a reactive process of resistance amid reconstruction.

This adaptive process entails that individuals and groups pick up the pieces of their practices, beliefs, values, and institutions and rearrange them into forms that may be new but nonetheless still make sense to them—in other words, that accord with their own *cultural logic*. As before contact, individuals and groups embed meanings in their "design for living," but in the face of unprecedented changes they are forced to engage in a continual process of redesign. The reintegrative process, then, which always involves a synthesis of indigenous, alien, and newly created elements, makes it difficult to conceive of anything remaining "traditional" much past the point of contact, because new meanings are embedded in the indigenous society from the moment the foreigners invade. Sometimes new meanings are embedded even before contact, such as in the case of the New Guinea Highlander and their response to the sighting of airplanes years prior to actual contact with Europeans. Marshall Sahlins, in an influential work focusing on early contact between Hawaiians and Europeans, has demonstrated very well the transformative potential built into frontier interaction: existing cultural categories take on new values, thus altering cultural meanings and transforming "traditional" structures (1985).

Continuity and change are essentially two sides of the same processual coin. Initially, the many obvious continuities that linked living Mardu to their recent "pre-European" existence dominated my research attention, but over time my research trajectory has shifted inexorably to one that foregrounds transformations in the analysis of Western impacts. Attempting to capture the major elements of

Jigalong Mission day cooks preparing ritual food

change and piece together their complex ramifications in a single account is a huge challenge. In the short term, particularly, a major problem for anthropological analysis lies in differentiating small organizational changes that prove to be temporary from those that later become structural and thereby more enduring and influential. The only effective solution is repeated fieldwork visits, or what anthropologists often call "the extended case method."

In this chapter I lay out both a rough chronology of change as it has affected and been accepted or contested by the Mardu over time. I also identify changes in both processes and structures of society that must be described if the nature of transformation is to be adequately understood. It is, of course, vital to acknowledge the disempowering and disfiguring effects of historical processes on Aboriginal people, and the huge disparity in power that has characterized relations between the British invaders and themselves. Yet it is equally important to emphasize the role of Mardu individuals and groups as conscious agents of change, actively participating in the process rather than inertly absorbing change.

A dramatic change in status from highly autonomous desert nomads to citizen constituents in a modern nation-state has been the lived experience of older Mardu adults. This often prompts them to make evaluative comments contrasting the present with the past. Yet Mardu tend not to philosophize about, analyze, or attempt to dissect and disentangle the many strands of change—individual and collective—that have engaged their attention and tested their adaptive capabilities since leaving the desert. Theirs has been a running battle, often emotionally fraught, to protect and maintain their cultural integrity in an adverse situation in terms of power relations. The core of the worldview bequeathed them by their religion and the Dreaming is one that discourages questioning and skepticism, and thus favors an absence of much self-reflection in people's discourse. As a result of relative isolation, and the retention of their language and cultural values, the Mardu are among the minority of indigenous Australians who display the most evident continuities with the traditions of their precolonial past.

THE MARDU IN A WIDER AUSTRALIAN CONTEXT

Many of the changes documented here have parallels elsewhere in Aboriginal Australia. Just as the traditional cultural landscape could be well described as a set of variations on a set of underlying similar themes, the outcomes of Western impacts throughout Aboriginal Australia show considerable likeness in both trajectory and contemporary manifestations. Aboriginal people comprise less than 2 percent of the total Australian population, and remain firmly at the bottom of the socioeconomic ladder. Members of the dominant society know little about how greatly racism and colonial history have contributed to the oppression, marginalization, and continuing chronic disadvantage that Aborigines suffer. People commonly tend to "blame the victims" and to resent as unfair the body of legislation aimed at correcting indigenous disadvantage lest it create two "nations," which in fact is what Australia already effectively has. Racist attitudes remain strong, though Aborigines in remote areas, like the Mardu, are much less aware of racism than their rural and urban counterparts. Their isolation often shields them from the most blatant and insidious forms of racism.

In general and historical terms, and inasmuch as non-Western peoples in small-scale societies have choices with respect to the acceptance or rejection of Western cultural elements, the Aborigines have tended to readily adopt many material cultural items, adapting them to traditional needs where appropriate. Their own traditional technologies, fashioned in the desert regions mainly from wood, stone, and bone, had to be lightweight, portable, and multipurpose, befitting their nomadic adaptation: wooden bowls and digging sticks for women; stone knives and adzes, spears, spear-throwers, clubs, boomerangs, and shields for men. Aboriginal Australia had no specialist manufacturers; every adult male and female possessed the skills necessary to fashion their own implements, and the status of such objects in the culture was practical and utilitarian, unembellished by any panoply of symbolic significances and rituals surrounding their use. When confronted with Western objects, the Aborigines were thus free to accept them as demonstrably useful, sometimes as clearly superior in durability or design to their own technologies, and in most cases no threat to any established and cherished values (Tonkinson 1994).

Yet, with regard to such culturally important elements as ideologies, ethos, religious beliefs, and values, all of which underpin and shape worldview, Aboriginal reactions have typically been conservative and resistant. A prominent example would have to be their response to Christianity, which failed, until relatively recently at least, to gain a solid foothold in Aboriginal Australia, in stark contrast to its rapid and widespread acceptance in nearby Oceania. Christianity seemed incapable of dislodging the Aboriginal religious system, which was so pervasive and strongly integrated that it was synonymous with, and inseparable from, the fabric of life itself (Tonkinson 1991; forthcoming).

Aboriginal religion in almost all of the continent centered on the "the Dreaming," a timeless "everywhen" embracing both a past creative epoch, in the course of which all things that now exist came to be as they are (cf. Stanner 1979; Berndt and Berndt 1988), and the present and future, because humans must faithfully reproduce its forms and obey its dictates if society is to continue and thrive (see Tonkinson 1991, chap. 1). The huge complex of beliefs and activities that comprise the Dreaming, together with the institution of kinship, are the twin pillars supporting the entire edifice of Aboriginal society and culture. In the creative era, a host of superhuman beings from an unspecified somewhere arrived and set out to populate and transform the previously flat and featureless Australian landmass. By their activities, many of which resemble the behaviors and experiences of humans good and bad, they created diverse, religiously charged landforms, richly imprinted mass with meaning and replete with fauna and flora. During their wanderings and numerous adventures, they established rituals and human institutions. These set in place for all time the various groups, their languages, and cultural characteristics, and bound the first humans to a kind of contract. Through obedience to the laws of the Dreaming and the proper and regular performance of rituals, living Aborigines were charged with keeping the whole cosmic system of order going. This would occur under the watchful and caring gaze of the creative beings, who are said to have withdrawn into the spiritual realm at the conclusion of their earthly activities, yet remain somewhere "out there." They monitor human affairs without direct interference, but stay in touch via spirit-being messengers through whom they channel new knowledge and ritual elements into human society. This connection ensures a lively and dynamic religious life and a society whose members remain keenly aware of the proximity and relevance of spiritual powers to their well-being and future existence. Failure by humans to uphold the human blueprint will cause the inhabitants of the spiritual realm to cut off the flow of power into human society and bring all life to an end, thus the spiritual imperative or contract is literally world-shattering in its import for the living.

Each succeeding generation is charged with the enormous responsibility for society's continuing reproduction. It is therefore little wonder that male initiation is such a protracted and culturally prominent process in Aboriginal societies, given that mature men are held disproportionately responsible for this vital task. Among all the Australian desert peoples, the complex of rituals surrounding male initiation was the most protracted and highly elaborated element of their religious life. Mardu boys' bodies were marked physically via a series of rituals, the most important of which were circumcision at puberty, then subincision a year or so later, which marked them as adult. As in many other parts of the world, circumcision was symbolically modeled on the death of the boy and his subsequent rebirth as a new adult person. Novices were then inducted through a series of named stages or levels that deepened and fixed their knowledge and understanding. This gave them greater religious responsibility until, around their late twenties, they were deemed ready for marriage, which brought full entry into social adulthood (see Tonkinson 1991).

The Aboriginal social system was one in which novelty and change emanating from outside the Dreaming would have been as unthinkable as were notions of revolution or progress. Thus the present was modeled exactly on the past, as ordained, and the changes that inevitably occurred were held to result from revelations emanating from the spiritual realm. These innovations were divorced from individual human intellectual effort and rapidly absorbed back into the realm of the Dreaming, which hovers somewhere just beyond the reach of either human memory or attempts to manipulate the transcendent spiritual powers for personal reasons (Tonkinson 1991; forthcoming). In the situation of the Mardu, as in many similarly remote areas of the interior and north of the continent today, the tenacity of the Dreaming as the key cultural symbol has been the most powerful and persistent continuity framing their adaptation over time.

As indicated previously, religion was one of two central pillars on which Aboriginal societies rested; the second was kinship, a network of social relationships radiating out from each person, and couched in a familial idiom ("father," "daughter," "mother's mother," etc.). Kinship was the major organizing principle for social behavior throughout Australia (see Tonkinson 1987). It is a key determinant of the who, when, how, why, and wherefore that guide an individual's actions, or inaction, where others are concerned. Traditionally, Aborigines lived in a universe of kin where virtually no relationship of deference, obligation, equality, or dominance was free from considerations of kinship; thus "strangers" could never interact until their specific kin relationship was reckoned and announced during a formal introduction. Although modifications have been made to this system of interaction, to a great extent Mardu still observe many of the kinship-derived rules of behavior. Every other person with whom one interacts is called by a kinship term, which establishes a set of expected behaviors between the two people so related. So you behave roughly the same toward all women you call "father's sister," though the emotional content of these behaviors will of course vary according to factors like age, biological closeness, and sentiment. These sets of behaviors range along a continuum from, at the least restrained end, totally uninhibited joking relationships, through to complete avoidance at the maximum restraint end.

Kinship provides a ready-made general guide to action, and one cannot begin to make sense of what is going on in a traditional Aboriginal society until one grasps the structuring and operation of its particular system of reckoning relationships. Marriage rules are also a function of kinship, and in every system there will be a kin category translatable as "spouse." Although children do not have to abide by the rules, they are constantly learning how the system works and will, before puberty and increasing self-consciousness, begin conforming without any external prompting. In small-scale hunting-gathering societies, most of which are egalitarian in spirit, the kinship system can comfortably handle the level of demand for direction and decision making. Not surprisingly, the system cuts right across factors of age, gender, and biological relatedness. It works out so that asymmetrical or unequal sets of obligation and responsibility obtain between members of adjacent generations. Symmetry and informality are the norm with same-generation members plus those of grandparents and grandchildren. Each adult person is at the center of a network of relationships. In the case of the asymmetrical relationships, these are divided equally between those that entail giving respect and deference and those in which one is on the receiving end of these behaviors. For example, women, as a category, have lower status and fewer rights than men as a category in Aboriginal societies; when in kinship terms they behave as "mothers," "fathers' sisters," "elder sisters," and so on they can exert considerable influence over those male kin who must defer to them.

EARLY CONTACTS WITH EUROPEANS: DEFINING THE "WHITEFELLA"

Many of the first contacts that occurred along the desert margins were initiated by the Aborigines, who appear to have been drawn toward the frontier of European settlement at least as much by curiosity as need. Of course, the desert people knew of the invaders long before they ever saw them, with the possible exception of a few explorers who had struggled across this harsh wilderness. Introduced species such as the rabbit, cat, and camel had already altered the desert environment. In addition, Aboriginal material culture was augmented by fragments of iron, cloth, tin containers, and so on, which had been traded into the heart of the desert from fringe areas.

It seems that the small groups who bravely made contact with the newcomers initially harbored no intention of permanently abandoning either their nomadism or their desert heartlands. Despite the fact that their hunter-gatherer adaptation necessitates a nomadic existence, they are powerfully anchored to their own territories by intensely spiritual and emotional bonds of belonging, attraction, responsibility, and homesickness when away from them (see Tonkinson and Tonkinson 2001). People recalling their homelands sound nostalgic for the happy times once spent there and speak of them as something akin to a Garden of Eden, full of wonderful food resources and teeming with game. They will always express sadness and regret when hearing a place-name from their country, which brings a painful reminder of their long separation from particular sites or localities. Throughout Aboriginal Australia, "belonging" brings with it strong religious responsibilities for, and obligations toward, the spiritual and physical upkeep of important sites. When people were unable to be physically present because of drought or distance, they could visit important sites in dream-spirit form and make sure that all was well (Tonkinson 1970). For them, such presence on, in, and over the land was "real" and tangible, not metaphysical. Dream-spirit travel also enabled Aborigines to fulfill important ritual responsibilities as, for example, when they visited special sites that are home to a particular species of plant or animal. These spirits wait in their multitudes for a ritual command from human guardians to emerge and go forth across the land, making themselves plentiful and amenable for gather or capture by the people whose sustenance and survival depend on them.

Inevitably, attachment to the heartland had to compete with the attractions of the contact situation, particularly the availability of foodstuffs and tobacco, which, especially in times of prolonged drought in the desert, proved too compelling. A scattering of pastoral leases on which cattle and sheep were raised and, later, the establishment of small towns and Christian missions in the late nineteenth and early twentieth centuries became powerful magnets for the desert people. The initial transformation that accompanied their migration from the desert was a massive one, which proved to be dramatic and far-reaching in its consequences.

As nomads the Mardu had enjoyed a high level of cultural autonomy, spending as much as 90 percent of their time living in small, highly mobile and labile groups of perhaps 15 to 25 people. Known in the hunter-gatherer literature as "bands," these groups comprised the basic economic unit and face-to-face social group in almost all foraging societies, and were characteristically flexible in their size and composition over time, increasing and decreasing in size according to a mixture of ecological and cultural factors. For example, good food and water supplies in the vicinity could encourage larger and less mobile bands, but a severe conflict within the band (which would have been a rare occurrence) could split it apart. These basic social groups were largely self-regulating, with age and gender the primary status determinants. In the absence of chiefs, the kinship system provided the overarching framework dictating the rules for interpersonal behavior and decision making. Men hunted large game such as kangaroos, emus, and bush turkeys, mostly alone or in pairs and often with the assistance of their dogs (dingoes). They shared communally the meat thus obtained according to a well-established etiquette that allotted designated parts of an animal to particular persons, determined by their kin relationship to the hunter. Women, mostly as a group, took the children out with them and gathered food, or hunted small game, notably lizards. This harvest was consumed by hearth groups because, with little or no "luck of the hunt" factor in gathering in the same area, all women normally returned to camp with food. Among the Mardu food staples, they gathered a wide variety of edible grass seeds, plus tubers, fruits, berries, edible grubs and honey ants, honey, and nectars, with some items more common than others. People snacked opportunistically during the day, and ate their main meal back at camp late afternoon or early evening. Unless a singalong or other ritual activity was planned for the evening, they typically retired early to "bed" (most often a brush windbreak and softened sand with a row of small fires for warmth in winter). The food quest seldom occupied more than a few hours a day, so they had ample leisure time, and men occupied much of this with discussion and planning that centered on the religious life. Women had rituals and important ritual responsibilities, but spent proportionately much less time than men engaged with such concerns; they spent more time in child care, food processing, and domestic pursuits.

The shift to settlements meant a much more sedentary existence, with greatly increased dependence on outsiders (despite the continuation of hunter-gatherer activities to supplement ration handouts) and the loss of their traditional band-based and highly autonomous economy and local organization. Frontier pastoralists drew many of the Mardu immigrants into an alien economic system that needed and valued their labor. It was a frontier from which white women were absent, and many Aboriginal women were sought not only for their labor but also for their sexual services (see Tonkinson 1990). Initially, returns to the desert were possible, as was escape from harsh employers, but it was a generally harmonious situation from which both parties obtained considerable benefit, according to older Mardu. As wants changed to needs and the immigrants eventually found themselves "captured by flour and sugar" (Tonkinson 1991, 162),

© Bob Tonkinson

Artist Yangkura Atkins and anthropologist Myrna Tonkinson at Jigalong

they became increasingly reluctant, and eventually unable, to face the arduous realities of a return to traditional desert subsistence.

For most of the Mardu, first contacts were with pastoralists or at a maintenance depot on the Number One Rabbit Proof Fence, called Jigalong. The fence, completed in 1907, was a futile attempt to halt the spread of these introduced pests. It later became a government ration station for the issue of food and clothing to local Aboriginal people who had begun to congregate there, and, beginning around the 1930s, to groups of desert immigrants from further east. The Mardu gradually displaced the original Nyiyaparli people (who moved westward and were absorbed into the pastoral economy). They settled at Jigalong, which would eventually become their home and the locus of a new kind of settlement-based identity, known as the "Jigalong mob." This nontraditional form of identity, the "mob" was forged by prolonged coresidence and increasing intermarriage between groups whose original territories in some cases may have been far apart but who nonetheless had much in common socially and culturally.

Once settled around the depot, many adults were given laboring jobs of various kinds in return for food, and their camp became a recruiting site for pastoralists looking for cheap labor. It is significant that first contacts for most Mardu in the pre-mission period were with these rough and ready frontiersmen, lone men who ran small, marginal cattle and sheep properties that teetered on insolvency. The Mardu constructed a stereotypical image of the whitefella as heavy drinkers, smokers, swearers, and womanizers who seldom interfered in internal Aboriginal affairs and who followed an ethos of "live and let live," as long as their orders were obeyed and the work got done. Whatever their moral pronouncements on Aboriginal personality and culture, these men sought no general reformation of Aboriginal beliefs and customs. Mardu judged them as individuals, either as "good" or "hard," and avoided going to work for the latter category. If they were badly treated on the pastoral properties, they would silently disappear in the night. These Mardu stereotypes of whites were to be seriously challenged by the arrival of a small group of fundamentalist missionaries.

THE MISSION AND ITS AFTERMATH: FROM MASTERS OF THE DESERT TO CHILDREN OF THE DEVIL

Jigalong came under the control of fundamentalist Christian missionaries in 1946, after the state government had closed down the maintenance depot and ration station there. As a cheap way of providing care and sustenance to the hundred or so Aboriginal people still living there, the government solicited the establishment of a mission. (Many more immigrants were to drift in from the desert, group by small group, over the following two decades.) From the outset, the missionaries encountered problems. Due to their relatively late arrival on the scene, the missionaries were viewed by the Mardu as a new, very different and separate category of person, labeled "Krijin" (Christian). By definition, and in sharp contrast to the whites they had previously known, these were people who did not swear, smoke, drink alcohol, or seek sexual relations with Aboriginal women, and knew little about the desert environment and stock work. More seriously, a Krijin was someone who, being firmly opposed to the Law, was determined to eradicate the many "sinful" aspects of Mardu culture and became intent on alienating Mardu schoolchildren from their parents. Thus, a largely negative view of the newcomers grew quickly among the Mardu. Local pastoralists reinforced this view as their relations with the missionaries soon soured over labor issues, especially over their recruitment of women as domestic servants. Deeply concerned about sexual relationships that often ensued from such engagement of labor, the missionaries sought to obstruct this recruitment.

Spatially and conceptually, the two domains—the settlement (*maya*, meaning "house") and the camp (*ngurra* "home, hearth")—were clearly separated, as they had been on pastoral properties. Missionary interference in camp affairs and trespass (in an attempt to view secret-sacred ritual performances, for example) were greatly resented as a domain violation, though evening prayer meetings that the missionaries held in camp on Sundays were tolerated as harmless diversions. In the space of the mission and school, however, white power and authority held sway. Many Mardu men, especially the able-bodied, spent much of the year away, working as cowboys for the many small, marginal pastoral properties along the semidesert western littoral. This left the women, preschoolers, and old people at Jigalong, along with the school-aged children, who lived in sex-segregated dormitories under tight discipline. Mardu parents resented the physical punishment of their children in the school and the dormitory, and angry parents sometimes

© Bob Tonkinson

Jigalong Mission ranch workers visiting.

transgressed the domain boundary to confront mission or school staff. Yet the Mardu appeared untroubled by concerted missionary attempts to indoctrinate the dormitory children, because parents saw their schoolchildren in their own domain daily, and continued to speak with them in their own language. This close contact is perhaps why parents did not appear to see education or Christianity as threatening to alienate their offspring. Boys still entered the initiation process soon after puberty, and moved smoothly into an Aboriginally defined adulthood and eventual marriage. However, older Mardu were often infuriated by missionary attempts to encourage teenage girls to resist arranged marriages or even to dissuade them from going to the much older men to whom many were betrothed; in fact, this was the beginning of an increasingly stronger assertion by women of their own autonomy. By the time of my first fieldwork in the early 1960s, older widows were refusing to remarry in accordance with the Law (Mardu society has no statuses akin to "spinster" or "bachelor"), preferring to live with one another in *kiriji* (single people's) camps. Also, young women increasingly rebelled against the betrothal system, and asserted themselves to be "free agents" regarding the choice of husbands and even the right to refuse to marry (Tonkinson 1990).

   During this period of strong paternalism, the Mardu were generally content to let the missionaries, as approved agents of "the government," handle bureaucratic relations with the largely mysterious world of the nation-state. By doing so, they maximized the time devoted to their own internal political and religious affairs. They were intent upon maintaining a strong firewall between their internal political and religious affairs and what they termed "whitefella business," of which Christianity was no doubt a part. The mission situation was one of "unstable accommodation," in which each party needed the other while exploiting unfavorable stereotypes of the other to justify their antagonistic stance (Tonkinson 1974). Relations were underlain by chronic tensions regarding the missionaries' strong urge to undermine and ultimately destroy Mardu culture, and the even more implacable Mardu determination to protect their core values while maintaining the strength and integrity of the Law.

In almost a quarter century of endeavor, the missionaries were unsuccessful in their goal to convert their charges to Christianity. Despite all their prayers seeking a sudden baptism of the Holy Spirit and their efforts to turn children against their parents and bring about the destruction of the traditional religion and "the old ways,"—which they regarded as "the work of the devil,"—they achieved only one avowed convert (for a detailed account of the mission era, see Tonkinson 1974). Dispirited by their failure to achieve conversions, the missionaries withdrew in 1969 after a scandal over the beating and detention of some young Mardu girls by the superintendent, which resulted in a widely publicized court case. Decreasing outside support and chronic staff problems plagued the mission for some years, forcing it to abandon the dormitory system and surrender its tight control over Social Security payments (pensions, child allowances, etc.) to the Mardu.

By the time the missionaries departed, the population of Jigalong had grown to about 350, and numbers continued to swell following job losses on pastoral properties in the wake of extending equal wages provisions to Aboriginal workers in 1968. Income from Social Security and other welfare payments thus became (and still remains) the backbone of the local economy, which switched to a cash base in the early 1970s. Having an assured income altered Mardu spending patterns and enabled more of them to purchase vehicles, thus increasing their mobility (which is still a very highly valued and conspicuous feature of desert Aboriginal cultures), but also their access to alcohol.

Within the Aboriginal political arena, meanwhile, much had changed. Kinship remained the blueprint for social behavior and the dominant factor in allocating roles and statuses and in decision making, but in altered circumstances. The band as the face-to-face group and economic unit of society had given way to a larger aggregation of people from many different local groups and several different language-named units (though they spoke dialects of a single language). They now identified themselves to outsiders as members of a single nontraditional entity, "the Jigalong mob," unified by strong bonds of kinship, intermarriage, shared Law, and associated ritual responsibilities. These ties transcended linguistic group boundaries and contributed to new kinds of solidarity between people who traditionally could not have achieved this closeness because survival dictated that they spend most of their time dispersed in small groups.

Their major adaptive strategy from desert days, that of maximizing resource use, was carried over into the mission milieu with considerable success. Sedentary living demanded creative responses of two related kinds: (1) to ensure the continuity of their Law while creating a new kind of viable community in a situation of culture contact; and (2) to cope with "Krijins" and other "whitefellas" in such a way as to adequately meet basic subsistence requirements while effectively shielding the core of their culture and their political relationships with neighboring Aboriginal groups from outside interference. Their "defeat" of the missionaries and the growth of Jigalong's regional reputation as the strongest "Law center" in the northwest were proof of the success of these strategies (Tonkinson 1998a).

However, despite some early peacemaking rituals and an ever-increasing rate of intermarriage between two of the biggest dialect-named groups ("tribes"), which was blurring and muting differences, some of the old antagonisms and suspicions (mainly concerning sorcery) lingered on. In the late 1960s, some of the Mardu's northern neighbors were able to exploit these lines of tension, persuading a large number of the Manyjilyjarra speakers to join their cooperative mining venture. This rupture exacerbated intercommunity tensions and had serious implications for the flow of religious lore among desert-fringe communities for about two decades. Ongoing tensions between the two communities continued to be a source of great concern to the Jigalong Mardu, because of its negative consequences for social relationships among kin and, more seriously, the flow of religious lore throughout the Western Desert.

"SELF-MANAGEMENT": THE PERILS OF WELL-MEANING GOVERNMENT POLICY

In the early 1970s, a period of governmental inactivity and neglect suddenly gave way to the advent of promising and positive new government policies of "self-management for Aboriginal people." The pace of change accelerated markedly, but unfortunately for the Mardu and many other Aboriginal people in rural and remote Australia at the time, they were quite ill-prepared for such a sudden transition. Virtually overnight, they lurched from the complete paternalism of a colonial situation to bureaucratic demands that they legally incorporate their communities and thus take on significant, and hitherto undreamed of, self-management responsibilities. The obligatory setting up of an elected all-Aboriginal community council vaulted the Mardu headlong into dealing with exactly the kinds of "whitefella business" from which they had formerly been excluded. The council and chairman structure was a nontraditional body that functioned according to state rules of incorporation and necessitated the assistance of white staff, so it took some time to accommodate the new governing structure to Mardu imperatives. After a time, both men and women were elected, generally middle-aged people who could read and write, plus one or two influential elders to keep an eye on things. The councilors dealt with most "whitefella business" and reported only culturally important issues back to the rather informal but nonetheless vital institution known as the "camp meeting," held in the Aboriginal domain and dealing with all matters pertaining to "Law business."[3]

The shock of the sudden onset of a post-paternalistic policy regime was not the only challenge to the Mardu people's capacity to cope. The inception of the new policies and concomitant huge increase in bureaucratic contacts between them and the outside world coincided with two decidedly negative developments: the severe curtailment of employment opportunities in the pastoral industry, and much easier access to alcohol. These developments had devastating effects on Mardu society and over time have clearly weakened their capacity to

© Bob Tonkinson

Mardu children at Parnngurr rockhole

keep the European domain at bay. Also, the much-vaunted new policies were a chimera in that governmental bureaucracies continued to firmly hold the purse strings, intent on preventing economic failures that would lead to adverse publicity. Thus they proved unwilling to allow Aboriginal people to make mistakes and learn from them. No training was provided to Aborigines to ensure such outcomes as good governance and the exercise of due diligence, and Aboriginal communities remained heavily reliant on the expertise of white staff, thus also blunting governmental expectations of a steady indigenization of local employment.

It should not be surprising, then, that by the mid-1970s some Mardu already spoke nostalgically about the mission era. The new self-management policies generated many problems, including an overreliance on the integrity and judgment of white staff, and difficulties in assessing their own job performance, especially in relation to the handling of cash. More perplexing still was conflict among the white staff arising from personality clashes, political and philosophical differences, and role conflicts, and the Mardu strongly resented attempts to draw them into arguments that they regarded as none of their business. Also, some staff took the self-management policy at face value, refusing to assume control in times of crisis. Instead they directed the onus back onto the council and community, both of which were ill-equipped to act decisively after decades of missionary paternalism that took care of all such trouble. A number of social problems emerged that the Mardu wanted white staff to deal with. Some of these difficulties were absent in the mission era; alcohol, for example, had been totally banned, and back then was in any case unobtainable within 150 miles of Jigalong. Other increasingly visible problems had been masked by firm missionary punishment of offenders, including breaking and entering, stealing, vandalism, and teenage promiscuity. On the plus side, though, social boundaries between Mardu and whites in the settlement began to erode, and the Mardu gained confidence in their new roles as employers and decision makers.

ON MOBILITY, DISPERSAL, AND AGGREGATION

All hunter-gatherer peoples, whose nomadism precluded the accumulation of material culture, were positively attuned to mobility for its variety, its widening of choices, the constant prospect of encountering other groups, and the expanded social horizon it occasioned. Their rhythm of life alternated between short periods of aggregation and intensification of social life and very long periods of dispersal in small bands, at least in the Western Desert. The love of movement and excitement at the prospect of reunions with kin and friends are cultural continuities that remain palpably important in the lives of desert people. Sedentarization, even under conditions of extreme paternalism and inadequate means of transportation, never brought people's mobility to a complete halt.

From Jigalong and similar settlements, families and small groups went on camping trips (on foot in the early days) out into the bush, to hunt and gather, collect raw materials, and enjoy a respite from the noise, conflicts, and general distractions of settlement living. Whenever possible, they also made longer visits to see kin in other settlements scattered around the fringes of the desert, sometimes in small groups, but more often in large convoys headed for "big meetings." These gatherings, the high points of the desert people's social calendar, were, and to some extent still are, also major nodes for the continued flow of information, objects, religious lore, male novices, and so on throughout and sometimes even beyond the culture area. Improved access to more reliable vehicles has not only facilitated such movements but also increased their range, so that "big meetings" (and now an ever-increasing tempo of funeral attendance) may draw people from as far as a thousand miles away from the opposite side of the desert.

The immigrants to Jigalong were fortunate in that they eventually arrived at a satisfactory accommodation with the original owners of the land around the settlement so that their tenure there remained unchallenged. They were thus spared the uncertain status of "visitors," which in many parts of northern Australia was a major factor precipitating dispersal of such people from large settlements since the 1970s. Still, many smaller kin-based groups took the opportunity afforded by the new self-management policy to increase their autonomy by establishing outstations back in their traditional homelands. Some groups of Mardu, including the last ones to come in from the desert in the 1960s, opted for dispersal from Jigalong and Strelley (the community to which many Manyjilyjarra people had moved from Jigalong). They have shifted toward their desert homelands, where they have reaggregated in smaller groupings. This is in part a response to growing social problems and a desire to distance their young people from alcohol, which is now readily available in the mining town of Newman just 100 miles to the west of Jigalong. Other motivating factors include a strong concern for the safety of their homelands in the face of increased incursions by resource developers, and a desire for greater autonomy and control over the resources expected to flow from the establishment of outstations. Many also wanted to teach subsistence skills to their settlement-born children, familiarize them with their ancestral territory, and, above all, impress upon the younger generation their responsibilities to care for their own country and keep their Law strong.

Three of the largest outstations made a successful transformation to independent incorporated communities, and much money has been spent on housing construction, and on improving facilities and communications. Each outstation has a store, school, clinic with resident nurse and visiting doctor, airstrip, telephone services including Internet access and e-mail, television, and twice-weekly mail service, and the main roads have been improved. In all three, however, the population seesaws wildly as more people spend longer periods away in towns and other communities in the region. Several small outstations that were established out from Jigalong are all now abandoned and their houses lie empty, some following conflicts or deaths, but mostly because of poor communications, a lack of facilities such as shops and garages, and a paucity of things to do for young people bored by tranquility.

At all the Mardu settlements, water supply problems continue to impede economic development, and local employment opportunities are minimal. A thriving but capital- rather than labor-intensive mining industry has tended to bypass locally available Aboriginal labor in favor of imported non-Aboriginal workers, but this neglect may be rectified now that native title has been granted. Employment creation remains a chronic problem in the desert interior, but even where training programs and jobs are available, a mixture of historical and cultural factors militates against trainees or workers remaining in long-term service. For example, a long history of ration handouts, dependence on government Social Security payments, plus low educational achievement levels, does not predispose many Mardu to desire employment. Also, with the strong cultural imperative to attend the funerals of relatives and associated ceremonials scattered in widely separated places, large numbers of people at any given time may be absent from their community. Chronic illness requiring treatment available only in cities or large towns also keeps people away, not only the patients, but often one or more family members who accompany and stay with the sick person for extended periods. At any one time, a significant number of Mardu adults, especially young men, are serving jail sentences for a variety of offences, most of them drink-related but also increasingly for failure to meet contractual financial commitments.

Despite these schismatic movements, much political activity in the past decades has focused on building alliances and uniting groups whose past relationships have featured more disputation than cooperation. Undoubtedly the struggle for land rights has been the catalyst for this. Although assuming great importance, this struggle is often more symbolic than real for the large majority of Aboriginal people throughout the nation whose lands have long since been alienated by the invaders and thus cannot be claimed under native title. In 1984, a number of Aboriginal groups on the western side of the desert agreed to form a regional land council to further their claims to their homelands and help keep the miners at bay. The Mardu native title claim had a long and often tortuous history, but in the course of it the Mardu and their northern neighbors settled their long-standing differences and became a single large claimant group, which was ultimately successful.

In 2003, Mardu claimants took an important step in the native title process when they established their own "prescribed body corporate." This representative body is required under the Native Title Act of 1993 to represent the interests of all constituent members in any negotiations with governments and other bodies interested in the claimed territory. Once adequately funded and staffed, the Mardu "PBC" is expected to play a vital intermediary and policy-making role in their internal as well as external political affairs. At no stage in the last decade have the Mardu known what rights and benefits might ultimately flow from the granting of native title, so they watch current developments with great interest and hope that considerable financial benefit from mining activities will accrue to them as landowners.

THE MARDU TODAY: ON THE ROAD TO SOMEWHERE

Most Mardu still live in their own communities, which have electricity, television, telephones, faxes, supermarkets, workshops, well-equipped schools, and adult-education facilities. These settlements are structured along Western-oriented administrative lines, nominally run by elected Aboriginal councils whose working time is increasingly taken up by bureaucratic dealings with the outside world. Every community has non-Aboriginal staff in key positions such as project officer, adviser, mechanic, bookkeeper, as well as government employees such as nurses, employment officers, and schoolteachers. More whitefellas now live and work in their communities than at any time in the past, which causes some Mardu and visitors alike to wonder whatever happened to Aboriginal "self-management." The Mardu could fulfill many of the jobs held by non-Aboriginal staff, but their enthusiasm for work at the settlement is muted; in addition to reasons outlined previously, "work for the dole" schemes pay almost as well as the available low-paid jobs, often entail minimal work, and expose them less to pressure from other Mardu seeking money or favors. The lack of interesting and rewarding employment possibilities is only one of many problems faced by Mardu who still live in their home communities.

At this stage in their history, the situation for Mardu remains so dynamic that it is impossible to predict accurately any endpoint—hence the subtitle of this chapter. There is much writing on the wall of social transformation, so it is possible to talk with varying levels of confidence about several different paths of significant change. One clear trend, decidedly negative, is the decline in health levels as a direct result of dietary change. Migration to settlements led to a dramatic shift from a low-fat, low-sugar, balanced diet to one based on "rations" heavy in sugars and fats, later exacerbated by increasing access to high-calorie, high-fat "junk foods" and takeaways. Today, despite considerable governmental expenditure aimed at alleviating Aboriginal health problems, Mardu of all ages suffer and die from Western lifestyle diseases. Diabetes, renal and liver failure are commonplace and many adults are kept alive with dialysis machines available only in distant cities. There is also a high incidence of cardio-vascular disease, often linked to childhood infections such as rheumatic fever. Many of these conditions are exacerbated or engendered by alcohol consumption, which has also contributed to a traumatic rise in serious injury and deaths from violence or accidents among the Mardu.

As a tiny marginalized minority encapsulated within a powerful nation-state, Aborigines have long been captive to policies and practices not of their own making, and for more than a century, based negatively on the firm "survival of the fittest" conviction that they would soon be extinct. They had to wait until the early 1970s for a self-management policy that projected a viable place for them in Australian society. Ironically a policy designed to increase Aboriginal self-reliance and control over their own affairs eroded the protective barrier they had erected to prevent "whitefella business" from intruding into the cherished "Law business" that was at the very core of their culture.

Although it is true that the Mardu have gained greater control over their own affairs, they are also now much more aware of their political and economic powerlessness in the dominant society, and more conscious of the impossibility of either disentangling or distancing themselves from its ever-tighter embrace. Their communities remain "closed," meaning that non-Aboriginal people require the council's permission to visit and reside, though this is no barrier to the inflow of people on government business, not to mention the exotic ideas and images that daily flood them in the form of television, videos, and DVDs. Tourism is still in its infancy in their region, but some Mardu are becoming more aware of its financial advantages, so visitors seeking gas, food, and Aboriginal artifacts and artworks are being welcomed.

A bigger threat to community survival continues to be the choices Mardu themselves make with regard to residence, though as yet young people are not well educated and therefore do not leave to seek good jobs in and beyond the region. Educational standards appear to have fallen since the 1960s, even though schools have become vastly better-equipped and more pupil-friendly learning environments. Truancy is rife because Mardu parents accede to their childrens' decisions to reject school, even as they affirm the value of education to a child's future. It is difficult to say whether or not in recent years there has been a stabilization in Mardu migration to towns that offer a greater range of services and facilities than settlements, but there is little doubt that the drift continues. The larger towns offer high schools, big supermarkets, a number of Christian churches, ready access to alcohol, greater freedom from censure over the choice of a wrong spouse or other infraction of Mardu custom, as well as attractions such as government-owned rental housing and unemployment benefits. Some Mardu move to towns because of serious medical needs that can be met only by staying close to hospitals, and a few are being cared for in nursing homes. Most town dwellers are unemployed, and many drink heavily and are thus in danger of increased involvement with agencies of the law. Yet despite periods spent in jail for alcohol-related offences, many seem to prefer town life and complain that the home settlements are boring, while at the same time affirming that their true "home" is where their parents and grandparents are buried.

Afternoon tea on the settlement

Explaining what "bores" younger people about the settlements leads us to the issue of greatest concern to mature Mardu: are they losing the battle to maintain their cultural integrity, or, as they put it, to "keep the Law strong"? Core activities associated with male initiation retain their prominence, and "big meetings" still attract hundreds of Aboriginal people from widely scattered communities and from the towns where Mardu continue to ensure that their teenage boys "go through the Law." However, it is clear that the male initiation process, once a 15-year learning curve, has been severely truncated. This means that the volume of knowledge being transmitted has shrunk dramatically, and young men are marrying at a much earlier age than traditionally. It is also true that the mature men responsible for the conduct of the religious life are less active than formerly, and there are fewer of them owing to the toll taken on Mardu society by premature deaths over the past three decades.

This has created gaps (particularly in the middle levels) in the ritual hierarchy that has driven their vibrant and complex religious system. The chain of interdependent links that made the system function efficiently as a whole and that is most vividly seen in the many different activities of the "big meetings" is now insufficiently active in other contexts. This is most evident in the induction of novices into higher grades, which entails the transmission of vital knowledge and assignment of religious responsibilities, and in the organization of ritual activities during the bulk of the year when no "big meetings" are occurring.

Although the Mardu have both male and female ritual-status hierarchies, senior males have the heaviest religious responsibilities in the Law. Initiated men move up a hierarchy of statuses, roughly age-based, that underpins a generalized division of labor operating in ritual contexts. The highest-ranking men are elders who function mostly as cooks for ritual feasts, guardians, caretakers, controllers, and directors of rituals. Middle-aged men are responsible for the mechanics of ritual activity. Below them are the "legmen" who assist the higher-status rank in many tasks and mainly function as hunters and supervisors of novices. At the bottom are the partially initiated novices (Tonkinson 1991, 138–142).

In a variety of ways, the power and the influence of mature Mardu men have been slipping. The mature men and the younger men trade accusations, in which the latter complain that the elders are lazy and will not teach them, whereas the older men accuse the younger of preoccupation with sex, drinking, whitefella ways, and of transgressions against the Law while drunk (such as using forbidden words and singing secret-sacred songs). Such interactions point to deeper problems that have weakened the integrity of the Law. Some of the younger and middle-aged men, conscious of the need for action, have enthusiastically attempted to gain as much knowledge as possible from their elders. Several are prominent leaders, with expertise in "whitefella business" and skilled as spokesmen for their people, and are painfully aware of what is happening, but they are insufficiently advanced in the ritual hierarchy to initiate the actions deemed necessary to get the Law back on track again.

Once a year-round activity, ritual performances are now largely confined to the summer "big meeting" season. At times, powerful counter-attractions have replaced these rituals, including hunting (from vehicles, with rifles), gambling, television, music, Australian-rules football, and carnivals. There are also trips to town to drink alcohol or shop for food and other consumer goods, including air conditioners, kitchen and laundry appliances, home entertainment units, furniture and motor vehicles. Virtually everyone is now housed, and increasingly people heat their dwellings in winter and cool them in the torrid summer, turning them into somewhere to spend time relatively insulated from the desert's extremes of weather. The nature and rhythm of mundane social life are changing from readily visible, open and permeable "camp" milieu to that of a much more closed and less permeable space, where much of daily life can be lived away from the direct gaze of others. The implications of this transformation, though undoubtedly considerable, are not yet clear.

A notable change with important implications for the integrity of Mardu social organization is occurring because the strict rules against marriage with partners not correctly related as "spouse" were relaxed. More and more young people are now marrying "all about," inevitably weakening the classificatory kinship system, the mechanism that structures each person's kin relationship to all other Mardu and provides the template for appropriate behavior. Traditionally, the kinship system dictated or guided behavior such as avoidance, restraint, easy familiarity, and joking relationships, and established certain roles to be filled in daily life and in ritual activity. Wrong marriages (that is, a union with anyone not related to you in kinship terms as "spouse") and a general relaxation of many rules result in increased ignorance, uncertainty, and inevitable breaches of those rules. This has implications for the filling of ceremonial roles and is also undermining the integrity and proper functioning of the associated social category system.[4]

Mardu teenagers favor sporting motifs on their shirts and long shorts, dress like many of their Australian and U.S. counterparts, adopt their hairstyles, listen to the same kinds of music, watch the same TV programs, cover surfaces with much the same teenage graffiti, and are schooled in a strongly Western curriculum (although their education tends to be a pale imitation of what their urban non-Aboriginal peers receive). Given these parallels, one could be forgiven for assuming that the younger Mardu also possess similar ambitions and world-views. One must ask, then: do all these contemporary changes add up to a "collapse" of Mardu society? Obviously, the answer is no, in the light of my earlier comments on the nature of social transformation. What, then, is the other side of the change coin among the Mardu? In my discussion of general anthropological understandings about social change earlier in this chapter, I mentioned the continuing power of culture and identity as acted out at the local level to resist global tendencies toward the erasure of difference. Our research to date suggests that such appearances of membership in a monolithic, Westernized world youth culture are deceiving. Young Mardu continue to live and find security in a world of kin, believe in the reality of the Dreaming as the foundation of the Law, and look forward to participation in ritual activities such as hunting and gathering, and camping out in the bush. They visit kin in other communities but otherwise remain close to their local kin and their home country (they are very homesick when away for any length of time). They live much the same kind of life as their elders do. Their very modest employment ambitions, which are realistic given their prior education, also reflect this inward-looking stance, one that above all sees security and predictably within the cocoon of familiar things: family, kin, and the desert environment. Most have seen the big city of Perth (800 miles south) and its bright lights, but have no desire to live or work there—it is too crowded, "full of whitefellas," and too big, whereas local towns are manageable and enjoyable places to visit and shop.

Despite 16 years of television, or maybe because of it, they see the wider world as a foreign and threatening rather than a beckoning place. Of state and Australian politics and current affairs they know or care very little; they see these events as remote from them and irrelevant to their lives. Their self-identity seems as firmly rooted as ever and they give no impression of being lost between two worlds. Younger Mardu are transforming their own world as they go, and show remarkably little curiosity about the hows and whys of Western "civilization," unless they have a strong case to seek knowledge—in the repair of broken-down vehicles, for example, or how to work a video recorder. The acceptance of obviously useful alien artifacts is as absolute now as it was in frontier days, but most such innovations offer no serious threat to cherished values in a culture that thoroughly disconnected property from the status or attributes of person.

Today, throughout the Western Desert, the major occasions drawing large numbers of visitors to a settlement are all too frequently funerals, which are increasingly Christian rituals. Given what has been said about a major decline in the richness and diversity of the traditional religious life, questions must be asked about the place of Christianity in contemporary Mardu life. After the departure of missionaries at the end of the 1960s, the spark of Christianity was kept alive by a few non-Mardu Christians still present in communities and nearby

© Bob Tonkinson

Youth looking at old photographs

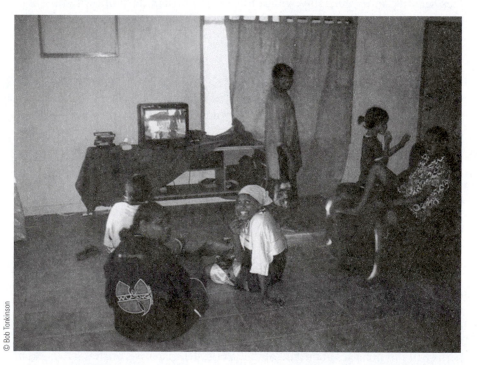

© Bob Tonkinson

Television in a Mardu house

towns. They built upon the fragmentary knowledge of Christianity that some Mardu had acquired, including many who were dormitory children during the mission era. The insistence of the early Jigalong missionaries on an all-or-nothing dichotomy between Christianity and Mardu culture has in recent decades given way to a more accommodating stance. Many of the Mardu now profess to be Christians, but most also claim to be "Law people" who follow both paths. Contemporary Christianity generally views this as allowable, as God "put" Aborigines and their religion here in the first place. Missionaries again reside in Jigalong, the number of professed Christians has increased, and the churches now active in the Mardu area seek to fill the large space left by unemployment, boredom, indirection, and the severe truncation of the traditional religious life. To date, however, they cannot claim any outstanding progress toward this goal. Young people, particularly males, are evincing little interest in whatever it is that Christianity has to offer them. There seems to be in many cases a clear connection between adherence to Christianity and being a nondrinker, and I suspect that in most such cases church membership is functioning as a way for Mardu to save themselves from themselves, by allowing them to refuse liquor on the grounds that it contravenes their church's teachings. Most avid Christian Mardu are reformed drinkers rather than lifelong teetotalers, and some still periodically suffer falls from the temperance wagon. However many churches are providing practical assistance in addition to spiritual guidance, and many Mardu particularly welcome this support for their attempts to distance themselves from "the demon drink."

CONCLUSION

Theorizing social change is never easy, but a central issue for anthropologists is to understand the workings of power: its control, manipulation, distribution, and discontents. From a moment very early on in their direct experience of whites, the Mardu knew that the invaders and their sources of power were located well beyond the bounds of what the Dreaming ordained. What they also must have realized quite early, though, was that the whites understood nothing of either their social organization or their religion, the building blocks of Aboriginal culture. From their perspective, disengagement and a return to the desert was impossible, largely because they had become seduced by food ration handouts. Their task was to exploit this new phenomenon to the best of their abilities while strenuously maintaining a barrier between the newcomers and their own cultural imperatives, an impermeable barrier that resisted encroachments by the whites into their cultural domain. Not until the arrival of the missionaries did the first direct threats become visible to them, and were duly and largely successfully resisted, despite a differential in both economic and legal power (in Western terms) favoring the whites. From their perspective, the Mardu had conceded little of value while effectively maintaining the integrity of their own domain.

The eventual penetration and compromise of the Mardu domain was gradual and largely invisible to them, not the result of any concerted frontal attack. Instead, a host of small elements of change and accommodation insidiously ate away at the barrier, but certainly did not destroy it. The Mardu appear reluctant to transfer into the whitefella domain the logistical skills they employed very effectively. These skills include organizing and running "big meetings," managing major affairs that require allocating resources, scheduling personnel, and coordinating different activities that are simultaneously ongoing. Much that gets done in the economic life and maintenance activities on the settlements still stems from the organizational and managerial activities of the non-Aboriginal workers. There is thus considerable scope for Mardu to exert much greater influence over these aspects of their communities.

It seems necessary for them to consciously bridge the two domains that they have for so long striven to keep separate. This would reverse the flow of influences from the dominant society, as the Mardu themselves breach the mental boundary they have erected, thus freeing knowledge, strategies, and power deriving from their Law to flow out from the Mardu domain into current circumstances that demand such skills. They are increasingly doing so with funerals, for example, but could also transform their new regional "prescribed body corporate" from an imposed and alien structural form into a truly Mardu institution in its functioning and cultural significance. Some Mardu have already expressed the hope that this regional forum will respond to pressing matters of Law and tradition in addition to managing economic and bureaucratic relationships with the outside world, most particularly the decline they perceive in the place and strength of the Law. What more appropriate context could there be in which to fuse the strands of both domains?

These various challenges to the future social and political integrity of their society may well be effectively addressed only through this suggested expansion of worldview. It is one that must draw the attention of the Mardu away from the ultimate sources of power (for example, as lying in the Dreaming, or with God, or in the whitefella secular political realm) toward a concentration on process, the various ways in which power can be marshaled and employed. This would have the effect of situating the urgent task of organizing and managing their representative body within a single undifferentiated domain of action. Power conceived of as having common properties regardless of its source would accord equal relevance and potential to both Law and law, and Business and business, and to the Dreaming and Christianity.

Yet it must be stressed that meeting these challenges is not simply a matter of the Mardu changing their mindset, given where they are currently located socioeconomically within the dominant society, remote and lacking entry to its stores of power. They and their communities remain heavily dependent on government monies. Most of them are unemployed, inadequately educated, and disadvantaged by their seriously compromised health levels and social circumstances. Compared to the situation 40 years ago, though, it is clear to me that much has been achieved, particularly in the level of confidence with which Mardu manage the elements of the non-Mardu world that confront them. Although still very poor by the standards of the wider Australian society, they are materially better off than at any time since they left their desert homelands. Yet, as most of them still see it, the major battle continues and will be uphill, to hold onto their Law and transmit it to the generations to follow. The Law and culture whose

Celebrating the opening of the gas pipeline

integrity they will be nurturing in 50 years' time will undoubtedly still be there but equally surely, will be very different from that which we see, and they experience, today.

REFERENCES

Appadurai, A. 1997. Discussion: Fieldwork in the era of globalization. *Anthropology and Humanism* 22 (1): 115–118.

Berndt, R. M. 1959. The concept of "the tribe" in the Western Desert of Australia. *Oceania* 30 (2): 81–107.

Berndt, R. M., and C. H Berndt. 1988. *The world of the first Australians*. Rev. ed. Canberra: Aboriginal Studies Press.

Cerroni-Long, E. L., ed. 1999. *Anthropological theory in North America*. Westport, CN: Bergin and Garvey.

Geertz, C. 1973. *The interpretation of cultures*. New York: Basic Books.

Gould, R. A. 1969. *Yiwara: Foragers of the Australian desert*. New York: Scribners.

Gould, R. A. 1971. The archaeologist as ethnographer: A case from the Western Desert of Australia. *World Archaeology* 3 (2): 143–177.

Hill, S. 1988. *The tragedy of technology*. London: Pluto.

Hogbin, I. 1958. *Social change*. London: Watts.

Linton, R. 1936. *The study of man: An introduction*. New York: Appleton-Century.

Nettheim, G. 1993. 'The consent of the natives': Mabo and indigenous political rights. In *Essays on the*

Mabo decision, 103–126. Sydney: The Law Book Company.

O'Connor, S., P. Veth, and C. Campbell. 1998. Serpent's Glen rockshelter: Report of the first Pleistocene-aged occupation sequence from the Western Desert. *Australian Archaeology* 46:12–22.

Ortner, S. 1984. Theory in anthropology since the sixties. *Comparative Studies in Society and History* 26 (1): 126–166.

Sahlins, M. 1985. *Islands of history.* Chicago: Chicago Univ. Press.

Stanner, W. E. H. 1979. *White man got no Dreaming: Essays 1938–1973.* Canberra: Australian National Univ. Press.

Tonkinson, R. 1970. Dream-spirit rituals in a contact situation. In *Australian Aboriginal anthropology,* ed. R. M. Berndt, 277–291. Nedlands: Univ. of Western Australia Press.

———. 1974. *The Jigalong mob: Aboriginal victors of the desert crusade.* Menlo Park: Cummings.

———. 1978. *The Mardudjara Aborigines: Living the dream in Australia's desert.* New York: Holt, Rinehart and Winston.

———. 1987. Mardudjara kinship. In *Australia to 1788,* vol. 1, *Australians: A Historical Library,* ed. D. J. Mulvaney and J. White, 196–219. Sydney: Fairfax, Syme and Weldon.

———. 1988a. One community, two laws: Aspects of conflict and convergence in a Western Australian Aboriginal settlement. In *Indigenous law and the state,* ed. B. Morse and G. Woodman, 395–411. Dordrecht: Foris.

———. 1988b. 'Ideology and domination' in Aboriginal Australia:

A Western Desert test case. In *Hunters and gatherers, vol. 1: Property, power and ideology,* ed. T. Ingold, D. Riches, and J. Woodburn, 170–184. Oxford: Berg.

———. 1990. The changing status of women: "Free agents" at Jigalong, Western Australia. In *Going it alone? Prospects for Aboriginal autonomy: Essays in honour of Ronald and Catherine Berndt,* ed. R. Tonkinson and M. C. Howard, 125–147. Canberra: Aboriginal Studies Press.

———. 1991. *The Mardu Aborigines: Living the dream in Australia's desert,* 2nd ed. Fort Worth: Holt, Rinehart and Winston.

———. 1994. Melanesia: Culture, technology and "tradition" before and after Western impacts. In *Traditional technological structures and cultures of the Pacific: Five papers,* ed. R.A. Stephenson, 32–66. Guam: Micronesian Area Research Center, University of Guam.

———. 1998. National identity: Australia after Mabo. In *Pacific answers to Western hegemony,* ed. J. Wassmann, 287–313. Oxford: Berg.

———. Forthcoming. Encountering the Other: Millenarianism and the permeability of indigenous domains—a Melanesian-Australian comparison. In *Cargo, cult and culture critique,* ed. H. Jebens. Honolulu: Univ. of Hawai'i Press.

Tonkinson, R., and M. Tonkinson. 2001. "Knowing" and "being" in place in the Western Desert. In *Histories of old ages: Essays in honour of Rhys Jones,* ed. I. Anderson, I. Lilley, and S. O'Connor, 133–139. Canberra: Pandanus.

Wallace, A. F. C. 1961. *Personality and culture.* New York: Random House.

NOTES

1. Desert Aborigines widely use the English word *Law* to denote the totality of their religion and culture, encompassing jural rules and moral evaluations of customary behaviors, as bequeathed them by the ancestral creative beings of the Dreaming. I use it here with a capital letter to distinguish it

from the law of the dominant society. The choice of this word by Aboriginal people indicates that they see parallels between the two systems and emphasize the use of rules and social control mechanisms in both (see Tonkinson 1974, 7; 1991, chap. 1).

2. For more detailed information about the nature and significance of native title in Australia, see Nettheim (1993) and the other contributors to this excellent volume of papers on the Mabo decision; see also Tonkinson (1998).

3. These meetings still take place at Jigalong, and retain their importance in community affairs, but appear to be convened less frequently than formerly, to the dismay of some older Mardu.

4. Mardu society is divided into four named "sections," which are useful labeling devices and an important basis for group formation associated with most ritual activity (see Tonkinson 1991, 72–78).

Fieldwork Biography
William C. Young

© William C. Young

William C. Young carried out his doctoral fieldwork with the Rashaayda Bedouin in eastern Sudan from 1977 to 1980. He spent these three years in the Rashaayda's nomadic encampments west of the city of Kassala, migrating with them during the rainy seasons. His task was to describe social relationships among nomadic households and explore the ways in which life-crisis rituals such as weddings and childbirth ceremonies shaped and constructed these relationships. He collected data about inter-household relationships and ritual through participant observation and interviewing. In 1992 he conducted fieldwork in Jordan with a sedentary kin group that has the same name—the Rashaayda—and that probably is related historically to the Sudanese Rashaayda. In 1999 he again returned to Jordan and visited yet a third group of Rashaayda near the city of Karak. His fourth research trip, in 2001, took him to Riyadh, Saudi Arabia, where he interviewed members of the Saudi Rashaayda. Dr. Young is currently a researcher at the University of Maryland's Center for Advanced Study of Language. He is shown in the photo above conducting an interview in Kassala in 1980.

11/From Local "Tribe" to Transnational Arab

The "New" Rashaayda Bedouin of Sudan

When I completed my fieldwork among the Rashaayda Bedouin, late in 1980, I felt that it was reasonable to describe them as one of many local societies in eastern Sudan. They had occupied local economic niches, had successfully laid claim—as livestock breeders—to local grazing territories, and had built networks of social relations that did not extend very far beyond Sudan's national boundaries. Most of them were pastoralists; that is, they fed their livestock on wild plants growing in desert pastures that were owned by no one. They were also nomadic. In other words, they lived in tents and moved to isolated desert pastures with their animals whenever rain fell on these pastures and triggered the growth of useful plants. Because they were nomadic pastoralists, the Rashaayda could produce most of their food and shelter by themselves, using the animal products (milk, meat, wool) from their herds. Because they were largely self-sufficient,

© William C. Young

Rashaayda Bedouin of Sudan, late 1970s

they did not depend on outsiders and kept to themselves, spending most of their time in campsites far from Sudanese cities.

True, some Rashaayda occasionally received visits from distant relatives who lived across the border in Eritrea, north of the port of Massawa along the Red Sea coast. Some other Rashaayda traveled to southern Egypt regularly to sell livestock and buy manufactured goods that could be resold in Sudan. A good many Rashaayda had also traveled to Saudi Arabia to work as unskilled laborers for two to three years, and during their sojourns had met members of the Bani Rashiid[1] "tribe" in Saudi Arabia whom they recognized as kin. But the majority of the Rashaayda whom I met had never been outside of Sudan and did not know anyone whom was not a Sudanese citizen. Although they spoke their own dialect of Arabic at home, they spoke Sudanese colloquial Arabic with non-Rashiidi Arabs. Some even knew a few words in Tu Bedawi, the local language of the neighboring Hadendowa tribe. In short, they were members of a local society whose most important social relations and economic resources were in Sudan.

This description is no longer accurate. At present (2003) the Rashaayda of Sudan have begun to represent themselves as members of a much larger social formation that is dispersed across Sudan, Eritrea, Kuwait, Saudi Arabia, Egypt, and perhaps, Jordan and Palestine. They are slowly adopting a new rhetoric of identity, according to which the scattered groups of the Rashaayda are all

© William C. Young

*Rashaayda Bedouin women dancing with swords during a wedding in the late 1970's.
Note the men in the audience in that era*

"branches" belonging to the same "tribe."[2] Some of them are even claiming to be
a "people" in diaspora—that is, not merely a tribe—with all the rights of ethnic
identity in a multiethnic state that such a peoplehood would imply.

It is no longer possible to carry out ethnographic field research in any one of
these scattered groups without taking into account its connections to "distant
cousins" in other countries, across national borders. The Bani Rashiid of Saudi
Arabia, for example, have exerted a considerable influence on the Rashaayda of
Sudan and Eritrea during the past two decades. To illustrate, in 1978, when I witnessed Rashiidi weddings in Sudan, they included a brief dance in which married
women, heavily veiled and wearing elaborately decorated costumes, performed in
front of men (see Young 1996, 124, and above). By 2003, however, this dance had
been deleted from the wedding ritual because it offended the sensibilities of the
Bani Rashiid. In Saudi Arabia, any mixing of the sexes outside of the house is
considered "un-Islamic." The Bani Rashiid told their "cousins" in Sudan that the
wedding dance was an embarrassment to them and harmed the collective reputation
of the Rashaayda and Bani Rashiid in Saudi Arabia. To improve their image in
Saudi Arabia, the Rashaayda of Sudan agreed to discard the wedding dance. This is
not the only important cultural change that has resulted from contact between the

Rashaayda on the western shore of the Red Sea with their kin on the eastern shore. Another change is the reformulation of their genealogies and histories.

To bring my case study of the Sudanese Rashaayda up to date, I cannot avoid describing some of the other, non-Sudanese groups that they are now recognizing as "kin." I should also try to explain why the various Rashaayda/Bani Rashiid groups are developing an overarching, unifying ideology that ties them all together. To take this new, expanded identity into account, therefore, I will begin by briefly identifying the Rashaayda who live outside of Sudan, including whatever information is available about their historical interrelationships. Next, I will describe the new, transnational forces that have brought some of these dispersed groups into actual contact with each other. I will argue that these same forces have disturbed the position of each group in its own national context (Sudan, Saudi Arabia, Eritrea), exposing it to new risks while at the same time offering it new opportunities. Finally, I will describe the new, pan-"tribal" ideology (as embodied in conversation and various publications) that the Rashaayda of Sudan and Saudi Arabia are producing, showing that many features of this ideology are strategic responses to changing political and economic conditions.

GEOGRAPHICAL AND HISTORICAL BACKGROUND

At least 11 different groups are scattered across the eastern Arab world (see Figure 11.1) that bear either the name *al-Rashaayda* or the cognate name, *Bani Rashiid*. Both names mean "descendants of Rashiid" and are eponyms for patrilineal descent groups. Each such group says that it constitutes a "tribe" (*gabiila* in Saudi and Sudanese colloquial Arabic; *'ashiira* in Jordanian and Palestinian colloquial Arabic). Groups calling themselves Rashaayda or Bani Rashiid are found in eastern Sudan, along the Red Sea coast in Eritrea, and in central Egypt. Still others are found in southeastern Israel, the West Bank/Palestine, northern Jordan, central Jordan, northwestern Saudi Arabia, and southwestern Saudi Arabia.[3]

By itself, the identification of these scattered groups by a single name does not prove that they have a common origin. The name is widespread and is used by many different tribal groups whose differing historical origins are well documented. For example, the Aal Rashiid of Haayil—a powerful family in northern Saudi Arabia that competed with the Aal Saud dynasty for mastery over the Arabian Peninsula in the early twentieth century (Habib 1978; Rasheed 1991)—are certainly not related, genealogically or historically, to the Bani Rashiid of Khaybar, in western Saudi Arabia. The Bani Rashiid of Khaybar do not seek to claim common descent from the ancestor of the Aal Rashiid, and the Aal Rashiid vehemently reject any suggestion that the Bani Rashiid are their relatives.

More solid evidence of common historical origin can be found by examining the names of the smaller, component branches that make up each local group of Rashaayda. For example, the Rashaayda of eastern Sudan consist of six distinct branches: the 'Awaazim, Qazaayiza, 'Uraynaat, Baraatiikh, Zunaymaat, and Biraa'asa (Young 1996, 87, 102). The members of the first branch, the 'Awaazim, say that they are not actually descended from the Rashaayda's eponymous ancestor, Rashiid al-Zawl, but are a separate descent group that has been closely associated with the Rashaayda for centuries (Hasan 1974, 11–13). This connection

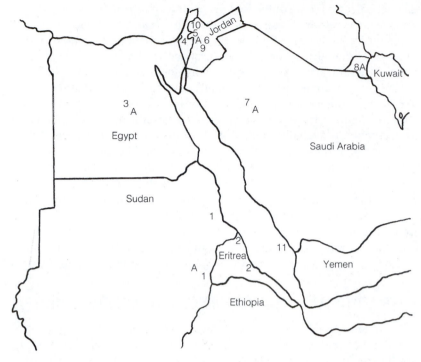

Figure 11.1 Geographical distribution of the Rashaayda, Bani Rashiid, and 'Awaazim "tribes." Locations inhabited by Rashaayda and Bani Rashiid are identified by numbers 1–11. Locations inhabited by "branches" of the 'Awaazim "tribes" are marked by the letter, "A."

between the Rashaayda and 'Awaazim is similar to the relationship between the Bani Rashiid and 'Awaazim in northwestern Arabia, near Khaybar. The two groups do not claim common descent but have lived as close neighbors for a very long time (von Oppenheim 1952, 85; al-Waa'ili 2002, 650–651, 1515). The Rashaayda of Kuwait—who live near the western border of the country in a region called al-Dabdaba (al-'Ubayd 1971, 60; al-Waa'ili 2002, 652)—are also neighbors of a separate "tribe" called the 'Awaazim. Some 'Awaazim live about 12 miles to the east of the Rashaayda in a village called Dalii' al-'Awaazim, whereas others live in the village of Thaaj, along with a group that is identified by the 'Aazimi author as "hutaym" (al-Hawaazini 1998, 170, 210, 231) but who are probably Rashaayda. What is more, some small descent groups known as "Rashaayda" and "'Awaazim" are found in central Egypt between the cities of Sohag and Qina (al-Hawaazini 1998, 110; al-Waa'ili 2002, 652, 1516). Finally, 'Awaazim live in the Jordanian village of Maa'iin, southwest of the town of Maadaba (al-Hawaazini 1998, 110, 333, 336), which is only 24 miles northwest of al-Simaakiya, a town where some Rashaayda live (Young 1999, 293; Young, al-Baqain, and Burnett 2001).

This combination of two identical names (Rashaayda and 'Awaazim) in five widely separated locations (see Figure 11.1) is probably not a mere coincidence.

It seems very likely that some ancestral confederation of Rashaayda and 'Awaazim originally shared a common territory. At some point, parts of this ancestral confederation left their territory in northwestern Arabia and spread out, eventually reaching Sudan, Palestine, and Kuwait. My guess is that this began in the sixteenth century and continued throughout the eighteenth and nineteenth centuries.[4] Unfortunately almost no documentary evidence exists to support this historical dispersion. The groups involved were illiterate nomads who did not attract the attention of government record keepers or tax collectors, much less that of chroniclers and historians. Only a few documents even mention the Rashaayda.

In light of these difficulties, we must leave the key historical questions— Where was the ancestral group located? When and why did it break up? How did each fragment of this ancestral group end up where it is now?—to the ethnohistorians, who will have to use nondocumentary evidence to try to answer them. I will not try to find and weigh the evidence here but will only say that I find the Rashaayda's argument convincing. It seems likely that all of the groups who now call themselves Rashaayda or Bani Rashiid were at some point members of a single society that initially included the ancestors of the 'Awaazim as well and that is now dispersed.[5]

Even if this story of common origins were not convincing to me, however, I would still have to acknowledge it as a cultural and social reality for the Rashaayda. Every group of the Rashaayda that I have visited (three groups in Jordan, one in Sudan, and one in Saudi Arabia) is fascinated by this historical reconstruction and is passionately committed to finding its place in history and reestablishing its broken ties to distant cousins elsewhere. Regardless of the historical accuracy of this reconstruction, it has become part of the Rashaayda's worldview and must be included in any ethnography of them. What I want to know is, why are the Rashaayda of Sudan no longer content to present themselves as a purely local society?

When I arrived in Sudan late in 1977, some of the Rashaayda mentioned that they had emigrated from Arabia and that their relatives there were known as "Bani Rashiid." They also acknowledged that "branches" of the Rashaayda were living in Egypt (Young 1998, 73–74). But they were not terribly clear about the identity of the Bani Rashiid and tended to confuse them with the powerful Aal Rashiid of Haayil, claiming, incorrectly, that it was the Bani Rashiid, not the Aal Rashiid, who had fought the Saud dynasty (Hasan 1974, 2, 6, 22). A researcher studying the Rashaayda in neighboring Eritrea heard the same story from elderly informants in 1985 (Mehari 1986, 5). So until 1985 many Rashaayda were content to claim a vague affiliation with either the Bani Rashiid or Aal Rashiid, not troubling to distinguish them. They merely wanted to establish a historical link of some sort with Saudi citizens, without tying themselves to the Bani Rashiid.

It was not until the mid-1990s that Rashaayda on the western shore of the Red Sea chose to affiliate specifically with the Bani Rashiid and try to rewrite their histories and genealogies to support this affiliation. This step is transforming them from a local society into a transnational social formation. I will argue that this transformation has been caused by the outbreak of war in eastern Sudan and Eritrea and the effects warfare has had on all of the "tribes" in these regions.

THE HISTORY OF "TRIBAL" AFFILIATIONS IN EASTERN SUDAN

The Rashaayda of eastern Sudan have not developed close alliances with any of the other inhabitants of the region. Most of the other "tribes" there—the Bani 'Aamir and Hadendowa—speak Cushitic languages, not Arabic. Urban Sudanese in Kassala speak Arabic, but in the countryside, only the Rashaayda and Lahawiyiin "tribes" are Arabic-speaking (see Young 1996, 30, 105–112). Generally, the Rashaayda do not feel threatened by neighboring "tribes." Since the early twentieth century they have occupied a portion of the inland savannah that cannot easily be utilized by the cattle-herding Hadendowa and Bani 'Aamir, because this area does not receive enough rainfall to support cattle. The neighboring "tribes" generally allowed the Rashaayda to exploit this niche unmolested. Thus the Sudanese Rashaayda have had little need for alliances with outsiders.

This is not to say that the Sudanese Rashaayda have been completely isolated from outside influences. During the late nineteenth century some Rashaayda were forced by warfare to flee from Sudan into Eritrea and did not return to Sudan until 1903. Some of them, in fact, did not return at all but remained in their camps along the Red Sea, in the Eritrean coastal lands (Young 1998). Later, during World War II, the Rashaayda near Kassala witnessed the battles that took place between British forces and the Italian colonial government of Eritrea in 1941, culminating in the extension of British colonial rule from Sudan into Eritrea. This briefly brought the Sudanese Rashaayda closer to their relatives in Eritrea, because it reduced barriers to travel and trade between the two regions. In fact, the British were in favor of partitioning Eritrea into two parts. They considered merging the part of the country inhabited by the Eritrean Rashaayda with Sudan. If this partition had taken place, the region's two groups of Rashaayda would probably have been blended together again. But the British military administration withdrew from Eritrea in 1952, when the United Nations made Eritrea part of a federation with Ethiopia (Encyclopaedia Britannica 1958, 690; Sherman 1980, 16–19, 23–26).

The withdrawal of Britain from Eritrea and the subsequent hardening of the border between British-administered Sudan and what became the Eritrean province of Ethiopia firmly encapsulated the Sudanese Rashaayda within the Sudanese state and cut them off from their relatives across the border. In that context, they became a truly local society. For the next 23 years—that is, from 1952 to 1975—their most important social relationships were with other citizens of Sudan.

THE ECONOMIC INTERNATIONALIZATION OF EASTERN SUDAN

Starting in 1975 an array of transnational forces began to undermine the boundary between Sudan and Eritrea and prompt the Sudanese Rashaayda to look for allies and trading partners outside of Sudan. The first force was economic. The Saudi oil boom, which began in 1974, dramatically increased the demand for labor in Saudi Arabia (El Mallakh 1982; Metz 1993). By 1975 thousands of Sudanese citizens, among them many Rashaayda, had responded to the lure of high-paying work in Saudi Arabia. They spent a year or so overseas and then returned to Sudan (Young 1998; Young 1996, 20). In other words, labor migration established relationships between the peoples of eastern Sudan and Saudi Arabia that transcended national boundaries.

While working in Saudi Arabia some Rashiidi men made contact with members of the Saudi Bani Rashiid "tribes." Although they were pleased to encounter their long-lost relatives, they did not enter into any business partnerships with them, because the Bani Rashiid generally were neither wealthy nor prominent in Saudi commerce and industry. However, the attraction of employment in Saudi Arabia kept the Sudanese Rashaayda coming back, year after year, and so increased the frequency and continuity of contacts between the Rashaayda and the Saudi Bani Rashiid. What is more, the Rashaayda soon discovered that, when they told Saudi customs officials that their ancestors had once lived in Saudi Arabia and that their distant kin still lived there, they received special treatment. The Saudi government facilitated their entry into the country, granting them visas more quickly than they did for other Sudanese citizens. One Rashiidi boy whom I met in 1979 was even granted a scholarship for study in Riyadh and went to live there at government expense for two years. Thus the Rashaayda had practical reasons for identifying with the Bani Rashiid, in addition to pure nostalgia for their original homeland.

The oil boom had another effect: it made more capital available to the Sudanese government. Saudi capital was used to help finance large public works projects. Unfortunately, the benefits of the oil boom for Sudan were offset by government corruption, unrealistic development planning, and soaring military spending (which increased dramatically after 1983, when the Sudanese civil war reemerged). These difficulties were compounded by two severe droughts and an influx of more than one million refugees from Eritrea, Ethiopia, Chad, and Uganda. After 1978 the gross domestic product of Sudan fell steadily. The money that the Sudanese migrant workers in the Gulf countries sent home was rarely invested in production but instead was spent on consumer goods and housing. Between 1978 and 1985, agricultural and industrial production had declined, and imports were three times the level of exports (Metz 1992; Nelson 1982, 142–146, 188–191).

The main effect of this economic crisis for the Rashaayda has been to reduce the value of pastoralism. Prior to 1975, most Rashaayda preferred to live simply, using the wild plants of the desert pastures to feed their animals and weaving the heavy cloth for their tents from the wool and hair that they sheared from their animals. All of these products could be had for free, and they gave the pastoral Rashaayda economic independence. But for the last 20 years, costly manufactured goods—many purchased with remittances that Sudanese migrant workers sent home from Saudi Arabia—have been pouring into eastern Sudan. Now the Rashaayda view them as necessities, not luxuries. The demand for expensive synthetic fabrics, for example, has greatly increased among the Rashaayda. Recent photographs of Rashiidi women, taken in July 2003 (Pelletier 2003), show them wearing brilliantly colored print cloth, tailored to conform to traditional clothing styles. Now Rashiidi men also wear brightly colored turbans and outer garments (or *thawbs*) that differ markedly in hue from their traditionally white clothing (see Young 1996, 36–39, 46, 53, 54, 71, 80, 81, 88–89, 134). Also, the Sudanese Rashaayda now use canvas for building their tents rather than weaving tent cloth out of a mixture of camel and sheep's wool, goat hair, and cotton (see Young 1996, 36–37, 46, 51). They have followed the example of Saudi Bedouin, who began replacing their hand-woven tent cloth with canvas when the oil boom started.

Subsistence livestock and grain production, formerly the basis of the Rashaayda's nomadic life (Young 1996, 34–42, 48–54), is no longer considered the ideal way to make a living. The expenses of pastoral production have soared since 1980, largely because of the introduction of mechanized agricultural schemes into what were formerly open pasturelands. Starting in 1975, the Sudanese government opened large tracts of government land in eastern Sudan to agricultural firms, in effect giving away government-controlled land to wealthy supporters and clients. Many of the wild pastures formerly exploited by nomads are now closed during the growing season. Although the stubble from crops is available as fodder after harvesting, it is not free; the cultivators sell it to the Rashaayda, who bring their livestock into the fields to eat the stubble. This food is not cheap. The average family has to sell three to four of its camels every year to get the cash it needs for a season's worth of fodder. A wealthy family that owned 100 camels had to pay 50,000 Sudanese pounds (about US$430) in 1990 to keep them fed. What is worse, the agricultural firms do not bother to correct the effects of such intensive cultivation on soil fertility and stability by using fertilizers. Instead, once the soil in a given plot is exhausted, they move on to new virgin territory, leaving behind them an infertile wasteland that is useful neither for pasture nor cultivation. This means that the pastures available to the Rashaayda are shrinking permanently, not just over the short run (Köhler-Rollefson et al. 1991, 73–75). More and more, the Rashaayda have to purchase fodder and grain to keep their animals alive during the dry seasons.

Another reason why subsistence pastoralism is no longer valued is the increase in demand for consumer goods and permanent housing, all of which cost money. One Rashiidi man in Riyadh complained to me bitterly in 2002 that his wife and children were still living in tents in the desert. He wanted to build a house in town for them; that was why he worked in Saudi Arabia. His attitude contrasted sharply with my Rashiidi friends' statements in 1979. At that time, they were afraid that their herd of camels might shrink because of illness and drought and worried that they might be forced to find a place to live near Kassala if they no longer had enough animals to move their tents during the rainy season migration. Rather than viewing this as an upward move, they thought settling in town would be a terrible defeat for them; even a temporary abandonment of pastoralism was seen as a calamity from which they might never recover.

Insofar as the expanding cash economy has made pastoralism less attractive for the Rashaayda, it also compels them, more than ever, to look for cash income outside of Sudan. Thus economic forces are pushing them out of the local economy into the international labor market.

A second influence from Saudi Arabia also impacted the Rashaayda: Usaama bin Laadin. In late 1991 bin Laadin came to Sudan after cementing a political alliance between himself and the two most powerful politicians in the country: President 'Umar Hasan al-Bashiir and Hasan al-Turaabi, the head of a religiously conservative party called the National Islamic Front. Bin Laadin soon set up an import company in the Red Sea port of 'Aqiiq—where some nomadic Rashaayda often spend the early months of summer (Young 1996, 31). His construction company, al-Hijra, began building roads and bridges. By the end of 1993 this company had constructed a new, more direct road from Khartoum to Port Sudan that was about 250 miles shorter than the old road (Bergen 2001, 79–81; Fisk 1993). More importantly—for the Rashaayda—the new road cut straight through their traditional grazing lands and linked Kassala directly to the center of the Khashm al-Qirba agricultural scheme (also known as the New Halfa scheme) (Macmillan 1999, 200–201; Young 1996, 30, 32).

One might ask whether the Rashaayda in these areas, who possibly came into contact with bin Laadin or his followers, were at all attracted to him. Certainly the Rashaayda and some of bin Laadin's Saudi disciples shared cultural and linguistic affinities because, culturally, the Rashaayda are more Saudi than Sudanese. When I met some Sudanese Rashaayda in Riyadh in 2002 I asked them about the political situation in eastern Sudan and bin Laadin's effect on it. They asserted that they were ready to resist bin Laadin and said they would gladly volunteer their services if asked to fight him. As we will see, their disinterest in bin Laadin's ideology and movement is consistent with their unwillingness to attach themselves too closely to the current Sudanese government. Bin Laadin is a partner of that government by virtue of his close ties with al-Bashiir and al-Turaabi. From the Rashaayda's perspective, then, he is an unlikely ally.

Bin Laadin's main construction project—the Khartoum-Port Sudan road—did have an effect on them, however. The increase of traffic on this road, in combination with the spread of mechanized agriculture in the region, transformed Kassala into a major road junction and invigorated its local commerce (Woodward 1990, 187–194), providing more opportunities for Rashiidi livestock merchants. It also made it much easier for the still-nomadic Rashaayda near Kassala to visit their semisedentary relatives in the New Halfa scheme (Young 1996, 29–30). This economic change also tended to draw the Rashaayda out of subsistence pastoralism into commerce. Like other Sudanese merchants, they became more interested in the import-export trade than in livestock breeding.

INTERNATIONAL POLITICS AND THE UNSTABLE NATIONAL BORDER BETWEEN SUDAN AND ERITREA

The other transnational forces that affected the Rashaayda were political. Ultimately they were generated by two civil wars: the clash between Eritrean nationalists and supporters of the Ethiopian empire, on the one hand, and the conflict between southern Sudanese and the central Sudanese government, on the other. Each of these civil conflicts had a different effect on the Rashaayda. The conflict between Eritreans and Ethiopians cut lines of communication between the Sudanese and Eritrean Rashaayda from 1952 to 2000—except for the period from about 1975 to 1985, when the border along the Red Sea coast was relatively open—and kept them isolated from each other. The civil war in Sudan, on the other hand, exposed the Sudanese Rashaayda to unprecedented dangers and forced them to seek new allies. In some cases these Rashaayda have had to leave Sudan entirely and find new homes in Eritrea.

The War in Eritrea

To see how the Eritrean conflict isolated the Eritrean Rashaayda we must first understand the impact of Eritrean geography on them. The Eritrean Rashaayda traditionally stayed in touch with their relatives in Sudan by traveling overland to visit them. They also brought their livestock to market in Kassala or Suakin. It was easy for them to reach Suakin from their camps along the Red Sea coast, and it was also possible for them to reach Kassala by migrating southwestward, crossing over the mountainous north-central zone of Eritrea to reach the town of Nak'fa, then following roads and established trails to the towns of Keren, Ak'ordat, Tesseney, and finally Kassala. Because this was a journey of over 200 miles it would not be undertaken frivolously. Yet it was no longer than the customary summer migration route of some Sudanese Rashaayda, who move from the Red Sea coast to the 'Atbara River during June and July (Young 1996, 31). These two land routes were the chief lines of communication. The war in Eritrea often disrupted or closed both of the overland routes, depending on the intensity of fighting. This in turn affected social relations between the two "branches" of the "tribe."

Armed warfare between the Eritrean insurgency movements and the Ethiopian Army began in the early 1960s and did not cease until Eritrea won complete independence from Ethiopia late in 1991. The course of the war was complicated by serious divisions within the ranks of the Eritrean fighters, internal changes in the Ethiopian government, and the government of Sudan's alternately warm and cool diplomatic relations with the Eritreans. All of these factors led to setbacks in the Eritreans' fight for independence.

An umbrella movement calling itself the Eritrean Liberation Front (ELF) initiated the fighting in the early 1960s. In 1967, however, the Ethiopian air force badly hurt the ELF by aerial bombardment of its home base. Well over three hundred villages in ELF-controlled areas in the west of the country were burned, sending some 30,000 refugees into Sudan. After three years, however, the ELF recovered and struck at Ethiopian Army bases again. In 1970, the Ethiopians counterattacked, again using air power, and completely depopulated the border zone between Sudan and Eritrea. At least 50,000 people from this area entered Sudan as refugees. Their numbers were probably higher, however; many of them were Bani 'Aamir nomads who simply crossed into Sudan without troubling to register with the government as refugees, because they could live with relatives on the other side of the border (Rogge 1985, 47; Sherman 1980, 76, 79–80). These battles certainly prevented the Rashaayda in coastal Eritrea from crossing the country to reach Kassala, although they did not stop them from visiting Suakin by boat if they so desired.

Ethiopian victories in 1970 caused the alliances that had held the ELF together to unravel. Two factions emerged: one that was largely Muslim and was based in the southwestern lowlands and another that had a largely Christian identity (although it espoused a secular, Marxist ideology). The latter group, after absorbing the followers of the Muslim leader Osman Saleh Sabbe, broke away from the ELF in 1972 and called itself the Eritrean People's Liberation Front (EPLF). Skirmishes between these two factions broke out between 1972 and 1974, even as they battled the Ethiopian Army. In 1972, a sudden rapprochement between the Ethiopian government and the Sudan weakened the ELF. Ethiopia's Haile Selassie succeeded in mediating Sudan's own civil conflict, giving Sudan its best chance of peace in decades. Out of gratitude for Ethiopia's intervention, Khartoum helped to undermine Selassie's Eritrean adversaries by preventing ELF forces from crossing the Sudanese border. The EPLF, who did not use the same supply routes, was less affected. In January 1974, when the EPLF soundly defeated Ethiopian forces at Asmara, it proved itself a better fighter than the weakened ELF. This enabled the EPLF to recruit even more followers, completely eclipsing the ELF (Morrison 1976, 7; Rogge 1985, 47; Sherman 1980, 42–46, 54–69, 85).

The Rashaayda were not completely oblivious of these divisions within Eritrean ranks. They realized that the two separate forces fighting Ethiopia also had fought each other between 1972 and 1974. But none of the Rashaayda were allied to either faction at this point, so the Eritrean gains and setbacks meant little to them. They merely observed while the EPLF scored more victories against Ethiopia. They heard about the intense fighting during 1975 and 1976 and knew that waves of Eritrea refugees—some 50,000 of them—were pouring out of the battle zones into temporary camps in eastern Sudan (Rogge 1985, 48). By the end of 1977, when I was in the field with the Rashaayda near Kassala, the Eritrean insurgents controlled 95 percent of their country and seemed to be close to victory. Suddenly, however, the Ethiopians hit back with overwhelming air power, supplied by the Soviet Union. Some of the Rashaayda who were in Eritrea at that time saw the aerial bombardments and told us about them when they visited us in 1978.

During 1978 the Ethiopians were once again on the offensive. The EPLF was forced to evacuate all of the cities and towns that it had taken and retreat to its home base in the mountains of northern Eritrea, near Nak'fa. The ELF, on the other hand, tried to hold on to its lowland territories in the southwest, where many of its members lived. Its more exposed positions were much more difficult to defend from air strikes than the EPLF's mountain base and, as a result, it suffered many casualties. Due to its vulnerability, the ELF felt compelled to try to negotiate with the Ethiopians in 1979. On its part, Addis Ababa was willing to strike a bargain; it offered the ELF a governing role in Eritrea if the ELF would consent to federation with Ethiopia. Before any agreement could be reached, however, the EPLF moved vigorously to prevent this. It attacked the ELF and defeated it, leaving the ELF fighters only two choices: join the EPLF or flee to Sudan. The EPLF was henceforth the only guerrilla force in Eritrea. In 1988 it captured Afabet, headquarters of the Ethiopian Army in northeastern Eritrea (Connell 1997, 173–82, 205–08, 228; Negash 1997, 160–163; Sherman 1980, 72, 92, 93) and effectively ended Ethiopian rule in Eritrea.

These events had important consequences for the Eritrean Rashaayda. Prior to 1988, they had been living in uneasy proximity to the Ethiopian Army's headquarters in Afabet, at the southernmost edge of their pasturelands, while they were also within easy reach of the EPLF headquarters in Nak'fa, only 50 miles to their east (Defense Mapping Agency 1982, 37, 507). Granted, the EPLF's headquarters were also some 6,000 feet higher in elevation, presenting quite a different target to Ethiopian bombers than the Rashaayda's tents far below on the Red Sea coastline. But the Rashaayda could not ignore the attacks and counteroffensives in the neighboring mountains.

During the 1980s the Eritrean Rashaayda tried to keep their distance from both sides. Despite this, the new socialist regime in Ethiopia tried to court them and by 1986 had reclassified them as "the Rashaida ethnic nationality in socialist Ethiopia." This Ethiopian government made some efforts to provide them with schools and medical facilities in order to win their loyalty (Mehari 1986, 25). When the EPLF took control of Afabet in 1988, it was prepared to make a similar offer to the Eritrean Rashaayda. They pledged to recognize the Rashaayda as an "ethnic group" with rights to full citizenship in the future independent state of Eritrea. Thus the Rashaayda developed a political relationship, if not a full-blown alliance, with the leadership of the EPLF. The EPLF fulfilled its promise in 1993, when national elections were held and Eritrea became an independent country. Now, even though the Rashaayda comprise only 1 percent of Eritrea's population, they are officially regarded as one of the nine "ethnic groups" in the country (Connell 1997, 49; Negash 1997, 168–170).

The War in Sudan

The Sudanese Civil War, which had begun in 1956 but had subsided in 1972, broke out again in February 1983 when President Ja'far al-Numayri tried to suppress an insurgency in the south. The insurgents initially were not successful, but al-Numayri made the mistake of sending northern Sudanese soldiers to fight them and transferring southern Sudanese troops—who he feared might not be loyal—to the north. This move, coupled with many long-standing problems, triggered negative reactions in the south and led more southerners to join the insurgency. Struggling to maintain his position, al-Numayri sought the support of religiously conservative northern Sudanese (including Hasan al-Turaabi, the leader of the National Islamic Front) by embarking on a thorough Islamicization of the country's legal system (Hamdi 1998, 4–5; Woodward 1990, 153–162). This further alienated the south, as well as secular northerners, and tied the government to an Islamic party whose previous role in national politics had been marginal.

Having isolated himself politically, al-Numayri was overthrown by a military coup in 1985. Successor governments also failed to make peace with the southerners, and in June 1989 Colonel 'Umar Hasan al-Bashiir carried out another military coup (Hamdi 1998, 6–7; O'Ballance 2000, 165–166), who also allied himself with Hasan al-Turaabi's National Islamic Front. Like al-Numayri, al-Bashiir was unable to resolve the conflict. Moreover, he and al-Turaabi alienated other northern Sudanese politicians to such an extent that some of them joined the southern rebels and formed the National Democratic Alliance in October 1989. This umbrella organization brought together many different opposition groups and parties, including the Democratic Unionist Party and the Umma Party

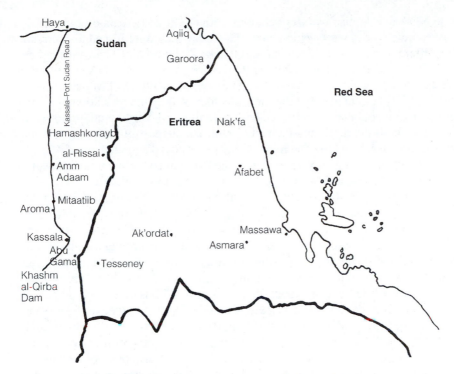

Figure 11.2 The unstable national border between Sudan and Eritrea

(both based in northern Sudan) and the Sudan People's Liberation Movement (the most prominent southern party). In addition, it included some specifically eastern Sudanese parties such as the Beja Congress (headed by 'Umar Muhammad Taahir) and the Free Lions Association (*tanziim al-usuud al-hurra*, headed by Mabruuk Mubaarak Saliim) (Web site of the National Democratic Alliance, www.ndasudan.org).

What mattered—from the Rashaayda's point of view—was that the National Democratic Alliance (NDA) has been using Eritrea as a base for military operations against the Sudanese government. International opponents of the Khartoum government, including the United States, have given the NDA the funding they need to train military units. Their raids across the border into Sudan, and the Sudanese government's counterattacks, have turned the border area, and with it much of the Rashaayda's traditional pasturelands, into a war zone.

This did not happen overnight. When the NDA was formed in October 1989, it at first called for a nonviolent campaign to overthrow the government in Khartoum. This proved impossible, as most of the opposition political parties inside the country had been banned and many opposition leaders were arrested in 1990. This stymied the NDA, because it had no alternative means—that is, armed paramilitary forces—for bringing down the al-Bashiir regime. Southern opposition groups, headed by the Sudan People's Liberation Movement (SPLM), had been waging war since 1983. They were much better qualified to mount attacks against government forces, but it took time for the northern political groups in the NDA to establish working relations with the SPLM. Years of mutual mistrust separated the two opposition blocs. However, they were forced to overcome their differences because of the many setbacks that both blocs had suffered between 1990 and 1993, including internal divisions within the NDA and military defeats of the SPLM forces in southern Sudan. By 1995 the SPLM had formally joined the NDA. Late in 1996, this step was followed by the formation of a Joint Military Command that was charged with planning and carrying out military operations in both the north and the south, with the support of both northern and southern Sudanese fighters. The Joint Military Command operated out of Asmara, using the Sudanese Embassy building that the Eritrean government turned over to the NDA in 1995 (Adar 2001; Lesch 1998, 149–152, 187–189, 262).

On October 8, 1996, the first NDA military operation in eastern Sudan was directed against a military garrison in Tuqan, "100 km [62 miles] from Aroma." It was followed by an attack on government troops "45 km [28 miles] southwest of Kassala" in November. In December a Sudanese government military helicopter was shot down near the Eritrean border. On December 28, about 1,500 rebels assaulted two brigades of government troops in Hamashkorayb, near the Port Sudan-Kassala highway about 65 miles north of Kassala.

Fighting intensified in January 1997 when the NDA launched a major offensive and captured many border positions in Blue Nile province, 200 miles south of Kassala. At the same time other NDA forces attacked the military garrison at Gadamayaib, northeast of Kassala. In April 1997 the garrisons of Gadamayaib and Tuqan—which had been attacked earlier but apparently had not been seized—were hit again and captured this time, along with garrisons in the Red Sea towns of Garoora and 'Aqiiq (Defense Mapping Agency 1989, 79, 438; O'Ballance 2000, 192).[6] The Sudanese Rashaayda frequented all of these garrison towns and villages, which lay within their traditional pasturelands.

For the next 10 months the NDA held back, neither gaining nor losing ground in eastern Sudan. But on February 3, 1998, it attacked al-Qaradha, "the largest of six garrisons guarding Kassala. . . ." Khartoum, however, claimed that government forces had been on the offensive near al-Qaradha and had wiped out a "rebel base." On the same day, according to Sudanese government statements, an artillery barrage from across the Eritrean border hit the town of Abu Gamal, barely 20 miles south of Kassala (Defense Mapping Agency 1989, 512; Young 1996, 32), killing three people and wounding 21. Skirmishing apparently continued until the end of February. On April 11, 1998, the NDA ambushed a government convoy on the road between Kassala and Khashm al-Qirba. In June they also attacked an army camp some 26 miles south of Kassala.

In June 1998 government forces counterattacked. They claimed to have defeated an "armed opposition group" near Kassala and said that the coastal town of Garoora, which opposition forces had captured the previous year, was now back in government hands. Opposition groups close to Kassala responded, sometimes by trying to shell government positions. On October 15, 1998, two children were killed and 132 were injured when the Wad Sharifai refugee camp, only 12 miles south of Kassala, was shelled. The International Committee of the Red Cross and Red Crescent, which released this news, stated that at least 55,000 people had moved from their villages along Sudan's eastern border with

Eritrea due to the fighting. In short, Kassala became a very dangerous place during 1998.

In 1999 the NDA began an effort to prevent travel to Kassala by attacking the roads leading to it. It struck a new Sudanese Army garrison that had been charged with guarding the road between Khashm al-Qirba and Kassala on April 11, closing the road for that entire day. On July 8, a truck belonging to the government petroleum company struck a land mine while traveling on the road between Sinkaat and Haya, about 225 miles north of Kassala. Two expatriates and one Sudanese were wounded. Government forces carried out a mine-clearing operation and found 80 more mines. To guard against such incidents, travel on this road was restricted for the next five months. Later in the year, attacks on the road between Kassala and Port Sudan forced the government to close the road entirely. Further north, fighting in Sitrab prompted local authorities to restrict travel on the road between Tokar and Port Sudan to daylight hours only.

In addition to these efforts to block the roads, the NDA conducted operations against other targets in 1999. In May, opposition forces launched an attack on the army garrison in al-Rissai, in Hamashkorayb province (north of Kassala), and captured it. NDA allies also attacked the barracks in Laffa, "13 km [8 miles] from Kassala" (Defense Mapping Agency 1989, 84) in that month. The opposition groups also tried to wreck the pipeline that carried refined oil from Port Sudan to Khartoum. On November 27, they blew up a section of it some 4 miles north of Erkowit—that is, some 280 miles north of Kassala.[7]

During most of 2000, opposition groups were completely in control of a 75 mile-long swath of territory along the Eritrean-Sudanese border, extending from the province of Hamashkorayb southward toward Kassala. It was not until November of that year that Sudanese government forces managed to take it back. The struggle for this territory caused heavy casualties on both sides. In the course of the fighting the NDA actually invaded the town of Kassala, on November 8, 2000, and held it for 24 hours before withdrawing. They said that they had accomplished their military objectives, that is, the seizure of military equipment, including 13 tanks, and the destruction of the military headquarters. Sudan accused Eritrea of supporting rebel groups and sending its own troops to northern Hamashkorayb where, it said, "they were 'extensively' deployed . . . near the areas of Gadamayet and Gergif. . . ." (Defense Mapping Agency 1989, 214).[8]

The struggle between the NDA (supported by its Eritrean allies) and the Sudanese government continued into 2002, when the NDA attempted to regain its lost positions in Hamashkorayb. In October 2002, skirmishes in the area "caused large-scale displacement of populations. Some 6,000 persons escaped from the war areas and resettled in Matatieb, Hadalia . . . [and other villages] . . . in the northern part of the state, increasing the number of internally displaced persons in the area by approximately 12,000" (Defense Mapping Agency 1989, 244). Fighting also erupted around al-Rissai and stopped the movement of traffic on the Port Sudan-Kassala road.[9]

Located in the center of this war zone, the Rashaayda near Kassala no longer had the luxury of remaining uninvolved in Sudanese politics. Some Rashaayda apparently had even participated in the NDA's military operations against Khartoum. They were members of the Free Lion's Association, one of the organizations that was included in the NDA and that in fact was headed by one of the leaders of the Baraatiikh "branch" of the Rashaayda "tribe." Judging from its name—the "Free Lions"—we can surmise that this association is exclusively for the Rashaayda. The notion that the Rashaayda are "free Arabs" is an important component of their identity (Young 1996, 108–112).[10]

Little is known about the association's history and goals. It does not appear to have existed prior to June 23, 1995, when most of the other member organizations of the National Democratic Alliance—including the Beja Congress—pledged to work for freedom of religion and political expression in Sudan (www.ndasudan.org/English/confer.religion.htm). One possible reason why the Rashaayda formed it may have been to counter the influence of the Beja Congress. The Beja Congress represents the Rashaayda's traditional enemies, the Hadendowa "tribe" (Manger 2001; Young 1996, 13, 30–31, 110–112). Both the Beja Congress and the Rashaayda are betting that the NDA might defeat the Sudanese government and form a new government of its own. In that case, both the Beja and the Rashaayda "tribes" will have influence in the new government. It would not be wise for either "tribe" to ignore this possibility. To safeguard their future, they both must share in the NDA's military and political activities against the Khartoum government now.

To sum up, civil wars in both Sudan and Eritrea have entangled the Rashaayda in national and international politics, forcing them into unsought allegiances with the ruling party in Eritrea, on the one hand, and the opposition parties in Sudan, on the other. Because of their relatively small numbers, the Rashaayda can only be marginal players in these political alliances and risk being pulled in directions that are not to their benefit. For this reason it makes sense for them to build partnerships with their Bani Rashiid kin on the eastern shore of the Red Sea. Years of warfare have also devastated the economies of both Sudan and Eritrea, so that the Rashaayda increasingly look elsewhere—that is, Saudi Arabia—for their primary sources of income. Economic factors, then, also provide a motive for the Rashaayda of Sudan and Eritrea to join with the Bani Rashiid of Saudi Arabia.

We can readily understand why the Rashaayda wanted to develop ties with the Bani Rashiid. What we still need to know is why the Bani Rashiid were so receptive. As I will show, the warm welcome that the Bani Rashiid gave to their Sudanese and Eritrean "cousins" was prompted by the social conditions in which they live in Saudi Arabia.

THE BANI RASHIID IN SAUDI ARABIA

Through no particular fault of their own, the Bani Rashiid of Saudi Arabia have been on the losing side of history for many centuries. Although there are a few indications that some of their ancestors might have held positions of power in southwestern Palestine during the sixteenth century (Young 1998, 77), in general the Bani Rashiid have lived in scattered, impoverished settlements in some of the most arid and undesirable parts of northwestern Arabia. Their settlements are all in or near a desolate mountainous area called Harrat Khaybar, which is covered with black fragments of basalt thrown up by an ancient volcanic eruption.[11] This blasted landscape is almost useless for both agriculture and pastoralism. Because their natural environment was so harsh, the Bani Rashiid could not sustain the large camel herds owned by wealthier Bedouin. Further, their poverty deprived them of the weapons and the large numbers of fighters that Bedouin groups need to defend themselves; they were regarded as weaklings who could be plundered with impunity. Their vulnerable condition forced them to seek protectors, who also exploited and ridiculed them.

As a consequence of their difficult circumstances, the Bani Rashiid have been categorized as *hutaym*,[12] a label for low-status groups in Arabia that has connotations of political weakness, poverty, and "mixed" or "impure" descent. The "hutaym" are said to have "forgotten" their origins; supposedly, they do not really know whom their ancestors were and cannot produce any long genealogies to link the living generation with known forefathers. They are also said to marry non-Arabs and, for this reason, none of the "pure" Arab "tribes" will give their daughters to "hutaym" in marriage (von Oppenheim 1952, 151). In fact, stereotypes do not really apply to the Bani Rashiid. The Bani Rashiid have not married non-Arabs. Furthermore, they can produce a fairly lengthy genealogy that links them to their eponymous ancestor, Rashiid al-Zawl. But most of the dominant "tribes" in Saudi Arabia do not accept this genealogy as genuine and refer to the Bani Rashiid as "hutaym" rather than calling them by the name that they themselves use.

Dominant groups have always applied the epithet hutaym to stigmatize those they wish to dominate or marginalize. It is a rhetorical weapon, a slur that marginal people in Arabia have to endure because they cannot persuade or force their oppressors to retract it. The Bani Rashiid were not the only inhabitants of northern Arabia who have been called "hutaym." Other "tribes," such as the 'Awaazim of Kuwait and the Sharaaraat of northwestern Arabia were also stigmatized in this manner. However, after they managed to arm themselves and demonstrate their military prowess, either by fighting off attackers or joining more powerful groups as allies in the nineteenth century, they won the respect of neighboring Bedouin "tribes" and were accepted as equals.[13]

The motivation for the Bani Rashiid's identification with the Rashaayda is now clear. They want to associate themselves with the Rashaayda of Sudan and Eritrea because they are arguably closer to the ideal of the "pure Arab" than the Bani Rashiid are themselves. The Rashaayda are "pure Arabs" in that they do not depend on anyone else for protection. Also, they control a territory and have extensive camel herds that give them economic self-sufficiency and mobility. Finally, they have occasionally joined with other Arab "tribes" (such as the Lahawiyiin) in conflicts against non-Arabic speakers, which indicates that other Arabs consider them equals. If the Bani Rashiid can prove that they are related to the Rashaayda—and this is easy to do—they can also argue that they are "pure Arabs," like the Rashaayda.

The Rashaayda of Sudan have something to lose by associating with the Bani Rashiid. They do not want to be classified as "hutaym" and recognize that the process of invidious labeling that has marginalized the Bani Rashiid is contagious and could possibly be extended to them. But they also have much to gain from this association. The government of Saudi Arabia has already given them

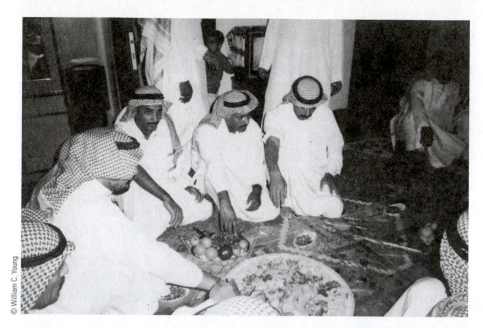

Members of the Saudi Bani Rashiid tribe enjoying the hospitality of Mr. 'Ata Alla Dyf Allah al Rashiidi. They have been served a traditional meal of cooked mutton on a bed of rice. Like most Bedouin, the men all use their right hands to eat and take their food from a shared platter.

preferential treatment with respect to visas, regarding them as Saudis in diaspora because their kin, the Bani Rashiid, are Saudi citizens. As long as jobs are more plentiful in Saudi Arabia than in Sudan, the Rashaayda will need this Saudi connection. So the Rashaayda have supported the Bani Rashiid's efforts to shed the label "hutaym" by joining forces with them ideologically.

THE BANI RASHIID CAMPAIGN TO REWORK GENEALOGIES AND HISTORY

What efforts are the Bani Rashiid making to shed this label? One of them involves publishing "correct" versions of their history and winning the support of respected Saudi scholars. In response to their questions about their origins, the prominent Saudi historian and genealogist, Hamad al-Jaasir, has affirmed that the Bani Rashiid are "true" Arabs whose roots can be traced to the ancient Arab tribe of 'Abs. He went on to say that "the Bani Rashiid are accomplished in religion, good morals, and generosity. They have brought warriors and leaders to the fields of battle and are known to be honorable. They have recognized lines of descent and have a place and good status and good relationships by marriage in the sedentary community. In the Bedouin community they are known to be honorable, of pure descent and good affiliations. They have preserved their honor and [Arab] origins throughout their migrations and have kept them intact, both in sedentary communities and Bedouin communities" (al-Jaasir 1970, 45, 229, 523, 526, 534;

The author with Mr. 'Ata Allah Dayf Allah al-Rashiidi. Mr. 'Ata Allah was the author's host during his visit to Riyadh and has supported the efforts of the Bani Rashiid to recover their history.

al-Muzayyini 1994, 95–96). With this support, al-Jaasir has encouraged the Bani Rashiid to keep struggling for equality with other Saudi citizens.

The ideological obstacles that they face are still substantial, however. To demonstrate that the Rashaayda/Bani Rashiid of Sudan, Eritrea, Kuwait, and Saudi Arabia are all members of the same "tribe," they must produce a genealogy (1) that links the eponymous ancestor of every component "branch" (Zunaymaat, Baraatiikh, etc.) to the eponymous ancestor of them all, Rashiid al-Zawl, and (2) that genealogical experts authenticate as true. Both tasks are difficult. The various "branches" in Saudi Arabia, Eritrea, Sudan, and Kuwait only agree on the name of their common ancestor (Rashiid al-Zawl); they do not agree about how to connect the Rashaayda/Bani Rashiid "branches" to him or to each other. Intervening names linking each "branch" ancestor to the common ancestor are missing. It was this problem that prompted one of the Bani Rashiid, 'Ata Allah Dayf Allah al-Rashiidi, to exclaim in 2002 that their past is a "history of an entire people (*sha'b*), not just a tribe (*qabiila*)." He said this during a gathering of Bani Rashiid elders in Riyadh who had assembled to meet some Eritrean Rashaayda visitors and exchange ideas about how to improve the Saudi public's perception of their "tribe" (Young, field notes in Riyadh, 2002).

Another part of this effort has been to commission translations of scholarly works about the Bani Rashiid/Rashaayda from other languages into Arabic. By making available to the reading public these works—which are not colored by the notion that the Bani Rashiid are hutaym—the Bani Rashiid hope they can present themselves in a new light and overcome Saudi prejudices against them.

One of the works they chose to translate, in part, was my own case study of the Sudanese Rashaayda (Young 1996). I was shown the preliminary translation of some sections of this book. I thought that the translation, in general, was accurate. In some places it is even eloquent. The editor has added some short notes, however, that were not in the original English version. He did this to make the book more useful for the Bani Rashiid and to support their effort to recover their historical identity.

One example of these additions is the preface, which was written by the man who commissioned the translation. He opened the preface by saying, "This is a study of the Bani Rashiid tribe in Sudan (*qabiilat bani rashiid fii al-suudaan*). . . . The book has been well-received by the members of the tribe and by people of other tribes who share the same ancestry in Saudi Arabia, Kuwait, Syria, Egypt, and Eritrea." His introductory remarks imply that the Sudanese Rashaayda are just a "branch" of a larger "tribe" that has spread across the eastern portion of the Arab world. This is probably correct; however, it was not a claim that I made in the original English edition. At the time when I was writing the original version, I did not have enough information about the history of the Rashaayda to support such a claim.

Another example of a socially motivated insertion is the following sentence: "The Rashaayda are the only tribe of pure Arabs in the area and want to be known as such *(al-rashaayda innahum hum al-qabiila al-wahiida min al-'arab al-aqhaah fii al-mintaqa fa hum yuriduuna an yu' arrifu anfusahum kadhaalik)*. . ." This is a mistranslation of my original text, "The Rashaayda did not say they were a 'tribe' solely because they wanted to identify themselves as such" (Young 1996, 26). I suspect that the translator, who was not familiar with the anthropological approach, did not understand what I meant. But his misunderstanding is not the only reason why his translation diverges so markedly from the original. He also wanted to insert his own understanding of the distinctive identity of the Rashaayda.

This translation project also demonstrates the scope of the Bani Rashiid's ambitions. They want to gather together all of the Bani Rashiid/Rashaayda communities in the Arab world under the rubric of "one tribe." This will not be easy.

Not all of the scattered Rashaayda groups are equally eager to blend into the emerging transnational network of "relatives." For example, the Rashaayda in the Jordanian village of Kufrinja, whom I visited in 1992, are not willing to identify themselves with their Bedouin "relatives" in Sudan. They were curious about the Sudanese Rashaayda and wanted to see my photographs of them. But when I gave them a slide presentation that showed Sudanese Rashaayda living in the desert—wearing dirty and unfashionable clothes, branding camels, herding goats and donkeys, and hauling water in cooking pots from desert wells—they were dismayed and embarrassed. Although they wanted to "discover their roots" in a proud and independent Bedouin past, the harsh realities of desert life clashed with their much more romantic images of Bedouin horsemen and tribal nobility. Thus the Sudanese Rashaayda were a disappointment for them. Although they want to establish ties with other, more prosperous Rashaayda in Jordan, Saudi Arabia, and Kuwait, they will probably draw the line at Saudi Arabia's eastern border. But their queasiness about including real Bedouin in their social circle may not protect them from the Sudanese Rashaayda's unwanted embrace. For the Sudanese Rashaayda have joined in the rewriting of Rashiidi history and may reach out for them, in print if not in person.

CONCLUSION

The Rashaayda of eastern Sudan and Eritrea no longer view themselves as just one of many local pastoralist societies moving in search of drinking water and pasture for their livestock. They have formed alliances with opposition parties in Sudan and the ruling party in Eritrea. In so doing, they have become aware of the disadvantages of being merely local. They now seek to impress their local allies—and hold their own against local enemies—by attaching themselves to the Bani Rashiid of Saudi Arabia. The Bani Rashiid, in turn, are trying to join them ideologically with other Rashaayda in Kuwait, hoping to create (or, putting it in terms that they would recognize) "prove the existence of" a transnational "tribe" whose members are spread across many Middle Eastern countries.

Increasingly, each local community of Rashaayda is representing itself as just one "branch" of this larger social formation. At the same time, actual contact—by cell phone, jet plane, and printed media—among the various Rashiidi communities is accelerating. Without doubt, the Sudanese Rashaayda will continue to use their international connections to find jobs in the Gulf states and also to market some of their purebred racing camels there (Köhler-Rollefson 1991, 71). Having "relatives" in Kuwait and Saudi Arabia will also remain important for the Sudanese Rashaayda for as long as the Sudanese-Eritrean border remains a war zone. Under such chaotic conditions, it is useful for them to forge alliances with the Bani Rashiid of Saudi Arabia and Kuwait.

The political and economic insecurity that characterizes life in eastern Sudan also encourages a form of conservatism, at least in the short run. That is, it compels many Rashaayda to remain nomadic pastoralists, even as pastoralism is becoming less and less viable economically. As long as the struggle between the Sudanese government and the Sudanese opposition groups in Eritrea continues, it makes little sense for Rashiidi families to purchase land and settle down. Why invest their resources in permanent housing when armed clashes might force them to abandon this housing and flee to safety in Eritrea?

Over the long run, however, nomadic pastoralism in eastern Sudan is probably fated to decline. Too much pastureland is being consumed by mechanized agricultural schemes to provide all of the Rashaayda with the pasture they need. My guess is that the number of Rashaayda who breed camels will drop steadily, with most families turning to wage labor in Saudi Arabia or in Sudan for their income. Some families will remain in their tents seasonally, herding camels only during the rainy season and returning to stationary homes in Kassala or the New Halfa agricultural scheme during the dry seasons. Others will become full-time city dwellers, working in commerce or making periodic trips overseas to work there. Camel breeding will become at most a part-time occupation.

How will this affect the Rashaayda culturally? Clearly, some of their specialized knowledge—for example, the proper diagnosis and treatment of livestock diseases (Köhler-Rollefson 1991, 72–73; Young 1996, 17–18)—will be lost.

Other skills, however, such as the ability to memorize and recite Arabic poetry will be kept and even developed. As they leave pastoralism and settle in towns and villages, more of their boys and girls will benefit from primary school education, a process that had already begun when I was last in Sudan. Primary education will open up the world of written literature to them. Furthermore, contact between the Rashaayda and the Bani Rashiid of Saudi Arabia will probably encourage them to adopt some Saudi styles of dress and behavior.

As they gain access to education, they will become conscious of their "rural" and "backward" habits and endeavor to replace them with what they regard as more sophisticated styles. They will lose some of their cultural distinctiveness but will gain access to a wealth of new ideas and values, some of which they will accept and some of which will be rejected. In other words, they will become more like "us," not in the sense of becoming more "Westernized," because their Arab language and identity will not disappear, but in the sense of having a much wider range of choices to make. Like all of us, in this new world of electronically and financially connected communities, they will become cosmopolitan, free to sample from the marketplaces of ideas and goods in the Arab world. But like all cosmopolitan peoples, they will have lost some of the security and certainty that comes from belonging to a small, relatively closed society that fancied itself able to survive on its own, without interacting very much with the outside world.

REFERENCES

'Abd al-'Aziiz, 'Iid Ruus. 2002. Al-Hukuuma al-suudaaniyya ta'tarif bi faqdaanihaa hamashkurayb wa al-mu'aaradha tatlubu bi al-i'tidhaar li ittihaamihaa bi 'al-khidhb [The Sudanese government admits that it has lost Hamashkurayb and the opposition demands an apology for its accusation of 'lying']. *Al-Sharq al-Awsat*, no. 8714 (October 7, 2002).

'Abd al-Siid, Muhammad, and 'Abd al-Haliim Hasan. 2002. Al-Mu'aaradha al-Suudaaniyya tu'akkidu istiilaa'ahaa 'ala Kassala wa al-hukuuma laa tastab'id tikraar al-hujuum fii al-Khartuum [The Sudanese opposition affirms its capture of Kassala and the government does not rule out the possibility of repeated attacks in Khartoum]. *Al-Sharq al-Awsat*, no. 8017 (November 9, 2002).

Adar, Korwa G. 2001. *Theocracy and state reconstruction in the Civil War-ravaged Sudan: In pursuit of an illusive national consensus.* Paper presented at the University of Pretoria workshop, "Politics of Identity and Exclusion in Africa," sponsored by the Konrad-Adenauer-Stiftung, July 25–26, 2001. See www.kas.org.za/ Publications/ SeminarReports/PoliticsofIdentityand Exclusion/adar.pdf.

African News. 2002. Sudan: Continuous Fighting—Peace Talks in Doubt—7 October. http://peacelink.it/anb-bia/ week_2k2/021010d.htm.

BBC News. 1998. Sudan accuses Eritrea of support for rebels. BBC News online, February 3. http://news.bbc.co.uk/1/hi/ world/middle_east/52890.stm.

BBC News. 1998. Sudan rebels claim major victory in east. BBC News online, February 26. http://news.bbc. co.uk/1/hi/world/middle_east/60490. stm.

BBC News. 1998. Sudan claims recapture of eastern town. BBC News online, June 30. http://news.bbc.co.uk/1/hi/ world/africa/122986.stm.

BBC News. 1998. Famine reports in eastern Sudan. BBC News online,

August 31. http://news.bbc.co.uk/1/hi/world/africa/162086.stm.

Bergen, Peter L. 2001. *Holy War, Inc.: Inside the secret world of Osama bin Laden*. New York: The Free Press.

Connell, Dan. 1997. *Against all odds: A chronicle of the Eritrean revolution with a new afterward on the postwar transition*. Trenton, NJ: Red Sea Press.

Defense Mapping Agency. 1982. *Gazetteer of Ethiopia*. Washington, DC: Defense Mapping Agency.

_____. 1989. *Gazetteer of Sudan*. Washington, DC: Defense Mapping Agency.

Doughty, Charles M. 1888. *Travels in Arabia Deserta*. Vol. 2. Cambridge: Cambridge Univ. Press.

Encyclopaedia Britannica. 1958. "Eritrea," 689–691. Volume 8 ("Edward to Extract") of the *Encyclopaedia Britannica*. Chicago: William Benton.

Fisk, Robert. 1993. Anti-Soviet Warrior Puts his Army on the Road to Peace. *The Independent* (London), no. 2225 (Dec. 6, 1993): 10.

Habib, John S. 1978. *Ibn Sa'ud's warriors of Islam: The Ikhwan of Najd and their role in the creation of the Sa'udi kingdom, 1910–1930*. Leiden: E. J. Bill.

Hamdi, Mohamed Elhachmi. 1998. *The making of an Islamic political leader: Conversations with Hasan al-Turabi*. Boulder, Colorado: Westview Press.

Hasan, 'Abd Allah Ahmad. 1974. *Al-Turaath al-sha'bi li qabiilat al-Rashaayida* [The folklore of the Rashaayida tribe]. Khartoum: Institute for African and Asian Studies and Khartoum Univ. Press.

al-Hawaazini, 'Abd Allah bin Muhammad Sa'd al-Harraan al-'Aazimi. 1998. *Lamahaat min akhbaar qabiilat al-'Awaazim* [Selected reports about the history of the 'Awaazim tribe]. Kuwait: D̲h̲aat al-salaasil.

al-Jaasir, Hamad. 1970. *Fii shimaal gharb al-jaziira* [In the Northwest of the Arabian Peninsula]. Riyadh: Daar al-yamaama li al-bahth wa al-tarjama wa al-nashr.

_____. 1980. *Mu'jam qabaa'il al-mamlaka al-'arabiyya al-sa'uudiyya* [Dictionary of the tribes of the kingdom of Saudi Arabia]. Vol. 1. Riyadh: Daar al-yamaama li al-bahth wa al-tarjama wa al-nashr.

Köhler-Rollefson, Ilse, Babiker Musa, and Mohamed Fadl Achmed. 1991. The camel pastoral system of the southern Rashaida in eastern Sudan. *Nomadic Peoples* 29:68–76.

Lesch, Ann Mosely. 1998. *The Sudan: Contested national identities*. Bloomington: Indiana University Press; and Oxford: James Currey.

Macmillan. 1999. *Macmillan centennial atlas of the world*. Rev. ed. New York: Macmillan Library Reference.

El Mallakh, Ragaei. 1982. *Saudi Arabia. Rush to development: Profile of an energy economy and development*. Baltimore: Johns Hopkins Univ. Press.

Manger, Leif. 2001. Pastoralist-state relationships among the Hadendowa Beja of eastern Sudan. *Nomadic Peoples*, n.s., 5 (2): 21–47.

Majtenyi, Cathy. 2002. Part 1—Sudan—Chronology. *AfricaNews—Sudan*, September 15–October 15. http://italy2.peacelink.org/africanews2/articles/art_543.html.

Mehari, Keshi Asfaha. 1986. *The Rashaida*. Asmara Univ., Institute of African Studies.

Metz, Helen Chapin, ed. 1992. *Sudan: A country study*. Washington, DC: Federal Research Division, Library of Congress. For sale by the Superintendent of Documents, Government Printing Office. See http://hdl.loc.gov/loc.gdc/cntrystd.sd.

_____, ed. 1993. *Saudi Arabia: A country study*. Washington, DC: Federal Research Division, Library of Congress. For sale by the Superintendent of Documents, Government Printing Office. See http://hdl.loc.gov/loc.gdc/cntrystd.sa.

Morrison, Godfrey. 1976. *Eritrea and the Southern Sudan*. 2nd ed. Minority Rights Group Report No. 5. London: Minority Rights Group.

Murray, G. W. 1935. *Sons of Ishmael: A study of the Egyptian Bedouin*. London: George Routledge & Sons, Ltd.

al-Muzayyini, Ahmad 'Abd al-'Aziiz. 1994. *Ansaab al-usar wa al-qabaa' il fii al-Kuwayt* [Genealogies of families and tribes in Kuwait]. Kuwait: Dhaat al-Salaasil Press.

Negash, Tekeste. 1997. *Eritrea and Ethiopia: The federal experience*. New Brunswick, NJ: Transaction Publishers.

Nelson, Harold D. 1982. *Sudan: A country study*. Washington: Headquarters, Department of the Army and U.S. Government Printing Office.

O'Ballance, Edgar. 2000. *Sudan, civil war and terrorism, 1956–1999*. New York: St. Martin's Press.

Operation Lifeline Sudan. n.d. Operation Lifeline Sudan weekly report. http://www.reliefweb.int/rw/dbc.nsf/.

Pelletier, Mark. 2003. http://www.markpelletierphotography.com/

Prunier, Gerard. 1997. Le Soudan au center d'une guerre regionale [Sudan's Regional War], trans. Lorna Dale. *Le monde diplomatique,* February 1997. http://mondediplo.com/1997/02/02sudan.

al-Rasheed, Madawi. 1991. *Politics in an Arabian oasis: The Rashidi tribal dynasty*. New York: I.B. Taurus.

ReliefWeb. *South Sudan Security Update*. January 30, 1997. http://www.reliefweb.int/w/rwb.nsf.

Reuters. 2000. Sudan state mobilizes against Eritrea "threat." *CNN.com,* July 20. http://www.cnn.com/2000/WORLD/africa/07/20/sudan.eritrea.reut.

al-Riihaani, Amiin. 1980. *Tariikh Najd al-hadiith* [The modern history of Najd]. Complete Works of Amiin al-Riihaani, Vol. 5. Beirut: al-Mu'assasa al-'arabiyya li al-diraasaat wa al-nashr.

Rogge, John R. 1985. *Too many, too long: Sudan's twenty-year refugee dilemma*. Totowa, NJ: Bowman & Allanheld.

Sherman, Richard. 1980. *Eritrea: The unfinished revolution*. New York: Praeger.

Sudan Catholic Information Office (SCIO). *Sudan Monthly Report*. Sudan Catholic Information Office, Bethany House. Kenya: Nairobi.

Sudan News and Views. http://www.sas.upenn.edu/African_Studies/Newsletters/snv21.htm.

Sudan Update. England: West Yorkshire. http://www.sas.upenn.edu/African_Studies/Newsletters/sdup98.html.

al-'Ubayd, 'Abd al-Rahmaan 'Abd al-Kariim. 1971. *Qabiilat al-'Awaazim* [The 'Awaazim Tribe]. Published by the author. Kuwait: Maktabat al-adaab.

United Nations International Children's Emergency Fund (UNICEF). 2003. UNICEF Humanitarian Action Report, Sudan, Northern Sector. April 30, 2003. http://www.unicef.org/emerg/Emergencies_Northern_Sudan_Donor_Update_300503.pdf.

Vigilance Soudan. 2000. Fourth Quarter, October-December 2000, English ed. http://www.vigilsd.org/articles/ba12/ab-12-5.htm.

von Oppenheim, Max Freiherr. 1943. *Die Beduinen*. Vol. 2. Unter Mitarbeitung von Erich Bräunlich und Werner Caskel. Leipzig: Otto Harrassowitz.

_____. 1952. *Die Beduinen*. Vol. 3. Bearbeitet und Herausgegeben von Werner Caskel. Al-Waa'ili, Abd al-Hakiim, ed. 2002. *Mawsuu'at qabaa'il al-'arab* [The encyclopedia of Arab tribes]. 6 vols. Amman, Jordan: Daar Usaama li al-nashr wa al-tawzii'. Wiesbaden: Otto Harrassowitz.

_____. 1967. *Die Beduinen*. Vol. 4. Bearbeitet und Herausgegeben von Werner Caskel. Wiesbaden: Otto Harrassowitz.

Woodward, Peter. 1990. *Sudan 1895–1989: The unstable state*. Boulder, CO: L. Rienner Publishers.

Young, William C. 1996. *The Rashaayda Bedouin: Arab pastoralists of Eastern Sudan*. Fort Worth, Texas: Harcourt Brace College Publishers.

———. 1998. From many, one: The social construction of the Rashāyida tribe in Eastern Sudan." *Northeast African Studies* 4 (1): 71–108.

———. 1999 'The Bedouin': Discursive identity or sociological category? A case study from Jordan. *Journal of Mediterranean Studies* 9 (2): 275–299.

Young, William C., R. N. al-Bagain, and G. W. Burnett. 2001. Al-Simakiya: Village formation on the Eastern Mediterranean's desert margin. *Journal of Mediterranean Studies* 11 (2): 341–354.

NOTES

1. The second vowel in "Rashiid" is a long vowel, which I have transliterated by doubling the letter *i*. I have done the same thing with other Arabic long vowels (aa, uu) in this article. To simplify typesetting I have not utilized the other special characters that I used in my case study of the Rashaayda (Young 1996, 2–3). A careful reader will note a few other inconsistencies. In my case study I spelled the name of the coastal Sudanese town, 'Aqiiq, differently: 'Agiig. I did so to represent the way in which this place-name was pronounced in colloquial Arabic speech, rather than using the *q* that appears in the classical, written form of this name. Some other Arabic names, such as the name of Usaama bin Laadin, are often spelled differently by the popular press. In bin Laadin's case I use a more accurate transliteration, whereas in other cases (such as the name of the town of Suakin), I have retained the popular, although inaccurate, transliteration to make it easier for nonspecialists to recognize them.

2. As we will see, it is not easy to determine the exact scope of the transnational arena in which these interactions among "tribal" branches occur. Is it restricted to eastern Sudan, Eritrea, and Saudi Arabia, or does it include Kuwait, Palestine, and Jordan? The Rashaayda of Sudan and Saudi Arabia do not agree about the identity and number of the groups who are indisputably members of the emerging, pan-tribal "society" (or "people").

Membership in this social formation is contested.

3. The general locations where "Rashaayda" or "Bani Rashiid" are found include: (1) eastern Sudan, near Kassala and Suakin; (2) Eritrea, along the Red Sea coast north of Massawa/Mitsiwa; (3) central Egypt, between Qina and Sohag; (4) southeastern Israel, near 'Ain Jidi/'En Gedi; (5) the West Bank/Palestine (in Bethlehem District); (6) southern Jordan, northwest of Ma'aan; (7) northwestern Saudi Arabia in Harrat Bani Rashiid and northeast of Khaybar; (8) Kuwait (al-Jaasir 1970, 45, 229, 523, 526, 534; Murray 1935, 269; von Oppenheim 1943, 128–129; von Oppenheim 1967, 114; al-Waa'ili 2002, 651–652); (9) central Jordan, next to the village of al-Simaakiya, northeast of al-Karak (al-Waa'ili 2002, 652; Young 1999, 293; Young, al-Baqain, and Burnett 2001); (10) in the north Jordanian village of Kufrinja (encountered by Young in 1993); (11) southwestern Saudi Arabia, in the Farasaan Islands (personal communication, 'Ata Allah Dayf Allah Muhammad al-Rashiidi, Riyadh, 2002). See also Figure 11.1.

4. One of the Rashaayda of Saudi Arabia, Mr. Ata Allah Dayf Allah al-Rashiidi, has suggested to me that the initial breakup of the ancestral Rashaayda tribe occurred in the tenth century in the course of the wars between the Qarmatian state (in what is now Kuwait) and the Buyid (Iraqi) and Fatimid (Egyptian) dynasties. This suggestion is intriguing but the

fragmentary character of the historical record makes it difficult to confirm (or refute) it.

5. I should point out that the 'Awaazim of Kuwait are quick to deny any genealogical or historical connection between them and the Rashaayda, despite the fact that the Rashaayda live immediately to the west of where the 'Awaazim are found. The 'Awaazim do not refer to the Rashaayda of Kuwait by their proper name but call them, instead, *hutaym* (al-'Ubayd 1971, 40). This term of abuse is applied throughout Arabia to many small groups who are not politically powerful.

6. Detailed and accurate information about the fighting along the Sudanese-Eritrean border during those years is hard to come by. Some of the sources used here include Prunier (1997), *Sudan News and Views* (no. 21–26, November 1996–May 1997), *SCIO Sudan Monthly Report* (October 15, 1996; January 15, 1997; February 15, 1997; July 15, 1997), and ReliefWeb (South Sudan Security Update, January 30, 1997).

7. For reports about armed conflict during this period, see BBC News Online, (February 3, 1998; February 26, 1998; June 30, 1998; August 31, 1998), *Operation Lifeline Sudan Weekly Report* (August 18, 1999; December 1, 1999), *Operation Lifeline Sudan [Northern Sector] Weekly Report* (July 14, 1999), *Operation Lifeline Sudan [Northern and Southern Sectors] Weekly Report* (September 22, 1999; October 6, 1999), *SCIO Sudan Monthly Report* (February 15, 1998; June 15, 1998; July 15, 1998; October 15, 1998; November 15, 1999; December 15, 1999), and *Sudan Update* (vol. 9, no. 8, May 15, 1998).

8. See 'Abd al-Siid and Hasan 2000; CNN.com 2000; Vigilance Soudan 2000.

9. See 'Abd al-'Aziiz 2002; *African News* October 10, 2002; Associated Press, October 4 2002; Majtenyi 2002; UNICEF 2003.

10. See www.ndasudan.org/English/ intro; Norwegian Support Group for Peace in the Sudan (SFS), http://www.sudansupport.no/sudan_konflikt/whoiswho/hva_er_hva.html#NDA; see also Young (1996, 87, 102).

11. The historian Amiin al-Riihaani describes this area as "that volcanic wasteland with its rounded pebbles and stone fragments that are as sharp as skewers. . . ." (al-Riihaani 1980, 69). The exact locations of the villages inhabited by the Bani Rashiid are al-Hulayfa (25°59'N, 40°49'E), Sufayt (25°36'N, 40°35'E), al-Murayr (25°25'N, 40°27'E), al-Raqab (25°46'N, 41°06'E), and al-Sulsula (25°44'N, 39°16'E). The area known as Harrat Khaybar is at 25°45'N and 39°11'E. See al-Jaasir (1980, 236–238) and http://www.multimap.com/.

12. See, for example, al-Riihaani, who refers to the inhabitants of the village of al-Murayr as "hutaym" (1980, 456). Information about the status of "hutaym" in and near Arabia can be found in Doughty (1888, 179, 239, 583), al-Jaasir (1980, 236–238), and Murray (1935, 269).

13. See al-Hawaazini (1998, 205–213), al-'Ubayd (1971, 73–84), von Oppenheim (1943, 126–127; 1952, 85, 151; 1967, 111–113).

Fieldwork Biography
Leo R. Chavez

Leo R. Chavez conducted his first fieldwork in Otavalo, Ecuador, a small town high in the Andes that was experiencing rural-to-town migration by its indigenous population, the Otavalos, who mostly lived in many small villages in the surrounding countryside. Since 1980, however, Professor Chavez has focused on transnational migration, beginning in San Diego, California. The ethnography *Shadowed Lives: Undocumented Immigrants in American Society* [1992/1998] was the result of over 10 years interviewing Mexican and Central American immigrants about their lives, integration into U.S. society, and access to medical services. In many ways, finding people to interview was easier in the small town of Otavalo, or in one of the surrounding villages, where all one had to do was walk around and meet people. Immigrants in San Diego, on the other hand, live in a wide range of places, from rural encampments in canyons near farms to apartments and houses in urban centers and suburban neighborhoods. They were not so easy to find! More recently, Professor Chavez has examined cultural, economic, and political issues related to breast and cervical cancer and the use of cancer-screening exams among immigrant women from Latin America in Orange County, California. His current fieldwork is among the adult children of immigrants and how well they are integrating into U.S. society, focusing on the greater Los Angeles area. It has now been about 25 years that Professor Chavez has been working to understand the immigrant experience, which he likens to a large jigsaw puzzle. Each research project helps to fill in one small piece of the puzzle.

12/Culture Change and Cultural Reproduction
Lessons from Research on Transnational Migration

Vignette 1: In San Diego, California, a number of men, recent immigrants from Mexico, stand on a street corner waiting for offers for work from the passing cars. Although they often find work cleaning up construction sites, at flower ranches, or gardening and landscaping, many people find their presence a problem. Complaints about the men's presence are often heard at city council meetings. Sometimes hiring sites are made available for the men and their employers. The men live in makeshift encampments hidden in the bushes and trees

Young Mexican migrant worker in his makeshift campsite next to the fields where he works.

not too far from where they look for work. Sometimes their homes are demolished, forcing them to pack up their few belongings and move to another site. What keeps them there is the work and the pay, often seven to ten times what they could make back in Mexico. Women also sometimes live in the campsites. They typically work in homes, as maids or taking care of children. As one woman told me: "I came here because there is no work over there. Oaxaca has no factories, no large businesses to employ people. When you do find work, it's very difficult. You work from nine in the morning to nine at night for little pay and it's hard to find another job. I was told that there were good wages here and that there was plenty of work for women. Right now I do housekeeping, but sometimes I do that and sometimes I don't. It's not stable [work]" (Chavez 1998). Many of these men and women will return to Mexico after a few months to a couple of years working in the United States. Some will stay longer, eventually forming families and settling in the United States. Although they may stay years, they often continue to maintain contacts with family and friends back home, even sending them some of the money they have earned. One of the things that impressed me most about this situation was the level of interdependence between Mexico and the United States, despite the often strong anti-Mexican attitudes expressed in public forums, especially on local talk radio programs.

Vignette 2: In Flushing, New York, Tony Sala, the owner of T.J.s Pizzeria & Restaurant watched as his neighborhood changed from mainly European immigrants and their children to predominantly Korean and Chinese immigrants and their children (Baum 2004). Seeing opportunity, the owner decided to innovate by putting kimchee, (hot spicy pickled cabbage favored by Koreans) on his pizzas. The Italian-Korean merger has been quite successful.

Vignette 3: In France, immigrants from the African countries of Senegal, Mali, and Mauritania bring with them the Muslim tradition of polygamy (Simons 1996). However, many of the immigrant's wives have rebelled at continuing this tradition in France, where they find the living conditions no longer tolerable for a man having multiple wives. Back in Africa, if a man could afford more than one wife, he could afford to place her in her own house. Even if they lived close to the other wives, they at least had some measure of separation. However, an immigrant male who manages to save enough money to return home to his village in Africa, acquire a second or third wife, and bring her back to France typically cannot afford to set her up in her own apartment. Consequently, two or three families may pack into a two-room apartment, a situation some wives indicate as difficult, making them feel "trapped" or that they are "losing their minds."

Vigenette 4: In Bellflower, California—a 13-square-mile section of Los Angeles—39 languages are spoken (Simmons 2004). A security guard at the local Department of Motor Vehicles speaks to customers with phrases in English, Spanish, Chinese, and Tagalog. Residents find that the cultural diversity makes learning about other cultures a way of life. As one observer in Bellflower put it, "Koreans are among the throng of customers having their eyebrows plucked by Indian beauticians. Japanese housewives have their nails clipped and polished by Vietnamese manicurists. Mexicans and Vietnamese dine on Vietnamese *pho* soup or Mexican *pozole* porridge at each other's eateries. And it is typical to find Indian spices being sold in Latino grocery stores" (Simmons 2004).

WHY IS TRANSNATIONAL MIGRATION IMPORTANT FOR ANTHROPOLOGISTS?

To pick up and move in search of a better life or security from a hostile environment is such an old pattern in human history that it is practically human nature. So is setting down roots in new locations, only to move on again should the opportunity or need arise. In today's theoretical discourse, humans have been deterritorializing and reterritorializing for almost as long as we have been a species (Gupta and Ferguson 1997). *Homo erectus* managed to migrate throughout Europe and Asia beginning more than a million years ago. And yet, despite the fact that migration and settlement are so fundamental a part of what it means to be human, the process itself is fraught with issues for both those who move and those whom migrants encounter.

The contemporary movement of people across national borders raises a whole range of issues, because migration creates the possibility of change in many directions: among those who move, among those where migrants settle, and among those left behind who often continue to communicate and maintain material relations with migrants (Basch, Schiller, and Blanc 1994). About 150 million people live outside the country of their birth (Stalker 2001). Although this accounts for only about 3 percent of the world's population, the importance of that movement is significant for those involved, that is, the migrants, those left behind, and those in the places migrants settle. Importantly, the forces propelling people from their homes and drawing them to live and work in primarily industrial societies will likely continue for most of the twenty-first century (Castles and Miller 1998). Thus, the sheer magnitude of, and the variety of, responses to the movement of people in the world today and in the next few decades makes transnational migration a topic of long-term anthropological interest.

The United States, long considered the preeminent immigrant-receiving nation, is now but one among many nations receiving large numbers of immigrants. For example, in 2003, 11.7 percent of the U.S. population was foreign-born, but the foreign-born accounted for 18.1 percent of Canada's population and 23.1 percent of Australia's population in 2001 (Institute 2004). In the last 25 years, millions of Eastern Europeans, North Africans, Turks, Albanians, and others have migrated into the industrialized nations of Europe. As a result, foreign-born populations in European countries increased, with at least 4.2 percent in the United Kingdom in 2000 (particularly from South Asia and the Caribbean), 2.2 percent in Italy in 1999, and 6.2 percent in Denmark in 2003 (Institute 2004). In 1999, the foreign-born accounted for about 9.8 percent of Germany's population (mainly Turks, Yugoslavs, and Poles),[1] and 7.4 percent of France's population (mainly Algerians, Moroccans, and Portuguese).[2] In 2001, the foreign-born accounted for 2.5 percent of Spain's population (Perez 2004). In 2000, Japan, not known for its openness to immigration, had about 864,000 foreign workers originally from Korea, China, Bangladesh, Pakistan, Iran, the Philippines, Peru, and Brazil, with an estimated 230,000 undocumented immigrants (Yamanaka 2000). In 2001, Russia had as many as 10 million undocumented migrants, mostly from former Soviet republics drawn by economic opportunities (*Los Angeles Times* 2001).

The paradox, however, is that although pressures may exist for more immigration, the presence of immigrants often raises fears associated with epochal change, especially in nations not accustomed to large-scale immigration. The integration of immigrants is not always an easy one. Immigrants pose challenges to dominant notions of what constitutes "the nation," that is, the people. People who had taken for granted that they were the standard bearers of national identity must cope with racial and cultural diversity in their society. Not surprisingly, then, immigrants and immigration often become ground zero in a battle over the perceived implications of change in contemporary societies around the world.

Immigration, and its counterpart, emigration, are often key symbols for a society (Ortner 1973). By this I mean that they are central and important concepts for how a people understand their identity. Some nations explicitly identify themselves as "immigrant nations," for example the United States, Canada, and Australia. Other countries have historically considered themselves "emigrant nations," because they have sent so many of their people to work and live in other countries (for example Italy and Spain). Other nations have not viewed themselves as immigrant nations at all because they have seen their identity as singular and not open to mixing with other people (for example, Japan, Germany,

Saudi Arabia, and many others) (Williams 2000a). An important aspect of key symbols is that they can refract multiple meanings. How any individual member of a society perceives the meaning of that symbol depends on that person's own personal status and history. Thus, immigration and being an immigrant nation (or not) can mean different things to different people at the same time. But the centrality of notions about immigration to a nation's identity is at the core of many of the issues raised by transnational migration, and thus a key source of anthropological investigation (Foner 2003).

A LOVE-HATE RELATIONSHIP WITH IMMIGRANTS

Vignette 5: In 1996, a black woman, a naturalized citizen who had immigrated from the Dominican Republic four years earlier, won the title of Miss Italy (Bohlen 1996). For a nation that had imagined itself as setting the standard in European beauty with international stars such as Gina Lollobrigida and Sophia Loren, the crowning of Denny Méndez as Miss Italy raised considerable controversy over the appropriate symbol of Italian female beauty. Suddenly, Italians questioned what it means to be Italian. One of the judges of the beauty contest asked "whether China would accept a Miss China without almond-shaped eyes, or if a non-black African could become Miss Senegal" (Bohlen 1996). However, Italy is changing. A nation that until recently sent emigrants out to other nations to work and live now receives many immigrants, mainly from North African, Albania, and the Balkans. As one person wrote in the Italian newspaper *La Republica*: "Italy became a land of immigration without ever deciding to, and in some cases, without ever wanting to" (Bohlen 1996). A year after Ms. Méndez was crowned Miss Italy, the guidelines for competing were changed so that at least one parent had to be "full-blooded Italian" (Rodriguez 2004).

Vignette 6: In Japan, Portuguese-speaking Japanese Brazilians find that they are looked down upon by the Japanese (Tsuda 2003). They came to Japan to work in factories, where they can earn more than in Brazil, even though many have experience in business or professional training. The Japanese wanted them because, after all, they are Japanese, and for a nation that values racial similarity rather than diversity, this was a huge plus for a foreign workforce. However, culturally, the Japanese Brazilians stand out because of the way they walk, the way they sit, and the way they express their emotions, all of which are more casual, open, and familiar than is customary in Japan. They also speak Japanese in a way that is noticeably imperfect, if they speak Japanese at all. The Japanese often treat the Japanese Brazilians with suspicion, as culturally inferior, and as people whose families must have been socially and economically unsuccessful if they had to emigrate from Japan in the first place. They are sometimes mocked as "country bumpkins" on television shows. As a result of their experiences, the Japanese Brazilians who migrate to Japan to work often wind up emphasizing their Brazilian, rather than their Japanese, identity. In Brazil they had emphasized their Japaneseness, rarely participating in events such as Mardi Gras parades. Once in Japan, however, it was clear that they had also acquired Brazilian culture, which they came to embrace and exhibit with pride. Japanese Brazilians now put on an annual Mardi Gras parade in Japan, complete with costumes and music.

In the United States, the often heated debate over immigration is about much more than just the number of immigrants coming to our shores and living in our communities (Lamphere 1992). Immigration is a very personal and emotional issue that touches fundamental, and often unconscious, beliefs about how we think of ourselves as a people, as a nation, and how we think of American culture (Chavez 1998). And despite immigration being central to how we identify ourselves as a nation, America has had a love-hate relationship with immigrants.

Since colonial days, Americans have desired the economic benefits resulting from immigrant labor while at the same time they have often worried about the negative influences of newcomers on American culture and society. In keeping with this love-hate relationship, Americans tend to denigrate this generation's immigrants, while remembering past immigrants fondly. Ironically, the same immigrants in the past were probably just as feared and reviled as some contemporary immigrants. Consider the alarmist sentiments that Benjamin Franklin's made about Germans in 1751:

> Why should the Palatine boors be suffered to swarm into our settlements, and, by herding together, establish their language and manners, to the exclusion of ours? Why should Pennsylvania, founded by the English, become a colony of aliens, who will shortly be so numerous as to Germanize us, instead of our Anglifying them . . . ? (Steinberg 1981).

Franklin's statement reflects concern that "Germanizing" would change and destroy what he viewed as a coherent Anglo-American culture in the colonies. This is a view of culture as static and inelastic, and thus as brittle and vulnerable to changes wrought by immigration. But despite such fears, other colonists desired more immigration to the colonies. Indeed, one of the main articles of the Declaration of Independence of July 4, 1776, was a complaint about England's unwillingness to let more immigrants come to the colonies:

> When in the course of human events, it becomes necessary for one people to dissolve the political bands which have connected them with another . . . a decent respect to the opinions of mankind requires that they should declare the causes which impel them to the separation. . . . The present King of Great Britain . . . has endeavored to prevent the population of these states; for that purpose obstructing the laws of naturalization of foreigners; refusing to pass others to encourage their migration hither.

Come hither immigrants did. The nineteenth century became *the* century of immigration, first from northern European countries such as the various countries making up the United Kingdom, Ireland, German, and Sweden. China and Japan also sent many immigrants beginning in the mid-1800s. By the late 1800s, immigrants were overwhelmingly from southern and eastern European countries, such as Italy, Austria, Hungary, Poland, and Russia. Because these "new" immigrants differed from the previous immigrants, they were often viewed with suspicion and ambivalence, as this article in the *Literary Digest* in 1892 strongly indicates:

> Ignorant, unskilled, inert, accustomed to the beastliest conditions, with little social aspirations, with none of the desire for air and light and room, for the decent dress and

home comfort, which our native people possess and which our earlier immigrants so speedily acquired, the presence of hundreds of thousands of these laborers constitutes a menace to the rate of wages and the American standard of living, which to my mind is absolutely appalling. . . . Taking whatever they can get in the way of wages, living like swine, crowded into filthy tenement houses, piecing out their miserable existence by systematic begging and by picking over garbage barrels, the arrival on our shores of such masses of degraded peasantry brings the greatest danger that American labor has ever known (Simon 1985).

Despite being thought of as biologically inferior to the stock of Americans at the time and thus unable to fully assimilate into American life, these immigrant groups fared well by today's standards. An Irish American became president (Kennedy), President Reagan liked to joke that his grandfather was an illegal alien from Ireland, and an Italian American is on the U.S. Supreme Court. In short, the descendents of southern and eastern European immigrants are integrated into every aspect of American life. The point is that immigrants once thought to be harbingers of the decline of American culture and people are now considered just plain Americans. Racialized immigrants (Asians, Africans and Afro-Caribbeans, and Latin Americans), however, may find their acceptance in the American mainstream less of a linear process (Pedraza 1996).

The current movement of peoples across national borders raises many of the same concerns as those of earlier periods. But less often is there critical reflection on the underlying causes of transnational migration. A nation can either produce the labor force it needs (by having babies) or import labor. Most of the industrialized nations of Europe, the United States, and Japan are experiencing large numbers of immigrants, partially due to low fertility rates and a demand for unskilled and semiskilled labor. According to the Population Reference Bureau's 2002 Population Data Sheet, the number of children per woman was at a low of 1.2 in eastern Europe, 1.3 in southern Europe, 1.5 in western Europe, and 1.6 in northern Europe. Particularly low fertility rates were the norm in the Czech Republic (1.1 children per woman), Spain (1.2), and Romania (1.2), with slightly higher fertility rates in many countries, including Italy (1.3), Germany (1.3), Austria, (1.3) and Russia (1.3) (Bureau 2002). In the United States, 1.23 children are born per woman between ages 18 and 44 (Bean, et al. 2000). Japan's fertility rate is 1.3, the lowest since 1947, and families who produce more than two children receive rewards (French 2000; *Newsweek* 2000).

With such low fertility rates, even modest economic growth can lead to a demand for immigrant labor. But the response to increased immigration has also been ambivalent and, at times, negative. Indeed, right-wing political parties have gained ground in many countries, especially in Europe.[3] For example, Denmark has witnessed increased anti-immigrant sentiments associated with the rise of the Danish People's Party (Williams 2000b). Despite Denmark's being among the 10 richest countries in the world, immigrants are blamed for the few economic ills that exist in that country. Especially troublesome is the need to import labor with computer skills from countries such as India and Russia. In other European countries, as well, right-wing political parties and leaders have gained popularity as a result of pandering to xenophobic sentiments toward foreigners (Los Angeles

Times 2000). Examples abound of such sentiment: Jean-Marie Le Pen in France, Joerg Haider in Austria, Pia Kjaersgaard and the Danish People's Party in Denmark, Filip Dewinter in Belgium, the British National Party and the National Front in England, and Pat Buchanan and a number of anti-immigrant organizations in the United States (Brugge 1995; Oakley 2001; Williams 2000b).[4]

Reaction to increased international migration has sharpened the debate over national identity and even the meaning of citizenship in many countries (Ong 2003). Nations that have not included immigration as a core element of their national identity suddenly see their taken-for-granted assumptions challenged. As a spokesman for Denmark's right-wing Danish People's Party commented: "We don't believe in Denmark turning into a multiethnic society. We have never been an immigrant country, and we will never be one" (Williams 2000b). Jean-Marie Le Pen's National Front Party in France views large-scale immigration "as a recipe for cultural suicide" (Tarmann 2001). In March 2001, Tory leader William Hague, speaking at the Tory party's spring conference in Harrogate, said that the United Kingdom was becoming a "foreign land" because of immigration. Hague went on to promise that, if elected, the Tories would "give you back your country" (News 2001a). In a similar vein, Italy's Silvio Berlusconi, leader of the center-right House of Freedom coalition that won a majority of seats in both the Chamber of Deputies and Senate, made reducing immigration one of his campaign themes: "Italy's borders are a sieve. The immigrants sail here across the Adriatic, or get over the border with Slovenia, and then they disappear. . . . That has meant a rise in crime. What we need to ensure is that any illegal aliens arrested for committing crimes are repatriated immediately. They cannot be tolerated" (News 2001b).

Even in countries like the United States that have historically received immigrants, some residents may believe that their national identity is under attack as the number of immigrants increase. For example, Peter Brimelow (1992) holds in disdain America's self-image as a "nation of immigrants," calling it something that children are taught in schools nowadays, "a sort of multicultural Pledge of Allegiance." He calls for an end to immigration into the United States: "It may be time to close the second period of American history with the announcement that the U.S. is no longer an 'immigrant country.'" it should be noted that Brimelow himself is an immigrant, from the United Kingdom.

Brimelow is not alone. Many have expressed concern about the large numbers of immigrants in the United States endangering the common values that defined the American way of life by bringing their plurality of differences, languages, and histories (Geyer 1996; Huntington 2004; Kadetsky 1994; Lamm and Imhoff 1985; Maharidge 1996; Tatalovich 1997). Patrick Buchanan, a nationally recognized conservative politician, provides us with perhaps one of the best articulations of contemporary American nativism (Bosniak 1997; Johnson 1997; Perea 1997). In a *Los Angeles Times* opinion piece, Buchanan (Buchanan 1994) expressed a deep concern for the future of the "American nation." His main anxiety concerned the very real possibility that, sometime in the near future, the majority of "Americans" would trace their roots not to Europe but to Africa, Asia, Latin America, the Middle East, and the Pacific Islands. He thus asked: What would it mean for "America" if, for example, south Texas and

Southern California became almost exclusively Latino?[5] He provided the following answer: "Each will have tens of millions of people whose linguistic, historic, and cultural roots are in Mexico," and thus "like Eastern Ukraine, where 10 million Russian-speaking 'Ukrainians' now look impatiently to Moscow, not Kiev, as their cultural capital, America could see, in a decade, demands for Quebec-like status for Southern California" (ibid., B7). For Buchanan, this prospect is not very appealing. He notes that the United States is already suffering for this trend toward cultural differentiation:

> Crowding together immigrant and minority populations in our major cities [is bringing] greater conflict. We saw that in the 1992 [Los Angeles] riots. Blacks and Latinos have lately collided in Washington's Adams-Morgan neighborhood, supposedly the most tolerant and progressive section of the nation's capital. The issue: bilingual education. Unlike 20 years ago, ethnic conflict is today on almost every front page (ibid.).

From Buchanan's perspective, the only solution to this problem of ethnic-cultural conflict is to put a stop to immigration: "If America is to survive as 'one nation, one people,' we need to call a timeout on immigration, to assimilate the tens of millions who have lately arrived. We need to get to know one another, to live together, to learn together America's language, history, culture and traditions of tolerance, to become a new national family, before we add a hundred million more" (ibid.). He concluded the article by noting that "Americans" must have the courage to make the decisions that affect "our" lives; otherwise, others will "make those decisions for us, not all of whom share our love of the America that seems to be fading away" (ibid.).

Newsweek's cover illustration on August 9, 1993, captured the image of America dying as a result of immigration. The cover depicts the Statue of Liberty drowning. She is barely visible above a flood of water. Only the top half of her head and her arm holding the torch remain above water. Dark-skinned people circle her in boats, unwilling to leave her alone in her torment. Her eyes are downcast, as if in shock and bewilderment, as she watches the coming peril but is powerless to act.

The meaning of the image is not difficult to read (Chavez 2001). The nation, in the guise of the Statue of Liberty, is in danger. The flood is a common metaphor for the flow of immigrants to the United States. And with floods come danger as the raging waters overwhelm people, land, and nations. The people in the boats represent the immigrants themselves, who are characterized as relentless in their pursuit of America (the Statue of Liberty) and who ultimately destroy that which they so eagerly seek. The image speaks clearly that the nation is at risk because of the uncontrolled movement of large numbers (floods) of immigrants. The text underscores the image's message: "Immigration Backlash: A Newsweek Poll: 60% of Americans Say Immigration Is 'Bad for the Country.'"

The image reflects a common view of culture and draws us to conclude that changes wrought by immigration spell the death of the nation. The theory of culture embedded in this message is that culture is static and nonresilient, that culture should reproduce itself, and that change can destroy a culture. Nothing in the image reflects change being transformative, or of the ability of American

culture to absorb that which is new and then to turn the newness into something quintessentially American. Many examples of this process exist in American history. American culture is neither static nor immutable; it has constantly recreated itself. And yet, the message this image conveys is that immigration is causing the impending death of the American nation and culture.

CULTURE CHANGE AND CULTURAL REPRODUCTION

Vignette 7: In Yolo County, California, Andres Bermudez is a successful tomato farmer (Mena 2001). He is so successful, in fact, that his compatriots call him the "Tomato King." He came to the Untied States illegally 30 years ago, but has since become a U.S. citizen. Long active in U.S.-based organizations that provided money for projects in his hometown of Jerez, Zacatecas, Mexico, Bermudez ran for mayor of Jerez and won on July 1, 2001. He became the first U.S. citizen to win elected office in Mexico. Mexico has been promoting a "dual nationality" program that allows Mexicans who become citizens in other countries to retain property and nationality rights (Mena 2001). Voting in Mexican elections has been another issue. Although Mexico promotes transnational civic engagement, the country has yet to implement a balloting mechanism for U.S.-based Mexican nationals to vote in Mexican elections. Bermudez's election was later overturned because he failed to meet Mexico's residency requirements, but he finally assumed the position of municipal president of Jerez in September 2004 (Pickel 2004).

Vignette 8: In New York, Indian American college students, both those born in the United and those who immigrated at an early age, are struggling with issues of identity and Indianness in the American context (Maira 2002). For these second-generation Indian Americans, issues of gender and sexuality are often a point of conflict when it comes to what it means to be "Indian" and what it means to be "Indian American." The tension arises because norms and values that immigrant parents bring with them can become hyper-emphasized, to the point of fossilization, in these immigrant families. For Indian American women, this means that control of their sexuality and public behavior is more important than controlling young men. Immigrant parents view Indian American women as the repositories of the family "izzat," or reputation. Even more, Indian American women are caught in the double bind of representing both tradition and modernity. By adhering to traditional behaviors, they represent authentic Indian ethnic identity. They are the stabilizing factor in cultural reproduction. However, if they change and exhibit "American" cultural behaviors and dress, then they represent change and modernity, and the loss of Indian identity in the American context. Thus, second-generation Indian American women face many pressures from family and community members who expect them to behave in ways that represent ethnic stability and continuity.

Vignette 9: In Long Beach, California, Riem Men, a Cambodian man, reflected on his culture shock at seeing young women taking responsibility in the public sphere. As he so eloquently put it (Yarborough 1996):

> In Cambodia, it was always taught that women must obey and respect men. Many of the old books that some Cambodians still read set out rules for a "good woman." She should always go to bed later than her husband and get up earlier than him, so she can attend to all household tasks. If he is a drunkard or adulterer or gambler, he is still always right. And even if he curses her, she should be quiet and respectful. If she follows these rules she'll be considered the best woman in the community and when she dies she'll go to heaven.
>
> When I grew up in Cambodia no one had any different ideas about that, so it all seemed natural and right. In my mind, women were a group of people who were there to take care of the house and raise children. They were regarded as very weak people, and they certainly had no chance to express opinions on such matters as politics.
>
> Therefore you can imagine my surprise when I first landed in San Francisco with a group of 350 other Asian officers and at our orientation an American girl [who looked] about 19 years old got on stage and talked in front of hundreds of high-ranking officers. She didn't even seem nervous, just normal, and I thought: Oh, my God! I've never seen anything like this before! Yet it was exciting to see a woman taking that kind of role and I felt admiration for her. Suddenly, it seemed appropriate. And as time went on, all my ideas began to change.

When people migrate they often come into contact with different nations, or people, who also often speak a different language and share different cultural views of the world and different ways of organizing their social lives. Today, nations are often associated with states with formal political borders. One of the most difficult problems migration raises is how to think about culture and what happens as people move and mix, or migrate and interact with people in different places. Too often culture is conceptualized as a "thing," as something that mechanically gets reproduced from one generation to the next. If novelty is introduced, or change occurs, and the system does not appear to reproduce itself, then fears arise that the culture is broken, failed to function properly, or is about to be destroyed. To parents, this could signal the breakdown of their way of life. Those experiencing rapid in-migration could view the newcomers as unwilling to learn about the welcoming society's culture. Immigrants might also desire that their children reproduce their parents' cultural beliefs and values and this can generate transgenerational tensions and conflicts (Espiritu 2003).

To a certain extent, anthropologists have had a hand in creating this problem of thinking of culture as mechanically reproducing itself. Anthropology became popular early in the twentieth century as part of a discourse on human societies. One of the prominent theories of culture and society at the time was functionalism, which later came to be known as structural-functionalism. In this perspective, the various elements of a society "functioned" in a way that produced or maintained the overall social system. Bronislaw Malinowski (1960 [1944]) believed that "each culture can be understood as an integrated whole of 'partly autonomous, partly coordinated institutions'" (cited in Salzman 2001, 14). Interdependence, maintenance, equilibrium, and continuity of the system as a whole were keys to functionalism and structural-functionalism. In this view, there is not so much change as cultural reproduction with little change.

Radcliffe-Brown, another leading theorist of the time put it this way: "The function of any recurrent activity, such as a the punishment of a crime, or a funeral ceremony, is the part it plays in the social life as a whole and therefore the contribution it makes to the maintenance of social structure" (Radcliffe-Brown 1948). Change, in this view, is not as important to understand as the coherent cultural system as a whole. Indeed, change was difficult to even articulate in this theory. Interestingly, functionalism contrasts with an earlier anthropological theory, diffusionism, which focused on the diffusion of cultural traits across wide geographic areas. But functionalism and structural-functionalism described cultures and societies as independent, self-sustaining, and autonomous cultures (Salzman 2001).

The arrows in Figure 12.1 represent the way particular cultural domains mutually reinforced the stability and coherence of the overall sociocultural system.

The seeming continuity and mechanical reproduction inherent in functionalism and structural-functionalism lead to the critique of functionalist theories as representing cultures and societies as static and ahistorical. As Eric Wolf (1982) argued, such thinking resulted in many non-Western peoples viewed as "people without history." However, societies and cultures are, or were even then, rarely secluded and cut off from their neighbors and the larger world.

Contemporary anthropological theory conceptualizes culture and change differently. Culture is still the system of meanings that people construct to give order to their world, and the material productions and social relationships that are part of that cultural world. However, cultural reproduction is not cloning. One generation does not transmit a culture in perfect formation to the next

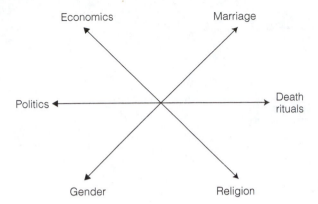

Figure 12.1 *Functionalist View of Culture*

generation because the individuals in the next generation are subject to flows of information from many directions at once: from parents, peers, teachers (formal and informal), and the many other interests and institutions in the society and beyond. Therefore, reproduction is never complete; cultural systems are not static. Cultures are dynamic and subject to historical processes, even though culture change is constrained by preexisting cultural understandings and social structures, but these too are subject to change.

Culture is not a fixed, thing-like concept, but is fluid, dynamic, processural, and constructed. Cultural understandings of the world are contested and open to new information so that, although some aspects of culture have continuity, change and even a lack of consensus also exist because of the multiple perspectives found among members of a society. Differences occur because members of social groups differ in terms of gender, age, relationships, where they were born, where they were raised, ethnic/racial identities, and many other ways. Moreover, a sociocultural system is subject to influences for change that originate both internally and externally to the system, which is really a system within systems, as Immanuel Wallerstein (1989 [1974]) argued. A model of culture change along these parameters would look very different from the previous functionalist one (see Figure 12.2).

Cultures and societies can change from internal dynamics, history, and societal pressures. On the other hand, people do not live in isolation. They are often in contact with other people who behave differently and have different ideas about the world. Sometimes people borrow from these others freely. Others times, these outside influences are imposed. Religion was one such transnational force. Whether brought by the sword or diffused more peacefully, major religions have moved from people to people and nation to nation. Conquerors and colonizers often imposed new religions and new ways of living on the people they conquered and colonized. This was as true in the past when "world" religions, such as Christianity and Islam, were spread across national borders, as it is today, when Christian evangelists pursue converts in U.S.-occupied Iraq.

But religion is not the only transnational force in history or in contemporary life. The spread of capitalism in the world today is another such transnational force (Ong 1999). Globalization is a term that refers to how the world and its

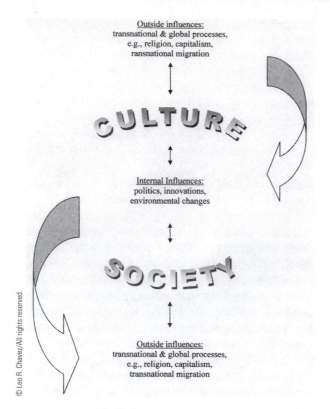

Figure 12.2 Culture change: cultural and social reproduction.

people are increasingly becoming integrated into one giant economic capitalist system. The spread of world capitalism also carries with it a spread of Western—often American—culture. One thing anyone who travels the world notices is how common American fast-food restaurants have become, a process often referred to as the McDonaldization of the society (Ritzer 2000). But globalization does not just refer to the movement of capital and the search for cheap labor. It is also about the movement of people, ideas, movies, music, "traditional" Chinese Medicine, and a whole host of flows unmoored from fixed national places (Zhan 2001). Jonathan Inda and Renato Rosaldo (2002) define a "world of globalization" as

> . . . a world of motion, of complex interconnections. Here capital traverses frontiers almost effortlessly, drawing more and more places into dense networks of financial interconnections; people readily (although certainly not freely and without difficulty) cut across national boundaries, turning countless territories into spaces where various cultures converge, clash, and struggle with each other; commodities drift briskly from one locality to another, becoming primary mediators in the encounter between culturally distant others; images flicker quickly from screen to screen, providing people with resources from which to fashion new ways of being in the world; and ideologies circulate rapidly through ever-expanding circuits, furnishing fodder for struggles couched in terms of cultural authenticity verses foreign influence.

New technologies that allow rapid electronic communication and faster transportation have made possible the increasing movement of people, capital, ideas, and cultures around the world and across national borders (Appadurai 1996). Although these powerful, worldwide trends may be occurring, they do not simply move around the world unimpeded. People living in local areas often have something to say about how global ideas and ways of life are integrated into local life. However, as some of the vignettes presented here indicate, change often results in backlash, as not everyone is pleased with change, especially if it upsets established relations of power and privilege. Forces for change and those resistant to change lead to a synthesis of new and old cultural beliefs and practices. This new crystallization of local life is not necessarily as hard and durable as the metaphor of a crystal suggests, because here, too, global life continues to influence. But at the same time, the local can effect changes in the global because change can occur in multiple directions, as the arrows in Figure 12.1 indicate.

In this process of change, the movement of people plays an important role. When people move from one social and cultural system to another, changes occur. Immigrants encounter new ideas and behavior while at the same time introducing their ideas and behaviors to the receiving society and culture. The next section examines specific examples of how migration and culture causes change in unanticipated ways. Over time, what was seen as new becomes routine and ordinary.

IMMIGRATION AND CULTURE CHANGE

Anthropologists often take the long view of culture change. Immediate reactions to newcomers (immigrants) in a society often focus on difference. New people in the neighborhood speaking a different language, practicing a different religion, and putting up signs on stores in foreign languages all raise ethnocentric responses and even fears. Over time, these differences may not be as pronounced because what was once new can become part of the accepted way things are, and even become central to a nation's identity and symbols of that identity.

Anthropologists are likely to speak of the culture changes that occur in a world of moving people, ideas, and cultural products as a blending, fusion, syncretization, hybridization, and creolization. These concepts reflect the multidimensional, multidirectional, and often unpredictable changes that take place as people and ideas, beliefs and behaviors collide and interweave into new cultural formations. Culture is always an emergent form of life (Fischer 2003). Anthropologists prefer these concepts to the more unidirectional flow of changes represented by models of assimilation, which are often inadequate to capture the complex process of culture change (Foner 2003, 34–35). A few examples make the point.

Food is often considered the symbol of a culture's identity and authenticity. Food is so closely associated with particular ethnic and national groups that this relationship is often taken for granted as natural, as if it always existed. People less often consider the history of food and its essential associations. In the United States, for example, burritos are considered Mexican food, but they were really invented in the United States. In Italy, Italianness is represented by food. The

John Wayne's statue at the John Wayne/Orange County airport.

very image of tomatoes, tomato sauce, and pasta conjures up connotations about what it means to be Italian (Barthes 1972). Carol Delaney (2004) notes that Italians are particularly identified with tomato sauce, what Americans often refer to as spaghetti sauce. Tomato sauce is a cultural force that holds generations of Italians together. However, before Europeans migrated to the Americas, Europe had no tomato sauce. It took years for the *tomatl* (as the Aztecs called the fruit in the Nahuatl language) to become accepted in European kitchens. Did the introduction of tomatoes destroy Italian culture (or cultures, as the state of Italy did not yet exist)? The introduction of tomatoes to the Italian peninsula actually resulted in tomato sauce eventually becoming the quintessential symbol of what it means to be Italian.

Another example starts close to my home. My local airport is John Wayne Airport in Orange County, California. For years, a statue of John Wayne, dressed as a cowboy, has been displayed prominently at the airport. But where does the "cowboy" come from? The image of the cowboy that John Wayne personifies has not always existed. The cowboy is a far cry from the image of Daniel Boone and the frontiersman of the colonial states in the late eighteenth and early nineteenth centuries. When whites and blacks from the colonial states moved West they encountered people in what is now New Mexico and Texas living a life well adapted to cattle and sheep ranching and herding. They were *vaqueros,* Mexican cowboys, from whom the Americans learned the cowboy way of life. Imagine how foreign the first American cowboys—with their big hats (*sombreros*), bandannas, ponchos, leather leggings over their pants, boots, ropes, and general demeanor—must have looked. And the words these new types of Americans used for the items and the techniques of their trade were essentially foreign, too, because many were words borrowed from Spanish (some of which were in turn borrowed from the Moors in Spain) (Graham 1994). Some cowboy words and their origin include,

Spanish	English
Vaqueros "men who work with cows"	buckaroos (cowboys)
chaparreras (pant leg coverings)	chaps
la reata (rope)	lariat
lazo (noose on rope)	lasso
reinda (ropes riders used to guide horse)	reins
mecate (rope made of horse tail hairs)	McCarty
Jáquima (bitless bridle to tame horses)	hackamore
broncos (wild horses)	broncs
mesteno (trained horse)	mustang
corral (pen)	corral
darle vuelta (roping and stopping cattle in their tracks by quickly snubbing a rope around the saddle horn)	dolly roping
rodeo	rodeo
juzgado (local jail)	hoosegow

But perhaps just as important as the words cowboys borrowed and adapted from the vaqueros was their lifestyle and personal characteristics: the strong, silent type whose time alone on the range made him manly (macho), independent, and self-reliant. Is this not the image John Wayne, the cowboy, exudes? In a few short years, the foreign-looking cowboy became the central figure in the myth of the West, and his qualities and characteristics came to epitomize the quintessential elements of what it means to be American. Did migrating West, encountering Mexican vaquero culture, and constructing the cowboy destroy American culture? Or did American culture change and in the process incorporate novelty? The answer is the statue standing at John Wayne airport.

Another example shows the unanticipated ways culture changes as a result of the immigration. Generations of Mexicans lived in Texas before it became part of the United States. As discussed previously, the cowboy was constructed out of the meeting of Americans and Texans in the early 1800s. However, another group of immigrants, Germans, had a profound and lasting effect on Tejanos (Texans of Mexican descent). Thousands of Germans migrated to Texas in the 1800s (Jordan 1966). They brought with them the accordion and their fondness of the polkas that they played during their parties. Locals heard the music and picked up the accordion, adapting it to fit their needs. Soon Tejanos were playing a new style of music in Texas that came to be known as "conjunto," "Tex-Mex,"

"Tejano," and "norteno" music (San Miguel 2002). To many Americans, it was "Mexican" music, and yet, this music was a real American invention, blending German polkas, Mexican ballads, and other song styles (see also the excellent PBS documentary *Accordion Dreams*). The late Texas singer, Selena Perez, was one of the most nationally famous performers of this style. In the long run, Tejanos did not lose their culture because they incorporated aspects of German culture into their lives. Their culture changed and was enriched in many ways because of such exchanges.

What are the lessons for anthropologists and others living in today's current world of movement? It is that migrations engender dislocations, opportunities, frictions, fears, and change. Most likely, the changes that occur will be unanticipated because transformations that cultures undergo are difficult to plan and predict. One thing is certain: the sets of cultural practices and understandings about the world that will emerge in the near future will make sense and seem as natural and enduring as the cultures and world we live in today.

REFERENCES

Appadurai, Arjun. 1996. *Modernity at large: cultural dimensions of globalization.* Minneapolis: Univ. of Minnesota Press.

Bandhauer, Carina A. 2001. *Global trends in racism: The late 20th century anti-immigrant movement in Southern California.* Ph.D., Binghamton Univ.

Barthes, Roland. 1972. *Mythologies.* London: Cape.

Basch, Linda, Nina Glick Schiller, and Cristina Szanton Blanc. 1994. *Nations unbound: Transnational projects, postcolonial predicaments, and deterritorialized nation-states.* Amsterdam: Gordon and Breach.

Baum, Geraldine. 2004. Queens pizzeria sells diversity by the slice. *Los Angeles Times,* May 31, E1.

Bean, Frank D., C. Gray Swicegood, and Ruth Berg. 2000. Mexican-origin fertility: New patterns and interpretations. *Social Science Quarterly* 81:404–420.

Bohlen, Celestine. 1996. Italians contemplate beauty in a Caribbean brow. *The New York Times,* September 10, A3.

Bosniak, Linda S. 1997. 'Nativism' the concept: Some reflections. In *Immigrants out! The new nativism and the anti-immigrant impulse in the United States,* ed. Juan F. Perea, 279–299. New York: New York Univ. Press.

Brimelow, Peter. 1992. Time to rethink immigration? *The National Review,* June 22, 30–46.

Brugge, Doug. 1995. Pulling up the ladder. In *Eyes right! Challenging the right wing backlash,* ed. Chip Berlet, 191–209. Boston: South End Press.

Buchanan, Patrick J. 1994. What will America be in 2050? *Los Angeles Times,* October 28, B7.

Bureau, Population Reference. 2002. 2002 World Population Data Sheet, Vol. 2004: Population Reference Bureau. www.prb.org/pdf/ WorldPopulationDSs02_Eng.pdf.

Castles, Stephen, and Mark J. Miller. 1998. *The age of migration: International population movements in the modern world.* 2nd ed. New York and London: The Guilford Press.

Chavez, Leo R. 1997. Immigration reform and nativism: The nationalist response to the transnationalist challenge. In *Immigrants out! The new nativism and the anti-immigrant impulse in the United States,* ed. Juan F. Perea, 61–77. New York: New York Univ. Press.

———. 1998. *Shadowed lives: Undocumented immigrants in American society.* 2nd ed. Ft. Worth: Harcourt Brace and Jovanovich College Publishers.

———. 2001. *Covering immigration: Popular images and the politics of the nation.* Berkeley: Univ. of California Press.

Dahlburg, John-Thor. 2000. EU bares its teeth over Austria 'crisis'. *Los Angeles Times,* February 3, A1.

Delaney, Carol. 2004. *Investigating culture: An experiential introduction to anthropology.* Malden, MA: Blackwell Publishing.

Espiritu, Yen Le. 2003. *Home bound: Filipino American lives across cultures, communities, and countries.* Berkeley: Univ. of California Press.

Fischer, Michael M.M. 2003. *Emergent forms of life and the anthropological voice.* Durham: Duke Univ. Press.

Foner, Nancy, ed. 2003. *American arrivals: Anthropology engages the new immigration.* Santa Fe: School of American Research.

French, Howard W. 2000. Japan fails to cope with its declining population. *Orange County Register,* March 14, news 19.

Geyer, Georgie Ann. 1996. *Americans no more.* New York: The Atlantic Monthly Press.

Graham, Joe S. 1994. *El Rancho in South Texas: Continuity and change from 1750.* College Station, TX: Texas A&M Univ. Press.

Gupta, Akhil, and James Ferguson, eds. 1997. *Culture, power, place: Ethnography at the end of an era.* Culture, Power, Place: Explorations in Critical Anthropology. Durham: Duke Univ. Press.

Huntington, Samuel P. 2004. The Hispanic challenge. *Foreign Policy* March/April: 30–45.

Inda, Jonathan Xavier, and Renato Rosaldo. 2002. Introduction: A world in motion. In *The anthropology of globalization: A reader,* eds. Jonathan Xavier Inda and Renato Rosaldo, 1–34. Malden, MA: Blackwell Publishers.

Institute, Migration Policy. 2004. Migration Information Source: Migration Policy Institute www.migrationinformation.org. http://www.migrationinformation. org.

Johnson, Kevin R. 1997. The new nativism: Something old, something new, something borrowed, something blue. In *Immigrants out! The new nativism and the anti-immigrant impulse in the United States,* ed. Juan F. Perea, 165–189. New York: New York Univ. Press.

Jordan, Terry G. 1966. *German seed in Texas soil: Immigrant farmers in nineteenth-century Texas.* Austin: Univ. of Texas Press

Kadetsky, Elizabeth. 1994. 'Save our state' initiative: Bashing illegals in California. *Nation,* October 17.

Lamm, Richard D., and Gary Imhoff. 1985. *The immigration time bomb.* New York: Truman Talley Books.

Lamphere, Louise, ed. 1992. *Structuring diversity: Ethnographic perspectives on the new immigration.* Chicago: The Univ. of Chicago Press.

Los Angeles Times. 2000. Anti-immigrant nationalist party gains in Flanders. October 10, A4.

———. 2001. Russia: Illegal migrants number 10 million, official says. 14.

Maharidge, Dale. 1996. *The coming white minority.* New York: Times Books.

Maira, Sunaina M. 2002. *Desis in the house: Indian American youth culture in York City.* Philadelphia: Temple Univ. Press.

Malinowski, Bronislaw. 1944/1960. *A scientific theory of culture.* Chapel Hill: Univ. of North Carolina Press.

Mena, Jennifer. 2001. Expatriates wild about 'Tomato King' mayor. *Los Angeles Times,* July 9, B3.

Migration News. 2001a. Vol. 8, no. 5 (May). Davis, CA: Univ. of California, Davis. http://migration.ucdavis.edu.

_____. 2001b. Vol. 8, no. 6 (June). Davis, CA: Univ. of California, Davis. http://migration.ucdavis.edu.

Migration Policy Institute. 2004. Migration Information Source: Migration Policy Institute www.migrationinformation.org. http://www.migrationinformation.org.

Newsweek. 2000. Perspectives, June 12, 23.

Oakley, Robin. 2001. Europe's tangle over immigration. *CNN.com,* February 20. www.cnn.com/2001/WORLD/europe/02/20/immigration.overview/index.html.

Ong, Aihwa. 1999. *Flexible citizenship: The cultural logics of transnationality*. Durham: Duke Univ. Press

_____. 2003. *Buddha is hiding: Refugees, citizenship, the new America*. Berkeley: Univ. of California Press.

Ortner, Sherry. 1973. On key symbols. *American Anthropologist* 75:1228–46.

Pedraza, Silvia. 1996. Origins and destinies: Immigration, race, and ethnicity in American history. In *Origins and Destinies: Immigration, Race, and Ethnicity in America,* ed. Silvia Pedraza and Ruben Rumbaut, 1–20. Belmont CA: Wadsworth Publishing Company.

Perea, Juan F., ed. 1997. *Immigrants out! The new nativism and the anti-immigrant impulse in the United States*. New York: New York Univ. Press.

Perez, Nieves Ortega. 2004. *Spain: Forging an Immigration Policy*. Migration Policy Institute. www.migrationinformation.org/Profiles/print.cfm?ID=97.

Pickel, Mary Lou. 2004. Mexican pauper returns to be a president. *Orange County Register,* September 15, news 17.

Radcliffe-Brown, A. R. 1948. *Structure and function in primitive society*. London: Cohen and West.

Reimers, David M. 1998. *Unwelcome strangers: American identity and the turn against immigration*. New York: Columbia Univ. Press.

Ritzer, George. 2000. *The McDonaldization of society*. 3rd ed. Thousand Oaks, CA: Pine Forge Press.

Rodriguez, Gregory. 2004. Europe's Implosion: The EU needs immigrants but feels threatened by them. *Los Angeles Times,* May 5, B13.

Salzman, Philip Carl. 2001. *Understanding culture: An introduction to anthropological theory*. Prospect Heights, Illinois: Waveland Press, Inc.

San Miguel, Guadalupe Jr. 2002. *Tejano proud: Tex-Mex music in the twentieth century*. College Station, TX: Texas A&M Univ. Press.

Simmons, Ann M. 2004. A melting pot that's brimming with alphabet soup. *Los Angeles Times,* July 1, B1.

Simon, Rita J. 1985. *Public opinion and the immigrant*. Lexington MA: Lexington Books.

Simons, Marlise. 1996. In France, Africa women are now fighting polygamy. *New York Times,* January 26, A1.

Stalker, Peter. 2001. *No-nonsense guide to international migration*. London: Verso.

Steinberg, Stephen. 1981. *The ethnic myth: Race, ethnicity, and class in America:* Boston: Beacon Press.

Tarmann, Allison. 2001. *The Flap Over Replacement Migration*. Washington, DC: Population Reference Bureau, June 13. ww.prb.org/pt/wooo/May June2000/flap_replacement_migration.html.

Tatalovich, Raymond. 1997. Official English as nativist backlash. In *Immigrants out! The new nativism and the anti-immigrant impulse in the United States,* ed. Juan F. Perea, 78–102. New York: New York Univ. Press.

Tsuda, Takeyuki. 2003. *Strangers in the ethnic homeland: Japanese Brazilian return migration in transnational perspective*. New York: Columbia Univ. Press.

Wallerstein, Immanuel. 1974/1989. *The modern world-system.* New York: Academic Press.

Williams, Carol J. 2000a. Citizenship reform has lost its punch. *Los Angeles Times,* January 8, A2.

———. 2000b. Danes cast cold eye on immigrants. *Los Angeles Times,* April 28, A1.

———. 2000c. Germans stand up to right-wing violence. *Los Angeles Times,* November 10, A4.

Wolf, Eric R. 1982. *Europe and the people without history.* Berkeley: Univ. of California Press.

Yamanaka, Keiko. 2000. "I will go home, but when?" Labor migration and circular diaspora formation by Japanese Brazilians in Japan. In *Japan and global migration,* eds. Mike Douglas and Glenda S. Roberts, 123–152. London: Routledge.

Yarborough, Trin. 1996. "I saw women go to school and have jobs." *Los Angeles Times,* March 2, B11.

Yee, Sonya. 2002. Far-right freedom party fizzles in Austrian election. *Los Angeles Times,* November 25, A3.

Zhan, Mei. 2001. Does it take a miracle? Negotiating knowledge, identities, and communities of traditional Chinese medicine. *Cultural Anthropology* 16 (4) :453–480.

NOTES

1. See Federal Statistical Office Germany, http://www. statistik-bund.de/e_home.htm.

2. See National Institute for Statistics and Economic Studies (INSEE) France in Facts and Figures, http://www.insee.fr/ en/home/home_page.asp.

3. There has also been an outcry against anti-immigrant politics and actions (Dahlburg 2000; Williams 2000c; Yee 2002).

4. The list of anti-immigrant organizations in the United States is too numerous to detail here, but includes the Federation for American Immigration Reform, American Citizens Together, Voice of Citizens Together, Stop Immigration Now, and California Coalition for Immigration Reform. See (Bandhauer 2001; Chavez 1997; Maharidge 1996; Reimers 1998) for a more thorough discussion of anti-immigrant organizations in the United States.

5. See Samuel Huntington (2004) for a more recent example of anti-Mexican discourse.

Fieldwork Biography
Susan Parman

Susan Parman began research in "Ciall" on the west side of the island of Lewis in the Scottish Outer Hebrides in 1970, and has maintained strong ties through visits, letters, and e-mail over the years. An elected "Fellow" of the Society of Antiquaries (Scotland), she is involved with numerous projects concerning Scotland and Europe (see http://anthro. fullerton.edu/sparman/). She earned a PhD from Rice University in 1972, and is currently at California State University, Fullerton.

© Courtesy of Susan Parman

13/Scottish Crofters

Narratives of Change among Small Landholders in Scotland

My journey into the world of Scottish crofters began 40 years ago when I did a year abroad at the University of Edinburgh as an undergraduate and listened to a story about a crofter named Murdo in a small community in the Highlands. The youngest son, Murdo had never left the community but had cared for his aging parents until they died; his siblings had settled all over the world—a doctor in Australia, a sociologist in Canada, two schoolteachers in Chicago—but they always came back at the New Year. When Murdo died, his brothers and sisters looked for the book he had always told them he was writing, because they wanted to publish it; the only book they could find was his daily journal, which consisted entirely of annotations of the weather.

My thought was: how could someone living alone in a small community spend time writing only about the weather? Five years later, and six months into a 14-month period of fieldwork in the village of Ciall on the west side of the island of Lewis in the Outer Hebrides, I remembered Murdo's journal and realized that it was about far more than the weather. *Blowing a gale today. Two fishing boats overdue. Five lambs lost from the late frost. Walked fourteen miles to deliver salted mackerel to the Widow MacDonald and was back before the summer dark came down.*

Scotland, sometimes referred to dismissively by the English as "North Britain," is about the size of South Carolina—a small country of about five million people. Scotland's weather is typically portrayed on tourist postcards as consisting of four seasons, all of them identical (cold rain). Crofters live in the northwest Highlands and Islands of Scotland, a region subject to frequent gale warnings and a higher level of rainfall than the east coast. In his book *West Highland Survey: An Essay in Human Ecology,* F. Fraser Darling (1955) sought the causes of economic decline and depopulation in the Highlands and described the region as devastated due to a combination of climatic, geographic, and historic reasons. Composed of "some of the highest, roughest, and poorest ground in Scotland" (Darling 1955, 15), the Highlands constitute a unique set of conditions affecting human adaptation.

The Outer Hebrides, today called the Western Isles (*Eilean Siar* in Gaelic), is a chain of islands between 15 and 40 miles west of the Isle of Skye and the Northwest Highlands. Composed of disintegrating Archaean gneiss, a hard and ancient rock, more than 200 islands scattered over 136 miles (most of them uninhabited) support a variety of wildlife such as seals, otters, birds, red deer, and salmon—the former three serving as fodder for naturalists, the latter two for tweed-wearing aristocrats, politicians, and international sportsmen. In addition, as Fraser MacDonald points out (2003), the Outer Hebrides served an important geopolitical function as a military complex during the Cold War of the 1950s— reflecting a common relationship in sparsely populated areas between the military and tourism (Lefebvre 1991 quoted in MacDonald 2003, 208). A very few of the islands are or once were home to crofters: Mingulay, Vatersay, Barra, South Uist, Benbecula, North Uist, Berneray, and the largest island of the north, "Lewis and Harris," often thought of as two islands because Harris, joined to Lewis by a narrow strip of land, is mostly mountain whereas Lewis is a relatively flat, open moor studded with marsh. The definition of the Hebrides as a wilderness for naturalists, sportsmen, and rocket launchers contributes to the perception of crofters as marginal in British society.

What is a croft? A croft is a strip of land (on Lewis, usually 3 to 5 acres) that encompasses both well-drained and boggy land, and adjoins a main road. The croft house sits next to the road and usually has a small garden patch behind it. The rest of the land may be planted in hay, oats, barley, or potatoes, and used for grazing by cattle, sheep, or in a few cases, llamas. Crofts are not owned but held in tenancy with security of tenure and fair rent. They are organized in crofting townships, which require communal action to support community needs (such as managing the common grazings, repairing fences and roads, and coordinating sheep fanks—the communal gathering of sheep from the moor). Thus a crofter is a member of a tightly integrated community with communal responsibilities. Shared language, kinship connections, and religious beliefs strengthen these ties.

Although Lowlanders often assume a croft to be a house, it is an agricultural smallholding in designated crofting counties in the Highlands and Islands of Scotland. A government agency called the Crofters Commission has managed and subjected the crofts to a diversity of changing laws over the years (to the extent that a croft is defined by some as "a piece of land entirely surrounded by legislation"). Crofting legislation was created in 1886 to protect a small tenantry from arbitrary eviction and excessive rents, prevent an uprising similar to Irish

Aerial view of a crofting township

land wars, and stem the flow through out-migration of what some have called the "cannon fodder" of the Highland military regiments. The legislation gave crofters security of tenure, fair rent, and hereditary succession to small pieces of land (initially no more than 50 acres, now 30 hectares or 74 acres). In 2001 the Crofters Commission reported 17,721 registered crofts, of which 6,087 are in the Outer Hebrides (*Eilean Siar*), and 3,611 on Lewis. About 11,500 households occupy the crofts, of which about 7,500 are considered to be headed by active crofters engaged in agricultural production, for a total crofting population of about 33,000. Thus although crofts occupy about one-third of the agricultural holdings in Scotland (17,721 out of 49,738), both the acreage and the population they represent are small in proportion to the total acreage of agricultural holdings and population; but they loom large in the Scottish imagination, as a symbol of the common man against the aristocratic laird, ecologically sensitive land management against big farming interests, and communitarian social consciousness against rapacious self-interest.

From my university friends at Edinburgh during my first encounter with Scotland, I gathered the impression that crofters were the Scottish equivalent of European peasantry (a connotation crofters themselves receive with disgust and disdain). The divide between Highland and Lowland seemed to be between past and future, rusticity and civilization, innovative dynamism and lazy backwardness. Stereotyped as clinging to the past (variously identified as Iron Age, medieval, and the nineteenth century), crofters represented the Celtic Twilight, or

Crofters picking potatoes

TABLE 13.1   CHANGES IN LAND USE (1891–1994)   PARISH OF BARVAS, ISLE
OF LEWIS AGRICULTURAL CENSUS SUMMARIES[1]

Year	Potatoes*	Barley*	Oats*	Milk Cows	Beef Cattle	Sheep†
1891	1105	1172	556	1771	—	17.7
1901	1281.5	1227.75	735.5	1947	—	20.28
1911	1146	959	1107	1951	—	19.5
1921	1126	1149	1039	1932	—	16.9
1931	1043	823	2045	1846	—	21.3
1941	679	401	2451	1544	50	22.7
1951	576	94	2327	1295	47	41
1961	413	14	1432	960	1273	37
1971	138.5	1.25	452.75	243	756	34.98
1981	89	.5	83.25	22	74	20.83
1991	36.75	7.5	16.5	1	115	20.17
1992	33.5	2.5	12.5	1	98	19.22
1993	28.5	—	12.5	—	82	19.28
1994	20.25	—	10.5	—	80	18.9

* In acres

† In thousands

were perceived to be Calvinists rigid in their fundamentalism (or, in the southern
Hebrides, Catholics out of sync with Scotland as a Protestant nation), and thus
helped to bolster Lowland Scots' identities as sophisticated, modern, and tolerant.

Almost every impression that I began with changed as I learned about crofting
communities. Far from being "peasants," a term implying primary involvement

in subsistence-based agricultural production, crofters constitute a rural proletariat that has worked at diverse jobs—kelp manufacturing in the eighteenth and nineteenth centuries, Harris Tweed weaving and fishing in the twentieth century, and wind farming and computer-related jobs in the twenty-first century. The agricultural use of the land has declined substantially over the past hundred years, and in recent years, nonagricultural activities have been recognized as significant aspects of crofting—the main purpose of crofting defined in socially conscious terms as an attempt to preserve a way of life.

DOING FIELDWORK

Trained in an era of community studies, structural-functionalism, and neoevolutionism, I set out to look at crofting townships as adaptive systems determined primarily by economic and ecological factors. I planned to study variations in crofting adaptations, or how social boundary systems changed in relation to whether the primary sources of work kept people away from the township (as in fishing and construction work) or kept them at home (for example, through work associated with the Harris Tweed industry). Thus, I chose the village of Ciall because it employed a number of Harris Tweed weavers and millworkers. In this chapter I attempt to tell some of the stories of Ciall in an organized framework of meaning, to capture contextualized speech events. (All quotes are derived from fieldwork; for the methods used, see Parman 2005, 21–23.)

Ciall is a crofting township of about 600 people that lies on three undulating hills along the shore in the parish of Barvas on the west side of Lewis, the northernmost island in the Outer Hebrides. Between 47°50'N and 58°30'N latitude, Lewis is as far north as Newfoundland and farther north than Mongolia. Bathed by the North Atlantic Drift, or Gulf Stream, Ciall rarely sees snow, but shivers in cool, windy wetness between a fairly narrow range of temperature—from an average of 55°F. in summer to 44°F. in winter. The wind is a relentless presence on the treeless northern islands, often reaching gale force; winds of 60 mph and more are common. Rain, which comes in heavy downpours or light mist, averages between 55 to 65 inches a year. The water may be held in colloidal suspension with decomposed organic matter in the compact, spongy material called peat, or pour as rivers and streams off the island's shelf of nonpourous Archaean gneiss into the sea. Of Lewis's total area of 437,200 acres, inland water comprises 24,863 acres (according to Murray [1966, 171]; the name *Lewis* actually derives from the Gaelic *leogach,* meaning marshy).

Lewis has a large town (Stornoway, with between five and six thousand people), an airport built in 1939, and a harbor to which come fishing boats and passenger ferries. Lewis also has a castle, where nineteenth-century crofters once brought annual "gifts" of chickens, but which was converted to a technical college and is now part of the emerging University of the Highlands and Islands. A circular, asphalt road and daily bus services link Stornoway to small villages scattered around the island's perimeter. The people of Stornoway refer to someone from the western side of the island as a *siarach* (west-sider), a term that connotes rusticity.[2] The location of these villages by the sea reflects the historical association of crofting with fishing, although today most villagers fish for sport

Stornoway Harbor, east side of town

and use the money they earn from weaving to buy fish from the local fish van (or, more often in 2003, from the petrol station in Barvas and the Co-op in Stornoway). Many no longer buy fish at all. The central core of the island—heather-cloaked, bog-soaked, and layered with an estimated 85 tons of peat—is uninhabited, except for sheep who use it as a vast, unfenced communal grazing land.

In 1970 and 1971 the Outer Hebrides were crosscut into separate government units linked with the mainland. For example, Lewis was linked with the county of Ross and Cromarty. The rural counterparts were considered peripheral. In 2003, symptomatic of the linguistic nationalism associated with regionalism in the European Union, the Outer Hebrides became a separate council area with the Gaelic name *Eilean Siar* (Western Isle). Road signs are in both Gaelic and English, and council members bristle at the connotations of periphery. Rurality has come to mean not rusticity but nature conservation, and crofting is touted as an ideal form of agriculture in the European Union (Parman 1993).

NARRATIVES ABOUT CROFTING

Residents of Ciall today still speak of some families as "outsiders" because they came to Ciall in the nineteenth century when landowners "cleared" excess families from land in the parish of Uig. The "clearances" were frequently mentioned in the Napier Commission's Report of 1884, the report that led to the passing of the Crofters Holdings (Scotland) Act of 1886 (usually referred to as the "Crofters Act" or "Crofting Act" of 1886) that created the crofting system.

One of the main purposes of the Crofters Act of 1886 was to provide small-holders with a "bit of land" to which Celts were thought to be fanatically attached.

"No people in the world have so great a value for land," wrote Mackinlay in 1878. In the 1870s, several hundred crofters on Lewis marched to the castle in Stornoway and demanded the return of their common grazing land. The land had been converted to deer parks and sheep farms as part of the agricultural revolution that swept through Britain beginning in the second half of the eighteen century and resulted in large-scale out-migration from rural areas to the industrial Lowland towns or overseas. The government, aware of the fomenting rebellion, appointed the Napier Commission to collect evidence and make recommendations. Ciall crofters gave evidence that families had been forced upon them from neighboring communities. Twenty-four families had been cleared from neighboring townships, five of them sent to Ciall, the rest "sent to America and to other places after they had but recently erected new buildings. Their fires were quenched. Had you seen it, you could scarcely bear the sight. Their houses were broken down and their fires were quenched" (Napier 1884, 962).[3]

When residents of Ciall narrate stories of the past, it is as if they were there themselves, experiencing the hurts, insults, and destruction. It sometimes took me a while to realize that the events they described occurred several centuries earlier, that the evil factor who quenched fires and stole cattle is long dead and that the still-rankling insult from the neighbor had been directed at the narrator's great-great-grandfather. In Ciall, the actions of kings, queens, princes, landlords, highwaymen, neighbors, and kinsmen are not abstract points on a timeline but actions felt in the present, with history riding a direct line from the emotional brain to the cortex.

In 1911 crofters were removed from special status and merged with small-holders all over Britain, but they were resurrected in 1955 with the passing of a new Crofters Act after the Taylor Report of 1954 argued that crofting communities should be maintained because they "embody a free and independent way of life which in a civilisation predominantly urban and industrial in character is worth preserving for its own intrinsic quality." The Taylor Report observed that "It was clear from the evidence put before us during our visits to the crofting areas that the history of the past remains vivid in the minds of the people and, in some measure, conditions their attitudes to current problems."

One Ciall crofter born in the 1930s describes the significance of the croft: "It was your security. You could always come home to the croft." The rents were low, and income was available through seasonal fishing, Harris Tweed weaving, and periodic construction work. Women packed their kits and moved as a group to mainland cities where they gutted and salt-packed herring or worked in the hotels. Families were large and outsiders were few; everyone was related, which might generate arguments but also assurance of mutual aid in times of need. The croft yielded potatoes, oats, barley, and hay, as well as carrots, kale, and turnips in small kitchen gardens protected by a stone wall behind the house. Before World War II, everyone kept cows that provided milk and cream.

Until as recently as the 1960s, a form of transhumance was practiced on Lewis. Cattle were taken away from the arable land to the central moorlands for several months during the summer. Those who stayed with them—usually the young people who looked forward to the opportunity for independence—lived in small huts whose locations duplicated neighborhoods within the village. The

© Courtesy of Susan Parman

Black house in snow

term *shieling* (*airidh* in Gaelic) refers to both the hut and the summer pasture on the moor.

Because women were responsible for milking, the mothers, aunts, and grandmothers of the young people came out in the evening to milk the cows and carry the milk back to the village. But during the day the young people kept lazy, carefree watch over the cattle—fishing for trout, gathering small blackberries, hunting the nests of grouse, and walking to visit friends on other shielings. The boys swam in the lochs, and sometimes the girls stole their clothes. From the tops of the hills many children learned for the first time about other parts of the island. If anyone got lost in snow or fog, they followed the cows home; the cattle knew their own shielings, and crowded close during the night, sometimes sticking their heads inside.

No one ever slept alone. Girls crowded in together between the narrow walls, and boys kept to separate shielings but sometimes came in groups to court the girls or make ghostly noises. No one ventured out on the moor alone at night. Although some light was always in the sky at these northerly latitudes, the moor was eerie with the sound of birds and the lowing of the cattle. Crowded in together in the small shieling with the cattle moving outside, the young people sang songs and told stories, some of them about the *each uisge* or water horse that lurked in nearby wells to capture laggards that walked alone across that eerie landscape.

On the weekends, the older boys and girls in their late teens and early twenties came out in their best clothes and chased the younger children home. It was a time of courtship and unrestrained talk, out from under the watchful eyes of the village elders and gossips.

The agricultural statistics for Barvas show the large numbers of cattle that were kept until the 1950s. During the Second World War, agricultural advisors introduced cattle bred more for beef than for milk, and subsidies were introduced to encourage the production of beef cattle.

After World War II, the government introduced an act that provided school-children with free milk, which a van from a farm near Stornoway brought. Ciall villagers first started buying milk from the school milk van. Weavers were earning more money, in part because of a strike during wartime, and did not need to keep milk cows. The cows were a lot of work (everyone had to keep several cattle to make certain they had at least one cow with milk), and as the tweed was more profitable, it was easier to buy milk instead. As the cattle became fewer, the market for bottled milk expanded. A dairy was started on the west side of the island in the mid-1960s, and during my fieldwork in 1970 and 1971 carried milk from Uig to Ness. Today milk is shipped from the mainland. When the townships started reseeding schemes, the shielings were no longer needed; the cattle could be kept apart from the crops on the croft land. A few continued to go out of habit, and for health reasons. ("The air is different there, more health-giving. On the hills there's no smoke fumes, just heather. The air is heavy by the sea.") In the early 1960s, when one couple in their seventies went out to their shieling, no one else was there. "We stayed for several days, it was a nice rest, and then we came back. My wife looked back at the dark empty hills and said, 'If I'd have known how dark it was on the shieling, I never would have gone out there.'"

The shielings that remain in use on Lewis today are huts of tin, wood, and concrete that were built within easy walking distance from the highway. They are holiday homes, used as weekend or summer retreats for harried urban dwellers. On the west side the shielings are in ruin, but remain in songs and nostalgic memories.

Between 1970 and 1971, the number of sheep the crofters kept exceeded the allowable number, whereas the number of cattle declined. As a result, crofting land deteriorated. Because people didn't have the rich feed that they can purchase today, a cow might have been four or five years old before she calved and had any milk. Therefore, one of the most significant contributions of cattle was not their milk, but their dung that helped to fertilize the croft. A major source of conflict in townships at that time concerned access to good pastureland among those who had cattle and those who had only sheep. As recently as the Napier Commission's collection of evidence in 1883, the terms *tacksman* (a powerful subsidiary of the laird in crofting communities) and *shepherd* were synonymous, reflecting the association that crofters still made between sheep and the clearances; but between 1970 and 1971 sheep were a relatively trouble-free complement to the loom. Today, the cattle have almost all disappeared (only 80 left in the parish of Barvas in 1994), and the number of sheep have dropped by about half.

In 2003, a man nicknamed Sgian Mhaol explained his decision to give his croft to his son, Uilleam:

> I never wanted to leave the island myself, so there was never a question about who would get the croft when I was growing up. I stayed on after leaving school while everyone else left to get married or get jobs on the mainland. For a while it was

Shieling with binoculars

crowded, with some of the kids still at home and my parents still alive, and my three aunties. The old man was the last to die, and suddenly the house was too big. I married a girl in the next village over and after Uilleam was born there was just the three of us. It wasn't a bad life, being a crofter—I raised a few cattle for beef, kept my share of sheep on the moor and a few on the croft, grew a few potatoes and some hay and oats for winter feed for the cattle. Of course my main income was from the tweed, but you couldn't count on getting tweed all the time. Uilleam did all right in school. There are some who would keep back their only sons to help with the croft, but I didn't mind it when he said he wanted to go to university. He said he had made up his mind what he wanted to do by watching the tellie. He was going to be an accountant, and so he was. But after a while of working away he came back to the island and got a job in Stornoway. We worked it out that I would take my house out of crofting and give him the croft. That meant he could build a new house on the croft. That's how he built the house across the road. No, he doesn't work the croft—I'm still the one who keeps a few sheep. He commutes to his job in Stornoway. But the croft is his base.

Sgian Mhaol's neighbors, three unmarried brothers in their fifties, have a different story of croft use. They are unusual in preferring cattle to sheep. Their croft is too small to keep many cattle, and too small to depend on grazing, so they rely heavily on hay purchased from the mainland, which they criticize for its poor quality. If they had access to large amounts of land, they would be successful farmers expanding their business every year. They enjoy experimenting with different breeds, have invested a lot of money in equipment, and follow the latest trends in livestock care. But given the limitations of croft sizes and the regulations preventing amalgamation of crofts, they are philosophical and call their investments a "hobby." When their parents died, the youngest son inherited the croft, but the three brothers have continued to live on and work the croft as a team, with one brother doing the housework and weaving tweed, another working in a trade that takes him all over the island, and the other focusing on croft work. The youngest brother has recently become engaged to a girl much younger than himself, who moved with her family to the village from the mainland (and who thereby attracts much doubt, curiosity, criticism, and gossip about her heritage). Long engagements are not uncommon, especially when they have the potential to disrupt existing household arrangements.

Sgian Mhaol's ability to decroft the land on which his house was located, thus freeing the remaining croft land for his son to build a house, is a recent development that has the potential to change forever the crofting community as it existed. A crofting community conferred status, security of tenure, and a subtle hierarchy (in which crofters with land were seen above squatters with land on suffrage, and the landless were on the bottom of the hierarchy). A crofting community had strong boundaries that prevented the incursion of outsiders. The community also preserved a way of life that in many areas was characterized by strong ties of kinship and shared customs, such as speaking Gaelic and the evangelical belief system of the Free Church. And a crofting community typically had an aging population whose young people were siphoned off to the mainland or overseas by jobs, education, and the paradoxical desire to both leave and return.

The Crofting Reform (Scotland) Act of 1976 gave crofters the legal right to buy their own croft. As an owner-occupier, the crofter could apply to have land decrofted, or taken out of crofting. This act was followed by the Crofters (Scotland) Act of 1993 that defined the circumstances under which land could be removed from crofting regulation. Sgian Mhaol now has a clear right to decroft his house site and garden. Or he could decroft land that would benefit the local community, such as for constructing a play area or community hall. But the overall effect has been to stimulate a new housing market in the crofting counties. The decrofted house eventually is put up for sale; the new houses built on croft land (to replace the decrofted house) may eventually be decrofted and available for sale themselves. The consumable, shrinking croft is today's family farm, tomorrow's housing development. Table 13.2 reflects the importance of the croft as a source of housing, and the policy of current crofting legislation to preserve population (statistics provided by the Crofters Commission).

The changes are evident. Where once a child ran in and out of every house on a street, now the child hesitates. Strangers are now in the village: a man from Wales, a family from England, Lowlanders. They build greenhouses, keep chickens, peddle eggs, and raise Highland cattle, horses, and llamas. Some are photographers, artists, and writers. Slowly people have realized that the croft is a source of wealth, and instead of assigning the croft to a member of the family they make under-the-table agreements whereby a croft assignation is "sold" to someone who wants the grants by which a house may be built.

It was my croft by right. It came to my cousin when his mother died, but he didn't want to move back to the village. I've been living in a council house and grazing

TABLE 13.2   DECROFTING APPLICATIONS
FOR LEWIS, 1992–2002

	Croft House Site/Garden	Part	Whole
1992	33	4	2
1993	45	7	2
1994	57	1	1
1995	35	5	0
1996	41	18	0
1997	53	37	0
1998	47	24	1
1999	49	32	0
2000	54	24	0
2001	39	22	0
2002	53	22	1

sheep on the croft for years. He wanted money for it and I offered him two thousand pounds, but he sold it to a man from Dundee for seven thousand pounds. I've put in a protest to the Crofters Commission. They're supposed to maintain the traditions of the islands, not let the croft go to the highest bidder.

The gossip whips around the community about the latest conflict over who will get the croft. Old stories are taken out and dusted off about various members of the family, with an effort toward proving that each person in the dispute is manifesting some characteristic inherited from some long-dead family member. No one acts as an individual; they are all submerged in the family, their behavior determined by blood.

"He's always been selfish. It's in the blood. He got it from his great-grandfather, who was hanged for sheep-stealing."

Some things never change.

NARRATIVES ABOUT SPEAKING GAELIC

Seonag Monadh has spoken Gaelic all her life, but when she was in school she was punished for speaking it. She prefers reading English to Gaelic books, and her Gaelic spelling is poor. When the grocery van pulls up to the door, she switches between English and Gaelic depending on the topic—English for measurements and descriptions of rising or falling barometers, Gaelic for gossip and graphic descriptions of heavy rain. When her children were little a Gaelic playschool was started in the village, and she sent her children; but although they can understand spoken Gaelic, they prefer to speak English. To avoid fights over the television, she bought them one for their bedroom, and they watch "Who Wants to be a Millionaire" while she listens to Gaelic songs. She regrets that Gaelic is declining, but isn't sure she wants her grandchildren to do the "Gaelic track" now available in school, because fewer Gaelic-speaking teachers are available to cover the subjects as are English-speaking teachers. On the other hand, she is proud that her children know Gaelic, saying, "It's very posh to speak

Gaelic playschool in the town Barvas on the west side of Lewis

the language of Scotland." She comments that many of the newcomers are picking up the language from their children.

Although Scotland was never totally Gaelic-speaking, Gaelic has for various historical symbolic reasons connoted the distinctive heritage of the Highlands and therefore (courtesy of Walter Scott and other promoters of Highland myths) of Scotland as a whole. "If you're going to understand what it means to be a crofter, you must have the Gaelic," I was told repeatedly. Although this is not entirely true (Shetland and Orkney, for example, are English-speaking crofting regions), the statement reflects a recurring theme: Scotland claims its unique identity on the European playing field of regionalism with distinctive characteristics such as speaking Gaelic and crofting. Gaelic (the language of the "aboriginal Celt") is linked with Scottish autochthony; Scots still invoke eighteenth-century linguistic claims that Gaelic was the language of Eden. The Crofters Commission is required to have at least one Gaelic-speaking member, and the Scottish Parliament has established a new post of Gaelic Information Officer.

Both the number and percentage of Gaelic speakers has been declining in Scotland since an official census was first taken, from 254,415 (6.3 percent) in 1891 to 65,978 (1.3 percent) in 1991. In 2001 the number of Gaelic speakers in crofting areas was 12,811 (organized in 4,725 households), or about 62.2 percent of the crofting population (Ekos Ltd. 2001, 19). Nancy Dorian uses the term *Language Death* (1981) to describe the process of destruction that is occurring in a Gaelic-speaking community in East Sutherland as a regional English dialect

TABLE 13.3   DECLINE IN GAELIC SPEAKERS ON
EILEAN SIAR BY CIVIL PARISH, 1891–2001

	Percentage of Gaelic Speakers, 1891	Percentage of Gaelic Speakers, 2001[4]
Barra	93.8	77.1
Barvas	95.7	80.9
Harris	95.4	78.0
Lochs	94.1	70.7
N. Uist	93.8	76.2
S. Uist	95.0	75.0
Stornoway	86.8	62.7
Uig	96.2	77.3

replaces the regional Gaelic dialect. The official census of 2001 reflects the decline in Gaelic speakers in the Western Isles since 1891.

Despite the decline in number of Gaelic speakers in the official census and Dorian's grim pronouncements of "language death," Gaelic has undergone a remarkable "renaissance" (Macdonald 1997) over the past 30 years. In 1997, the Local Government (Gaelic Names) (Scotland) Act was passed that enabled local authorities in Scotland to take Gaelic names. William Gillies (1987, 38) warns of the dangers of festivalizing Gaelic rather than using it. Gillies applauds the regional reorganization of the mid-1970s that produced the Western Isles Council (*Comhairle nan Eilean Siar*) for providing new hope for the Gaelic language. In 1975 the council adopted a policy of bilingualism in the schools; middle-school children in Ciall today have the option of taking a Gaelic-language track, whereas their parents and grandparents were punished for speaking it on the playground.

June Jonnie Ruadh, in her twenties, describes her decision to attend the Gaelic College, Sabhal Mor Ostaig:

"My mother insisted that I join the Gaelic Playschool and go through the Gaelic track from P1 to P6. After that I wanted to take French, but by then I had started singing and I wanted to sing in the Mod[5] so I continued with the Gaelic. You have to be pure to win in the Mod—singing without accompaniment, correct pronunciation. It helps if you're a member of the Free Church, but no one talks about that. I had dreams when I was little about being a famous singer and traveling all over the world, but when I got to the Mod I realized my voice wasn't all that special. My mum wanted me to study something practical and I was good at math and I like the computers. My cousin went to the Gaelic college Sabhal Mor Ostaig so I tried it out for a year and I liked it. I could keep up my Gaelic and study computers at the same time. They don't make you feel like you're taking a step back in time. And the secretary is a famous Gaelic singer! You'll be walking to class and her voice floats up through the halls.

Sabhal Mor Ostaig is a Gaelic-medium College of Further Education founded in 1983 and dedicated to teaching everything from statistics to export marketing, in addition to Gaelic arts, literature, and history. The poet Sorley MacLean was a cofounder, trustee, and first writer in residence. The University of the Highlands and Islands supports a community-based approach to population retention that recognizes the significance of Gaelic. (See Thomson's 1980 "assessment and prognosis" of Gaelic in Scotland, and Sharon Macdonald [1997, 57–59] for a comprehensive review of pro-Gaelic developments between 1950 and 1990.) It would be reasonable to say that more people are now influenced by and conscious of Gaelic than there were 30 years ago, although the actual number of fluent Gaelic speakers has declined.

Macdonald (1997) addresses the ambivalence that Gaelic speakers feel about the increased artificiality of promoting Gaelic as a marker of identity. It is more likely that Scots abroad and in the cities, and the "white settlers" (Jedrej and Nuttall 1996) moving into rural communities, identify Gaelic as a means of distinguishing their uniqueness from English speakers and English (as opposed to Scottish) culture, whereas Gaelic speakers in primarily Gaelic-speaking environments speak it because it feels right and natural. "The jokes are better in Gaelic," as one Ciall resident expressed it, "and the church services more frightening. 'Death' is just death, but *bas* reminds me of my doom." For many, Gaelic remains the language of home and community, and English is the language of "out," "away," "getting on," and the majority culture.

Promoters of Gaelic are caught between a rock and a hard place. Accused of being part of a "Gaelic Mafia" if they become too aggressive, they run the equal risk of being identified as "dreamy Celts" if they glorify the language without providing concrete solutions to its revival. Establishing Celtic studies departments, providing classes for Gaelic learners (including tapes and Internet instruction for people living abroad), and supporting Mods and other Gaelic festivals, are alone insufficient. A language comes alive only in the context of community interaction—in the playground, the workplace, the sheep fank, and at the wake.

The Western Isles Council has built an office building in Ciall that currently stands empty. If it is used to house telephone attendants who interact only with callers and not with each other, the effort is wasted as a means to promote Gaelic in the workplace.[6] A woman in her forties observes that when she was in school, all the children spoke Gaelic on the playground; now they tend to speak English on the playground, and although they might understand their Gaelic-speaking parents, they respond in English. When developing programs for teaching Gaelic, planners scratch their heads over which Gaelic to use—the dialectic variation is so great. It would be worth studying whether the increase in Gaelic on TV has generated a "BBC Gaelic" that is working to standardize dialects, just as English as spoken in London and on the BBC (British Broadcasting Company) worked to standardize the speaking of English. The question would be, which dialect is used to standardize Gaelic educational instruction, especially in rules of spelling and grammar? Although such choices are sure to infuriate some segments of the Gaelic-speaking community, they are a natural and inevitable part of linguistic change; survival of Gaelic does not ensure survival of all forms of Gaelic. Some criticize the vigorous perpetuation of Gaelic at Sabhal Mor Ostaig as the perpetuation of a distinctive form of Gaelic that does not match the Gaelic spoken elsewhere ("It's an enclosed universe apart, a little Gaelic Eden," observed one Gaelic speaker); but in fact it has taken seriously a mission to integrate and coordinate the different versions of Gaelic, and is an important agent of both change and linguistic survival in the Gaidhealtachd (the region of Scotland where Gaelic has traditionally been spoken).

Scottish churches, especially the Free Church and the Church of Scotland, have contributed enormously to the conservation of Gaelic. Although associated with a more stilted, formalized version of Gaelic (Bible Gaelic versus fireside Gaelic[7]), the Gaelic spoken in sermons has nevertheless contributed to the linguistic webs of meaning and symbolic reference in Gaelic speakers' minds. In Ciall between 1970 and 1971, all services (two on Sunday, a prayer meeting on Wednesday, and services twice a day for the week of Communion) were in Gaelic, except for the rare occasion when an English speaker was present. Today, because of the influx of English speakers, only one service on Sunday is in Gaelic. Notably absent during English services is the distinctive Gaelic psalm-singing, with individualistic interpretations of the song that are rendered communally as cacophony.

If there were a scale of conservation of Gaelic, the churches would exist at one end, and the efforts by various educators to encourage a looser, more creative approach to the maintenance of Gaelic in a changing world would be placed at the other. An example of the latter is *An Leabhar Mor* (*The Great Book of Gaelic*), a celebration of 1,500 years of Gaelic poetry and art from Ireland and Scotland (Maclean and Dorgan 2002). Educational materials based on the book will be circulated in Gaelic-medium schools and are intended to encourage pride and more creative expressions in contemporary forms of Gaelic, as well as change attitudes toward the Irish/Gaelic connection across the Catholic/Protestant divide.

NARRATIVES ABOUT THE FREE CHURCH

"There's less fear of Christmas as a papist plot," says a friend as we walk through the streets of Stornoway. I have just commented on the display of Christmas decorations in the windows.

The Free Church is an evangelical offshoot of the Church of Scotland and reflects the ideology of Calvinist Scotland. The Church of Scotland was established during the Reformation, recognized by the Scots Parliament in 1560, and legally made the national church in 1690. Its austere, puritan policies were established first in the cities and supported by the gentry. For several centuries the Church of Scotland had very little effect on the Highlands, which continued the Catholic practices introduced from Ireland.

Lowland missionaries entered the Highlands in the eighteenth century in part to suppress Jacobitism, paganism, and episcopacy in the forfeited estates following the Jacobite Rebellions. Brown (1997, 91) notes that the Highlands and Islands were Scottish Presbyterianism's "first 'foreign' mission, and a 'dry run' for the great work in Africa and Asia." He also notes the irony of the fact that the church was a vehicle to absorb Highland into Lowland culture and that today it is the Gaelic-speaking Highlands that uphold "the religious heritage of the seventeenth-century Lowlands" (ibid., 92).

Today residents of the northern half of the Outer Hebrides (North Uist, Lewis, and Harris) are Protestant, mostly worshipping with the Free Church, Free Presbyterian, and Church of Scotland. The southern part of the Outer Hebrides (South Uist, Barra, and Eriskay) is Catholic. Catholic townships are considered less strict with regard to recreation: church-sponsored dances may be held on Sundays. In the sterner north, many a fiddler broke his instrument over his knee when he converted to the evangelical Protestant churches.

The important thing to remember is that, unlike Catholicism that has maintained a remarkable unity for hundreds of years because of its elaborate priestly hierarchy, bureaucracy, and procedures to maintain conformity (from threats of excommunication to the Inquisition), the Reformation is about reform and has therefore generated continuous fragmentation. The Free Church formed during the Disruption in 1843 and was conceived as a purification of the Church of Scotland, which, through "Moderatism," had lost sight of its mission and was enforcing patronage, or the right of the state to choose ministers, onto resistant congregations. In 1893 the Free Church itself fragmented, with thousands of Gaelic-speaking Highlanders deserting to form the Free Presbyterian Church. In 1900 the Free Church split again over a proposal to unify the Free Church with the United Presbyterian Church of Scotland to form the United Free Church of Scotland. Twenty-six ministers and some 50,000 people remained in the Free Church. Additional realignments occurred during the twentieth century, of which the most recent is the formation of the Free Church (Continuing) (see Collins 1974; MacDonald 2000; MacLeod 2000; Stewart and Cameron 1989; Wylie 1881.) The sense of personal enlightenment, purity, and power that infuses reform movements may be found not only in the formation of new churches but all the way down to the lonely dissenter who withdraws into his house and is rarely seen for the rest of his life. The life of one such dissenter in Ciall is captured by another Ciall resident in the following narrative:

> After a life of hard drinking he began following the church—twice a day on Sunday, Wednesday night prayer meetings, following the Communion services around the island. But when a certain person was allowed to take Communion that he knew didn't deserve it—he hadn't really stopped drinking although he said he had—well, that was it. He started holding his own prayer meetings, and there were a few who came. But then he took to arguing with them over scripture, and one by one they dropped off. You can hear him on Sundays if there's no wind—his voice carries out to the hills.

Beliefs and practices found today in the Highland Free Church were common throughout Lowland Scotland but gradually declined there. For example, such values included the belief in the base sinfulness of human beings (including children) and the belief in the doctrine of predestination, that almost everyone is doomed to damnation and only a few are saved. Practices included stringent adherence to the Sabbath, the view that theatrical and musical forms of recreation are worldly temptations of the Devil, and distaste for ornamentation. In addition, believers publicly condemned sinners, such as forcing women who had conceived or given birth to children outside of wedlock to confess and be lectured for their sins before the congregation, as well as having ministers and elders give scriptural examinations of congregational members in their homes. The Highland

Free Church appropriated these beliefs symbolically as part of an evangelical movement, which, although widespread throughout Scotland in the late eighteenth and nineteenth centuries, was particularly prevalent in the Highlands that were reeling from a series of devastating economic ills.

Although some families in Ciall today belong to the Church of Scotland and other Protestant churches, and a few describe themselves as agnostic or atheist, most villagers attend the Free Church, which is the only church now in the village. All members of the community participate in some or all of the religious rituals that mark the passage of life from birth to death. Sermons remind the congregation that the Bible contains everything that man needs to know, that it never needs to be updated or revised. Many people in the village use the Bible as a historical framework in which all events in all cultures can be placed, since the dawn of creation to modern times. Like those who prefer to use encyclopedias, or those who claim there is a healing plant for every illness, there is an assumption of the fixity and containment of knowledge, a finite wholeness that can be packaged and held in the hand.

The church also plays an important role in maintaining social control. Just as Robert Ekvall (1952, 1964) argued that Tibetan lamas serve as "research centers" for processing the gossip that flows rapidly through the countryside and use it in divination, the minister once described the manse as the office to which everyone brought information. Through the channels of gossip, the village has extensive knowledge about sinful behavior, such as about a man who impregnates a woman besides his wife, a couple who conceives a child out of wedlock (even if the child is miscarried), or a woman who conceives a child with someone other than her spouse. Although this knowledge is still used to determine who shall be allowed to take Communion, it is no longer used to restrict access to other church-related rituals. For example, parents who conceive a child out of wedlock no longer have to stand and be lectured by the minister in front of the congregation before their child is allowed to be baptized. This requirement, dreaded by people for whom maintaining a low profile is a strong value, caused some couples to leave the island or have their children baptized in Glasgow before they would endure the shame of standing in church.

Those who are "following"[8] (*leantail*) the church also attend a Wednesday-night prayer meeting. Communions (*na h-orduighean*, the ordinances) are held twice a year, at which time those who are converted (*curamach*) and whose requests to join the communicants have been accepted by the kirk-session (church council), partake in the "Lord's Supper" of bread and wine. The Gaelic term for communion, *Na h-Orduighean* (pronounced "ordion," as in "accordion"), refers not only to the act of consuming bread and wine but to a set of rotating five-day ceremonial periods held twice a year (in fall and late winter). For five to six weeks, communion services are held among Free Church congregations, and many members move from village to village to follow the services, staying in the homes of villagers who open their doors to communicants.[9] For the five-day period, services are held twice a day, usually in Gaelic, and reach a crescendo of intensified separation between converted (*curamach*) and unconverted on Sunday, when the *curamach* take communion under the watchful and envious eyes of the unchosen (see Parman 1990).

Parents teach catechism to their children at home (catechism refers to memorized questions and responses about religious doctrine); children also practice their catechism at Sunday School, which is taught primarily by *curamach* women who may or may not be trained as teachers. Before the Second World War, classes were taught in Gaelic. After the war it was decided to give instructions in English. Catechism was once taught in the schools as well, and the ministers visited the schools regularly to examine the children. This practice has recently been discontinued. In the past, teachers preceded class with prayer practice. "Catechism nights" were held on every street, in which the minister drilled parents on their knowledge of the correct answers to questions. For example, according to *The Shorter Catechism*, Question 19 is "What is the misery of that estate whereinto man fell?" The correct answer, which must be recited exactly, is, "All mankind by their fall lost communion with God, are under his wrath and curse, and so made liable to all miseries in this life, to death itself, and to the pains of hell for ever".

In 1971, I wrote this entry in my journal:

> I volunteer to visit the school and show the children how to make "*ojos*" (God's eyes) from toothpicks and yarn, a Christmas decoration I learned to make growing up in New Mexico. The teacher gets to her feet and clears her throat nervously. The children scramble to their feet. The minister enters the room. He is a big man dressed in black with the white collar at his throat. He stands at the front of the classroom and beckons to one of the children, who comes slowly forward with his eyes fixed on his feet. The minister places his hand on the child's shoulder and says, "Remember . . . what does that remind you of?" The boy beneath his hand is as still as a statue, but from the back of the room comes a small, piping voice, "Remember-the-Sabbath-Day-and-keep-it-holy."

These memorized phrases, learned during home training, school drills, and examinations by the kirk-session for baptism and Communion, lay the foundation for later experiences of "talking with God" and conversion. They are deeply embedded, and surface sometimes as unbidden thoughts, as a voice external to themselves. This uncontrolled flow has the thumbprint of supernatural intervention, as something non-normal, as proof of the divine. My bedside reading in 2003 included sermons, meditations, John Bunyan's *Pilgrim's Progress,* and daily devotionals that informed me that I was debased, that sin had invaded every part of my nature. "The heart is deceitful above all things, and desperately wicked. . . . Out of the heart of men proceed evil thoughts. . . . Hell is factual, fearful, final, and fair. Religion can never satisfy God. All our righteousnesses are as filthy rags. God demands perfection."[10]

Tourist brochures warn visitors of the strictness with which the Sabbath is maintained in the rural parts of Lewis. Most Ciall families contrast the laxness of the present day with their father's time when the hot food for Sunday was prepared the previous night, no children could be out past twilight on Saturday, and Sunday was spent attending two church services and reading the Bible inbetween. As a Ciall woman in her fifties recalled, "No cooking or washing, not even knitting. You shined your shoes for church the previous night." Lewis girls working in mainland hotels refused to celebrate New Year's Eve if it fell on a Saturday night; Lewis men were fired for refusing to work on emergency construction jobs on Sundays. A Ciall woman in her forties recalled that "When television came to the island, my father went to bed and pulled the bedclothes over his head when my brother—still living at home but too old to smack—watched it on Sunday." One mother, who allows her children to watch TV on Sunday, "keeps an eye out for the holies. We draw the curtains and turn down the volume." Wherever people are, they are very conscious of the restrictive presence of Sundays. A Ciall woman who once worked in hotels on the mainland jokes that, "Wherever I am, I always stiffen up on Sunday. Once a Glasgow fellow took me to a dance and I sat there as rigid as a post, certain I would be sent straight to hell."

In the twenty-first century, the hold of the churches appears to be less strong. Stornoway now has public art (for example, fountains and boat structures planted with flowers) and puts up Christmas lights and decorations (the commercial aspects of Christmas having bypassed the papist connotations). The Stornoway airport has recently begun flights on Sunday, and has also begun bar service, to the consternation of the Lord's Day Observance Society. More people live together without getting married. Sweets still circulate during the sermon and no woman would enter a church without a hat, but English sermons are replacing the Gaelic, no precentor stands to lead the English psalms, and the music is tamely melodic rather than fiercely individualistic. It is possible to hang your washing out on a Sunday without receiving a delegation of church elders at your door, and instead of sleeping on Sunday afternoon, people read or watch television.

At the same time, the church retains its passionate intensity for reform, an extremism that is both hated and admired. One Church of Scotland minister expressed his feelings about the position of the Free Church in theological puritanism: "The Church of Scotland is always looking over its shoulder at the Free Church." Many perceive the Protestants on Lewis as evangelical giants, and many theological mendicants make their pilgrimage to Lewis.

The Gaelic psalm-singing provides one of the best metaphors of Highland life. The power of psalmody is in the grace notes. Given the emphasis on kin and community, one might expect harmony, but nothing could be further from the reality. Each member of the congregation tackles the tune with intense personal concern—with sharp, forceful, personal interpretation. The result, as a whole, is cacophony—a metaphor for community as a loud, raucous whole: all individuals strong and beautiful, forming their own version of the universe, and by intent brushing hard against their neighbors under the veil of worship. Psalm-singing in the Gaidhealtachd is the essence of William Robertson Smith's totemism, better known to sociologists and anthropologists as Durkheim's church-as-society. As the Gael sings, so is his society—piercing, intense, lyrical, and full of grace. The harsh bitterness, the dense musical individuality, is part of the piercing sound, like Sorley Maclean's black bog, "the darkening sourness of the spirit," pierced by radiance (MacLean 1999, 76–77).

NARRATIVES OF HOME AND EXILE

As documents attest the world over, you can't go home again. But the intensity of belonging that permeates life in small communities characterized by close kinship ties, shared stories, and a common sense of "us" versus "them"

(Gaelic/English, island/mainland, poor/rich, etc.) generates an ambivalence of feeling among people who call themselves "exiles." The ambience of longing to return is captured in the following poem, the "Canadian Boat Song"[11], written in the nineteenth century. Though probably not written by a Highlander at all, this poem is widely quoted among émigrés:

> From the lone shieling of the misty island
> Mountains divide us, and the waste of seas—
> Yet still the blood is strong, the heart is Highland,
> And we in dreams behold the Hebrides!

One such "exile" is Hilda MacLeod, a Detroit schoolteacher whose father had emigrated from Ciall to the United States in the 1930s, married the daughter of a German immigrant, and retired to Ciall after her death. In 1971 we sat in the kitchen of her father's house where she smoked one cigarette after another. It was midsummer and the horizon of moorland hills was still visible through the window although it was after midnight. I wrote her comments in my journal:

> When I'm away from here I remember the light—it's sort of opalescent, isn't it?— and I can hardly wait to come back for a visit; but when I'm here I freeze, and I feel that everyone's looking at me all the time, and I suddenly look around and wonder where all the young people are.

The population of crofting townships is distinguished by a disproportionately large number of aged people, a pattern that is mirrored throughout Scotland as a whole: in 2001, the population of Scotland was 5,062,011, a decline of about 2 percent over the past 20 years, with the greatest decline occurring in the age groups 0–14 and 15–29, and increases occurring in the older age groups. An age-sex "population pyramid" of the Highlands is not so much a pyramid as a top-heavy hourglass, and Ciall is no exception.

In the 1961 national census, Ciall was listed as having a population of 598, and in 1981, 564. In 1970, I counted 515 residents in the village, 83 of whom considered themselves to be a significant part of the community, although not living in Ciall—17 young people were attending school in Stornoway, and 66 people between the ages of 25 and 54 who were working away from the village, contributed to the income of their relatives in the village, and returned periodically to weave or work in the mill, care for aged parents, and visit for a while until they became restless and set off again. Their roots were in the village, and when they were absent they were nevertheless present in the electrical storm of the village gossip system. To many villagers, the concept of "holiday" has no meaning other than the time when these "exiles" return.

In 1841 the population of the Highlands and Islands as a whole reached its peak and began to decline. Lewis was unique in that its population continued to increase throughout the nineteenth century. In 1911 the population of Lewis peaked at 29,603. After that it declined steadily, reaching 20,622 in 1969 (about 70 percent of its 1911 peak). The 1981 census reported a slightly higher population of 20,726, but by 2001 it had decreased to 18,489. The dominant cause of population decline is emigration. According to some estimates, 60 percent of the young between the ages of 15 and 24 leave rural Lewis. They take their memories with them, and contribute to the idealization of place and ethnicity in music, writing, and conversation when they return.

An example of an "exile" whose heart remained at home although she spent many years working on the mainland is Seonag Thormoid, who was born in 1917. When she was 16 years old she left the island to work in hotels on the mainland, just as her mother had done before the First World War. As she described her choice, "You were raised with the idea that you would go away. I've prepared my children for the same thing. Any work that exists here is temporary. You can't depend on it."

Seonag went to Glasgow with three other girls from Ciall and stayed with her aunt until she found a job. The wages were extremely low—about two pounds a month—and wealthy families typically had five or six servants. She remembers that she was "treated like scum. You worked in the kitchen fixing roast beef and fine puddings for them, and then sat down to a dinner of salt herring and potatoes. Those fine houses are gone now, broken down into smaller flats, and it does my heart good to see that when I'm in Glasgow."

She moved from one job to another, and finally, when she was 37 years old, married her fiance who had returned from the war. They were both from Ciall, and had pursued a sporadic courtship whenever they happened to be home on leave. He had joined the Naval Reserve before the war. She stated that "There was always a sign up in the Stornoway Labor Exchange for men to join the Naval Reserve, because the islanders were such good seamen. They were fisherman or had been in the Merchant Service." He had spent five years in the navy during the war and was glad to leave the sea for the croft. He was the second son and fourth child in the family, and got the croft because he had stayed home to take care of his parents. His elder brother, who had emigrated to the United States, returned during the Depression and built a house on the common grazing. Another brother married into a croft in a neighboring village, and a fourth brother settled in Glasgow. A sister married an islander who became a policeman in Glasgow.

Seonag and her husband have four children. The eldest is in the Merchant Service, and the second son is a teacher. A daughter is studying domestic science in Aberdeen, and the youngest, Anna, is attending the Nicolson Institute, the secondary school in Stornoway at which rural children who do well in exams board during the week. Anna wants to study French and German at a university in Aberdeen, which would involve spending a year on the European continent. "Leave the island?" she replies, when asked about her eventual plans. "Of course. I've always had the idea that I was going away."

In bitterness and hope, in search of memories and identity, some members of the community return—at least for a little while. There are also those who return in search of the community that they remember only from their childhood. In 2005 a man named Aonghas Aobronn bought a croft and moved to Ciall. In his late thirties, he lived most of his life on the Scottish mainland in large cities but spent childhood summers in Ciall where his mother was born. He describes Ciall as "a place of memories and ghosts," of "intense love and palpable eeriness." To live in Ciall is to smell burning peat, walk through a dense carpet of summer flowers, and look out over a landscape so familiar that it has a life and a personality of its own. As he walks down the road he knows that people watch him and judge him and yet at the same time, he feels at home, submerged in a network of people who know him, of relatives who welcome him back. He is eager to play the full role of crofter: assume his share of township duties, attend meetings, write for grants, and stock his croft with the proper sheep/cattle ratio. He considers the pros and cons of solid fuel, plans to cut peat but not depend on it (oil burners are cleaner), and scans the Internet for "traditional" designs of Highland houses. He e-mails friends around the world about the call of blood like a tide in his soul.

SUMMARY OF CHANGES

Forty years of doing fieldwork in Scotland have reinforced the maxim, "The more things change, the more they stay the same." Scottish crofters, like a body in which almost all the cells have changed after seven years, retain distinctive styles of cultural construction.

Nevertheless, a number of changes have occurred in Ciall between 1970 and 2003, some of them superficial and some with significant potential for deep-rooted change. Some aspects of transportation have improved, such as the replacement of the single-lane track between Stornoway and the west side with a two-lane road over which cars speed through the community, stopping less often to offer lifts. The bus service is better than it was in 1970 but not as good as it was in the 1930s. The community has a sewage system, and water from the taps comes out clear rather than peat-brown.

As services improve, the community is at the same time more vibrant and lonely. Almost every house has a phone and at least one television (at a cost of £110 per year in tax, in addition to payments for special channels and programs), which has cut down on the visiting on the one hand, and has provided new opportunities for humor on the other. Television divides even the members of a household, as a wife listens to *Coronation Street* in the kitchen, her husband to sheep trial news in the parlor, and their daughter to *So You Want to Be a Millionaire* upstairs. The hills now sprout cellular phone towers. On New Year's Eve, instead of using a torch to find your way through the pitch-black dark from one lighted house to another, streetlights cast a dim orange glow along the road. The small lights of houses on the dark moor were beacons of hospitality. Now the orange spotlights only exacerbate the loneliness of the dark.

Another startling change is the disappearance of the "junk" (old cars, tractors, harvesters, and other machinery) that has served the community as a source of recyclable parts. The Western Isles Council has placed "skips" (large dumpsters) all over the island, and has purchased a mobile car crusher to clean up the countryside. Ancient stone brochs, old houses, and old machinery do not register as items of historical significance; all are subject to easy destruction. The debate continues of which aspects of history to retain and which to reject.

The village has a new school, which has computers, Gaelic-medium classes, and a swimming pool that is open for community use. The old school is being converted into a community center.

The sense of the exile persists at many levels: "Exiles" who live on the mainland or abroad return at New Year and during the summer for short, intense visits and are nostalgic in between. Also exiled are the semi-Gaels who, isolated from the language by a generation or two, dream of the Gaidhealtachd with that peculiar intensity of the diasporic refugee. The term "exile" can also be used to refer to many deeply religious Presbyterian Scots who with their depressed critical intellect and overactive conscience feel exiled from paradise; they meditate on lost perfection and the glorious union of mind and heart embodied in a supernatural being (Christ the only perfect man), compared with whom they are imperfect and doomed.

The commercialism of international business penetrates here as elsewhere. Bathrooms are filled with aromatherapy candles and soaps, electric-heated showers have replaced the water heated at the back of the fireplace, and touch-lights illuminate the dark. A few people are traveling to places where they don't have relatives, just for the sake of travel. Children choose careers based on what they see on television. Soon-to-be parents draw upon a wealth of outside experience to name their children. Words like *wow* and *brilliant* punctuate Gaelic speech. Policies promulgated by the Western Isles Council on bilingualism and tourism result in bilingual signs for streets, banks, and communities, and self-conscious signs combine English and Gaelic that direct tourists to local sights: "Welcome to (Gaelic version of village name)." A sign, "To the Shore," directs tourists to the beach where picnic tables have been set up. Posts mark the walking trails that local people have walked, unselfconsciously, for generations. An entire black-house street has been resurrected in Carloway that, when you come over the hill and see it leading down to the shore, has all the appearance of a reappearing Brigadoon; the houses have been modified to serve as meeting places and bed-and-breakfast services for tourists.

Harris Tweed continues to be woven, but the number of weavers in Ciall is diminishing as the weavers switch from single-width to double-width looms (although in certain areas of the island, such as Ness, weavers have switched to the new looms and increased in number). The sight of single-width tweeds sitting on fence posts to be picked up by the tweed van is gone; for the heavier double-width tweeds, a forklift comes to the door.

Sheep remain the primary focus of crofting activity, but the interisland fanks have declined, replaced by fencing of allotments near the township. Most hay is imported from the mainland in plastic-wrapped bundles. The amount of work done on the croft appears to be inversely proportional to the number of vehicles (tractors, vans, four-wheel drive vehicles) now available to do the work. Whereas one tractor might have done the work of two townships to bring in the hay in 1970, many households now have their own tractors that they use to move the imported hay, feeding units, and sheep from one part of their crofting land to another.

New businesses have emerged: fish farms and wind farms, the harvest of water and air. Foreigners—Germans and especially Norwegians—own many of the businesses on the island. The new "farms" are much more capital-intensive than the old farms; farms take at least five years of intensive investment before returns can be seen. The fish farms are not cottage industries but major industrial investments, with all the pollution, expense, thievery, and dangers of a fluctuating market threatening the value of the investment. Even though grants are available, local investors find it difficult to enter the market.

© Courtesy of Susan Parman

Salmon farming in a loch on the west side of Lewis

Fewer fishing boats leave from Stornoway harbor, and they catch shellfish for the mainland rather than herring that was once delivered by fish van, salted, and hung over the Aga stove in local communities. Contrary to Lord Leverhulme's dream of Lewis and Harris serving as the center of a vast fishing fleet in the North Atlantic, the major locus of fishing in Scotland is in the northeast, and it is this region that will be most affected by the recent decision of the European Commision's Council of Fisheries to reduce the haddock quota from 104,000 to 51,000 tons to protect stock.

Few people now cut peat, although some still take pride in their peat (two Ciall residents commented, "The incomers buy tons of coal, whereas we're more economical"; "I almost called off the wedding when I saw how poor the quality of his village's peat banks were."). Instead, coal, electric heating, and central heating with oil have replaced the beautiful and economical peat- or coal-burning Aga stoves—the centers of warmth in the kitchen. The use of oil makes it difficult to tell if people are in and prepared for visitors, as fewer chimneys smoke.

Funerals and wakes are still held, and the men still "take the lift" in sharing the burden of carrying the coffin to the hearse or graveyard. The local community now handles people with depression who once went in "for the treatment" to Craig Dunain, the mental hospital near Inverness. Old people whose siblings or spouses have died, or whose children have left, continue to receive support from neighbors and community services, but many are now choosing to live in retirement homes in Stornoway.

Some of the same sources of conflict exist. Poachers still thumb their noses at the laird (but the peat lunch is no longer the stage on which to display your impudence by serving salmon, because even families that cut the peat go home for lunch in their vehicles). And Lochs, because of its rich fishing resources and history of poaching, is still identified (by other parishes) as the parish most likely to produce stories in the *Stornoway Gazette* about conflicts with the police. But as more cars come and go on the ferries, and as the world changes, the stories of scandal and shame include a new element: drugs (everything from Ecstasy to heroin).

The bachelors, "boys" until they marry, still prowl the night highways, traveling between dances, finding privacy in their cars and behind the diminishing peat stacks. Musical talent continues to spring up in local bands. The bands listen to and borrow from the tangled, inventive multinational musical trends that create, for example, the Leningrad Cowboys—a Finnish band popular in the Baltic that mocks both the Americans and the Russians—and Scotland's own Battlefield Band that plays jazz and polkas with bagpipes. The New Year remains a time of visiting, renewing friendships and rehashing feuds, and taking steps to make new alliances. It is a time when declarations of marriage are made, as well as the beginning of slights and missteps, irrational explosions that can reverberate down the generations.

Although there is some sense that times have changed, the communitarian spirit of mutual aid remains strong, as it does generally throughout Scotland. Neighbors do what they can to help neighbors, despite the occasional feud and dispute. And the fire of hospitality burns bright, along with the rich humor from which new nicknames, anecdotes, and histories are generated.

Eventually the economic value of land as a source of housing will change the cultural profile of crofting forever as land, housing, heritage, and beauty become commodified. In a white paper titled *Crofting Reform Proposals for Legislation* submitted to the Scottish Parliament on July 4, 2002, consultants recommended that the price payable to the landlord for a croft intended to be used to construct a house should reflect the full market value of the house site, not limited to 15 times the value of the rent, as is currently the case. Many under-the-table agreements are being reached whereby a croft assignation is "sold" to someone who is not a member of the family but who wants the land because of the value it holds for access to grants to build a house. For example, by paying the crofter £7,000, the non-family member gets access to a house for which £12,000 in grants is available, thus coming out £5,000 ahead. The Crofters Commission is now dealing with arguments from relatives who want the commission to deny such assignations, and to give the land to them—not because they're willing to pay competitive prices but to "maintain the tradition." Does the commission act on the basis of the croft being an economic unit, or to preserve a way of life? Symbolizing an ancient way of life, the crofter stands as a Celtic island, surrounded by protective legislation, embroiled in the active process of creating meaning out of an image of romantic extinction. The Celtic island of Hebridean crofters is slowly being eroded, as much by tides of linguistic change as by the small, subtle earthquakes of land reform that will both remove protective legislation and provide opportunity.

© Courtesy of Susan Parman

Woman by peat stack

Scotland is more than a blocked-out space on a map, more than a collection of kilts and bagpipes or a list of battlefields. It is an ongoing story with many characters and plots. Hitchcock, an Englishman, portrayed the crofter in his film *Thirty-Nine Steps* as a narrow-minded, penny-pinching, wife-beater. Scotland's filmic self-presentation reflects more complex perceptions: of the rural fey Highlands (the silkies and environmental beauty of *Local Hero*) and gritty urban Lowlands (*Trainspotting* and *Shallow Grave*).

When I travel to Scotland, I prefer to go in winter when the tourists are gone and the days are short, when people gather inside during the long dark, when the water cascades from the cliffs in frozen waterfalls, and the frozen bog lines the narrow roads reminding me that life exists on narrow margins, and that those who remember poverty are most likely to appreciate generosity, and those who have been cruel most appreciate kindness. Scotland is wealthier than it was 40 years ago, but its social conscience is shaped by decades of poverty. The mountains of Scotland are not so much tall as vast, deep-rooted, and ground down. America's peaks still soar—the innocence and beauty for which, as Yeats said, only time is the enemy. Scotland is both old and young: its age is bitter, its youth brazen. Between the new Scottish Parliament and the cleared glens, children experiment with drugs and alcohol, seek purification and reformation through adherence to the Word (but whose word, and in what language?). In England, the Scots are thought of as still Celtic, but as a kind of "reliable Irish"; the Queen Mother distances herself from troublesome issues by identifying herself as Scottish. In some ways Scotland may be seen as a historical precipitate of English internal colonialism—reactively proud, comparatively class-free, and unified by shared alliances (France and America) and shared enemies (England and the laird).

Scotland is a land that continues to be imagined by its exiles in historic terms but that continues, stubbornly, with integrity, and into the full force of the wind, to evolve its own future.

REFERENCES

Cameron, Ewen A. 1996. *Land for the people? The British government and the Scottish Highlands, c. 1880–1925.* East Linton, Scotland: Tuckwell Press.

Brown, Callum G. 1997. *Religion and society in Scotland since 1707.* Edinburgh: Edinburgh Univ. Press.

Cheape, Hugh. 1997. The Communion Season. *Records of the Scottish Church History Society* 27:305–316.

Collins, G.N.M. 1974. *The heritage of our fathers.* Edinburgh: The Knox Press.

Darling, F. Fraser, ed. 1955. *West Highland survey: An essay in human ecology.* Oxford: Oxford Univ. Press.

Dorian, Nancy C. 1981. *Language death: The life cycle of a Scottish Gaelic dialect.* Philadelphia: Univ. of Pennsylvania Press.

Ekos Ltd. 2001. *The acquisition of crofting data: A baseline study.* Final report for the Crofters Commission. Inverness: Ballantyne House.

Ekvall, R. B. 1952. *Tibetan skylines.* New York: Farrar, Strauss and Young.

———. 1964. *Religious observances in Tibet: Patterns and function.* Chicago: Univ. of Chicago Press.

Gillies, William. 1987. Scottish Gaelic— The present situation. In *Proceedings of the third international conference on minority languages,* ed. G. MacEoin, et al. Philadelphia: Clevedon.

Jedrej, Charles, and Mark Nuttall. 1996. *White settlers: The impact of rural repopulation in Scotland.* Newark, New Jersey: Hardwood Academic Publishers.

Lefebvre, Henri. 1991. *The production of space.* London: Blackwell.

MacDonald, Fraser. 2000. Scenes of ecclesiastical theatre in the Free Church of Scotland, 1981–2000. *Northern Scotland* 20:125–148.

———. 2003. *Geographies of vision and modernity: Things seen in the Scottish Highlands.* PhD thesis, Univ. of Oxford.

MacDonald, Sharon. 1997. *Reimagining culture: Histories, identities and the Gaelic renaissance.* Oxford: Berg Publishers.

Mackinlay, D. 1878. *The island of Lewis and its fishermen crofters.* London.

MacLean, Malcolm, and Theo Dorgan. 2002. *An Leabhar Mor: The great book of Gaelic.* Edinburgh: Canongate Books.

MacLean, Sorley. 1999. *Eimhir.* Trans. Iain Crichton Smith. Stornoway, Scotland: Acair.

MacLeod, James Lachlan. 2000. *The second disruption: The Free Church in Victorian Scotland and the origins of the Free Presbyterian Church.* East Linton, Scotland: Tuckwell Press.

Meek, Donald. 2000. *The quest for Celtic Christianity.* Edinburgh: Handsel Press.

Murray, W. H. 1966. *The Hebrides.* London: Heinemann.

Napier, Lord. 1884. *Report of the commissioners of inquiry into the condition of the crofters and cottars in the Highlands and Islands of Scotland.* HMSO.

Needler, G. H. 1941. *The lone shieling: Origin and authorship of the Blackwood 'Canadian Boat-Song.'* Toronto: Univ. of Toronto Press.

Parman, Susan. 1990. Orduighean: A dominant ritual symbol in the Free Church of the Scottish Highlands. *American Anthropologist* 92:295–305.

———. 1993. The future of European boundaries: A case study. In *Cultural change and the new Europe: Perspectives on the European community,* ed. Thomas M. Wilson and M. Estellie Smith, 189–202. San Francisco: Westview Press.

Smout, T. C. 1969. *A history of the Scottish people 1560–1830*. London: Collins.

Stewart, A., and J. Kennedy Cameron. 1989. *The Free Church of Scotland: The crisis of 1900*. Edinburgh: Knox Press.

Taylor, Lord. 1954. *Report of the commission of enquiry into crofting conditions*. HMSO.

Thomson, Derick. Gaelic in Scotland: Assessment and Prognosis. In *Minority languages today,* eds. E. Haugen et al., 10–20. Edinburgh: Edinburgh Univ. Press.

Wylie, Rev. James A. 1881. *Disruption worthies: A memorial of 1843*. Edinburgh: Thomas C. Jack, Grange Publishing Works.

NOTES

1. Information from West Register House, Edinburgh. Various changes affect comparison of agricultural statistics because information first began to be collected in 1866. Information collected in the first series (1866–1911) was given voluntarily. The Agricultural Acts of 1925 and 1947 made census returns statutory and compulsory. The parish is the lowest unit of consolidation of information. Ciall is located in the parish of Barvas, which after 1933 was identified by the number 753. In 1970 the basis of calculating minimum holdings was altered from one acre to holdings with a labor requirement of 26 standard man-days or more per annum; in 1973, it was changed to 40 or more standard man-days per year. In 1976, metric measurements replaced acres with hectares (2.471054 acres = 1 hectare); I have converted hectares to acres in the chart. The numerical categories in the agricultural census used to indicate amounts (of acres/hectares, of milk and beef cattle, and of sheep in thousands) are as follows: potatoes (24, 25, 26), barley (16, 18), oats (20), milk cows (100, 102, 104, 106, 111, 115), beef cattle (101, 103, 105, 107, 112, 116), and sheep (145). In 1993, the number of holdings was added; thus it is possible now to know not only the total acreage and livestock numbers but also the total number of holdings responsible for these figures (for example, in 1993, 13 holdings in the parish of Barvas were responsible for cultivating five acres of oats, whereas in 1994, only 9 holdings cultivated a total of 4.2 acres of oats).

2. Battles over images of rusticity seesaw back and forth between east and west, north and south, as in the old saw about why Highlanders are called *Teuchtars*. In the Aberdeen version of the joke, the Aberdonians killed and ate the invading Romans, Vikings, and English, all except the invading Highlanders who were "ower teuch tae eat" (too tough to eat). What to the English was a signifier of mispronunciation was to the Highlander a form of recognition of his status as tutor or teacher, a civilized man among the barbarians.

3. Cameron (1996) provides a carefully reasoned analysis of the "interplay of politics and ideology" in the history of land policies between 1880 and 1925 that contribute to the ambiguities and contradictions affecting crofting policy today.

4. These figures were calculated by subtracting the number of people identified as having "no knowledge of Gaelic" from the total population for each parish, as listed in the 2001 Census, Table UV12 "Knowledge of Gaelic" at www.SCROL.gov.uk. Thus "percentage of Gaelic speakers" includes any variation on speaking Gaelic, from "understands spoken Gaelic" to "speaks, reads, writes Gaelic" to "writes, can't speak or read," and so on, resulting in a figure for "Gaelic speaking" that is generous.

5. *Mod,* Gaelic for "meeting, assembly," is a Gaelic festival highlighting the purity of Gaelic in song and storytelling.

6. Smout (1969, 32) argues that the introduction of Flemish, Norman, Anglic, and Scandinavian tradesmen and merchants into the burghs established by David I in the twelfth century led to the decline of Celtic languages in the Lowlands; Gaelic was no longer the vehicle of economic transactions in everyday life.

7. *"G idhlig a' Bhiobaill"* versus *"G idhlig taobh an teine"* (Cheape 1997, 307).

8. From Mark 8:34, to take up the cross and follow Jesus. In Gaelic usage, to "start following" refers to a new convert.

9. For example, in 2002, the communion dates as described in *The Monthly Record: The Magazine of the Free Church of Scotland* (February 2002) were as follows: March 3—Glasgow-Dowanvale, North Tolsta, Lochbroom, Urquhart, Kiltarlity, Kilmallie, Dumfries, Carloway; March 10—Cross, Park, Scalpay-Harris, Portree, Knockbain, Livingston, Lennoxtown, Glasgow-St. Vincent Street; March 17—Dunbarton, East Kilbride, Barvas, Kinloch, Inverness-Greyfriars, Creich, Kincardine and Croick, Rogart, Bishopbriggs, Dunblame, Dornoch; March 24—Greenock, Lochs, Olrig, Roschall; and March 31—Back, North Uist.

10. *The Monthly Record: The Magazine of the Free Church of Scotland* (February 2002), reviewed the film, *The Lord of the Rings,* comparing it to *Pilgrim's Progress* and the Narnia books in its treatment of basic Christian themes of evil, sin, forgiveness, sacrifice, redemption, faithfulness, and love. It criticized the film for its "postmodern tendency toward psychobabble" (Aragorn would never have the self-doubts shown in the film; he knew "the right and wise path"), and for its portrayal of Arwen saving Frodo from the Black Riders ("The whole point of that scene . . . is that little Frodo of the Shire stood alone and resisted temptation"). On the other hand, the Harry Potter books are attacked as being based on real occult practice.

11. This famous poem, which has for over one hundred and fifty years evoked the intense sense of longing for home among Scots abroad, is usually attributed to John Galt (1779–1839), who opened up land for immigrants in Canada. The poem, titled "Canadian Boat Song (from the Gaelic)," was published anonymously in *Blackwood's Edinburgh Magazine* in 1829. In a cleverly argued treatise based on analysis of metrics, G. H. Needler (1941) argues that the poem was not a boat song, was never originally in Gaelic, and was probably written by a Scottish friend of John Galt, David MacBeth Moir, who had never been to Canada. I am indebted to Gordon Adams for having called my attention to Needler's book.

Fieldwork Biography
Ernestine Friedl

I have had a variety of fieldwork experiences, the earliest working with Native Americans. First I conducted research in a field school with the Pomo tribe in California in the summer of 1941. Next I worked with the Chippewa tribe in Wisconsin during the summers of 1942 and 1943. I started fieldwork on the Greek village of Vasilika in 1955 and began to focus on the urbanization of villagers there during 1964. Since then I have returned to Vasilika several times, and have now followed the fortunes of the people of that small village for more than 50 years.

© Ernestine Friedl

I am the James B. Duke professor emeritus of anthropology at Duke University, and have served as the president of the American Anthropological Association.

I dedicate this chapter to the memory of Triandaphyllos Athanasios Triandafyllou, the son of my original village host, who died several months after my last visit to Vasilika.

14/A Village in Greece
Vasilika Then and Now

Driving into Vasilika on a warm sunny day in June 1998, 22 years after I had last visited the village, a new road sign read only "Vasilika"; "Krevasaras" (its former appellation under Turkish rule) had disappeared. As we drove into the village on much-improved roads, reflections from freshly whitewashed houses and a church were dazzling. The cemetery was more ordered than it had looked in earlier years, with stone slabs over the graves and photographs of the dead at each grave site. Flower gardens in many front yards added bright color to the scene. There were some unoccupied houses but very few dilapidated ones. Some outbuildings for storage were relatively new constructions. A few automobiles were parked near some of the houses. The fields of the village were planted in tobacco and cotton and there were some small vegetable gardens. There was little movement in the street or on the main road but this was not surprising as it was close to noon.

Although Vasilika was still there, not deserted as many communities had become in other parts of Greece, it was a community much diminished as we subsequently learned.

The forces of change on both the national and local level in 1955 continued to influence the fates of the villagers. The love of the city, or *astifilia*, has lasted as a significant value and has impelled more and more boys and girls in the

Vintage snapshot of a Greek village: Vasilika with Parori and Mount Parnassus in the background, mid-twentieth century.

village to seek a gymnasium or secondary education and then to find jobs in Athens. Parents have continued to seek urban sons-in-law for their daughters, giving urban housing as dowries. Dowries are gifts given by the bride's family to the groom at the time of the marriage.

Traditionally in Vasilika, and Greece more broadly, dowries consisted of land, animals, and linens woven by the bride and her mother in preparation for marriage. In recent years, dowries have also included money and an apartment in Athens. Giving dowries used to be required by law but no longer is a legal obligation. Nevertheless, the bride's father and brothers still tend to give substantial gifts to the new couple.

During the 1950s, increasing numbers of young women left Vasilika to further their education in Athens. Afterward they took jobs and eventually married in the city. Men who stayed in Vasilika to farm were compelled to seek brides in more distant communities; however, the reluctance of women to marry farmers meant smaller dowries for Vasilika grooms. Because the greater Greek economy was strong, Vasilika's migrants to Athens were able to find employment. Only for a short period in the 1960s did one or two local families leave the country to find work.

As a result of these forces of change, in the 43 years from 1955 to 1998, Vasilika's population dropped from 216 to about 40, and its functioning family farm households from 27 to 5. Several additional households consisted only of elderly couples who opted not to join their married children in Athens.

© Ernestine Friedl

Vasilika women laboring in the fields, early 1960's.

By 1998, there were too few young children remaining in the community to keep a school functioning with a regular teacher, so the village school was no longer in operation. Children were forced to go to school elsewhere. The town no longer had a resident priest; a visiting priest came every few weeks. A government-appointed secretary kept records on local population and crop yields.

Although the cultivation of crops was heavily mechanized by 1998, the types of crops grown were substantially unchanged. Grapevines were an exception, because they were no longer planted to supply the households' retsina wine. And wheat was now cultivated less than before. The functioning farm households still planted cotton and tobacco as their major sources of cash, and household gardens produced tomatoes and fresh vegetables during the summer. Farming households continued to raise sheep, too; they sold the wool and used the milk for cheese. What also persisted was their system of values that led the villagers to work hard to ensure the welfare of their children. Although the dowry was by now no longer a legal requirement and parents no longer arranged most marriages, families still gave substantial gifts to their daughters at marriage. Standards and styles of consumption remained very important as symbols of worth and prestige, and these were still derived from association with Athenian relatives. However, now television had globalized tastes, so that those who remained in Vasilika were subject to the same influences as the rest of the Greek population.

Vasilika was not in 1955, nor has it been since, a pristine community isolated from the national, and indeed, global forces that impinged on its population. After my original fieldwork I wanted to probe further into the detailed mechanisms and conditions of migration from the village. I conducted research on

© Ernestine Friedl

Men at work roasting lambing for a village festival in Vasilika, mid-twentieth century.

these matters during the summers of 1964 and 1965, and again in 1976. My original interest in the dowry led me to continue to focus on gender relations in the village at a time when the study of women's roles was coming to the forefront. The next sections of this chapter are devoted to the consequences for the villagers of migration and to further discussion of changing gender roles.

I conclude with an epilogue devoted to some additional details on the Vasilika of 1998 and some comments on my professional and personal reactions to more than 40 years of intermittent association with a group of people who were so important to my life.

MIGRATION AND THE FATES OF MIGRANTS

The small size of the community made for an ideal setting in which to study individuals who left the village: I was able to discover the particular personal, social, economic, and political circumstances under which they left, the relevant conditions prevailing in the nation, and the ultimate place of the migrants in the urban setting of Athens. By 1965, almost half of Vasilika's 48 household heads had relatives who had grown up in the village and were now living in Athens. They had left the village as individuals and not as families. It is these kin I learned most about. An obvious question is why, given a similar set of values, did some leave and some stay at home? The efforts of families to improve the conditions for their children certainly played a part, but then, all the families agreed on that goal. Every village family seemed to have examined the particular resources available to them and made fairly rational calculations of the risks and rewards of moving to Athens. As it turned out, their predictions were quite good.

I traced 53 migrants who had left the village for Athens between 1930 and 1965 and interviewed all but five of them, usually in their homes. Six of the migrants left in the 1930s, 10 shortly after the end of World War II and the Greek Civil War, and 37 between 1951 and 1965. They had therefore left under different conditions, and ranged similarly in age and in length of urban experience at the time of the study. In all cases they went to Athens to improve their economic circumstances and to escape what they saw as the drudgeries of farming and the monotony of rural life. Many left as adolescents with the help of their parents and relatives who supported them as they gained skills and experience. The young people and their families had specific criteria for what they aspired to and, eventually, for judging whether they had succeeded.

The villagers had their own rank order of occupations and social positions they considered possible for their migrating sons and prospective sons-in-law. At the top were the posts requiring education beyond secondary school, such as the liberal professions (law, medicine, engineering, university or secondary school professorships), upper-level civil servants, managers in industry, and commissioned posts in the armed services or police. The second level also required a secondary degree, here for use in middle-level civil service posts, noncommissioned places in the armed services or police, elementary school teaching, or village priesthood. At this level, ownership or management of a retail store or other commercial enterprise or brokerage paid a respectable income that compensated for the absence of a secondary education. The third level from the top was one in which income was lower, and required fewer educational qualifications. Examples included low-level civil servants, office workers, proprietors of small stores, artisans, or clerks. Finally, the fourth and lowest level was one in which academic education was not needed, such as skilled construction or factory work, unskilled factory work, or farm labor. Proprietors of farms between 40 and 100 stremmata (4 stremmata equal 1 acre) were rated as equivalent to the second level. Those with fewer than 10 acres had to do some wage labor or be sharecroppers on the farms of others. Vasilika's families with the largest landholdings hoped to enable their sons to complete the education required for the higher-ranked occupations in Athens. For their daughters they wanted to provide dower properties in the form of houses or apartments in Athens. In short, men needed skills, women needed real estate. A secondary avenue to improvement for girls was also to acquire a secondary education or some skill such as dressmaking, and to work before marriage to contribute to their own dowries. Marriage to a farmer with substantial landholdings was also a step in the right direction, but it meant staying on a farm and therefore was considered not as prestigious a situation as a good post in Athens. For those with less land, further education was still a goal, but work opportunities other than sharecropping or low-level jobs in the village were also enticements.

In general, the movements out of the village were related to the economic standing of the farmers in the local economy, the presence or absence of kin already established in Athens, and the economic and political conditions of the nation that were favorable or unfavorable to the possibility of employment. The 18 households that had the largest landholdings were the ones whose sons and daughters were the first to leave and they continued to be the most heavily represented. The children of the lowest-level households were the last to leave, and the ones in the middle economic group were in between. Such generalizations, however, do not convey the drama of the apprehensions, vicissitudes, and satisfactions of the change from rural to urban life.

I shall begin the story of the depopulation of the village with the first phase of the migration between 1932 and 1936. I have identified five men and one woman as the pioneers. Because education beyond the six years of the village school was required for higher-level occupations, the families of the five men decided to send their sons for further education. They calculated that their resources were sufficient to maintain the boys while they studied, and each of the boys had one or more brothers old enough to furnish the labor for the maintenance of the farm under 1920 conditions. Those who stayed also helped to accumulate the dowries for their unmarried sisters. If one of the highest-level families had only one son, he did not leave the village during those years. The education of the boys was construed as a part of their inheritance and it left viable landholdings available to the other children. (The total living children of the pioneer families ranged from four to seven.) The son's choice to go was not based on his rank in the family, but on his age at the time and his promise of academic talent.

Indeed, the village schoolteacher was often responsible for touting the educational opportunities and encouraging the villagers to take advantage of them. At the time, a larger village five miles away had a Middle School (three years beyond the six years of village school). This obviated the need to find some social support for these 12-year-old boys in a community further away, especially as no relatives of the villagers resided there. There were no transportation costs; the boys walked the five miles back and forth to the village each weekend where they picked up enough bread and cheese to last them the entire week. They did require money for lodging, books, and school supplies. The men later reminisced about the long walk back and forth in all kinds of weather. They remembered how cold and sometimes rain-soaked they frequently were through the fall and winter. They told of their fear of the dark and of ghosts and evil spirits. They delighted in telling how one time they were frightened out of their wits and ran in terror for a few miles before they discovered that they were running from a stray dog.

After completing the Middle School in 1926 four of the pioneering boys went on to a secondary school in a provincial town 12 miles away for an additional three years of schooling. Transportation and more expensive lodgings added to the expenses their families had to bear. Their families also feared that without kin to supervise them, their 15-year-old sons would get into bad company and habits. However, at that time, all secondary school students were required to wear uniform caps and they were subject to the discipline of their teachers even during their free time in the town. This surveillance helped to reassure the parents. They were also encouraged by the state of the national economy, which seemed favorable to their sons' prospects for eventual employment in Athens.

In 1922 about one and a half million refugees from Asia Minor arrived in Greece and about one hundred and fifty thousand settled in Athens. They increased the labor force at a time when low industrialization and the disarray of the Greek economy after the First World War left no market for common laborers from rural villages. However, new civil service administrative personnel were needed to help in the settlement of the refugees. The prospects for Greek young men with secondary degrees were therefore propitious.

The fifth pioneering boy did not complete secondary school but instead went to a police academy in Athens. About 10 years later, he had an urban job and brought a Vasilika bride to Athens. I have thought of her as the sixth pioneer. Her memories of her terror in a strange impersonal city with a new husband were vivid. She recounted her story to me with verve and drama.

The other five boys of this cohort finished secondary school. One went to Athens following his sister (our sixth pioneer). He boarded with her, had a job during the day to help pay expenses, and went to school at night. He and the three others of the original five opted for further university education to increase their chances for better posts. The police officers training was supported by the government, the other three lived on remittances from their families back in the village. Between the end of their schooling and the outbreak of World War II in 1939, the three men searched for jobs with intermittent success and returned to the village for short periods. But after the sacrifices their families had made for them and the superfluity of farm labor in a period when farming was beginning to need even less labor, the honor of their families depended on their success in getting a post in Athens.

By the mid 1940s, all the men had taken civil service examinations and achieved permanent salaried places in Athens. They had built a network of friends in Athens who helped them learn of vacancies. Perhaps because of the miniscule numbers of migrants from the village, the men were not helped by any association of migrants from their region, as were so many migrants from other parts of Greece. The men originally formed a small group living near each other in rented quarters, but settled in different parts of Athens once married.

The pattern of marriages was interesting. When they had reached their early thirties, two of the men married without parental arrangement to rural schoolteachers who had come to Athens to teach. These women supplemented their husbands' initially meager incomes as the dowry of the Vasilikan bride helped her husband. The remaining two men, like many middle-class Athenians, married late, one at forty and one at fifty. The first found a rural wife by arrangement and the second married an urban friend. Also like many Athenians, none of these men had more than two children.

By 1965 all five who began as frightened little boys on their way to middle school had been promoted in their organizations, and three were close to or already had retired. They anticipated the pensions for which they had worked so hard. They all owned either a house or an apartment in good residential neighborhoods in Athens and not in the rapidly growing outlying sections. They had acquired these through their wives' dowries or a generous loan program for civil servants, or a combination of the two. They all had daughters who either had or were expecting to acquire secondary diplomas.

One of the most important consequences of the settlement of these pioneers in Athens was that they became the links in a chain through which their Vasilika nieces and nephews went to Athens. They took on the obligation of helping their brothers' and sisters' children leave the village. Their presence in Athens accounted for 34 percent of all the later migrants from the community. So important was the kin linkage that it makes sense to divide all subsequent village migrants into those who had kin in Athens and those who did not, because the experiences of the two groups were distinctly different. The adventures of these pioneers also illustrate the principles of choice and the sets of conditions that both motivated and constrained migration from the village.

Just before the outbreak of the Second World War and during the German occupation that ended in 1945, no one left the village for Athens. Despite the unsettled conditions during the Greek Civil War between 1945 and 1950, four men and one woman—all kin of the pioneers—set out for Athens. The young woman, like the men, continued her education and eventually acquired a civil service job in Athens.

These years also marked the beginning of the migration of those from the lowest economic levels from the village. One young man whose family could not support him in town was kin to one of the pioneers. With few land resources, only one sister on the farm to dower, and a talent for studies, his prospects in Athens were better than in the village. He worked during the day and went to school at night. A second man with few resources and no kin in Athens was the first to leave without further education in mind; because he had two brothers and a father at home in Vasilika, he left to try his luck in the city.

One woman, whose parents were in the second economic level, represented the most frequent avenue for women's migration: she married an artisan who had set up shop in Athens. With the aid of her dowry, she and her husband eventually built a house in the outlying sections of the city.

Three sisters from the lowest economic category also left the village during the postwar years. They had one younger brother and the family had too few resources for adequate dowries for the girls. The eldest went to Piraeus first, probably because a woman acquaintance of her parents lived there. She chose to live at the terminus of a railroad line where she could receive food sent from home. She started secondary school but she left it to take a factory job. She soon married her landlord's son, who was an office worker. She then helped her two sisters come to town. One got a job in a factory, the other learned dressmaking.

The four migrants from the top economic group and the one less advantaged man all had kin connections to the original pioneers and all had educational and employment histories that paralleled those of that earlier generation. One of the men was still unmarried in 1965, two were over thirty when they married, and the other two were in their late twenties. Two of the marriages were arranged with women from a rural village. For all the married men, their wives' dowries were the source of their housing. The young woman in this group married in her mid-twenties, chose her own husband, and he provided their dwelling place.

The careers of the four migrants from the least advantaged families exemplify patterns common to some of the later migrants from this economic group. The girls were younger when they married, some in their early twenties, and they also chose their own husbands. They eventually accumulated enough money so that when supplemented with their fathers' limited dowry contributions, they were able to build houses in the outlying sections of Athens. After their marriages two of these women left Greece to find work. One woman and her husband worked temporarily in Switzerland. One man stayed in Canada for many years. I visited him briefly one afternoon in Montreal at a pizza restaurant that he ran with a partner. The menu included French pastries, as befits French Montreal. He spoke of long years of separation from his wife and hard physical labor in northern Canada to acquire the money for his business. Our conversation was in Greek and English, but he lamented the need to know French as well, as his customers all spoke French.

From 1951 to 1965 Greece began a gradual recovery from the ravages of the wars and the country started on a course of economic growth and development. Twenty-five village men and 12 village women established themselves in Athens. Several new circumstances were now conducive to migration from Vasilika: all the villagers could now expect help from relatives settled in Athens, and Greece was experiencing an expanding economy with no substantial increase in the size of the labor force. As before, the largest number of migrants (19) came from the highest economic group in the village, seven from the middle, and 11 from the least advantaged households. For those in better circumstances, the government gave credit for machinery and fertilizers to increase yields and make it feasible to lease land for sharecropping. In the meantime, the size of dowries required for girls to marry townsmen increased. Revenues from the land were used to build urban housing and dower daughters, leaving less for sons. These men could not expect to recoup their farm income from their wives' dowries, because only poorer girls with small dowries were willing to marry Vasilika farmers. As a result, four households encouraged all their sons to migrate. The families of the six women with relatives in Athens counted on them to help them find reliable grooms in what were still arranged marriages. Two of the women at this income level had earlier married men in provincial towns and were later able to move to Athens. Two of the men were encouraged to take up military careers.

The youth from this upper economic stratum who remained in the village were young men who enjoyed farming and had sufficient resources to support a reasonably good standard of living, or were young women who had started secondary school in provincial towns and were waiting to see what marriage prospects lie ahead.

In one anomalous situation, a charitable foundation offered a scholarship to a son who had completed secondary school in Athens to attend Columbia University in New York. His parents permitted him to accept the award. He graduated from Columbia, married and has two children, and worked as a computer specialist on Long Island in New York State.

During the 14 years of this period, from 1951 to 1965, many of the men and husbands of the women were still building careers. Some were still attending secondary school or university. Among the rest, all the men had education or training beyond the secondary school level. One man had a top-ranked job, the others were employed in jobs that ranked just below. The six young men and one woman from the second tier of village families now had slightly more income to support the education of their boys, and two used the military and police training route to urban support. Half the men were still students in training in 1965 and the others were in second-tier occupations in Athens, as was the husband of the one woman who married into Athens.

As we have come to expect, the families on the lowest level of the Vasilika economic ladder sent the smallest proportion of their young people to migrate. Because of the earlier exodus from the village, new opportunities for wage labor or sharecropping in the village were equal to what unskilled or semiskilled work in Athens would have provided. If they had attempted schooling they would have deprived their families of both their labor power and the resources needed to help support them through school. Several started additional schooling but suffered small setbacks that discouraged them and they returned to the village.

In the 20 years between 1945 and 1965, more than half of the men who had left the village and had finished their schooling were still unmarried. They ranged in age from 26 to the early 40s; most were in their middle 30s. In this cohort, those with the best jobs in Athens married the latest. They waited for advancement to the point where they could command higher dowries or marry educated urban women. Both routes enhanced their standard of living and their prestige. The three men with the highest standing who did marry, chose to exemplify the Greek proverb, "it is best to find a shoe from your home town even if it is patched." They acquiesced in the efforts of their Vasilika relatives to find them wives from neighboring villages. One of the least advantaged men also married a rural girl. In each case, the women brought with them enough wealth to provide housing.

During this same period a higher proportion of those from the lowest echelons married in their twenties. Several of them found girls who thought them attractive and persuaded their parents to let them marry. They were the urban version of the in-marrying son-in-law. In the beginning, the parents offered the couples housing and some even offered their sons-in-law employment and training. This fortunate marriage pattern enabled a few of these men to develop exceptional careers.

The migrant women from the upper-level households married later than the others. A higher proportion of the women from the lowest level came to Athens alone, arranged their own marriages, and married early. For one woman, acquaintance with her spouse began in telephone conversations over business matters. Another interesting marital outcome was that one-quarter of all the married women migrants married men whose parents were already in Athens. In each of these cases the young couples lived with the grooms' parents as they would have in the village. In other words, independent households were not a new urban value; rather they developed in part from the absence in Athens of the parents of migrants from Vasilika and elsewhere.

The importance of establishing independent homes in the city appeared repeatedly in these narratives. A dwelling was necessary for marriage and most migrants were able to provide one. The migrants' success in achieving that goal was dependent on the forces that influenced the building of houses in Athens in the 1950s and 1960s. The city was growing in an ever widening semicircle from the Acropolis, and houses had started creeping up the hillsides surrounding the city. In the meantime the value of previously existing housing was increasing. One-room homes built without sewers or piped water on unpaved roads, were being improved or demolished to build apartment houses in their place.

The migrants from Vasilika, both married and unmarried, lived in more than a dozen different districts in the Athens-Piraeus area. As always kin linkage played its part as migrants settled near their relatives. In 1965 three regions of the city had more than two kin-linked households from Vasilika. The majority of the most advantaged migrants settled in old and new standard middle-class housing not far from the center and which were equipped with the amenities of running water, electricity, baths, and water closets. None of those in the lowest village economic level had these amenities with the exception of electricity. Nevertheless, all occupants owned their houses, some even occupying them as soon as the walls and roofs were completed. Their owners scrimped and saved to complete the houses and gradually to add to their amenities (electric refrigerators were among the first desired), often using additional dowry installments for this purpose. Real estate taxes in Greece were low for those of low income, and costs of upkeep were limited to garbage collection and water.

Despite the absence of piped water and flush toilets, such housing did not create unsanitary, crowded slum conditions. Usually a married couple and no more than two children lived in the dwellings. The houses were widely spaced, and backyard latrines had only a small number of users. Electric or kerosene heaters were sufficient for the few months when heating is needed in Athens, and cooking was done with bottled gas. The women maintained the orderly standards of village housekeeping and added the touches of elegance they were accustomed to in the village.

In short, Vasilika's families encouraged their children to migrate in relation to the resources available to them, both material and emotional. Over time, relatives or godparents in the city gave worried parents some assurance that their children would be safe. Once settled in Athens, friends became a source of support and information. The timing of the moves was related to the economic circumstances of the villagers as defined by the relative quantity of land their households owned. They not only determined when their children would migrate but also influenced the occupational level they were able to reach in Athens. All the migrants improved their economic circumstances but, interestingly, they remained in the same position relative to their fellow villagers. With rare exceptions, the wealthiest of the villagers had the best economic and social positions in Athens compared to those of their less advantaged fellow villagers. Nevertheless, the military was an available substitute for those without urban kin. Those better off married later and acquired better housing than their fellow Vasilikans.

Economic and political conditions in Greece between 1950 and 1965 were favorable for migration to Athens. Indeed, economic development was a national goal. Increased income from agriculture, in spite of increased costs for rural labor, added to the resources of the family back home. Employment in Athens was available, whereas in the village there were few provincial industries which might keep young men and women at home. Fiscal policies maintained the value of the drachma and limited inflation. Finally, a cheap system of bus transportation with routes that extended into the outlying areas of the city made it possible for people to get to work in Athens.

For the people of Vasilika, the move into the city was fraught with drama and hardship but not with social disorganization or disintegration. Studies of migration from other parts of Greece tell the same story. The unemployed in Athens during the period were not migrants from the countryside.

GENDER ROLES

Once in Athens, the mutual dependence of men and women on each other on the farm, and decisions about agricultural production, the practices in which men, women, and children participated, were no longer relevant. The shared economic interdependence was replaced by a mutual concern for the maintenance of appropriate consumption standards for the family and the education and welfare of the children. The quality of the housing, the appliances used, the fashions for interior decoration, and the quality and forms of hospitality were joint interests and together they tried to conform to the latest urban standards.

Nevertheless, men lost some power over their own lives. On the family farms, in spite of the constraints of national farm policy, discretion and skillful planning were possible in the organization of each family's time and labor. They could assign land for sharecropping and they could hire labor. By contrast, in Athens, many of the men had salaried jobs in bureaucratic organizations in government or business. They did not control their own time, the tasks they performed, nor the personnel with whom they worked. Unless they were in executive positions, they also did not have to make as many decisions. In Athens, men worked with female fellow employees, women who were not part of their families (either as wives or as daughters), and they were not responsible for supervising the sexual behavior of these female coworkers. Men did acquire male friends in their new workplaces, and these became companions for outings. Another contrast with life in Vasilika was that men's living quarters in Athens were often their wives' dower houses or apartment.

For women the changes in the urban setting were in some ways more profound. The strict segregation of men and women characteristic of the village was maintained in the men's coffee houses in Athens, but was mitigated by the availability of sweet shops where men and women could eat ice cream and pastries together.

Certainly women could move about the city more freely without supervision. Those who went for advanced education worked independently in office settings, and some continued to work after marriage. Their male relatives did not continually supervise their activities. They took greater control of their own lives, including their sexuality.

Married women who stayed at home continued to be responsible for cooking, cleaning, shopping, and caring for the children. They also still attended the graves of their kinfolk buried in Athens' cemeteries. Many continued to embroider, sew, and crochet.

Within the family, the women acquired a new task: they became responsible for helping their children with schooling. They could not work outside the home after they had children, some women said, because they felt responsible for helping them with their homework and seeing that they settled down to their school obligations.

In the village, women had been in the habit of consulting with other women about carrying out the most routine tasks. In the city, women's relatives did not live nearby, and newly married women complained of loneliness and even boredom, especially if they had young children. In Athens the Vasilikans did not live together in enclaves that might have perpetuated their village world through community organizations. Women were isolated in their houses or apartments, with few opportunities for unstructured visits with other women, unlike in their village, where church attendance and comings and goings from the field provided these. As some compensation, husbands occasionally took their wives to the sweet pastry shops or even for a dinner at a taverna, and those who owned cars went for family excursions to the seaside or countryside. For married women, this indicated a good husband.

In time, the village origins of the people of Vasilika were subsumed into the life of Athenian Greeks at different economic levels. The loss of the cooperation between husbands, wives, and children on the family farm decreased men's control over their families. Relations between men and women were close to European patterns with some bias, as in the rest of Europe, toward advantages for and deference to men.

EPILOGUE

Throughout my years of association with the people of Vasilika from 1955 to 1976, my husband, Harry L. Levy, accompanied me. He was a classicist whose knowledge of ancient Greek gave him an advantage in spelling modern Greek; he acted as scribe and helped with interviews and conversations with the men of the community. He was a quick wit, a teller of stories in his own tongue, and enthusiastically learned the idioms of verbal exchange in the village. Harry loved Greece. At one time we even thought of spending part of each year living there. After he died in 1981, I was reluctant to go back alone. Although I spent a week traveling in Greece with a friend who had never been to Europe in the late 1980s, and I taught an American summer program near Poros in the summer of 1992, I did not go back to the village at either time.

I married again in 1990. My husband, Merel Harmel, an anaesthesiologist, learned quickly of the deep imprint the people of Vasilika had made on me, and wanted to see for himself. It was time to revisit Vasilika, however briefly. My only knowledge of the village after 1976 came from a sociologist who telephoned to tell me of his visit in the mid-1980s, and from brief reports by Roland Moore, an anthropologist who had passed through the community twice in the 1990s.

We planned to visit the village in June 1998 and by great good luck discovered that Peter Allen, another anthropologist and good friend who worked in Greece for many years, was free to come with us. I wrote Triandaphyllos Triandafillou, the son of our original village host, about the date we were coming and asked him to leave a message for us at the College Year in Athens program office. He called in his telephone number and invited us to visit with them that evening, at the home of their newly married daughter in Kato Petralona, a suburb of Athens. Peter, with his-six-year-old son, Jeremiah, drove us from our hotel to their home.

For me, it was an emotional reunion. Takis, the nickname for Triandaphyllos, had been 18 years old in 1955; he was now 60. He looked exactly like his father who had been close to that age when we first met the family. His mannerisms, humor, and pride in his daughter and her home were reminiscent of his father's personality. Mina, Takis's wife, had grown from the thin young girl she had been into a fine-looking woman. His daughter, little Sophia, or Foula as she was called, was a lovely modern young bride. What was most moving was how many memories of our first visit to Vasilika we shared: Takis remembered me, stringing tobacco with them, the jokes about the "spaghetti tree," the time his father referred to his mother emerging from the house as Lazarus emerging from the tomb, and many more. We talked about how Harry "(my husband)," who was a colonel in the U.S. Army Reserves, had managed to get Takis a free afternoon during his army service in Athens so that we could visit with him during one of our brief visits to Vasilika.

Compared to the village amenities even as late as 1976, the present circumstances of the family were impressive, indeed. In 1997, without her parents' arrangement, Foula had married Dimitris Gallanti, whom she had met in Athens. He was a graduate of the Pantios School in Athens where he had studied political science and sociology. He had heard of my book on Vasilika from one of his teachers. At the time, he was doing odd jobs and hoping for a civil service position. Foula had learned about computers in Athens and was working in a computer firm. They had a computer in the house and young Jeremiah settled in for the evening playing computer games. The apartment was reasonably spacious, newly refurbished with new furniture, decorative stonework, glass cabinets with attractive nicknacks, and windows with electrically powered shades. They also had the latest kitchen appliances. Takis and Mina pointed out the features of the house with great pride. Takis said he had given them the apartment as a dowry, presumably now not as an obligation but as a free gift.

The hospitality of the house followed a familiar pattern; after a tour of the apartment, we were seated and offered a drink and a sweet, in this case a slice of cake. We chatted for quite a while, and Foula and Mina went to the kitchen to prepare a sumptuous meal of pasta, stewed beef, salads, bread, wine, and fruit. It was after midnight when we left, and we agreed to meet the next day in Vasilika.

Accordingly the next day Peter and Jeremiah drove us up to the village following the old road through Thebes that we had taken before the new national road from Athens had been built. On our arrival, Takis and Mina, and their 26-year-old son, Athanasios, greeted us. According to Greek custom, Athanasios, was named after Takis's father, just as Sophia (Foula) was named after his mother. In the yard next to the house were two cars, one a green Ford van and the other a small yellow sporty Spanish car. The second belonged to Athanasios, who had decided to stay on the farm rather than leave for the city. We were told that he would settle in Tithorea, a nearby town, and that if he could not get a house as part of a dowry, Takis would build him one.

After a drink and a sweet at a table under a grape arbor, they gave us a tour of the house. The front yard facing the street was now a lovely rose garden, with potted plants against the wall of the house. The home itself had been refurbished and reorganized. A handsome metal railing topped with a wooden banister ran up the side of the stairs. The second-story veranda had a new wooden ceiling. The upstairs rooms were divided into a large saloni or salon and bedroom, with the old shallow sink still in the room. New furniture with photographs of Takis's parents were on the wall. The ground floor had a bathroom with a commode and shower, and the kitchen now had stainless steel sinks, a clothes washing machine, running water, and a heater. Athanasios's bedroom was there adjacent to the kitchen and could be made into a dining room. Indeed, it was there we later enjoyed a midday meal. Again, Takis and Mina much enjoyed my pleasure as they displayed so many amenities and conveniences.

Just as his father had done before him, Takis delegated to his son the task of taking us on a tour of the village. They had a storehouse for farm machinery including a tobacco- and tomato-planting machine that could be ridden by women as well as by men, a large Ferguson tractor, and cultivating equipment of different kinds. All looked new and shiny. We also saw storerooms and three tobacco sheds for flu-curing tobacco (no more threading and hanging in the sun). Takis shared one of these sheds with another farmer. The old loom was stored but does not seem to be used any longer. Athanasios took us to the family vegetable garden planted with zucchini, cucumbers, tomatoes, and other vegetables—all grown organically without chemical fertilizer. Athanasios said not even the tobacco was cultivated with artificial fertilizers. The family had chickens, a rifle and a shotgun, as well as a hunting dog they used for hunting birds. Their sheep were in the mountains for the summer season.

Takis later explained that he farmed about 50 acres, 20 acres of his own and 30 acres that he rented from farmers living in the city. Rents were paid in cash, not by shares in the crop. In addition to himself, Mina, and his son who all worked in the fields, he joined with the other farmers in the village to hire five Albanian men who came every year. They did agricultural work for all of Vasilika's remaining farmers and were provided with food and housing in a place set aside just for them.

We stopped by the homes of Mina's parents (she was a Vasilika girl) and one or two other old couples still in the village. It was on this tour that we also met the mother of Athanasios Tassopolos, the young boy who in the 1960s, had left for Columbia University and was still in the United States. It was extremely hot, and most people were indoors, so we met fewer people than we might have otherwise.

When we arrived back at their house we were served an ample and delicious meal of pork and lamb chops, fried zucchini and eggplant, tomatoes, bread, and a light village-resinated wine, just the right complement to the meal. We faced the television set as we ate and suddenly realized that we were watching a video of Foula and Dimitri's wedding and reception. It had taken place in Vasilika, at the smaller church of the Agi Anaryiri. We watched the traditional Greek Orthodox ceremony, and some two hundred guests as they danced the traditional dances of the region after the ceremony. To everyone's glee, the officiating priest joined in the dance. Weddings in Athens were more common among those who had left the village for the city, so the village as a setting was all the more special. The guests included all the family members and many other villagers I had known. They had aged of course, and Takis and Mina had to tell me who many of them were. Also there were all the new children I had never seen before. The video did not include the finale of the festivities, a trip to a taverna for a meal. We left soon after to return to appointments in Athens.

What was a sentimental and personal journey nevertheless revealed the consequences for some individual farming families of the political—and

1990's Vasilika: author's friend in front of a modern village house.

economic—situation in Greece. The relative prosperity and political stability of the country in the 1980s and 1990s enabled them to fulfill their dreams of an urban setting for their children and more sophisticated living conditions in the countryside. How long the current situation can last is not predictable. Greece profits from the commercial crops grown in the Boeotian plain where Vasilika is situated. Vasilika farmers may continue to cultivate land profitably with the help of outside labor, but the urban landholders of the village return for holidays and vacations less and less frequently as their parents die. Many prefer to go to Atalanti, a nearby town on the sea. They might eventually sell their land to agribusiness and displace the few farmers left in the village.

But whatever the future holds, let us hope it will be a good one. It has been a privilege for me to have known and followed the fortunes of the people of this small village of Vasilika. I am forever in their debt.

REFERENCES

Friedl, Ernestine. 1967. The position of women: Appearance and reality. *Anthropological Quarterly* 40:97–108. Reprinted in *Gender and power in rural Greece,* ed. Dubisch, Jill, 1986. Princeton: Princeton Univ. Press.

———.1995. *In a different place: Pilgrimage, gender, and politics of a Greek island shrine.* Princeton: Princeton Univ. Press.

———.1976. Kinship, class, and selective migration. In *Mediterranean family structures,* ed. 7. G. Peristiany, 363–387. Cambridge Univ. Press.

ADDITIONAL WORKS ON VASILIKA

Friedl, Ernestine. 1964. Lagging emulation in post-peasant society. *American Anthropologist* 66:569–586.

Friedl, Ernestine. 1970. Fieldwork in a Greek village. In *Women in the field,* ed. Peggy Golde, 195–217. Chicago: Aldine Publishing Company.

RECOMMENDED READING

John Campbell (in 1964) and Julie DuBoulay (in 1974) published their classic ethnographies of Greece based on fieldwork conducted earlier. Beginning in the 1980s anthropologists have published a virtual flowering of excellent works on Greece. The list that follows is a sampling of these. The particular subject of the books can be gleaned from the titles.

Campbell, John. 1964. *Honour, family, and patronage.* Oxford: Clarendon Press.

Cowan, Jane. 1990. *Dance and the body politic in Northern Greece.* Princeton, NJ: Princeton University Press.

DuBoulay, Juliet. 1974. *Portrait of a Greek mountain village.* Oxford: Clarendon Press.

Danforth, Loring M. 1982. *The death rituals of rural Greece.* Princeton: Princeton Univ. Press.

———.1995. *The Macedonian conflict: Ethnic nationalism in a transnational world.* Princeton: Princeton Univ. Press.

Dubisch, Jill, ed. 1986. *Gender and power in rural Greece.* Princeton: Princeton Univ. Press.

———.1995. *In a different place: Pilgrimage, gender, and politics of a Greek island shrine.* Princeton: Princeton Univ. Press.

Hirschon, Renee. 1989. *Heirs of the Greek catastrophe: The social life of Asia Minor refugees in Piraeus.* Oxford: Clarendon Press.

Herzfeld, Michael. 1982. *Ours once more: Folklore, ideology, and the*

making of modern Greece. Austin: Univ. of Texas Press.

———.1985. *The poetics of manhood contest and identity in a Cretan mountain village.* Princeton: Princeton Univ. Press.

———.1992. *The social production of indifference.* Chicago: Univ. of Chicago Press.

Karakasidou, Anastasia. 1997. *Fields of wheat. Hills of blood.* Chicago: Univ. of Chicago Press.

Seremetakis, C. Nadia. 1991. *The last word: Women, death, and divination in Inner Mani.* Chicago: Univ. of Chicago Press.

Stewart, Charles. 1991. *Demons and devils: Moral imagination in modern Greek culture.* Princeton: Princeton Univ. Press.

Loizos, Peter, and E. Papatachiarchis, eds. 1991. *Contested Identities: Gender and Kinship in Modern Greece.* Princeton: Princeton University Press.

Panourgia, Neni. 1995. *Fragments of death, fables of identity: An Athenian anthropography.* Madison: Univ. of Wisconsin Press.

Fieldwork Biography
Toshiyuki Sano and Mariko Fujita

As Japanese anthropologists and a married couple, Toshiyuki Sano and Mariko Fujita conducted their joint fieldwork during the mid-1980s in the Midwestern town they call Riverfront in Wisconsin. "Our first son was born during our two-and-a-half years of fieldwork in Riverfront. His presence dramatically changed our relationship with our informants. After fieldwork, we returned to Japan to establish our professional careers. We revisited our field site in the late 1990s and again in 2003. It was such a rewarding experience for us to reencounter our friends who not only remembered us but also cherished our shared memories."

Toshiyuki Sano is a professor in the school of human life and environment at Nara Women's University in Nara, Japan. Mariko Fujita is a professor on the faculty of integrated arts and sciences at Hiroshima University in Higashi-Hiroshima, Japan.

Courtesy of Mariko Fujita-Sano and Toshiyuki Sano.

15/Through Japanese Eyes
Culture Change in a Midwestern Town

In Japan, the last decade of the twentieth century was termed the "lost decade." Originally coined to designate the aftermath of the burst economic bubble of the late 1980s, the term can also be applied to our own lives. Upon our return from extensive ethnographic fieldwork in "Riverfront," Pine County, Wisconsin in 1987, we experienced major transitions—personally, professionally, and academically. Originally we had planned to write our ethnography of Riverfront soon after completing our fieldwork. Instead we waited to publish until 2001.

First we had to establish ourselves in our careers as professional anthropologists and academics in Japan. In addition, we knew we needed to develop a new perspective and framework to analyze the data from our fieldwork in Riverfront and write our ethnography about culture change there. We avoided revisiting Riverfront during the 1990s, because we expected that more changes had occurred since we left. We knew that if we learned about these, we would be forced to deal with even more complex material in writing about life and culture change in Riverfront. Toward the end of the 1990s, we finally situated our experiences from 1980s Riverfront in broader and deeper historical contexts. We began to realize the significance of our research on an American town in transition during a specific historical period. Among many changes, residents lost their downtown and gained postmodern consumer sites. In this chapter, we describe the shift in our cognitive perspective that enabled us to contextualize the changes that occurred (and are occurring) in the town of Riverfront and the surrounding rural area.

CHANGING EYES—FROM ANALOGUE TO DIGITAL

When we first arrived in the Riverfront area of central Wisconsin in a California-licensed car in October 1984, the downtown was changing. Workers were replacing sewage pipes under Main Street. A crew of workers was relocating an old building on the public square to widen an entranceway to a new shopping mall. During two-and-a-half years of fieldwork in the Riverfront area in the mid-1980s, we saw many changes underway in the town and surrounding farming community, but we believed these changes were specific to this region.

The construction of downtown shopping malls was a trend we had observed in central Wisconsin on our first visits in the late 1970s and early 1980s. We had a sense that the changes we saw would soon be fixed in local history, set in a past, distant from the present. This is what "analogue" images make us think. A still camera that we used at that time helped to create such images. Waiting a week for prints to be developed, we felt somehow detached from the images that we had captured on film of the changes underway in Riverfront. Such images, we felt, needed to be placed in sequential order.

By contrast, when we revisited Riverfront in 1999, we were able to conceptualize changes within a "digital" framework. At first glance, downtown Riverfront appeared to be much the same. Downtown businesses seemed as slow as they used to be.[1] However, as we walked to the public square, we noticed most of the old wall paintings of European design had disappeared. Then we unexpectedly encountered an Asian grocery store at a corner of the square. The disappearance of the traditional European wall paintings and the appearance of an Asian store on the public square seemed unconnected to each other at first. Soon we realized that they were connected, but first we had to shift our perspective from analogue to digital imagery. By digital images, we mean those provided by a digital camera. With such a camera, we could immediately see on-site the pictures that we had just taken. Once downloaded onto a computer, the images could be easily scanned, searched, and combined on the screen. Digital images are easier to print, change, and rearrange, compared to analogue ones. Our experience has shown us that we can gather much more information and in a shorter time using digital technology. Pictures can be stored within the compact space of a memory chip of less than an inch.

To describe all the changes and developments that have occurred in the Riverfront area and to analyze how they were generated and maintained, we will try to read between seemingly unconnected images. To us, it appears that local people now make connections between symbols, entities, and social institutions more intentionally and abruptly than before. In other words, Riverfront people seem to be constantly engaged in reorganizing their own culture. If their culture is indeed changing in this way, then we as anthropologists must change our way of conceptualizing culture, and come to see it more as a newly woven, still-emerging web of symbols. To capture such cultural changes, anthropologists must be flexible, able to move through the different levels, domains, and spheres of people's everyday lives.[2]

TWO VIEWS OF DOWNTOWN AND THE PUBLIC SQUARE

Standing at the center of the public square in the 1980s, we saw the Polish Catholic Church, the paintings of eastern European design, a newly opened European delicatessen, the Riverfront Bakery selling homemade breads, a half-vacant grocery store operated by Jewish brothers, a few bars, a pharmacy owned by an old Polish pharmacist, a sports shop with a front sign with a Polish name, a bank along Main Street, and a women's clothing store. Such places seemed somehow connected in a way analogous to a culture that is conceived as an ordered web of symbols. Even at the close of our first fieldwork in the late 1980s, we still had a sense that everything was related to local people's lives, and that we could connect one thing with another in Riverfront.

Standing at the same spot in Riverfront in the early 2000s, what we now saw were things seemingly unconnected to each other, or to people's everyday lives. Only a portion of the top of the Polish Catholic Church could be seen over the roof of the shopping mall that was built in the mid-1980s. Vacant stores were everywhere, although vendors were busy at the Farmers Market. There were store signs without Polish names. A trendy tattoo and piercing shop had opened, bright with colorful lights and walls decorated with sample tattoo designs (Figure 15.1). In early 2000, we had the sense that everything in Riverfront was disconnected, that nothing related to the lives of local people.

"Polish town," a term that referred to Riverfront through the 1980s, had become a misnomer in the 1990s; "ethnically mixed" was now a more accurate characterization. Riverfront was formerly known as "Polish town" because more than half of its residents were of Polish descent. Riverfront now was ethnically mixed, not because its current inhabitants were people of diverse European origins (as in other towns), but because of the substantial addition of people of Asian backgrounds—especially Hmong people.

The shift in the town's ethnic composition started gradually, but by the 1990s had become the new reality. The Hmong population increased to the point where one young Hmong man was able to open an Asian grocery store in the public square downtown. His clients seemed to be exclusively Hmong, because he carried only items from Southeast Asia, and he did not use any English signs and advertisements to attract the general public. Three years later, in 2002, we found that the store was already gone, but we also learned that more Hmong people lived in town than before. A year later we found two Asian grocery stores, not in the tranquil public square, but in small commercial zones adjacent to a residential area. One store was jammed with goods, and local Hmong people came and

Courtesy of Toshiyuki Sano, August 2003.

Figure 15.1 A trendy tattoo shop at a corner of the public square, Riverfront downtown (August 2003).

went while we were there. Another store, a general Asian grocery that a young Hmong family from Minneapolis owned, also carried diverse Asian foods and goods. The fact that Asian foods had become locally available suggests that the Hmong population in Riverfront will increase even more in the coming years.

We asked ourselves what the disappearance of the wall paintings from the public square could mean? It appears that from the 1980s to the 1990s, local residents became less interested in simply expressing their cultural heritage, and more interested in employing that heritage as a cultural resource, to attract outsiders and revitalize the town. Riverfront had no obvious ethnic markers except the wall paintings of eastern European design in the public square. Kataryna Baszka had initiated that painting project after she emigrated in the 1950s from Poland to Riverfront, where she married the editor of a weekly Polish newspaper. In the late 1980s, although she still had a voice in town affairs, with age it had become less dominant. The wall paintings lost their founding spirit. By the 1990s, they had been taken down, perhaps by people who did not care about their historical significance and emblematic meanings.

The symbolic power that the public square had exercised was almost gone too.[3] Its role in creating town cohesiveness ceased when the shopping mall was constructed, blocking the northbound traffic, both physically and symbolically, from the Public Square to the north side. We had expected the square's significance would continue, that someone else would make use of it, as Kataryna Baszka had decades earlier. However, during our follow-up visits in 2002 and

Courtesy of Toshiyuki Sano, August 2003.

Figure 15.2 Several young Hmong children sell produce in the farmers market at the public square in the Riverfront downtown (August 2003).

2003, we realized that the downtown businesses were not thriving. The news that the *Riverfront Journal,* the local newspaper, had been sold during the 1990s came as a complete surprise to us. The fact that its headquarters were located downtown had exerted a strong symbolic power, creating a sense of community by providing local news. The new newspaper, published by an international media company, did not carry as much local flavor as the previous one. Concerned local people began to publish their own weekly tabloid gazette that provided news of only local people and issues.

In the new public square of 2003, changes in the farmers market seemed especially significant. It had survived for more than two decades, and the vendors still numbered about a dozen. Its continuity was impressive, but perhaps not too surprising, because farmers' markets have become popular across the United States, promoted in many places because they bring new life to downtown business districts.

What the farmers market did reveal about changes in Riverfront was the fact that young Hmong families had established their own agricultural enterprises. Half of the vendors were Asian children, all apparently of Hmong background. The peaceful setting of the Riverfront downtown allowed them to help their parents sell produce at the farmers market. The rest of the vendors were white men and women of various ages, who were friendly with the Asian child vendors (see Figure 15.2). The ethnic and age composition of the vendors struck us. We realized that it was a common experience for the children of immigrants to help their parents sell produce—first Polish children in the 1930s, now Hmong children in 2003.

Similarities in the experiences of Polish immigrants and their descendants and of Hmong in the Riverfront area are much greater than we would have expected at the time of our first fieldwork. When Polish people began to arrive in Riverfront and its surrounding farming area in the late-nineteenth century, ethnic substitutions occurred: as more Polish immigrants arrived, the early-comers, mostly of western European origin, were in the process of moving out of the area. More than a century later, in the mid-1980s, another ethnic change occurred. We learned that Vietnamese had moved to central Wisconsin, but then relocated to the southern states, because (according to popular opinion) the winters in Wisconsin were too cold for them. The Hmong had in effect replaced the Vietnamese. They came and stayed, contrary to speculation that they, too, would soon move out of the area. We realized that the reason the Vietnamese left the area was not because of the climate, but because appropriate job opportunities were not then available to them in Riverfront. For Hmong, job conditions were better than they were for the Vietnamese, in part due to the economic growth in the local area during the late 1980s and 1990s. For Polish people, too, similar changes had occurred around 1900, when new job opportunities became available in Riverfront's new downtown factories. At that time, many Polish people were recruited as factory workers.

Networking among members of the same ethnic group seemed important for both Hmong and people of Polish background. The Polish Women's Alliance, headquartered in Chicago, has long been one of the nationwide organizations that provides aid for Polish Americans. Kataryna Baszka herself had headed its local chapter, stepping down when we were still in Riverfront. A few years later, however, she again became head of the local chapter, because she felt dissatisfied with her successor. She was dedicated to the welfare of Polish Americans (as well as people in Poland), and was energetic about helping them. Through word of mouth, people from distant towns heard about her. Some came to Riverfront to ask for her help; for instance, she translated letters people received from family and friends in Poland.

The network among Hmong was a commercial one that seemed to have been established in a relatively short time, during just the last decade. The flyer we found at one of the Hmong grocery stores advertised seminars for starting business ventures. Their network appeared to be expanding across Wisconsin, as we saw flyers with the names of contact persons posted in many towns. This suggests that Hmong people had settled throughout the region and were trying to actively engage in the life of local towns. Many Hmong were also taking English language classes.

A religious place was important for early settlers in Riverfront, both Polish and Hmong, as well as for other ethnic groups. Once the Polish immigrants had established a parish in the late-nineteenth century, they built a Catholic church on Riverfront's north side, only a few blocks from the public square. Afterward, the north side became Polish "territory," and was designated so through the 1980s. Similarly, the Hmong established their own Christian church, a building long used by a different Protestant congregation. Because of its location—at the margin of the residential area in Riverfront—the existence of a Hmong church was hardly noticeable to outsiders.

Although spiritual support was important for Polish and Hmong immigrants during the early years of their adjustment to their new environment (and still is), the visibility and location of their churches suggests differences in their experiences: Each group lived under different conditions and held different attitudes about living in Riverfront. Until World War II, Polish people competed with people of other European backgrounds. They had to establish a new niche, "Polish territory," in an already-established community. By contrast, Hmong people were not trying to contest but instead to coexist with European American inhabitants. They created their own sphere in town life, at a time when the town was losing its cohesiveness and ethnic boundaries were becoming less physically marked.

The problems confronting newcomers today may not be much different from those that Polish and Hmong immigrants faced. However, what their problems mean to the different generations of townspeople appears to differ. As the Hmong population grew through the 1990s, their problems became increasingly difficult to solve on an individual basis. Local townspeople (mostly Americans of European descent) decided that social intervention was necessary. One group of such townspeople that we came to know in 2003 was a nonprofit organization offering English-language classes to Hmong adults. Identifying the English-language deficiency of the newcomers as a social problem requiring community intervention was certainly new. This kind of town response did not greet the Polish immigrants a century ago.

This difference in community response to newcomers suggests that Riverfront had been fundamentally transformed. From our own Japanese cultural viewpoint, we did not expect that problems immigrants faced would be treated as community problems requiring social intervention. Based on what we know of American culture and town life, we assumed that it was typical of Riverfront residents to leave newcomers (immigrants or not) to solve their own problems. If help were indeed necessary, it would be provided on an individual basis, case by case. This is of course a cultural stereotype, and social assistance for new immigrants is now not unusual in towns across the United States. Riverfront was no exception.

From our own experience in the 1980s, we came to know the people of Riverfront as a concerned and caring community. Nevertheless, we still believed that the general attitude was that newcomers could and should solve their own problems themselves, without community assistance. Our belief is based on our own personal experience as newcomers. Before we came to Riverfront from California's San Francisco Bay Area in 1984, we worried about the acceptance of Asian people within the Riverfront community. While checking the statistics of the town, we found only a handful of inhabitants with an Asian background out of more than 20,000 residents in Riverfront. Based on this fact, we of course assumed that people in central Wisconsin did not have enough contact with Asian people to be receptive to them. This assumption, however, was not born out in our own experience. We had to revise our assumption: we now believe that, because Riverfront residents had not had personal experiences with Asian people, they were simply open to them.

During our fieldwork, we came to feel accepted by the local community as we began to make acquaintances and friends. We found some individuals very familiar with Japanese people and culture. They showed us that they had positive images of our culture, and this made us feel comfortable living in Riverfront. Our neighbor in Riverfront, a man of Polish descent who had been a marine stationed in Japan immediately after World War II, obviously wanted to befriend us, and we often talked together in the backyard.

Still another case is Kataryna Baszka herself, whom we occasionally visited. One day she told us that she had read an article about Japanese customs in a Polish magazine and had then realized that Japanese and Polish cultures had many similarities. A retired 70-year-old postman, whom we had met through a mutual friend, remembered that a Japanese American had been a minister of his Methodist church in Riverfront and was one of the town's historical figures, whose picture had even been published in the centennial issue of the local newspaper. Although the minister and his family eventually moved away, his wife returned to Riverfront after her husband's death to be close to her children and grandchildren.

During our fieldwork in Riverfront, the experiences that we shared with friends and acquaintances were powerful enough to leave us feeling that we could live our lives as members of this town. We felt a sense of acceptance from people in Riverfront—and we seemed to readily solve (on our own) the problems we encountered living there as new arrivals.

The situation that we knew then has apparently changed for newcomers in Riverfront today. The lively and yet cozy American town that we had come to know has changed, as Riverfront has undergone many of the same changes affecting other American towns. What does its future hold?

A TRANQUIL PLACE AND AN INTENSE SITE

Away from the public square and downtown area, driving around the town and its environs in September 2002 and August 2003, we were impressed with the tranquility. We drove on several renovated roads but saw little traffic on them. The shopping zone at the north end of the town, which used to be one of the busiest zones, was now quiet, the pace slow, in part because it was summertime. Also, a supermarket was gone, and a gas station stood closed, as if abandoned. We found that within this commercial zone, a new-style supermarket had been built, and the YMCA buildings had been expanded and redecorated with pastel colors. However, the residential area that spread across most of the town was still full of its old houses, and as peaceful as had been before.

The contrasts among brand-new, relatively new, old, and very old elements made the town "cool" in a postmodern sense. To us, the town seemed at once both an intimate place, as well as somehow distant, remote. This mosaic quality of Riverfront compelled us to shift our focus from different scenes, a mix of old and traditional scenes, new and modern, and in-betweens in different degrees. This is similar to the pictures that a digital camera captures and stores. Because digital cameras are easy to operate, we found ourselves inclined to take more pictures of more varied subjects than we had done before with our analogue camera.

To understand the mosaic quality of life and culture in today's Riverfront, we found it useful to think in a digital mode, where everything is connectable and reconnectable. When we were in Riverfront in the 1980s, we were still thinking in the analogue mode, where everything is ordered in a sequence. For example, when we used an analogue video camera to film social interactions and events at a day care center and a senior center, the camera itself reinforced our belief that events followed on previous events, and that social interactions took place like a chain of actions. We unconsciously extended this mode of cognition to a place like the public square, and even imagined the whole town in this way. Thus, even as we still studied the culture of Riverfront, by midpoint in our first fieldwork, we felt that we had already captured it. However, although we thought we had captured the culture, we hadn't. Looking back, we now reinterpret our earlier impression of Riverfront culture, which was even then shifting, changing, and becoming more pluralistic.

Returning to Japan after fieldwork, we continued to use an analogue mode of viewing and describing Riverfront culture to frame our interpretations. During the post-fieldwork period, the distance separating Riverfront in the United States and us in Japan seemed to grow larger. Eventually the distance became too vast for us to feel we were still attached to the world of Riverfront, its people and culture. That bothered us, because Riverfront was in one sense our "hometown," the place where our son was born. We wanted to keep alive the sense of connection with Riverfront, both for professional and personal reasons.

One incident suddenly made the mental distance between the American Midwest and Japan very small. At a supermarket in Japan in the early 1990s, we saw stacked cases of "ice beer" brewed in Wisconsin. Major Japanese supermarket companies had begun to import foods, wines, and beers from all over the world. Globalization seemed to prevail. The media in Japan announced that now economic activities were no longer confined within borders, but had become trans-regional and transnational.[4] We were surprised to find that a mere can of beer with a Wisconsin brewery label had such an impact on our worldview. Seeing the Wisconsin "ice beer" every time we shopped at our Japanese supermarket made us feel that people in Riverfront and "we" in Japan consumed the same product at the same time. We began to feel as if we were next-door neighbors. At about the same time, Internet and e-mail were also becoming popular. As these things entered our everyday life, our sense of a faraway Riverfront left us.

By the middle of the 1990s, agencies and organizations in Riverfront began to use Web sites. From our home in Japan, we were able to learn about Riverfront activities, past and future events, and people, as if we were there in Riverfront, reading their bulletin boards or the monthly newsletter. Using a search engine on the Internet, we were surprised to hit the Web sites of Riverfront government agencies and the Chamber of Commerce, welcoming visitors to the Riverfront community. We even found Web sites of bed-and-breakfasts, a brand new form of business in Riverfront. For towns across the United States, the Internet had become a major means of advertising their community and businesses. However, moving from Web site to Web site, it isn't easy for viewers to distinguish features of a specific town from those of the others, because the categories of information are similar everywhere.

Thanks to economic globalization and Internet technology, we have regained a "closeness" and sense of community with Riverfront. Because of this, we realized that we needed to decide whether we should see changes in Riverfront as happening within a range of Midwestern regional change, or as happening in the greater context of a globalizing world. For instance, bed-and-breakfasts did not exist in Riverfront in the 1980s and did not fit our image of Riverfront as a Midwestern town. Should we consider them as part of the local culture, or as introduced from the outside? We decided they were from outside the region, that they were part of national or perhaps even global cultural movements. Although a change may appear local and initiated by a grassroots movement, this may not in fact be the case. Because of new communication technologies, people in different places can simultaneously and readily share ideas about change, even specific changes. Thus, in the context of Riverfront, the bed-and-breakfasts were different from older grassroots movements, which were perhaps best exemplified by Kataryna Baszka's personal initiative to paint eastern European designs on building walls in the public square, symbolically celebrating the cultural heritage of Riverfront and its pride in immigrants' contributions to the community.

Through our eyes, as local and regional colors continued to fade away, a more generic color—perhaps a more global or universal color—began to prevail in Riverfront. In 1999, we were intrigued that a grand opening ceremony was held for a supermarket that was part of a locally based, but regional company. The new store was located in a recently developed commercial zone, along a state highway, just beyond the intersection with a federal freeway. The new commercial zone was intended to serve as a strategic site for the region's commercial activities, as well as for local ones. Formerly an agricultural area, this zone was now lined on both sides of the road with large-scale stores. Many were open 24 hours a day. Some of them were nationwide companies, whereas others were regional ones.[5] The supermarket company based in Riverfront had consolidated its smaller old branches to make one giant store, following national commercial trends. It was built alongside other large company stores.

To us, both the outward appearance and interiors of the stores were the same as ones in other places, such as California, where we had lived during graduate school. They did not carry any regional Midwestern signs or marks. We felt lost and asked ourselves, were we still in California, Wisconsin, or somewhere else altogether? We wondered who came to shop at midnight in the stores that were open 24 hours a day. Apparently people came from all over the region—not just Riverfront—because now all the roads were upgraded, and the stores that used to be scattered were now concentrated in this shared zone.

Such commercial zones could be identified as sites into which labor and money are intensively poured, concentrated in the form of employment and investment. This kind of site, which we refer to as an "intense site," contrasts with the town's sense of tranquility, as we have experienced and described it. Here, we do not use the term *intensity* to refer to a level of noise. We mean the level of human energy invested in a specific place.[6] Before the establishment of the "giant" shopping zone, Riverfront had four distinct commercial areas located in town: the downtown, north end, east end, and south end. Still earlier in Riverfront history (in the first half of the twentieth century), many small or family-owned grocery stores had been scattered in residential areas all over town. These changes distinguished Riverfront as a town from places outside it.

We have seen changes in the commercial domain of the town and found the "intense site" as context for the whole tranquil town. In the domain of housing in

Riverfront, we have seen parallel changes. Nationwide in the 1980s, there was a construction boom in apartment building. Riverfront was no exception. Local investors and real estate developers funded new apartments as additions to the old residential area. In contrast, by the early 2000s, a huge vacant space beside the federal freeway just at the edge of the town was developed for residents, but the new houses were large and painted with bright colors. These houses were not in a Midwestern style, but similar to the ones we had come to know and recognize in California. The developers must not have been local. We wondered who would buy so many large houses? Then we learned from our former neighbor that most of them had already been sold. Because vast sums of money must have been invested into this new residential "district" of town, we would also identify this district as an intense site, similar to the giant shopping zone. The two new developments seemed to go hand in hand.

We asked ourselves, what would happen to the old residential area, full of old houses? It seems clear to us that as the local inhabitants age and leave, younger people are moving into the older houses, which they repair, renovate, and remodel. Without them, many older houses would fall into ruin and become vacant. The experience of middle-sized towns such as Riverfront seem to mirror the changes in larger cities—differentiating into an inner city of lower-income people and suburbs of middle-income residents.

Given this general direction of change, we wondered who would become the primary inhabitants of downtown Riverfront? It seems likely that in the future these residents will be Hmong, who are now increasingly settling there. Two Asian grocery stores in different residential areas suggest that Hmong will continue to stay in Riverfront. We are inclined to think that the course of the town's development will once again return to an earlier pattern, when neighborhood stores served local residents. Of course, this time we expect that the small grocery stores will coexist alongside giant shopping zones.

CHANGES IN FARMING PRACTICE

The contrast between intense and tranquil sites found in town can also be found in the surrounding farming area. The farming families that we had occasionally visited during our fieldwork seemed to have survived the so-called "farm crisis" of the middle 1980s. In 2002, we revisited members of two of those families: Ronald (who is of Polish descent) and Gale (of Norwegian background). We met each of them at their respective farms. Although we had not been in contact with them for more than a decade, they remembered us and readily talked to us about changes in farm and family during the 1990s.

Ronald told us that in our absence a critical change took place on farms in this area, in effect dividing farmers into two types: those who abandoned farming altogether and those who intensified their farming enterprises, enlarging their holdings and operations. The latter type doubled their farming acreage. Ronald is representative of the first type. In 1987, he farmed about 240 acres of land, renting 80 acres from a neighboring farm family. He decided to quit farming in the early 1990s.

Before he had taken up farming, he had held a job in town. When his father died in 1976, he inherited his family's dairy farm. He was then 27, and his mother had continued to work on the farm with him. When we first met this family, his mother had told us that farmers of the day needed more management skills, and that her son had good ones to help him succeed at operating their relatively large farm. Although his mother knew how to drive a tractor and a few hired men helped out, Ronald himself was the primary worker and the one who managed the farm. Ronald's wife had her own full-time job in town, and therefore was not involved in running the farm. Although his only brother lived close by, he had had no interest in farming. Ronald had depended on community goodwill to overcome the difficult times; when milk prices were flat, many farms were at risk, and his own farm's operating expenses were increasing.

Remembering his plan to keep the farm, we had expected continuity in Ronald's farming enterprise when we visited him in 2002. Entering from a local highway into the farmlands northeast of Riverfront, we were relieved to feel the same tranquil atmosphere as before. We saw the familiar house, where Ronald's mother lived, and the same barns, too. As we arrived, Ronald was loading hay into the old truck, and his son was helping him. It seemed that they were still farming, and had managed to keep the family business. Loading hay was part of Ronald's regular farmwork; his son had come home to help from Milwaukee, where he was a graduate student in business administration. We were curious to learn about Ronald's experiences managing the farm during the intervening years.

The story Ronald told us was totally different from what we had expected. Ronald now kept only a few cows. Growing and harvesting hay was not a demanding part of his job any more. Now he worked as a professional photographer, with his own studio located at the farm. He told us that in the early 1990s, when in his early forties, he faced a turning point in his life. A Vietnam veteran, Ronald wondered what he would do if he quit farming, because he was supporting his wife while she completed her doctorate.

As he began searching for alternative work, he started taking classes offered to nontraditional students at the state university in Riverfront. All the while, he gradually began to minimize his farming operation. He first considered training in the natural sciences, but because he was already in his forties, he realized this was not a realistic career choice. While scanning through a list of courses, a photography class caught his eye, and he signed up. Encouraged by praise from his instructor and classmates in response to his class projects, he realized that photography could become his new profession. With his family in full support of his decision, he entered a one-year training program for professional photographers at a school in Colorado. After finishing school, he opened his studio at home on the farm. As his reputation as a good photographer spread, his business flourished, and he found himself well satisfied with his new job.

Ronald's case is an example of a successful career change. Of course, a shift from farmer to studio photographer is unusual. When we met Ronald and his family for the first time in the mid-1980s, we had not predicted this change. However, considering the developmental stage of his family at the time of his decision, his career change was not wholly unpredictable. We heard about another case, a farmer who was a generation older than Ronald and a man also of Polish descent. He took over his father's farm and became a farmer, but later left farming to become a politician. This case and Ronald's have one point in common: both men wanted to keep their parents' farm, even after quitting farming. This may be important in maintaining a sustainable and satisfying life in a rural area today.

Many farmers sell their farmland when they quit or retire from farming. Some of them retain a small parcel on which to retire. Still others leave the farm holdings to live in town. Their neighbors who want to expand their farming take this opportunity to acquire more land, often at sale prices. In some cases, younger relatives, like nephews, buy up the family farm. Occasionally one of the farmer's own children, usually a son, takes over his parents' farm. In Ronald's case, his only son was pursuing a business administration degree, and his daughter was a medical school student. As long as Ronald kept the farm, his son (or his daughter's future husband) might at some future time take up farming, when farming again becomes an attractive economic enterprise.

In contrast to Ronald, Gale retired from farming in the 1990s at age 60. One of his sons later decided to develop the family farming enterprise. Both of Gale's sons, after graduating from high school, began to help their father on the farm. When we first visited them during our fieldwork, Gale told us in an interview that he planned to let one of his sons take over the management of his farm when he retired.

When we visited them again in 2002, Gale had retired and he and his wife had moved into a house in the woods, on the edge of town and near the farm. Chris, his younger son, lived with his wife and two young children in Gale's former house on the farm. Gale's older son became a local fire department chief and lived in a town close by. His daughter, a student in pharmacology in the middle 1980s, now worked as a manager at a pharmacy in the giant commercial area. As we expected, Gale's family had continued to develop their farming enterprise.

In the 1990s, when he took over his parents' farm, Chris was in his early twenties. Unlike Ronald who eventually abandoned farming to take up a new career, Chris sought to develop a new way of farming. He studied new technologies, planned and tried what he thought would be good for a new era of farming, and even consulted with university professors. For these contacts, Chris drew on his father's connections in agriculture at the University of Wisconsin. In the end, Chris finally decided on a plan to combine dairy farming with a recycling plant for processing cow waste. An automated and systematized milking plant was needed, and a new system of storing milk had to be developed. The whole idea was designed to create a more effective and competitive milk production enterprise, beyond the conventional mode of dairy farming. The new intensive operation required new electronic, mechanical, and biotechnologies and expertise, in addition to traditional agricultural know-how. Gale was still assisting this son, while the older son (when off duty from the fire department) came to help with the technical aspects of the operation.

Between 1961 and 1984, Gale had expanded his farm holdings from 200 acres to about 450 acres, in part over concern about local farming conditions. He tried to prevent the price of farmland from dropping by participating in farm auctions, which were taking place in his neighborhood as farmers quit farming. At these auctions, farmers sold everything, including houses and furniture, agricultural machinery and tools, as well as the farmland itself. Gale's own earlier expansion had served as a platform for his son's plan, which required large holdings that could support the construction of a family "factory."

Approaching Gale's farm, we saw a huge concrete building, which did indeed appear to be a factory. We speculated that Gale's family had sold their lands to a large corporation, perhaps during the 1990s. It looked so different from the traditional image of the family farm that we remembered. However, when we found that the family had kept the farm, we were simply amazed by how the farm had been developed. We were even more amazed, as we followed Gale's pickup truck to the huge roofed cowshed, similar in appearance to the huge stores built in the giant commercial area in Riverfront.

The intense site on this farm stood in vivid contrast to Ronald's tranquil farmlands. Intensive and sophisticated farming operations like Gale and Chris's are now busy crossroads of the new and old skills and technologies, machines and know-how, systems and labor. The workers we met at the farm confirmed the fact that now the family could not run the farm on their own, but needed outside workers. Before, it had been customary to hire extra hands from neighboring farms, usually young men of European backgrounds. Now the hired workers were Spanish-speaking people.

In the mid-1980s, retired seniors in Riverfront had told us that local farmers had traditionally hired migrant workers to help out during the harvesting season. They worked on the cucumber and other vegetable farms south of Riverfront. We had no chance to see them at work, but we saw signs in Spanish on the wall of a Catholic church, built in the middle of a farming area. Now Chris employed several migrants for the milking plant and other farming operations. We were intrigued that they were working in the plant, but we assumed that they were only temporary, seasonal workers. It became increasingly clear, however, that this was their regular job. That fact made us feel that we were "getting lost" again, and we wondered whether we were in Wisconsin, California, or somewhere else.

We weren't anxious about the changes we saw that were transforming the Riverfront we had known in the 1980s. Rather, we were becoming aware that the recent changes in the area's ethnic map would have a major impact on the town in the future. The new arrivals, bringing their different, rich cultural heritages, would profoundly reshape everyday life and culture in Riverfront. We listened to a 2003 National Public Radio program that reported on similar changes occurring in another Midwestern town. A small town in Nebraska had undergone a major shift in its ethnic composition. As the senior generation of residents aged, the junior generation moved to urban areas, and new residents arrived from Mexico.

Another example of broader trends in cultural change in the Riverfront area was provided by the case of the local Amish. We had visited their community during the 1980s and were relieved to find that their farms had survived the recent decade of rapid change. Although a slower-paced lifestyle seems everywhere to be gaining in popularity, the local Amish have managed since the 1970s to continue to live their comparatively tranquil rural lifestyle, even as changes radically transformed farming practice in the communities around them. As non-Amish farmers began to quit their farms, selling off their land, Amish farmers acquired new land and expanded their farms.

In 2003, we attended the Amish quilt auction that was held at the local fairgrounds (see Figure 15.3). In the 1980s, we had also attended their auction, but

Courtesy of Mariko Fujita-Sano, August 2003.

Figure 15.3 Amish men help with their quilt auction in a rural town (August 2003).

it had been held outside in the middle of a farm field, not at the fairgrounds. At the time, that fairground had no roofed facility, just the wide-open skies. Many buyers came to look at the colorful handmade quilts hanging from poles. Non-Amish venders sold drinks and sandwiches. We tried to take pictures of the gathering from a distance, but a member of the auction committee immediately noticed us and announced over the speaker system that, "photos are not allowed." They sold all kinds of baked goods, which seemed quite popular. Inside a kitchen house, a group of young women made donuts from scratch, selling fresh ones at the window counters. Young Amish helped out by showing off the auctioned goods. They were cheerful, and our image of the Amish as a poised and quiet people seemed confirmed by what we saw. We were probably hoping to see "authentic" Amish on that first visit, but both Amish and other people at the auction mixed so naturally, that we soon got used to what contemporary Amish people are really like. The auctioneers seemed like family members, and we were told that their family name was an Amish name established in the area.

On both of our visits to the Amish quilt auction, we found the Amish themselves actively engaged in the organization of the event. They assumed roles as auctioneer's assistants, bakers, ice-cream makers, quilters, salespersons, van drivers, and vendors. On both occasions, they wore traditional clothing and head coverings, which served to distinguish them as members of a different ethnic group, and in a sense established them as "authentic" Amish. They did not, however, arrive in one-horse carriages. Probably the biggest difference we observed between our first Amish auction in the 1980s and the one in 2003 was that at the more recent event, the Amish seemed more intensively involved in the auctioning of items from their cultural archive, primarily of course their quilts, but also other handmade and homemade items and foods. We felt they were actively engaged in generating income from the sale of these cultural goods, much more intensively on this last occasion.

The culture business itself is not unique to the Amish, of course. The Riverfront Chamber of Commerce organized a Polish festival downtown in 1985. (We used a picture of a Polish dancing group that we took at that festival for the cover of our case study, *Life in Riverfront* [Fujita and Sano 2001].) Both the Polish festival and the Amish quilt auction are good examples of how ethnicity can be employed to generate income, as well as reaffirm ethnic identity in an era of rapid culture change. Thinking back over the difference in the Amish auctions of two eras, we now feel that the Amish may no longer be able to escape from engaging in activities at intense sites (even if only temporarily) and using these sites to sustain their tranquil lifestyles.

A CHANGING ETHNIC AND ECONOMIC MAP

When we left Riverfront in the mid-1980s, we speculated that it would remain a town of predominantly Americans of European descent. Hmong and Spanish-speaking people seemed to be but temporary residents, and there seemed to be no specific reason for them to choose to settle in Riverfront. We assumed that Wisconsin towns would not experience the population shifts undergone in California towns in the 1980s, during which immigrants of Asian, Mexican, or Latin American origins increased their populations substantially. We anticipated that the African American population might increase, because we knew about the new demographic trends in Milwaukee and Madison in the mid-1980s. We therefore expected to see a similar growth in that population in central Wisconsin, but not an increase in the Asian- and Spanish-speaking communities. Contrary to our predictions, however, the number of African Americans in Riverfront did not increase.

From our perspective, we are tempted to say that in the areas of ethnic and economic change, a "Californiazation" has taken place in Wisconsin. In a reverse of the population shift that took place more than a century ago, now the trend is for people to move eastward from the West. Further supporting our thesis is the recent arrival in Wisconsin of the California-style huge commercial zones, built of nationwide chain stores. In the area of economic change specifically, we feel that the term *globalization* might be more appropriate than *Californiazation,* because many of the nationwide corporations originated in Midwestern and Northern towns, not the West. Also, workers arrive in the Midwest from the South, even beyond the national border, from rural towns in Mexico. This movement is described as the northerly flow of immigrants from Mexico to the United States.[7] We are suggesting that the narrower term *Californiazation* (rather than globalization) might be even more helpful in understanding the specific culture changes we saw happening in Wisconsin.

By *Californiazation,* we mean that encountering people of European, Asian, and Mexican backgrounds is now becoming a dominant feature of people's everyday lives in Riverfront, especially in public places such as schools, churches, shopping centers, the workplace, and at community events. Economically it means that goods carried by local chain stores are of modern design, durable, functional, and inexpensive—all qualities that meet the needs of both Riverfront newcomers and long-term residents. With regard to the local economy, Riverfront has long been considered a place lacking in suitable opportunities for young people. This does not mean that jobs haven't been available for young workers, but that the jobs that were available were unattractive to younger generation of Riverfront Americans of European descent. There were jobs to be had, however, and Hmong- and Spanish-speaking people arriving in Riverfront discovered economic opportunities.

The term *Californiazation* also suggests a time lag between the population shift that was experienced earlier in the West and only now in the Midwest. Until recently, Americans of European descent in the Riverfront area had been trying to maintain a lifestyle established when the first generation of immigrants settled in the area. In other words, Riverfront and its environs had until very recently retained a Wisconsin-ness and Midwestern-ness. In contrast, California has long had the more diverse ethnic composition characteristic of a cosmopolitan place.

How had Riverfront kept such Midwestern-ness? We think that the retiring generation of Riverfront residents, whom we met and interviewed in the mid-1980s, was probably the last one to play a role in maintaining the distinctly Midwestern culture and community. Most of them had chosen to live, work, and retire in the same place as their own parents. This commitment to remain in the Midwest contrasts with the choices made by members of the next generation—who feel unconstrained to remain in Riverfront and free to relocate upon retirement. We believe that we have witnessed the last generation that will actively produce and maintain traditional Midwestern culture. Even if members of the next generation of retirees choose to stay in Riverfront, as a cohort they are highly mobile and more likely to up and move whenever and wherever the fulfilled life seems to beckon. They are as a generation more detached from Riverfront, the place where they were born and raised. To us, it seems no new generation is in place that will live and recreate the distinctive culture of Midwestern-ness. This is true of both the town of Riverfront, as well as the surrounding farming area, as we have seen. Interviews at the senior center in Riverfront, which we often visited during fieldwork, revealed more about the changing local culture.

THE TRANSFORMATION OF THE SENIOR CENTER

In August 2003, we visited senior centers in Riverfront, as well as in San Francisco's Bay Area in California. The senior centers in both places have undergone similar transformations. As a major trend, retired persons, who formerly were the primary users, seem less interested in senior center programs and activities today. In general, the seniors of this generation are healthier, enjoy more active lives, and are engaged in a wide range of activities outside of senior centers.

Courtesy of Mariko Fujita-Sano, August 2003.

Figure 15.4 In 1985, participants at a meal program in the senior center that has just been reorganized as the Aging and Disability Resource Center

The senior center movement in the United States began in the 1970s, reaching its height during the 1980s, when its senior meal program and social activities enjoyed peak popularity. At the Jefferson Center in Riverfront in the 1980s, more than 100 senior citizens came to the center for lunch every day, and the atmosphere was lively. By the late 1990s, however, the number of meal program users dropped by almost half, and the new lunchtime atmosphere was decidedly more tranquil (see Figure 15.4). In its place, however, a new program has risen in popularity in Riverfront and in the Bay Area—the "home delivery" senior meal program. In addition, today senior centers in both places have continued to find other ways to meet the needs of its new seniors, especially by establishing more exercise classes (see Figure 15.5) to keep pace with the growing concern over health and fitness among the new generation of seniors.

As we learned from our interviews in Riverfront, the largest transformation in senior services at Jefferson Center occurred during the late 1990s with the reorganization and expansion of its program to accommodate the needs of disabled seniors through assisted living arrangements. This transformation was accomplished with county participation, and resulted in the remodeling of the old center and construction of the new two-story building complex. Into this new program and building, both funds and staff were heavily invested, thus making it another intensive site. This marked the end of one era, but the beginning of another: The era of the senior center as a drop-in meal and service provider had passed. In a sense, one idea—the senior center as a tranquil place—had been

Courtesy of Toshiyuki Sano, August 2003.

Figure 15.5 Exercise class in the early morning at Riverfront's senior center (August 2003).

merged with another idea—the center as an assisted living facility, an intensively managed site. Such transformations in the senior center are parallel to other recent changes we have described for Riverfront and its surrounding area. None of these changes were local grassroots movements, but instead followed trends occurring nationwide.

CONCLUDING REMARKS

When we first encountered it, Riverfront was a changing world. We found that the most pervasive and profound cultural changes were occurring in the areas of ethnicity, employment, commercial activities, and services for the elderly. The combined impact of these changes is the fundamental transformation of local culture. In Riverfront, the celebrated family-centered lifestyle, a hallmark of Midwestern culture in general, does not now seem to characterize culture at the community level, but remains powerful at the family level. Although the image of a community of families has not lost its symbolic power, we expect that the major shift in ethnic composition in Riverfront heralds a future in which diverse peoples will celebrate the family, each according to their different cultural heritage.

To capture the rapidly changing local culture of Riverfront, we employed the imagery of digital (as opposed to analogue) camera technology. In our earlier fieldwork, the technology and capabilities of the analogue camera that we used shaped our very interpretation of local culture change: events and actions seemed to occur in an ordered, historical sequence. A decade later, our return field trips showed us the limitations of both analogue camera technology and the world-view that it created. Setting out with our digital camera, we found that we were better able to capture the fast stream of changes occurring simultaneously at multiple sites and in different domains of social life. In addition, we discovered that our new perspective on change could be best conveyed using the digital camera as a metaphor: the plethora of local changes created a mosaic quality to contemporary Riverfront life and culture, in which images were seemingly unconnected to one another; with digital technology these images could be recombined and the connections between them revealed. We also found that digital photography (both as method and metaphor) could be employed to capture change as intensifying and tranquilizing movements occurring at various sites both in town and in the rural areas. *Intensive* and *tranquil* sites are of course two terms we employ to describe a changed sociocultural landscape. We predict that the social benefits created by new intensive sites—with their intensive energy and information flows and heavy financial investment (all in a compact space)—can perhaps best be enjoyed alongside tranquil sites. We expect that tranquil sites will in the future continue to sustain and enhance the quality of life for people in Riverfront.

We have found the term *Californiazation* to be especially useful in describing the nature of changes occurring in ethnic composition in Riverfront. The arrival of significant populations from Asia and Mexico, together with the departure of Americans of European descent, has profoundly reshaped life and culture in Riverfront. This ethnic shift has been accompanied by commercial changes that support the new cultural diversity. We think it is inevitable that some people will experience these changes as a loss of community and identity. Together with other changes in its "local" cultural characteristics, Riverfront is increasingly becoming one of America's "universal" towns. We think that in the context of such towns, the concept of ethnicity itself will inevitably change. In the 1980s, we conceived of ethnicity as something to be expressed, a response to the historical suppression of ethnic markers. More recently, we have found ethnic identity and practices employed as cultural resources. In Riverfront, ethnicity today is not only a symbol of the town's historical and cultural heritage, but it is increasingly becoming an economic enterprise to attract tourists and promote local business.

REFERENCES

Fishman, Robert. 1996. Re-Imagining Los Angeles. In *Rethinking Los Angeles*, ed. M. J. Dear, H. E. Schockman, and G. Hise, 251–261. London: Sage.

Fujita, Mariko, and Toshiyuki Sano. 2001. *Life in Riverfront: A Middle-Western town seen through Japanese eyes*. Fort Worth, Texas: Harcourt Brace College Publishers.

Grey, Mark A., and Anne C. Woodrick. 2002. Unofficial sister cities: Meatpacking labor migration between Villachuato, Mexico, and Marshalltown, Iowa." *Human Organization* 61 (4): 364–376.

Harvey, David. 1989. *The condition of postmodernity: An inquiry into the origins of cultural change*. Oxford: Blackwell.

Kelly, Marjorie. 2003. Projecting an image and expressing identity: T-shirts in Hawaii. *Fashion Theory* 7 (2): 191–212.

Sassen, Saskia. 1995. On concentration and centrality in the global city. In *World cities in a world-system,* ed. Paul I. Knox and Peter J. Taylor, 63–75. Cambridge: Cambridge Univ. Press.

Schneider, Mary Jo. 1998. The Wal-Mart annual meeting: From small-town America to a global corporate culture. *Human Organization* 57 (3): 292–299.

Spindler, George, and Louise Spindler. 1990. *The American cultural dialogue and its transmission.* New York: Falmer Press.

NOTES

1. The Japan Society for the Promotion of Science supported our revisit to Riverfront in 1999, as well as our additional field research trips in 2002 and in 2003.

2. To understand changes in the early 1990s, we think it is important to examine cultural dialogues in people's decision making. See Spindler and Spindler (1990).

3. Among the major concerns for those who rethink the larger cities like Los Angeles are a community's downtown and "market square"; see Fishman (1996).

4. For an example, see Harvey (1989).

5. The contrast between chained and rooted businesses is mentioned to show the recent changes in Hawaii's consumer cultures; see Kelly (2003). One of the chained corporations has a history of early years in a small town; see Schneider (1998).

6. A similar concept to *intense* is *concentration* in the larger cities derived from globalization; see Sassen (1995).

7. See Grey and Woodrick (2002).

Index

Aborigines. *See* Mardu
Acquired Immune Deficiency Syndrome. *See* AIDS
African Americans
  culture of, 80, 81
  gang membership among, xx–xxi, 74, 89.
    See also Gangs
  oppression of, 74, 77
African immigrants, 285. *See also*
    Immigrants/Immigration; Migration/Mobility
Agriculture/Horticulture/Pastoralism
  in Aztec Empire, 3, 15–17
  by Canela, 25–26, 29, 30, 36, 37, 39–40, 41
  by crofters, 307–308, 310–312, 327, 328
  gender roles and, 345, 346
  in Greece, 336, 338, 339, 342, 345, 346
  by Ju/'hoansi, 146–148, 150, 153–155
  by Mardu, 235, 237–238, 241
  in Melemchi, 200–203, 206–207, 210, 211,
    214, 216, 218
  by Minangkabau, 130–131, 132, 139, 140
  by Rashaayda Bedouin, 256–257, 262, 263–264,
    273, 277
  in Riverfront, 355–356, 361–366
  by Sambia, 98, 113–114
  technology in, 363, 364
  in Yucatán, 175–178, 180, 182–183
AIDS
  in Africa, 145, 156–169
  alcohol use and, 161, 162, 163, 164, 165–167,
    168, 169
  deaths from, 157, 162–163
  history of, 157
  incidence of, 144, 157, 158–159, 168
  prevention of, 159–160, 163, 167, 168–169
  rape and, 167
  transmission of, 157, 161–164, 168
  women's autonomy and, 159–161, 167
Alcohol use
  AIDS and, 161, 162, 163, 164, 165–167,
    168, 169
  by Canela, 33–34
  by Ju/'hoansi, 148–149, 151, 152, 154, 161, 162,
    163, 164, 165–167, 168, 169
  by Mardu, 228–229, 242, 243, 244, 246,
    248, 251
  sexual activity and, 161, 162, 163, 164, 165–167,
    168, 169
Altepetl, 4, 10, 11, 20–21. *See also* Aztec Empire,
    political organization of
Amish, 364–366
Anthropology/Anthropologists
  on culture, 229
  on culture change, xix–xxvii, 294–295, 297,
    300, 308, 351–352, 353

ethnography and, xvii, xxiii, 79
on globalization, xvii, xxiii, 173–174
on immigrants/immigration, 285–287,
    297, 300
on power, 251
on small-scale societies, 229, 230
on social change, 229–231
Asian immigrants, 285, 286, 288, 293, 353–354,
    355–357, 361, 366, 367, 370. *See also*
    Immigrants/Immigration; Migration/Mobility
Australia
  aboriginal peoples of. *See* Mardu
  colonization of, 226, 228, 231, 235, 241
  gender roles/hierarchy in, xix–xx, 97–116.
    See also Sambia
  migration to, 286
  mobility within, xxii–xxiii, 225–255.
    See also Mardu
  tourism in, 246
Aztec Empire, xxi–xxii, 1–23
  agriculture in, 3, 15–17
  conquest of, 1, 2, 8–9
  development of, 2–4
  disease in, 9–10
  economy of, 6–7, 13–15, 20
  end of, 9, 15
  ethnic groups in, 11–12
  military action by, 3, 5–6, 9
  political organization of, 3, 4, 10–11, 15, 20
  religion in, 7–8, 18–19, 20
  social stratification in, 5–6, 10–12, 20
  Spanish influences on, 15–19, 20
  territory of, 3, 4

Bani Rashid (of Saudi Arabia), 261, 272–277
Bedouin. *See* Rashaayda Bedouin
Berdan, Francis, xxi–xxii, 1
bin Laadin, Usaama, 265
Bishop, Naomi, xxi, 199–200
Blackwood, Evelyn, xxii, 117
Botswana
  agriculture in, 154–155
  AIDS in, xxii, 144, 156, 157. *See also* Ju/'hoansi,
    AIDS among
  history of, 168
  independence of, 146
  tourism in, 155
  water supply in, 148, 155
  wildlife conservation in, 154–155
Brazil
  migration from, 287
  native peoples of, xix, 24–52. *See also* Canela
Buddhism, 205, 208, 210, 214–215, 216, 219
Bushmen. *See* Ju/'hoansi

California (migration to), xxi, 283–284, 285
Canela (of Brazil), xix, 24–52
  agriculture/horticulture by, 25–26, 29, 30, 36, 37,
    39–40, 41
  alcohol use by, 33–34
  clothing of, 26, 35, 47
  cultural influences on, 26, 29, 31, 32, 34, 35, 41,
    43–44, 45–46, 47–48, 48
  diaries of, 27–28, 31–32, 39, 41
  disease among, 30, 48
  economy of, 29, 30–31, 32, 34, 43–44, 48–49
  education of, 29, 31, 32, 35, 38–39, 40, 41, 45, 49
  environment of, 24–25, 28–29, 34, 48
  government influence on, 28, 30, 31, 35–36,
    37, 40, 48
  history of, 29–31, 48
  housing of, 26
  language of, 28, 37–38, 39, 44, 47
  plucking facial hair by, 26, 29, 32, 34, 35, 41,
    44, 46–46, 49
  religion of, 29, 30, 31, 37, 39, 49
  sharing by, 25–26, 29, 30, 48
  social stratification of, 30–31, 32, 34–35, 37,
    38, 39, 40–41, 42–44, 45–46, 47–48
  study of, 26–28
  violence against, 25, 30, 36, 40, 47, 48
Capitalism (as transnational force), 295–296.
    See also Economy/Economics
Catholicism, 175, 307, 320. See also Christianity
Chavez, Leo, xxi, 283
Chicago, xx, 73, 89
China, xxi, 53–72
  crime in, 65
  cultural diversity in, 53–54, 56, 58, 59, 67
  economy in, 54, 59, 62–63, 64, 65, 66
  ethnic identity in, 53, 54, 55–56, 61–62, 63.
      See also Han population; Uygur nationalists
  foreign policy of, 62–63
  future of, 67–68
  globalization in, 56
  government in, 53, 54, 56, 59, 60, 62–63,
    65–66, 67
  history of, 56, 59, 64–65, 67
  human rights in, 56
  Jews in, 63
  languages in, 56, 59, 62, 64, 65
  migration from, 64
  migration within, 54, 64, 65
  military in, 67–68
  Muslims in, 54, 55–56, 62–63, 68, 69
  national security in, 53–54, 63, 67–68
  nationalism in, 53, 54–56, 57–58, 61, 67, 69
  population of, 61
  religion in, 54, 55–56, 59–60, 62–63
  separatism in, 67–70
  social stratification in, 61–62
  terrorism and, 53–54, 67
  tourism in, 63
  violence in, 54–56, 63, 65
Christianity. See also specific denominations
  colonization and spread of, 8, 18–19, 118–119,
    175, 295
  among Mardu, 232, 235, 238–241, 242, 249–251

  missionaries of, 97–98, 106, 108, 113, 115, 232,
    235, 238, 240–241, 242, 249–251, 319
  in Sumatra, 118–119
Church of Scotland, 319. See also Free Church
Ciall (Scotland), 308. See also Crofters
Clothing
  of Canela, 26, 35, 47
  of Rashaayda Bedouin, 263–264
Colonization
  of Australia, 226, 228, 230, 231, 235, 241
  Christianity and, 8, 18–19, 118–119, 175, 295
  disease and, 9–10
  of Mexico, xxi–xxii, 1, 2, 8–9, 174, 175. See also
    Aztec Empire
  of Namibia, 150–152, 153
  religion and, 8, 18–19, 118–119, 175, 295
  of Sudan, 262
  world systems theory and, 173–174
Communism (in China), 54, 59, 65–66
Commuting (in Yucatán), 190–193
Condom use (and AIDS prevention), 159–160,
    163, 167
Cordemex, 180, 181, 184, 191
Cortés, Hernán, 2, 8
Cowboy (origin of word), 298–299
Criminal justice system (and gangs), 77–78, 82–83,
    87–89, 95
Crocker, William and Jean, xix, 24, 26–28
Crofters (of Scotland), xx, 304–333
  agriculture by, 307–308, 310–312, 327, 328
  cultural change experienced by, 326–327
  cultural traditions of, 314
  definition of, 305
  economy of, 305, 325, 328, 329
  as "exiles," 324, 325, 326–327
  fishing by, 308–309, 327–328
  gender roles of, 311, 322–323, 328, 329
  government influence on, 305–306, 309–310,
    312, 314, 329
  history of, 305–306, 309–312, 314
  language of, 309, 315–319, 322, 327
  migration by, 310, 323–326
  music of, 323
  population of, 306, 324–325
  religion of, 306–307, 314, 319–323, 327
  social stratification of, 306–308, 310, 314,
    315–316
  tourism and, 322, 330
  weaving by, 308, 327
Cultural change. See Culture change
Cultural logic, 230
Culture. See each chapter for specific cultures.
  of African Americans, 80, 81
  definition of, 80, 229, 294, 295
  of gangs, 74, 79–81
  migration and, 288, 290–292, 293–300
  passing on knowledge of, 219–220
Culture change. See each chapter for specific
    cultures.
  definition of, xxiii (n1), 229–231
  dimensions of, xviii–xix
  migration and, 288, 290–292, 293–300, 334–337
  study of, xxiii–xxiv (n1), 294–295

Davidson, R. T., 77, 78
Democracy (in China), 54, 65–67
Denmark (migration to), 289, 290
Disease
  AIDS. *See* AIDS
  in Aztec Empire, 9–10
  among Canela, 30, 48
  colonization and, 9–10
  among Mardu, 228–229, 245–246
Dobe Ju/'hoansi. *See* Ju/'hoansi
Drug use, 77, 82, 89. *See also* Alcohol use

Economy/Economics
  of Aztec Empire, 6–7, 13–15, 20
  changes in, xix
  of Canela, 29, 30–31, 32, 34, 43–44, 48–49
  of China, 54, 59, 62–63, 64, 65, 66
  of crofters, 305, 325, 328, 329
  of Greece, 335, 338, 339–340, 342, 343, 344,
    345, 348–349
  of Ju/'hoansi, 148–149, 150, 152, 153, 154,
    166, 167
  of Mardu, 236, 240, 244, 246, 252
  of Melemchi, 201–203, 206–207, 208, 209–212,
    217–219
  migration and, 288, 289
  of Minangkabau, 132, 134, 135–136, 137
  modernization and, xix
  of Rashaayda Bedouin, 256, 262–265, 277
  of Riverfront, 359–360, 361, 363, 367, 370
  of Sambia, 106–107, 113–115
  of Yucatán, 174, 176, 177–178, 179–181,
    182–189, 191–195
Education
  AIDS and, 164–165
  of Canela, 29, 31, 32, 35, 38–39, 40, 41, 45, 49
  gender differences in, 107–109, 114–115, 124–125
  in Greece, 335–336, 338, 339, 340, 341, 342, 345
  of Ju/'hoansi, 149–150, 155–156, 164–165
  of Mardu, 246
  in Melemchi, 206, 209, 212–214
  migration and, 195, 214
  of Minangkabau, 123–125, 127, 131
  of Rashaayda Bedouin, 268, 278
  in Riverfront, 362, 363
  of Sambia, 106, 107–109, 113, 114–115
  in Yucatán, 191, 192, 193, 195
ELF. *See* Eritrean Liberation Front
Emigration, 286. *See also* Immigrants/Immigration;
    Migration/Mobility
Encomendero, 10, 11
England. *See* United Kingdom
EPLF. *See* Eritrean People's Liberation Front
Eritrea, 262, 265–268, 272
Eritrean Liberation Front (ELF), 266–267
Eritrean People's Liberation Front (EPLF), 267–268
Ethiopia (war with Eritrea), 266–268
Ethnicity/Ethnic identity
  in Aztec Empire, 11–12
  in China, xxi, 53–72. *See also* China
  food and, 297–298, 359
  language and, 315–319

  of Rashaayda Bedouin, 258, 261, 263, 268, 273,
    274–277
  in Riverfront, 353–354, 355–358, 364, 366, 370
Ethnography, xvii, xxiii, 79
European immigrants, 285, 286, 288, 325, 353, 354,
    355–357, 358, 364, 366, 367, 370. *See also*
    Immigrants/Immigration; Migration/Mobility

Farming. *See* Agriculture/Horticulture/Pastoralism
Fertility rates (and immigration), 289
Fieldwork, xxiii, xxiv–xxv (n6). *See also*
    Ethnography
Fishing (by crofters), 308–309, 327–328
Food (and ethnic identity), 297–298, 359
Fort, Jeff, 88, 89
Free Church (Scotland), 314, 319–323
Friedl, Ernestine, xx, 334, 336–337, 346–349
Fujita, Mariko, xx, 350

Gaelic language, 315–319, 322
Gangs, xx–xxi, 73–96. *See also* Vice Lords
  culture of, 74, 79–81
  functions of, 78
  legitimate enterprises of, 76, 87
  media coverage of, 75–76, 77–78
  research on, 79, 80
  resources of, 86–87
Gangster Disciples, 76, 77, 78. *See also* Gangs
Geertz, Clifford, 81–82, 229
Gender roles/hierarchies
  agriculture and, 345, 346
  AIDS and, 159
  of crofters, 311, 322–323, 328, 329
  education and, 107–109, 114–115, 124–125
  in Greece, 335, 337, 345–346
  influences on, xviii
  of Mardu, 236
  in Melemchi, 204, 205
  of Minangkabau, 118–119, 120, 125–126
  of Sambia, 97–116. *See also* Sambia
  in Yucatán, 179, 180–181, 184–185
Germany (migration from), 299–300
Gladney, Dru, xxi, 53
Globalization
  anthropologists' perspective on, xvii, xxiii,
    173–174
  capitalism and, 295–296
  in China, 56
  definition of, 295–296
  effects of, xvii, xxiii, 89, 295–297
  in Greece, 336–337
  in Melemchi, 218, 220
  resources about, xxiv (n1)
  in Riverfront, 359–360, 366
  technology and, 297, 359, 360
  Western culture and, 296
  in Yucatán, 173, 174, 195
Government (influence of)
  on Canela, 28, 30, 31, 35–36, 37, 40, 48
  in China, 53, 54, 56, 59, 60, 62–63, 65–66, 67
  on crofters, 305–306, 309–310, 312, 314, 329
  on Ju/'hoansi, 148, 150–152, 163–164

Government (influence of) (*continued*)
  on Mardu, 239, 241–243, 252
  in Melemchi, 206, 209–212
  on Minangkabau, 127–128, 129, 132, 137–138, 140, 141
  on Rashaayda Bedouin, 263, 268
  on Sambia, 105, 107, 109
  in Yucatán, 178, 181, 186–187, 188–189
Great Britain. *See* United Kingdom
Greece, xx, 334–350
  agriculture in, 336, 338, 339, 342, 345, 346
  cultural change experienced in, 334–337
  economy of, 335, 338, 339–340, 342, 343, 344, 345, 348–349
  education in, 335–336, 338, 339, 340, 341, 342, 345
  gender roles in, 335, 337, 345–346
  globalization and, 336–337
  housing in, 343–344
  kinship in, 340–341, 342, 343–344
  marriage in, 335, 336, 338, 339, 340, 341, 342, 343, 344, 345–346
  migration to, 339–340
  migration within, 334–335, 336–344
  population of, 335–336
  social stratification in, 336, 338–339, 341, 342, 343, 346

Hagedorn, John, 79, 80, 81
Hammock industry, 185–186
Han population, 53, 54, 56, 57, 59, 61, 63–65
Henequen cultivation, 175–178, 180, 181, 191
Herdt, Gilbert, xix–xx, 97–98
Hmong immigrants, 353–354, 355–357, 361, 366, 367. *See also* Asian immigrants
Hoover, Larry, 76, 77, 78
Horticulture. *See* Agriculture/Horticulture/Pastoralism
Houses/Housing
  of Canela, 26
  in Greece, 343–344
  in Melemchi, 200
  of Minangkabau, 120–125, 132–140
  of Rashaayda Bedouin, 264
  in Riverfront, 360–361
Hull, Cindy, xxii, 172–173
Human rights (in China), 56
Hunting–gathering societies
  Ju'hoansi as, 144, 146, 148, 150, 151, 155
  Mardu as, 235–236, 243

Identity, xviii, xxiv (n3). *See also* Ethnicity/Ethnic identity; Nationalism/National identity
Illegal immigrants, xxi. *See also* Immigrants/Immigration; Mexican immigrants; Migration/Mobility
Immigrants/Immigration, 283–303. *See also* Migration/Mobility
  anthropologists' study of, 285–287, 297, 300
  attitudes toward, 283–284, 285, 286, 287–292, 297, 357

  children of, 355
  cultural influence of, 288, 290–292, 293–300, 364
  cultural traditions of, 293–295
  economy and, 288, 289
  examples of, 283–285, 287, 292–293, 297–300
  fertility rate and, 289
  kinship and, 340–341, 342, 343–344
  languages of, 285, 286, 357, 364
  national identity and, 286–288, 290
  population and, 324–325
  prevalence of, 285–286
  race and, 289
  reasons for, 284, 285, 286, 287, 289, 325, 337–338, 344
  religion of, 356–357, 358
  to United States, xxi, 64, 283–285, 286, 288, 290, 299–300, 324, 342, 353–354, 355–358, 364, 366, 367, 370
India (migration from), 293
Initiation rites
  of Mardu, 232, 247–248
  of Sambia, 97, 98, 100, 101–102, 103, 104, 107, 108–109, 110
Inner city, 75, 76–77, 78
Islam. *See also* Muslims
  in Saudi Arabia, 265
  in Sudan, 268
  in Sumatra, 118–119
  Vice Lordism as, 90–92
  women's role in, 129, 136
Italy (migration to), 287, 290

Japan (migration to), 286, 287
Jews (in China), 63
Jigalong (Australia), 237, 238, 240, 241, 242, 243. *See also* Mardu
Ju'hoansi (of Botswana/Namibia), xxii, 144–171
  agriculture by, 146–148, 150, 153–155
  AIDS among, 145, 156–170. *See also* AIDS
  alcohol use by, 148–149, 151, 152, 154, 161, 162, 163, 164, 165–167, 168, 169
  cultural influences on, 144–145
  economy of, 148–149, 150, 152, 153, 154, 166, 167
  education of, 149–150, 155–156, 164–165
  government influence on, 148, 150–152, 163–164
  history of, 146–154, 155–156
  as hunting–gathering society, 144, 146, 148, 150, 151, 155
  military and, 150, 151–152, 162, 164
  self-government by, 153–154
  social stratification of, 146
  study of, 144–145
  war and, 151–152
  water supply of, 146, 148, 154

Kathmandau Valley (Nepal), 214–215, 216, 218–219, 220
Keiser, Lincoln, xx–xxi, 73–75

Kinship
    in Greece, 340–341, 342, 343–344
    among Mardu, 234–235, 243, 248
    migration and, 340–341, 342, 343–344
    among Rashaayda Bedouin, 259, 276–277
!Kung San. *See* Ju/'hoansi

Langtang National Park (Nepal), 206,
    209–212, 218
Language(s)
    adaptations to, 298–299
    of Canela, 28, 37–38, 39, 44, 47
    in China, 56, 59, 62, 64, 65
    of crofters, 309, 315–319, 322, 327
    of immigrants, 285, 286, 298–299, 357
    in Melemchi, 200, 207, 210, 212, 219
    of Rashaayda Bedouin, 257, 262, 275, 278
    religion and, 319
    in Yucatán, 192, 193
Law enforcement (and gangs), 77, 82–83,
    87–88
Lee, Richard, xxii, 144
Lewis (Scotland), 308–309. *See also* Crofters
Liebow, Elliot, 80, 81
Lloyd, Willie, 75, 76, 77, 78, 93
Lutherans, 106, 108, 109. *See also* Christianity

Mardu (of Western Australia), xxii–xxiii, 225–255
    agriculture/pastoralism by, 235, 237–238, 241
    alcohol use by, 228–229, 242, 243, 244, 246,
        248, 251
    "big meetings" of, 227, 252
    colonization and, 226, 228, 231, 235, 241
    cultural influences on, 228–229, 231, 232–234,
        238, 240–241, 251–252
    cultural traditions of, 226–227, 232, 247, 251
    disease among, 228–229, 245–246
    economy of, 236, 240, 244, 246, 252
    education of, 238–239, 246
    environment of, 225–227
    gender roles of, 236
    government influence on, 239, 241–243, 252
    history of, 226, 227–229, 231
    as hunter–gatherers, 235–236, 243
    initiation rites of, 232, 247–248
    kinship among, 234–235, 243, 248
    as laborers, 236, 237, 238
    land ownership by, 228, 245
    marriage by, 234, 239, 241, 248
    media influence on, 229, 249
    migration of, 238, 246
    political organization of, 240, 241, 244–245, 252
    population of, 232
    religion of, 232–234, 235, 238–241, 242,
        247–248, 249–251, 252
    self-management by, 241–243, 245, 246
    social organization of, 226–227, 236, 251
    social stratification of, 232, 234–235, 247–248
    tourism and, 246
    violence among, 228–229, 246
    youth of, 238–239, 249

Marriage
    in Greece, 335, 336, 338, 339, 340, 341, 342,
        343, 344, 345–346
    by Mardu, 234, 239, 241, 248
    in Melemchi, 204
    by Minangkabau, 125–127
    by Rashaayda Bedouin, 258–259
    by Sambia, 99, 102, 103–105, 112
Matrilineal system, 117–120, 133–134,
    137–140, 141
Mayans (in ancient Mexico), 174–175
Media
    coverage of gangs, 75–76, 77–78
    influence on Mardu, 229, 249
    influence on Minangkabau, 128–130, 131
Melemchi (Nepal), 199–224
    agriculture/pastoralism in, 200–203, 206–207,
        210, 211, 214, 216, 218
    cultural influences on, 206–214
    cultural knowledge in, 219–220
    economy of, 201–203, 206–207, 208, 209–212,
        217–219
    education in, 206, 209, 212–214
    future of, 215–220
    gender roles in, 204, 205
    globalization in, 218, 220
    government influence in, 206, 209–212
    history of, 200
    housing in, 200
    language in, 200, 207, 210, 212, 214, 219
    marriage in, 204
    migration from, 203, 206, 207–209, 214, 215,
        216, 217, 219–220
    military in, 210, 212
    patrilineal system in, 204
    population of, 215–216
    religion in, 204–206, 208, 210, 216
    social–political organization of, 204
    tourism in, 210
Mesoamerica, 2. *See also* Aztec Empire
Mexican immigrants, xxi, 283–284, 285, 288,
    292–293, 299–300, 364, 366, 367, 370.
    See also Immigrants/Immigration;
    Migration/Mobility
Mexico
    colonization of, xxi–xxii, 1, 2, 8–9, 174, 175.
        See also Aztec Empire
    gender roles/hierarchy in, xxii, 172–198.
        See also Yucatán
    indigenous peoples of. *See* Aztec Empire;
        Mayans
    migration from, xxi, 283–284, 285, 288, 292–293,
        299–300, 364, 366, 367, 370. *See also*
        Immigrants/Immigration; Migration/Mobility
    relationship with United States, 177, 178,
        179, 284
Migration/Mobility. *See also*
    Immigrants/Immigration
    AIDS and, 163–164
    in China, 54, 64, 65
    by crofters, 310, 323–326
    education and, 195

Migration/Mobility (*continued*)
  effects of, xviii–xix
  to/within Greece, 334–335, 336–344
  kinship and, 340–341, 342, 343–344
  by Mardu, 238, 246
  from Melemchi, 203, 206, 207–209, 214, 215,
    216, 217, 219–220
  by Minangkabau, 133–134
  oil production and, 262–263
  population and, 324–325, 335–336
  by Rashaayda Bedouin, xxi, 257, 261,
    262–263, 264
  reasons for, 284, 285, 286, 287, 289, 325,
    337–338, 344
  resources about, xxiv (n4)
  to Riverfront, 353–354, 355–358, 364, 366
  by Sambia, 106–107, 112
  types of, xviii–xix, 194–195, 203, 206, 207–209,
    217, 285–287
  in Yucatán, 193–195
Military action/organizations
  AIDS and, 162, 164
  in Aztec Empire, 3, 5–6, 9
  in China, 67–68
  Ju/'hoansi and, 150, 151–152, 162, 164
  in Melemchi, 210, 212
Minangkabau (of West Sumatra), xxii, 117–143
  agriculture by, 130–131, 132, 139, 140
  economy of, 132, 134, 135–136, 137
  education of, 123–125, 127, 131
  extended-family households of, 120–125, 140
  gender roles of, 118–119, 120, 125–126
  government influence on, 127–128, 129, 132,
    137–138, 140, 141
  marriage of, 125–127
  matrilineal system of, 117–120, 133–134,
    137–140, 141
  media influence on, 128–130, 131
  migration by, 133–134
  modernization and, 125–126
  population of, 117
  religion of, 118–119, 129
  single-family households of, 123–124, 132–140
  social stratification of, 117–120, 122–123,
    126–127, 128, 130–131, 133–135, 137,
    138–140
  women's changing role among, 123–130, 140
Modernization
  economic transitions in, xix
  effects of, xix
  Minangkabau and, 125–126
  resources about, xxiv (n5)
  in Yucatán, 178, 179
Music (of crofters), 323
Muslims. *See also* Islam
  in China, 54, 55–56, 62–63, 68, 69
  migration by, 285
  Vice Lords as, 90–92

NAFTA. *See* North American Free Trade
  Agreement
Nahuas, 9, 12, 13–19. *See also* Aztec Empire

Namibia
  agriculture in, 148
  AIDS in, xxii, 144, 156, 157. *See also* Ju/'hoansi,
    AIDS among
  education in, 155–156
  history of, 150–154, 155–156, 168
  independence of, 150, 152, 155, 156, 162, 163, 168
  tourism in, 155, 161
  water supply in, 148
  wildlife conservation in, 155
National Democratic Alliance (NDA), 268, 269–272
National Islamic Front, 265, 268. *See also* Islam
Nationalism/National identity
  in China, 53, 54–56, 57–58, 61, 67, 69
  migration and, 286–288, 290
NDA. *See* National Democratic Alliance
Nepal (migration in), xxi, 199–224. *See also*
  Melemchi
New Guinea (gender roles/hierarchy in), xix–xx,
  97–116. *See also* Sambia
New Spain. *See* Aztec Empire; Mexico,
  colonization of
NNDFN. *See* Nyae Nyae Development Foundation
  of Namibia
NNFC. *See* Nyae Nyae Farmers' Cooperative
Norms (of culture), 80
North American Free Trade Agreement (NAFTA),
  178, 179, 187
Nyae Nyae Development Foundation of Namibia
  (NNDFN), 152–153, 155
Nyae Nyae Farmers' Cooperative (NNFC), 153, 155

Oil production (in Saudia Arabia), 262–263

Papua New Guinea. *See* New Guinea
Parman, Susan, xx, 304
Pastoralism. *See* Agriculture/Horticulture/
  Pastoralism
Patrilineal system, 204
People's Republic of China. *See* China
Police (and gangs), 77, 82–83, 87–88
Polish immigrants, 353, 354, 355–357, 358.
  See also European immigrants
Politics/Political structure
  of Aztec Empire, 3, 4 10–11, 15, 20
  of Mardu, 240, 241, 244–245, 252
  of Sambia, 103, 105–106
  of Vice Lords, 78–79, 83–85, 89–90, 93
Polygamy, 285
Population
  of China, 61
  of crofters, 306, 324–325
  of Greece, 335–336
  of Mardu, 232
  of Melemchi, 215–216
  migration and, 324–325, 335–336
  of Minangkabau, 117
  of Riverfront, 361, 367–369
  of Sambia, 98
Power (influences on), xviii
Prison, 77–78, 88–89, 95
Protestantism, 307, 320, 321. *See also* Christianity

Rashaayda Bedouin (of Sudan), xxi, 256–282
  agriculture/pastoralism by, 256–257, 262,
      263–264, 273, 277
  Bani Rashid and, 261, 272–277
  branches of, 259–262, 276, 277
  clothing of, 263–264
  cultural influences on, 259, 262, 263–264, 265, 278
  cultural traditions of, 277–278
  economy of, 256, 262–265, 277
  education of, 268, 278
  environment of, 259, 261
  ethnic identity of, 258, 261, 263, 268, 273, 274–277
  government influence on, 263, 268
  history of, 256–257, 259–262
  housing of, 264
  kinship among, 259, 276–277
  languages of, 257, 262, 275, 278
  migration by, xxi, 257, 261, 262–263, 264
  social stratification of, 273–274
  transnational forces and, 262, 265
  war and, 262, 265–272
  weddings of, 258–259
Religion/Religious organizations. *See also*
      specific religions
  in Aztec Empire, 7–8, 18–19, 20
  of Canela, 29, 30, 31, 37, 39, 49
  in China, 54, 55–56, 59–60, 62–63
  colonization and, 8, 18–19, 118–119, 175, 295
  of crofters, 306–307, 314, 319–323, 327
  of immigrants, 356–357, 358
  indigenous types of, 18–19, 29, 30, 31, 37, 39,
      49, 59–60, 205–206, 232–234
  language and, 319
  of Mardu, 232–234, 235, 238–241, 242, 247–248,
      249–251, 252
  in Melemchi, 204–206, 208, 210, 216
  of Minangkabau, 118–119, 129
  in Riverfront, 356–357, 358
  of Sambia, 97–98, 106, 108, 113, 115
  social control and, 321
  of Vice Lords, 90–92, 93, 94, 95
Riverfront (Wisconsin), xx, 351–371
  agriculture in, 355–356, 361–366
  commercial zone of, 358, 360–361, 366
  culture change in, 351–352, 364, 366–367, 369–370
  downtown of, 352, 353–355
  economy of, 359–360, 361, 363, 367, 370
  education in, 362, 363
  ethnic groups in, 353–354, 355–358, 364, 366, 370
  globalization in, 359–360, 366
  housing in, 360–361
  local identity in, 360, 367
  migration to, 353–354, 355–358, 364, 366
  population of, 361, 367–369
  religion in, 356–357, 358
  senior center in, 367–369
  social interaction in, 358–359, 360, 362, 370
Russia (migration to), 286. *See also* Soviet Union

Sambia (of Papua New Guinea), xix–xx, 97–116
  agriculture by, 98, 113–114
  cultural influences on, 108–109

  economy of, 106–107, 113–115
  education of, 106, 107–109, 113, 114–115
  gender roles of, 98–102, 104, 110–112, 115
  gender segregation among, 98–100, 104
  government influence on, 105, 107, 109
  history of, 98, 104, 105
  initiation rites of, 97, 98, 100, 101–102, 103, 104,
      107, 108–109, 110
  marriage of, 99, 102, 103–105, 112
  migration by, 106–107, 112
  political organization and, 103, 105–106
  population of, 98
  religion of, 97–98, 106, 108, 113, 115
  sexuality of, 103–105, 112
  social stratification of, 98, 102–103,
      109–112
  socialization of, 99–100, 108, 109
  war and, 97–98
Sano, Toshiyuki, xx, 351
Saudia Arabia
  Bani Rashid of, 272–277
  oil production in, 262–263
  Usaama bin Laadin in, 265
Scotland, xx, 319. *See also* Crofters
Separatism (in China), 67–70
Seventh-Day Adventists, 106, 109, 111, 113, 192.
      See also Christianity
Sexual activity/Sexuality
  AIDS and, 161, 162, 163, 164, 165–167,
      168, 169
  among Sambia, 103–105, 112
Shamans (of Yolmo), 205–206
Social stratification
  in Aztec Empire, 5–6, 10–12, 20
  of Canela, 30–31, 32, 34–35, 37, 38, 39, 40–41,
      42–44, 45–46, 47–48
  in China, 61–62
  of crofters, 306–308, 310, 314, 315–316
  in Greece, 336, 338–339, 341, 342, 343, 346
  of Ju/'hoansi, 146
  of Mardu, 232, 234–235, 247–248
  of Minangkabau, 117–120, 122–123,
      126–127, 128, 130–131, 133–135,
      137, 138–140
  of Rashaayda Bedouin, 273–274
  of Sambia, 98, 102–103, 109–112
  of Vice Lords, 89–90, 91, 93
  in Yucatán, 177–178, 182–183
Socialization (of Sambia), 99–100, 108, 109
Sonam Losar (Tibetan New Year), 221–222
South Africa
  colonization of Namibia by, 150–152, 153
  democratic elections in, 156
Soviet Union
  fragmentation of, 54, 66, 69
  nationalism in, 66
  war in Eritrea and, 267
Spain (colonization by), 1, 2, 8–9, 174, 175.
      See also Aztec Empire
Stolpe, Birgitte, xix–xx, 97, 98
sub-Saharan Africa (AIDS in), 156.
      See also AIDS

Sudan
    colonization of, 262
    migration in, xxi, 256–282. *See also* Rashaayda
        Bedouin
    war in, 262, 265, 266, 268–272
Sumatra (gender roles/hierarchy in), xxii, 117–143.
    See also Minangkabau

Taiwan
    migration to, 208, 217
    separatism by, 66–67, 70
Terrorism, 53–54, 67
Tibetan Buddhism, 205, 208, 210, 214–215,
    216, 219
Tonkinson, Robert, xxii–xxiii, 225
Tourism
    in Australia, 246
    in Botswana, 155
    in China, 63
    in Namibia, 155, 161
    in Nepal, 210
    in Scotland, 322, 330
    in Yucatán, 179, 192, 193–194
Transnationalism
    capitalism and, 295–296
    economic forces and, 262, 295–296
    migration and, 285–287
    political forces and, 262, 265
    religion and, 295
    study of, xxiv (n1), 285–287

Undocumented workers. *See* Illegal immigrants
United Kingdom (migration to), 287, 290
United States
    history of, 288–289
    migration to, xxi, 64, 283–285, 286, 288, 290,
        299–300, 324, 342, 353–354, 355–358,
        364, 366, 367, 370. *See also* Immigrants/
        Immigration; Migration/Mobility
    relationship with Mexico, 177, 178, 179, 284
    terrorism and, 53–54
Uygur nationalists, 55–56, 63, 67, 69–70

Vasilika (Greece), 334. *See also* Greece
Vice Lords, 73–96
    conflict/discipline within, 83, 85–86, 87, 91,
        94–95
    culture of, 74, 79–81
    drug dealing by, 82, 89
    history of, 73–74, 82–90
    leadership within, 84, 86, 89, 90
    legitimate enterprises of, 87
    media coverage of, 75–76, 77–78
    meetings of, 94
    political–economic context of, 74, 75, 79, 85,
        87–88
    political involvement by, 87
    political organization of, 78–79, 83–85, 89–90, 93
    prison and, 79, 89, 95
    religion of, 90–92, 93, 94, 95
    resources of, 86–87

social interactions of, 79
social stratification in, 89–90, 91, 93
splintering of, 85–86
symbols/rituals of, 92, 93, 95

War/Violence
    in Aztec Empire, 3, 5–6
    against Canela, 25, 30, 36, 40, 47, 48
    in China, 54–56, 63, 65
    among Ju/'hoansi, 151–152
    among Mardu, 228–229, 246
    and Rashaayda Bedouin, 262, 265–272
    against Sambia, 97–98
    in Yucatán, 175, 177
War on Poverty, 87
Weaving (by crofters), 308, 327
Wildlife conservation (in Botswana/Namibia),
    154–155
Wisconsin, xx, 80, 351–352, 366. *See also*
    Riverfront
world systems theory, 173–174
World Trade Organization (WTO), 70
WTO. *See* World Trade Organization

Yaxbe (Yucatán, Mexico), 172–173, 179–196.
    See also Yucatán
    agriculture in, 180, 182–183
    commuting in, 190–193
    economy of, 179–181, 182–189, 191–195
    education in, 191, 192, 193, 195
    gender roles in, 180–181, 184–185
    globalization in, 195
    government influence in, 181, 186–187, 188–189
    henequen production in, 180, 181, 191
    history of, 179–182
    industry in, 184, 187–189, 190, 191, 195
    language in, 192, 193
    migration from, 193–195
    social stratification in, 182–183
    tourism in, 192, 193–194, 195
    women's role in, 180–181, 184–189, 191, 193
Yolmo, xxi, 199–224. *See also* Melemchi
Young, William, xxi, 256–259
Yucatán (Mexico), xxii, 172–198. *See also* Yaxbe
    agriculture in, 175–178, 180, 182–183
    climate of, 174–175
    commuting in, 190–193
    economy of, 174, 176, 177–178, 179–181,
        182–189, 191–195
    education in, 191, 192, 193, 195
    globalization in, 173, 174, 195
    government influence in, 178, 181, 186–187,
        188–189
    henequen cultivation in, 175–178, 180, 181, 191
    history of, 174–178, 179–182
    indigenous labor in, 174, 175, 176
    industry in, 184, 187–189, 190, 191, 195
    migration within, 193–195
    modernization in, 178, 179
    tourism in, 179, 192, 193–194
    war in, 175, 177